The Western Desert of Egypt

An Explorer's Handbook

CASSANDRA VIVIAN

Maps and illustrations by
Vivienne Groves and **Lyla Pinch Brock**

The American University in Cairo Press

This edition is dedicated to my two great friends
Mohamed Shebl and Marilyn Garcia-Mora,
whom I spoke to or saw almost every day for nearly
twenty years: Egypt is not Egypt without them.

Readers can help us keep future editions of this book accurate
by writing to us with information updates to cass5@verizon.net

Sixth printing 2007

An earlier version of this book was published as
*Islands of the Blest: A Guide to the Oases
and Western Desert of Egypt* in 1990 by Trade
Routes Enterprises. Maps and illustrations were
by Vivienne Groves. Additional maps
and illustrations have been prepared for this
edition by Lyla Pinch Brock.

Dar el Kutub No. 3978/99
ISBN 978 977 424 527 5

Printed in Egypt

Contents

Acknowledgments   **xv**
Preface   **xvii**

1 The Natural World   **1**
North Africa   2
Sudan   4
Geography and Geology   4
    Archean Era   6
    Paleozoic Era   5
    Mesozoic Era   6
    Cenozoic Era   6
Depressions and Oases   9
Sand and Sand Dunes   10
    Dune Fields   11
    Sand Seas   13
Water   13
    Birs and Ains   14
    Out of Water   14
    Fog and Rain   14
Wind   15
    Sandstorms   16
Stones, Oils, and Gases   16
    Oil and Gas   17
Fossils   17
    Petrified Wood   17
Plants and Animals   18
    Insects and Reptiles   18
    Mammals   19
    Birds   21

2 The People and Explorers of the Desert   **23**
The People   24
    Garamantians   24
    Goraan   25
    Tebu   25
    Tuareg   25
    Berbers   26

Kababish 26
The Oaseans 26
The Bedouin 26
The Sanusi 27
Caravans and Roadways 28
Taghaza Road 29
Ghadames–Air–Kano Road 30
Garamantian Road 30
Fezzan–Kawan Road 30
Tripoli–Benghazi–Waidai Road 30
Darb al-Arbain 31
Explorers and Travelers 31
The Classical World 31
The Middle Ages 32
The Early Europeans 33
The African Association 33
The Americans 34
Muhammad Ali Opens the Door 35
The Germans 37
The Geological Survey of Egypt and its Desert Survey Department 39
Royal Geographical Society 42
A Hungarian 43
The Women 44
The Egyptians 45
The Warriors 47
Mapping Egypt 49
Egypt from Space 50

3 Kharga Oasis **53**

Asyut to the Kharga Escarpment 53
Wadi al-Battikha 53
Checkpoints 53
Naqb al-Ramliya 54
Kharga Oasis 54
History 54
Pharaonic 54
Roman Period 55
Christian Era 56
Islamic Era 58
Muhammad Ali 58
European Travelers 58
British Occupation 59

The New Valley   60
Geography and Geology   61
  Mountains   61
  Water   61
  Sand Dunes   63
  Yardangs   63
Caravan Routes and Roadways   64
  North–South Routes   64
  East–West Routes   64
  Passes (Naqbs)   65
  The Forts   65
The People   66
  Agriculture   67
  Food   67
The Crafts of the Oasis   67
  Baskets   67
  Pottery   69
  Wall Paintings   69
  Dresses   70
  Jewelry   70
The Tour   71
  Tour #1 Qasr Kharga   73
  Tour #2 Hibis, Bagawat, and Environs   76
  Tour #3 Qasr Kharga to Dush   80
  Tour #4 Al-Deir, Qasr al-Geb, and Qasr al-Sumaria   90
  Tour #5 Qasr Labeka and Ain Umm Dabadib   95
  Tour #6 Ain al-Dabashiya (Ain Tabashir), Ain al-Tarakwa
    (maybe), and Beleida   102
  Tour #7 Ain Amur   104

4 Dakhla   **107**

Kharga to Dakhla along the Darb al-Ghabari   107
History   109
  Pharaonic   109
  Roman and Christian Periods   110
  Islamic Era   110
  British Occupation   111
  Today   112
  Explorers   113
Geography and Geology   113
  Mountains and Passes (Naqbs)   114
  Water   114

Caravan Routes and Roadways   115
The People   116
  Food   116
The Crafts of the Oasis   117
  Baskets and Rugs   117
  Pottery   118
  Decorative Arts   120
  Dresses   121
  Jewelry   123
The Tour   124
  Tour #1 Mut   125
  Tour #2 Eastern Dakhla   127
  Tour #3 Mut to Qasr Dakhla   134
  Tour #4 Around Qasr Dakhla   136
  Tour #5 Loop Road from Qasr Dakhla to Mut   140

5 Farafra   **143**

Dakhla to Farafra via Darb Abu Minqar   143
To Qasr Farafra from Bahariya Oasis   145
  Farafra   147
History   147
  Old Kingdom   147
  New Kingdom   147
  Third Intermediate and Late Periods   147
  Roman Period   150
  Islamic Era   150
  Modern Times   150
  The New Valley in Farafra   151
Geography and Geology   152
  Mountains and Hills   152
  Water   152
Caravan Routes and Roadways   153
The People   153
  Agriculture   154
The Crafts of the Oasis   154
The Tour   154
  Tour #1 Qasr Farafra   155
  Tour #2 Toward Abu Minqar   158
  The White Desert   159
  Tour #3 Easy Access White Desert   160
  Tour #4 Inselbergs, Hummocks, and Monoliths of the White Desert 161
  Tour #5 Quss Abu Said, al-Ubeida Playa, and Ain Dilla   162

Tour #6 Mushrooms, Acacia, and Ain Hadra   167
Tour #7 Ain al-Wadi, Wadi Hinnis, and Twin Peaks 169
Tour #8 Qarawein   170
Additional Tours with local guides   172

6 Bahariya   **175**

From Cairo to Bahariya   175
History   177
  Middle and New Kingdom   177
  Third Intermediate and Late Periods   177
  Roman and Christian Periods   178
  Islamic Era   178
  Nineteenth and Twentieth Centuries   179
Geography and Geology   180
  Mountains   181
  Dunes   181
  Water   181
  Fossils, Ferns, and Earthquakes   181
Caravan Routes and Roadways   182
  Passes (Naqbs)   182
  Darbs   182
The People   184
  Agriculture   185
  Food   186
The Crafts of the Oasis   186
  Dresses   186
  Jewelry   187
  Tour #1 Bawiti   191
  Tour #2 Qasr   194
  Tour #3 Tibniya and Environs   197
  Tour #4 Mountains, Desert, and Far Gardens   200
  Tour #5 Northern Bahariya and Environs   203
  Tour #6 Sahara Suda (the Black Desert)   206
  Tour #7 Al-Hayz   208
  Tour #8 Darb Siwa   210

7 Fayoum   **223**

History   213
  Pharaonic   213
  Greek Period   215
  Roman Period   215
  Christian and Islamic Periods   216

Fayoum from 1798 to 1882   216
British Occupation   217
Fayoum Today   217
Geography and Geology   217
Mountains and Wadis   218
The Lake   218
Fossils   219
Water   225
Caravan Routes and Roadways   225
Darb Wadi Natrun   225
Darb al-Rayyan I and II   225
The People   226
Agriculture, Fishing, and Industry   226
The Crafts of the Oasis   227
Baskets   227
Pottery   228
Dresses and Jewelry   229
Roman Fayoum Portraits   229
Wildlife   230
Tour #1 Eastern Edge of Fayoum   231
The Lake District   237
Tour #2 North of Lake Qarun   238
Tour #3 Southern Shore of Lake Qarun   242
Tour #4 Western Edge of the Fayoum   243
Tour #5 Medinet Fayoum   246
Tour #6 Hawara Pyramid   249
Tour #7 South of Medinet Fayoum   250
Tour #8 South to Tebtunis and Environs   252
Wadi Rayyan   254
Geography and Geology   256
Tour #1 The Waterfall   256
Tour #2 Magic Spring and the Monastery   256
Tour #3 Gebel Guhannam and Wadi Zeuglodon   258
Wadi Mawalih   260

8 Al-Diffa (the Northern Coast)   **261**

History   261
Pharaonic   262
Greek and Roman Periods   262
Islamic Era   263
British Occupation   263
The World Wars along the Northern Coast   265

Today   267
Geography and Geology   267
   Water   267
Caravans Routes and Roadways   267
   Alexandria–Sollum   267
   Interior Road   267
   Wadi Natrun–al-Alamein Road   268
   Maryut Railway   268
The Tour   268
   Alexandria to Mersa Matruh   268
   Tour #1 Agami to al-Alamein   269
   Tour #2 The Battlefield of al-Alamein   281
   Tour #3 Qattara Depression   284
   Tour #4 Qara (Gara) Oasis   287
   Tour #5 Sidi Abd al-Rahman to Mersa Matruh   289
   Tour #6 Mersa Matruh   291
   Tour #7 Mersa Matruh to Sollum: Agube Major   298

9 Siwa   **303**

From Mersa Matruh: the Masrab al-Istabl   303
From Bahariya along the Darb Siwa   303
   Siwa   305
History   305
   Ancient Egypt   305
   Alexander the Great   305
   Christian Era   306
   Islamic Era   306
   Muhammad Ali and the Europeans   307
   The Twentieth Century   309
   Today   311
Geography and Geology   311
   Mountains and Hills   312
   Water and Salt   312
Caravan Routes and Roadways   313
The People   314
The Crafts of the Oasis   318
   Baskets   318
   Wooden Bowls and Boxes   319
   Pottery   320
   Clothing   321
   Jewelry   322
   Headdresses   324

Bracelets   325
Rings   326
Tour #1 Shali   327
Tour #2 Loop the Loop from Shali to Shali   329
Tour #3 Fatnas at Sunset   335
Tour #4 North and West of Shali   336
Tour #5 East of Shali   340

10 The Darb al-Arbain Desert   343

History   343
Geography and Geology   344
Limestone Plateau   344
Nubia Pediplain   344
Selima Sand Sheet   344
Tushka Canal   344
Al-Sheikh Zayed Canal   345
Caravan Routes and Roadways   346
Darb al-Arbain   346
Darb al-Galaba   346
Darb al-Tamanin   347
Darb al-Tarfawi   347
The Darb al-Arbain, the Forty Days' Road   347
Tour #1 Riding the Darb al-Arbain   358
Tour #2 Darb al-Galaba   360

11 The Uwaynat Desert   364

History   364
Zerzura   365
Exploration History   366
Geography and Geology   367
Mountains   367
Craters   368
Wind   369
Caravan Routes and Roadways   369
Darb al-Tarfawi   369
Dakhla to Kufra   369
Gilf Kebir to Kufra   369
The People   369
Rock Art   370
Location   371
Themes and Style   371
Origin   372

Who Found What   372
Pottery   373
The Tour   374
Middle Arbain Desert   374
From Dakhla Oasis to the Gilf Kebir   375
Gilf Kebir   380
Between the Gilf and Uwaynat   389
Gebel Uwaynat   389

Practical Information   **393**

Selected Reading   **411**

Index   **415**

Acknowledgments

The following people and organizations were helpful in gathering information for this book.

In the Matruh Governorate: the director of tourism, Abd al-Hamid Fahmy al-Gammal, and Ahmed Ali Haida and Abdulla Baghi, residents of Siwa Oasis.

In the New Valley: the director of Egyptian antiquities, Bahgat Ahmed Ibrahim and his assistant Magdy Hussein, who provided much expertise and assistance while I was in Kharga, as did Mahmoud Youssef, director of the Kharga Museum. Also thanks to Ibrahim Mohamed Hassan, director of the Tourist Information Office at Kharga Oasis, and his assistant Omar Ahmed Mahmoud in Dakhla, who, as usual, provided his time, his expertise, and his kindness.

In Bahariya and the Giza Governorate: Dr. Zahi Hawass, director of antiquities for Giza and Saqqara, Mohamed al-Taib, inspector of antiquities in Bahariya Oasis, Mohamad Abd al-Kadar, director of the Tourist Information Office, Salah Abdulla, Mahmoud Eed, and Mohamed Kilani, all helped in one way or another.

In Farafra: Mohamed Raifat Amin, mayor of Farafra, enthusiastically provided information about the past and future of the oasis. Saad Ali of Farafra renewed my appreciation for his desert once more and made every desert journey fun. He and Josiane Chopard, his partner at the Farafra Bedouin Village, graciously provided true desert hospitality.

For this edition Peter Wirth was guide, driver, interpreter, procurer, translator, and friend. Probably the best part of the desert journeys was sitting around the fire in the evening cuddled deep into my sleeping bag while Peter read and translated Gerhard Rohlfs' book and the German edition of Almasy. It led to a lot of interesting discussions.

Samir and Wally Lama took me to the Gilf Kebir and then provided the opportunity to meet Theodore Monod and Peter Clayton. This type of cooperation and unselfish spirit is seldom seen among travelers in the Western Desert and is much appreciated.

In the same spirit, Giancarlo Negro of Sahara Magazine (simonis@tin.it) shared important information on silica glass and southwestern Egypt.

Jim and Sandy Sorenson took me into the world of the GPS and then to Abd al-Fattah Khalifa and the United Consultant Group in Nasr City, who provided me with a Garmin 140 GPS.

Additional thanks to Danny Hamilton of Telson USA, at 111 Washington Avenue, Dumont, New Jersey (www.telson.net), for the outright grant of a Garmin GPS III with external antenna.

My thanks to Casio, Inc. who gave me their PRT40K-IV module no. 1470 watch, which, in addition to normal watch functions, provides a digital compass, an altimeter, a barometer, and a thermometer.

David and Susan Torgerson and their two sons Marc and Paul gave me their home twice in two years, the second for a four month stint. This was a most appreciated sacrifice.

For hospitality in the desert I am indebted to the Kamil Group of Bahariya Oasis and the Farafra Bedowin Village in Farafra.

Fellow travelers who helped show the way: Izz al-Din Khalifa Hamza, Mabrouk, Nasser of Dakhla, and SEEgypt (especially May).

For use of their libraries I would like to thank: Chicago House, The American Research Center in Egypt, and Sandra Gamal, librarian at Cairo American College, who kept me abreast of events in Egypt while I was in the States.

A special mention must be made of the wonderful inter-library loan system established in libraries throughout the United States. Without the use of this incredible opportunity, more than half of the references in this book would have been out of reach. Special thanks to the library staff at the Community College of Allegheny County, and the Monessen Public Library and District Center. Their continuous efforts over a three-year period, when hundreds of books and magazine articles were ordered, is not only appreciated, but was essential to my research.

. . . the desert smiles and there is no place worth living but the desert.

Ahmed Hassanein

Preface

Perhaps the most exciting aspect of traveling in the Western Desert is the feeling that the great age of desert exploration is not over. Making your way into the interior of the desert and riding the wind to an ancient fort is one of the few great adventures left in the world. Knowing that the last time someone visited the area was years ago produces a euphoria that is unparalleled. The strain of wading through old records means nothing once you are standing in the desert, feet firmly planted in the sand. The eye searches the horizon looking for the ghosts of the past: the amazing Kufra refugees, the slave caravans, the great religious community of the Sanusi, the nineteenth-century explorers, and soldiers of war.

Change is inevitable in the desert. It has always changed. It changed in prehistory when people scribbled graffiti on the rock surfaces at Gebel Uwaynat. It changed in the Middle Kingdom when someone built a temple along the shores of the lake in Fayoum and when someone else, surely amid great protest and apprehension, changed the level of the lake. It changed when the Romans built a string of forts in Kharga Oasis, when the underground water systems were introduced in Bahariya, Kharga, and Farafra oases, when the medieval rulers of Cairo established villages in Dakhla, and when the British and Italians created the national borders. Surely, as each new change came it was met with controversy.

The current round of changes in the Western Desert have been greeted with a lot of criticism. They began in the 1970s when the government connected the oases with asphalt roads. They continued with the creation of the New Valley, the laying of the infrastructure, the immigration to Farafra, the emergence of East Uwaynat, and the construction of modern hotels in the oases. This book, first published in 1990, has been a part of the growth. It explained the desert. It built a bridge between the people of the desert and the travelers who ventured there. It brought about change.

Some are angry because of these changes. They do not want tourists in the desert, yet they lead safaris. They do not want people to follow after them into remote regions, yet they want to earn their living from the desert. It does not work that way. In the 1920s, Byron Khun de Prorok was appalled to find, on his return visit a year after making Neolithic discoveries in the Fayoum, that his trackless desert between Cairo and the Fayoum was "covered with motor tracks and countless sardine tins." It would not be surprising to find a papyrus on which some scribe in ancient Egypt chastised Egyptian tourists for similar things, or Roman tourists for hauling precious cargo back to Rome.

Some are not so much angry at change as at how change is materializing in the Western Desert. This, too, is an eternal conflict between ideologies. Critics bring their own prejudices, their own shortcomings, their own agendas, when they pass judgment on desert development. They may find change not within their financial interest, not up to their moral standards, not within their environmental expectations. Surely they must realize that there is more than one way for this desert to blossom. Surely they must realize that no one person or idea will be the salvation of this desert, just as no one person or idea is responsible for all the problems that development and change bring. Although some abhor them, the modern changes are improving the quality of life for the desert people. Thanks to the government there are better roads, better schools, hospitals, telephones, televisions, and imported goods from the Nile Valley. How the desert people adapt these changes to their lifestyles and traditions is their most important task. They can lose their identity, as many in the world have done, or they can create a balance, making the new work with the old.

Today we are writing a new chapter in desert adventure. We are the inheritors of a great tradition that has shown respect for the desert, its dangers, and its beauty. We owe a debt to every person whose name is associated with this place: to the Oracle of Siwa, who predicted the future; to the soldiers of the Persian Army, who are lost forever in its sands; to Gerhard Rohlfs, who stepped off into the unknown; to John Ball, Hugh Beadnell, and Patrick Clayton, who mapped the desert inch by inch; to Ahmed Hassanein, who trekked over 1,000 miles to discover new places; to the Englishman Ralph Bagnold, the Frenchman Théodore Monod, and the German Hans Rhotert, who epitomize the international concern for the desert; to the intriguing, romantic spirits of travelers like Count Ladislaus Edouard de Almasy, who add not only history but also glamour to the desert; and to Ahmed Fakhry, who explored the desert's antiquities.

It is our honor-bound duty to protect their desert, to keep it clean from modern debris, unpolluted by cities and their clutter, and safe from human destructiveness. We must maintain its wildness and natural splendor to hand down to those who come after us.

Allah ma'ak wa ma'a salama (Go with God and with safety).
Cassandra Vivian
Maadi and Monessen, 1999

Global Positioning System (GPS) waypoints are given to all onroad and a limited number of offroad sites in this book. There are no GPS points to remote sites or unguarded archaeologial sites. This is intentional. The waypoints are here for the enjoyment of the traveler, but not to the detriment of the desert. Nor are the GPS points to be considered as life saving devices. How well a traveler knows his or her equipment, understands how GPS works, and makes logical decisions are all factors in GPS travel. Always maintain a backup. Do not consider these GPS points as 100 percent reliable: nothing is.

The GPS receiver can be set to receive waypoints in a number of ways. The first is Lat/Lon dd.mm.ss format. This format gives the waypoint in degrees, minutes, and seconds. This format seems to be more popular in the United States. The second format is dd.mm.mm, sometimes called the metric format, which is used by most people throughout the world. The waypoint is in degrees, minutes, and 100 parts of a minute. All the waypoints in this book were calculated in this manner. The third format is the UTM (the Universal Transverse Mercator) or MGRS, the newest type of system developed by the US government. It is considered to be more accurate than the traditional longitude and latitude systems. In the future it will probably be the system we all use. For a full explanation on how to use UTM, go to *www.maptools.com/index.html*. There is a complicated formula to translate formats, but there are also electronic calculators that can do it for you. One of the easiest to use is on the Jeep homepage at *www.jeep.com/details/coord/* (one more exciting GPS page to explore). A click of the mouse will move you from one system to the other.

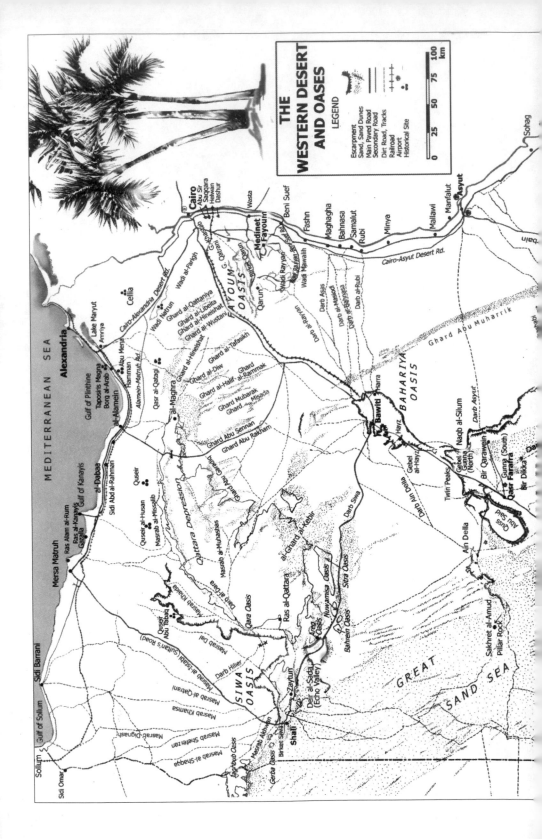

THE WESTERN DESERT AND OASES

LEGEND

Escarpment
Sand, Sand Dunes
Main Paved Road
Secondary Road
Dirt Road, Tracks
Railroad
Airport
Historical Site

0   25   50   75   100
km

MEDITERRANEAN SEA

Alexandria

Sollum
Gulf of Sollum
Sidi Barrani
Sidi Omar
Mersa Matruh
Ras al-Rum
Ras al-Kanayis
Gazala
Gulf of Kanayis
al-Dabaa
Sidi Abd al-Rahman
al-Alamein
Borg al-Arab
Gulf of Plinthine
Taposiris Magna
Lake Maryut
Amriya
Abu Mena
Hammam
Qasr al-Qatagi
Qaret al-Husan
Masrab al-Hissalib

Cairo-Alexandria Desert Rd.
Alamein-Matruh Rd.

Wadi Natrun
Celia
Wadi al-Farigh
Ghard al-Qattaniya
Ghard al-Libeita
Ghard al-Hineishat
Ghard al-Wustani
Ghard al-Hineishat
Ghard al-Tafasikh
Ghard al-Diw
Ghard al-Halif   Ghard
Ghard al-Rammak
Ghard Mubarak
Ghard. Misqada
Ghard Abu Serman
Ghard Abu Rakham

Qaret al-Maghra
al-Maghra

Qattara Depression

Ghard Abu Muharrik

Cairo
Abu Sir
Saqqara
Helwan
Dashur
Wosta
Beni Suef
Fashn
Maghagha
Bahnasa
Samalut
Rubi
Minya
Mallawi
Manfalut
Asyut
Sohag

Medinet Fayoum
FAYOUM OASIS
Qarun
Birket Qarun
G. Qatrani
Wadi Rayyan
Wadi Mawalih

Darb Asas
Darb al-Haasod
Darb al-Bahnasa
Darb al-Rubi
Cairo-Asyut Desert Rd.
Darb Asyut

BAHARIYA OASIS
Bawiti
Harra
Hayz
Gebel al-Hayz
Gebel Gunna (North)
Gunna (South)
Twin Peaks
Naqb al-Silum
Bir Qarawein
Qasr Farafra
Bir Dikka
Dar
Oasis ABU SAID

Ain Della
Darb Ain Della
Darb Siwa

al-Ghard al-Kebir
Nuwamisa Oasis
Sitra Oasis
Areg Oasis
Bahrein Oasis
Ras al-Qattara
Qara Oasis
Qaret Umm al-Hush

Masrab al-Munashes

Darb al-Dora

Masrab Dal
Qusur Abu Tabaq
Masrab al-Istabl (Sultan's Road)
Darb Hilier
Masrab al-Qatani
Masrab Khamsa
Masrab Shelaizan
Masrab al-Shagga
Masrab Dighnash
Tabghubub Oasis
Gerba Oasis
Birket Siwa
Masrab Menhun

SIWA OASIS
Zaytun
Deir al-Sada (Echo Valley)
Shali

GREAT SAND SEA

Sakhret al-Amud
Pillar Rock

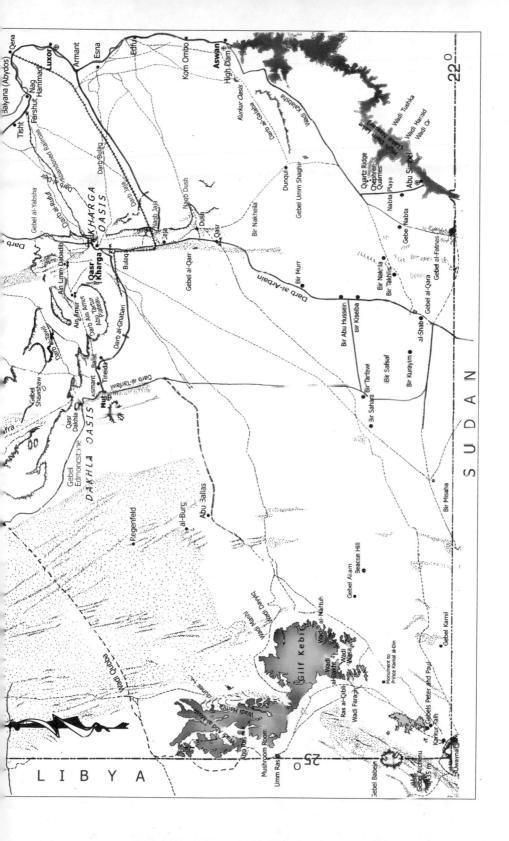

1

The Natural World

This desert has always been a mysterious land. The ancient Egyptians made it the home of the evil god Seth, who like Cain, killed his brother. The classical world braved its terrors to visit the Oracle at Siwa. The Greeks believed the desert was the home of Medusa, the gorgon with hair of writhing snakes and a look that turned men to stone. Caravans loaded with slaves and ivory traversed its dunes and suffered its perils. Entire armies disappeared into its belly, while individuals have made incredible treks over its hundreds of desolate kilometers and eagerly dug up its sands in quest for buried treasures. One man thumped his way through the desert on camels laden with Bibles, which he distributed throughout the hostile oases. Another carried a boat into the desert in his search for hidden treasure. A third crossed and recrossed its dunes in an airplane looking for a lost oasis. The Italians ran a barbed wire fence from the Mediterranean Sea to Kufra Oasis to keep some people in and others out. The desert has beckoned to explorers from around the world, eager to discover what lies over the next sand dune, or beyond the next plateau.

But the Western Desert does not really exist. The name was invented by the British to label their share of the North African wasteland. Mountains separate the Libyan Desert from the Sahara Desert, but no natural barrier distinguishes the Western Desert from the Libyan Desert. The Western Desert exists only as a political demarcation.

One cannot totally condemn the British, for the Romans had done the same thing centuries earlier. When Octavian saw the last of Antony and Cleopatra, he changed his name to Augustus Caesar and separated Egypt from the rest of Rome's empire by giving it a separate status: it acquired a separate ruler, separate legions, and, ultimately, a separate history. As Augustus, Octavian was no fool. Roman politics were too full of intrigue and Egypt too rich a plum for Augustus to allow an ambitious appointee too tempting an opportunity. Egypt was too rebellious for him to let its leaders mix with those of Rome's other conquests. Egypt's granaries were too vital to Rome's sustenance to have them used as pawns in a Middle Eastern power play. Thus, everything in Egypt became, of design, isolated and self-contained, reporting directly to Rome and bypassing the normal hierarchy. This one brilliant maneuver separated Egypt from the rest of North Africa and the Middle East for the next twenty centuries.

Today, scholars follow the same patterns. Roman scholars study North Africa and the Middle East and for the most part ignore Egypt. Egyptian scholars study Egypt and seldom look west to Libya or east to Sinai or Palestine for answers to perplexing questions. North African scholars do not look to Egypt as a continuation of their desert civilizations. Egypt stands alone, and so does its desert, a fact that makes unraveling its mysteries more difficult.

In Arabic, the word *sahara* means 'desert.' The Western Desert of Egypt, one of the many deserts that straddle the earth along the tropics of Cancer and Capricorn, is a *sahara*, but it is not *the* Sahara. The term Sahara Desert was given to the entire desert of North Africa by Europeans before they knew much about the interior. During the era of exploration, it was discovered that there were two distinct deserts in North Africa: the western desert of Morocco, Algeria, and Tunisia, which the French called the Sahara Desert; and the eastern desert of Libya and Egypt, which the Italians called the Libyan Desert. In the north the high plateau of the Fezzan, in Libya, forms a wedge that divides the Sahara Desert in the west from the Libyan Desert in the east. Starting in Sudan, mountains run west to meet the Fezzan. They include the Ennedi, Erdi, and Tibesti mountain chains. These high points cut the Libyan Desert off from the Sahara.

So, in point of fact, the Western Desert falls out of Egypt into Libya in the west and into Sudan in the south, and just keeps going. To understand it, one must understand what happens to the Libyan Desert when it rolls out of Egypt. We should know a bit about the people and places.

North Africa

In North Africa the northern coast from Tripoli to the west is called the Barbary Coast and from Tripoli to the East, al-Diffa. Moving south are the two deserts, the Sahara and the Libyan. South of the deserts is a stretch of semi-desert called the Sahel. At this point, the entire continent from the Atlantic Ocean in the west to the Red Sea in the east—5,500 kilometers (3,500 miles)—is the Bilad al-Sudan, the Land of the Blacks.

Libya is divided into a number of provinces. **Cyrenaica** abuts Egypt along the 25th meridian and shares its desert. It was founded by the Greeks in the seventh century B.C. when the Oracle of Delphi commanded the emigrants from the overpopulated island of Thera to colonize North Africa. In the 630s B.C. they founded Cyrene. Soon Barce,

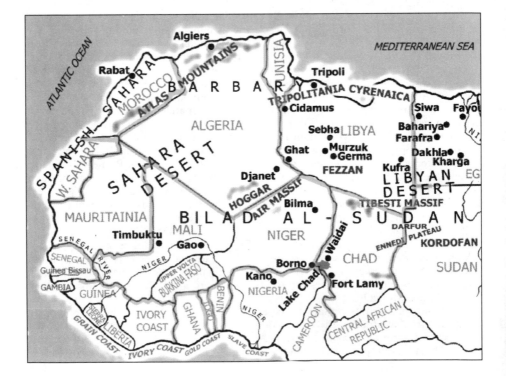

Rock art of ancient desert chariot

Euhesperides (ancient Berenice, current Benghazi), Teuchira (Arsinoe, then Tuhra) and Apollonia (Susa) followed. Collectively, they were called Pentapolis, the five cities. The entire region was Cyrenaica. When Alexander the Great conquered Egypt, the Cyrenaicans simple surrendered to him. Under the Ptolemies, a large Jewish community revolted against Rome in Jerusalem in A.D. 70. In 115, they revolted again, and this revolt spread to Egypt. Cyrenaica was wasted, Cyrene sacked, the northern coast of Egypt devastated, Alexandria burned. In medieval times, Cyrenaica languished on the perimeter of Egypt's Islamic state from the rule of Salah al-Din to the fall of the Ottoman empire. In the twentieth century, Italy lusted after its ancient colony once again, dreaming of creating the 'Fourth Shore' to the Italian peninsula. It eventually did, only to lose it again in World War II.

Tripolitania abuts Cyrenaica on the west. In its early history, the Phoenicians established a number of colonies along the North African coast and were the first, as far as we know, to establish trade with the caravans of the desert. When Carthage overtook the Phoenician ports, it also took over trade with the caravans. By this time, three of the great north–south African trade routes had been established: Gabes to Ghadames, Wayat to Fezzan, and Lept to Tibesti and Waidai. The Romans, around A.D. 200 created Tripolitania, the three cities. Tripolitania was conquered by Touareg ancestors around 366. Then the Vandals took over around 440. In the next century, the area fell to Byzantium. The Arabs were at Tripoli in 647. In the Middle Ages, Tripolitania was the seat of piracy along the Mediterranean Coast, which continued into the nineteenth century. In 1714, the Arab Ahmad Karamanli took Tripoli away from the Turks and his family ruled until 1835. It took the Italians to join Tripolitania to Cyrenaica.

The Fezzan is a fertile plateau corridor that separates the Libyan Desert from the Sahara. Early civilizations knew that the routes south through the Sahara via the Fezzan linked interior Africa to the Mediterranean Sea. Along these routes is an abundance of ancient rock art including pictures of horses and ancient chariots, ascribed by scholars to the Garamantians. The Garamantians were a formidable foe to the Romans, who never quite conquered them. Rome came to the Fezzan as early as 20 B.C., when Pliny tells us that the consul Cornelius Balbus tried to overthrow the Garamantians and occupy Ghadames. In the fourteenth century, the Moroccans took over the Fezzan and established their capital: Murzuk. It lasted through the Ottoman era. The Turks came to the Fezzan from Egypt in the person of Sherif al-Din Karakosh, who occupied its oases. The Turks used the Fezzan as a place of banishment and many young men languished amid its dunes and oases. The Fezzan was a difficult adversary for twentieth-century Italy, just as it had been for ancient Rome.

Sudan

Two provinces of Sudan are important to our discussion, **Darfur** and **Kordofan**, both northern provinces and part of the Libyan Desert. Darfur is a huge plain of 444,000 square kilometers (170,000 square miles). In prehistory the people of Darfur were Nile Valley dwellers and it is probably correct to assume that the ancient Egyptians traded with Darfur, via caravan trails. Darfur figured prominently in the slave trade with Egypt. The people of Darfur caught the slaves, held them, and sent them north along the Darb al-Arbain, the slave route to Egypt. Kordofan lies between Darfur and the Nile. The history of Kordofan is similar to that of Darfur. Kordofan was part of the Kanem-Bornu empire. Slavery was an important economic factor in Kordofan. Eventually it was ruled by the Mahdi and fell to the Egyptians. It covers 390,000 square kilometers (150,000 square miles), its north being desert and its south savanna.

Geography and Geology

The Libyan Desert is the most arid region on earth and is the site of some of the highest recorded temperatures. A shocking 58° C (136° F) was recorded just south of Tripoli in Azizia on September 13, 1922, which is the highest temperature ever recorded.

From near Kordofan in Sudan, the Libyan Desert covers 1,600 kilometers (994 miles) as it extends north through Egypt to the Mediterranean coast. Beginning at the Nile Valley it stretches west for 1,760 kilometers (1,093 miles). The first 500 kilometers (310 miles) are within the Egyptian border, the desert thereafter extending far into Libya. Covering 2.8 million square kilometers (1 million square miles), including two-thirds of the area of Egypt, it is the largest desert in the world.

Scientists once believed that the desert was expanding, moving ever southward. However, with the advent of satellite technology, several decades of monitoring indicate that the desert moves south when rain is scarce and north when rain is abundant. This has probably been the case since as early as prehistory, when four wet periods occurred. Geology and climate have changed very little since the Roman Period.

How did it all happen? How did the mountains and valleys of the desert come into being? Within the cliffs of the barren and exposed mountains can be found a chronology of events that changed the surface of the earth. For age after age the environment that is now the Libyan Desert was lifted up, sank, was submerged, was hot, cold, moist, or dry. As it evolved, debris piled up, level after level, that can now be identified as coming from a particular age. These strata, exposed in the cliffsides of the mountains and escarpments, were laid into place over billions of years, locking into the rock the secrets of life on earth.

Life on earth began about two and a half billion years ago. About six hundred million years ago life forms began to leave traces behind in the form of fossils. These were trilo-bites, and some 2,500 species have been found, many, we are discovering, originating in an even earlier time. The Libyan Desert is rich in fossil history, perhaps the richest desert in the world.

Archean Era

The Archean Era, 'ancient age,' which began four thousand million years ago, was a period of great disturbance, when under great pressure the earth's surface folded and cracked along fault lines. These upheavals laid the foundation from which the oldest and strongest rocks in Egypt can be dated: the granite of the Red Sea Mountains, the base rock of the first cataract of the Nile at Aswan, and the lofty summits of Gebel Uwaynat in the southwestern corner of Egypt. These mineral-bearing strata contain gold, diorite, white silver, copper, and iron. At the end of the Archean Age, the Precambrian period saw the development of the land masses, the seas, the atmosphere, and simple plants, fungi, and algae. The Sea of Tethys, the ancestor of the Mediterranean Sea, probably formed at this time with its southern shore somewhere around modern day Fayoum.

GEOLOGICAL TIME

EPOCH		PERIOD	ERA	
Holocene				
Bronze	2,000			
Neolithic	6,000			
Terminal Paleolithic	9,000			
Pleistocene	10,000	Quarternary	**Cenozoic**	
Aterien	9,000			
Paleolithic	50,000			
Acheulen				
Pre-Acheulen	900,000			
	1,800,000			
Pliocene				
Miocene		Tertiary		
Oligocene				
Eocene				
Paleocene				- 65
	136 –	Cretaceous	**Meso-zoic**	
	190 –	Jurassic		
	280 –	Triassic		- 225
	320 –	Permian	**Paleozoic**	
	345 –	Carboniferous		
	395 –	Devonian		
	430 –	Silurian		
	500 –	Ordovician		
		Cambrian		
		Precambrian		-570

millions of years ago

Paleozoic Era

Scientists divide the Paleozoic Era, 'age of ancient life,' into six periods. For much of the **Cambrian** period, over a hundred million years, most of the earth, including Egypt, was submerged, and the fossils from this period, the first signs of life on earth, consist of simple algae, worms, and mollusks.

The **Ordovician** period, when life existed only underwater, and the Silurian period, which lasted for twenty million years, saw the reshaping of landmasses. Drifting continents clashed, creating mountains, until finally two super continents were formed, Laurasis in the north and Gondwanaland in the south.

During the **Devonian** period the earth's climate warmed and land masses collided to form a single continent, called Pangaea. This collision happened somewhere in the Libyan Desert, probably in northern Sudan. Although called 'the age of fishes,' fossils found in Egypt include evidence of forests, ferns, corals, and the first land animals—spiders, millipedes, and insects.

As its name suggests, the **Carboniferous** period saw the beginning of coal formations. Throughout the world there were shallow seas and swamps. Egypt was submerged by the first of three inundations. Uplifts at the end of this era caused the first sea to recede and Egypt to reappear as a landmass. Reptiles and amphibians such as snails, centipedes, scorpions, and giant dragonflies began to emerge. Carboniferous formations exist near Gebel Uwaynat in the southwestern corner of the Western Desert.

The **Permian** period, from 320 to 280 million years ago, saw Pangaea move north and glaciers move south. Mountains, ancestors of existing ranges, formed. The climate became cooler and dryer. Reptiles replaced amphibians as the dominant life form on earth and an insect group emerged.

Mesozoic Era

The Mesozoic Era, 'age of middle life,' is divided into three periods: Triassic, Jurassic, and Cretaceous. It was a time of reptiles, birds, mammals, flowering plants, and trees like elm, oak, and maple. Named for three *(tri)* strata of rocks, the **Triassic** period, forty-nine million years, saw the first mammals, dinosaurs, sponges, and protozoans. Only 50 square kilometers (31 square miles) in Eastern Sinai at Gebel Arif al-Naga contain evidence of this arid period. The Libyan Desert has no sediments from this period and so, it too, was probably arid and dry.

The **Jurassic** period lasted forty-six million years. The super continent Gondwanaland, of which Egypt was a part, broke into smaller continents. The climate was warm and moist and it was the age of the dinosaurs: the sauropods, stegosaurs, and theropods. Mammals and birds also began to emerge. Though much of Egypt continued to be uplifted, the northeastern section was now under water.

Named because of the massive chalk *(creta)* layers that were created during this time, the **Cretaceous** period lasted for seventy-two million years. Continents began to take shape. Mountains like the Rockies and Andes were created. Dinosaurs, which had existed on all continents and in Egypt at Maghra and Bahariya oases, became extinct. Oak trees and flowering plants like hickory and magnolia developed. Much of Egypt was submerged. Rock formations from this period, the Nubian sandstone south of Kharga and Dakhla oases and chalk north of Kharga to Bahariya Oasis, comprise two fifths of Egypt's landmass. At the end of this period upheaval occurred once more. This upheaval created an anticline, evident in southern Bahariya and northern Farafra (see Bahariya Oasis for details).

Fossils

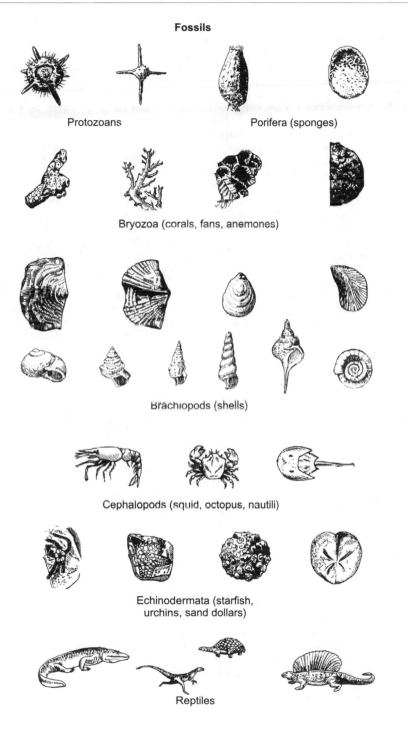

Protozoans   Porifera (sponges)

Bryozoa (corals, fans, anemones)

Brachiopods (shells)

Cephalopods (squid, octopus, nautili)

Echinodermata (starfish,
urchins, sand dollars)

Reptiles

Cenozoic Era

The Cenozoic Era, 'the age of recent life,' the current geological era, is divided into two periods the Tertiary and the Quarternary. In the **Tertiary** there are five epochs: Paleocene, Eocene, Oligocene, Miocene, and Pliocene. At last the earth warmed, modern continents formed, and mammals became the dominant species on earth. The first epoch of this era, **Paleocene**, 'old recent life,' saw the seas retreat, new mammals emerge, and gastropods and bivalves dominate the seas.

The 'dawn of recent life,' the **Eocene** epoch, lasted twenty-two million years and, although the climate was warm and mild, involved great upheavals. North America was cut off from Europe, South America from Antarctica. Familiar forms of life came into existence: true rodents, rhinoceroses, the early horse, giant pigs, ancestral camels, mastodons, saber-toothed cats, the first whales, and sea cows. The Eocene sea, which varied in size, covered Egypt as far south as Aswan, and the Old Libyan River of the Western Desert was formed. The mud left behind from the Eocene period is called Esna Shale and extends from Esna to Cairo along the western portion of Farafra and the plateau above the Kharga–Dakhla depressions. The latter stretches north to the Qattara–Siwa depressions. Eocene debris includes limestone, marl, and clay with marine fossils. Thebes limestone can be found on the fringes of the Farafra Depression.

The **Oligocene** epoch, 'few kinds of recent life,' lasted eleven million years. Antarctica became isolated. The climates cooled. Grazing and browsing animals multiplied. The outline of Africa emerged. It was a time when Egypt saw much faulting, folding, and volcanisms, accompanied by massive rainfalls. The land mass of the Western Desert reached north beyond the Fayoum Depression. Oligocene deposits of sand, fluvial gravel with fossil plants, petrified wood, and fossils of elephants, crocodiles, *Arsinoitherium* (a large, two-horned mammal), and other animals, were left between Fayoum and Bahariya. It is believed that the corpses of these animals were carried by the massive drainage system of the Old Libyan River to be deposited in bone beds. During the Eocene epoch the mouth of the river was near the western edge of Lake Qarun in the Fayoum, by the dawn of the Pliocene it was at Wadi Natrun (although by the end of the Pliocene the river was gone). When the Oligocene ended, Egypt, which was near the equator, drifted northward and rainfall ceased.

The 'less recent age,' the **Miocene** epoch, lasted twelve million years. During this epoch the Mediterranean Sea extended to Cairo. This was not a time of great change in Egypt. There was subsidence, but no tectonic activity of note. Miocene deposits cover most of the northern portion of the Western Desert including the Qattara Depression. The mastodon fossil found in the Maghra Oasis of the Qattara Depression is from this era. As the period drew to a close an uplifting of the land caused the sea to retreat and the Nile River to form.

The **Pliocene** epoch, 'more recent age,' also lasted twelve million years. There was a great glacial age in Europe, during which the Alps were formed. In Egypt, the gulfs of Suez and Aqaba were created by great rifts in the earth's crust. Typical Pliocene formations of marine, fluviomarine, and continental debris are rare in Egypt, but the second can be found in the northern escarpment of the Fayoum. Fossilized elephants, giraffes, and crocodiles have been found at Wadi Natrun. Despite glacial formations in Europe, moisture was not increasing in the Libyan Desert. The Old Libyan River disappeared. The landmass underwent periods of subsidence followed by periods of faulting and folding. This upheaval is evident in Bahariya Oasis in the form of a large fold that cuts through the entire depression. Once created, the depressions were covered by a lake and later, maybe, by a sea.

In the **Quarternary** period there are two epochs, the Pleistocene and Holocene. The

Pleistocene, 'most recent age,' lasted until 10,000 years ago. The Ice Age gripped Europe and the levels of the oceans fell, allowing more land to emerge from the water. Combined with the heavy rainfall were the beginnings of human beings and the extinction of many mammals like mammoths and saber-tooth tigers. It was during this epoch that the depressions of the Western Desert took their present form. The dry desert climate began around 8000 B.C.

The earliest traces of human beings in the Libyan Desert are found during the Pleistocene period, in the period we call the Paleolithic. From the scientific investigation we have learned that the Libyan Desert had (at least) four periods when it was wetter than present: Pre-late Acheulian, Acheulian, Paleolithic, and Post-Aterian Hyperarid Interval, all in the Pleistocene. One of these, the Paleolithic, brought a substantial population of cattle herders and hunters to the southeastern desert. Settlements throughout the desert from the Fayoum to the Sudanese border, from the Nile Valley at Maadi to the southwestern corner of the country at Uwaynat, tell us about these early peoples.

The **Holocene** epoch, 'the recent age,' is the present age. South of Kharga Oasis the Western Desert is composed of sandstone and is called the Nubian Sandstone Plateau. This plateau, recently named the Darb al-Arbain Desert, begins at Gebel Uwaynat and ends in the depressions of Kharga, Dakhla, and Abu Minqar. The Nubian Sandstone Plateau is then replaced by the limestone of the Gilf Kebir Plateau, which continues north until it, in turn, is replaced by the limestone Miocene Plateau, just south of the Qattara Depression. Called al-Diffa, this final landform continues to the coast.

The Holocene has three periods: Terminal Paleolithic, Neolithic, and Bronze. They lasted from about 10,000 years ago to 1,000 years ago.

Depressions and Oases

The depressions formed in the Pliocene epoch contain the famous oases of the Western Desert. Some Christian sects believe that Ham, the son of Noah, created the oases of the Libyan Desert. Called "Islands of the Blest" by Herodotus, the oases are seldom what visitors expect. They are not small areas of the desert offering scrub for animals, a few trees for shade, and enough water to quench one's thirst and fill a waterbag. This type of oasis exists, of course, at places like al-Shab in the southeastern section of the Western Desert. But the major oases are not like that at all. Nor is each depression a single continuous oasis, all lush and green.

The depressions are the same as the desert terrain that surrounds them, the difference being that they have fallen below the average surface of the desert and are near or at sea level, where subterranean water is easily accessible. Where this water comes to the surface plant and animal life can exist more easily than in other parts of the depression or the desert at large. In these places, either thanks to natural springs or tapped underground water, oases have come into existence. In each depression there may be dozens of such places. Some have become towns, others are used only as day stations by farmers.

There are seven major depressions in the Western Desert (the Libyan Desert has many more): Qattara, Kharga, Dakhla, Farafra, Bahariya, Siwa, and Fayoum. In addition there are minor depressions including Kurkur, Wadi Rayyan, Wadi Natrun, and Qara. All the depressions tend to be near a geological boundary and are surrounded totally or in part by a cliff called an escarpment or scarp, the top of which is at the level of the normal desert floor. The major depressions in Egypt all have northern escarpments, with Bahariya and Fayoum completely hemmed in. The first line of defense for the people who live in the oases, it wasn't until modern roads were built that the scarps were penetrated with ease.

How these depressions were formed has been a matter of great speculation, but the general consensus among geologists is that they are the result of the combined action of structural weaknesses, salt weathering, and wind erosion during the Pliocene epoch.

Sand and Sand Dunes

Sand is the final form of rock. The small grains come from quartz, sandstone, or igneous rocks that have been pounded round and smooth by the wind. In the Western Desert they are primarily 40 percent quartz. Sand is the final menace. Nothing stops it. The Great Sand Sea steadily moving south has begun to infiltrate into several high valleys in the northeastern corner of the Gilf Kebir. Slowly the sand is piling up in great waves against one of the sides of each valley. In January of 1998, climbing over each other piggy back style, a few dunes had actually reached the top of the plateau encroaching on Lama Point and Almasy Mountain. It is a horrific yet awesome view, as it becomes evident that a barrier the height and size of the Gilf Kebir cannot forestall the moving sand. It makes one believe that sand is truly the final form to which all things will be reduced.

Sand dunes, which exist only when there is enough fine-grained material to allow them to form, cover 40 percent of the Western Desert. Beginning around an obstruction, most sand dunes are constantly moving, their size, form, and speed determined by the force and direction of the wind. Without a good unidirectional wind, a dune isn't going anywhere. With a good wind, dunes will move at a rate of up to ten meters (32 feet) a year and rise as high as 156 meters (500 feet). That does not mean all sand dunes move. Some do not, as we shall see. Others behave without any logic at all. When Almasy, Clayton, and Penderel were exploring the Gilf Kebir in 1934, they found a series of dunes along its northwestern side 'guarding' the entrance to a pass. Upon their return a few days later, everything had changed. Their tracks were gone. Seif dunes had become whale dunes, whale dunes seif. New dunes had formed, smaller ones had vanished. There was no logic to it at all.

In the early 1970s, photographs of the earth's dune fields taken by Skylab 4 were studied by scientists, who then made a global classification of dunes. The object of the project was to compare dune fields around the globe with those found on Mars in an effort to better understand that planet. They categorized five major dune types: parallel straight dunes, parallel wavy dunes, star dunes, parabolic dunes, and sheets and stringers.

The **parallel straight dune** is long and slim with slipfaces on both sides and waves on top, just like a sea. In the past, scientists referred to them as longitudinal dunes. In the North African deserts they are called *seif*, sword, dunes because they look like the long, slender blades of Arab swords. They are formed by a unidirectional wind. Seif dunes are found mostly in the northern portions of the Libyan Desert, around the

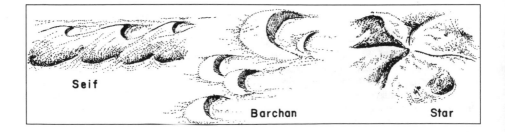

Seif   Barchan   Star

Qattara Depression in Egypt and in the Great Sand Sea in Egypt and Libya. Some of the seif dunes in the Great Sand Sea are as much as 145 kilometers (91 miles) long. When these dunes fall over something as big as an escarpment and reform at the base, they reform as crescent-shaped, or barchan, dunes. This is why seif formations dominate in the north of Egypt and crescent dunes dominate in Kharga and Dakhla. The dunes fell off the mountain.

Parallel wavy dunes are crescent-shaped dunes formed into straight lines that march like soldiers in a specific direction. Also called barchan dunes, their width is equal to their length, they have a single-sided slipface, and are often equidistant from each other. Corridors appear between them. In the Libyan Desert these dunes occur mostly in the south, in the Kharga Depression in Egypt (especially at Ain Umm Dabadib and Dush), and near Ghat in Libya. They can go as high as 94 meters (300 feet), extend for 375 meters (1,200 feet), and even while climbing over a large object, like a building, remain the same height. There are no bulges to indicate something is underneath. Barchan dunes can travel as much as 19 meters (60 feet) per year and change direction if the wind pattern changes. In Dakhla, individual dunes can be seen falling down the cliff of the escarpment only to reform and continue marching south once on the desert floor. The ends, or horns, of a barchan dune usually remain parallel and baby dunes are reproduced downwind from one of the horns of the parent dune. This is how chains of dunes are formed.

The **star dune** has been known by a number of names including polypyramid, mastodons, oghurds, khurds, draa peaks, and stellate roses. They do align in chains, but more often they are found in isolation. Star dunes are created by a wind that often changes direction. These dunes do not move forward, but turn round and round in the same spot, the sand accumulating from point to point in a constant circle. Star dunes have been found in the Erg Oriental of Algeria in the Sahara and in the northern Namib Desert of South West Africa. They are seldom seen in the Libyan Desert, but the Apollo–Soyuz team recorded one in the upper part of Wadi Bakht at the Gilf Kebir in 1979.

Giant crescent dunes are called whalebacks or megabarchan. These magnificent mountains of sand are created when a series of dunes pile together, one on top of the other. When they collide, the smallest dune simply climbs up the back of the others. The sides of the dunes point in various directions and reflect the light like the facets of a diamond. A particularly fine grouping of whale dunes can be found on the way to Ain Umm Dabadib in Kharga Oasis.

Parabolic dunes are U- or V-shaped dunes also called upsiloidal. The edges of the arms are held in place by vegetation. None are known in the Libyan Desert. There are also compound parabolic dunes, some as long as 40 kilometers (25 miles). Skylab found some of these monsters in the Thar Desert of India and Pakistan, but none in the Western Desert.

Sheets and Stringers are flat, hard, sheets of sand that go on for miles. The north-western coast of Africa including Mauritania and the Spanish Sahara has sand sheets and stringers. The Darb al-Arbain Desert in the southeast corner of Egypt has the Selima Sand Sheet.

Dune Fields

Dunes do not move alone, they travel in groups. According to Farouk al-Baz of the Center for Remote Sensing at Boston University, there are 32 dune fields in the desert area in North Africa. He has concluded that the sand came to the desert because of running surface water. The wind reshaped the sand into dunes.

John Ball, in 1898, believed a dune field would move at about 15 meters (48 feet) a

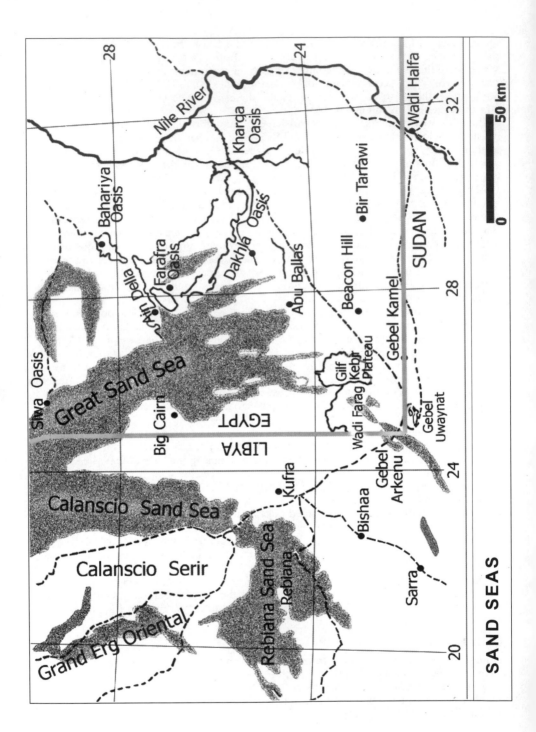

SAND SEAS

year, with large dunes moving slower and small dunes faster. He estimated the Abu Muharrik belt (see Western Desert map) at 350 kilometers (219 miles) was not only one of the largest dune fields in Egypt but that it was moving at 10 meters (32 feet) a year and was about 35,000 years old. A more recent study by N. S. Embabi, with the use of aerial photographs, space images, and new topographical maps, further defines the dune belt. In 1996, almost a hundred years after Ball's observations, the dune field measured 500 kilometers (300 miles) and covered about 6,000 square kilometers (3,750 square miles). In the north the chain is seif dunes, but once they fall from the Kharga escarpment they become barchan. These dunes moved at a rate of 9 meters (29 feet) a year from 1930 to 1961. Embabi estimates that the "last dunes at the southern margins of Kharga, which lie at about 200 kilometers from its northern scarps, entered the depression 22,000 years ago."

One cannot wander long in the Western Desert without running into a dune field. They are scattered everywhere. In the north they flow in a north-northwesterly direction, while in the south they move north–northeasterly. Dunes are especially prominent southwest of Fayoum, Areg, Wadi Rayyan, Wadi Mawalih, north of the Giza Pyramids, and between Bahnasa and Mallawi near the Nile Valley. The Western Desert map at the beginning of this chapter shows most of the dune fields in the Western Desert.

Sand Seas

Then there are the sand seas. These are great expanses of sand. In Algeria, in the Sahara, there is the Grand Erg Occidental in the northwestern part of the country, south of the Atlas Mountains in Morocco, and the Grand Erg Oriental in the northeastern part of the country, which runs into Tunisia. There are three major sand seas in the Libyan Desert, the Rebiana Sand Sea and the Calanscio Sand Sea, both in Libya, and the Great Sand Sea, the largest, which falls out of Libya into Egypt.

The Great Sand Sea enters Egypt just to the west of Siwa and continues southeast, staying to the west of Ain Della, Farafra, and Dakhla. It splits into three major fingers, the eastern one ending above and to the east of Abu Ballas, the middle one ending to the northwest of Abu Ballas, and the western one splitting into a number of paths but all ending north of the Gilf Kebir.

In 1981 imaging radar on NASA's Space Shuttle found ancient river beds under the sand. (For more details on the Great Sand Sea see Uwaynat).

Water

Generally, deserts don't have a lot of water; that is the missing ingredient. Not so the Libyan Desert. There is plenty of water. The trouble is, it is not easily accessible. In 1927 John Ball, in "Problems of the Libyan Desert," concluded that water is trapped in subterranean chambers throughout the thousands of kilometers of the Libyan Desert. He was right. It is easily accessible in the depressions, where the floor of the desert is near or below sea level and water gushes from natural springs or can be tapped by drilling wells. Here the land is productive, while the rest of the desert lies barren.

This underground water is believed to originate in the rains of Equatorial Africa. Taking thousands of years on its journey north, the water works its way through underground fissures to the Mediterranean Sea. The more southern the source, the fresher the water. Kharga, Dakhla, and Bahariya oases have the sweetest and most plentiful water supply, while Siwa, in the north, has highly saline water. That does not mean that all the springs in an oasis are sweet. Many are brackish and unpleasant to the taste, but all contain gases and minerals of great medicinal value.

Birs and Ains

The oaseans extract trapped water by drilling artesian wells. These wells, providing the very lifeblood of existence, are of three types: modern; *Romani*, ancient wells drilled by the Egyptians and Romans; or aqueducts, of which we will hear more later. There are an amazing number of them—420 *Romani* wells in Dakhla Oasis alone and a similar number in the other oases. Drilling a well is a laborious process taking up to six months. Often the expense and labor are shared by the farmers expected to use the well. Although there are plenty of cold water wells, the majority of the wells in the Western Desert are hot, with temperatures sometimes exceeding 100 degrees Fahrenheit. That means they are deep, for deep wells produce hot water. Wells that produce hot water are described as thermal.

The village wells were once centers of the community where the people met to exchange news. The hot springs were used to wash clothes and dishes (one spring in Dakhla was used to boil eggs), and hours were specified for bathing. Bathing was usually at night, when the stars twinkled like tiny lights, the Milky Way hung heavy as clotted cream in the sky, and the moon sent an unforgettable halo of color over the land. That was ten years ago, and had probably been the same for thousands of years before that. Today modern plumbing is reaching the oases and fewer and fewer people use the wells as gathering places.

In each oasis at least one spring has been set aside for tourists. Almost every new hotel opening in the desert features a hot spring either on the facilities or nearby. It is one of the great pleasures of the desert.

Out of Water

When will the water run out? This question hangs over life in the Libyan Desert. For the past quarter of a century it has been the consensus view that the water under the desert is nonrenewable. When it runs out it will be gone forever. It is predicted that the water will be gone in 100 years if consumption remains at the current rate. However, some new studies maintain that the water is in fact replenishing itself regularly. If this is true, then there is no problem with water in the desert, but skeptics doubt its accuracy.

A related concern for Egypt is the huge water scheme undertaken by Libya in the last decades. The underground water at Kufra Oasis has been tapped to create 'a river in the desert.' The artesian water level in Egypt is falling a meter per year, some believe as a direct result of the Libyan project. This is serious. Rushdi Said, former director of the Geological Survey, acknowledges that this is a complicated problem, but he does not believe the Libyan scheme is a threat. "The underground water is not in a single reservoir, but in many reservoirs," says Said, who believes the Kufra water is separate from the Western Desert water.

Fog and Rain

Although there is practically no rain in the Western Desert, there is fog and dew. Fog is most common in the fall, but can occur even in the middle of summer. Heavy morning mists create an eerie atmosphere and gently drop life-giving moisture like a blanket on the sands. This moisture provides drinking water for insects, reptiles, and mammals. It also waters the plants that grow in the highly saline soil. Although salt is the primary factor affecting desert waste, it is also the salt that helps natural desert flora survive. Moisture is attracted to the salt where it accumulates, allowing plants to drink. High on the Gilf Kebir the dew freezes on the sand dunes overnight as the temperature falls, then in the early dawn the dunes, looking like icicles lying on their sides, slowly shed the moisture as the sun rises.

And in fact it does rain. Seldom, but when it does the desert comes alive. Rain is reputed to have saved the Rohlfs expedition in the winter of 1874. English-language texts maintain they were locked into the Great Sand Sea, out of water and out of time. And it rained. This is the equivalent of snow falling on Aswan or icebergs forming in the Caribbean. It rained enough to fill their water tanks, refresh their camels, and save their lives. That is a lot of rain. (For the Rohlfs water controversy, see People.)

H. E. Winlock recorded a similar rain on May 18, 1908, while he was at Deir al-Hagar in Dakhla, not too far from where Rohlfs met his rain. "It grew warmer in the afternoon, clouds gathered, at 2:20 p.m. rain began to patter, and 10 minutes later we were in the midst of a cyclonic disturbance that kept things lively around the tent for half an hour."

The same thing happen to this author on February 20, 1998. We had a deluge for about 20 minutes while we were at Deir al-Hagar. Everything was soaked. Then the sun came out and so did a rainbow. Yes, a rainbow. Could anything be more spectacular? That was the same day we had rain between Abu Minqar and Dakhla. The previous month, on January 19, 1998, at 5:13 in the early dawn, it began to gently rain at our camp in the Great Sand Sea. The patter continued on our tents until 5:20. Throughout our entire trip we saw evidence of rain in places where it was not supposed to rain for ten to twenty years at a time. The top of the Gilf Kebir had had rain, as had the Wadi Abd al-Malik.

During 1998 weather patterns all over the world were affected by El Niño, a hot water spot in the Pacific Ocean that affects weather around the globe. El Niño was unusually large and warm during the winter of 1997–98. Could El Niño, lying off the coast of South America and devastating the west coast of the United States with rain and mudslides, be affecting the desert in North Africa?

Wind

Wind is the alpha and omega of the Western Desert. It creates and destroys the landscape, blasting against mountains and carving out depressions. Its unrelenting movement establishes the direction of the dune belts, dehydrates the plant and animal life, and pulverizes mountains until they breakdown and turn to sand. It prematurely ages the skin and is the main factor in heat stroke.

When moisture dominates, it erodes the land, but here in the Western Desert, where it has been arid since at least 5000 B.C., the wind creates and destroys. Farouk al-Baz and R. W. Wolfe tell us that the wind in the Libyan Desert is influenced by two factors, the seasonal high pressure areas and the Inter-Tropical Convergence Zone (ITCZ). The latter follows the path of the sun and "may play the greatest role in determining the winds of southern Egypt and the Western Desert." In the winter, from December to February, it is to the south. In the spring, from March to May, it moves northward. In summer, from June to September, it reaches northern Sudan, and in autumn it retreats south again. All of this affects the direction of the wind. The winter winds are north–northwesterly, except in northern Egypt where they are south–southwesterly. In spring, sandstorms arrive, brought on by the strong southern winds. In summer, the winds are northerly, and in autumn, as the ITCZ retreats, the winds are at their lowest.

The wind is constant in the desert, sometimes merely a breeze, but often a steady blast. When it does die for a few minutes at dawn and dusk each day the silence is almost unbearable, similar to the time just before a great storm.

Sandstorms

Blowing slightly west of north, the wind carries the sandstorm. Sandstorms can happen at any time and come in varying degrees of intensity, from slight gusts that swirl sand over the road and create wind devils—*zazaya bi-l-gebel*—to terrifying gales that can sand blast the paint off a car and get into every crease and crevice imaginable. In the Western Desert sandstorms are to be expected during November and December, but may occur anytime.

In the spring, from March to May comes the special sandstorm, the *khamasin* (the 50). The season lasts for 50 days, and most storms are a few days in duration. Called *siroccos* in Morocco, *qibli* in Libya, *cheheli* in the northern Sahara, *irifi* along the coast, and *ouahdy* in the central Sahara, the storms of North Africa each have their own special personality. Some, like the *khamasin*, are hot winds, others cold winds, but all are laden with sand and dust. The *khamasin* blows from the south to the northwest, in opposition to the prevailing winds. The *harmattan* in West Africa is a cold northeasterly wind that blows in November through February. The *simum*, 'poison wind,' is hot and dry and temperatures reach $55°$ C or $130°$ F. The *habub* is hot and moist and is prevalent along the southern edges of the Sahara and in Sudan. It carries sandstorms and duststorms, but can also be the harbinger of thunderstorms and small tornadoes. With each storm lasting about three hours, the *haboob* is mostly a summer affair. Its wall of sand and dust can be as high as 900 meters (3,000 feet).

Like the regular sandstorm, all of the storms can be minor irritations that affect the sinuses and make the day uncomfortable, or they can last for days, turning the sky dull yellow and laying low everything in their path. In the open spaces of the desert one can often see the storm coming. The air grows still and in the distance a huge dull yellow or black wall of sand and wind stretches into the sky, sometimes thousands of feet high.

Stones, Oils, and Gases

Egypt has an abundance of minerals, including, says Rushdi Said, former director of the Geological Survey, "gold, copper, tin, tungsten, lead, zinc, nickel, chrome, iron, titanium, beryllium, talc, barite, asbestos, graphite, phosphate, marble, and alabaster."

The Eastern Desert is loaded. The Western Desert, dramatically larger, considerably more inhospitable, far more barren, far less studied, has yielded less. Although there is the dolorite for Chephren's immortal statue, there is no wonderful porphyry for statues or bowls. There is iron ore at Bahariya and it has fed a steel industry for several decades. There is phosphate in Kharga Oasis and its development is underway. Said says it is not that the minerals are not there, but that the sands of the Libyan Desert have covered them up.

Through the centuries different desert stones have been held in esteem. The ancient Egyptians of the Old Kingdom used basalt from Abu Rawwash and Widan al-Faras (Fayoum) to pave the funerary temples. Of course, granite was used throughout all the phases of the ancient civilization, as were the salts and natron (sodium carbonate) from Wadi Natrun. Even ancient Egyptian cosmetics came from the deserts: limestone and gypsum produced white, ochers yielded yellows and reds, malachite created green, azurite was blue, and black was created by burned woods mixed with oils. For adornment, the ancient Egyptians had 90 gold mines, none of which were in the Western Desert. Today we know that gold is found in the southwestern corner at Gebel Kamil. Lapis lazuli is found in the remote regions of Gebel Uwaynat. Silver was, and is, imported.

During the Middle and New Kingdoms, sandstone became the stone of choice for buildings. And in Ptolemaic times the iron deposits in Bahariya Oasis were used. The Greeks also enjoyed emeralds and peridot. They were found in the Eastern Desert and the islands in the Red Sea. The Romans imported Egyptian alum found in the southern portion of the Western Desert. And it was during this time that glass became a major Egyptian product. Alexandria became the center of the glass-making industry, which relied heavily on the salts from Wadi Natrun.

In Islamic times the deserts were almost shut down and Egypt imported its gold from the caravans of West Africa. But alum was definitely mined in the oases until it was discovered in Asia and imported. Gypsum, mined in the Fayoum and along the northern coast near Alexandria, was used for architectural ornamentation in many mosques.

Oil and Gas

By 1974, the Egyptian General Petroleum Corporation had contracted 100 agreements with 40 companies, and the Red Sea became the main oil producing area of the country. Oil exploration did not begin in the Western Desert until 1940 and no oil was discovered in the Western Desert until 1955, when the al-Alamein field began to produce. By 1983, 223 exploratory wells had been drilled and over 150,000 kilometers (94,000 miles) of seismic work had been completed. Yet, while Libya enjoys large deposits, oil remains the most elusive of treasures in Egypt. In 1996, 32 companies were operating in Egypt, 12 in oil and 20 in gas.

Natural gas is abundant in the Western Desert. With a reserve of 21 trillion cubic meters (67 trillion cubic feet), 421 billion cubic feet were produced in 1994. Gas represented 35 percent of the country's total energy consumption and was used for 80 percent of the fuel for electricity. Plans for expansion in both domestic use and exportation are underway. Foreign companies have been offered incentives to explore for natural gas.

Fossils

The Libyan Desert is host to a multitude of fossils, the remains of plants or animals that have been preserved in sedimentary rocks. Fossils can be a variety of things: a cast or mold of an object, a piece of a skeleton, a footprint, animal droppings and trails, or, rarely, a complete organism. They are classified into type, class, order, and families, with each individual organism bearing a scientific name. Fossils of prehistoric animals have been found in many areas of the Libyan Desert, with spectacular finds in the Fayoum and the Qattara Depression. (See individual sections for details.)

Petrified Wood

Medusa has been held responsible for turning the great trees of the Libyan Desert to stone. One look from her frightening eyes was enough to petrify any living thing. In truth, however, the petrified forests of the North African deserts are the remains of thousands of trees that existed in the distant past. Through a natural process over an extended period of time they have been turned into silica. They retain their original shape, down to the fine splinters of wood and the central rings that mark the age of the trees, but the wood has been replaced by a hard, almost glassy substance. This is done in one of two ways: bubbles or replacement. In the former, bubbles of silica (or calcite, pyrite, or marcasite) dissolve and seep over and into the oxygen-denied, decaying wood. The silica gradually fills the pores, turning the tree to stone but keeping its form and texture. In the latter, the molecules of the tree are completely replaced by the silica. Either process is thought to take millions of years, although recent experiments in

Yellowstone National Park in the United States have shown that in a rich silica environment, under certain conditions, the process can be relatively short.

There are many petrified forests in the Sahara and Libyan deserts and a short walk in any spot will produce a small specimen of petrified wood. One must not expect standing trees with their roots firmly planted in the ground, however. These are fallen forests, with trees fragmented into millions of pieces, leaving an occasional large log that has not disintegrated.

There are dozens of mountains throughout both the Eastern and Western deserts bearing the name Gebel Khashab, Wood Mountain, and the desert track running due north from Asmant in Dakhla Oasis is called Darb al-Khashabi, the Wooden Road. Petrified wood can be found here in quantity. There is a great deal of petrified wood along the route to Bahariya, and at Qattara it is so plentiful that the Bedouin use it to outline graves. The routes to Ain Amur and Ain Umm Dabadib have scattered heaps along the way. Within 80 kilometers (50 miles) of the Giza Pyramids lies a forest where, according to R. A. Bagnold, "They [the tree trunks] were scattered everywhere over the country, sometimes singly, sometimes in tumbled heaps, mostly intact save for the leaves and smaller branches. One could see the details of the bark, the very pores of the wood and the knots from which big boughs had parted . . . for all this tropical life had been turned ages ago to a stone so permanent that untold centuries of driving sand have not defaced it."

Plants and Animals

The Libyan Desert is the most sterile desert in the world. Flora has to be sturdy to survive, for in some areas it has not rained for thirty years. Yet, when the occasional rain does fall, the dormant seedlings burst into bloom and the desert floor is a carpet of beauty. During the short lifetime of the bloom, complete cycles that would normally take a full season are completed in a few days so that the seedlings can be replenished. This is when the desert is at its most surprising, when it smiles. The most typical flora of the desert includes acacia and palm trees, salt bushes, and sage, together with varieties of bushes and plants that have adapted to the harsh environment.

Water is and always has been a determining factor for life in the desert. Adaptability is another. Animals living in desert climates develop features unique to their species that enable them to withstand the harsh conditions. As with the flowers and plants, the lifecycles of smaller animals and insects are shortened and their eggs lie dormant over long periods awaiting a great burst of life.

Most of the fauna is nocturnal, so do not count on seeing much and put your food away in sealed containers at night unless you want visitors. Even if you do not see them, in the morning you will find plenty of trails left by insects, and sometimes larger animals, in and around your camp.

Insects and Reptiles

In 1874 P. Ascherson collected 400 different types of insects. The children of the oases would follow behind him and bring him plants and insects. He must have asked them for unusual things because they came bearing a lizard with a broken tail, a cricket with three legs, or a mouse with no ears. Among the insects are varieties of ants, beetles—including the famous scarab beetle of ancient Egypt—moths, spiders, ticks, wasps, centipedes, snails, scorpions, and locusts. Scorpions will sting, but the sting is usually not fatal. Locusts have been a plague since biblical times.

White snails are prevalent along the northern coast and throughout the Qattara Depression. They may not look it but, as one of my traveling companions discovered, they are alive. She put two shells in her jacket and upon returning to Cairo put her jacket in the closet. The next time she took out her jacket the snails had made a mess in her pocket. They had survived on some famous Mersa Matruh pumpkin seeds. In R. S. Gwatkin Williams' book *In the Hands of the Senussi* we are told that the English soldiers captured from the *Tara* had only these snails for survival.

The locust of the Western Desert comes in two varieties, the solitary locust, which creates little harm, and the migratory locust, which can devastate an area in a matter of minutes. The former is small and pale, while the latter is dark with orange and yellow markings. Interestingly, both can come from the same nest of eggs. Lack of food may be a factor for migration, but we are not really sure. What we do know is that the locusts' flight ends in death. The swarm gathers prior to mating and begins its journey after the female has deposited her eggs. There is no pattern to the yearly flights, and the swarm may take off in any direction.

There are thirty-seven varieties of snakes in Egypt and seven are poisonous. Among the poisonous varieties are the cobra, spitting cobra, and horned viper. Although one seldom sees a snake in the desert, precautions must be taken. Some live in the dunes, many burrow under the sand and are not visible at all. They are waiting for some unsuspecting target to pass by. They also live in crevices and cool places, like caves. Snakes come out to drink at night and hibernate in the winter.

Mammals

Among the smaller animals are weasels, hares, gerbils, mice, and rats. Two of the most fascinating animals in the desert are the fennec fox, with its large ears and big eyes, and the tiny hedgehog. The fennec is an excellent example of how animals adapt to desert life. The large ears and huge eyes that make it so endearing to humans enable the fennec to hear and see better than most desert animals. A nocturnal creature, the hedgehog lives on insects and can sometimes be seen, or heard, foraging around a camp at night, grunting and snorting as it looks for food. When frightened, the hedgehog rolls itself into a spiky ball.

Although most visitors seldom see large animals in the desert, they do exist. Among the largest are the Barbary sheep, mainly found around the Gilf Kebir; cheetah, oryx, and jackals in the Qattara Depression; and hyenas, gazelles, and cats roaming throughout the Libyan Desert. William Eaton saw an ostrich along the northern coast on his journey to Libya in 1805. Archibald Edmondstone said there were "lions and tigers (hyaenas?)," in Dakhla around 1820 and they were not uncommon; but "there are no ostriches." Wally Lama saw two ostriches heading for Egypt while she was in northern Sudan in 1984. Ball, in 1897, said that jackals "abound in Dakhla, especially near Qasr Dakhla, Birbaya and Ufaima, where they are frequently a great source of annoyance owing to the din they make at night." G. W. Murray claims to have seen cheetah footprints only 100 miles west of the Great Pyramid in the 1920s and "knows" that "Abu Fideil killed the last addax in Egypt by running it down with his car

Hedgehog

Fennec Fox

Barbary Sheep

near al-Shab while on Clayton's 1931 expedition." As late as 1998, workers on the new al-Sheikh Zayed Canal in the Arbain Desert needed sharpshooters on the lookout at night to protect them from marauding wolves.

On his 1938 trip to Gilf Kebir and Gebel Uwaynat Bagnold encountered a *waddan* or wild sheep at Karkur Murr. When he approached one of the huts, it came rushing out. "As he trotted away I saw that his mane of chest hair reached to the ground, trailing between his forelegs. It has recently been said in Cairo that these animals were extinct at Uweinat, but we saw many." He goes on to say there was plenty of wildlife at Karkur Talh too, including gazelle and foxes, and that at Gebel Kissu the plants were in full flower in March. As for the Barbary sheep there was plenty of evidence that they were roaming the top of Gilf Kebir on our expedition in January 1998. Small circular patches of dusty sand peeked through the blackish earth where they had stopped to roll in the sand and their sandy-colored footprints were easily seen in the open areas of the Gilf.

If you see any wild animal in the desert, it is most likely to be a gazelle. There were once herds of gazelles throughout all the deserts of Egypt. P. A. Clayton found twenty-three of them dead or dying in the Qattara Depression. They had fallen off a cliff after what Clayton surmised was a chase by a cheetah. Now one is lucky to glimpse one or two scurrying away.

African elephant remains have been found at Bir Kiseiba and in Kharga Oasis, both places at Neolithic sites. Probably the last area of North Africa where elephants existed was the Atlas Mountains in Morocco; but alas, that, too, was long ago, probably in the Byzantine period. Their disappearance was partly due to the Roman hunger for exotic animals to die in the arenas. In one set of games sponsored by Augustus, 3,500 African animals were slaughtered.

It was the camel that made desert travel possible, and it came late to North Africa. According to Bovill in *Caravans of the Old Sahara*, the first news of the camel comes at the Battle of Thapsus in 46 B.C., when Julius Caesar took twenty-two as booty. By A.D. 363, four thousand of them were demanded by the Romans for Leptis Magna, which sat at the head of the Garamantian Road in what is now Libya. These sturdy, violent beasts have natural defenses against harsh conditions.

Everyone knows that a camel can go for long periods without water, but they are especially suited to the desert in other ways too. Their feet are covered with pliable sturdy pads that travel as well on sand as gravel. Their knees are padded so they can rest on them. Their noses have filters and their eyes have a second membrane and extra lashes to keep out sand. Their lips thicken when they eat thorny plants.

Most camels stand over 2.1 meters (7 feet) high and average over 122 kilos (400 pounds). They live an average of forty-five years. Their thick hairy coat keeps them warm in winter and sheds to keep them cool in summer. They walk at a pace, moving both legs on one side at the same time. Although mostly domesticated, some camels live in the wild in Farafra. Their hump is made of fat, not water, and it stores the energy needed for long periods without food or drink.

The Bedouin have names for their camels at every stage of life, variety of color, size, strength, stubbornness, and valor. The Rashida of Sudan train their camels to crawl forward and backward on their knees, to race, to move without making a sound, and to carry up to 262 kilograms (800 pounds) of cargo. One of the last enclaves of nomadic lifestyle and master camel trainers, the Rashida still come to the southern oases from time to time to pasture their animals, and sometimes they stay at Wadi al-Gamel in

Bahariya. The Tuareg camels are taught to move quickly through the desert at a gait of 6.4 kilometers (4 miles) an hour, traveling in a straight line without losing direction.

Archibald Edmondstone saw a curious thing in Dakhla Oasis in 1819. When a baby camel was born the Bedouin beat its legs against the ground very hard. When he protested he was told this harsh treatment would make the joints supple. Hassanein tells us that the camel will instinctively continue to move to safety during a sandstorm, but as soon as it rains it sits down. The idea being that a sandstorm will bury it, but the rain will provide sustenance.

In Egypt, there aren't as many camels as one might suppose. There never were. Most of the camels are brought north by the Rashida over caravan trails like the Darb al-Galaba close to the Nile Valley (see Kharga Oasis and Darb al-Arbain for details). It takes them sixteen days to get to Daraw, just south of Kom Ombo, where camels are sold in the market. Whereas a few years ago they continued their journey north to Cairo, now camels are mostly shipped by truck and train up the Nile Valley. They do not use the ancient Darb al-Arbain because it is too far west for their needs.

Birds

The ancient Egyptians had a special fondness for birds, which they used as hieroglyphic symbols and as manifestations for some of the gods. It is no wonder, since they were so abundant. Egypt is on one of the world's major migratory paths. These visitors, combined with the abundance of resident birds, make the country a bird lover's paradise. Mass migration takes place in the fall when the birds leave the cooling climates of Europe and Central Asia, and in the spring when they return to enjoy the summer in the north. Most birds that follow the broad front migration across the Mediterranean continue their journey south down the Nile Valley, but many continue over the desert, a frightening barrier. Some stop in the southern oases of Kharga and Dakhla to spend the winter, but most continue south of Egypt into Central Africa.

Schweinfurth tells of a caravan out of Darfur along the Darb al-Arbain that got lost and as it unknowingly approached Baris in Kharga Oasis found a pool of water filled with wild geese. Rohlfs comments on migrating swallows near Kufra in 1879. Archibald Edmondstone saw coveys of partridges along the Darb al-Tawil on his journey to Dakhla in 1819. Each season around 1900, André von Dumreicher saw thousands of quail in markets along the northern coast, captured by Bedouin with nets during migration. When in season they were served in every restaurant in Alexandria.

On his trek from Kufra to Darfur via Gebel Uwaynat, Hassanein actually had a small bird land on his head and shoulder, mistaking him, Hassanein supposed, for a tree in this barren place. He gave it water and it began its southern journey again. One April in the 1930s, Robert Clayton-East-Clayton and Count Almasy encountered migrating plover moving north around Bir Mesaha. Almasy actually stayed behind when Sir Robert went back to Kharga for petrol, "to see what it felt like to be alone in the desert for a few days."

In 1929, west of Ain Della in the Great Sand Sea, Bagnold found a 16-foot-high rock pillar. Its sides were white with bird droppings and at its base were dozens of skeletons of hawks, jerboas, and little birds, mostly pied wagtails. The same thing was found near Selima just beyond the Egyptian border with Sudan, where there is a rock called Burg al-Tuyur, Tower of the Birds. At this spot in 1927 Shaw and Newbold collected the skins of the Abyssinian white-eye, European golden oriole, hoopoe, chiffchaff, red-throated pipit, and a martin.

In early March of 1938, Bagnold spent a few days by himself at the Gilf Kebir while his party went back to Kharga for supplies. "Each evening the solitude was broken by loud and deep-throated talk coming from far up in the sky where, on their leisurely migration northward to the African coast, flights of cranes circled and recircled while waiting for their laggard friends. Farther south, just east of Uwainat, we found flights of these great birds rallying daily some three hours earlier in the afternoon."

On the same trip Bagnold saw more cranes on his way to Selima to pick up petrol: "We also passed a large flight of cranes resting on the sand like a party of tourists on a beach. There were many single birds too, from other migrations."

Bird watchers will enjoy spotting birds all over the desert. Birds of prey, such as hawks and vultures, are found everywhere: at Wadi Natrun, along the northern coast, and especially in the Fayoum and the agricultural fields of Dakhla Oasis. The Fayoum has so many water birds they cannot be counted. In Wadi Natrun special sightings include Kittlitz's plover and blue-cheeked bee-eaters. Around Abu Simbel one encounters rare species: long-tailed cormorants, pink-backed pelicans, yellow-billed storks, African skimmers, pink-headed doves, and African pied wagtails.

2

The People and Explorers of the Desert

In prehistory the desert was not a desert. The climate was mild, and there was plenty of rainfall. People established villages around rivers and lakes, and lived, probably contentedly, as hunters, gatherers, and eventually farmers. The oldest known village in all of Egypt, and perhaps all of Africa, is found at the Nabta Playa in the southeastern desert south of the Chephren quarries and north of Abu Simbel. In almost every major oasis and along the entire southern desert from Gebel Uwaynat and Gilf Kebir to Lake Nasser and the Nile River there is rubble left behind by people during these hospitable times. Then the climate conditions changed, the waterways dried up, habitation decreased, and the people emigrated.

We know of four such cycles in prehistory. The earliest known to date is Acheulian (see chart in Chapter 1). Although the final word is not in, two Late Acheulian sites have been found in Dakhla and another, Final Acheulian, at Bir Sahara in the southeastern section of the Darb al-Arbain Desert.

We have more evidence of life during the Middle Paleolithic. In fact, the desert, where few people have disturbed the terrain, is yielding more information about early life than the Nile Valley, which has been under almost constant habitation. At Bir Sahara, at least five periods of occupation have been identified. This research is still in the very early stages and it has not yet been possible to compare these sites with discoveries outside the Western Desert. But by the Middle Paleolithic there were rhino, buffalo, giant camel, ass, gazelle, and antelope. This was about 44,000 years ago. Then another dry period came, and this one lasted a long, long time.

As far as we know, the Western Desert was abandoned from the end of the Middle Paleolithic to the beginning of the Holocene, when rainfall made it habitable again. During the Holocene, round hut settlements developed, as did industry. Evidence of Terminal Paleolithic, the last Old Stone Age existence, is found in Kharga, Nabta, and primarily at Bir Kiseiba. In Kharga, the sites are from 7850 B.C. and 7855 B.C.

The next phase of habitation is the Neolithic, still in the Early Holocene. Now the desert became more densely populated and this period provides an important record of the spread of agriculture and food production. In addition to nomads, the people lived in Siwa, Kharga, Dakhla, Farafra, Fayoum, Nabta Playa, Bir Kiseiba, Gilf Kebir, and Uwaynat.

The lineage of these early peoples is hard to identify. For the most part they are the ancestors of many of the current occupants of the Libyan Desert. They may well be the ancestors of the Garamantians, Goraan, Tebu, Tuareg, Berber, and Kababish. There is no doubt that some of them are the ancestors of the current inhabitants of the oases. They may even be ancestors of some Nile Valley peoples. One thing we know for sure, they are not the ancestors of the Bedouin, for the Bedouin came to the Libyan Desert centuries later.

The People

The harsh environment of the desert forged the character of desert people. Food and water were scarce, so they subsisted on very little. Strangers needed to survive too and often took what they wanted, so strangers were not welcome. The desert sun and wind were debilitating, so cloth was wrapped about the head and down the nape of the neck to hold moisture. Loose, layered, garments were worn, which absorbed the rays of the sun and allow the breeze to circulate, cooling the body.

Nature was the teacher. People traveled by the stars at night and known landmarks by day, using their own shadow as a compass. Tracking became a highly developed skill. A good tracker knew who, what, when, where, and even why. They were able to tell not only the time a person passed, but sometimes identified the person. They could tell the direction and origin of the journey, including its destination, and could also estimate the weight and contents of the load.

Dumreicher in *Trackers and Smugglers in the Deserts of Egypt* tells of a Bedouin woman at Wadi Natrun. She had been watering her flock of sheep and goats and they had mingled with four other flocks, each with about 100 animals. After the flocks had departed, the woman returned to the well, studied the tracks, and went in search of three missing animals. She picked the right tracks and returned with her animals in tow.

In this manner, the people discovered, named, and moved over the tracks that today link the towns and villages in the desert. They crossed these tracks as invaders who assaulted not only the fortress towns established in the oases but Nile Valley towns as well. They were also called upon to serve as caravan leaders, responsible for the lives of thousands of people. They were superstitious and often sought good omens. A caravan was considered lucky if it found dates along the trail, so friends would often sneak out and place dates in the path of the caravan as it got underway.

Two elements combined to bring about the death of the nomadic way of life: the establishment of modern nations and the motorized vehicle. Nations contained them and wanted them to stay in one place, as is the case in Egypt. The car, truck, and airplane diminished distances, and made the camel obsolete. A decade ago, most of the tribal peoples of the Libyan Desert lived permanently on the fringes of the cultivated land. They no longer roamed the desert as they had done for thousands of years. They had bowed to the pressures of the modern world and had become dependent upon it. It, in turn, provided them with a subsistence existence. If one wanted to know anything about the desert, it was to the their elders one had to go because the young men no longer traveled the desert routes.

Today this is changing. Throughout the oases the young men are exploring the desert once again. Using 4x4s and GPSs they are rediscovering the old routes traveled by their grandfathers. This time they are learning the routes not to lead camel caravans to the Nile Valley for food, but to lead foreigners into the desert in search of adventure. They are buying camels and re-learning the ancient ways.

Garamantians

The Garamantians were a tribal people who lived in the Fezzan, specifically the Wadi Ajal, before 1000 B.C. Their capital was Garama (the modern oasis of Germa or Djerma in Libya), and from it they controlled the famous caravan route from what is now

Tripoli to Lake Chad. The Carthaginians traded with them and employed them to lead their caravans into the desert. The Romans were never able to subdue them and also hired them as caravan leaders to the interior of Africa. They are probably responsible for many of the rock carvings found throughout the Libyan and Sahara deserts. Some of these depict them on their many raids in a much milder desert, probably a savanna, on chariots led by horses. In their necropolis at Garama there are over 40,000 graves and one hundred pyramid tombs. We do not know how this relates them to the Nile Valley, but it probably does. Their tombs reveal a tall people, with straight profiles, and small noses. They may have been fair skinned, some blond. By the Middle Ages they were known as the Gorhani or Gorham.

Goraan

The origin of the Goraan was in the Tibesti Mountains. When the French gained control of Tibesti, they fled. They also occupy the Fezzan. Some argue they are the descendants of the Garamantians. They were found inhabiting Uwaynat when Hassanein discovered it. But by the time the Italians used it as an outpost during their tenure in Libya and the Sudanese Defense Force established store huts at Karkur Murr, they were gone. Gongoi, one of the last warring Goraan chiefs, raided throughout the desert as late as the 1930s.

Tebu

The Tebu, with their homeland in Tibesti, are pastoralists, herders, and traders. They were known in the past as raiders throughout the desert, preying on settlements in Waidai, Chad, Cyrenaica, Kordofan, the Western Desert, and the Nile Valley. When the people of Dakhla destroyed the wells to the south and west of the oasis to halt invaders, they were probably protecting themselves from the Tebu. Today their wandering and raiding is all but over—the French saw to that. About 200,000 Tebu live in Chad, with 16,000 in southern Libya and another 300,000 scattered through Niger and Sudan. In Egypt, they are often visitors to the south and southwestern sections of the country around Gilf Kebir and Gebel Uwaynat, mostly on a temporary basis. They come to graze when water is available. Hassanein saw a small number of Tebu herdsmen at Uwaynat. In fact, he owes his discovery of rock art at Uwaynat to a Tebu. They are probably the people Harding King described as coming from Zerzura. When Rohlfs' men saw three black men who told him they were from Zerzura, they were probably Tebu.

Tuareg

The Tuareg are commonly associated with the Western Sahara, especially Timbuktu in Mali, but they belong in the Libyan Desert, too, especially in the Fezzan in Libya. Traditionally, no Tuaregs lived in Egypt; they just raided or grazed here. They are sometimes called the Veiled People or the Blue People from the blue veils the men use to cover their faces. Great caravan drivers, the Tuaregs, at one time or another, controlled three of the four major caravan roads of North Africa. They maintained and protected the wells, served as contractors for merchants, and levied tolls. According to Bovill (1933), "that the wealth of the far interior [of Africa] was always accessible to the mercantile communities of the western world was due to the Tuareg and constitutes their greatest contribution to the history of civilization." When they were not leading caravans, they were extracting protection money from them, or plundering them in a raid. One of their basic forms of survival, the raids were carried out mainly to steal stock, women, and food. Almost every group of people in North Africa went raiding. Unlike the lush oases of Egypt's Western Desert, there was never enough food or enough clothing in the desert. Raids were a way of replenishing the communities.

Berbers

The Berbers once dominated life in North Africa. They were in North Africa long before the Bedouin. In all probability, a great number of Berbers came from the southern Arabian peninsula, but invaders beginning with the Greeks have intermarried with them. As each invasion came, they were pushed one way or another until they were squeezed into the most inhospitable land. They came into Egypt and were repulsed century after century, until only the interior of the desert was theirs.

Kababish

Once numbering about 70,000, the Kababish are nomadic Arabs, the largest group in Kordofan. Great caravan leaders and camel owners, they often carried cargo from the Nile to Darfur, or assessed a fee for any caravan crossing their territory that was not theirs. Groups of Kababish joined the Mahdi revolt. They graze their livestock over a huge area, mostly in northern Sudan, but as far west as Lake Chad, and crossed, at some point, areas in the extreme south of Egypt.

The Oaseans

The farmers of the oases are the people who live in the cultivated areas, mainly in the depressions. Some of them immigrated from the Nile Valley, some may well be descended from the ancient peoples of the desert, and others settled in the oases from other lands. The farmers were never interested in roaming the desert. They remained in their small world, cultivated their crops with primitive tools, and were born, lived, married, and died in the same place unless they were carted off in a raid. In this they are similar to the farmers in the Nile Valley.

The Bedouin

The Bedouin are the Arab nomads of the desert. They are descendants of the Arab invasion of Egypt and Libya, which began in 643. They are primarily the Bani Hilal, originally in Egypt, but now mostly in Tunisia and Tripolitania; the Bani Sulaym, mostly in Cyrenaica (in Libya); and the Awlad Ali, who migrated to Egypt under pressure from other Bedouin groups in the nineteenth century. The Awlad Ali dominate the northern coast of Egypt and in the 1960s numbered about 100,000.

During the Islamic period the desert declined. Newbold in *Rock Pictures and Archaeology of the Libyan Desert* maintains that the Arabs did not know how to dig and maintain wells as well as the Libyans and therefore many oases that had been occupied were abandoned when the water ran out.

The Bedouin roamed the desert in small groups looking for grazing for their herds of goats and camels, stopping in some areas long enough to cultivate a small crop. All of their possessions were portable and they lived in tents which could be transported on the back of a camel whenever it became necessary to move. Their movement was always restricted by territorial ownership among the people of the desert.

When Muhammad Ali came to power in Egypt he called upon the Bedouin to keep peace in the deserts while he battled the Mamluk Beys in the cities. This they did and in reward for their service, when he and his descendants conscripted an army the Bedouin were free not to answer the call.

If one does encounter a rare Bedouin encampment today, it will probably be along the northern coast between Siwa or Qattara and the sea. The black tents are the same as they always were, held up by nine poles to a height of seven feet, divided into a men's side and a women's side with a rug on the ground, and facing away from the winds and storms.

Perhaps some insight into their character can be gained from the following story by Ahmad Hassanein. A Bedouin named Bukara told him this tale one evening around a campfire at Gebel Uwaynat.

"Why don't you ride, Bukara?" I [Hassanein] asked. "There are several unloaded camels."

"What would my washoon (wife) say if she heard that her Bukara had ridden between Arkenu and Ouenat [Uwaynat]?"

He told me that on one occasion he had been entrusted with some fifty camels to take to Ouenat for grazing. He was alone and ran short of food.

"For twelve days I ate no meal, except the pips of colocynth, which upset my digestion," he replied simply. "Then I reached Kufra. The men at Kufra who had sent me for the camels had forgotten to send me food. They had expected me at Kufra earlier."

"But why didn't you slaughter a camel?" I inquired.

"Should I permit the men of Kufra to say that Bukara could not endure hunger and had killed a camel?"

The Sanusi

No other modern group has had such a profound effect on life in this desert as the Sanusi. Ahmed Hassanein, who had considerable help from them, defines them as "not a race nor a country nor a political entity nor a religion. They have however, some of the characteristics of all four. In fact they are almost exclusively Bedouins; they inhabit, for the most part, the Libyan Desert; they exert a controlling influence over considerable areas of that region and are recognized by the governments of surrounding territory as a real power in the affairs of north eastern Africa; and they are Moslems."

Al-Sayyid Muhammad bin Ali al-Sanusi Khatibi al-Idrisi al-Hasani, a devout Muslim mystic, was born into a wealthy Algerian family in 1787. After studying religious teachings at Qayrawan University and in Mecca, he returned to the Libyan Desert and when he was in his seventies established a religious order. The Grand Sanusi, *al-Sanusi al-Kabir*, came at a time when religious principles were lax among the tribes of the desert and he restored strong religious beliefs once again. The people of the desert considered him a *marabout*, a wandering holy man.

Al-Sanusi al-Kabir acquired a following for practices that would today be called fundamentalist: resistance to Western ideals, no tobacco or alcohol, no gold or jewels for men, no music, dance, or song in religious observations, no contact with Christians, Jews, or bad Muslims, and strict adherence to the Quran. Disobedience was met with severe punishment.

*Zawya*s, religious centers, were established throughout the oases, first at Siwa in Egypt, and soon at Jalo and Aujila in Libya. The *zawya*s consisted of a mosque and three rooms: a schoolroom for children, which was very important as it was the only educational facility in the desert; a guesthouse for travelers, which offered the traditional three days' hospitality; and the private quarters for the *ikhwan*, the Sanusi teachers. The *zawya*s were established near important wells along the main caravan routes, and in the oases. Eventually the Sanusi controlled most of the northern portion of the Libyan Desert.

In 1854, a *zawya* was established at the uninhabited and isolated Jaghbub Oasis (now in Libya, but at that time in Egypt), which became the center of the movement. Here an Islamic university was established. Jaghbub was selected because it was central to the feuding tribes of the desert whom the Grand Sanusi wished to unite. It also sat at the crossroads of the pilgrimage route to Mecca and the trade route from the sea to Sudan. When the Grand Sanusi died in September 1859, most of the tribes were counted among his followers and thirty-eight *zawya*s had been opened in Cyrenaica, eighteen in

Tripolitania, twenty in Egypt, and additional ones all the way from Fez across Africa to Damascus and from Istanbul as far east as India.

Sayyid al-Mahdi
The Grand Sanusi's son, Sayyid al-Mahdi ruled for forty-two years. (In Islam it is believed a Mahdi [a rightly guided one] will appear at the end of the world. He will attain his majority on the first day of the Islamic month of Muharram, be the son of parents with the names Muhammad and Fatima, and have lived several years in seclusion: Sayyid al-Mahdi fulfilled all these conditions, but never proclaimed himself Mahdi.)

During al-Mahdi's leadership the sect grew to three million followers and expanded west into Libya and Algeria and south into Sudan. The religious center was moved to Kufra, headquarters to the brigands who roamed the desert. The Sanusi had to control them in order to bring peace to the desert. Hassanein tells us that "each caravan going through Kufra north or south was either pillaged or, if lucky, compelled to pay a route tax." The Sanusi protected the caravans from such extortion. Under their reign, the caravan trail from Kufra to Sudan became heavily used because it was safe.

Sayyid Ahmad
Sayyid al-Mahdi died in 1900 and was succeeded by his nephew Sayyid Ahmad. The Sanusi now dominated the North African deserts. At the same time the Libyan Desert began to attract the attention of the European powers. It was becoming impossible for Sayyid Ahmad to continue the apolitical stance of his predecessors. He refused to help in several conflicts in the area, disappointing not only the Turks but Ahmad Urabi in his rebellion against the British in Egypt, and the Sudanese Mahdi in his rebellion against the British in Sudan. But invaders of North Africa viewed the Sanusi as a threat. Finally, during World War I, the Sanusi sided with the Turks.

Sayyid Muhammad Idris
The next ruler of the Sanusi was Sayyid Muhammad Idris, the son of al-Mahdi. He lived in Egypt while his predecessor's battles were being fought. He was elevated to leader after World War I and reconciled the Sanusi with the Egyptians. However, the Italians still had intentions to colonize Cyrenaica. Sayyid Idris could not fight back. Although the British had successfully thrown the Sanusi out of Egypt, he exiled himself to Egypt once again. His followers scattered throughout the desert living in caves and underground cisterns far away from Italian and British eyes and ears.

In the second Italo–Sanusi war, beginning in 1923, Omar Mukhtar rose to power and fought the Italians. He was eventually killed and his amazing band of warriors destroyed. By 1938, the Italians had dominated the country and joined Cyrenaica, Tripolitania, and the Fezzan into what they called Libya, reviving the name given to the area by Diocletian 1,500 years earlier. When the Italians entered World War II, Sayyid Idris, from Egypt, aligned himself with the British.

Caravans and Roadways

There are a number of great north–south routes leading from the northern coast of Africa through the North African deserts to the Bilad al-Sudan that are important to a discussion of the Libyan Desert. Great nations rose and fell by their ability to keep these routes open and working. In one century one route dominated, in another century another route rose in prominence.

Operating well before the arrival of the Romans, modern trade along all the routes reached its peak between the eleventh and fourteenth centuries. In the sixteenth century a decline set in and by the nineteenth century only two major routes remained.

Once Europe was able to defeat the Barbary pirates, the European exploration of Africa began in earnest. New ports were needed for European goods. Trade items were brought to Africa by European merchants who got as far as the coast, where they had to stop. Once in Africa, the goods were hauled through the desert by local merchants. They included such things as cloth, sugar, brass, horses, and even books. Out of Africa would come three major items: gold, slaves, and in some places, ivory.

The secrets of these routes and their wells were carefully guarded. No foreigners were permitted to travel south from the northern coast. Hanns Vischer tells us his trip from the Mediterranean to Lake Chad around 1906 "had been long forbidden to European travelers." In fact, as he was assembling his entourage, objections were raised in Tripoli. People said, "Why should the Christian dog be permitted to cross the Sahara? . . ." and saw "the sure foreshadowing of European occupation." They were so opposed to his travel into Africa that "arrangements had been made with Tuarek [Tuareg] and Tubbu [Tebu] robbers to attack my caravan."

With variations there were six great north–south routes. Running west to east they are the Taghaza Road, the Ghadames–Air–Kano Road, the Garamantian Road, the Fezzan–Kawan Road, the Tripoli–Benghazi–Waidai Road, and the Darb al-Arbain.

Taghaza Road

The most westerly of these routes, the Taghaza Road, began in the amazing city of Sijilmasa (completely destroyed in the Moroccan Civil War in the eighteenth century) in the oasis of Tafilelt at the base of the Atlas Mountains. From Sijilmasa, where the caravans were supplied and packed, the trail moved due south to the salt mines at

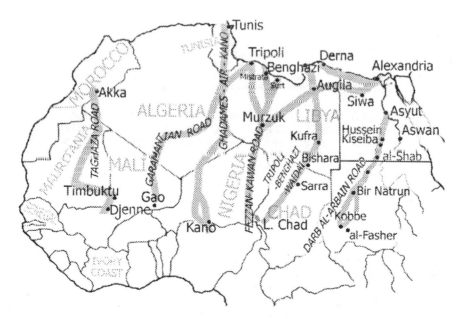

Major North African trade routes

Taghaza, a journey of three weeks. The journey continued south to Walata, where a number of caravan routes converged. The caravans could go to the Atlantic, or to the fabled and legendary towns of Djenne and Timbuktu (both in modern Mali).

Ghadames–Air–Kano Road

The Ghadames–Air Road began in Tunis along an ancient Roman road running south through the al-Qantara Gorge, Biskra, and Tuggurt. It proceeded south through Ghat (in modern Libya), Azawa, and Iferuan in the Air Mountains, to Agades (in modern Niger) and on via either Zinder or Katsina to Kano, Nigeria. There are grooves in the rocks of this road that attest to its ancient age. Over the centuries the route varied now and again, but ran pretty much as described above. The gold trade between Tripoli and Gao (in modern Mali) came along a variation of this road. The cargo going north was gold and slaves, cloth from Kano (Nigeria), kola nuts from Gwanja (at $1.00 a piece), salt from Bilma (in modern Niger), and natron from Lake Chad, while silk from Tripoli and France, cotton from Manchester, glass beads from Venice, paper, mirrors, needles, and sword blades from Nuremberg, and spices, sugar, and tea went south. By the early nineteenth century this route was the most important. It was under the control of two Tourag tribes.

Garamantian Road

The third north–south caravan route, perhaps the most famous, was the Garamantian Road. It was an ancient track, at least partly known to Herodotus who was able to tell the distance from the coast to Roman Phazania (modern Fezzan) where the Garamantians lived. It was a trade route as early as the Carthaginians who received carbuncles, gold, and slaves from the Garamantians. (Carbuncles were precious gems to the Garamantians.) It ran from Oea, now Tripoli, on the coast, through the Fezzan and the Hoggar Mountains to Gao on the Niger River.

Fezzan–Kawan Road

The Fezzan–Kawan Road dominated African trade for centuries. Following it from the south, it moved almost due north from Chad through Waidai to Murzuk in the Fezzan. From Murzuk there were a number of routes to follow: to the coast at Misrata; via Surt or Jalo to Benghazi; or from Jalo to Jaghbub, Siwa, and Alexandria. This route also went to Kerdassa near Cairo.

As with all the desert routes this was a slavers' road, and many of the slaves were sent to Egypt. Bovill says, "The Taghaza and the Ghadames–Air roads were both used by slave traders, but the part they played in the trade was small compared with the Fezzan–Kawar road; so much was this so, that in Denham's time foreign merchants trading with Bornu refused to accept payment for their trade goods in anything but slaves which consequently became the chief currency of the country."

Tripoli–Benghazi–Waidai Road

The next great road was the Sanusi road, the most important road of the late nineteenth and early twentieth centuries. In 1805, the Waidai power secured the Fezzan–Kawan Road. But by the 1840s and 1850s the Awlad Sulayman were waging war with Bornu in the south and the Bedouin tribes in Cyrenaica were fighting the Tebu of Tibesti in the north. The sultan of Waidai, keen to find a route via Kufra to Benghazi, sent the merchant Shehaymah of Jalo to blaze a new trail. He traveled 480 kilometers (300 miles) to Uwaynat, then pushed on to Kufra. Then he returned to Waidai with a caravan. It was on Shehaymah's third trip to Kufra that he found the more direct route between Waidai and Kufra that was used from that time forward. The problem was a waterless

576 kilometers (360 miles) between Tekro and Kufra. When they rose to power, the Sanusi took control of this route and solved the water problem by digging two wells, one at Bishara, 160 kilometers (100 miles) south of Kufra, and another at Sarra, 160 kilometers (100 miles) beyond. From Cyrenaica, the famous trade route moved south via Benghazi to Kufra and through the Tibesti Mountains and Bornu to Waidai, and on to Darfur. Benghazi grew from a population of 5,000 in 1817, to 16,500 in 1911.

Darb al-Arbain

The sixth road lies a thousand miles to the east. The Darb al-Arbain, Road of the Forty or the Forty Days' Road, is the major north–south route through the Western Desert in Egypt.

The Darb al-Arbain is the main caravan track linking Fasher in the Darfur Province of Sudan to Asyut in the Nile Valley in Egypt, a journey of 1,721 kilometers (1,082 miles). It cuts through the heart of Kharga Oasis which it enters at Maks Qibli. In Kharga, it came under Egyptian control and goods were subject to taxation (see Kharga Oasis for details). It continued and continues north, straight through the oasis to Naqb Ramliya where it ascended the scarp and continues to the Nile Valley following the modern macadamized route of today. (See Darb al-Arbain chapter for a fuller discussion of this route, slavery, and the slave trade.)

Eventually, all the caravan routes declined. The European colonization of North Africa ended the importance of the trans-Saharan trade routes. The French moved in from the west and occupied Morocco, Algeria, and most of West Africa. The British took over Nigeria and Egypt. The Italians dominated Libya. The great European squeeze was on. After the Europeans dominated North Africa, they found their own way, often by sea, and eliminated the middlemen: the desert tribes who controlled the trade. The Timbuktu route died out completely. The French occupation of Algeria in 1839, enabled them to pass a law in 1843, forbidding products from Sudan to enter the country. Waidai killed two other routes. The Italian occupation of Libya killed the Sanusi route. After centuries of domination, the North Africans were out of business.

Explorers and Travelers

The Western Desert, except for Cambyses' soldiers, has been kinder to humankind that its mother the Libyan Desert and its sister the Sahara. The latter two have claimed too many explorers and adventurers, mostly at the hands of the incredible Tuareg: Alexine Tinne, Father de Foucauld, Gordon Laing, Colonel Paul Flatters and his men, and more. No, unless you want to count the 10,000 soldiers killed in World War II, the Western Desert was far more hospitable. Perhaps, if the truth be told, the people of the Western Desert, most of the time victims to marauders, but seldom marauders themselves, were less willing or less able to stop what was happening to them and to their surroundings.

The Classical World

Herodotus of Halicarnassus (c485–25 B.C.) visited Egypt and the Libyan Desert for a period of three and a half months in 450 B.C. On his map, the Mediterranean is the center of the known world with the three continents of Europe, Asia, and Libya surrounding it. He called the Western Desert the Region of Wild Beasts and marked the Gulf of Plinthinete (Arab's Gulf), Plinthine, along the coast, and interior places like Crocodilopolis (Medinet Fayoum), Ammonium (Siwa), and Augila. He wrote his famous *History* about Asia, Europe and Africa, which he called Libya.

Strabo (c. 63 B.C. to c. A.D. 24) came to Egypt as the guest of his friend the prefect

Aelius Gallus, Augustus's hand-picked ruler for Egypt. He presents us with a much more in-depth geographical picture of Egypt in antiquity and includes more of the Libyan Desert in his descriptions. Strabo is the first known geographer to mention Bahariya and Kharga. He tells us that oases dotted the Western Desert "like the spots on a leopard."

The Middle Ages

Arab travelers in the Middle Ages wrote about the Western Desert as early as 641, though many of the writers never visited the area. **Ibn al-Wardi** reported on a journey in 708 by Musa Ibn Nusayr, the Omayyad governor of North Africa, in his book **Kharitat al-Ajaib**. The pilgrimage to Mecca instigated many geographical treatises, as the way people journeyed from North Africa and from the Bilad al-Sudan was through the Libyan Desert. **Al-Masudi**, a Baghdadi scholar, traveled nearly twenty years through the Islamic world, spending a great deal of time in Egypt where he died around 956. He wrote a book called *Meadows of Gold and Mines of Precious Stones* which contained not only the geography for which he became famous, but also everyday knowledge, like an encyclopedia. He called the Atlantic Ocean the Green Sea of Darkness. Some portions of Al-Masudi's maps are amazingly correct, especially his positioning and details of the Nile Valley.

Contemporary with Al-Masudi was **Ibn Hawqal** (?920–90), another geographer from Baghdad. From 947 to 948 he crossed North Africa, returning in 951 to take the Taghaza Road south to modern Mali. When he saw the Niger he thought it was the Nile. Ibn Hawqal then undertook the formidable task of recrossing Africa on his way to Egypt. He arrived as the Fatimids were invading the country and was accused of being a Fatimid spy. He traveled for over thirty years and wrote a book first called *Of Ways and Provinces* in 967 (reissued in 977). The second and definitive edition was published in 988 and called *On the Shape of the World*. He was the first, to our knowledge, to explore western Sudan.

Abu Ubayd al-Bakri came from Cordoba in the eleventh century. Among his prolific writings was a multi-volumed geographical work which had a huge section on North Africa. Remarkably accurate in his descriptions, he never left Spain.

Muhammad al-Sharif al-Idrisi (1100–66) was born in Morocco of a wealthy family that ruled North Africa and southern Spain. He studied at Cordoba and traveled extensively through the Middle East and North Africa. He was invited to the court of Roger II, the Norman King of Sicily, where he lived from 1099 to 1154. There, over a fifteen-year period, he produced a silver globe and map of the world accompanied by the now famous *Book of Roger* or *Rogerian Description of the World*. It is considered the most important geographical work of the Middle Ages and the most accurate account of the Mediterranean world in the twelfth Century. Today only six original copies are known to exist.

Abu Abdallah Ibn Battuta (1304–69), of Berber stock from Tangier, is perhaps the most well-known Arab traveler and geographer. His travels in the fourteenth century took fourteen years. He started his journey by crossing North Africa, which took him ten months. Then he went as far as China. After his return, he took one more trip of note, across the deserts of North Africa to Sudan, thus completing his visits to Islamic countries and covering 120,000 kilometers (75,000 miles) in the process. That last journey began in the Atlas Mountains and went down the Taghaza Road. When he returned to Morocco he began the task of writing his memoirs. In two years he produced the *Rihla*, also known as *A Gift to the Observers Concerning the Curiosities of the Cities and Marvels Encountered in Travels*.

Ibn Battuta's contemporary **Ibn Khaldun** came from Tunisia. In 1384 he was in

Cairo where he served as a Mufti, and by 1387 was in the Fayoum where he probably wrote the bulk of his work.

The Early Europeans

In the wake of Western expansion emerged that most romantic of figures, the professional explorer. By the late seventeenth century, Europeans, eager to discover unknown territories, were setting out in hordes to march across barren terrain in search of their place in history. Egypt was one of their goals.

These travelers were headed into the unknown. They were invading territories where they were mostly unwelcome. They discovered little that was not already known by local peoples, but they had the scientific know-how to share their knowledge with the rest of the world. What they did was bring modern technology to the desert, enabling them to locate, identify, and record places in reference to a larger world order. This is no mean feat and it was then, and still stands, as a major contribution to the world's understanding of the planet. Only in that sense do we use the word discovered.

Despite the fact that they were not the first, their journeys were formidable undertakings that tested their very fiber. They had no idea if they would return alive from their desert wanderings and many did not. They knew oases existed, but there were not sure exactly where, how many there were, which was which, and what to expect when they did find one. They were on the verge of understanding some of the last outposts on earth as we are on the verge of understanding the moon, our sister planets, and our solar system.

Charles Jacques Poncet, a French physician, traveled to Kharga Oasis in 1698. And if we are to believe the English-language source, by accident. This was over a century before exploration began in West Africa when Mungo Park explored the Niger River in 1805. Mistakenly thinking he was headed down the east bank of the Nile, Poncet turned west, intending to meet the river. But traveling instead down the west bank, by turning he headed for the desert. He also traveled the Darb al-Arbain headed to Abyssinia (Ethiopia) by request of the French Consul in Cairo, Mr. Maillet. He wrote *A Voyage to Ethiopia*.

A century later **William George Browne**, an Englishman came to Africa. His primary goal was to visit Sudan, which he did by traveling the length of the Darb al Arbain in 1793. But first he went in search of Siwa in 1792, which he reached after twelve days via Bareton (Mersa Matruh). He was looking for the Temple of Jupiter Ammon and was never quite sure if he had found it or not. He wrote *Travels in Africa, Egypt, and Syria in 1799.*

The African Association

The African Association was formed over a dinner at The Saturday's Club in St. Alban's Tavern in London, England, on June 9, 1788. First called The Association for Promoting the Discovery of the Interior Parts of Africa, it was not long before it became The African Association. It lasted for nearly half a century until it was absorbed into the Royal Geographical Society. Always high on enthusiasm and short on cash, it managed to send some of the most prominent explorers into Africa, and through its persistence, it pushed the British government to do the same.

Abolition of the slave trade was a serious motive for The African Association, as were the quest for the source of the Niger River and investigations into geography and natural history. But the major consideration was the need to find customers for Europe's growing Industrial Revolution. With the American colonies lost to England, new outlets had to be found. There was an additional consideration, too. According to Adu Boahen in *Britain, the Sahara, and the Western Sudan 1788–1861*, Britain also had too many prisoners and no place to send them, so they were looking for a penal colony and like the ancient Egyptians and the Romans before them, they looked to the North African deserts.

One of the first objectives of The African Association was the Libyan Desert. Three weeks after the Association began, they sent the American **John Ledyard** to Egypt. He was to cross Africa, find the Niger, and visit the towns and countries along the way. He arrived in Cairo on August 19, 1788, and died there in October from overmedicating himself. Only two months after Ledyard departed England, the Association sent **Simon Lucas** to the Fezzan. He was to return to England via Gambia. He arrived in Tripoli in October, got 100 miles east of Tripoli, got caught in a rebellion, and returned to London the following July. **Major Daniel Houghton**, the Association's next explorer, reached the mouth of the Gambia in November, 1790. After a tortuous journey along the Gambia River, Houghton was either killed by the local inhabitants (including the French who were attacking British traders), or died of hunger in the desert. His mandate had been to find the source of the Niger. **Mungo Park** left England on the same mission in May, 1795. It took him a year, but he found the Niger and returned to England on Christmas Day 1797.

At the same time as Mungo Park was exploring West Africa, the German **Friederich Konrad Hornemann** was sent to the other side of the continent. He arrived in Cairo in September 1797, and remained there to study the language. When Napoleon arrived in Egypt it looked as if Hornemann's journey had come to an end, but the French ruler gave him protection and sent him on his way. In 1798, Hornemann and his associate, Frenderburg, joined a pilgrim's caravan crossing the Libyan Desert from Tripoli to Bornu. Having studied Arabic for a year in Cairo, he disguised himself as Yousef ibn Abdulla, an escaped Mamluk. They were the first Europeans to disguise themselves successfully as Arabs. His route took him through Siwa and the Fezzan. At Murzuk— they were the first Europeans to visit this oasis—the locals were at war with the Tuaregs. Here Frenderburg died and Hornemann had to return to Tripoli. He remained there for eighteen months and had the foresight to send his papers back to London before he joined a second caravan headed for Bornu. He died on November 17, 1798, near Bornu. All the papers of this second journey were lost. His book, *The Journal of Frederich Hornemann's Travels from Cairo to Mourzouck*, was published in 1802. It covers his first trip. We know nothing about his second journey. With the French invasion of Egypt, the activities of The African Association were curtailed.

By this time the limited resources for The African Association had dwindled drastically. They sent off **Henry Nicholls**, who headed for the Guinea coast and died there in early 1805. The Association languished for the next few decades, sending off **Jean Louis Burckhardt** and **A. Linant** in 1826. In 1831, it merged with the Royal Geographical Society. The British government now took over the exploration of Africa.

The Americans

The colonists were barely Americans when the French came to Egypt. But by 1804, as a possible solution to the Barbary pirates' interference in American trade, they landed the first authorized American overseas expedition in Alexandria. It was led by **William Eaton**, a flamboyant, persistent, problematic New Englander who some have called America's Lawrence of Arabia. These writers enveloped him in flowing Arab robes, gave him the gift of the Arabic tongue, and placed a whirling scimitar in his hand. Although the image is romanticized, Eaton was America's first hero in Egypt. He led a small group of Marines under **Lieutenant Presley Neville O'Bannon**, a boastful Irish–American. This was the first military action on foreign soil by the newly formed United States Marines. Their formidable task was to find Hamet Karamanli, deposed and rightful ruler of Tripoli, trek across the northern coast, depose Yusef Karamanli, the current ruler, and set Hamet on the throne of Tripoli. It was a journey into hell. (See al-Diffa for details.)

This encounter along the Barbary Coast set many precedents for the United States. It helped establish the US Navy and set the military tradition of the US Marine Corp. It is immortalized in the opening line of the Marine Hymn: "From the halls of Montezuma to the shores of Tripoli," and the sword worn by Marines at full dress symbolizes the North African sword given to O'Bannon by Hamet at Derna, complete with duplicate engravings on the shaft.

Muhammad Ali Opens the Door

The golden age of nineteenth-century professional exploration began with the arrival in Egypt of a number of scientists who answered the call of Muhammad Ali. When Muhammad Ali came to power the oases had been left to their own devices for a long time. He brought them back under Egyptian control, and then requested explorers to find out just what was in the desert.

G. B. Belzoni, the two-meter (six-foot seven-inch) Italian strongman and circus performer came to Egypt to convince Muhammad Ali his hydraulic engines would be good for Egyptian irrigation, and stayed to scavenge for antiquities. Belzoni went to Bahariya via the caravan route from Beni Suef, arriving on May 26, 1819, for an eleven-day stay. Unfortunately, Belzoni thought Bahariya was Siwa, mistaking the Triumphal Arch at Qasr as the Temple of the Oracle. Ahmed Fakhry tells an amusing tale about Belzoni. When Belzoni's notes kept disappearing he discovered that the people, believing they were magical, were buying them from his servant each day to keep the evil spirits away. Belzoni published *Narrative of the Operations and Recent Discoveries Within the Pyramids, Temples, Tombs and Excavations, in Egypt and Nubia* in two volumes in 1820.

Frederic Cailliaud, a French mineralogist in the employ of Muhammad Ali, explored most of the Nile Valley including Meroe in Sudan in two visits: 1815–19 and 1819–22. Also called Murad Effendi, he searched for sulfur and visited the emerald mines along the Red Sea Coast. In the Western Desert, he visited Fayoum, Siwa, Bahariya, and Farafra in search of ancient mines. He claims to be the first European to visit Kharga Oasis and in a lengthy inscription he carved on the Temple of Hibis in Kharga he credits himself with its discovery. According to him, he left the Nile at Esna in June, 1818. His book, *Voyage à Meroe, au Fleuve Blanc, au-delà de Fazgol dans le midi du Royaume de Sennar, à Syouah et dans cinq autres oases*, published in Paris in 1826, is a masterpiece in four volumes. The outstanding and important plans and drawings were executed by the painter Letorzec, his traveling companion. Upon his return to France he became Curator of the Museum of Natural History in Nîmes.

Bernadino Drovetti, an Italian, was a lawyer and diplomat who arrived in Egypt soon after Napoleon left and was appointed French Deputy Commissioner of Commercial Relations at Alexandria on October 20, 1802. Drovetti, strongly anti-English and a formidable force against the American expedition led by William Eaton, was in turn ill-treated by English-language sources, but is one of the main architects of modern Egypt. Not only did he play a significant role in elevating Muhammad Ali to a position of power in Egypt, he accompanied the conquering army of Muhammad Ali to Siwa in 1820. Drovetti eventually became French Consul and assisted many travelers and scientists on their various missions in Egypt. He lived in Egypt for many years, amassing much wealth including property in the Fayoum.

But he is equally guilty of promoting French interests over English and was not above stretching the truth to accomplish his ambitions. In the book, *Journal d'un voyage a la vallee de Dakel par M le chevalier Drovetti, Consul General de France en Egypte, vers la fin de 1818*, Drovetti appears to have visited Kharga in 1818, and announced that he was the first European to reach "the farther Oasis" (Dakhla).

Archibald Edmondstone had other thoughts. He claims the year was not 1818, but 1819, and that on February 21, 1819, they met while Drovetti was entering Dakhla and Edmondstone was on his way back to Kharga from Dakhla.

Edmondstone writes, ". . . on our arrival at Siout [Asyut] on the 7th of February, being informed that M. Drovetti had set out for the Oases from hence three days before, we resolved to lose no time in following him." Perhaps this information led Edmondstone to chose the Darb al-Tawil, a direct, but seldom used, link to Dakhla. He wanted to beat the Frenchman and claim the glory.

Accompanied by his friends Houghton and Masters, Edmondstone visited the southern oasis of Dakhla from Asyut over the Darb al-Tawil in 1819. He left Cairo on January 14, arrived in Balat on February 16, and was at Ain Amur on the February 22. The only mountain in Dakhla Oasis was named after him in 1874, by the members of Rohlfs' expedition. Edmondstone wrote a very well-researched and informative narrative: *A Journey to Two of the Oases* published in 1822.

Another Englishman who traveled in the Western Desert at the same time as Cailliaud was **I. Hyde**. In fact this was the Englishman John Hyde who traveled in Egypt from November, 1818 to August, 1819. Hyde kept a private journal, now in the British Museum, and in addition he chiseled his name on most of the monuments, especially in Kharga and Dakhla. After he left Egypt he went on to India where he died in 1825.

Baron Heinrich von Minutoli, a Prussian army officer, visited Siwa from October 26 to November 12, 1820. His original plan was to travel along the northern coast to Cyrenaica. It was not to be, so he settled for Siwa where he drew the temple and walls of Umm Ubayd. Because the temple was destroyed in 1897, his work remains the best record of this site. It is preserved in his book *Reise zum Tempel des Jupiter Ammon*. One of his companions, Victor Ehrenberg, an avid rock hound, published *Mikrogeologie und Reisen in Ägypten*. Minutoli stayed in Egypt for only ten months but during that time he managed to accumulate an important Egyptian collection, which formed the basis of Berlin's Egyptian Museum. He was the first European to view the interior of the Step Pyramid. He encouraged the creation of the first chair of Egyptology in Berlin. He was influential in sponsoring Karl Richard Lepsius' work in Egypt. His bride, Baroness Wolfradine Menu von Minutoli, in addition to collecting exotic animals, published *Recollections of Egypt 1820–21*.

Also included among these early travelers is **Jean Raimond Pacho**, a French explorer–botanist who came to Egypt in 1818 and again from 1822–25. Although he had a brother in Egypt working as a merchant, his travels were supported by a number of patrons. He traveled from Alexandria in November, 1824, and stayed pretty much to the area of the Northern Coast of the Western Desert. He accompanied Jean Jacques Rifaud, a Frenchman employed by Drovetti, to the Fayoum to survey the lake and look for the Labyrinth. We have a number of engravings he did of North African sites, but he is very elusive and little is known about him. A mountain near Sitra and Bahrein oases is named in his honor. His traveling companion was Frederick Muller, who did publish a book entitled *Lapie'schen Karte Kufra*, which included a map. Fragments of Pacho's observations were included in his work, including an essay on vocabulary and language and another on Syouah (Siwa). They were in Dakhla in the summer of 1824. He committed suicide.

Bayle St. John journeyed from Alexandria to Siwa and visited many sites in the oasis in 1847. He left Alexandria September 15, with six donkeys, two mules, a pony, and a number of cattle, and ventured into the 'Desert of Dogs.' St. John used historical names for sites along the northern coast, many of them long out of use today. His description of his party when they were looked upon by Siwans for the first time is well worth remembering:

"Had they [the Siwans] laughed at our appearance I should have forgiven them: four such guys as we were had never before surely entered their territories. One sported a nightcap surmounted by an old gray hat much the worse for wear, and a brown Holland suit, which at starting scarce contained his portly form, but now hung loose about it; another had decked himself out in a tarboosh and an indescribable summer coat; the brows of a third were surmounted by a huge turban, and he was wrapped in a flannel jacket, in which, according to the necessities of the journey, he had slashed innumerable extempore pockets; whilst your humble servant was overshadowed by an enormous truncated cone formed by a beaver hat with a brim six inches broad, and a white linen covering stretched tight over from the crown to the outer edge. True that there was some attempt at respectability in the shape of clean shirts and trousers, but these could not conceal the fact that we had been knocking about for nearly three weeks in the desert, generally sub divo, and always too fatigued at our halts to pay much attention to the toilet: as to shaving, nobody ever thought of such a thing; our faces, too, were burned black with the sun, and several noses were regularly skinned."

The Germans

Georg August Schweinfurth (1836–1925) lived in Helwan and worked in Egypt for over thirty-five years. He was the single most important influence in the study of Egyptian geography and geology of the era. Under the auspices of the Khedive Ismail, he founded the *Société Géographique d'Egypte* (Royal Geographical Society of Egypt) still located on Sharia Qasr al-Aini in Cairo. President of the *Institut d'Egypte* (also on Qasr al-Aini), he was an archaeologist, geologist, and botanist. Through the latter part of the nineteenth century he labored in the Eastern and Western deserts and the Nile Valley. Among his credits in the Western Desert are the discoveries of fossiliferous rocks in Abu Rauwash, and fossil exploration in the Fayoum, including the discovery of the famous *Arsinoitherium*, a large, two-horned mammal, and *Zeuglodon*, a large whale. (See Fayoum for details.)

The Germans played a major role in the exploration of North Africa. **Heinrich (Henry) Barth** explored the Sahara and the western and central Sudan, the Bilad al-Sudan. He traveled along the northern coast of Egypt from 1845 to 1847. Barth's scientific observations and adept records make his expedition from 1850–55 from Tripoli to Agades, Kano, Kanem, Sokoto, and Timbuktu most important. He is credited with having discovered and recorded more information about Africa than any other European. In 1857, he published a five-volume work, *Travels and Discoveries in North and Central Africa in the Years 1849–1855*. Heinrich Barth died in 1865 at the age of 44. Today in Germany, he is remembered by the Heinrich Barth Institute at the University of Cologne. The institute has continued his work since its inception in 1989. It concentrates on the Eastern Sahara with special focus on cultural and ecological changes and adaptations in arid zones and documentation and analysis of rock art.

Gustav Nachtigal explored eastern Sudan and almost single-handedly created a German protectorate in West Equatorial Africa. Nachtigal was a medical doctor living in Tunis when Gerhard Rohlfs asked him to carry out a mission to deliver presents to Sultan Omar in Bornu for the king of Prussia. These presents were in recognition of the sultan's assistance not only to Rohlfs on a previous journey, but also to the German traveler Moritz von Beurmann. Nachtigal left Tripoli on February 18, 1839, and sashayed down the caravan trail. Five and a half years later, far beyond Bornu, Nachtigal ended his journey in Egypt after passing through Waidai, Darfur, and Kordofan. He was the first European in many of these places, including the Tibesti

Mountains. He was the first to journey to Waidai and Darfur from the west. He died of malaria in West Africa in 1855, at the age of 51.

For Egypt, one name looms above the rest of the Germans in reference to the Western Desert and that is **Gerhard Rohlfs** (1831–96) Rohlfs, a geographer, presented a proposal to Dr. von Jasmund, the German consul to Egypt in 1872. He wanted to explore and record information about the unknown territories of Egypt. Jasmund received LE4,000 for Rohlfs from the Khedive Ismail in 1873. The original itinerary was to go from Asyut to Kufra through areas that were mostly unexplored and unknown to Europeans. Kufra was a known place, but no European had ever been there. No one on the expedition knew the Great Sand Sea stood in the way.

Rohlfs was not a newcomer to North Africa. He began his African adventures in 1855, when he arrived in Algiers as a French Foreign Legionnaire. He was to accomplish six outstanding journeys into the unknown deserts of North Africa. The first journey was through Morocco from 1861 to 1862. The second was a crossing of the Atlas Mountains, which made him the first European to accomplish such a trek, and the first European to discover the oases of Tafilet, Tuat, and Tidikeit, major stops on the ancient caravan trails of Algeria. The third journey, in 1865–67, made him the first European to cross West Africa from north to south. After passing the mantle to Gustav Nachtigal, Rohlfs took his fourth journey from Tripoli, Pentapolis, and Cyrene, to Siwa and Alexandria.

His mandate from Ismail was twofold: to find the old riverbed of the Nile, the *Bahr bila ma* ('river without water'), and to ascertain if the desert was suitable for agriculture. It took him five months of preparation in Germany before he set out for Cairo. Included in his baggage were 500 iron water tanks built by Stieberitz and Muller in Apolda, each able to contain fifty liters of water. The square tanks, sealed with screws, each weighed 25 pounds empty and 125 pounds full. One camel could only carry two tanks. It was just such tanks that got Alexine Tinne killed, as her Tuareg guides thought gold was inside. During his journey, Rohlfs discarded a good number of these tanks. What became of them is another desert mystery.

The expedition caused quite a stir in Cairo. There was a conference at the Institut d'Egypte, where the plans were carefully laid out. From their headquarters at the Nile Hotel the team gathered information and planned their work.

The Rohlfs Expedition was the first crossing of the Western Desert by a European (the first crossing of the Sahara by Europeans was the Denham, Clapperton, and Oudney Expedition in 1822–25 from Tripoli via Murzuk, Bilma, and Kano, to Sokoto), the first multidiscipline expedition, the first to fix the exact geographical positions of major landmarks, the first to leave us good maps of natural sites and villages, and the first to unravel the geological wonders of the Western Desert. Many of the geographical names we use today were given to us by this expedition. One could say the Rohlfs expedition was the birth of modern Egyptian exploration.

The expedition consisted of several prominent scholars. **Professor Karl Zittel** was a Munich geologist who published *Palaeontographica (Beitraege zur Geologie und Palaeontologie der libyschen Wüste)*, still one of the most important works on the Western Desert and the first to contain a geological map of the area. This was no mean feat. **Wilhelm Jordan**, the topographer, was the first to map the area. His geographical and meteorological expertise measured sea levels and recorded topographical information in the oases. **Ph. Remele**, the expedition's photographer, took the first pictures of the Western Desert. **P. Ascherson**, the botanist, collected flora and named four species after Rohlfs. Ascherson was the only member of the team to visit Bahariya. The geological map produced by this expedition remained the standard until 1910, when the first Survey map, relying heavily on the former's information, was produced.

Attempting to go to Kufra, English-language sources maintain, the expedition nearly perished in the Great Sand Sea (for details on this controversy see Uwaynat), but, incredibly, it rained. They replenished their supplies, left their cairn, named the place Regenfeld (Rainfield), and headed north to Siwa. They left Siwa on February 25, and returned to Kharga Oasis, where Schweinfurth was waiting, and then on to the Nile and down to Cairo, which they reached April 15, 1874. It was an amazing adventure.

Rohlfs published *Drei Monate in der libyschen Wüste* in Berlin in 1876. Complete with photographs, it is the definitive work on the Western Desert.

Although Rohlfs then spent a few years at home, his adventure in the deserts of North Africa was not over. The sixth and final journey was the Kufra Expedition. Under the sponsorship of the Afrikanische Gesellschaft zur Erforschung Äquatorialafrika (African Society for the Exploration of Equatorial Africa), Rohlfs was to enter the Sahara and journey to the African Congo. He was accompanied by the zoologist Stecker. They left Tripoli in December, 1878, and arrived in Kufra, the first Europeans to do so, in September, 1879. Like so many travelers in the desert, they were not welcome. Their belongings were confiscated and they returned to Benghazi, failing to complete the original mandate. According to H. Abel in "Gerhard Rohlfs – Life and Work" in the *Annals of the Geological Survey of Egypt,* no European entered Kufra again until Ahmed Hassanein and Rosita Forbes visited in 1920.

Gerhardt Rohlfs died June 2, 1896, at 65, a ripe old age for an African explorer, in Bad Godesberg, Germany. In 1974, his efforts were acknowledged in a conference celebrating 100 Years of Geological Research in Egyptian Deserts organized by the Geological Survey of Egypt.

Georg Steindorff, a German Egyptologist, visited Siwa, Bahariya, and the Fayoum around 1901. In the meantime, exploration continued in Libya. In 1818, **Lyon** and **Ritchie** set off on Sunday, February 7, 1819, for the interior. Ritchie died of fever in Murzuk. Joining a slave caravan on January 10, 1820, Lyon made it to Tripoli and got back to England. Lyon went on to explore the Arctic, Mexico, and South America, He died at sea October 8, 1832, at 37 years of age. In 1823, **Denham, Clapperton,** and **Oudney** were the first Europeans to enter Lake Chad area and Bornu. In 1826, **Major Gordon Laing** went west to Timbuktu, in the first crossing of the desert. He was killed on his return, papers lost. Also in 1826, **Rene Caillie** arrived at Timbuktu (The French had launched a contest offering a reward for the first person to reach Timbuktu. Caillie won.) In 1817, **Paolo Della Cella**, an Italian doctor, explored Cyrenaica.

The Geological Survey of Egypt and its Desert Survey Department

In 1893 and 1894, **Henry George Lyons** (1864–1944) surveyed the southern portion of the Libyan Desert for the British government. On his return to Cairo, Lyons pleaded for greater scientific investigation of the area, and as a result the Geological Survey of Egypt was founded in 1896.

With Lyons at the helm, the survey began a systematic, detailed exploration of the desert. Its staff originally included Thomas Barron, H. J. L. Beadnell, and Leigh Smith. John Ball and W. F. Hume joined in 1897. The British were concerned about protecting Egypt, but knew nothing about the desert. The Sudanese knew the desert and there had been several attacks on the desert in recent years. So, the British had to know the desert. From October, 1897, to June, 1898, men and machines triangulated, astrolated, measured, and produced maps of the four major oases.

By 1900, Lyons became the director general and appointed Hume the director of the Geological Survey. The latter remained in that position until 1928. Lyons had created the Helwan Observatory and went on to establish the British Museum's Science Department. In 1906, the Geological Survey placed the international frontier with

Turkey between Taba on the Gulf of Aqaba and Fara on the Mediterranean. They created their first geological maps in 6 sheets at a scale of 1:1 million in 1912.

In 1904, the **Egyptian Geological Museum,** part of the Geological Survey, was opened in a building designed especially for it on Sheikh Rehan Street across from the campus of the American University in Cairo. In 1982, it was demolished to make way for the underground and the artifacts were moved to temporary headquarters on the corniche near Maadi.

In 1934, the Geological Survey surveyed the route along Latitude 27° North through the Great Sand Sea that was later to play a significant role in World War II. In 1938, they were responsible for the establishment of the border and the erection of beacons along the frontier between Egypt and Libya. In the 1950s, the Survey worked extensively with the rescue of Nubian monuments during the construction of the High Dam. In the 1980s, when Egypt and Israel were negotiating for the town of Taba on the Red Sea, the strongest argument the Egyptians produced to support their ownership of Taba was the report done by the Geological Survey in 1906. It fixed the international frontier between Turkey, which controlled the area in question, and Egypt, placing Taba in Egyptian territory.

William Fraser Hume served as director of the Geological Survey from 1909 to 1928. He was a Cambridge graduate with a DSc, a degree few people had at that time. He published copious articles on everything from the "Iron Ores of Egypt" and "The First Meteorite Record in Egypt" to reviews of other books. Hume placed the work of the Survey in his own three-volume book, *The Geology of Egypt.* He died in England on February 3, 1949.

John Ball (1874–1941) was an important part of the Geological Survey of Egypt. He founded the Desert Survey Department and served as its director. He was a nearly deaf geologist who came to Egypt for treatment for tuberculosis at Helwan. Once there, he joined the Survey. Bagnold called him the Father of Egyptian Exploration. He joined Prince Kamal al-Din on his two great desert journeys. He was the first to find Abu Ballas, Pottery Hill, where ancient pots were used to store water. It was Ball who discovered that underground artesian aquifers underlay all of the Western Desert. A bachelor and chain smoker, he traveled with the Light Car Patrols of World War I. Ball explored Egypt's deserts for thirty-four years. He died in Port Said on July 11, 1941. In addition to his survey work, Ball published a number of books including *Egypt in the Classical Geographers*, and numerous articles in the *Geographical Journal.*

Hugh Beadnell (1874–1944) did not stay long in Egypt, but his work is among the best of the Desert Survey. He was one of the first men to join the Survey. Unfortunately, when Lyons appointed Hume to head the Geological Survey, Beadnell though he should have had the position (many people concurred). He left Egypt and went to work in South America. Eventually, he came back to Egypt with the expeditionary forces of World War I. He published a number of books in addition to his survey work including *The Wilderness of Sinai* and *An Egyptian Oasis: An Account of the Oasis of Kharga in the Libyan Desert with Special Reference to its History, Physical Geography and Water Supply*, but never again for the Geological Survey.

The maps and topographical information on the Western Desert produced by these early expeditions are among the most important documents we have. The Survey first went to Bahariya in 1897, then to Kharga in January, 1898. They measured the Darb al-Dush between Esna and Kharga inch by inch with a measuring wheel, set the exact location of many sites using the heavens and barometric readings to find the absolute level of the oasis. In Kharga, they mapped the Ain Umm Dabadib area for the first time, defined the true shape of Gebel al-Tarif, established the latitude of Baris, recorded many wells, delineated the east scarp, and positioned archaeological remains. Out of this project came a bevy of books including individual ones on the topography and geology

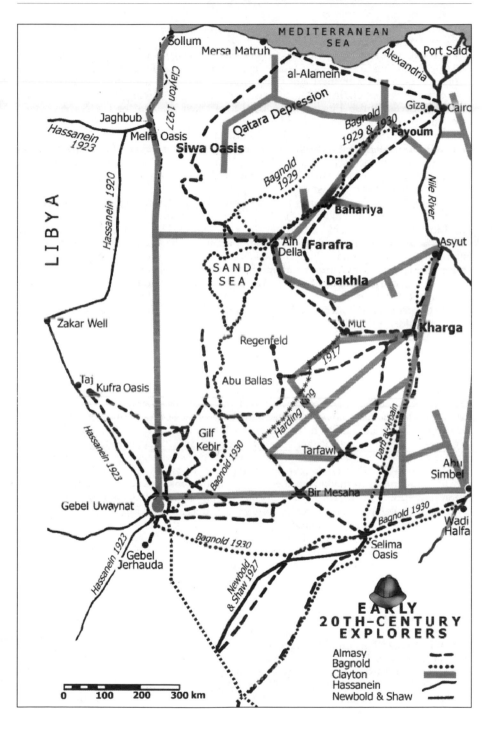

Sollum
Mersa Matruh
al-Alamein
Alexandria
Port Said
MEDITERRANEAN
SEA
Clayton 1927
Jaghbub
Melfa Oasis
Siwa Oasis
Qatara Depression
Giza
Cairo
Bagnold
1929 & 1930
Fayoum
Hassanein
1923
Bagnold
1929
Hassanein 1920
Bahariya
Nile River
LIBYA
Ain
Della
Farafra
Asyut
SAND
SEA
Dakhla
Zakar Well
Mut
Kharga
Regenfeld
1917
Taj
Kufra Oasis
Abu Ballas
Harding
Darb al-Arbain
Gilf
Kebir
Bagnold 1930
Tarfawi
Abu
Simbel
Hassanein 1923
Bir Mesaha
Gebel Uwaynat
Bagnold 1930
Wadi
Halfa
Hassanein 1923
Gebel
Jerhauda
Bagnold 1930
Selima
Oasis
Newbold
& Shaw 1927

EARLY
20TH-CENTURY
EXPLORERS
Almasy
Bagnold
Clayton
Hassanein
Newbold & Shaw

0   100   200   300 km

of Farafra, Dakhla, Bahariya, Kharga and the Fayoum. The books are accompanied by excellent 1:50,000 scale maps.

P. A. Clayton joined the Geological Survey as an inspector in 1920. By 1923, John Ball appointed him to the Desert Survey as a field surveyor. One of his first jobs in the Western Desert was with the Light Car Patrols of the Frontier District Administration to the western frontier. In 1927, he was responsible for placing the markers on the frontier between British Egypt and Italian Libya when the two foreign powers established the border. (In 1938, when more permanent markers were placed, Clayton was there again.) In 1931, he discovered Wadi Sura and some of its rock art. He received the Gold Medal of Merit and a thank you from King Fuad for helping the Kufra refugees who were dying in the desert between Kufra, Uwaynat, and Dakhla oases. (See Tineida in Dakhla Oasis for details.) In 1933, along with Lady Clayton-East-Clayton, he crossed the Great Sand Sea for the first time.

By 1940, Clayton was a member of the Long Range Desert Group (LRDG) of the Eighth Army and commanded its T Patrol. He was captured by the Italians on a raid into Libya in 1941 and sent back to Italy as a prisoner. Of his work with the LRDG he said in a letter to his sister-in-law from prison, "I had a good run and cannot complain—I was much more likely to be killed or maimed: after all I took two forts and an aerodrome and burnt Murzuk fort and blew up lorries north of Aujila."

Rushdi Said says **George William Murray** was the greatest of them all. He came early and did not leave until 1948. He lived in Maadi, had no children, but had a famous dog that accompanied Murray and his wife into the desert. He was head of the Survey from 1932–48.

With the Revolution of 1952 the Geological Survey was handed over to the Egyptians who continued the work in Egypt's deserts.

Royal Geographical Society

The Royal Geographical Society of England began as the Raleigh Travelers' Club in 1827, became the Geographical Society of London in 1830, and was incorporated as the Royal Geographical Society in 1859. At some point in these transitions it absorbed the African Association, which was in existence as early as 1788. Its mandate was to advance geographical knowledge, which it accomplished through lectures and its two publications: *The Geographical Journal* and the *Geographical Magazine*. The *Journal* is a bonanza to anyone interested in researching the Libyan Desert. Article after article provides in-depth information on the area. A second mandate was to support exploration and research, which it accomplished with gusto throughout the nineteenth century. It figures prominently in the history of exploration in Egypt and the Western Desert. In 1995, it merged with the Institute of British Geographers.

Harding King explored the desert around Kharga and Dakhla on three expeditions for the Royal Geographical Society at the beginning of the twentieth century. He fixed the location of Abu Minqar, mapped the eastern boundary of Farafra, explored the small depressions to the north of Ain Amur, and marched south of Dakhla toward Uwaynat looking for Zerzura and mapping new terrain. King did a lot of ethnographic work and recorded songs and poems.

Sir Robert Clayton-East-Clayton had a short career in the Libyan Desert. Educated at Dartmouth he was with the Royal Navy, serving as a pilot. He bought a Gypsy I Moth and his thirst for adventure led him to Egypt. Meeting up with Almasy, P. A. Clayton, on loan from the Desert Survey Department, and Squadron Leader Penderel of the Royal Air Force, they went in quest of Zerzura "with three motor-cars and one light aeroplane." Jumping off from Kharga Oasis on April 12, Sir Robert flew over the wadi while Almasy was off at Kufra visiting the Italians (he brought back 12 bottles of Chianti). He died two months after returning from the Gilf Kebir in September of 1933, of "a rare form of poliomyelitis." His ashes were scattered over the English Channel.

A Hungarian

Ladislaus Edouard de Almasy (1895–1951), a Hungarian count, did a little of everything in the Western Desert, including spying. He was fearless, some said suicidal. Speaking six languages, he first came to Egypt as a representative of the Austrian Steyr off-road car. He was an engineer by profession and had a brother, Janos, who inherited the family fortune. They were the sons of Gyorgy Almasy, a famous zoologist and explorer of Central Asia. "Laszlo" met Prince Hussein Kamal al-Din while the prince, an avid horseman, was hunting in Hungary and his brother Janos had just purchased Emperor Karl's stables. In 1929, after one abortive attempt to be the first, he succeeded in crossing the Darb al-Arbain by motorcar, with the prince of Liechtenstein.

He had a great love of flying and owned a de Havilland Gypsy Moth. Between 1923 and 1938, first under the leadership of Prince Kamal al-Din, he crisscrossed the dangerous terrain of the Libyan Desert by airplane, seeking to solve many of its mysteries. Though unsuccessful in his search for the lost army of Cambyses, many discoveries are credited to him. In 1931, he was the first to find his way to the top of the Gilf Kebir via a gap now called Aqaba near Wadi Firaq.

In 1932, Almasy was traveling with Sir Robert Clayton-East-Clayton and Wing Commander Penderel on a Zerzura quest up the western side of the Gilf Kebir. He went to Kufra while they winged over "an acacia-dotted wadi in the Gilf Kebir," which later became known as the Wadi Abd al-Malik. Clayton-East-Clayton died before he could return to explore it on foot and his wife, Lady Dorothy Clayton-East-Clayton, although she mounted an expedition to find it, did not succeed. It was Almasy who actually explored the wadi by foot. They all believed that this, along with Wadi Hamra and Wadi Talh, was "the true Zerzura, the Oasis of the Blacks." (See Uwaynat for details.)

Almasy discovered at least two sets of rock art: the Cave of Swimmers at Ain Sura and the drawings at Ain Doua. (See Uwaynat for details.) The Wadi Sura is located along the western side of the Gilf Kebir. The paintings were part of the central theme of the movie *The English Patient*, which brought them into prominence. Almasy was present when the drawings at Ain Doua at Gebel Uwaynat on the Libyan side of the mountain were found. Professor Caporiacco of the Italian Army was the first to publish them.

His next adventure took him to the dunes southeast of Siwa with Baron von der Esch, looking for the lost army of Cambyses. In World War I, he was a flying ace and in World War II he joined the Hungarian Air Force, which lend-leased him to Rommel's Panzer Armee Afrika. This lend-lease got him into trouble with his former friends. Photos he had taken on one of his Western Desert journeys were later used by Rommel in the Afrika Korps handbook *Nord Ost Afrika* and landed Almasy in jail after the war.

He was, still under lend-lease, a key figure in the German spy ring operating in Cairo during World War II, which inspired the novel *The Key to Rebecca*. Actually conceived by the Brandenburg Brigade (see below) it was known as the Kondor Mission. Its role was to supply Rommel with intelligence information on British military action in Egypt, especially in the Western Desert. Almasy went into the desert under Operation Salam, which he claimed was an anagram for his name. He led the two German spies, Eppler and Monkaster, to Asyut from Tripoli by going south to Gebel Uwaynat, over Gilf Kebir via Aqaba Pass, and on to Dakhla and Kharga, where he fooled the sentries on duty along the desert routes. He returned to the desert while his charges headed for Cairo and a houseboat on the Nile. No one chased him through the desert. None of his old buddies knew he was there. However, according to Peter Clayton, the son of P. A. Clayton, one lady did: Jean Howard. She worked for Ultra.

Ultra was part of the British intelligence system responsible for breaking the Enigma Code of the German army. The Enigma Code was a ciphering system used to transmit military messages throughout the Third Reich. Enigma, Greek for 'puzzle,' was based on an enciphering machine for radio transmission invented in the 1920s. Germany modified Enigma for military needs during the same decade and built a top-secret factory for the manufacture of the machines in East Germany. Howard, who spoke Hungarian, had been assigned to Almasy and she followed his every move. She knew he was on Operation Salam. In fact, the British, thanks to breaking the Enigma Code, knew of the entire plot.

When P. A. Clayton of the Long Range Desert Group, Almasy's old traveling companion in the Western Desert, was in a prisoner of war camp in Italy, Almasy went to visit. He told Patrick he had found the land mines meant for him at the Gilf Kebir and moved them to other locations. (Shaw says these mines never existed.) Peter Clayton believes Almasy may have helped his father by seeing that he was put into a more liberal prison camp instead of the dreaded Campo Cinque, where he was reputedly scheduled to go. Almasy himself was not so lucky. He was a prisoner of the Russians, suffered chronic amoebic dysentery, lost all his teeth, and by the time his friends were able to extricate him from a Russian prison his health was completely shattered.

In addition to helping fill in the voids in cartography, Almasy was important to civil aviation in Egypt. He set the record in 1949 by towing a glider plane from Paris to Cairo. He buzzed Cheop's pyramid in another glider. He was appointed head of the Desert Institute, housed in the villa of his now deceased friend Prince Kamal al-Din, in 1951, the same year of his death.

He has a number of publications to his credit including *Récentes explorations dans le désert Libyque (1932–36)* published by the Societé Royal de Géographie d'Egypte in Cairo and *Unbekannte Sahara: mit Flugzeug und Auto in der Libyschen Wüste* published by F. U. Brockhaus in Leipzig. There are also two travelogs.

Almasy's life was filled with controversy. Did he find Zerzura or didn't he? Was he the first European to see the rock art at Ain Doua or wasn't he? Was the Cave of Swimmers his discovery or P. A. Clayton's? Was he a willing German spy or wasn't he? Two fellow Hungarians, Janos Gudenus and Laszlo Szentirmany, even want to take his aristocratic status away. They are supported by Gert Buchheit, who maintains the Almasys were ancient magnates "whose title of count was abrogated after their participation in the 1849 Kossuth revolution." So, was he a count or wasn't he?

All these controversies make him a most intriguing figure. And now he has become a romantic one, glamorized as the mysterious burns victim in Michael Ondaatje's book and the movie *The English Patient*, winner of the Best Picture at the Academy Awards of 1996. When it is all said, Almasy was important to the exploration of the Libyan Desert. Among the Bedouin of Egypt, he was affectionately known as Abu Ramla, Father of the Dunes. One hopes that pleased him!

The Women

Undoubtedly the most famous woman explorer or traveler in the Libyan Desert is **Alexine Tinne** (1835–69) Alexandrine Pieternella Françoise Tinne was a wealthy Dutch adventuress who first came to Egypt in the early 1860s. She came looking for the source of the Nile and brought along her mother, aunt, servants, and like Napoleon, a number of scientists. Hoping to meet with British explorer John Speke, she got as far as Gondokoro and waited. When he did not arrive, she headed toward central Africa (present Zaire). Then she went back to Gondokoro, but again no Speke, so she headed back to Cairo. Her mother, aunt, and two scientists died on this journey. That did not daunt Alexine Tinne. In 1867, she moved to Algiers, and in 1869 wanted to be the first woman to cross the Sahara Desert. She took the Tripoli route through Libya. In Murzuk, she took a side trip to visit a Tuareg tribe and was robbed and murdered by her guides.

Rosita Forbes was not liked very much by the "in" crowd in British Cairo. One could understand why. She was a spirited adventuress who really did not care much for precedence. If she wanted something she found a way to get it. Most history books maintain that she accompanied Ahmed Hassanein to Kufra Oasis in November 1920. It is more correct to say that he accompanied her. She organized the trip and Hassanein came along. It was Rosita who hopped from one continent to another getting all the proper documents and permissions for the journey. It was Rosita who financed the trip, outfitted it, and got all the logistics in order. Traveling under the name of Sitt Khadiija, she was the first foreign woman in Kufra and wrote *The Secret of the Sahara: Kufara,* the first book to describe the region to Europeans. For her exploits she received recognition by the Royal Geographical Society.

After North Africa, Forbes when to Arabia, then to Ethiopia where she again went on an adventure described in her book *From Red Sea to Blue Nile.* A list of her publications speaks of the scope of her travels. There were over 20 books including six novels and an autobiography, *Gypsy in the Sun.* She died in the United States in 1967.

A character somewhat based on **Lady Dorothy Mary Clayton-East-Clayton** died in the Cave of Swimmers in the Gilf Kebir in the film *The English Patient.* The real Lady Clayton-East Clayton accompanied her husband Lord Robert on some of his expeditions in quest of Zerzura and continued the journeys after his premature death in 1932. On her only solo quest for Zerzura she was joined by Commander Roundell, perhaps her boyfriend, and P. A. Clayton, whom she met through the efforts of Ahmed Hassanein. They journeyed from Bahariya to Ain Della, the Great Sand Sea, the Gilf Kebir, Kufra Oasis, back to Siwa, and on to Cairo. No Zerzura. She was the first woman to drive into the Great Sand Sea and the Gilf Kebir.

She, too, died prematurely, in 1933, but not in a cave surrounded by rock art in the Libyan Desert. While taxiing her airplane in Brooklands airfield in England, she suddenly jumped out of the cockpit and fell to the ground. She probably hit some part of the airplane during her fall, as she fractured her skull. Her death was ruled death by misadventure.

Today a number of women are making their way to the Egyptian desert. **Waltraud 'Wally' Lama,** a German-born adventuress married to the desert explorer Samir Lama, not only drives her own vehicle kilometer by kilometer with her husband through the deep desert, but also does all the cooking and cleanup. She works closely with museums and scientists in Germany and France and is always on the lookout for new places for them to explore. **Arita Baaijens** trekked the Libyan Desert by camel, making several journeys that she writes about in her book *Kameelentochten door de Egyptische Woestijn,* written in Dutch. And myself, who first went into the Western Desert on a visit to Bahariya as a guest of the village of Mandisha in June, 1978. I had been to the Fayoum and northern coast earlier, but this was my first oasis. It changed my life.

The Egyptians

The true history of the Egyptians and their desert will probably never be written, for most of it was never recorded. From the days of the pharaohs the vast empty spaces of the desert provided not only mineral wealth, but a buffer that put off all but the most hearty invaders. Many a hieroglyphic inscription written on tombs in the Nile Valley tells tales of ancient exploits. Yet we know so little about them. The modern Egyptian has continued his ancestors' relationship with the desert, traveling its empty spaces to explore, record, and map. This time, for now, we have a record. It, too, may disappear in the distant future. It seems, when it comes to this desert, nothing is forever.

In 1923, **Ahmed Hassanein**, the first of the modern Egyptian explorers, made a remarkable journey of 3,572 kilometers (2,220 miles) from the port of Sollum on the Mediterranean Sea via the oasis of Kufra (now in Libya) past Uwaynat into Fasher in Sudan. It was the first recorded crossing of the Libyan Desert in modern times and is one of the greatest desert journeys in history. On this expedition Hassanein fixed the true positions of Zieghen and Kufra oases in Libya, discovered the existence of Gebel Arkenu, also in Libya, and Gebel Uwaynat in the southwestern corner of the country, and discovered a route from southwestern Egypt to Darfur in Sudan. The 1923 expedition was actually his second major desert trek. In 1920, he went from the Mediterranean to Kufra Oasis accompanied by Rosita Forbes.

Hassanein brought a duality that had been missing in desert exploration. He was an Egyptian educated in Europe. He was able to combine European scholarship with Middle Eastern diplomacy and expertise. His journey was blessed by the king of Egypt and he came as a friend to the Bedouin and Sanusi. They opened the way with their hospitality and desert knowledge. He knew the desert. He knew the desert people. He knew the language, the superstitions, the taboos. He understood the protocol. On the unknown part of his journey he encountered tribesmen who became his guides, not his enemies. On the day he was taken to the rock drawings at Uwaynat his Tebu guide told him of more drawings half a day's journey away. He did not go. In his book he says, "I did not want to excite suspicion, I did not go to them." Only a person sensitive to the culture will understand Hassanein's savvy.

Prince Kamal al-Din was a great sportsman. He loved horsemanship and his great love for hunting led him into Egypt's deserts. Soon he began to explore the Western Desert in earnest. In 1923, the same year that Hassanein made his journey, using Citröen caterpillars that were specially adapted to travel in the desert, the prince took a team of scientists, doctors, mechanics, and servants with him to the desert.

One of the prince's dynamic Citröen cars was found by the Geological Survey at Bir Kiseiba in 1965 and brought back to Maadi, where it stayed for some time in Rushdi Said's garden on Road 12. Unfortunately, Egyptian bureaucracy being what it was, the Survey Department could not license the vehicle because they could not prove ownership. It was eventually sold.

In 1923–24, Prince Kamal journeyed via Bahariya and Farafra (the first motor car in this oasis) with three caterpillars to search for the Rohlfs expedition's cairn at Regenfeld (Rainfield). He found it. (See Arbain Desert for details.) The following winter, 1924–25, Prince Kamal was again in the Western Desert. This time he journeyed south along the Darb al-Arbain via Bir al-Shab and Bir Tarfawi on his way to Gebel Uwaynat and the oasis of Merga, 360 kilometers (223 miles) east of Uwaynat, in Sudan. Hassanein had discovered Uwaynat the previous year, but it was left to Prince Kamal to map the peaks and springs of the mountain. Throughout his journey he fixed geographic positions and altitudes.

The following year, the prince continued his work in the southwestern corner of Egypt. He was the first to map the Gilf Kebir, which he named. He also supervised a map of the Libyan Desert prepared in Paris, and in 1928 was awarded the Gold Medal of the Geographical Society of France for his extensive work in the Western Desert. This is impressive work, and even more impressive given that the prince had an overwhelming handicap: he was without the use of his legs.

Prince Kamal al-Din was the son of the King Hussein Kamal and was in line for the throne. He did not want it, however, and when his father died it passed to King Fuad. He died in France on August 6, 1932, at 57 years of age. His extensive library is now housed in Cairo University. His palace, sequestered after the revolution, is the home of the Desert Institute. Almasy (see above) was his protégé and the prince funded many of his expeditions.

Prince Omar Toussoon (1872–1944) had a staff of researchers who worked with him and he did a lot of work about the Nile, including collecting hydrology records published by the *Institut d'Egypt*. He did a lot of exploration for the Geographical Society of Egypt using six-wheeled Renaults. In the Western Desert his work was mainly in Wadi Natrun, Abu Mena, and along the northern coast. His library is at the Geographical Society.

Rushdi Said is a son of the Cairo suburb of Maadi. He went to Cairo University and then to Harvard University in the United States. In 1962, Said published *The Geology of Egypt*. Later he published *The River Nile*, which was translated into Arabic, and hundreds of articles. His most recent book is *The Desert and the Rise and Fall of Ancient Egypt*. Said was Director of the Geological Survey from 1968 to 1977.

He decided that there were three areas that needed extensive study: the southeastern desert, the Gulf of Suez, and the Quaternary period. Said launched an expedition to the southeastern desert. Fred Windorf came along and a huge project, lasting to this day, began.

Samir Lama calls himself a desert man. His fellow Egyptians call him a legend. At the age of nine he was taken into the desert to hunt by his famous filmmaker father, Ibrahim Lama. He shot his first lion at age sixteen, and has been exploring Libya, Egypt, and Sudan ever since. He visited the Gilf Kebir for the first time in 1946 and in 1947 he led his own expedition there. He found a new way up the Gilf, and at the halfway point he named the spot Lama Point. He found a way down the Gilf Kebir in the north west which he named the Lama/Monod Pass.

Now nearly 70 years old, he is a gruff, tough, taskmaster in the desert where he gives no quarter to travelers as he determines how wide a window should be open, how early a person should awaken or sleep, who should sit where, ride where, and walk where. He guards his secrets from the prying eyes of writers like me and does not want his desert overrun with amateurs who will get killed trying to find their way around the Gilf Kebir and Gebel Uwaynat. He believes that they will despoil the desert by taking all the silica glass, the ancient spearheads, and ancient tools. He is right.

Despite his gruffness, he has a kind heart, a warm smile, and twinkling eyes.

The Warriors

The modern soldiers, Axis and Allied alike, who lived and died in the Libyan Desert during the first half of this century were explorers by necessity. Armies needed water, escape routes, and battle plans. Through the years the men who met these needs did more in less time to discover the ins and outs of the Libyan Desert than any other single force. A great deal of work was done by the Light Car Patrols and the Long Range Desert Group of the British Army. Egypt was defensible in almost all places but one: Uwaynat. And Uwaynat led to Aswan and the Aswan Dam. These patrols had to keep Uwaynat safe.

Light Car Patrols

The Light Car Patrols were the first. In 1916, the British Army launched a number of motor cars mounted with machine guns to guard the 1,280 kilometer (800 mile) frontier of the Western Desert against the Sanusi of Libya. This was the first major attempt to tame the desert by automobile. It worked very well. The Ford became the vehicle of choice and its narrow rubber wheels soon began leaving marks throughout the desert, some still visible today. The men included Lieutenant Colonel Llewellyn Partridge (thus Partridge Gap), Captain Claude Williams (thus Williams Dunes, Williams Pass, Williams Mountain), Major Wilfred Jennings-Bramly (founder of the new Burg al-Arab), Doctor John Ball (thus Ball's Road), Major Owston (thus Owston's Dunes) and Lieutenant Colonel Nowell de Lancey Forth (with no geographic claim to fame). These names will not be found on desert maps today, but they existed in 1915–16, and identify key locations in the Italo–Egyptian Accord that established the border between Egypt and Libya.

Although intended as a reconnaissance group of the army, the Light Car Patrols explored the unknown territories of the Libyan Desert with gusto. They rediscovered and opened the old desert routes, mapped much of the northern and northwestern sections of the desert, named many of the landmarks like Gebels Peter and Paul and Ammonite Hill. When World War I came to an end, so did the Light Car Patrols. Exploring the desert fell from high priority.

Long Range Desert Group

The Libyan Desert was a major theater of operation during World War II. The intense activity culminated in the Battle of al-Alamein (see al-Diffa for details), but the activity of the armies, both Axis and Allied, went far beyond the coastal plains of the desert. Every inch of the desert was under observation, especially remote Uwaynat, which was the corridor to the Aswan Dam.

The Long Range Desert Group (LRDG) was the brainchild of then Major Ralph A. Bagnold of the British Troops in Egypt (BTE) Signal Corp. It was patterned after the Light Car Patrols of World War I. Its primary objective was to maneuver through the desert behind enemy lines causing as much disruption as possible. Anthony Eden called it his "mosquito army."

With headquarters at the Citadel in Cairo, it was officially formed on July 3, 1940. The group was divided into patrols of 10 trucks and 30 men each. In a Cairo junkyard Bagnold found old World War I steel channel sections, originally used as dugout roofing, which he used to get cars out of the sand. We still use the same design today. They had dumps at Uwaynat, Big Cairn in the Great Sand Sea, and Ain Della, with a few other places in between. The LRDG was disbanded on August 1, 1945. After the war a LRDG Association was formed.

Among the men who worked in and with the LRDG and whose names became synonymous with the desert were W. B. Kennedy-Shaw, the intelligence officer; P. A. Clayton, a cartographer; Douglas Newbold, a diplomat; Harding-Newman; and Guy Prendergast, a captain of the Royal Tank Corp. Many of them lived in Maadi and planned some of their trips from a villa on the corner of Fuad al-Awwal and Road 15.

The personnel were mainly New Zealanders, bivouacked in Maadi, originally under the command of Major-General Bernard Freyberg. One hundred and fifty donned the uniforms of the LRDG, which was distinguished by Arab headdress and desert sandals. Their insignia became a scorpion within a wheel.

Ralph A. Bagnold was probably the most prolific writer of the group. During the pre-war days he organized two major expeditions into the desert: 1929–30 and 1932. In the first, he was accompanied by Newbold and Shaw and they traveled to Uwaynat and the Great Sand Sea. In the latter, eight men and four cars went from Kharga to Uwaynat and Sarra Wells, then up the Darb al-Arbain from al-Fasher, al-Atrun, Merga (a detour), Laqiya, and Selima. This trip was supported by the Royal Geographical Society and Shell Oil. Bagnold was awarded a Gold Medal by the Royal Geographical Society in 1934 for this effort.

His 1938 expedition had a purpose, too. It was to confirm his theories about blowing sand, especially wind tunnel results. Again the Royal Geographical Society helped sponsor the expedition. The expedition was joined by scientists of the Mond Expedition and together they traveled to the Gilf Kebir, which they reached in February, 1938. In 1939, Bagnold was back in the army in East Africa. He was recalled to Egypt and, under the wise guidance of General Wavell, formed the LRDG. Bagnold wrote extensively on the Western Desert. Among his publications are *Early Days of the Long Range Desert Group*, *Libyan Sands: Travel in a Dead World*, *The Physics of Blown Sand and Desert Dunes*, and *Sand, Wind and War: Memoirs of a Desert Explorer*.

W. B. Kennedy-Shaw (Shaw) was educated at Oxford and in 1923 accepted a post as forester in Sudan. He and soon to be governor of Kordofan, Douglas Newbold, an Arabic scholar, explored much of the southwestern part of the Libyan Desert, especially in Sudan. In Sudan, the two of them mapped Merga Depression and discovered Burg al-Tuyur, Hill of Birds. They "explored the desert between Merga and Selima on the last scientific camel expedition in the Western Desert" in the 1920s. It wasn't long before Shaw gave up forestry and worked full time as an archaeologist.

Newbold's and Shaw's articles in both *Sudan Notes and Records* and the *Geographical Journal* are invaluable for anyone interested in the Darb al-Arbain and the southwestern portion of the Libyan Desert. On one journey to the Great Sand Sea and Uwaynat, in 1936, Shaw traveled over 6,000 miles including Wadi Howar and Wadi Hussein, again in Sudan. On this trip he discovered a number of rock paintings in Wadi Howar. It was Shaw that presented the plight of the Kufra refugees to the world in a meeting of the Royal Geographical Society in 1931. (See Dakhla Oasis for details.)

When called to the LRDG he was with the Palestine Department of Antiquities. He published the book *Long Range Desert Group* in 1945. He died April 23, 1979.

Axis Groups

Of course, the LRDG had rival units among the Italians and Germans. The major German unit was the **Brandenburg Brigade**. It was composed of German expatriates who had lived abroad, knew the terrain and languages of other countries, and, Peter Clayton politely says, were "penetration agents." One of its function was to infiltrate Egypt with German intelligence operatives. It was responsible for Operation Kondor and as a part of that big operation, Operation Salam, which was Almasy's dash through the desert to place two spies in Cairo.

The Italians had the **Auto Saharan Companies**. One company was captured at Sidi Barrani in 1940 which Peter Clayton says, "should have been at Murzuk awaiting my father." Another, based at Kufra actually caught Clayton at Abu Sherif Automobiles and airplanes worked in tandem, the latter spotting the enemy and the former attacking. It was not unusual for the airplanes to land and assist the ground forces whenever necessary. These companies were well organized, and good at what they did. Once the French captured Kufra, they were out of business.

Mapping Egypt

The mapping of the Libyan Desert has been going on for some time. Very early in Mediterranean history the coast of Africa was mapped. Among the earliest and probably best of early cartographers was **Claudius Ptolemaeus**, known throughout the world as Ptolemy. He lived in Alexandria during its glory years. Although he was not the first Egyptian to know the Western Desert, he was one of the few that opened it up to the Western World.

H. Hagedorn in "The African Map in the 18th and 19th Centuries" in *Annals of the*

Geological Survey of Egypt acknowledges that seamen's charts of the fourteenth century, Italian cartographers' maps of the fifteenth century, and Diego Ribero's maps for Charles V of 1527, were remarkably accurate in their portrayals of the area. Even the mapping of the Nile to the fifth cataract was acceptable. It was the interior of the desert that was unknown.

The French Geographer **Bourgignon d'Anville** in 1749, produced what Hagedorn calls "probably for the first time in history, a map." When the French came to Egypt, Jacotin produced forty-seven sheets of maps of Egypt. This set African exploration in motion. In the 1800s, as soon as a new European discovery was made, a new map was produced. Between the English Royal Geographical Society and the German **August Heinrich Petermann**, cartography exploded. The maps of C. Mauch's South African journey and Gustav Nachtigal's voyage to Tibesti were published in 1870. The Rohlfs Expedition in Egypt and the map of Stanley's Lake Victoria were published in 1875. The Rohlfs geological map was "the first reliable geological map of the extensive deserts to the south of the latitude of Fayoum." It remained the standard until the Survey published their own maps.

The French didn't do so badly either. They published forty-seven maps done by triangulation by **Edmé Jomard** and reissued them again in 1882. In 1855, **Linant de Bellefonds** published the Nile Valley. The French also did excellent maps of Algeria and Tunisia from 1864 to 1899.

The Geological Survey and its sister organizations the Egyptian General Survey Authority, the Topographical Survey founded in 1903, the Desert Survey founded in 1920, and the Geodetic (eventually they all merged) are primarily responsible for the mapping of Egypt in modern times. H. G. Lyons supervised the first Cadastral Survey of the country.

Despite Napoleon's savants making Egypt the best know country in the world, maps of remote regions were lacking. In fact, John Ball had been asked to make a contour map of the Libyan Desert for the International "Million" map of the world, but could not do so for so much of the area was unknown territory and could not be contoured. By 1925, only 20 percent of Egypt had been mapped, 24 percent was known from reconnaissance, and 56 percent was totally unknown. By 1948, the percentages were 40 percent, 26 percent, and 34 percent. By 1970, 22 percent of the land of Egypt was still unknown territory and most of the unexplored terrain was in the Western Desert. That is a staggering amount of unknown territory in the late twentieth century.

The Survey published the first topography map of Egypt in 1910. Based on reconnaissance surveys, it appeared in six sheets. In 1911, they published the first geological map. By 1914, a new map on the scale of 1/250,000 was published based on a systematic survey. In 1922, a map scaled 1 to 2 million, prepared by P. A. Clayton was published. In 1971, after several improved editions of the 1922 map had been published, a new geological map was published. In 1981, the first colored version of the 1971 map appeared. The Survey has been making maps ever since. Once the first satellite began circling the globe there were soon no more unknown territories in Egypt. By 1995, a different kind of exploration was underway.

Egypt from Space

Today exploration has become much more specialized than in the past. Many of the early riddles have been solved and explorers, geologists, botanists, and other enthusiasts venture into the desert with specialized tasks, including exploration from space.

Photographing the Western Desert has been on the agenda of manned missions of Gemini IV to XII, Apollo 7 and 9, Skylab 2, 3, and 4, the Apollo–Soyuz Test Project, and Landsat. Formerly, the only known aerial photographs of the Western Desert were a few from Kharga Oasis dune fields and World War II reconnaissance photographs of the northern coast. With space travel, it all changed. Bit by bit, aerial views of such unknown areas as Gilf Kebir, Gebel Uwaynat, and the Great Sand Sea are defining some of the last frontiers of the world. It is called remote sensing.

Remote sensing merely means "collecting information about an object without the use of physical contact," like taking a picture. Today, it means taking those photographs from space. The man who sits at the center of this amazing industry is **Farouk al-Baz**, an Egyptian–American. Al-Baz formerly established and directed the Center for Earth and Planetary Studies at the National Air and Space Museum of the Smithsonian Institution and is currently Professor of Remote Sensing and founding director of the Center for Remote Sensing at Boston University.

Remote sensing from space became possible when technology developed new methods of photographing with minimum light, created computers powerful enough to deal with the process, and placed "carrier platforms" aboard such vehicles as Skylab, Spacelab, Landsat, Seasat, and Meteosat. Each is taking pictures of a specific place like the sky, space, land, sea, and meteors.

The first aerial views of Egypt's desert were of the southwestern regions of the desert by the Gemini missions. They gave us a clear view of the directions of the sand dune belts and a vertical view of Gebel Uwaynat. Apollo 7 gave us an unprecedented view of the southern half of the Gilf Kebir showing its flat top and many wadis. From this view it was clear that the wadis were made by water erosion. Apollo 9, in addition to new views of Uwaynat and its dune belt areas, gave us impressive images of the southeastern desert showing ancient lake beds. Skylab continued the work in the southeast. By this time the southwestern deserts similarities with Mars were apparent and the Apollo–Soyuz Test Project gave high priority to photographing the Egyptian desert once again.

Landsat began in July of 1972. Unmanned and working at an altitude of over 900 kilometers (562 miles), Landsat has a near-polar orbit and takes eighteen days to cover the earth. The data can be enhanced to 1:250,000. To date, five Landsat satellites have been launched each more sophisticated and faster than the last. Landsat 4 and 5 are about 705 kilometers (440 miles) above the earth and circle it every ninety-eight minutes. Landsat 6 was launched in 1993, but did not succeed and Landsat 7 was launched early in 1998. In Egypt, it takes about sixty landsat frames to cover the entire country, this is better than the former 1,300 aerial photographs (at 1:40,000).

In 1978, al-Baz led a team of sixteen scientists from Kharga Oasis to Gilf Kebir and Gebel Uwaynat as part of an Apollo–Soyuz project to verify photographs taken from space. He is a pioneer in applying space photography to arid terrain, especially in search of water resources. The Western Desert has benefited from his research.

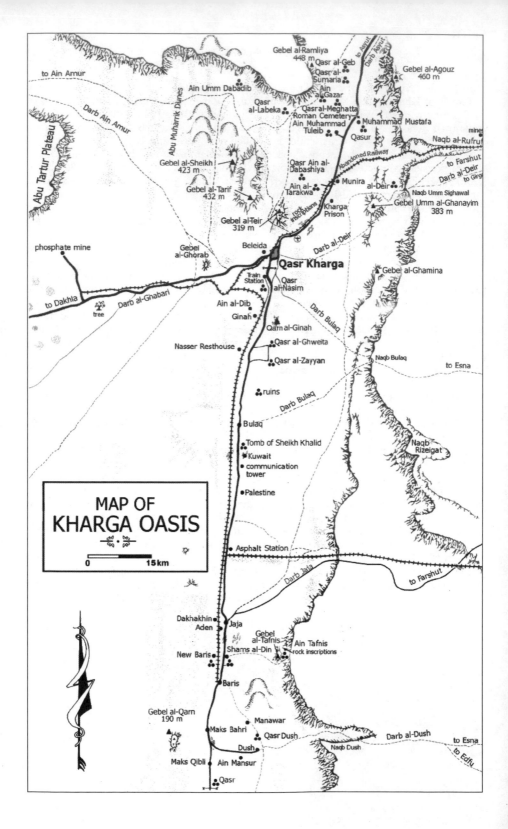

MAP OF
KHARGA OASIS

0   15km

3
Kharga Oasis

Asyut to the Kharga Escarpment

			km	total km
Cairo/Asyut Rd	N 27 06 485	E 31 00 519	0	0
Wadi al-Battikha	N 26 27 217	E 30 47 320	75	75
Checkpoint	N 26 19 366	E 30 43 196	7	82
Naqb al-Ramliya (top)	N 25 57 275	E 30 42 497	42	124

A major change has taken place since the first edition of this book: the Cairo–Asyut Desert Road has opened. There are now two paved roads leading to Kharga Oasis from the north. The original route follows the river and almost always requires an overnight stop at Asyut. The new road, which begins on the Fayoum Road and runs south through the desert, is faster and does not require an overnight rest. The two roads merge just after the Asyut road has climbed out of the Nile Valley, approximately 25 kilometers (16 miles) into the desert and 350 kilometers from Cairo.

Once the two roads join, the traveler is on the famous **Darb al-Arbain**, used by traders and travelers since the earliest of times. No sooner do you catch your breath than the Asyut airport appears on the left. Today the drive from Asyut to Kharga takes about four hours, but when the road was unpaved and the mode of travel was the camel, the journey took thirty-eight hours—and another four to descend the escarpment.

Wadi al-Battikha

The desert to Kharga is uninspiring and strewn with unattractive stones until about 75 kilometers (47 miles) into the journey. Here the first of three small valleys, collectively called Wadi al-Battikha, Valley of the Melons, appears on the east (left) side of the road. The first and second valleys are separated by a small hill topped by a primitive desert outpost. The third, and best, is a few kilometers down the road. This third wadi runs west as far as the eye can see and is a good place to stop and wander. The unusual Lower Eocene stones are a fairly common feature of wind erosion and can be found in various places in the Western Desert, of which this is the most accessible. The name Wadi al-Battikha comes from the stones, which are locally called *battikha* (melons) because of their similarity to the Egyptian variety of watermelon. The stones are subspheroidal siliceous concretions, gray in color and often polished to a good shine by sand blasting. Some of them have been split in half by temperature extremes.

Checkpoints

There is a military checkpoint (*taftish*) at the resthouse just beyond the Valley of the Melons. For those who wish to pause, tea and biscuits are available, but in any event all vehicles must stop for the military authorities. The officer records the license-plate number, asks the destination of the vehicle, inspects the car papers, and asks to see the passports of all passengers. This is the first of many checkpoints the traveler will encounter in the desert. These checkpoints, which mark the points at which vehicles leave one area and enter another, are for the protection of the traveler. It is good to know someone is aware you have entered the desert.

Naqb al-Ramliya

The road enters Kharga Oasis through Naqb al-Ramliya, Pass of the Sand Dunes, also called **Naqb Asyut** because the road terminates in Asyut in the Nile Valley. Used by a bevy of nineteenth-century explorers including Schweinfurth in the 1870s, Blundell in the 1890s, and

Moritz in 1900, the descent, in the past knee-deep in sand, offers wonderful panoramas. When the escarpment was unpaved it took four hours to descend; now it can be done in a matter of minutes. On a clear day some of the Roman forts that dot the depression floor are visible to the west. The road snakes 9 kilometers (5.6 miles) down the scarp to the floor of the depression.

There are a number of passes along this eastern escarpment. Only 13 kilometers (8.1 miles) south of Naqb al-Ramliya is **Naqb Yabsa**, where a track exits the oasis and later joins the road to Asyut. It has an easier ascent than Ramliya, but not for cars. Two tracks leave the oasis from Yabsa Pass. The first joins the Darb al-Arbain here at Ramliya Pass, while the second, south of the first, heads north to al-Ghanayim over 180 kilometers (112 miles) away.

Kharga Oasis

Kharga is the seat of the New Valley Governorate and the most populous oasis of the Western Desert. Although it offers a variety of sites of interest to the visitor, including ancient fortresses and villages, in Kharga it is the landscape that most overwhelms the traveler. For it is in Kharga that we encounter the desert as we had always imagined it to be.

History

Two points emerge over and over when investigating life in the desert. In times of prosperity in the Nile Valley its control reached into the oases. In hard times, the oases were left to fend for themselves, and were often invaded and influenced from the west. When water was plentiful, the oases thrived; when water was scant, they did not.

Evidence of early human presence can be found throughout the Kharga depression, including along the escarpment. Most settlements occur around water sources including playa lakes and springs that are now fossilized. In Kharga there are springs at high elevations, and ancient settlements have been found in the passes leading out of the oases. This is especially true along the eastern scarp at such sites as Naqb al-Rufuf.

Pharaonic (2686–332 B.C.)

Details of life in Kharga Oasis in pharaonic times have been hard to come by. Recent excavations indicate major settlements in Dakhla Oasis during the Old Kingdom, but in Kharga, nearer to the Nile Valley and situated between it and Dakhla, surprisingly little has been found. There are references to the oasis region as far back as the Sixth Dynasty of the Old Kingdom, when Harkhuf, a governor of Aswan, undertook several expeditions into the Western Desert, but it has not been possible to firmly identify his 'Oasis Road.'

New information about the Middle Kingdom has recently been found around the

Luxor–Farshut road at the fringe of the Nile Valley. This route and all the roads that lead into the Western Desert from it are now under study by the Oriental Institute of Chicago. Desert pottery from as early as the Middle Kingdom has been found in the area. The route is, in all probability, the major ancient Theban route to Kharga and the rest of the desert.

One stela records information about a Middle Kingdom policeman named Kay who made an official visit to the oases from Qamula to round up "criminals and renegades." There must be a wealth of information about the oases and oasis travel in ancient Egypt awaiting discovery along this road.

The area was investigated by Schweinfurth in 1909 and again by the Mond Expedition in 1938. Perhaps the present study by the Oriental Institute of Chicago will solve some riddles about ancient life in the desert.

New Kingdom (1570–1070 B.C.)

More information is available about Kharga during the New Kingdom. Tomb inscriptions in Thebes record taxes paid by the inhabitants of the Western Desert in the form of produce such as dates, grapes and wine, and minerals like ocher. They also tell of punitive expeditions sent into the desert to control the rebellious oaseans. We know too that Kharga was used as a place of exile, a practice which continued well into the twentieth century. So far most of our information has come from Nile Valley sources. Hopefully, the sands of Kharga will soon begin to tell their own story of life in the oasis during the New Kingdom.

Late Period (525–332 B.C.)

By the Twenty-second Dynasty there were Libyans on the throne of Egypt, and the Western Desert became a place of great interest since it lay between the Nile Valley and the Libyan capital. Shoshenq I, the first ruler of the Twenty-second Dynasty, sent officials to Kharga to improve desert tracks and bring the rebellious oaseans under control. By the time of Darius I (521–486 B.C.) the oasis was important enough to merit the construction of two great temples. Thereafter Kharga was permanently attached to the Nile Valley, and the increasing number of monuments attests to the growing activity in the area.

Roman Period (30 B.C. to A.D. 323)

We know most about Kharga in Roman times, when all the oases enjoyed their greatest prosperity. Linked to Dakhla and called the Oasis of the Thebaid and later the Hibis Nome, Kharga was well protected by the Romans. According to Naphtali Lewis in *Life in Egypt under Roman Rule*, Rome usually had two legions in Egypt for a total of 17,000 to 18,000 men. These were accompanied by provincial units composed mostly of non-Romans supervised by Roman officers. This number varied during the centuries of Roman rule. At some point the Romans manned Kharga and Dakhla with two battalions, each containing between 500 and 1,000 men. In Kharga, the Abasgi Battalion was stationed at Hibis, and men from this military force manned the various forts in the oasis. Dakhla was manned by the Quadi Battalion. The soldiers and Bedouin in their hire also patrolled the various desert tracks leading in and out of Kharga. These tracks had garrisoned fortresses, many of which are still standing. They also had watering holes along the routes, where mounds of pottery can still be found, as well as inns along the more heavily traveled routes.

During the Roman occupation new wells were created throughout the oasis, perhaps including some massive aqueducts (see Dabadib below for a discussion of these controversial water systems). They also erected temples, mostly in strategic positions overlooking the main caravan routes. These caravan routes were part of the massive road system built by the Romans in Egypt. They built civil as well as military roads in their provinces. In all, the Romans built 103 roadways, over 4,000 kilometers (2,500 miles) in Egypt. The civil roads were wide, paved, and commonly used by travelers and the post. The military or frontier roads, like those throughout the Libyan Desert, were narrow, had watering stations and post stations and went in a straight line from fort to fort. No one could use the roads without permission, and travelers were issued a passport.

All this building required people. New communities sprang out of the desert and older ones grew in population. The oasis must have bustled with activity, much as it does today. We have yet to discover any papyri here—as we have found in the Fayoum—to give us a bird's eye view of life in Kharga at that time, but we can imagine it to be similar to life in the Fayoum, only a little more provincial, being on the frontier.

The Romans secured the oasis against invasion and internal strife by establishing a series of forts. From the south they first feared invasion by the Maeories, then the Blemmyes, the people Pliny maintained had no heads, but eyes and mouths below their shoulders.

The ancient Egyptian practice of using Kharga as a penal colony was continued by the Romans. One of the most famous victims was Juvenal (60–130), the satirist who spoke against Rome's corruption and vices. Beadnell tells us that Juvenal was first banished to Syene (Aswan) and then to Kharga for "his attacks on the Court [of Hadrian]." Once the emperor died, Juvenal returned to Rome and freedom.

Christian Era (323–642)

All one has to do is look at the grand cemetery of Bagawat to see that Kharga was not only Christian, but Christian in a big way. There were churches and hermitages every-where. At almost every ancient site either a church was built, or an existing structure was converted into a church. Christianity stuck around longer here than it did in the Nile Valley. When Islam did come, it came mostly from the west, via Libya.

Christians, too, were banished to the oases when different sects were fighting for control of the church in Egypt. Banishment to the oases was a punishment that had existed since pharaonic times, when Dakhla Oasis was known as the 'Oasis to Which We Deport.' Since no one was expected to escape into the desert and find the way back to civilization, banishment was in effect a death sentence. If the person lived in Lower Egypt they were deported to the oases near Upper Egypt, that is Kharga and sometimes Dakhla. If they lived in Upper Egypt, they were deported to Siwa, and sometimes Bahariya.

Among the prominent men who were exiled to Kharga in the fourth century was **Athanasius** (298–373), a native of Alexandria who had served as patriarch of the Christian Church in Egypt and was probably the most important Christian theologian of his time. Constantinus, the successor to the Emperor Constantine, who deposed Athanasius shortly after the establishment of Constantinople, set in motion a period of turmoil within the Egyptian Church that saw Athanasius banished at least five times, due to his support for the Nicaean position of the church. This position believed that the Son of God was one and the same with God the Father. Nicaeanism stood in opposition to Arianism, which held that the son of God was not one with God, but separate. "The Arians," wrote Athanasius, "[have] exceeded the Emperor's orders, in exiling old men and bishops to places unfrequented and inspiring horror; for some were sent from Libya to the Great Oasis, and others from the Thebaid to that of Jupiter Ammon."

Athanasius was exiled to France in 335. In 339, he was exiled to Rome. In 346, he was exiled to the desert, probably to Kharga, where, in 358, he wrote *Discourses against the Arians*. In 362, he was exiled for the fourth time. In 365, he wrote *On the Incarnation of the Word of God and against the Arians*, for which he was sent back into exile. In all, Athanasius spent fifteen years and ten months of his forty-five years as Bishop of Alexandria in exile.

In the desert Athanasius took refuge with hermits, including, according to tradition, the Christian community in Kharga Oasis. In Kharga, Athanasius lived at Bagawat, from where he continued his efforts to reunite the Christian church in Egypt. He had a long association with the Christian community of Kharga. Even before he was banished, Athanasius wrote letters to disciples in Kharga. According to Edmondstone, he died in 373 in the territory of the Ammonians (Siwa). This may be evidence of another banishment. Perhaps his position in Kharga had become so strong, or so comfortable, that another oasis was chosen.

Another Christian banished to Kharga Oasis was **Bishop Nestorius**, Patriarch of Constantinople from 428 to 431. He was exiled to Kharga in 435 by Patriarch Cyril of Alexandria for not accepting the doctrine of the immaculate conception. Nestorius believed that Christ was two-fold—divine and human—and that Mary gave birth to the man and therefore could not be called the Mother of God. This belief led eventually to the establishment of the Nestorian church.

Nestorius was originally banished to Petra in modern-day Jordan, but he converted too many of its citizens to Christianity so he was moved to Kharga. In his papers (most were burned by order of Theodosius II), Nestorius mentions raids against southern Kharga by the Blemmyes of the Nile Valley and tells of his own capture and subsequent release: "After the oasis was . . . taken by the barbarians [Blemmyes] and completely laid waste and devastated by fire, those who, for what cause I know not, carried me off, suddenly took compassion and dismissed me, adding threats. . ." Nestorius eventually died in exile sixteen dreadful years later, some sources say at Panopolis (Akhmim), others at Kharga. He endured extreme persecution at the hands of the Blemmyes.

The bishops Ammonios and Markos were banished, as were the priests Eugenius and Macarius, who arrived in Kharga in 362, having been banished by Julian the Apostate. Peter the Fuller and Caandio of Antioch were banished to Kharga in 471. The monk Dorotheus of Alexandria was banished in 484, and Macedonius Patriarch of Constantinople in 512.

By 390, both Kharga and Dakhla were completely Christian. The community in Kharga, judging by the cemetery at Bagawat, was large, and, with important and charismatic leaders, it thrived. Several monasteries were established and hermits lived in the surrounding desert. The old temples and forts were converted into churches, monasteries such as that of Mustafa Kashif were built, and churches and hermitages were developed in the mountains, especially at Gebel al-Teir. These are among the earliest known Christian religious buildings in Egypt.

By the fifth century, increasing threats from Nubia, Sudan, Chad, Libya, and marauding desert tribes had led to the fortification of many villages, though this did not prevent the destruction of Qasr Kharga by Nubian raiders. The Blemmyes' raid that captured Nestorius took place around 440. Another tribe, the Mazices, from Libya, raided and pillaged throughout the Egyptian portion of the Libyan Desert in the fifth and sixth centuries. They were so bold that around 580 they invaded Wadi Natrun, killing or capturing the monks. They hit Kharga the same year, killing many of the Christians.

Christian influence in Kharga continued until the fourteenth century, yet information about these later years is scarce. Beadnell tells us that Christian customs and festivals were still celebrated in Kharga in 1907.

Islamic Era (641 to 1798)

The earliest reports of an Arab presence in the oases date to the seventh century, though there is no way of knowing exactly when the oases came under the direct control of Egypt's medieval rulers. By the Middle Ages, the oases were once again neglected and as the population declined many of the wells fell into disrepair. In fact, the Arab geographer al-Idrisi tells us Kharga was "laid waste and without any population." Al-Maqrizi, in the fifteenth century, says that the oases were too far away to belong to any province from the Nile Valley and that in 943 their ruler was the Arab Abd al-Malik ibn Marwan. Local legend holds that the grave of the Arab general Khalid ibn al-Walid is to be found near Bulaq.

By the Mamluk Era (1250–1517) Kharga had fallen under the direct control of the central government in Cairo. Soldiers were sent to garrison the towns and fortresses, and emigrated to the oasis along with their families. Their major responsibilities were the defense of both villages and caravan trails and the assessment and collection of taxes.

The Ottoman Period saw the oases mostly under the control of the Turks. They appointed Kashifs to oversee their interests and janissaries to enforce their edicts. The oases were peaceful enough to permit foreign travelers. The French traveler Poncet, who visited Kharga in 1698, reports the oases were in good order with clear flowing wells and a Turkish administration. They remained so for two centuries; as late as the eighteenth century both Kharga and Baris were administered by Ibrahim Bey al-Kebir, a Turkish official.

Muhammad Ali

When the French invaded Upper Egypt large caravans of Mamluks and peasants escaped to the oases for protection. Muhammad Ali reconquered them, then left them virtually independent, on condition that they paid tribute, usually rice, to their nominal ruler. Hoskins, who visited Kharga and Dakhla in 1832, comments on the rule of Muhammad Ali:

> When he [Muhammad Ali] invaded the territory of these people, many of them made an obstinate resistance, but his arms were victorious; and the fruit of his success is a considerable tribute, collected from each oasis, without either trouble or expense. If he had left large garrisons in each district, their maintenance would have absorbed a great portion of the revenues of the place, their tyrannical conduct would have excited the indignation of the inhabitants, and doubtless many of his soldiers would have fallen victims to the baneful diseases often fatal to the natives, and much more so to strangers.

Hoskins found the merchant class thriving on the sale of dates to the Nile Valley and by importing wheat, spices, coffee, arms, clothes, ornaments, mirrors, and glass beads, which they sold at great profit.

In 1893, the Dervish invaded Kharga and Dakhla via the Darb al-Arbain, occupying Baris in July. Kharga then briefly resumed its place as a post for exiles, this time for Nile Valley robbers, one of whom came as late as 1914.

European Travelers

We know of one European who visited Kharga in the seventeenth century, the French physician Monsieur Poncet. He was headed for Abyssinia along the Darb al-Arbain and arrived at Kharga in 1698, calling it Helaoue, Country of Sweetness. He believed Kharga to be the border of Egypt at that time and found it garrisoned with 500 Janissaries and 300 Spahis, some of them undoubtedly in the fortresses strung along the Darb al-Arbain.

In the eighteenth century, W. G. Browne followed the Darb al-Arbain south, and in June, 1793, he was in Kharga. (For details about Browne's journey as well as other explorers and travelers along the Darb al-Arbain see the chapter of the same name.)

Two foreigners are thought to have arrived in Kharga in 1818. The French mineralogist Frederic Cailliaud published the first known descriptions and illustrations of Kharga's antiquities. He traveled from Esna to Jaja along the Darb al-Jaja to enter the oasis, and left via Darb al-Rufuf to Farshut in 1818. He is credited with the discovery of the Temple of Hibis. He returned in 1820, after visits to Siwa, Bahariya, Farafra, and Dakhla. The second traveler is reported to have been the French consul Drovetti, but this date is suspect. He traveled the Darb al-Arbain all the way to Dongola in Sudan and returned to Kharga. Then he went to Dakhla and took the Darb al-Tawil back to the Nile Valley. (For the controversy about Drovetti and Edmondstone and who came first see *People*.)

Sir Archibald Edmondstone visited Dakhla and Kharga in 1819. Frederic Muller was in Kharga in 1824, and Sir Gardner Wilkinson arrived in 1825. Hoskins, who arrived in 1832, fleshes out our information on the oasis and provides many illustrations of the antiquities and scenery. He came into the oasis via the Darb Bulaq from near Thebes. Hoskins was followed by the German Egyptologist Heinrich Karl Brugsch, who visited Egypt regularly from the 1850s to the 1880s. He wrote a book, *Reise nach der grossen Oases al Khargeh* (1878), a few decades after his trip to Kharga. He was followed by Grey in 1843.

When Rohlfs arrived in Kharga, via Dakhla and Ain Amur, in 1874, his friend and relative by marriage Georg Schweinfurth was there to meet him. Rohlfs was impressed with the work of Hoskins and did not tarry long in Kharga. Schweinfurth wrote accounts of antiquities in Petermann's *Mittheilunger* in 1875. He was followed by another German, Golenischeff. Then Captain Lyons arrived in the winter of 1893–94, while on military patrol. Finally, Hugh Beadnell and John Ball came to Kharga and Dakhla with the Geological Survey. They created detailed maps on a scale of 1:50,000, which formed the basis of all maps thereafter. One of the best sources for information about travelers to Kharga is Hugh Beadnell's *An Egyptian Oasis*.

Many of these travelers left their graffiti on the monuments. It becomes a game to find their signatures and keep a tally of who was here when and whose signature is bigger, better, and more obvious.

British Occupation (1882–1954)

During the British occupation of Egypt, Kharga was vulnerable to the Dervish army in Sudan, and Baris was captured by the forces of Abdulla Tashi in 1893. The British built a system of towers, *tabia*, in the south of the oasis at Maks Qibli, Baris, and Fuq al-Dum to protect the oasis from the invading Dervish, and established a telegraph connection that was in operation by 1895. In an attempt to develop the resources of the oases, several British citizens formed the Corporation of Western Egypt, Ltd., initially to search for oil. Finding water instead, much of their attention turned to cultivation. It was this organization that built the first railroad (see below). Local citizens claim that the organization excavated at Bagawat and Hibis and took away many antiquities.

In 1916, during World War I, the Sanusi (see People) entered Dakhla in force and the British Army came to Kharga to set up defensive positions. Until that time, the British had managed to keep an eye on things in the Western Desert by airplane; but after a decisive battle on the northern coast at the beginning of 1916, the Sanusi were on the run and General Sir John Maxwell manned the oases to curtail any raids on the Nile Valley.

The soldiers in Kharga stayed mainly near Bagawat and al-Deir, where a plethora of graffiti attests to their presence. Murray tells us they had two swimming baths for men and officers. They also occupied Bahariya and Siwa. De Casson estimated than 35,000 troops were deployed in all. The army set to work extending the railroad to Dakhla, but after a bombing raid in Dakhla, the Sanusi retreated and the railroad was abandoned after only 30 kilometers (18.7 miles).

It could well be that the Sanusi were headed for Sudan via the Darb al-Arbain, but in May the British defeated the sultan of Darfur and put an end to Sudan as a safe haven. The British army returned to the Nile Valley, leaving behind a small defensive troop. A Kharga–Dakhla governorate was established called al-Sahara al-Ganubiya, the Southern Desert, and was run by six successive British governors between 1917 and 1924. After 1924, the oases came under the jurisdiction of the Border Police.

Kharga was a tourist attraction during the British occupation. Travelers had the option of visiting Kharga by train, car, or caravan. Trains ran twice a week in either direction, with accommodations at the Kara Resthouse, which offered tents and supplies for desert excursions.

The New Valley

After World War II the oases fell into decline again. Having become dependent on the Nile Valley, they were in trouble because the valley was having problems of its own. Who could take care of the perimeter when a new nation was being born and a new war was being fought? Irrigation systems throughout the desert got clogged and the fields were unproductive. People began to leave the oases in a pattern that by this time was thousands of years old.

Then things began to improve. In 1958, President Nasser declared the New Valley by joining the oases of Kharga, Dakhla, and Farafra. Covering 458,000 square kilometers (286,000 square miles), it extends to Egypt's western and southern borders. This was done, in part, because the Syrians, who had joined with Egypt in the United Arab Republic, were concerned that the Egyptians would come to Syria in great numbers because the Nile Valley was overpopulated. To appease the Syrians and keep Egyptian pride intact, Nasser acted. He established a Desert Authority with military officers and scientists. They went to the totally isolated oases, where there were no roads and the only contact with the outside world was a single car with a single driver who visited once a week (the Geological Survey paid the driver's salary).

Things changed rapidly. First, the road from Asyut was paved, an airport constructed, and a hotel established. Then, a research project was organized to determine the amount of water under the desert. Next, wells were cleaned and reclaimed and 30,000 acres of new land were placed under production. Farmers from Upper Egypt came to Kharga.

The next move was to build the High Dam. A new government committee, the General Desert Development Organization, was created and a five-year plan emerged. By 1964, over 150 new wells were dug, more land was brought under cultivation, and fourteen new villages were created in Kharga Oasis. Roads were paved and villages were electrified.

The New Valley is the biggest governorate in Egypt, and with plans for the Toshka and Sheikh Zayed canals, it may soon be divided into three governorates. Although the population is increasing, it is still underpopulated in comparison with the other governorates of Egypt. Plans are underway to modernize and industrialize the area. Development is occurring in three areas: agriculture, industry, and mining. Agricultural plans include increasing production on available lands, expanding resources through desert reclamation, exporting products to both the Nile Valley and abroad, and developing related industries like the existing date and tomato factories.

Industrial development, largely in the form of mining, is presently centered on the new phosphate mining complex at Abu Tartur, though additional mining is planned for clay and alabaster.

Tourism is of primary importance to the development of the New Valley, with monuments, villages from the Ottoman period, hot springs, and sand dunes all targeted as tourist attractions. To this end, new roadways are proposed and at least four new tourist villages are under construction.

The first phase, the infrastructure for developing the New Valley, has already been implemented. All villages in the three oases have been electrified. Each village has a clinic and major hospitals exist in larger towns. Primary and preparatory schools are available, usually within a pupil's own village, with secondary schools serving a cluster of villages. Specialized industrial, technical, commercial, nursing, and trade schools exist at Mut in Dakhla and at Qasr Kharga in Kharga.

Future development includes: increasing production and population; reclaiming 100,000 feddans in Farafra Oasis, where new villages are being developed; opening tourist offices, cafeterias, and services at monuments; opening new resthouses and camping facilities; and upgrading roads to all monuments.

Geography and Geology

The Kharga Depression is shaped like a frightened seahorse with its tail curling toward the Nile Valley and its face looking toward Dakhla and the Great Sand Sea. Bound by escarpments only along its eastern and northern borders, the depression, lying north to south between E 30 and E 31, is 220 kilometers (137.5 miles) long north to south and barely 15 to 40 kilometers (9 to 25 miles) wide east to west. At one point, where the open mouth of the seahorse gapes aghast at the desert that lies before it, the oasis is 80 kilometers (50 miles) wide. A fault runs the entire length of the depression.

Although Kharga's fossils are not as prominent, or as much studied, as those of Fayoum, Kharga does lay claim to a dinosaur, *Ornithischian*. There are also plenty of sea fossils within the ash-gray clays of the Upper Danian sections of the escarpments. The beds run from less than 20 meters (64 feet) to not more than 40 meters (127.6 feet) thick. Zittel, during the Rohlfs Expedition, found a wide assortment of fossils.

At one time covered by a great sea, evident from fossils found in the depression and on the escarpment, it is believed that the depression was created by the natural forces of wind and water, assisted by upheavals and tectonic action in the Tertiary Period. The eastern escarpment is a 371 meter (1,187 foot) Eocene wall of limestone, which is extremely steep and difficult to traverse.

Mountains

There are many impressive mountains in Kharga Oasis, particularly in the north where they not only determine access routes, but dictate the personality of the oasis. **Gebel al-Ramliya**, Mountain of the Sand Dunes, at 448 meters (1,433 feet), is located near the northeastern edge of the depression just above the escarpment. **Gebel al-Aguz**, Old Man Mountain, is connected to the escarpment, but protrudes above it, just south of the modern descent into the oasis. **Gebel Umm al-Ghanayim**, the Mountain of the Mother of Spoils, follows along the eastern edge of the escarpment. **Gebel al-Ghanima**, 14 kilometers (8.7 miles) south of Gebel Umm al-Ghanayim, and due east of Qasr Kharga, is 5 kilometers (3 miles) west of the edge of the eastern scarp. Running north to south it is 2 kilometers (1.2 miles) long with a 250 meter (800 foot) wide flat top and is 383 meters (1,225 feet) above sea level. **Gebel al-Teir**, Mountain of the Birds, is the most elusive mountain in the oasis. When one searches for landmarks it is never where you think it should be. Located near Qasr Kharga, Bagawat is found in its foothills. **Gebel al-Tarwan**, just south of Gebel al-Teir, is much smaller, being 0.05 kilometers (0.03 miles) long and only 32 meters (102 feet) above the depression floor. It is currently being mined for its white limestone, and is destined to disappear altogether if mining continues. To the south of its western side is Bagawat. **Gebel al-Zuhur**, Mountain of Roses, is less than a mountain and even a poor excuse for a hill. Located to the west of Gebel al-Tarwan and Bagawat, just to the east of the main road, its only claim to fame is the unusual rock formations, called Desert Roses, that give it its name. Desert Roses are selenite.

The most impressive mountains in the entire depression are **Gebel al-Tarif**, Mountain of the Border, and its small neighbor **Gebel al-Sheikh**. The pair form the western border of the oasis. To their west and really out of Kharga Oasis, the small hill called **Gebel Ghurabi** has no distinction other than as a landmark for finding the beginning of the ancient desert road to Ain Umm Dabadib and Ain Amur.

In the south stands the rugged **Qarn al-Ginah**, a rugged sandstone hill 14.5 kilometers (9 miles) southwest of Qasr Kharga. Standing alone on the depression floor it is visible from most locations and serves as an excellent landmark. **Gebel al-Tafnis** is located on the scarp due east of Baris. **Gebel al-Qarn**, Horn Mountain, a 204-meter (652-foot) double-peaked black anticlinal hill surrounded by sand dunes, is located 16 kilometers (10 miles) southwest of Baris and is the southernmost mountain in the oasis.

The **Abu Tartur Plateau**, Plateau of the Cone Shaped Hat, separates Kharga and Dakhla oases, and covers 1,200 square kilometers (750 square miles). Its oval-shaped, flat-topped summit is surrounded by high scarps on three sides and is joined to the escarpment in the northwest by a small saddle. Rich in phosphate, the Abu Tartur Plateau is attracting modern mining ventures. The fabled Ain Amur is located on one of its northern slopes.

Water

Most of the water in this oasis and throughout the Western Desert comes from rainfall in tropical Africa that saturates and penetrates the ground and moves north through two layers of Nubian sandstone. The sandstone, which composes most of the depression floor, is 700 meters (2,240 feet) thick. The water gushes forth from the depression floor at a rate of 11 million gallons a day, watering the cultivated area of the oasis, which is only 1 percent of the total area of the depression.

The water flows from a spring, *ain*, if it bubbles up naturally and only needs to be cleared from time to time, or a well, *bir*, if the source had to be tapped by a drill. There are hundreds of springs and wells in Kharga and most of them have been running non-stop night and day for thousands of years with no sign of abating. Some date as far back as Acheulean times. In 1832, the French mining engineer LeFèvre worked in Kharga drilling wells, and new wells are constantly being dug.

Ancient springs are called *Ain Romani* in Kharga. But they may in fact be Persian, as the Persians developed considerable water resources in Kharga too. The ancient springs still retain their old wooden linings of *doum* or date palm or acacia wood. Built water tight they are still in good working order after 2,000 years.

There is another method of obtaining water which was used in ancient times, probably developed by the Chinese or the Persians and possibly brought to Egypt by the Romans. An elaborate underground aqueduct system tapped trapped water in limestone ridges below, but near, the surface. Once tapped the water was channeled through a massive system of tunnels to lower lying areas where it was used for irrigation. Sometimes these tunnels went on for kilometers. Three systems were known to exist in Kharga: at Ain Umm Dabadib, Qasr al-Labeka, and Qasr al-Geb. Now a new site must be added, for the French Mission at Dush has found an extensive system at Manawar.

These amazing systems exist in many areas of the ancient world and are still used in Afghanistan and Iran (Persia), where they are called *qanat*; in Libya and Algeria, where they are called *foggara*; in Oman, where they are called *falaj*; in southeast Asia where they are called *karez*; and in Egypt's Western Desert. These systems are found in Bahariya, Farafra, and Kharga and in each place under a different name. In Bahariya they are *manafis*, in Farafra, *jub*, and in Kharga *manawal*.

Their origin in Egypt is somewhat questionable. It has been suggested they came late to North Africa and could have been introduced to the Western Desert well after the classical era. Ahmed Fakhry, excavating at Bahariya, where similar aqueducts exist, found that a Twenty-sixth Dynasty tomb had to be redug because it collided with one of the existing aqueducts. That means that particular system may have been in existence before the Persians came to Egypt. The variety of names raises the possibility that different people introduced the systems to different parts of the oases.

There is also ample evidence of fossil springs at Kharga. It was these springs that provided water for prehistoric people and evidence of their existence goes down as far as 4 meters (13 feet) around these springs. They appear as "crater-like mounds with concave tops of hardened sand-rock."

Sand Dunes

If mountains were not the dominant feature of the oasis, then sand dunes would be. These long rows of marching soldiers cascade down the northern scarp onto the depression floor, reform, and continue their march south. They are mostly barchan dunes falling into three belts: the western group accumulating around Gebel al-Tarif and Gebel al-Sheikh (cutting the Kharga–Dakhla road) are part of the massive 300 plus kilometer (187.5 mile) Abu Muharrik belt. They would have obliterated Qasr Kharga long ago if it wasn't for the mountains. According to Winlock they formed the border of Kharga "throughout historic times and . . . during this period the desert has changed very little if at all." The middle belt runs to the east of Gebels al-Teir, al-Tarwan, and Nadura and to the north of Gebel al-Qarn. It cuts the Asyut–Kharga road, and runs from Qasr Labeka to Nadura. Someday it will crash into Gebel Umm al-Ghanayim. The eastern belt runs from the scarp opposite Gebel Yabsa south to the Baris plain, all the way to Dush. The most massive dune formation is the first.

Local lore maintains that the Romans erected a brass cow atop the northern escarpment to act as a talisman and that it swallowed up the sand; therefore there were no dune fields in Kharga in Roman times. This, of course, was not true. The Abu Muharrik belt alone is estimated to be over 35,000 years old.

Despite their beauty, sand dunes pose a serious threat in Kharga. Cultivated land and villages are all vulnerable to dunes and in some places, like Baris, villagers have built additional stories to their homes as the dunes encroach. Poorly planned newer settlements, erected as part of the New Valley project, have been completely obliterated, leaving modern ghost towns, buried under the sand and expected to reemerge once the dunes pass on their way. No Roman fortress in Kharga is threatened by these dune fields.

Yardangs

One other unique geological form must be mentioned in reference to Kharga and that is the yardangs, or mud lions, found in the north along the Kharga–Asyut road. Yardangs are formed by erosion as are the inselbergs of Farafra. But unlike the inselbergs, the yardangs are little hills that have remained by withstanding the blast of wind erosion while everything around them has been blown away. Inselbergs have eroded away from the natural escarpment.

Caravan Routes and Roadways

Kharga has well over a dozen desert tracks linking it to all points in all directions. The major ones are described here. There are a number of darbs that go from the eastern escarpment to the Nile Valley. They are listed in the tour below.

North–South Routes

The only north–south route in Kharga and the most remarkable desert track of the Western Desert is the **Darb al-Arbain**. It comes into the oasis in the south, runs the length of the depression, and exits in the north. It was a trail of agony for the tens of thousands of slaves who moved along its route. The portion of the Darb al-Arbain that runs from Kharga to the Nile Valley at Asyut is locally also called the Darb Asyut. Beadnell calls it "the last and worst portion of the Derb [Darb] el Arbain, or forty days' road." (See chapter on Darb al-Arbain Desert for a full description, and tour #3 below.)

East–West Routes

The **Darb al-Ghubari**, the Dust Road, runs south of the Abu Tartur Plateau, linking Kharga to Dakhla. The modern roadway follows approximately the route of this ancient track. This waterless and difficult passage was 190 kilometers (118 miles) long, the longer and southernmost of the two roads which linked Kharga and Dakhla oases. It took four days to go between the two oases by camel with the howling northern wind pounding broadside most of the way. The road began in Kharga, passing a series of small sand dunes. All along the traditional route are found an amazing number of rock inscriptions left by ancient travelers. They include hunting and battle scenes, boats, camels, magical signs, game boards to idle away the time, and tribal camel brands, *wasm*s, by the dozen. They attest to the heavy traffic in what is normally considered a remote, uninhabitable area. The *wasm*s are among the most interesting graffiti here. Every Arab tribe has its own *wasm* with which it brands its camels, marks storehouses, and announces to the world that it has passed. The Darb al-Ghabari was mapped by the Geological Survey of 1898. They measured it step by step with a 20-meter (64-foot) steel tape.

Darb Ain Amur, Road of the Lovely One, a second east–west route connecting Kharga to Dakhla, may have been the western continuation of the Darb al-Arbain. It is the northernmost of the two tracks which joined the two oases and is 10 kilometers (6.25 miles) shorter than the Darb al-Ghubari. In addition, it has a water source, at Ain Amur, half way along the journey. Although more strenuous, it was an attractive alternative to the longer, waterless, Darb al-Ghubari. One more important fact about this road is that a traveler can reach the Nile without having to show up at Kharga at all. From Ain Amur it is 40 kilometers (25 miles) to Ain Umm Dabadib, then 24 kilometers (15 miles) to Ain Labeka, then 25 kilometers (16 miles) to Umm al-Ghanayim.

For those of us traveling the paved desert routes today, where we cover a day's journey by camel in an hour by car, the need for cutting an hour off a journey does not seem so great, nor does the importance of access to water along the way. But the logistics of carrying an extra day's water supply for hundreds of people and animals make easier, but longer, routes impossible.

The Darb Ain Amur cuts west across the depression floor from Qasr Labeka at the foot of the northern scarp to Ain Umm Dabadib, and Ain Amur. (For details of these sites see below.) Before ascending the Abu Tartur Plateau to Ain Amur, where the only water is to be found, it is joined by a second track coming north from Qasr Kharga. Then it begins its climb up the slopes of the plateau, crossing the massive and flat high ground, descending into Dakhla Oasis via Naqb Tineida, and continuing through another Wadi al-Battikha on its way to Tineida. A Roman *mahatta* or watering place, covered with pottery, exists near the end of the journey after descending the escarpment. This route was used by H. E. Winlock when he was returning from Dakhla in 1908 and by Harding King in the 1910s.

Passes (Naqbs)

There are at least seven passes, called *naqb*s, in the cliffs, which form access routes to the Nile Valley. In 1925, Bagnold tells us, there was no way to bring a car down any of the passes that entered Kharga. **Naqb al-Ramliya**, also called Naqb Asyut, is at the head of the modern asphalt road leading to the Nile Valley. **Naqb Yabsa**, 13 kilometers (8.1 miles) south of Ramliya, was considered by Beadnell the easiest route over the escarpment, though the next pass, **Naqb al-Rufuf**, was used by Archibald Edmondstone on his journey into the oasis in 1819, and later by a now abandoned railway. **Naqb Abu Sighawal** (or **Umm Sighawal**), located near Gebel Umm al-Ghanayim along the Girga–Farshut track is at the beginning of the shortest route to the Nile Valley. **Naqb Bulaq**, passing the escarpment opposite the village of Bulaq, was used for the road from Kharga to Esna; **Naqb Jaja**, in the south of the oasis opposite the village of Jaja, is the pass chosen for a new paved road to the Nile Valley as well as the new railroad. **Naqb Dush**, in the extreme south of the oases, is at the head of a track with two branches, one going to Esna and the other to Edfu. (For more information on these roads and passes see the individual entries below.)

Hoskins, in 1832, called the eastern escarpment Hagel Bel Badah, and it took him fifty hours to reach it from the Nile. He estimated that at 2.5 miles per hour, his journey was 200 kilometers (125 miles) long.

The northern scarp is the higher of the two great cliffs hemming in Kharga Oasis. It reaches 371 meters (1,187 feet) and is topped by white Cretaceous limestone. Its western portion is topped by white chalk, then dark colored clays and sandstone. The plateau above is strewn with siliceous concretions, *battikha* like those found along the Kharga–Asyut road in the Valley of the Melons. (See Asyut to Kharga for details.) The best descent of the northern scarp is in the northeast corner at Naqb Ramliya.

The Forts

There are so many unanswered questions about these mostly understudied structures that it would require an encyclopedia to deal with them in the manner they deserve. The fortress towns like Zayyan, Ghweita, Hibis, and Dush do not pose as many riddles as the long string of structures from Qasr in the south to Dabadib, Labeka, Sumaria, and Geb in the north. The former have been studied by archaeologists over an extended period of time. The latter have not, and they have few inscriptions or designs to tells us about them. John Ball and Hugh Beadnell, who were among the first to describe, measure, and record them were already confused in 1897. Why were they there? They were perplexed by the location, and suggested they were arranged in a long string for "fear of invasion" or to prevent the escape of prisoners. Invasion was indeed likely, as the Darb al-Arbain was a major desert caravan route. Prisoners were also likely, as Kharga had been used as a penal colony for centuries.

Are they Roman? All the litter around them suggests they are: most pottery dates to Roman times, most burials date to Roman times. From what we can see, Roman forts existed throughout the empire in a variety of sizes, some sites—like Dabadib—large enough to accommodate an entire legion (5,000 persons), others—like Geb—merely outposts guarding a specific road. Their shape and function changed with time (Rome ruled for hundreds of years), so we have different architectural styles. Kennedy and Riley in *Rome's Desert Frontier from the Air* define Roman forts as "all military installations which fall in function between the bases for legions and the towers garrisoned by a handful of soldiers as a watch post."

All of this exists in Kharga Oasis. Why have the Roman scholars ignored them? Along the eastern (Palestine to Persia) frontier these scholars point to dozens of forts. All rubble. They do the same thing with the few forts in the Eastern Desert of Egypt. They too, are rubble.

Here in the Western Desert, where the forts stand tall and magnificent, scholars are mute. Kennedy and Riley have an entire chapter on Roman forts in the Middle East, but practically ignore Egypt as part of Rome's frontier. The text discusses and shows aerial views of ruins that stand less than a meter high, but ignores completely structures in Kharga that rise over 30 meters (96 feet). *The Limits of Empire* by Benjamin Isaac, published in 1990, makes no mention of Roman forts in Egypt. Richard Alston in *Soldier and Society in Roman Egypt: A Social History*, published in 1995, talks of Roman forts erected early in the Nile Valley and Eastern Desert, but in the Western Desert, where he dates all military installations to the late empire (fourth and fifth centuries), he mentions only two forts: the fort at Dionysius in the Fayoum and the one at Dush (Kysis) here in Kharga. These are amazing omissions.

Along the caravan routes in Libya, from the Mediterranean to Lake Chad, the Third Augustus Legion built huge forts at Bu Ngem, Ghadames, and Ghat. The forts, obviously military in nature, also served as customs houses. In Kharga, the Romans probably did the same thing with the Darb al-Arbain. First they explored it, then they controlled it, manned it, and exploited it.

The Third Augustus Legion of 12,000 men were the army engineers of Rome. They remained in the desert for over 200 years not only building forts, but building and controlling roads and fighting wars. They were also good at underground water tunnels. According to Wellard in *The Great Sahara*, when they came into an area they marked the borders with a ditch, set up camps at key locations, linked them with roads, and finally erected forts. The forts that they built in what is now Libya are exactly like the forts in Kharga. Did the Third Augustus come to Kharga Oasis? Or, more intriguing, did the people of the desert, long students of things Roman, come into Kharga from the west and build the forts?

The People

There is evidence that people inhabited Kharga from the earliest of times. Acheulian, Aterian, Terminal Paleolithic, and Neolithic people inhabited many of the passes leading into the oasis and lived along the scarp and, although fewer in number, along the desert floor. The artifacts, including flint cores and tools found in situ, were first unearthed by G. Caton-Thompson's expedition in the 1930s, and later by the Combined Prehistoric Expedition. The flint mines of these early peoples cover many miles along the plateau edge. The most recent excavations have been carried out by teams working with the Canadian Institute.

In 1832, Hoskins found the people of Kharga to be hospitable, unlike the experience of many explorers in Siwa. Well-dressed sheikhs with "fierce mustachios" brought him dates, pomegranates, limes, and "flavourless" oranges. (Hoskins was correct in his description of oranges in Kharga; they lack the flavor and juices of oranges and tangerines in the other oases.)

The men wore brown woolen gallabiyas, which were spun and sewn in the oasis. The sheikhs and the wealthy wore red shoes and tarboushes wound with yellow, blue, green, or white scarves; the poor wore only a white skull cap. The women did not cover their faces. Hoskins says, "A man here thinks there is no danger if his neighbour admires, and feels no uneasiness if the whole town sees his wife's good looks. Love and friendship are the only locks on his harem door." Hoskins found the women of Kharga better looking than their sisters in the Nile Valley. He also found they possessed great influence over their men, and they often handled the money in the family. "Our servants were obliged to apply to them for every article that they required. They complained most bitterly that the females were very sharp in making bargains." The women wore long robes profusely decorated with embroidery and ornaments like shells. The rich wore gold earrings, nose rings, bracelets, and necklaces.

The modern inhabitants of Kharga came to the oasis from a variety of places. Immigrants from Saudi Arabia, Tunisia, and Libya, they were primarily of Bedouin and Berber origin. Once settled, they seldom married outside their clans. In fact, one family in Kharga is still identified in oral tradition as having a female ancestor who married a Roman soldier, and entire villages in both Kharga and Dakhla, admired for their fair skin, are still thought of as Turkish immigrants though they arrived during the Mamluk and Ottoman periods. Villages are divided into farmers and Bedouin. New Bedouin settlements are found on the desert fringes and it is to these sedentary Bedouin that one must go for information on trade routes and desert passes.

In 1897, there were 7,856 inhabitants, 10,000 in 1908, and in the 1930s, 8,000. Today there are 30,000 people in Qasr Kharga alone. If current plans are realized the immigration of thousands of people from the Nile Valley is expected. These people will fill the villages that are being established throughout the New Valley.

Agriculture

Agriculture is still the main occupation in Kharga. The major crop is dates, wheat the second. Rice, alfalfa, and other vegetables are exported to the Nile Valley. Fruit trees have recently been introduced. Taxes in the oases have always been assessed on the number of palm trees over a certain age and the amount of water used from the wells and springs. In past centuries ocher and alum were mined; today phosphate is mined along the edges of the Abu Tartur Plateau and alabaster along the road to Asyut.

Food

Kharga is noted for its *firik*, green wheat that has been roasted. It is delicious when used as a stuffing for chicken or turkey or served like rice. The bread is baked like the Upper Egyptian *eish shamsi*, bread of the sun. In the morning the dough is prepared and patted into loaves which are placed on individual plates and set in the sun to rise. After the fire has died, the bread is placed in the oven and five minutes later a delicious flatbread is ready. The drink of choice, as in all the oases, is tea, the stronger and the sweeter the better. It has always been an imported item and through the centuries has represented quite an expense for the poor people of the oases.

The Crafts of the Oasis

Whereas Siwa stands alone in the style of its crafts, the four southern oases share many of the shapes and motifs found in their traditional ware. Baskets and pots are of similar design and are often called by the same name from one oasis to the other. For a description of most of the pots, see Dakhla Oasis. Wall paintings, although individualized, share common motifs.

Baskets

Hand-woven baskets are a special item throughout the oases. Like clay pots they serve a variety of purposes both in the home and in the fields. Most are woven from the small

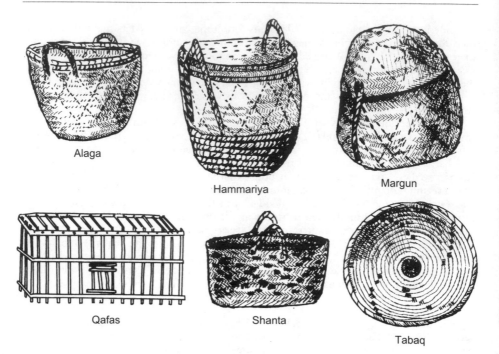

Alaga

Hammariya

Margun

Qafas

Shanta

Tabaq

leaves of the palm tree and their shapes and names vary according to their task.

The *alaga* is a plain, deep basket without any decoration made of palm leaves and used as a carry all for just about everything. The *hammariya* is a workman's basket reinforced with hemp for durability. A version of the *hammariya* is the *maqtaf*, a deep, wide-mouthed basket, existing in Dakhla, Kharga, and Bahariya oases. Used originally for crops, it is reinforced with sturdy ropes wound in coils around the base and up the sides, giving it a special charm. The handles are made of the same rope, which is woven from the fibers of the palm tree. This sturdy basket can be seen straddling the backs of donkeys, often laden with dates, onions, or earth.

The wonderful little *margun* basket, complete with an attached domed lid, is a wedding basket and part of the trousseau of the bride. Used by the new bridegroom to carry his lunch to the fields, it is often gaily decorated with yarns and pieces of cloth. Older ones are sturdy, non-flexible baskets with a coil weave, newer ones are flat, woven, and pliable.

Traditional throughout Egypt, but in the oases made only in Kharga and Siwa, is the *qafas*, which can be dated to the pharaonic era. These sturdy open square and rectangular boxes, sometimes with a lid, are created from the strong ribs of palm fronds. The *qafas* is so well designed that it stays together by itself without the use of nails or pegs. Used mostly for hauling produce and poultry to market, the *qafas* can be adapted for just about anything.

Probably a newcomer, the *shanta*, meaning 'bag,' made of palm leaves and fibers, is flat-bottomed and oblong with an open-mouthed top and two fiber handles. The *tabaq* is a large flat tray with slightly elevated sides made of palm leaves and used for bread, fruit, and other items served during a meal.

Miniature traditional pots   Modernized traditional pots   Mabrouk statue

Pottery

As part of the development scheme of the New Valley, a pottery factory has been estab lished in Qasr Kharga. Here, in addition to traditional pots, a new industry is emerging (see the Crafts section in Dakhla Oasis for a description of traditional pots). Under the auspices of the Ministry of Culture a pottery studio has been erected at the Tourist Home Village, where young artists use traditional pots as a base, decorating them with modern designs. They also create excellent terracotta figures using people in the oasis as subjects. These figures are a specialty of Mabrouk, who has earned an international reputation for his artistry. Both these items are for sale at the pottery factory.

Wall Paintings

Egyptians have been decorating the outside of their homes since pharaonic times. Although there are some traditional motifs connected with these wall paintings, each area of the country has unique designs and a local artist usually adds a touch or two of his own. The most widespread motif throughout Egypt is the *hagg* painting. This painting commemorates the pilgrimage to Mecca, one of the duties of each Muslim during his or her lifetime. While the pilgrim is in Saudi Arabia, an artist is commissioned to illustrate the journey around the main entrance to the home. When the pilgrim returns, his voyage has been immortalized for his arrival. The painting serves as a blessing on the home and its inhabitants and as an announcement that a pious person lives within. In a *hagg* painting certain elements must be present: the Kaaba, the sacred stone in Mecca, is the central motif, while the method of the journey—airplane, boat, at one time camel—and a number of personal details, complete the composition.

In the oases, wall paintings are often on all the exterior walls of a home. These murals have geometric forms, embellished animal motifs, and scenes from daily life. In Kharga a medallion, either square, round, or oval, and containing verses of the Quran, is added to the red and/or blue geometric strip of Quranic verse that runs around the exterior walls of the home. (For illustrations of wall paintings see Farafra and Bahariya oases.)

None of the newer buildings have the traditional wall paintings. This means of expression is disappearing.

Dresses

Dress motifs are simpler but distinctive, with styles varying from village to village. Despite a plethora of design, in all crafts shapes are consistently exciting, colors vivid and natural, and the local craftsmen are beginning to adapt traditional designs for the modern tourist industry.

The traditional dresses once worn by the women of Kharga are long gone, replaced by Nile Valley type garb. Today, the more conservative women wear a long black loose fitting dress over a more colorful garment, although many of the younger women have adopted western style clothes. However, the tight sleeved, delicately embroidered black dress that was once worn by all the women of the oasis can still be seen from time to time on older women.

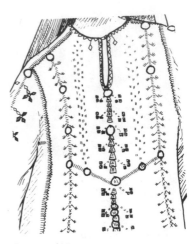

Bodice of Kharga dress

Jewelry

Shenifa

There is little exotic, precious metal jewelry in the southern oases. One reason is that the population shifted to the use of gold very early, perhaps because of the trade along the Darb al-Arbain. In hard times the gold was sold. What there was is long gone, and although one occasionally sees a design in base metal, on the whole what is worn today is glass and plastic beads. (See jewelry in Dakhla Oasis for illustrations.) The women of Qasr Kharga once wore an unusual necklace called an *uqd* or *lowisin*, which was made of bone. It is a choker, worn around the neck, consisting of varying sizes of rectangular bones. The largest was placed in the middle.

The traditional Kharga bracelet, an *aswira*, is similar to the one worn by women in the Nile Valley, except that in most instances it is of base metal rather than heavy silver.

Throughout the southern oases one piece of jewelry exists that is unique to traditional societies, the nose ring or *shenifa*. In Kharga, the *shenifa* has a circular design, usually of gold, which had a series of small golden balls dangling from the bottom. Sizes vary, but unlike in Bahariya Oasis, where nose rings are large enough to hang over the entire mouth, those of Kharga and Dakhla are usually quite small.

Most raw material for jewelry had to be imported. Peter W. Schienerl in *Spanish/Mexican Dollars in Egypt: Currency—Raw Material for Silversmiths—Ornament—Amulet*, tells us that a favorite way of importing silver was through Spanish coins—any antique necklace, earring, bracelet, belt, horse adornment, sword hilt, mirror frame, tray, coffee urn, or candlestick was probably manufactured from the silver of Pillar and Maria Theresa dollars. European coinage, unlike that of the Ottoman porte, was never debased and therefore was used in international trade. Of all the European coinage, the Spanish coin was preferred. Barbary pirates not only paid tribute, but also ransom, with Spanish and Mexican coin. Cairo merchants dealing in spices, coffee, cloth, and other trade goods sought and got the Spanish and Mexican coins. The slavers, when not trading slaves for salt, or gold, or ivory, probably took a coin or two.

Ascherson tells us that when the Rohlfs Expedition received letters, the fee for delivery was one Maria Theresa coin. When the expedition arrived in Siwa after its perilous journey through the Great Sand Sea, a servant persuaded the Siwans the iron water boxes contained Maria Theresa coins and watches.

Mexican pillar dollar

André Raymond tells us that from 1690 to 1720 over a million Spanish dollars a year left the port of Marseille in France bound for Egypt. Most of the coins were melted down. If you hold any old silver in your hand, part of it may have been from the ransom used to free the American and European sailors and merchants from the ships that were captured by the Barbary pirates along the North African coast, or it may have been carried across the Sahara by merchants on their way to the great *wakalas* of Cairo, or it may have once adorned the neck of a concubine in one of the harems of the East.

Eventually, the coins themselves became popular as adornment and one can still see necklaces, especially in Sudan, with a Maria Theresa dollar as its central pendant.

The pillar dollar, issued in Mexico under Charles III from 1759 to 1788 and Charles IV from 1788 to 1808 became an amulet central to the *zar*, a ceremony practiced to exorcise evil from a person. It became known as the *abu madfa* coin. The *sheikha*, the woman performing the ceremony, slept with the coin under her pillow for three nights in a row, then during the ceremony she dipped it into the blood of a sacrificial animal and gave to the patient to keep for a certain length of time, or forever.

The trade for pendants became so lucrative that forgeries began to appear. The jewelers in Cairo signed their names to the imitations, making them primary sources for the study of Egyptian traditional jewelry, since the names of jewelers were not recorded on any other silver ornaments.

The Tour

Ninety-nine monuments were recorded in Dakhla and Kharga oases by Ahmed Fakhry, one of the last persons to visit the oases by camel. That was over half a century ago, but few have yet been explored. We mention the major sites here, most with something for the tourist to see, but Kharga is so full of ancient artifacts that every inch of dirt tells a story.

Bahgat Ibrahim, the director of antiquities for the New Valley, tells us there are so many sites that need excavation that a lifetime of digging will not uncover them all. Most sites have tombs, towns, and temples, mostly buried. There are residential structures of prehistoric peoples north of Kharga at Gebel al-Teir. There are over fifty sites, mostly Roman, that have never been touched such as Bir al-Gebel, Ain Haran, Ain Yasim, Kanafis, Ain Hussein, and Ain Byramdi, all in the north and Ain Aska, Gebel Siwa, Gebel Sharfa, Ain Mansur, Wakfa, Badran, Mabruka, and Qasr Baris, all in the south.

The long range plan for the New Valley includes tourism as one of its major goals. The infrastructure of new roads, new hotels, and tourism offices in all the oases is nearly complete. Now the monuments are being prepared for visitors. As more travelers respond to the lure of the oases, more and more sites will be on their list of 'must sees.' That means these sites must, at least, acquire guards.

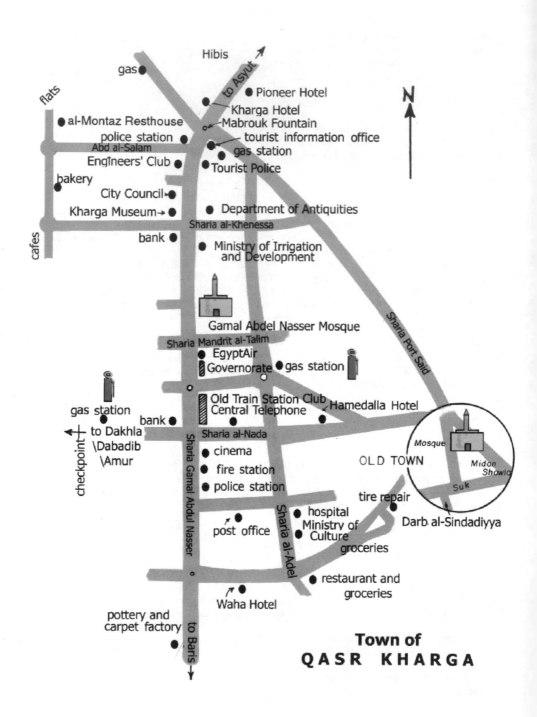

Town of
QASR KHARGA

TOUR #1

Qasr Kharga

Qasr Kharga, 86 meters (275 feet) above sea level, became the capital of Kharga Oasis during Islamic times, replacing Hibis a few kilometers away. Located in the center of the depression, it stands due south of Gebel Tarif which not only protects it from the howling northern winds, but deflects the bands of marching sand dunes of the Abu Muharrik dune belt which tumble down the northern escarpment around Ain Umm Dabadib.

Founded by a little over thirty families, the community had an influx of additional families around A.D. 300 (A.H. 1316). These families were mainly from the Nile Valley. Hoskins, in 1832, found Qasr Kharga to be inhabited by 3,000 people, only 600 of them male. (This is an unusual head count. The villagers often believed that travelers represented the Pasha in the Nile Valley and did not want them to know the exact number of men in the village.) The town was "prepossessing," and its greatest asset was "a magnificent thick forest of date trees, which extends probably a mile toward the north and south and is surrounded by a brick enclosure, like the wall of a park." He found a cemetery to the north and a second to the south. He found the town as "difficult for a stranger to pass through. . . without a guide, as it would have been to thread the mazes of the Cretan labyrinth."

Harding King described Qasr Kharga as built of mudbrick and riddled with tunnels "so low that it is impossible to stand upright in them, and of such a length as to be completely dark." In 1898, John Ball found it an "uninteresting collection of mudbrick dwellings . . . with dark covered-in streets resembling tunnels." He also reported it had no shops or bazaars.

The Qasr Kharga of today is very different. The covered fortress town described by nineteenth-century travelers expanded north and east during the British occupation. The English governor's residence to the east of the Darb al-Sindadiya (the original town) is still in existence, as is the British compound, a series of gardened bungalows shaded by lofty palm and casuarina trees, and the Kharga railway station, now a sporting club. In the 1960s, the oases underwent great changes: new housing, wide streets, clubs, indoor plumbing, and electricity. The population grew to over 16,000. As the seat of the governorate of the New Valley, the city has grown in all directions.

Today 30,000 inhabitants live in Qasr Kharga. Hotels, schools, a hospital, a museum, municipal and governorate buildings keep increasing. Factories exist on the outskirts of the town. More and more residents are abandoning the gallabiya for western dress and women, once hidden away in their homes, are seen walking the streets, shopping, and working in government offices.

Mabrouk Fountain

One of the first sites to greet the traveler is the Mabrouk fountain in the midan near the Tourist Information Office. The statues decorating the fountain were completed in three days by the local artist Mabrouk. The large breasted woman is intended to symbolize Egypt as she drags her reluctant child, the people of Egypt, behind her to a new destiny. The statues are made of cement, alabaster, and gypsum.

Suq

The suq is the traditional marketplace of Qasr Kharga and although visited by tourists its main purpose is to serve the local population. That does not mean there is nothing for the tourist to buy—hand-woven baskets, scarves, and other items used by residents make excellent and authentic souvenirs.

Darb al-Sindadiya

Despite the fact that its people lived in isolation, hundreds of miles from any other inhabited area, almost every village that was built in the Western Desert during the Middle Ages was in the form of a fortress. The Darb al-Sindadiya, the original village of Qasr Kharga, is no exception. Centered around the Ain al-Dar, a now dry spring, it is the best preserved of all the fortress cities in the oases. The narrow, covered streets described by European travelers, in some places only a meter wide, kept out invaders mounted on horses or camels. Twists and turns provided good ambush in case the enemy did manage to penetrate the town. The multi-storied houses with no windows to the outside formed formidable walls that could not be scaled. Although the interior was pitch black and even at high noon the passages had to be lit by oil lamps, the darkness provided cooling shade from the brutal desert sun.

The name came from a family that once lived there and it originally designated the main street of the village. Today it represents the entire structure. As a street, it once ran for 4 kilometers (2.5 miles). It no longer does, but enough of it exists to give visitors a picture of what life was like in a medieval oasis town. Although tourists are encouraged to visit the site, it is not recommended they journey too far into the interior without a guide for one could easily become lost. Minimally inhabited by people, the passages are used primarily as barns for domestic animals. Built entirely of mudbrick with palm trunks as beams, this tenth-century city is one of the treasures of Qasr Kharga and plans are underway for its restoration.

Pottery Factory

Two factories were established in the early sixties to produce traditional pottery and carpets in the hopes of establishing new industry in the oasis. Through the years the work has expanded to include a variety of products. Local artists, using modern pottery methods make not only traditional pots, but candlesticks and flatware. Two types of carpet are made in the carpet factory, knotted *siggada*s and woven *kelim*s.

Kharga Museum

The stunning Kharga Museum, housed in a new building constructed to resemble the tombs at Bagawat, contains both Pharaonic and Islamic antiquities found in the New Valley. Located in the center of Kharga, along the main street, Sharia Gamal Abd al-Nasser, it is easy to find.

There are three levels, two currently open to the public and a third for a future library. The museum contains a great quantity of coins and jewelry from all periods of Egyptian history. The first floor is devoted to ancient Egyptian, Greek, and Roman antiquities. Among other things, it contains ostrich eggs, prehistoric tools, masks, Roman glass items, and Greek and Roman coins from Muzawwaqa, Zayyan, and Kharga. Its most important antiquities include:

First Floor

1. Sarcophagus of Badi Bastit This Roman sarcophagus made of sycamore was found at Labeka by the French Mission. It has a complete design and full color. This is the interior coffin—the mummy is still inside, but in very poor condition.

2. Ba Birds These wonderful birds were discovered in Dush by the French Mission. Ba birds were buried with the person to assure the person would move to the other world. There were five elements, each represented by a bird: the Ba, which is the soul; the Ka, which is the double image of the person; the Ren, which is the name of the person; the Khet, which is the physical body of the person; and the Akh, which is the shadow of the person. If only one piece of the person was missing, he or she could not enter paradise in peace. The birds assured that the entire person reached its destination. They are 7–10 cm (3–4 inches) long, painted, and made of wood.

3. The Tomb of Im-Pepi of the Sixth Dynasty is the outer parts of a tomb discovered by the French Mission in Dakhla Oasis.

4. False Door Stela of M Khent-ka Khent-ka was governor of the oasis during the Sixth Dynasty (2700 B.C.). This limestone door found at Balat carries the earliest reference to the oasis so far discovered: *Wahet*, which means 'oasis' in ancient Egyptian. This word is the origin of both the English word *oasis* (via Greek) and the Arabic word *waha*. The director of the museum, Mahmoud Youssef, himself an Egyptologist, believes this is the most important piece in the museum.

5. Double Statue of Ima Bibi and Wife This painted, color statue of a governor of the oases was discovered in Balat. It is 30cm by 25cm.

6. Kellis Wooden Panels Discovered at Kellis in Dakhla by the Canadian Mission, these sycamore tablets contain documents that list marriage contracts, the buying and selling of goods, letters, and even some fiction writing. They provide us with a glimpse of everyday life in Dakhla during the Roman period. They were found in the home of the craftsman who fashioned the wooden tablets for people to use as we use notebooks today.

Second Floor

The second floor of the museum is devoted to Islamic and Coptic items and is heavy with jewelry, coins, and personal items. Many of the items on this floor are on loan from other museums in Egypt. An entire room is devoted to silver service, plates, tablecloths, and other items from the Manial Palace in Cairo. There is also a coin display of the Muhammad Ali dynasty, rounding out the museum's very interesting coin collection.

With all the archaeological work going on in the New Valley it won't be long before the museum is filled entirely with interesting items from the desert and oases.

1. Coptic Textiles There are three panels of Coptic textiles on view, dated from the seventh to the ninth centuries. They carry floral and animal patterns and consist of a woolen head covering, a jacket, and a panel. All are on loan from the Coptic Museum.

2. Icons These eighteenth-century wooden icons are of the Virgin Mary and Jesus, and the martyr Mari Girgis stabbing the Dragon. On loan from the Coptic Museum.

3. Arabic and Coptic Books A display of Arabic and Coptic books show various scripts and designs.

4. Islamic Coins There are a number of interesting coins displayed here from almost all periods of Islamic history. They include gold dinars, silver coins of the Mamluk sultan Baybars, glass coin-weights of the Fatimid caliph al-Aziz al-Zahir, tenth- and eleventh-century glass measures for lentils, cumin, oil, and more. A very interesting display.

TOUR #2

Hibis, Bagawat, and Environs

- walk, 2x2, some 4x4 behind Bagawat
- 2–3 hours
- entrance fee

			km	total km
Tourist Office	N 25 27 531	E 30 32 931	0	0
Hibis	N 25 28 589	E 30 33 527	1.5	1.5
Bagawat	N 25 28 963	E 30 33 293	1.3	2.8

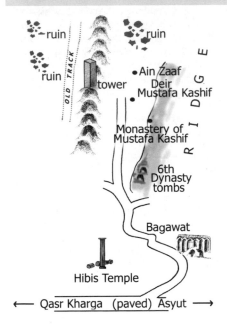

Tour #2
Hibis, Bagawat, and Environs

Nadura

The Temple of Nadura, the lookout, is visible atop a 133 meter (425 foot) hill and, as its name implies, commands a superb view from this strategic position. Dating from 138–161, during the reign of Caesar Antoninus, it is typical of the temple/forts which were built to protect the oases. The outside wall has disappeared in places. The interior contains a large open space with a sandstone temple with hieroglyphic inscriptions in the center. It was later used as a Turkish fortress.

The main entrance to the complex is through a sandstone gate in the southern wall with a smaller entrance in the northern wall. Within the wall stood the temple, with three rooms. A church once stood within the enclosure wall, but outside the temple itself. Near the bottom of the hill toward Hibis is a second, uninscribed temple, also Roman.

Getting There: Nadura is southeast of the Temple of Hibis and 1.5 kilometers (1 mile) north of the tourist information office at Qasr Kharga. Turn right (south) on the paved road and park at the base of the mountain. Enjoy the climb!

Hibis

Hibis, known as the Town of the Plough in ancient times, was the garrisoned capital of the oasis. Easily covering a square kilometer, it lay in the valley between the foothills of gebels al-Teir and Nadura. We know little of the town, for much of it is buried beneath cultivated land, but excavations by the Metropolitan Museum of Art in 1909–10, uncovered a few houses with vaulted ceilings and fresco paintings.

In the center of the town stood the Temple of Amun-Re, a sandstone temple, with an

Bagawat

east/west axis, which is the best preserved temple in the Western Desert (partly because it was buried in sand until the Metropolitan team dug it out). It was begun by Apries in 588 B.C., during the Twenty-sixth Dynasty, continued by his successor Amasis II, and completed by Darius I in 522 B.C. The temple is one of two built by the Persians in Egypt, both in Kharga Oasis. Further additions were made by later pharaohs and a fourth century church was built along the north side of the portico.

Today the temple is located in a picturesque palm grove in front of what was once the sacred lake. It is approached through a Roman gate with inscriptions that have contributed greatly to our understanding of Roman rule. Created in A.D. 68, they provide information on a variety of topics including taxation, the court system, inheritance, and the rights of women. Modern graffiti found in the hypostyle hall includes the names of nineteenth-century European travelers: Cailliaud, who claims to have discovered it, Drovetti, Rosingana, Houghton, Hyde, Schweinfurth, and Rohlfs.

The temple is dedicated to the Theban triad Amun, Mut, and Khonsu, and reliefs are in very good condition. There is also a large wall relief of Seth, the god of the oases, with a blue body and the head of a falcon. Here he is slaying a serpent with his spear. Recently the temple has been the object of a five-year epigraphic survey carried out by an American team led by Eugene Cruze-Uribe. In front of the temple are Greek and Roman tombs.

Getting There: Hibis is 1.3 kilometers (0.8 miles) after the turn off for Nadura. You can't miss it.

Bagawat

Entrance Fee. Cascading down the southern foothills of Gebel al-Teir are the desert brown, domed mausoleums of one of the earliest and best preserved Christian cemeteries in the world, Bagawat. In the center of the cemetery stands a Christian church that still had "traces of saints painted on the wall" when Edmondstone passed this way in 1819. Numbering 263 in all, with many pit burials between the chapels, most of the tombs are a

Chapel ceiling

single room. Some are larger and six have domed roofs. Evidence indicates the area was a burial site long before the Christian era, but the current structures date from the fourth to the seventh centuries (some sources say only until the fifth century). Each chapel once had a wooden door with lintels of wood or stone at the entrance. Most have plain interiors, but there are several with wall paintings and graffiti. Two stand out: the Chapel of the Exodus and the Chapel of Peace.

Chapel of the Exodus
One of the earliest chapels in the necropolis, the interior of the Chapel of the Exodus is

decorated with scenes from the Old Testament, which run in two circles around the interior of the dome. The upper register shows Moses leading the Israelites, the Israelites on their journey through Sinai, Pharaoh and the Egyptian army, Noah's Ark, Adam and Eve, Daniel in the lion's den, Shadrach, Mishach, and Abednego in the furnace, the sacrifices of Abraham, Jonah in the whale, Jonah out of the whale, Rebecca at the well, Job in a chair, Job suffering, Susanna and Jeremiah at the temple of Jerusalem, Sarah in prayer, a shepherd, the martyrdom of St. Thekla, seven virgins, and a garden.

In addition to the original paintings, there is graffiti in this chapel dating from the ninth century to the present day, including the scribblings of Turkish soldiers, whom historians believe may have been garrisoned here 200 years ago.

Chapel of Peace
Located in the southwest corner of the necropolis, the domed Chapel of Peace also has a richly decorated interior. Vines, peacocks, and allegorical figures, all in Byzantine style and reminiscent of paintings in the catacombs in Rome, are found throughout. The most exciting frescoes are around the central panel of the dome. Identified in Greek, they are, starting from the panel above the entrance: Adam and Eve after the Fall; the Sacrifice of Isaac; Eirene, the Allegory of Peace; Daniel in the lions' den; Dikaiosyne, the Allegory of Justice; Euche, the Allegory of Prayer; Jacob; Noah's Ark; The Annunciation of the Virgin Mary; and the apostle Paul instructing Thekla.

Behind Bagawat
Passing through the gate at Bagawat the road skirts the western (left) side of the cemetery past the small house once used by Ahmed Fakhry when he was working in the oasis (perched on the edge of the Bagawat hill). It continues northwest to the Sixth Dynasty Tombs, the Monastery of Mustafa Kashif, Ain Zaaf, Tahunet al-Hawa, and a few other ruins.

Sixth Dynasty Tombs
Although named after a dynasty of the Old Kingdom, the mostly unexcavated Sixth Dynasty Tombs have not really been identified as belonging to the ancient Egyptians and to date little evidence has been found to suggest that the ancient Egyptians maintained any significant presence in Kharga Oasis. The rock tombs are cut into the side of the foothills behind Bagawat and run for nearly a kilometer.

Monastery of Mustafa Kashif
Just beyond the tombs and a kilometer north of Bagawat, commanding a magnificent view of the valley, is the Monastery of Mustafa Kashif, Mustapha the tax collector. Named after a governor of the oasis during Mamluk times, the site, now in ruins, was occupied during the Middle Kingdom, the Roman Period, and the Christian era, when the current structure was built. A Mamluk army general dug the nearby well, which is now silted up.

With two entrances on the northern and southern walls, the building, part monastery, part hostel for travelers, was erected over an ancient tomb and once had five levels. Home to Christian hermits, it contains a church, where inscriptions dating to the fifth and sixth centuries are found on the ceiling. The western side is the oldest.

Despite its ruinous state, the monastery is still a magnificent structure. Shards cover the ground around the ruin. On the depression floor below the monastery are several additional ruins.

Monastery of Mustafa Kashif

Ain Zaaf
Ain Zaaf, Spring of Palm Fronds, is tucked into the base of the foothills of Gebel al-Teir, a kilometer north of the Monastery of Mustafa Kashif. It contains three structures:

a Christian burial chapel that could have jumped out of the cemetery of Bagawat, a barrel vaulted tomb, and a recently excavated Christian church that archaeologists believe could be the church of the banished Bishop Athanasius. Today, roofless and standing less than a meter high, the church is a labyrinth of tiny rooms. Along the northwest corner is Coptic graffiti. For the naturalist and rock hound the cliffs around Ain Zaaf hold various clays and colored stones.

Tahunet al-Hawa

On the west side of the road, visible from Ain Zaaf but accessible only by 4x4, as it is surrounded by sand dunes, is the well-preserved Roman mudbrick watchtower of Tahunet al-Hawa, the windmill. Standing 11.5 meters (36 feet) tall with a southern entrance, the building rises to four stories but is only 5 meters by 6.5 meters (16 feet by 21 feet) at its base. The floors, perhaps built of wood, have collapsed. Like the Monastery of Mustafa Kashif, it guarded the crossroads of the oasis.

Just before it is an ancient desert track (N 25 30 802 E 30 32 061) and beyond are two more ruins dominating the plain below Gebel al-Tarif, the largest mountain in the oasis (see Ain Umm Dabadib below for details), which dominates the horizon at this point.

Another ruin, which first appears to be within the dunes but is actually beyond Ain Zaaf, is a small chambered structure of two stories of arches. It may well be Ain Khussa.

Gebel al-Teir

Gebel al-Teir, Mountain of the Birds, an outlier mountain, is located 8 kilometers (5 miles) north of Qasr Kharga. Along its southern side it is 3 kilometers (1.8 miles) long, 1 kilometer (0.6 miles) wide, and 319 meters (1,020 feet) above sea level. On its northern side it is 5 kilometers (3 miles) long and 600 meters (1,920 feet) high.

Gebel al-Teir is a true wilderness. It is the home of foxes, wild dogs, snakes, including the deadly horned viper, and a lot of fossils. Because of the quarrying roads that have been created recently, a trip into the wadis of

Rock inscriptions at Gebel al-Teir

Gebel al-Teir is complicated and should not be undertaken without a local guide.

Located about 2 kilometers (1.2 miles) north of Bagawat in one of the wadis of Gebel al-Teir are three different sets of rock inscriptions and graffiti covering a time span from prehistory to this century. The first set of graffiti is on the eastern facade of the mountain, at the very entrance to the wadi. Hunters with bows and arrows, giraffes, gazelles, a boat, ancient Egyptian gods, and Demotic, Greek, Coptic, and Arabic script collide in a topsy-turvy jumble of writing and drawing in this timewarp motel, a billboard still in use after thousands of years.

The second set is located 155 meters (496 feet) further into the wadi along the same side. Here in addition to more of the same, we have a great deal of hieroglyphic writing and inscriptions to the ancient Egyptian gods. Located across the wadi from an ancient stone quarry, this site was heavily inscribed during pharaonic times.

The third set of inscriptions, mostly Coptic, is harder to reach. On the western side, a path leads to the top of the mountain through a grotto. Here Coptic paintings, prayers, and invocations dating from the fourth, fifth, and tenth centuries are the dominant motif. There is also Demotic and Greek script. Most of these inscriptions, often identified by a cross, were left by the hermits who lived in these caves.

At the top of the mountain is the Cave of Mary, which must have been a revered place during the Christian era. Amid a multitude of graffiti, some predating the Christian era, is a painting of the Madonna and Child and a prayer in alternating red and yellow lines.

TOUR #3

Qasr Kharga to Dush

- 2x2 (4x4 beyond Dush or long walk)
- all day
- entrance fees at Zayyan, Ghweita, and Dush.
- no petrol

			km	total km
Tourist Office	N 25 27 531	E 30 32 931	0	0
Train	N 25 23 480	E 30 33 314	7	7
Ginah (at rd)	N 25 19 184	E 30 33 242	8	15
Ain al-Dib	N 25 19 144	E 30 33 386	0	15
Ghweita/Zayyan (at rd)	N 25 17 692	E 30 32 724	3	18
Sheikhs' tombs	N 25 10 719	E 30 32 188	13	31
Luxor road	N 24 48 823	E 30 34 825	39	70
New Baris/Shams al-Din	N 24 31 747	E 30 35 897	12	82
Baris	N 24 40 543	E 30 36 061	4	86
Qasr/Checkpoint	N 24 30 225	E 30 36 949	20	106
Dush (at main road)	N 24 33 318	E 30 27 222	varies	

The southern portion of the Darb al-Arbain in Kharga is in sharp contrast to its northern counterpart. Where the north is surrounded by escarpments, the south with only an eastern scarp is open to the rest of the desert. Where water is very scarce in the north, it is readily available in the south. Unsurprisingly, in this century it is the south that has seen extensive development. New villages, all with electricity, primary schools, and health clinics, have been established, bearing names such as Algeria, Kuwait, and Aden, in tribute to neighboring Arab countries.

The journey from Qasr Kharga to Dush, the last ruin in the oasis, covers about 110 kilometers (69 miles) one way. It moves along a well paved highway and is therefore accessible to all vehicles. Some of the sites are located along desert tracks, 3 to 10 kilometers (1.8 to 6 miles) off the main road, but most of these secondary tracks are paved (at least to the major monuments), or are easily traveled by regular vehicle. Since there is no petrol along the route, travelers must carry enough for the return trip.

Train Station

Now Kharga has a new train. Officially opened in 1996, it currently has three routes: Kharga to Qena (and on to Luxor), Kharga to Baris, and Kharga to Dakhla (under construction). The train is part of the infrastructure for the new development in the south which will bring a lot of water to the oasis and is intended to link the train routes being developed in the Eastern Desert and Delta. The train from Qena in the Nile Valley arrives Thursday around 3:30 pm and leaves Friday at 8 am, to give tourists time to visit the major sites at the oasis. The trip to Qena covers 410 kilometers. It takes about six hours with an additional two hours to reach Luxor, the most popular destination. Currently passengers are few in number.

It also has a new train station and it is a work of art. Designed to resemble an Islamic building with a domed center hall, the interior is all marble. It is very extravagant and quite a statement about the future of the New Valley. (For the original railway built by the British see Naqb al-Rufuf below.)

Five kilometers after the train station, the village of Port Said is on the right (west) side of the road.

Qasr al-Nesim

Qasr al-Nesim, the Fortress of the Breeze, is 14 kilometers (8.7 miles) along a dirt track to the west of the main road 6 kilometers (4 miles) south of Qasr Kharga. Little is known about this ruined ancient fortress but the Egyptian Antiquities Organization, who recently began excavations here, think that it is probably Coptic. There is nothing to see. Access is also available from the Kharga–Dakhla road.

Ginah

Sand dunes, proceeding from the northwest, are slowly inundating Ginah, 15 kilometers (9 miles) south of Qasr Kharga. Free of dunes only to the south, the village has been in existence since the Roman era. Since it is possible only to guess at its extent in ancient times, we have no way of gauging how much is buried under the mounds of sand. Hoskins found 250 people living in the village, with 50 of them men (for the same reason as in Qasr Kharga, above). The streets, uncovered but shaded by fruit trees, were so narrow his camel had to be unloaded to pass through. According to Beadnell, the Ain Estakherab, found in Ginah, is "the finest well in the Libyan desert and has been running for hundreds, if not thousands of years."

Ain al-Dib

N 25 19 848 E 30 30 427 (at site)

Just beyond the village is Ain al-Dib, an ancient Roman site with several mudbrick ruins. There are four Roman mansions and an ancient cemetery in the area, none in a good state of preservation. Hoskins tells us it was also known by the names Ain al-Zahama and Ain Hanadi. No archaeological work has been done at this site.

Getting There: Turn right (west) from the main road at the village of Ginah. Pass through the village; at the fork take a left around the modern graveyard heading for the ridge. Once over the ridge turn right and head for the dunes. Pass in front of the dunes, passing two of them. Circle the last

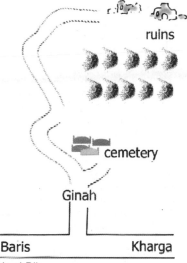

ruins

 cemetery

Ginah

Baris   Kharga

Ain al-Dib

dune on its far side and Ain al-Dib is just beyond. It is less than 4 kilometers from the main road.

Qasr al-Ghweita

N 25 17 280 E 36 33 566 (at temple)

Qasr al-Ghweita, Fortress of the Small Garden, is located 18 kilometers (11 miles) south of Qasr Kharga, atop a high sandstone hill to the east of the main road. This beautiful and picturesque fortress commands a strategic view of the entire area and was once the center of an extensive agricultural community. Little remains of the buildings of the village, which once tumbled down the hillside and onto the plain below, or of the vineyards that once supplied wine to the royal court in the Nile Valley. Inscriptions in the tombs at Thebes attest to the excellent quality of the grapes of Ghweita. This means the ancient Egyptians inhabited the area long before the erection of the present fortress and some other type of fortification must have existed on the top of the hill. In fact, there is evidence that the site was inhabited in prehistory.

The fortress dominates the hilltop. It could well have been the headquarters for the garrison in Roman times. Within its walls is a well preserved sandstone temple dedicated, like its sister at Hibis, to the Theban triad of Amun, Mut, and Khonsu. The present temple was originally constructed by Darius I with additions by Ptolemies III, IV, and X, and is a three-room temple with a courtyard, hypostyle hall, and sanctuary. Within the hypostyle hall, on the lower register circling all four walls are scenes of Hapi, god of the Nile, holding symbols of the nomes of ancient Egypt. The sanctuary has plenty of decorations, some ruined by the black soot of many fires. Around the exterior are several areas where ancient houses are being excavated and a small sand dune hugs one of the exterior walls.

In 1819 Drovetti and Edmondstone, separately, found the ruins of an Arab village inside the large temple. Excavated by Ahmed Fakhry in 1972, the yellow sandstone temple has undergone more recent excavations by the Egyptian Antiquities Organization.

Qarn al-Ginah

4 kilometers (2.5 miles) to the north of Qasr al-Ghweita is the rugged mountain of Qarn al-Ginah. This mountain, which looks as if it erupted from the desert floor, is located 13 kilometers (8.3 miles) south of Qasr Kharga and 4 kilometers (2.5 miles) east-southeast of Ginah. It is a 2 kilometer (1.2 mile) long range of sandstone and is 161 meters (515 feet) above sea level.

Getting There: To reach the temple, a macadamized road on the left (east), marked by a sign, winds its way from the main road. The route is easily traversed by regular vehicles. Zayyan is a few kilometers later along the same road.

Qasr al-Zayyan

N 25 15 054 E 30 34 279 (at temple)

The Roman temple of Qasr al-Zayyan, one of the major monuments of Kharga Oasis, was situated in the village of Tkhonemyris in A.D. 140, when the village was, as now, full of life. This Roman temple, like those in the north, was dedicated to Amun-Re. Facing

Qasr al-Zayyan

south, it is entered through a sandstone gate erected in the mudbrick enclosure wall. Three rooms lead to the inner sanctuary. As with Qasr al-Ghweita, the temple is only a part of the fortress, the remaining areas being given over to living quarters. The present temple, built during the Ptolemaic period when it was known as the Great Well, was restored by the Roman Emperor Antoninus Pius in 138. Schweinfurth, who found pottery, coins, glass, and cast bronzes in the area, recorded that one of the village families kept a bronze as a fertility amulet and the villagers believed it possessed great powers.

The temple went through an extensive restoration in 1984–86. New excavations were recently begun by the Egyptian Antiquities Organization who reconstructed parts of the temple, cleared a portion of the interior, and discovered kilns, a water cistern, and a cache of Roman coins.

The plain below Qasr al-Zayyan, 18 meters (57 feet) below sea level, is the lowest point in the oasis. It is here that the cemeteries of the ancient community are to be found.

After returning to the main road the Nasser Village Camp is across the road. Turning south (left) Saudia village is 2 kilometers (1.2 miles) beyond on the west (right) of the road.

Bulaq to Jaja
Bulaq   N 25 12 745 E 30 32 159

Bulaq is 4 kilometers (2.5 miles) beyond the Nasser Resthouse, 28 kilometers (17.5 miles) beyond Qasr Kharga and 3 meters (0.9 feet) above sea level. On the right, immediately before the town is the tourist house. The old village, surrounded by ancient wells, cemeteries, and defensive fortresses, lies to the west of the road, while the larger but uninteresting new village is on the east.

Bulaq was one of the largest villages in the oasis. In 1832, Hoskins recorded 250 people, with 50 men. In 1897, when Ball was here, the population had grown to 838, and when Harding King visited in the first quarter of this century, it had over 1,000 inhabitants. At that time it was noted for its weaving industry, primarily mats and *zambil*, wide-mouthed baskets used by farmers all over Egypt.

To the east of the village is the **Darb al-Bulaq**, ascending the escarpment via the sand filled **Naqb Bulaq**. The darb makes a 176 kilometer (110 mile) journey to Esna in the Nile Valley. It meets the Darb Jaja (see below) about a day and a half by camel out of the oasis at a point called al-Mafariq, and they move together toward the Nile Valley at Farshut and Rizagat. Just before reaching the escarpment it links up with the caravan route from Farshut. Within the Naqb additional artifacts of prehistoric humans can be found, including perhaps the largest ancient industry sites to be found in this oasis.

Sheikhs' Tombs
Four kilometers (2.5 miles) south of Bulaq are two Sheikhs' tombs. The first is of a local holy man, the second, about a kilometer south, is the ruin of the tomb of Sheikh Khalid ibn al-Walid, a large, whitewashed tomb surrounded by a mudbrick wall erected in honor of an amir who died here while traveling in a caravan on his way to Mecca in the seventeenth century. The sheikh has a huge following as he is associated with the famous general of the same name who conquered Palestine, Syria, and Iraq for the early Muslims. Some of the material used to build the tomb was taken from nearby ruins and bears inscriptions from other eras. The area is 38 meters (121 feet) above sea level.

The new Bulaq train station is on the right. Now come a series of villages erected in the past decade. Algeria stands 2 kilometers (1.2 miles) south of the tomb of Sheikh Khalid along the east side of the road. After 3 kilometers (1.8 miles) is Sanaa, on the west (right). Mud lions (yardangs) begin to appear to the west of the road 4 kilometers (2.5 miles) south of Sanaa, followed by a tea shop on the east, a pleasant place to stop for a drink. Then another series of modern villages follows: Kuwait, a white-domed village on the east of the road, followed in 5 kilometers (3 miles) by Palestine, again on the east, and 12 kilometers (7.5 miles) later by Jeddah on the west. Eight kilometers (5 miles) later the new road to Luxor turns left (east), less than a kilometer before Jaja.

Jaja
N 24 47 836 E 30 35 150
A little under 75 kilometers (46.8 miles) south of Qasr Kharga is the ancient village of Jaja, located in a verdant oasis on the east side of the road. (The new village of Baghdad is on the west, or right side.) In 1898, seventeen people lived in Jaja. Today the community is larger, but still sparse. With the advent of the new paved road to the Nile Valley, Jaja is expected to thrive once again.

East of the town is **Naqb Jaja**, the ascent up the escarpment. The darb bearing the same name was an easy crossing from Kharga to Farshut in the Nile Valley, a 224 kilometer (140 mile) journey. In recent years this access route was used by the Pharaoh's Rally, and created so much interest that it was decided to pave the way. Jaja is followed 5 kilometers (3.1 miles) later by Aden, on the west and yardangs follow 3 kilometers (1.8 miles) later.

Dakhakhin
Dakhakhin is a small village hidden from view by a small sandy hill near Jaja. At the turn of the century, it had 43 people. Its most famous landmark is the Ain Dakhakhin, which once flowed at 110 gallons per minute. Some of the wells in Kharga have ancient wooden casings. This and Ain Jaja do not, at least not at ground level. Beadnell believed the origin of the well was much lower than the present ground level, and the ancient casings will be found at that level.

New Baris (Hassan Fathy Village)
New Baris lies 2 kilometers (1.2 miles) north of the ancient community of Baris. It is on the west side of the Darb al-Arbain which is 76 meters (250 feet) above sea level at this point. The abandoned project of New Baris, a visionary community that was never completely built, was designed by the renowned Egyptian architect Hassan Fathy for the Egyptian Administration of Desert Development. The community was to be a model for all the new villages to be built in the oasis. Building began in 1967 and when it was interrupted that same year by the Six

Day War several structures had been completed. After the war the project was never resumed. A few families lived here for a single year; some say they were banished to the oasis for smuggling activities near Suez.

Fathy, known for his traditional designs, studied the medieval fortress towns of the oasis and planned a modern version of the same: narrow lanes, covered passages, inner courtyards, domes, and all the details of traditional design. Today, standing desolate and haunting, a sad reminder of the frustrations of a great man, one can see the market place complete with cooling wind shafts, a bus terminal abutting the main road, the workshop, and two villas. Fathy, who died in 1989, built two additional projects in Kharga, the Narpin Resthouse and the Hotel Rebat, neither in use today.

Shams al-Din
Across the road from New Baris is the ancient settlement of Shams al-Din, Sun of the Faith. Called Water of Isis in antiquity, Shams al-Din contains a necropolis and a fourth-century church, one of the oldest in Egypt. In the vestibule of the church is more graffiti, this time Greek, and dating from the fourth century. The scribbles tell of soldiers and travelers who passed by this spot along the ancient caravan trail.

Gebel and Ain Tafnis
Due east of New Baris and Shams al-Din, sticking out from, but joined to the escarpment, is Gebel Tafnis. Half way up the northern slope of Gebel Tafnis and a good three-hour climb from the depression floor is Ain Tafnis, not to be confused with the spring bearing the same name located near Shams al-Din. What is unusual about this spring is that it is 260 meters (832 feet) above sea level and 180 meters (576 feet) above the desert below. Most of the springs in the oases lie on the floor of the depression, close to sea level, where underground water is easily accessible. This spring and Ain Amur in the north are the only two springs in the oasis that are located on the cliffs and fed by ground water.

Southeast of the spring amid the caves

IC

ⲡⲁⲩ   ⲗⲟⲥ

Ⲃⲉⲱ Ⲁⲥⲇⲱⲣⲩⲟ

Christian graffiti at Ain Tafnis

along the northern slope of Gebel Tafnis is a series of graffiti that confirms the use of the area over several centuries. In addition to the Greek, Coptic, and Arabic inscriptions, the area is rich in potsherds dating from the Byzantine and medieval Islamic periods.

Getting There: The road to Gebel and Ain Tafnis leaves the main road on the east between Shams al-Din and the new communications tower. It is an easy track to follow heading toward the scarp past a cluster of yardangs and the valley well that is also called Ain Tafnis. It circles south around the mountain and turning north continues between it and the main escarpment. The total distance to Ain Tafnis is 14 kilometers (8.7 miles) from the main road and requires a 4x4 or dirt bike.

Old Baris

In antiquity Baris was an important trading center along the Darb al-Arbain. In 1832, Hoskins found 600 inhabitants in Baris with 120 of them men. They carried on a healthy trade directly with the Nile Valley at Esna. They exported dates, rice, and fruit, and brought back wheat, which was sold to the caravans along the Darb al-Arbain. Located 86 kilometers (54 miles) south of Qasr Kharga, local inhabitants still consider it a separate oasis.

By the eighteenth century the caravans from the south no longer stopped at Maks Bahri and Maks Qibli (see below) but here at Baris. The Darfur caravan, according to Hoskins, rested here a few days to trade and rest the camels before going south. In 1893, during the Dervish invasion, the British established a military camp, which was still standing in 1898. The barrack was located east of the village. There were also three small blockhouses, one north of the village, another to the west, and a third protecting the spring, Ain Anfala.

The government plans to build fertilizer factories somewhere south of Baris. The new Sheikh Zayed canal system currently under construction will enter the Kharga depression here at Baris.

Maks Bahri N 24 35 659 E 30 35 591
Maks Qibli N 24 33 792 W 30 36 503

Maks Bahri, 54 meters (173 feet) above sea level, meaning Customs (as in duty) North, and Maks Qibli, Customs South, are two villages divided by a sand ridge 103.5 kilometers (64.4 miles) south of Qasr Kharga and 10 kilometers (6 miles) south of Baris. When Hoskins was here in 1832, 100 people lived in the two Maks, twenty of them men. Forty people lived at Maks Bahri when Ball passed through in the late 1890s and 82 lived at Maks Qibli.

There are plenty of wells here. Ain Lebakh, Ain Fuq, Ain Dakkal, Ain Abd al-Sid, and al-Ayun, 'the wells,' which lies about 2.25 kilometers (1.3 miles) to the west of Maks Qibli amid the dunes. Twenty-one people lived at al-Ayun in 1897. Additional wells exist to the south: Ain Fakhura, Ain Dab, Ain Gaffr, Ain al-Hamra, and Ain Agil. The existence of so many wells made it a good place for caravans to stop.

It was here that caravans traveling along the Darb al-Arbain came under the control of the Egyptian authorities and were subject to taxation. Those going north were taxed in one village, those going south in the other.

In Roman times all desert routes were subject to tolls. Although we do not have assessments for trade goods along the Darb al-Arbain, we do have fees for the Coptus toll house leading from the Nile Valley through the Eastern Desert to the Red Sea in A.D. 90. One must assume the tolls were similar, but the Coptus fees do not mention slaves. According to Naphtali Lewis, the tolls were: "For a skipper in the Red Sea trade, 8 dr.; guard, 10 dr.; sailor, 5; artisan, 8; prostitutes, 108; sailors' women, 20; soldiers' women, 20; permit for a camel, 1 obol; seal on permit, 2 ob; donkey, 2 ob; covered wagon, 4 dr; funeral, round trip, 1 dr, 4 ob."

By Ottoman times, duty was 9 percent of the price of the slave. According to Ehud R. Toledano in *The Ottoman Slave Trade and its Suppression: 1840–1890*, if a slave died within fifteen days of assessment, the duty was returned. There was plenty of bribery and illicit traffic in the slavery business; no one was immune—governors as well as customs officials were corrupt.

In March of 1825, Wilkinson saw a caravan of 600 slaves and 600 camels, half the slaves having perished from the cold and hunger along the Darb. Nearly all the survivors were women and children.

In 1832, during the reign of Muhammad Ali, Hoskins observed that the Darfur caravan came every autumn on its way north and returned south in the spring. At that time it took the caravan twenty-six days to go from Maks in Kharga to Darfur; Maks to al-Shab, five days; al-Shab to Selima, three days; Selima to Seligna (W. G. Browne's "Lighen") four days; Seligna to Monjerone, five days; and from Monjerone to Darfur, nine days. However, no caravans passed the Darb once Muhammad Ali began his altercation with Sudan.

It is hard to imagine the activity that must have surrounded these sandy cities when a caravan arrived. Caravans from the north laden with goods from Europe and Cairo and caravans from the south bringing slaves, ivory, and spices out of Africa unloaded their cargo, had it examined and assessed, paid their tariffs, and reloaded the goods onto the awaiting camels. Camps had to be set up nearby to accommodate both men and beasts. Food was provided. Imagine a caravan with thousands of people. It must have stretched from Dush to Geb, through the heart of the oasis. It must have taken days to complete customs, weeks to exit the oasis. Wisely, a system was set up whereby when a caravan arrived at Qasr Kharga, a courier was sent to Asyut so the people could prepare for its arrival.

There was certain to be debris. One traveler broke a pot, one lost a trinket, one finished an ostrich egg and discarded the shell (a single ostrich egg could feed eight people and the sturdy shell could later be used as a water container). At the regular resting places loads were sorted and unwanted items were discarded or fell into the sand. When the caravans reached villages like the two Maks and Qasr Kharga they paused for a few days camping near the springs. Scattered along caravan routes and at watering holes are the remains of artifacts that tell the history of travel in the desert.

By the twentieth century the Darb al-Arbain had all but vanished, or so the authorities thought. When André von Dumreicher of the Camel Corps visited Kharga Oasis, he knew he had all the smugglers' roads covered. But here, among the southern wells of Kharga, he found enough camel tracks to arouse his suspicions. The villagers confirmed his worst thoughts; the Darb al-Arbain was alive and well and numerous caravans were arriving from Sudan laden with salt dug up at Bir al-Sultan and Bir Natron. He immediately "occupied a certain well where the camels had of necessity to be watered." He does not tell us which well. (For details about the Darb al-Arbain see the chapter by the same name.)

A small Islamic fortress called Tabid al-Darawish, erected by the British during the Dervish invasion of the oasis, still stands at

Tabid al-Darawish at Maks Qibli

Ruins at Dush

Maks Qibli. It is a two-story structure and until recently was used as a home by a member of the village. The British, through the Egyptian government, had structures like this one erected at most wells in the southern part of the oasis for protection.

Qasr

Qasr, the fortress, 5.25 kilometers (3.2 miles) south of Maks Qibli, was the last outpost of the oasis in antiquity as well as today. In Roman times it was guarded by a garrison that lived in the mudbrick fortress which is now a ruin in the palm grove on the east side of the road. It is hardly visible today. No one lived here in 1832 when Hoskins came to visit. Now the little hamlet of Tafayyia is here.

The Egyptian Antiquities Organization began excavations at Qasr in 1983, and discovered over 150 Ottoman tombs with Islamic pottery and some silver, glass, and ivory jewelry in the area.

We know that the Ottomans kept a garrison in this area, but we do not know if it was intended to protect the southern frontier or to guard the trade route.

At the southern edge of Qasr is a military checkpoint. Although the paved road continues to the newly developed areas of the southwestern desert, foreigners are not permitted to travel beyond Qasr without special permission. There is no petrol along the route. The last water in the oasis is at Ain Mabruka, 3 kilometers (1.8 miles) further south and 22 kilometers (13.8 miles) from Baris (see Darb al-Arbain for details).

You must return to Maks Qibli to take the paved road to Dush. Turn east.

Dush (Kysis)

N 24 34 942 E 30 42 803 (at Dush)

Entrance fee. While the main route of the Darb al-Arbain goes south from Baris to the two Maks and Qasr, another goes southeast to Dush and then east to the Nile Valley. Dush is the ancient Kysis, and lies 13 kilometers (8.1 miles) south of Baris on this route. Located, yet again, on a strategic hill, Dush is a border town and held a garrisoned fortress to protect the community, the cultivated areas, and the southern frontier of the Roman Empire. A major military installation, it was guarded by Roman troops sent from Esna and Edfu along the Darb al-Dush.

Today thousands upon thousands of potsherds cover the site and two sandstone temples and several cemeteries have been excavated by the Institut Français d'Archéologie Orientale, whose dig house is at the base of the hill.

There is evidence that the town existed before Ptolemaic times. From papyri found in the area dated to the third century, and archaeological evidence just coming to light, it is apparent that the site was of great importance. Kysis was a bustling community with merchants filling the needs of the populace and trading with the caravans that passed both north–south and east–west. Daily needs were met by potters, jewelers, metal-workers, and other craftsmen. There were schools for the children and bawdy and gaming houses filled with good food and wine from the excellent oasis grapes for the soldiers. Farmers, cultivating the fields, provided produce and meat for the area, and some of it, especially the grain, was loaded onto caravans for export to other communities in the oasis, the Nile Valley, and perhaps to Rome itself. Evidence indicates the town was abandoned in the fifth century.

The Fortress
The fortress stands atop the highest hill in the area about 2 kilometers (1.2 miles) northeast of the modern village of Dush. It is 79 meters (253 feet) above sea level. The oldest building found so far on this site, the fortress dates from the Ptolemaic era. The ruined walls, rising to 6 meters (19.2 feet) enclose a rectangular space. Four or five stories lie underground. Recent theories postulate that the fortress at Dush was garrisoned to keep the Darb al-Dush open. Thus Dush may have been more important to the east–west connection to the Nile Valley than to the north–south Darb al-Arbain.

The Temple
The sandstone temple of Osiris, built by Domitian between 81 and 96, abuts the fortress on the east. Trajan added a court in 117 and Hadrian added other portions of the temple. Although there are few decorations, parts of the temple are believed to have been covered in gold. The temple comprises several areas including two courts, a small hypostyle hall with only four columns, and a sanctuary. Full of inscriptions to the Roman emperors Hadrian and Trajan, the gateway was also used by nineteenth-century travelers, who did not hesitate to join their names with those of their illustrious ancestors. They include Cailliaud, who claimed to be the first European to visit the site.

Numerous artifacts have been unearthed in and around the temple area including pottery, coins, ostraca, and jewelry. Among the most interesting finds have been letters, receipts, garrison lists, and bills. They help us to piece together life at Kysis. A second temple, probably from the Roman period, lies 200 meters (640 feet) west. It has vaulted ceilings, small rooms, and a staircase.

Ancient cemeteries surround the town on the north and west. Although the Roman cemeteries running southeast almost to the escarpment are the largest, the most impressive is a tiny version of Bagawat that lies to

the north of the fortress. Dating from the late Ptolemaic period, the tombs are undecorated. The ruins of Tell al-Dabba al-Sarqiya, home to a farming community which cultivated the region between the fortress and the cemetery, lie along the route to the Naqb and Darb al-Dush.

The modern village, perched atop a smaller hill to the south of Kysis, is still a good-sized community, which has maintained the feel of a frontier town. It sits well into the middle of the Western Desert and the major trade routes to and from have been abandoned for over a century. In 1898, only 161 people lived in Dush but with the paving of the Darb al-Arbain and the future possibility of paving the Darb al-Dush the village could once more develop into a thriving community.

Naqb and Darb al-Dush
The Naqb al-Dush ascends the 400 meter (1280 foot) scarp as a series of passes, none easy. Today, without pack animals to worry about, the ascent on foot can take around two hours. The passes are covered in sand and full of ridges. Cairns help to keep one on course, but no vehicles can ascend.

The Darb al-Dush is the old caravan trail leading due east from the village of Dush to the Nile Valley. Immediately after the ascent from the depression floor the road is difficult, full of gullies and desolate terrain. But the road is marked by cairns. It diverts into two tracks about two thirds of the way, the northern route going to Esna, a major market town during Roman times (perhaps before), and the southern route going to Edfu, a center for trade from the Western Desert. Ball and Beadnell used this route to measure the longitude of Kharga Oasis in 1898.

The French Mission has been working at Dush for over twenty years.

Getting There: The approach to Dush is spectacular, a place where one truly senses the remoteness of the area. The dominant feature is the incredible field of golden barchan dunes, marching for over 10 kilometers (6 miles) in silent formation south into the emptiness beyond. The oasis road to Dush, now paved, begins at Maks Qibli and runs east for ten kilometers past the village of Ain Mansur. The asphalt leads you to the site. Dush is visible from a distance situated atop a hill amid moving sand dunes. An alternate route to Baris is a beautiful 13 kilometer (8.1 mile) journey through the dunes.

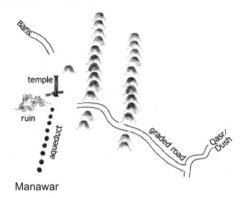

Manawar

Manawar

In the dunes at the foot of Dush is the newly discovered site of Manawar. It spreads out amid the dunes with several ruins including a temple, pottery mounds, and a village. At lease nine lines of aqueducts, some of them excavated and relined in mudbrick, have been found so far. It is most impressive. Also impressive is the fact that the dune fields are directly in line to obliterate the excavations. They are heading toward the site.

Getting There: To reach Manawar, return along the asphalt road to Dush. Just after the gardens as the road is making a bend a well-graded road takes off toward the dune fields. Follow it through the dune field. Manawar is only a few kilometers away. After your visit return to the graded road and turn north, follow it for about 10 kilometers through the dunes to Baris. Baris is marked by the radio tower in front of you at west-northwest.

Aqueduct irrigation system

TOUR #4

Al-Deir, Qasr al-Geb, and Qasr al-Sumaria

- walk, 2x2, 4x4
- 1/2 day
- easy

			km	total km
Tourist Office	N 25 27 531	E 30 32 931	0	0
Yardangs	N 25 31 401	E 38 36 834	10.4	10.4
Al-Deir (at rd)	N 25 36 822	E 30 38 871	10.4	20.8
Umm al-Qusur (at rd)	N 25 45 330	E 30 39 922	15.2	36
Geb (at rd)	N 25 49 844	E 30 39 296	8.3	44.3
Geb (at site)			c3	47.3
Qasr al-Sumaria			c2.5	49.8

All the sites on this tour are restricted and free of charge, and you need permission to visit them from the Director of Antiquities' Office across the street from the Kharga Museum. They require one of their officers to accompany you. This is not a hardship, as they can answer your questions and provide you with interesting information. DO NOT VISIT THESE SITES WITHOUT PERMISSION OR YOU WILL BE BREAKING THE LAW.

Yardangs

These unusual outcroppings on the desert floor are called mud lions, or yardangs. Scientists come from all over the world to study this particular group of yardangs. They are filled with debris including sands, silts, shells, pottery, and animal skeletons. There are a number of theories as to what they actually are. Beadnell in 1909, the first person to discuss them, thought they were deposits left by an extensive lake. Caton-Thompson and Gardner in 1932, thought they were well deposits. Now we know they are caused by wind erosion. Farouk al-Baz tell us mud lions are, "wind sculpted yardangs of lacustrine deposits with blunt fronts and aerodynamically shaped bodies." This collection of yardangs is the largest in the Western Desert.

Getting There: The mud lions are 10.4 kilometers (6.8 miles) north of Qasr Kharga on either side of the road.

Al-Deir

1–2 hours, 4x4 at end. Easy.

If there is time to visit only one of the Roman fortresses in this area, this is the one. Tucked

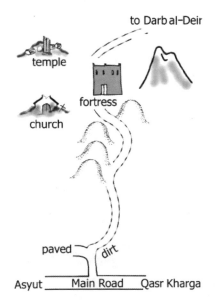

to Darb al-Deir

temple

fortress

church

paved   dirt

Asyut ____ Main Road ____ Qasr Kharga

at the foot of the eastern scarp in a picturesque setting, the fortress is not only pretty, but up to the last kilometer is accessible by regular vehicle.

The Fortress
Built of mudbrick, the imposing Diocletian fortress sits at the end of a once paved road just north of Gebel Umm al-Ghanayim. The building, 73 x 73 meters (233.5 feet) square, has twelve towers, one round one at each corner and two semicircular ones within each 3.6 meter (11.5 feet) thick mudbrick wall. The southern wall is the best preserved. The towers are connected by a gallery atop the 10 meter (32 foot) walls. The interior, where a well once stood, is almost totally gutted except for rooms along the southern wall. Here in room after room is wonderful graffiti, most written by soldiers who were stationed in the Western Desert. There are drawings of Turkish soldiers with tarbushes, airplanes and tanks from British regiments, and many names in Arabic, Coptic, Turkish, and English.

Water posed no problem to the inhabitants of the fortress for the well was located in the central courtyard. From there the water was channeled through three tunnels to the outbuildings and fields, yet another Roman engineering marvel. The existence of these tunnels was unknown until they were unearthed by accident at the beginning of the twentieth century. Trenches were dug, then large flat slabs of stone were placed over the trenches before everything was covered up again. This allowed for free-flowing water. A system was put in place to block the entrance

Graffiti on fortress walls at al-Deir

to the tunnels in the well so that the water level in the well would rise enough for use within the fortress. To allow the water to reach the outlying areas, the tunnels were simply unblocked.

The Church
After the decline of the Romans the site may have been used as a Christian monastery, which would account for the name al-Deir, which means 'monastery.' There is a necropolis and the ruins of a church to the west of the fortress. There is evidence that it was used in World War I by the British when they were defending the oasis from the Sanusi of Libya. There are additional buildings from a modern British settlement nearby which was abandoned when the well in the courtyard of the fortress went dry.

The Town
The town, which once surrounded the temple, is located between the two ruins, a kilometer away to the north. Here, there are two buildings still standing. The one toward the escarpment is a small temple which was later used as a church. It contains some Coptic, Greek, and Arabic graffiti in the sanctuary. The second building is unidentified at the present time. Between these two buildings and the main building is an area with some dead palm trees which was once used for agriculture.

Fortress at al-Deir

Gebel Umm al-Ghanayim

The monastery is to the north of Gebel Umm al-Ghanayim, Mountain of the Mother of Spoils. This free standing 388-meter-high (1,241-foot), flat-topped mountain guards the escarpment and the **Naqb Abu Sighawal**. Caton-Thompson found extensive evidence of Microlithic humans at the pass when she camped here from February 27 to March 6, 1931.

The pass is the beginning of the **Darb al-Deir**. At 167 kilometers (104 miles) it is the shortest route from the oasis to the Nile Valley, which it reaches at both Girga, near Abydos, and Farshut, near Luxor. For centuries, before the building of the Asyut road, it was the most important connection between the oasis and the Nile Valley. Its Girga terminus was definitely the shortest, only 160 kilometers (100 miles). The Samhud, Karnak, Farshut terminus is 174 kilometers (109 miles). Along this route the first telegraph lines to the oasis were erected.

Beyond the pass, the Darb al-Deir moves through rough limestone country called *Mishabit*. That is followed by an area called al-*Battikha*, the watermelons, where concretions like those along the main Asyut highway can be found. That is followed by a limestone hill, called al-*Maghribi*, where, according to tradition and Hugh Beadnell, the people from Kharga killed (decapitated) a Maghribi Arab who had stolen a woman from the oases. Then come the Rocks of al-Burayg, a Roman watering station where plenty of pottery identifies the site (the water was brought from Kharga).

Imagine such a road during Roman days. If there were soldiers there were also items which serviced soldier's needs. In *The Roman Army and Long Distance Trade*, Paul Middleton tells us that the army brought the Roman way of life with it. Soldiers demanded wine on a daily basis and it had to be brought from someplace. Two legions would need 3.5 million liters a year. Oasis wine could have been used, but on special occasions a touch of home would have been expected. This single product would account for a considerable amount of caravan traffic.

Excavations by the French Mission started at al-Deir in the fall of 1998.

Getting There: al-Deir is less than a half a kilometer south of the checkpoint at Munira and 20.8 kilometers (13 miles) north of Qasr Kharga. Enter the desert just south of Munira on the first asphalt road going east. When the asphalt turns left, turn right past the mudbrick building. Head toward the mountain. At 1.4 kilometers from the beginning of the asphalt road one hooks up with the now decomposed asphalt of the old road to al-Deir. There is more than one track leading into the desert here, as elsewhere, and the correct one shows signs of paving and heads for the sand dunes to the north of Gebel Umm al-Ghanayim. The track ends at the dunes and al-Deir is on the other side. These dunes can be climbed by a 4x4 or dirt bike, which provides easy access to the entire site, but a regular vehicle can traverse the desert to the base of the dunes. The fortress is a kilometer away. Travelers have found the way through the dunes. Follow the tracks.

Return following the same route. At the highway turn right, north. Munira and the checkpoint are just ahead.

Munira

Munira, less than a kilometer from the turn into the desert at al-Deir, was the first stop of the railroad station in Kharga. Today there is a checkpoint. Used primarily by the British, Munira sits on the depression floor without any type of protection except a few casuraini trees.

Naqb and Darb al-Rufuf

At **Naqb al-Rufuf**, there are more traces of ancient peoples than in any other pass in Kharga, especially debris fields of their tools. Caton-Thompson found plenty of chert workings stretching over several square miles here. This was a large ancient factory where primitive implements were manufactured. Within the area are to be found the remains of at least thirty stone shelters, all open to the south (away from the wind). There are also fossil springs in the area.

Darb al-Rufuf has two routes. The first was the pass used by the railway, the second led to Sohag. One simply follows the railroad tracks to this pass. The railway came to Kharga on a 75 centimeter (3 foot) gauge on January 17, 1908, after two years of construction. It was built by the Corporation of Western Egypt, Ltd. (Western Desert Corporation), a company which intended to carry on extensive work in the Western Desert through trade and irrigation. It was called the Western Oases Railway and was under the direction of Albert M. Lythgoe. The Nile Valley terminal was at Muwasalat al-Kharga, Kharga (or Oasis) Junction. It is situated along the railroad tracks in the desert between the villages of Abu Tisht and Farshut, 195 kilometers (122 miles) north of Luxor. It ran along the valley edge to Gara, where travelers usually breakfasted at the resthouses. Then it ascended the escarpment at Wadi Samhud. Heading southwest it passed through the Naqb al-Rufuf in the Kharga escarpment, taking 16 kilometers (10 miles) to reach the bottom. Trains ran twice a week, Tuesdays and Fridays from the Nile Valley and Mondays and Thursdays from Kharga.

The train was specifically designed for desert travel. Martin S. Briggs, in *Through Egypt in Wartime*, tells us the roof was double with deep eaves to shade the windows from the harsh sun. In turn, the windows were double and partially tinted blue. The first class saloon had basket chairs. When the first train arrived in Kharga, the *umda* (mayor) climbed aboard and headed for the seaside at Alexandria, in order, he said, to promote desert travel. In Kharga the headquarters were at Sherika and they included a hotel with a garden and swimming pool. Today this railroad has been abandoned. From the outset it fought a losing battle with the dunes. The railway stations at Kharga and Munira still stand. Instead a new rail system has recently been developed that links Kharga not only to the Nile Valley, but also to the Red Sea.

The Darb al-Rufuf route was used by Archibald Edmondstone in 1819, and again by Gertrude Caton-Thompson in the 1930s. Beadnell tells us the southern route leads to al-Tundaba, "a deep shaft in the centre of the plateau, at kilometre No. 92 on the railway." Caton-Thompson tells us there is plenty of evidence of Roman mining for alum along the route and a great number of watering stations.

Umm al-Qusur and Almasy Hideout

Still following the main road from Qasr Kharga to Asyut, one comes to the Ezbat Muhammad Mustafa. It is simply a garden on the right (east) side of the road. Reportedly, Count Almasy, after depositing several spies at Asyut for the German army, stopped here. (See People for details.)

The desert in this area is being used to grow watermelons. There is also a cement factory. Beyond the garden is the dirt track to Umm al-Qusur. We know there is a Roman cemetery here, and the Egyptian Antiquities Department has unearthed some tombs with pottery, caskets, and beads on the west side of a small mountain. There is nothing of note to see.

Qasr al-Geb and Qasr al-Sumaria

• **Off road** • **Easy**

These two small fortresses, or watchtowers, were probably erected by the Romans, most likely around the fifth century. They were later used by the Turks during the Ottoman period. Both have ample mounds of large shards and some nearly complete pots have been found. Neither of these fortresses has been excavated.

Qasr al-Geb and Qasr al-Sumaria

Qasr al-Geb

Qasr al-Geb is the last outpost in the oasis. It is named after the ancient Egyptian god of the earth. It is a small, square fortress sitting atop a sandstone hill which offers a strategic view of the surrounding area. Around its base a small community once existed, but Geb is an outpost, not a village.

Qasr al-Geb is constructed of mudbrick. It

Qasr al-Geb

currently measures 15 x 16.5 meters (48 feet x 53 feet) and has 2.5 meter (8 feet) thick exterior walls. It once had circular towers with parapets, but they are gone now. There are arched entrances on the eastern and southern walls, but the top story of the eastern wall has collapsed. The bottom story is under rubble. The main entrance is along the southern wall, where there are also two windows. The interior, now collapsed, contained garrison rooms. An underground gallery and aqueduct system exists here.

Qasr al-Sumaria

Only 2.5 kilometers (1.5 miles) to the south of Qasr al-Geb is Qasr al-Sumaria, accessible across the desert floor in an almost straight line. Looking much like its neighbor, the fort is a square building that once had round buttresses in the corners and entrances in the center of the southern and northern walls. The western wall has collapsed. The interior, cluttered with debris and mostly collapsed, is a series of rooms. The easiest access to the interior is via the southeast corner. It is 14 meters (45 feet) square.

The difference between the two sites is that Geb is an outpost, but Sumaria is a village. South of the fort are the ruins of several

houses and an extensive Roman cemetery.

Getting There: Access to the two forts is 6.24 kilometers (3.9 miles) south of the bottom of the scarp. The turn west off the main road is clearly marked just before the main road makes a major bend. Qasr al-Geb is visible in the distance. There is no track, but one must head directly toward the fortress. Distance into the desert is approximately 5 kilometers (3 miles).

One can see Sumaria from Geb. Between the two is rough ground, so to reach Sumaria arc either southeast or southwest. After visiting all the sites at Sumaria, turn toward the eastern escarpment. The high tension wires that mark the road in this area are clearly visible east-northeast of the fortresses. Head in that direction. There are plenty of tracks to follow. Note that the high tension wires do not always mark the road in the desert. Here, north of Qasr Kharga, they do.

Additional sites

The entire plain in this area was inhabited at one time or another in antiquity. There are dozens of known villages and cemeteries. To the south of Sumaria is **Ain al-Gazar**, a village with a spring and cemetery. There have been no excavations here and nothing is standing above the ground, so it is not worth seeing at this time.

A second site, further south still, is **Qasr al-Mughatta**. Here, too, everything is buried. The ancient community covers a huge area and contains rock cut tombs. This site was discussed by early travelers, who tell us it was plundered and the mummies, buried in wooden or pottery coffins dating to the Roman time, were exposed.

Qasr al-Sumaria

TOUR #5

Qasr Labeka and Ain Umm Dabadib

- off road
- full day
- very rough
- no entrance fees

			km	total km
Tourist Office	N 25 27 531	E 30 32 931	0	0
Labeka Road	N 25 41 759	E 30 39 100	39	39
Tuleib	N 24 41 837	E 30 38 469	1	1
Labeka (site)			10.5	11.5
Dabadib (fortress)			c23	34.5

You must have permission to visit these sites from the Director of Antiquities' Office across the street from the Kharga Museum. They require one of their officers to accompany you. This is not a hardship as they can give you a lot of interesting information. DO NOT VISIT THESE SITES WITHOUT PERMISSION OR YOU WILL BE BREAKING THE LAW.

Ain Muhammad Tuleib

The only northern fort directly accessible from the main road, Ain Muhammad Tuleib can be visited without an off-road vehicle. Located in a Roman–Byzantine settlement, the fortress gets its name from the man who once owned the land in the area. This fort appears to be in good condition when viewed from the road, but only two walls are stand-

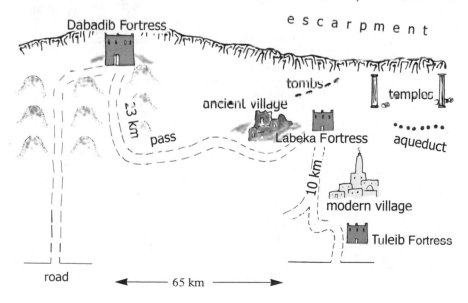

Fortress at Ain Muhammad Tuleib

ing and the interior is rubble. It is a rectangular structure 22 x 16 meters (70 x 51 feet) with mudbrick walls, once rising to at least two stories.

Getting There: Ain Muhammad Tuleib is 7.2 kilometers (4.5 miles) north of Munira. The turn west off the main road is via a paved road. It leads to the village of Muhammad Tuleib. The fortress, visible to the north of the village, is surrounded by soft sand and the immediate approach must be on foot or by dirt bike.

Qasr al-Labeka

One of the most spectacular complexes in Kharga, Qasr al-Labeka is tucked into a beautiful wadi at the base of the northern escarpment. The ruins are impressive with three marvelous buildings, two aqueducts, several rock tombs, and plenty of shards. Labeka had one of the largest fortresses in Kharga. There must have been plenty of activity here when it served as a guardian along the Darb al-Arbain. Despite the broiling sun of summer and the bitter cold of winter nights, despite the slaves that were paraded past its lofty towers, there must have been quiet, peaceful moments when the scarp glimmered pink and white in the winter sun and the stars illuminated the crystal clear sky at night.

The Northern Temple (1st/2nd cent.)

The most northerly building at the main site of Qasr al-Labeka is a 12 meter square (38 feet square) mudbrick temple perched upon a rock outcropping. Three walls are standing, while the fourth, the eastern one, has begun to collapse. There are three entrances, on the western, southern, and eastern walls respectively and the small, cluttered interior has

three arches and a vaulted room. On the lintel of the first arch is a small bit of plaster fresco that shows the wings of a vulture, representing the protective goddess of ancient Egypt. Along the sides of this arch is some graffiti.

The Roman Tombs

Along the ridge beside the temple are a number of Roman tombs dated from the first to the fifth centuries. One has been completely excavated and sits in the side of the hill like a mini Abu Simbel minus Ramses II's giant statues. Additional tombs have been located in the mountains west of the fortress and more cemeteries have been found.

The Fortress

The fortress, some distance away, has four circular towers, one at each corner of the 12 meter (38 foot) mudbrick walls. The interior, filled with sand, but accessible by a door in the eastern wall, is divided into chambers with domed ceilings. At one time there were several buildings surrounding the fortress. Between the two buildings, surrounded by a modern mudbrick wall, is an ancient spring.

Fortress at Qasr Labeka

Sanctuary of Piyris

This temple, 250 meters south of the northern temple, was rediscovered by Adel Hussein of the Egyptian Antiquities Organization during the 1991–92 season. John Ball described it in 1898 as a well preserved, unburnt brick, battered wall Christian chapel with three rooms, three windows on either side, and traces of painted stucco on the doorways. It has now been dated to the third century.

There is evidence that this temple may be dedicated to Hercules. If it is, this is the second temple in the Western Desert now known to be dedicated to Hercules. The other, also unpublished as of the summer of 1999, is at Bahariya.

After Hussein the site was investigated further by the French Mission. A limestone hawk statue was found here, now in the Kharga Museum.

Aqueducts

There are at least two aqueducts, called *manafis* at Labeka. (See Dabadib for details.) Today the source is dry and silted up, but the surrounding vegetation indicates the presence of water below and locals maintain the water can be tapped.

The French mission has been working at Labeka for the past five years and they have discovered wonderful things.

Getting There: After passing Tuleib the paved road enters the village and becomes a dirt track. At the mosque bear left and curve around it. The track now heads for the desert. This is rough terrain. Although only 5 to 8 kilometers (3 to 5 miles), depending on zigzags, from the main road, rough undulating sand sheets that cut and tear at tires mark some of the way. 4x4 or dirt bike only. After the visit, the traveler has a choice: to return to the main road by retracing the route or to do some off road travel to Ain Umm Dabadib.

Offroad from Labeka to Dabadib
• 1 hour   • Difficult

There are two routes that lead to Dabadib from Labeka. The first is the cavalry and monks' route that hugs the escarpment and can only be accessed by camel, on foot, or, perhaps, by dirt bike. There is a lot of ancient graffiti here from prehistory through the Pharaonic, Persian, and Coptic periods. The second route is longer because it runs further out into the plain to avoid the long fingers of the escarpment. Because of that, it is accessible by 4x4s.

This is the most fascinating offroad journey in Kharga and one of the most beautiful in the entire Western Desert. It has everything: dunes, mountains, narrow passes, and grand, spectacular vistas. It will test the mettle of any driver and vehicle. A GUIDE IS REQUIRED BY THE AUTHORITIES

AND IS A MUST FOR ANYONE WITH A BRAIN.

From the fortress at Labeka bear east a short distance to hit a well-graded ancient track. Turn south onto the track for about 3 kilometers (1.8 miles). There are many tire tracks to follow.

The dune chain is 4 kilometers (2.5 miles) later. The route weaves through the small hills at this point until it narrows into a small pass, approximately 2 kilometers (1.2 miles) later. The most difficult part of the journey is this pass, where boulders are strewn about. The route is very well defined as the hills continue.

Four kilometers (2.5 miles) after the pass are more dune fields. Travel is now up and down passes and through and over dunes. Follow the tire tracks. If 50 tire tracks bear right and 4 bear left, FOLLOW THE RIGHT TRACKS OR LIKE THE FOUR BEFORE YOU, YOU WILL END UP IN TROUBLE.

Approximately four kilometers (2.5 miles) after the dune fields a valley of yardangs appears. Head for the rise. As you turn the corner the fortress of Ain Umm Dabadib is visible at the escarpment (north-northwest) to the left of a sand dune about 4 kilometers (2.5 miles) dead ahead. The sight will take your breath away.

Ain Umm Dabadib

About 20 kilometers (12.5 miles) west of Qasr al-Labeka, 40 kilometers (25 miles) east of Ain Amur, and about 40 kilometers (25 miles) north of Qasr Kharga sits a most spectacular site. It nestles at the base of an escarpment that is 380 meters (1216 feet) above sea level and 225 meters (720 feet) above the desert floor. Dabadib stretches its ancient arms over more than 60,000 acres, and three major desert tracks converge on the plain in front of it, all offshoots of the Darb Ain Amur. Called the Abbas Oasis by M. de S. Abargues, it was an important settlement for thousands of years.

Geologically, Dabadib is also very interesting. Dry river channels are evident as they fall from the escarpment onto the plain below, leading one to suspect that waterfalls

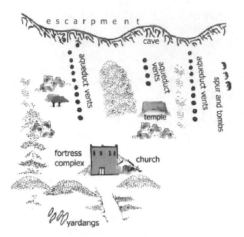

Ain Umm Dabadib

may have existed here. The plain is a playa, a dried-up lake. This is all Neolithic. The river channels are probably Acheulean. Here, in the lake bed, we see the action of the wind, which has, as Beadnell says, "truncated and diluted" every "cobble and boulder."

Someone, probably the Romans, had a major settlement at Ain Umm Dabadib and the complicated aqueduct system makes one believe it was inhabited and functional long before the Romans. With the escarpment as dramatic backdrop and the entire oasis lying to the south, Dabadib must have been a paradise. It was an excellent location, far less remote when garrisoned and when the tracks meeting in the area were maintained.

Fortress at Ain Umm Dabadib

The Fortress

The towering mudbrick fortress at Ain Umm Dabadib is located 0.5 kilometers (0.3 miles) southeast of the ruins of the town. The enclosure wall measures 90 to 100 meters (288 to 320 feet). The entrance, flanked by two square towers, is on the south. This fortress does not have the rounded towers of al-Deir and Qasr al-Labeka. Here the towers are square. It is more in keeping with the Monastery of Mustafa Kashif. Like other fortresses at Kharga, it is made of mud brick, each 35x17x9 cm in size. All the forts have very thick walls, not only good for defense, but for keeping cool in summer and warm in winter. Here at Dabadib the interior, now a ruin, was once filled with cells with vaulted ceilings.

The Church

The ruins of a church, complete with several arches, abut the east side of the fortress. The apse contained Greek, Coptic, and Arabic graffiti. Although a portion of the western external wall had collapsed, most of the structure was still standing in 1997. The interior contained various rooms. But no more. The church has recently been damaged by a local person looking for treasure. He came, not on a motorbike, not in a 4x4, not even in a truck. This clever fellow came to Dabadib in a forklift with caterpillar tracks. He drove that gigantic monster all the way from Qasr Kharga in the belief that he would be a rich man on his return journey. He did not get lost. He did not run out of petrol. He found his way. And when he got here he pushed that forklift against this church again and again until he had destroyed an important piece of history.

We have discussed the quest for buried treasure before. It is a mania in the desert. Some of the local people find it hard to believe that someone would work hard for several months only to look at and record broken buildings. They are sure riches are being looted and taken away. This type of belief has caused the death of more than one explorer through the years. (See Alexine Tinne.)

Western village

Lying to the west of the fortress, along the channel of the more westerly aqueduct as it makes its way toward the mountain are the substantial remains of a village. Along its western side are a number of sunt trees, a good place to have lunch.

Aqueducts

Despite the grandeur of the fortress, the most spectacular ruins at Ain Umm Dabadib are the aqueducts. Obviously such huge settlements needed a constant water supply. During antiquity, an extensive 14.3 kilometer (9 mile) twisting and turning underground system of galleries was created. There are four main aqueducts that run parallel to each other with man holes for maintenance along each of them. The longest is the westerly one at 4.6 kilometers (2.8 miles). The one to the north is 53.5 meters (175 feet) deep, runs for 2.9 kilometers (1.5 miles), and has 150 shafts spaced at 19 to 20 meters (64 feet) apart It falls at a rate of 1 meter (3.1 feet) per 2.5 kilometers (1.5 miles). Altogether, the builders excavated 4,875 cubic meters (15,595 cubic feet), 600 to 700 vertical shafts, and cut and moved over 20,000 meters (64,690 feet) of solid rock. It is an amazing feat of construction.

Although the design and manner of the aqueduct system is probably Persian, the construction of this and similar aqueducts in the Western Desert is still a mystery. Caton-Thompson, in the 1930s, suggests a Libyan, possible Garamantian, connection at a much

Air vents of Ain Umm Dabadib aqueduct

earlier date. Her observation is a valid one, especially in light of Ahmed Fakhry's discovery in Bahariya that the aqueduct there was in place before a Twenty-sixth Dynasty tomb was dug.

The Romans did extensive work on water systems in the Western Desert, constructing huge cisterns along the northern coast and underground galleries and aqueducts in most of the oases. However, none of the Roman work looks like these systems. Instead Dabadib's waterworks are identical to the *foggara* found in Libya and Algeria. In both countries dozens of such systems exist. As mentioned previously, they are also found in Iran (Persia), Afghanistan, Oman, and China, from where they may have originated. In the Western Desert they are plentiful. (see Water, this chapter)

These aqueducts were explored by Ball (1898) and Beadnell (1898, 1905). They were also visited by Ahmed Fakhry in the 1930s. Today they are still intact, snaking north from the town to the source in the escarpment. Along the route, every few meters, is an air vent and access hole which permitted maintenance of the underground galleries. This is very important as the aqueducts are labor intensive. They were always filling with sand and it was necessary to clear them out.

Ball and Beadnell, when examining the northern scarp near Ain Umm Dabadib, questioned whether another depression lay to the north of Kharga. Although they did not explore the area, they noted several factors to support their hypothesis. There was enough sand to suggest a depression beyond the escarpment and ample evidence of caravan routes headed north to an unknown destination. (Could Cambyses' army be on one of them?) Sala Abdulla, a Khargian, told Beadnell that an old, well-traveled road leading to a place called Ain Hamur moved northwest over the escarpment. Although Sala had heard about it, he tried to find it and failed. (Could this be Ain Amur?)

Even more compelling is the story told by the inhabitants of Kharga of travelers from Asyut who discovered an unknown oasis while heading for Kharga. They maintained it was nine hours away from Ain Umm Dabadib (by camel) and completely surrounded by escarpment and high mountains. Could the tunnel penetrating the escarpment have been a conduit for water to this second depression?

One of the aqueducts was cleared of debris by eighty men from the oases directed by Sheikh Hassan Hanadi, brother of the *umda* (mayor) of Kharga. Water began to flow once again through the tunnel. Immediately a small community of farmers moved to Dabadib.

In 1905, Beadnell explored the tunnel. Thirty to 35 gallons a minute were flowing and land was under cultivation. He found the 1.5 meter by 0.75 meter (4.7 feet by 2.3 feet) shaft well cut through solid sandstone rock to a depth of 40.3 meters (132 feet). It led to a tunnel approximately 1.5 meters (4.8 feet) high and 60 cm (24 inches) wide at the top. It was hot and sultry but after a few attempts Beadnell traced it to its end hoping to find an inscription that would date the construction and name the builders. He found nothing.

He leaves us a record: "On more than one occasion I sank exhausted into the water, the huge gasps of breath which I took seeming powerless to relieve the horrible sensation of stifling, and with the unpleasant prospect of getting drowned if I escaped suffocation. Yet there seemed to be ten thousand devils tempting me onwards, and although I did not know how long life could be supported under such conditions, a mad desire possessed me to see the thing through; so that whenever I was able to progress a few yards it was toward the head of the tunnel."

There are three more systems lying close together over the ridge to the east of the fortress. Two are easily found, the fourth is elusive. These shafts are dangerous to the visitor. Snakes and scorpions, not to mention bats live there. Use your brains.

Eastern Village

Almost directly behind the fortress and mudbrick buildings at its base are the ruins of another section of the town. Beyond, toward the escarpment is the temple, very small in comparison to the fortress and easily recog-

nizable as the exterior walls do not rise in a straight line but slant inward from the base. Beside the temple is the second aqueduct. To the east of it, past some vegetation, which makes getting to it a little bit tricky, is the third aqueduct, sitting at the base of a spur of the escarpment.

Rock Tombs

To the east of the third aqueduct, all along the spur, are tombs. Some have been mutilated, the mummies desecrated and their remains scattered about. These tombs are not to the west of the town as in the Nile Valley.

The richness of Ain Umm Dabadib, although it has failed to lure archaeologists, has lured farmers throughout the centuries. In the 1910s, when Harding King visited the area two families were living at Ain Umm Dabadib and in recent years a small number of men cleared one of the springs, which began to yield sufficient water to cultivate the area. Unfortunately, the projects have always been abandoned.

Excavations are finally underway at Ain Umm Dabadib. The first season was in 1998.

Dunes

Dunes dominate the route to Ain Umm Dabadib. They form three 30 to 40 kilometer (18 to 25 mile) parallel lines of tall mounds following one another in a seemingly never ending parade south. Most are barchan, or crescent dunes, but there are whale dunes, where the smaller dunes have crashed together to form a mountain of sand with many facets, as formidable as any granite or limestone barricade. They are impressive.

A climb up the escarpment north of Ain Umm Dabadib is well worth the effort, for from this height one can see the various dune fields making their way south.

Gebel al-Tarif

Gebel al-Tarif, Mountain of the Border, at 432 meters (1,384 feet) the highest and largest mountain within the oasis, sprawls in its full majesty to the east of the track to Ain Umm Dabadib. It runs for 10 kilometers (6 miles) north to south and 2 kilometers (1.2

miles) east to west. Along its flanks, covering a 100 meter (320 foot) span of Nubian limestone, are tons of sand banks built up over the centuries as Abu Muharrik makes its way south. Ancient mining sites honeycomb the mountain. Ball and Beadnell tell us north of Beleida and west of Labeka the rocks are almost volcanic. The hills are honeycombed with tunnels that "penetrate for long distances underground." The entrances to these mines are often designated by dumps where the useless rock was left behind when the alum was extracted. It was exported to Greece and Rome and was still in production in the Islamic era. We do not know when the mining stopped, but it was reopened by the British. Aptly named, the mountain divides the open desert from the more habitable eastern section of the oasis.

Gebel al-Sheikh

Gebel al-Sheikh, Mountain of the Sheikh or Chief, is a small, circular mountain tucked into the northwestern side of Gebel al-Tarif. Pink and white, it is not as formidable as its parent, but nevertheless is a welcome landmark for anyone on a desert journey.

Off Road from Dabadib to Qasr Kharga (the way back)

	km	total km
Fortress	0	0
Graded road		
15 kms	15	16
High tension wires	c15	30
Gebel Ghurabi	c4	34
Dakhla/Kharga rd N 25 23 948	c7	37
E 30 26 859		

Getting There: The route to Ain Umm Dabadib lies to the west of gebels al-Tarif and al-Sheikh through a single narrow corridor surrounded by sand dunes. The route is extremely difficult for any type of vehicle, and a digression east or west will put one into the massive north–south dune fields. The journey is only 35–40 kilometers (22–25 miles), less if one does not get caught in a dune field, more if one zigs and zags too much. It cannot be done in less than two hours. **A local guide is essential**.

From the fortress look for the well-graded road probably built by the Romans. It is only a short distance away between the second and third dune field (the third is the most eastern). Follow the road as long as you can for it is the direct route back. However, it is often obliterated and is hard to find again. There are dozens and dozens of tracks to follow too and they make a fairly straight line to home. Follow the majority, leave the one or two tracks headed off by themselves alone.

About 15 kilometers (9 miles) later the mountains should be on your left; you have crossed a dune or two and have negotiated between a few. As long as the mountains stay on your left and the escarpment behind you, you are OK.

Another 15 kilometers (9 miles) later, high tension wires appear on the left. They are *not* along the main road at this point. They will ride with you on your left for a while before they join the highway. The sign to the road is high tension wires with telephone poles beneath them directly in front of you.

A few kilometers later (maybe 4) whale back dunes will appear and a small mountain, more of a hill, appears ahead on the right. This is Gebel Ghurabi. It is the marker for the beginning of the Dabadib road and sits just beside the highway. Head for it and you will find the well graded road again. The highway is just beyond. When you hit the highway turn left (east). You are 14 kilometers (8.7 miles) from the checkpoint at Kharga.

TOUR #6

Ain al-Dabashiya (Ain Tabashir), Ain al-Tarakwa (maybe), and Beleida

- 2x2, 4x4
- all day, or 2 half days
- easy to difficult

			km	total km
Tourist Office	N 25 27 531	E 30 32 931	0	0
Dabashiya (rd)	N 25 33 646	E 30 37 624	14	14
Dabashiya (site)			6	20
(Return to Kharga)				
Beleida	N 25 29 416	E 30 30 616	6	6

You must have permission to visit these sites from the Director of Antiquities' Office across the street from the Kharga Museum. They require one of their officers to accompany you. This is not a hardship as they can give you a lot of interesting information. DO NOT VISIT THESE SITES WITHOUT PERMISSION OR YOU WILL BE BREAKING THE LAW.

Ain al-Dabashiya (Ain Tabashir)

As with so many of the ancient sites along the northern plain in Kharga, Dabashiya was a community at some time in the

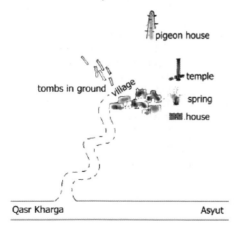

Ain al-Dabashiya

remote past. When all the excavations are complete we may find it was one of the largest communities in ancient Kharga. There are a number of Roman sites here, including a village, a temple, an ancient pigeon house (colombaria, dovecote), and tombs.

The site was excavated by the local antiquities office over two very successful seasons in 1994–95.

The Temple

The mudbrick temple lies directly on the desert floor. It is quite substantial, measuring 29.70 meters (95 feet) by 8.30 meters (26.5 feet). The walls along the outside are 85 cm (34 inches) thick. The temple interior of four rooms was once filled with huts.

The Columbaria

The pigeon house is the best preserved in either Kharga or Dakhla oases. Ball found it and a few more scattered around the oasis in the 1890s. In 1897, three outer walls remained. This is still true over one hundred years later. It measured 5.5 by 4.5 meters (18 feet by 14 feet) and rose 6–7 meters (17–22 feet) high. The outer walls were rounded at the corners and the interior filled with small recesses of about 20 centimeters (8 inches) for pigeons to roost. There were steps in the center of the building so the guano could be harvested.

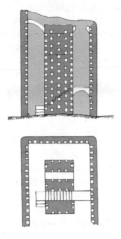

Columbaria

Town and Tombs

Archaeologists have been working here for a number of seasons and have discovered an entire community. They found 68 tombs, one complete and unmolested. Among the items unearthed was a 60 cm wooden statue of Osiris, a canopic jar box, and two coffins. One of the coffins was a complete burial with an outer and inner decorated coffin and a wrapped mummy with mask dated to the first century, very old for this oasis.

Getting There: From Kharga go north for 14 kilometers (9 miles) to a small village. Turn left (northwest) on a paved road that leads through the village. The pavement ends after the village. Continue ahead, avoiding the soft places. Dabashiya is about 6 kilometers (3.7 miles) into the desert.

Ain al-Tarakwa

Ain al-Tarakwa, Spring of the Turks, is currently buried. Here, after a sandstorm in 1949, the desert yielded one of its mysteries, the top part of a sandstone temple once standing along the Darb al-Arbain. This decorated temple is unexcavated. Decorations indicate that it was dedicated to Amun Re. Now it is buried again. It certainly leads us to wonder how many other treasures lie under the sand.

Getting There: Let your guide lead you

cemetery and pigeon house

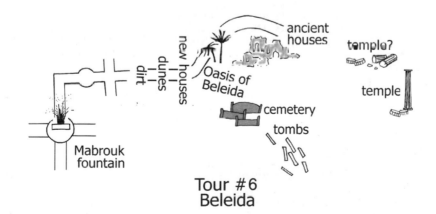

Tour #6
Beleida

Beleida

to al-Tarakwa; if it is exposed there is something to see; if not, return to the asphalt road and head back to Qasr Kharga. At Qasr Kharga, go one block past the Mabrouk fountain and turn right. You are headed to Beleida.

Beleida

Seven kilometers (4.3 miles) north-northwest of Qasr Kharga in the southern foothills of Gebel al-Tarif lies Beleida, a most amazing site. The first thing you notice is that the ground is red. The sand itself is not red, but the ancient pottery is piled so thick at this site it looks that way.

Dated from the first to the fifth centuries, this Roman, and perhaps Greek, site stretches over a large area and includes a number of mudbrick buildings, a small fortress, two possible temples, two cemeteries, a village, and a pigeon house.

Schweinfurth visited Beleida in 1874 and remarked upon the houses. He found a large number of small vaulted buildings closely packed together forming the remains of a large village to which the Arabs gave the name Balad, 'the village.'

Excavations have been carried out at Beleida by the local antiquities department and a number of the ancient homes have been cleaned out. It is an amazing look at how people lived in ancient times.

Getting There: Pass the Mabrouk fountain in Qasr Kharga and turn right at the next block. Continue through the city. The road will turn into a dirt road and pass through some construction. Keep going. The oasis of Beleida is dead ahead. At the fork, bear left to pass around the oasis. The ruins are on the far side.

TOUR #7

Ain Amur

- **4x4**
- **all day**
- **very difficult**

You must have permission to visit these sites from the Director of Antiquities Office across the street from the Kharga Museum. They require one of their officers to accompany you. This is not a hardship as they can give you a lot of interesting information. DO NOT VISIT THESE SITES WITHOUT PERMISSION OR YOU WILL BE BREAKING THE LAW.

Ain Amur

Ain Amur, Spring of the Lovely One, is not within any oasis. Kharga lies to the east and Dakhla lies to the west. Its significance is that it was the only water source on the Darb Ain Amur, one of two desert tracks connecting Kharga to Dakhla. Because of its strategic importance, a stronghold was established at Ain Amur.

Ain Amur is totally isolated. It is not a place that one stumbles across, and how it was ever found in the first place is baffling. It is dominated by the elements. When the wind blows there is a howling which seems to penetrate the very soul and when it dies the silence is unbearable. In the stillness, if one places pencil to paper the graphite sounds like running a fingernail down a chalkboard. Ain Amur is awesome.

The spring, called Muallekeh, 'the hanging,' by Cailliaud, is found in a slight depression two thirds of the way up the side of the 371 meter (1,187 foot) northwestern cliffs of the Abu Tartur Plateau. It is 525 meters (1,680 feet) above sea level, an unusually high elevation for any spring. There are two springs in the Western Desert that do not lie on the depression floor, close to underground water sources—this one and Ain Tafnis, also in Kharga. Neither is fed by underground water, but by surface water trapped in the limestone scarp.

The area surrounding the spring is unexpectedly flat with several palm trees and ancient ruins. The most impressive are the ruins of a Roman temple/fortress which is only decorated on the back wall. There is graffiti on the jambs of the main gateway. In fact there is plenty of graffiti to be found at Ain Amur, some dating as far back as Paleolithic times. The Coptic graffiti found on the jambs of the temple was left there by hermits living in the caves around Ain Amur during the Christian era. Part of this graffiti tells of an Arab traveler in early Christian times who took on the Darb Ain Amur by himself and on foot. He was "faint from thirst" and "came to [Ain Amur] in the latter part of the night . . . and it saved him."

Winlock found the entrance and back chambers well preserved in 1908. They are made of sandstone blocks excavated from the escarpment. The roof and lintels were of larger limestone blocks.

Explorers of the nineteenth century also left their mark. Among the most noteworthy are A. Edmondstone in February 1819 and I. Hyde, 17 December 1819, Drovetti—Rosingana, one above the other with only the year. There is one other name here at Ain Amur worth talking about, that of Ismail Abu Shanab. He traveled with Frederic Cailliaud, was French by birth, but became a soldier for the Pasha. These men were called French Mamluks. He chose the name Ismail Abu Shanab as his Islamic name. It means, Ismail, Father of a Moustache (that is, he had a moustache). Here he signed his name Le Torzec, Ismael Bouchenape, 1820, a bastardized French version of the Arabic.

Ain Amur has yet to be adequately excavated and a plethora of artifacts await the archaeologist, including tombs with mummies, and a great quantity of shards. There is a temple that once measured 53 feet 10 inches by 25 feet (English team) or 70 feet long (French team). Sculptures covered the back of the building. There were a few houses, too.

Getting There: The journey is too difficult at this time for anyone to try it alone. Depend on your guide to get you there. Everything about the trip to Ain Amur is strenuous. The route cannot be traversed in less than three hours. Approximately 48 kilometers (30 miles) from the main road, it weaves and twists its way through soft sand, sand waves, rock-strewn gullies, and foothills. One leaves the Darb al-Ghubari, heading for the northern side of the Abu Tartur Plateau on the same desert track leading to Dabadib. Penetrating the foothills surrounding Abu Tartur is probably the most difficult job, for these long fingers extend a good distance into the plain below. It is a journey for 4x4s, dirt bikes, or camels. No regular vehicle should try to navigate this route. A local guide is essential.

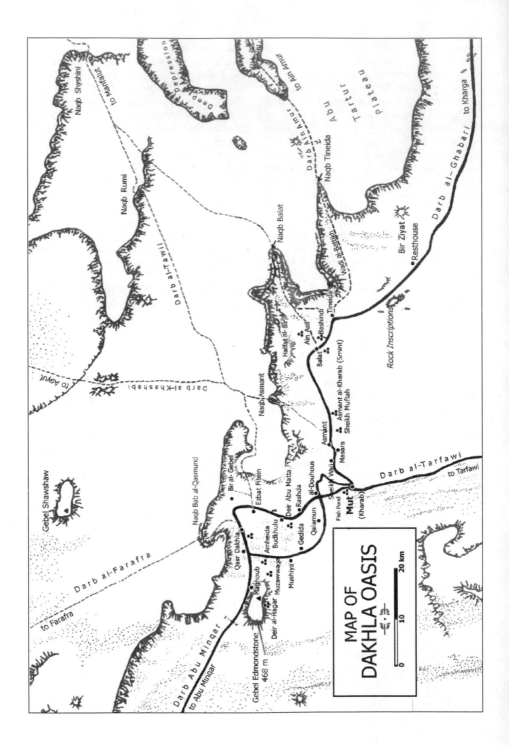

MAP OF DAKHLA OASIS

4

Dakhla

Kharga to Dakhla along the Darb al-Ghubari

			km	total km
Kharga checkpoint	N 25 26 648	E 30 31 927	0	0
Dabadib/Amur rd	N 25 23 524	E 30 26 100	14	14
New Valley Phosphate	N 25 14 635	E 30 04 415	30.5	44.5
Conical Valley	N 25 14 635	E 30 04 152	5.5	50
Ziyyat checkpoint	N 25 13 486	E 29 43 606	45	95
Rock inscriptions	N 25 27 782	E 29 20 862	40	135

The route to Dakhla leaves Kharga at Banque Misr on the corner of Sharia Gamal Abd al-Nasser and Sharia al-Nada and travels west over the Darb al-Ghubari. Although Kharga is slowly creeping west, one almost immediately enters the dune fields that are marching south from the escarpment. Although the scenery is varied and interesting, when the northern wind hits the car broadside, which it does most of the time, and the hot sun beats relentlessly (even in winter it is intense), the trip can be uncomfortable. It is best to make this journey in the early morning. It is 151 kilometers (94.8 miles) to Tineida, the first village in Dakhla Oasis.

A mere kilometer out of Kharga along the Darb al-Ghubari the road passes a checkpoint and begins to cut through the spectacular dune fields that are moving slowly south through the desert. Only 14 kilometers (8.75) from Kharga is the desert track to Ain Umm Dabadib and Ain Amur. Neither should be pursued without two 4x4s and a guide.

New Valley Phosphate Project
About 44.5 kilometers (27.8 miles) from Kharga is the New Valley Phosphate Project, a new industry that is mining phosphates from the Abu Tartur Plateau, the huge mountain that sits between Kharga and Dakhla. Given that the plateau holds one of the largest phosphate deposits in the world, an entire village has grown in the area. This phosphate bed was discovered in 1958 by the Geological Survey. In 1968, under Rushdi Said, the true depth of the beds was assessed.

Conical Hills
Less than 5 kilometers (3 miles) after the phosphate mine the terrain changes dramatically, and conical hills appear to the north and south of the road. They seem to extend into infinity. These hills, so reminiscent of the pyramids along the Nile Valley, lie in a quiet, sometimes misty, always windblown, valley.

Bir Ziyyat
95 kilometers (59.3 miles) into the journey

is a resthouse and Bir Ziyyat checkpoint, quickly followed by a series of yardangs. The checkpoint is currently open but one may be requested to present car papers. There is rock art in the area.

Rock Inscriptions

At 135 kilometers (84.3 miles) from Kharga, just as the road bends to Tineida, the terrain changes and a series of sandstone outcroppings appear on both sides of the road. Some resemble familiar animals like the camel and sphinx. One, among the closest rocks to the south side of the road, contains a series of prehistoric rock inscriptions.

This valley is at the terminus of two major routes to Kharga, the Nile Valley, and Sudan. The first is the Darb al-Ghubari, which followed pretty much the present day asphalt road (in some places it runs further north, hugging the base of the plateau). The second is a now lost track which linked Tineida with Baris and the Darb al-Arbain in Kharga Oasis. The spot was a major halting place for caravans.

The impressive rock inscriptions, recorded by Hans A. Winkler in 1939 and Ahmed Fakhry in 1942, cover the entire base of the rock, especially on the side facing the road. They include both prehistoric and modern drawings of giraffes, camels, hunters, and Bedouin tribal symbols (*wasm*s). The rock itself is soft sandstone blasted by the harsh northern wind for centuries, a fact that made Harding King and others question the early date of these well preserved drawings. Winkler calls the artists Early Oasis Dwellers and points out that pictures of pregnant women are seen here. There is a massive buildup of sand at the base of the rock, which may be covering additional inscriptions and could well have covered and preserved those we see today.

At the eastern end of the large rock is a small pot-shaped outcropping. It also has prehistoric inscriptions and two other interesting features. The name of Jarvis, once the British governor of Kharga and Dakhla oases and an avid explorer of the deserts, is carved into the base of the

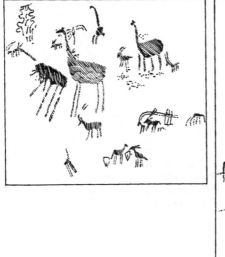

Rock art at Tineida

stone. Below it swirls of yellow and reddish-orange sandstone form wonderful patterns.

The most disturbing aspect of this site is that valuable prehistoric inscriptions, containing important information, are being destroyed by modern travelers who are so stupid as to carve their own graffiti directly on top of the ancient ones.

To travel from Farafra to Dakhla see Farafra chapter.

Dakhla

After trekking over nonexistent roads to visit Roman forts strung across the desert along the north–south Darb al-Arbain, Dakhla's prehistoric cemeteries, Old Kingdom villages, and Islamic fortress towns, lying east to west near the edge of the escarpment along the Darb al-Ghubari, come as a welcome change. Where Kharga is the administrative center of the New Valley, Dakhla is the breadbasket, its fields and orchards lush with produce. The beige and brown landscape of Kharga is replaced with golden sand, red earth, a pastel escarpment, and vibrant green fields. Dakhla bathes in spectacular color, especially in winter when the air is clear of the haze that plagues the horizon in summer, and at early morning and sunset when the long rays of the sun drown the earth in golden light.

History

Recent discoveries tell us that Dakhla Oasis has been populated for over 10,000 years. In Neolithic times (5500–2500 B.C.), the climate of Dakhla was similar to that of the African savanna. Buffaloes, elephants, rhinos, zebras, ostriches, and hartebeests wandered around the shores of a huge lake, on whose southern bank primitive people had settled to herd goats and cattle. But with a breakdown in the environment which caused the lake to dry and the region to become arid, there was massive migration south and east, which helped to populate the early Nile Valley. The sands of the oasis covered the ancient sites and kept them safe for centuries. Now those same sands are eroding the surface and ancient cemeteries and villages are popping out of the ground like rare blossoms. Archaeologists, who are just beginning to explore the area, are being well rewarded for their efforts.

Dakhla has been known as al-Wah, the Inner Oasis, Oasis Magna, and Zeszes, place of the two swords.

Pharaonic (2686–332 B.C.)

Dakhla Oasis had contact with the Nile Valley as early as the Archaic Period (c.3150–2686 B.C.) and this contact continued through the Third (c.2686–2181 B.C.) and Sixth Dynasties (c.2345–2333 B.C.) of the Old Kingdom. Over a hundred ancient cemeteries have been recorded by the Dakhleh Oasis Project, in operation since 1978. Covering a span of time from prehistory to the Roman period, their excavations have told us much about life during these eras. The Institut Français d'Archéologie Orientale, working since 1977, has been excavating in the area of Ain Asil, where they have uncovered what is believed to be the Old Kingdom capital of Dakhla Oasis.

It is likely that during the Old Kingdom Dakhla Oasis had a direct link to the Nile Valley via the Darb al-Tawil and was not dependent on the route through nearby Kharga Oasis. In fact, evidence suggests Dakhla may have been much more important to the Nile Valley pharaohs than Kharga.

During the New Kingdom, settlement moved further west and Mut became the capital of Dakhla. We know from inscriptions on tombs in the Nile Valley that taxes from both Kharga and Dakhla were paid in wine, fruit, minerals, and woven products. We also know that throughout history the oases were difficult to bring under control. So far away from the Nile, with so inhospitable a journey, few people went willingly to the desert.

A stela from the Twenty-second Dynasty found near Mut by H. G. Lyons in 1894, now known as the First Dakhla Stela, tells us that Sheshonk I sent a man to "the two lands of wahat [oases]" to "regulate disputes over water rights." At that time a "cadastral register of the wells and orchards took place." In the pharaoh's fifth year he sent one of his royal relatives "to restore order in the Oasis-land, after he had found it in a state of war and turmoil."

No evidence has yet emerged to indicate a heavy Greek presence in the oasis, but several Ptolemaic structures have been found.

Roman (30 B.C.–A.D. 323) and Christian (323–642) Periods

Like all the oases in the Western Desert, Dakhla was very heavily populated during Roman rule. Roman farms, villages, and cemeteries litter the landscape, with major sites discovered at Smint, Amheida, and Qasr. A heavy influx of Roman immigrants occurred during the first century, possibly coming from the Fayoum, where the agricultural community was in decline. The Romans grew wheat, barley, and cotton. They had presses for olive oil and wine, and raised chickens and pigs.

It must be remembered that Dakhla was an agricultural area in the farthest corner of the Roman Empire. Unlike Kharga, dotted with dozens of Roman fortresses, only a few ruined fortresses have been found in Dakhla. The Kharga fortresses guarded the Darb al-Arbain, the major economic link to the interior of Africa. Although there is one route going south from Dakhla, the Darb al-Tarfawi, there is little to suggest that it rivaled in importance the Darb al-Arbain. It must also be remembered that Rome expected one third of its annual supply of grain from Egypt. If the Fayoum was being abandoned, the grain had to come from somewhere. Dakhla is as likely a place as is the Nile Valley.

Egypt was not treated like other conquered countries. Octavian, now Augustus Caesar, after he defeated Antony and Cleopatra, separated Egypt from the rest of the empire and oversaw its affairs himself through the appointment of a prefect, not the usual proconsul. Augustus, according the Naphtali Lewis in *Life in Egypt under Roman Rule*, used members of the equestrian order (his own) as prefects. He forbade any ranking public figure, including senators or equestrians, holding a higher rank than a prefect from entering the province without his permission. He kept the thirty nomes intact, but changed the power structure. Where the Ptolemaic era saw soldiers who were farmers living with their families, Roman soldiers lived in fortified camps and outposts. Small detachments rotated to key places on the frontier. The Romans never achieved a sense of belonging to Egypt.

After the Roman period the population declined dramatically, but grew again when Christians came to Dakhleh and occupied some Roman sites. There are ruins of Coptic churches and communities dating back as late as the seventh century. A. J. Mills, head of the Dakhleh Oasis Project, believes this may be the single most important archaeological fact in Dakhla. Many of these sites have been buried for centuries and once uncovered and examined may "provide rare evidence for the development of late Roman/Byzantine periods." We will be able to see the transition between these two eras, a transition now shrouded in the mists of the past.

Islamic Era (641–1798)

Closer to our era, the period from the seventh to the eighteenth centuries has left a permanent mark on this oasis. Threatened by invaders from the south and west it was at this time that the fortified towns like Qasr Dakhla, Qalamun, and Budkhulu were constructed. Built in places selected for their natural defensive positions, usually a hill or a cliff, these Islamic towns were divided into quarters, with gates that were locked at night against invaders. Buildings in Qasr Dakhla have been identified as existing during the Ayyubid Period, 1171–1250. That is well before the Mamluk era, so someone was out here doing something.

In recent years, these villages have spread beyond the protective walls to the now secure plains below, and have become electrified and modernized, but in villages like Mut, Qalamun, Qasr, and Balat one is still able to view the original buildings. All the domed tombs found throughout the oasis have their origins in Islamic architecture and some of the facades, especially in Qasr, are still in Islamic style.

Raiders came out of the west to loot and plunder the villages in annual raids or *ghazya*s (the word that has entered English as 'razzia'). They all did it: Arab, Tebu, and Tuareg. Edmondstone was told of just such a raid by Mograbin or Barbary Arabs three years (1816) before he arrived. There were 400 of them, and just like the pestilence, they hit and ran. It was probably very similar to a raid described by Vischer that took place on the road to Bornu: "The Arabs had chosen the hottest part of the year and swooped down on Tibesti when the Tubbus [Tebu], themselves probably on a raid of their own, expected nothing. Without much trouble they took all the camels, women, and children they found, burnt villages, cut down palm trees in the most approved fashion, and hurried off before the husbands had any news of the disaster."

The raids into Dakhla were so severe that during Mamluk times the government established a military colony of Surbaghi (Chourbghi) in Qalamun. It was their job to stop the raids. Qalamun, established as the main administrative center of Dakhla Oasis during the Mamluk era, became the center of Turkish influence. In fact, some families still insist on their Turkish origins. The Surbaghi destroyed the wells along the caravan route leading to the west (probably the Abu Minqar–Kufra camel track, or a lost track to Kufra) to a distance of seven days. This made any travel to Dakhla impossible by this route. The trail fell out of use and was lost. It existed only in rumor. The stories of the raiders also diminished.

This was the situation when the European explorers began searching for Zerzura. This information was given to Ascherson of the Rohlfs Expedition by Hassan Effendi, the mayor of Dakhla in 1874. He said the raiders were Bedajat, a name Henrich Barth used for the people of Ennedi north of Wadai, but Ascherson believed they were actually from Bornu. Hassan Effendi actually had one of the iron boomerangs, called *kurbaj*, that were used by the raiders. He gave it to Rohlfs as a gift and it looked just like a Tebu boomerang found by Nachtigal.

Muhammad Ali subdued the oasis by force. Edmondstone tells us ". . . their tribute, which is paid in kind, not only varies every year, according to his [the pasha's] caprice, as they affirm, but four or five soldiers are now sufficient for levying it, whereas four hundred were necessary for that purpose when they first came under his dominion." It was during Muhammad Ali's reign that the first Europeans came to Dakhla.

British Occupation (1882–1954)

During the Mahdist uprising in Sudan, Dakhla fared better than Kharga. A few Dervish raids, a rebuilding of the Mut fortifications, and the threat was over. Dakhla did have a *zawya* and was occupied by Sanusi forces in 1916, when the British were chasing the Sanusi through the Western Desert. Some of the people of the oasis joined the Sanusi, others considered them just another set of invaders. The oasis was taxed and forced to supply provisions for the army. One of the villagers from Gedida remembers how difficult the occupation was, maintaining that no supplies came via the Nile Valley and commodities, such as fabric, became scarce. The occupation lasted until October 16 of the same year.

The British, who were in control of Egypt at that time, evacuated all British personnel from Kharga in anticipation of a takeover. According to W. T. Massey in *The Desert Campaigns*, they sent a reconnaissance plane to Mut on October 9–10, and it observed that the Sanusi were on their way out of the oasis. On October 15, three lieutenants (Armstrong, Lindsay, and Gayford), six light patrol cars, three Lewis guns, a Ford delivery van with signalers, and ten motorcyclists took off for Dakhla. One can almost see them charging down the Ghubari Road, circling sand dunes, with the Union Jack snapping in the wind. They were met by an armored car and tender at mile 73, a former Sanusi post. Two sections of Australian Imperial Camel Corps soon joined them.

They occupied Tineida on the 16th. On the 17th, Armstrong and four patrol cars went to Balat and Budkhulu. Nearby they encountered some Sanusi and attacked. They surrendered to the Lewis guns. Armstrong moved on to Rashida and "arrested ten Senussi in the Omda's house." Wright went to Bir Sheikh Muhammad and captured forty Sanusi while he burned the farm building. In all, in three days, 181 Sanusi were captured including seven "Egyptian coastguards who had traitorously left their posts in the coastal section." The remainder of the Sanusi headed for Siwa where, by this time, they were unwelcome.

In colonial days the road from Dakhla was open to motorcars, but the journey took nine hours. The more adventurous traveler could go by camel which took three to four days.

Today

There are sixteen villages in Dakhla Oasis. (When Edmondstone was here in 1819, there were twelve.) Mut, named after the ancient Egyptian goddess of the Theban triad, is the capital. Today there are 127,000 inhabitants in the entire New Valley with 75,000 in Dakhla. Of these 11,000 reside in Mut (in 1874 there were 17,000 in all of Dakhla).

Agriculture is the main industry in Dakhla and its olives, dates, onions, and dried fruit are exported to the Nile Valley. By government decree each farmer must cultivate wheat and rice, and orchards must have a variety of trees including dates, oranges, apricots, and olives. Recent years have seen the introduction of a number of modern innovations: diesel pumps, certified seeds, chemical fertilizers, mechanization, and commercial pest management. Modern pest management, including pesticides, which some claim compound the problem, have been introduced at Mut especially in post-harvest storage of grains. These pests, including insects, weevils, *sus*, and rodents, *firan*, have been formidable enemies for centuries. In some instances farmers lose 50 percent of their crops to pests, either in the fields or in storage.

Traditional methods of post-harvest pest control include burying grain in the sand, which has worked for centuries, to keep grain not only insect free, but dry. The second method is storing the crops in granary rooms inside of houses. A final method is storing grain in specially built mud silos, *souma*. Anne M. Parrish, with the University of Kentucky field team, reports, "Some farmers say that 'in the old days' there were no *sus*. One even said that there were no *sus* until the Ministry of Agriculture came to the oasis. But others explained that 'the old days' were also 'the poor days.' Food was consumed before insects could cause serious economic losses." She also tells us an interesting story about rats: "One farmer said: 'Rats are so clever that they send their young in to eat first. If they don't die, then the old ones come in to eat.'"

Primary and preparatory schools exist in all villages, with three secondary schools at Mut, Balat, and Qasr Dakhla. In Mut commercial, teaching, industrial, and agricultural schools have been established in the past few years. Each village has a clinic (with a hospital in Mut), a post office, electricity, tap water, and telephone service with foreign exchange.

Marriage usually takes place in summer. Men marry when they are 20 to 25 and women at 17 to 20. Families which have always averaged five to ten children are stream-lining to four or fewer.

Explorers

Sir Archibald Edmondstone is believed to be the first modern European to visit Dakhla. He came in February of 1819, over the Darb al-Tawil from Beniadi, near Asyut, to Balat and returned via Darb Ain Amur and Kharga to Farshut via the Darb al-Rufuf. Understand, Dakhla was only a theory. There was no proof it existed at all. He provided us with a good map of the two oases, their escarpments, and villages. He made mistakes, but we had nothing before him. In fact, Dakhla had been forgotten. Edmondstone arrived in Balat at eight o'clock in the evening on the 16th having taken sixty-four hours. By his calculations, that was 178 miles.

Following quickly on his heels was M. Drovetti. Make no bones about it, this was an all out rivalry between an Englishman and a Frenchman for the right to say, "I was the first." The French had won the battle for most of North Africa and the prize of Dakhla would only add to their West African kingdom. Edmondstone deliberately came via the shorter Darb al-Tawil directly, bypassing Kharga and thus saving precious time. Along with a forced march on the last night, it took him five days. This was done to beat Drovetti to Dakhla. Winlock confirms our suspicions: "Edmondstone, with his two friends Houghton and Master, getting wind of the fact that the French Consul General Drovetti was starting westward from Esna, organized a caravan at Asyut, to be the first in the race to the rumored oasis beyond el Khargeh."

Edmondstone and Drovetti were followed by Cailliaud in 1819, Frederic Muller in 1824, and John G. Wilkinson in 1825. Then came the Rohlfs' Expedition in 1874. In Dakhla, the Rohlfs' expedition mapped the topography, named Gebel Edmondstone in honor of the first explorer in the area, named Bab al-Qasmund after the German consul in Cairo, and Bab al-Cailliaud after the French explorer who did so much to open the desert.

Captain H. G. Lyons joined the list of explorers to Dakhla in 1894 and the Geological Survey sent Hugh Beadnell and company to survey in February of 1898. In 1908, the Americans H. E. Winlock and Arthur M. Jones of Boston made the journey and Winlock published his account of the journey in 1936. Only 400 copies were printed. Just when the explorers' era came to an end and the archaeologist and anthropologist era began is hard to say. Winlock and company were probably among the first of the latter. Harding King came in 1909. He was definitely an explorer. Once the railroad was opened in 1908, Dakhla was a tourist destination.

Geography and Geology

Dakhla lies at N 25 28 and N 25 44 latitude and E 28 48 and E 29 21 longitude. Located 120 kilometers (75 miles) west of Kharga, Dakhla, at 410 square kilometers (256 square miles), shares the same northern escarpment as its eastern neighbor. The scarp runs for 200 kilometers (125 miles) east-southeast to west-northwest along the northern edge of both depressions. The 300 to 400 meter (960 to 1,280 foot) high scarp is composed of a top layer of white chalky limestone followed by a mid-section of "greenish and ash-grey leafy clays" (the terms used by Rohlfs) and has a base of brown and black beds containing gypsum and scattered deposits of fossils. In fact, there are fossils and bone beds throughout the oasis. Between the scarp and the cultivated areas from Qasr Dakhla in the west to beyond Tineida in the east is the Sioh Ridge, a 2 to 3 meter (6.4 to 9.6

foot) thick dark-brown bone bed of fish, fish teeth, bones, and vertebrae. These bone beds create phosphate, which is used as fertilizer. Other minerals found in the area include ocher, cobalt, nickel, salt, and barytes. There are also black and red clays, the latter containing iron oxide. Most of the mudbrick buildings in the oasis are tinged with the red of iron oxide.

The escarpment, which is eroding in a northerly direction, helps to break the harsh winds, allowing for rich agricultural development along the floor of the depression. It has a number of bays, one near Qasr Dakhla at Bab al-Qasmund where the Darb al-Farafra exits the oasis, one northeast of Balat where the Naqb Balat leaves the depression, and another east of Tineida where Naqb Tineida leads up the cliffs of the Abu Tartur Plateau to the Darb Ain Amur.

The northern escarpment is the major cliff in Dakhla. The eastern part of the oasis is open to Kharga, the west is blocked, not by a cliff but by the massive dunes of the Great Sand Sea, and the south drops over a minor escarpment and then runs free and clear for hundreds of kilometers past the Gilf Kebir and into Sudan. Higher than Kharga, the lowest point in Dakhla is 100 meters (320 feet) above sea level. More fertile than Kharga, 45 percent of the total area is under cultivation.

Mountains and Passes (Naqbs)

The only mountain in the depression is **Gebel Edmondstone**, 17 kilometers (10.6 miles) west-southwest of Qasr. Named by members of Rohlfs expedition after Archibald Edmondstone, the base of the mountain is composed of fossil beds and the yellow and white flat-topped limestone cap contains scattered reef corals. Just above the scarp, heading north to Farafra is the **Gebel Shawshaw**, a 415 meter (1,328 feet) high mountain located between the Darb al-Farafra and the Darb al-Khashabi above the depression.

There are several passes in the scarp. Starting in the west is **Bab al-Qasmund** on the Darb al-Farafra. Continuing east are **Naqb Asmant, Naqb Balat**, and **Naqb Tineida**. On the plateau to the northeast along the Darb al-Tawil are **Naqb Rumi** and **Naqb Shyshini**.

The oasis is divided into two fertile areas: the east around Tineida and Balat and the west, Mut to Qasr. They are separated by 15 kilometers (9.3 miles) of barren desert.

Water

As with all the oases, water is the key ingredient in Dakhla. Prehistoric lakes once covered most of the cultivated area of this oasis. Today an artificial lake has been created just north of Mut in the hope of developing a fishing industry, but the main water source remains the wells. Deep wells are characteristic of this depression. As in Kharga, they are drilled to great depth so that the water can be extracted from Nubian sandstone. This drilling process is an expensive and time consuming affair and it is disastrous when a well runs dry. Farmers go to great lengths to keep the source open and clear of overgrowth.

At the beginning of the twentieth century there were 420 ancient wells, known by the natives as *Ain Romani*, and 162 modern wells, called *bir*, or *abyar* in the plural. Rohlfs, in 1874, reported that a Hassan Effendi, originally working with the French mining engineer LeFèvre, had drilled sixty wells in Dakhla in thirty years. The wells form only the first part of the irrigation system, since the farmers must also dig irrigation canals to transport the water to the fields. Today 600 wells exist in Dakhla with more on the way. It takes one million Egyptian pounds to create a new well. The springs and wells contain iron, magnesium, sulfur, and chloride and their healing waters are good for rheumatism, colds, skin diseases, and kidney stones.

No aqueducts have been found in Dakhla. A member of the Canadian team suggests that the geology of the oasis is not conducive to the construction of such systems.

Golden colored barchan sand dunes stretch along the edges of the depression. The 2 kilometer (1.2 mile) wide western field, almost true magnetic north–south, runs for 14 kilometers (8.7 miles) between Gebel Edmondstone and the scarp. The road to Abu Minqar and Farafra Oasis, often blocked by blowing sand, passes directly over one of the dunes. The view north at this point is spectacular, with dozens of crescent shaped golden dunes marching south from the pink and white scarp over which they tumble to reach the depression floor.

Caravan Routes and Roadways

Darb Ain Amur, Road of the Lovely One, passes east through Tineida and the Wadi al-Battikha over the scarp through Naqb Tineida to the Abu Tartur Plateau and Ain Amur, Ain Umm Dabadib, and Qasr Kharga. Used by Archibald Edmondstone in 1819 on his way back from Dakhla and by Rohlfs in 1874, it is the shortest distance between the two oases. (See Kharga Oasis for details.)

Darb al-Ghubari, the Dust Road, is the second major route that crosses east–west from Kharga at Qasr Kharga to Dakhla, entering the depression at Tineida and forming the main road through the oasis. (See Kharga Oasis for details.) There is a cut off from this route that leads to Baris in the south of Kharga Oasis.

The **Darb al-Farafra** links Dakhla Oasis to Farafra Oasis in the north. It begins at Qasr Dakhla where it goes north over the scarp at Bab al-Qasmund, veering west over dunes to Bir Dikker and Qasr Farafra. It continues on to Bahariya, Siwa, and Fayoum.

Darb Abu Minqar begins at Qasr and moves northwest between Gebel Edmondstone and the northern scarp to Ain Sheikh Marzuq, and to the northwest of Farafra Oasis. It is the modern roadway. (See Farafra Oasis.)

Darb al-Tawil, the Long Road, bypassing Kharga completely, is the only direct connection from Dakhla Oasis to the Nile Valley. Like most of the desert tracks, it is an old route and there is evidence that it was used extensively during the Old Kingdom. In 1908, Winlock tells us, tea, sugar, and coffee came with the caravans over this route. In this century it was still a viable route, often used by caravans loaded with dates on their way to market in the Nile Valley. The Darb al-Tawil has several starting points in the oasis. The westernmost route begins just east of Qasr Dakhla in the western part of the oasis. It quickly climbs the escarpment near Qasr and joins the Darb al-Khashabi, which works its way north from Asmant. Shortly thereafter the Darb al-Tawil turns northeast. At the Naqb Rumi, the Darb al-Tawil is joined by a third route from Balat and Tineida. (Some sources consider this the main route of the Darb al-Tawil in Dakhla.) This route begins at Balat and moves northeast 15 kilometers (9.3 miles) to a bay in the 350 meter (1,120 foot) scarp. Here it is joined by a track from Tineida.

They climb out of the depression at Naqb Balat and continue northeast along the desert to Naqb Rumi. The Darb al-Tawil, now complete, continues northeast through Naqb Shyshini and heads to Manfalut near Asyut in the Nile Valley. Edmondstone took five days to reach Dakhla, setting up camps along the way. Just as along the Darb al-Arbain, he was struck by the number of dead camels along the way. The trip took him sixty-four marching hours which he calculated as 178 miles.

Darb al-Khashabi, the Wooden Road, begins at Asmant and passes over the scarp at Naqb Asmant, heading almost due north where it seems to disappear. It is named the Wooden Road because it passes through a grove of dead trees.

The **Darb al-Tarfawi** is the only southern route in the oasis. Used in 1893–4 by Captain H. G. Lyons, it begins at Mut and heads south through the empty and seldom used southwestern desert to Bir Tarfawi and then on to Merga and al-Fasher in Sudan. A spur goes to the Gilf Kebir and Gebel Uwaynat. This isolated area is currently the focus of a major development program and plans are underway to launch a large agricultural project in the area. The Darb al-Tarfawi is receiving attention and is now paved for over 300 kilometers (187 miles). It will eventually be a major artery linking Dakhla to the southwestern corner of Egypt.

The People

There is evidence to suggest that Dakhla has been inhabited since prehistory and maybe as long as 200,000 years ago. Recent studies carried out by the Canadians indicate that the ancient inhabitants suffered from arthritis, tuberculosis, and iron deficiency anemia. The average life expectancy of men was twenty-four, while women lived to be around thirty-seven.

By studying Late Roman remains they have also discovered the antibiotic tetracycline was present in many of the bones. It helped protect the health of people in this oasis those many centuries ago. Further investigation showed that it was naturally ingested and not synthetically manufactured. In all probability, it was produced in contaminated grain which was consumed during hard times.

In 1819, the population of the entire oasis was estimated at between five and six thousand. Cailliaud found the people of Dakhla to be much more friendly and curious about Europeans that those of Kharga, Bahariya, and Siwa. They were more willing to show him around.

Today's population is an amalgam of peoples who have traveled to the oasis through the ages. There are elements of Libyan, Nubian, and Sudanese heritage, but mainly the people are Berber and Bedouin. Among themselves they make distinctions from village to village: al-Mahub is of Sanusi origin; Balat and Tineida are Moroccan; Qasr is Saudi Arabian; Qalamun, Turkish; and Mut is Asyuti and Bedouin. Sheikh Wali is considered a new village populated by the people from Gedida.

As in all the oases in the Western Desert, people marry within the extended family. Although patterns vary, educated men marry at twenty-five to thirty and uneducated men at twenty to twenty-five. Women marry at a younger age. The head of every village must be invited to every wedding (and when someone dies, each village must send a representative). Life expectancy for men in the oasis today is sixty to seventy-five, for women seventy-five to eighty.

When problems arise in a family, the eldest man still makes the decisions. If the dispute cannot be solved within the family, then the matter is brought before the mayor of the town. Police are never involved in these matters. This type of discipline can only work if there is respect among relations.

Today, the villages retain many distinctions, even in dialects. At Qasr they pronounce the *l* like an *n*, saying *unna* for *ulla*, the water jug. In Tineida, they use the classical "Qaf." In Asmant *ei* as in 'bay" is pronounced "oy" as in "joy," so "Enti fein?" (where are you?) is pronounced "Enti foyn?"

Food

The bread of Dakhla is the *eish shamsi*, sunbread, of Upper Egypt but called *aghif* in Dakhla. It is baked the same too. The oven, *tabuna*, here in Dakhla, has a symbol to ward off the evil eye at the top of the oven door. Known as 'the man,' *al-rais*, it looks like a little man. Bread is eaten as the morning meal.

In the fields, at midmorning, leftovers, dates, or fresh vegetables are eaten. Lunch is a mid-afternoon affair, around 2 or 3 o'clock. It is usually bread, rice, and vegetable stews.

Poultry and meat are eaten on special occasions. Rich families have it once or twice a week. Rice and macaroni are common.

Millet pudding is a specialty of Dakhla, as are date honey and date paste. Palm wine is not unknown.

The Crafts of the Oasis

Dakhla's heritage is both rich and representative of the four other oases in the central desert. As in the Nile Valley, women use *kohl*, powdered antimony, to accent their eyes. They also use *henna*. Young girls get a rich burgundy color from using black henna, while old women, with silver hair, become carrot tops when they use red henna on their hair. Henna is also applied to the soles of the feet and the palms of the hand. It means protection and good luck. It keeps the evil spirits away. Orange henna handprints were once seen everywhere, on doors, walls, and even the sides of donkeys.

Tattoos are also a method of personal adornment that have a symbolic purpose. Tattoos bring luck if done at the grave of a favorite sheikh. They also bring strength to aching hands, poor eyesight, or broken bones. Three dots at the corner of the eyes make the eyes strong. A bird at the temple helps too. Tree branches are often seen on women's chins for fertility. All these customs are beginning to wane.

However, it is in other crafts, especially baskets and pottery, that Dakhla excels, and exceptional items are still being made. The best place to see the crafts of Dakhla Oasis, including the elusive necklaces and dresses once worn by the women, is the small but exciting Ethnographic Museum in Mut. (For details see Mut below.)

Baskets and Rugs

Qasr Dakhla, Mut, and Gedida are the main basket making villages in Dakhla, though baskets are made in all the oasis's villages. Many of the baskets illustrated in the Kharga Oasis chapter are also part of the Dakhla crafts industry, but some Dakhla baskets are unique. The *marguna* is a woven basket with a sturdy lid and ornamental decorations similar to the *margun* basket of Kharga in shape. The *marguna* is stronger, being made of palm leaves that wrap around thin twigs. In Kharga the palm leaves are simply woven together. An additional difference is that the Dakhla version, made mostly at Qasr, is decorated with strips of ribbon or material, whereas the Kharga basket is decorated with colorful wool yarn. (See Kharga Oasis for illustration.) The *maqtaf* is a pliable basket used as a carry-all and often seen strapped to the side of a donkey laden with produce. Especially fine *maqtaf*s are made in Gedida.

Other woven items made from palm leaves include the *shamsiya*, a broad brimmed hat unique to Dakhla, worn by the men in the fields as protection against the hot rays of the sun, and the *fakhkh* (*asyad al-ghazal*), a hunting trap used to catch small birds and gazelles.

Although all villages in the oasis make *bursh*, mats, Gedida is the center of the mat making industry. These decorative mats come in a variety of sizes and some are ornamented with variations of green and red geometric patterns. Special *bursh* include the *bursh al-arusa*, mat of the bride, a special oval mat used in the wedding ceremony. The *bursh al-tin*, mat for clay, is a circular mat heavily entwined with ropes ending in four handles at the sides of the circle, used to gather clay, rice, and other produce. The ends pull up to use as a carry-all.

One of the most spectacular kelims of the Western Desert is the *khurg*, a Bedouin kelim used to cover camels. The wool of the *khurg* is naturally dyed in orange, red, black, and white and then woven into geometric patterns by Bedouin women on portable desert looms. The long strips are then sewn together for added width. Although

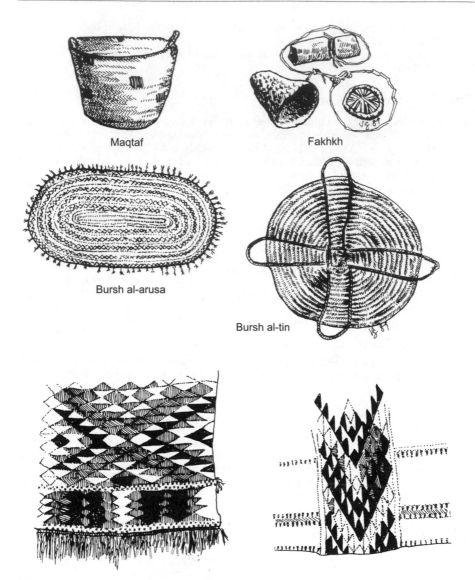

Maqtaf

Fakhkh

Bursh al-arusa

Bursh al-tin

Khurg

there are a variety of traditional designs in the Bedouin kelims, the colors tend to remain the same.

Pottery

Of the two southern oases, Dakhla, with its large deposits of high quality clay around the village of Qasr Dakhla, is far and away the largest producer of pottery. Ancient kilns in this area attest to the long life of the craft. One of the potter families originally came

Magur

Ballas

Hanab   Manshal

Qadus

Sumaa

Garra

Tisht

Zabdiya

Ulla

Turshiya

Labuk

Mahlab

from Qena in the Nile Valley in the early part of the seventeenth century. Today, the Qasr potters, located at the bottom of the hill, work in a dark, mudbrick hut on foot-powered wheels, much as their ancestors did tens of centuries before. Unlike in Kharga, where modern designs are used as decoration on traditional pots, in Qasr the same pots that have been created for centuries can be found. The garden around the kilns is arrayed with pots drying in the sun before being fired.

The variety of pots is amazing. The *asriya* or *magur* is a large-mouthed, deep-sided bowl used for kneading dough when making bread. The *ballas*, the traditional pot of Upper Egypt, is imported into the oasis, but instead of being used to carry water, it is used for storing dates. The *hanab*, known to have existed during the Middle Ages, is a wide-mouthed, handled pot used to store butter, salt, and almonds. It is hung on the wall by a cord. The *manshal* is a long, thin pot with a wide lip and handles, used for storing water, while the *mahlab* is a wide-lipped pot used to store fats. Lashed to the sides of the vertical part of the *saqiya*, a waterwheel that originated in the Nile Valley, are the *qadus* or *aduz*, small, wide-lipped pots with pointed bottoms and no handles (since the advent of the electric water pump one is more likely to find a *saqiya* in the oases than along the river).

Additional pots include the *qidra* (not shown) used for cooking *ful* (fava bean) and rice; the *sabil* (not shown), a long, thin pot with a rounded bottom and no handles, tied with a rope to hang on the wall and used to store water; the *sumaa*, a large, flat-bottomed pot used to store grains such as rice, lentils, and beans and sometimes, when round peep holes are cut into the sides, used to keep baby chicks; and the *siga* (not shown), a small pot with a lid also used for water.

One of the most singular pots in all of Egypt is the *garra*, found only in Dakhla Oasis. Originally catalogued by Flinders Petrie, its bullet-shape can be traced to predynastic times. Used to gather water, its unusual form makes it easy to carry when the women balance it on their heads or tuck it under their arms. According to Colin A. Hope in the "Dakhla Field Reports" of the *SSEA Journal*, pots of this type are found in hieroglyphic inscriptions dating to the reign of Thutmose III, when they were used to store honey and transport wine from the oases to the Nile Valley.

Finally there are four Islamic influenced pots: the *tisht* and *abriq*, a large jug with a handle and spout (*abriq*) which sits on top of a large bowl (*tisht*) used for washing before and after meals; the *turshiya*, an elongated pot with a wide mouth and pointed bottom used to store cheese; the *zabdiya*, used to store melted butter; the *ulla*, a small water jug; and the *zir*, a large-mouthed pot with a pointed bottom also used to hold water (See Fayoum Oasis for illustration.) Because the clay is porous, the water in the *zir* and *ulla* remains cool and pure. *Zirs* are found on many public streets and desert tracks where anyone may drink from them. Naturally cooled, the water tastes better than water from a refrigerator.

Decorative Arts

The decorative arts of Dakhla, wall painting and woodwork, are among the finest in the Western Desert. The first is an ongoing tradition handed down from father to son which exists throughout the central desert and the Nile Valley. The latter is a type of decoration that exists only in the Islamic villages of Dakhla and is a skill no longer practiced in the oasis.

The tradition of painting the exterior walls of a house dates back to the pharaonic era when friezes of cobras and other scenes decorated not only the tombs, but also the houses of ancient Egypt. Throughout Egypt today traditional homes are still beautified in this manner. Local artists often add their own touches to these paintings, sometimes illustrating famous heroic poems, although the most often used motif is the *hagg*. Wall

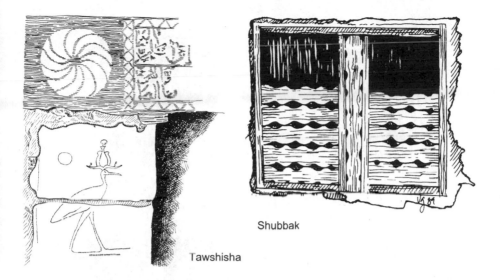

Shubbak

Tawshisha

paintings take two forms in Dakhla: bands of script, and medallions with drawings. The former consists of a band of blue and red script from the Quran, encased top and bottom in geometric designs. It runs near the top of the wall all the way around the outside of a house. The latter have multicolored paintings including human figures, village scenes, the traditional Hagg paintings, flora, and fauna (see Farafra and Bahariya oases for illustrations).

Of the two decorative arts, woodwork is by far the finest. The most interesting woodwork in Dakhla, and perhaps of the entire Western Desert, is the *tawshisha*, hand carved Ottoman wooden door beams measuring 15cm x 100–220cm, which are placed above the doors of certain houses in the villages of Qasr, Qalamun, Budkhulu, Balat, and Mut. These beams seem to have been reserved for homes belonging to important people in the village: clan leaders, scholars, craftsmen, and the like. The writing, in decorative Arabic script, begins with the traditional invocation, "In the name of God, the Compassionate, the Merciful" and is followed by a quote from the Quran, a blessing, and then the name of the owner of the house, followed by the date. The oldest beam found so far, discovered in Qasr, dates from 1518. A complete survey of these beams was done by the Institut Français d'Archéologie Orientale in 1981. It was discovered that the beams were often reused, with parts of inscriptions being recarved.

Another ancient wooden item in Dakhla is the *shubbak*, a wooden shutter which is cut in geometric patterns. The *shubbak* allows light to filter into a room but maintains the privacy of the people within.

Dresses

Most of the fabric in the oases is, as it always has been, imported from the Nile Valley, originally from weaving villages, like Kerdassa, that were located at the end of desert caravan trails. However, the women of Dakhla embroider designs unique to the area. Today the traditional scarves, *tawb*, and dresses, *tauba*, have given way to Nile Valley Islamic fashions, but some of the women still do the traditional embroidery.

The dresses that are prized by visitors are the black, in some cases blue, outer garments worn by women on festive occasions, usually weddings. Cross-stitch embroi-

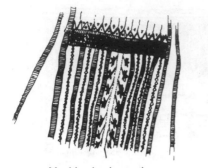

Mushiya back panel

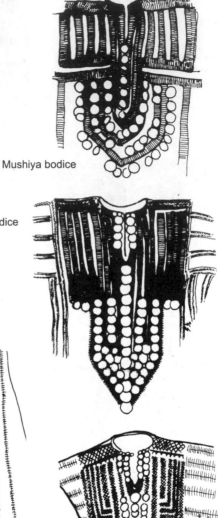

Mushiya bodice

Bashindi bodice

Balat back panel

Balat bodice

dery runs down the body and sleeves in straight lines. The most distinctive design is around the neck. The bodice is heavily embroidered and decorated with tassels and coins, which on the better dresses are authentic, old, dated, five piaster pieces. Others are imitations, made during this century. Buttons may also be used in decoration, the better being of mother of pearl, the worse, plastic. One may find an amulet sewn into the design. These amulets, varying from tiny fabric sacks with Quran sayings written inside to small blue stones, are used to ward off the evil eye. The designs on the bodice vary from village to village, each having distinctive features.

Older dresses, often faded and torn from years of use, have muted colors of deep red, burnt orange, and dull yellow, indicating natural dyes; the newer versions have bright, shocking, synthetic threads, which are now available at the local stores. Dresses can occasionally be purchased at the villages of Bashindi, Mushiya, and Balat.

Jewelry

Jewelry is not the most interesting of the crafts of Dakhla. Around the neck, decorations are mostly plastic or glass beads, coming in a variety of shapes, from a choker to a strand that hangs to mid-bodice. One popular necklace has individual plastic pieces that may be the modern version of animal teeth (see [A] below). One glass necklace consists of two rows of gold-covered glass separated by imitation amber (see [B] below).

The women wear earrings of a type mostly found in the Nile Valley. However, in the

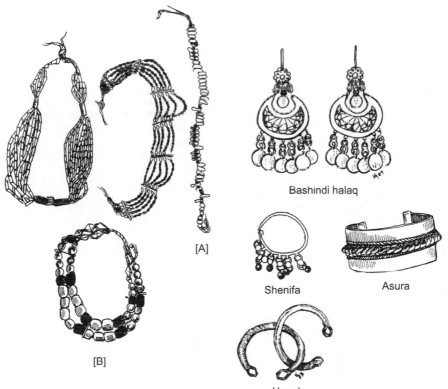

Bashindi halaq

[A]

Shenifa

Asura

[B]

Hagala

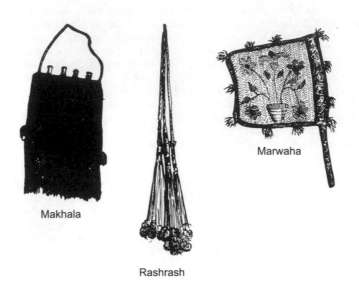

Makhala

Rashrash

Marwaha

village of Bashindi they wear a striking 7-centimeter (3-inch) long filigree and bangle earring called the *halaq*, often made of brass and then gold plated. In the nose a *shenifa* is worn. This is of silver or base metal and consists of a wire circle from which small balls fall. On the arm the most popular bracelet is the *asura*, a stunning design found in the Nile Valley, especially around Luxor. It is a 5-centimeter (2-inch) wide band interrupted in the center by a plaited, heavy wire. At the ankle are *hagala*, the *khulkhal* of Dakhla. Worn by married women around both ankles, they are made of silver or base metal. Where some *khulkhal*s are highly ornate, in Dakhla they are plain, with a knob at the end.

The jewelry may be uninspiring compared to other areas of Egypt, but the kohl pots used to hold eye shadow and liner and the false hair plaits of the women of Dakhla, are among the most decorative craft items in the Western Desert. The *makhala*, a *kohl* pot, varies in design and size, but is always decorated with bright, often red, yellow, green, and blue, bead work. It is suspended by a beaded handle and hangs on the wall. The *rashrash* consists of woven strings of red plaits that end in tassels, worn by women on the back of the head. It is very similar in design to pieces worn in Bahariya. The final decorative item in Dakhla is the *marwaha*, a small, highly decorated fan woven of threads and appliquéd with varying designs.

The Tour

The concept of the safari as in the other oases on the desert loop is limited in Dakhla. Most of the sites are either on the paved road or so close to it that few travelers need a 4x4. There are two safari companies that, in addition to the tours below, offer limited off-road travel to sand dunes and other desert sites. The tours below use Mut as the center and radiate out.

TOUR #1
Mut

N 25 29 685 E 28 58 797

Named for the ancient Egyptian goddess of the Theban triad, the city of Mut, the capital of modern Dakhla, was called Back of the Oasis in pharaonic times. Today, Mut is growing rapidly into a modern city.

When Rohlfs was here in 1874, there were many craftsmen in Mut, organized into guilds: tablemakers, millers, blacksmiths, and tailors. There was even a distillery for date wine and a cotton press. There were also Islamic doorbeams like those in Qasr. Today, the Dakhla Oasis Training and Archaeological Conservation Project helps the people of Dakhla learn to honor and conserve their own heritage. Funded by the Royal Netherlands Embassy Cultural Fund

and supervised by the Dakhleh Oasis Project, it will train men and women in cultural conservation and restoration including recovery, handling, and storage of artifacts.

In 1909, when Harding King visited Mut for the Royal Geographical Society, it was still a fortified town. In 1897, 1,078 people lived here.

Ethnographic Museum

Small entrance fee. Following the ground plan of a traditional Islamic home with a *haramlik*, women's quarters, and *salamlik*, men's public room, the wonderful, small Ethnographic Museum is a must. It contains items used in Islamic times in the oasis including pots, rugs, dresses, baskets, and jewelry. In addition there are figurines by the artist Mabrouk showing scenes from daily life.

The Ethnographic Museum is located next to the cinema. (Naming streets is a new concept in the oases towns, and many streets, although named, are not known by those names by the local inhabitants.) There are no set hours for this museum, which is opened on request. For admission call the Tourist Information Office or Culture Office. (See Practical Information for details.)

Old Mut

Falling to ruin, yet intriguing and full of the ghosts of past centuries, the old part of Mut, along with its main square, is another journey into twisting, narrow, dark passages offering cool shade and protection. The all but windowless facades of the houses once formed a defensive wall. The city is situated on a hill and divided into quarters which, in true Middle Eastern tradition, are separated by gates which were once bolted at night. In the 1890s, the mayor had a wall built around the village when he heard that the Mahdists had invaded Kharga and captured the Mamur of the Wells and other officials. Old Mut is still inhabited.

Mut al-Kharab

Mut al-Kharab, Mut the Ruined, southwest of Mut, was the temple area of the ancient town, the remainder of which is probably buried under the modern city. Mut al-Kharab has been plundered again and again, but extant ruins date from all major periods. The site has little to attract the visitor, but plenty to excite the archaeologist. It is enclosed by a Roman wall and contains the ruins of a temple. Winlock defines it as 300 meters (960 feet) north to south and 200 meters (640 feet) east to west. He also tells us that Drovetti saw a temple here, Rohlfs mentions pieces of sandstone columns, and Lyons took two stelas of the Twenty-second Dynasty to the Ashmolean Museum in Oxford. All Winlock describes is a dried up ancient well about 40 meters (128 feet) in diameter, and a short water tunnel. In 1897, 1,341 people lived here.

King Farouk's Resthouse

King Farouk's Resthouse is located at the southern edge of Mut and is owned by the government and used by public officials when they visit the oasis. Although a tour of the premise may not be possible, a visit to the site is.

TOUR #2

Eastern Dakhla

- 2x2, 4x4 (very little)
- all day
- easy

			km	total km
Tineida	N 25 30 627	E 29 20 346	0	0
Bashindi	N 25 31 613	E 29 17 738	4	4
Balat	N 25 33 950	E 29 15 534	5	9
Sheikh Muftah	N 25 31 744	E 29 06 822	21	30
Asmant	N 25 31 422	E 29 04 406	5	35
Masara	N 25 30 761	E 29 03 288	3.4	38.4
Sheikh Wali	N 25 30 860	E 29 01 240	5	43.4

Unfortunately there is no resthouse or hotel in eastern Dakhla at the present time, so everyone is hard pressed to see all the sites here. There are too many things to see to attach the tour to the Darb al-Ghubari crossing. To travel to and from Kharga and see eastern Dakhla as well requires too many hours. It is recommended that the sites here be seen in a day trip from Mut, returning to Mut for an overnight. The villages are in a line from east to west, so it is also recommended to go to the furthermost point, Tineida, and work back toward Mut. There is a gas station at Balat, but one must carry all other provisions including food and water.

Tineida

The village of Tineida was part of an incredible drama played out in the southwestern section of the Western Desert in the first half of this century. In 1930, five hundred Bedouin and their families, rejecting the sedentary life offered by the victorious Italians, attempted to make the 322 kilometer (200 mile) journey from Kufra, a cluster of oases in Libya, to Gebel Uwaynat in the southwest corner of Egypt. Their story is the stuff of legend.

Most of the inhabitants of Kufra at that time were Bedouin of the Zwaya tribe. Like so many Libyans they set out to live in the desert rather than under the harsh rule of the Italians. When the Italians approached Kufra, they machine gunned and bombed the oasis from airplanes. Their machine guns, light artillery, and armored cars easily defeated the Bedouin, who were armed with only rifles. The Bedouin headed south. Some went to Lake Chad, others to Sudan, and some to Gebel Uwaynat. Many perished.

For those bound for Gebel Uwaynat, the terrible ordeal of crossing the Great Sand Sea and skirting the Gilf Kebir was just the beginning of an even longer journey. On arrival at Uwaynat the Bedouin discovered that there had been no rain for years, and there was insufficient food and water for even a handful of people, let alone a large group.

The refugees sent three men to Dakhla Oasis, another 580 kilometers (360 miles) away. While the remainder were waiting at Uwaynat, a Desert Survey team under the leadership of P. A. Clayton came into the area. The surveyors, astounded by the mass of people gathered at the mountain and appalled by their condition, encouraged the remainder of the refugees to begin the journey to Dakhla. Through the use of an old, broken down car and a petrol dump that had been established nearby, Clayton and his men proceeded to help those who could not make the additional journey. He fixed the car and took ten nearly dead women and children to Wadi Halfa in a raging sandstorm. Clayton tells us, "The women's feet were so raw that they could only crawl to us on hands and knees." They had never seen a car before and were terrified.

Upon his return to Uwaynat, Clayton found twenty-five other refugees headed in the wrong direction. He sent his driver, Abu Fudail, 500 kilometers (313 miles) to Wadi Halfa for food and water. It was a perilous journey, especially for a single vehicle and a solo driver. But Fudail came through. *The Egyptian Gazette* of June 4, 1931, picks up the story: "A party of 27 persons and 7 camels [were found] north of Bir Meddha, which they had missed. Their leader was Salah al-Ateiwis, a well-known Arab chief of Cyrenaica, who was still dressed in magnificent red and gold ceremonial robes, although he was almost at death's door through lack of water and food." This group was sent to Kharga Oasis.

In the meantime, the three refugees, half-dead from their ordeal, arrived at Tineida. A mercy expedition, organized by the Egyptians, was sent to find the main group of refugees. Three hundred people were found by the Egyptians and Clayton's survey cars. They were brought into Dakhla and Kharga, and given food, water, and lodging. To quote the London newspaper *The Times*, "The total number of Arabs reaching Dakhla was about 300. The first arrivals must have covered 420 miles [675 kilometers] between water over arid desert, a feat of endurance which can have few parallels in the history of desert travel."

Existing since ancient Egyptian times, Tineida is the most eastern village in Dakhla Oasis. At some point, the people of Tineida manufactured indigo, but the village was in ruins when Bernadino Drovetti, the French consul to Egypt, visited the oasis in 1819. It had been plundered so many times by marauding tribes that it had been abandoned. By 1897, when Beadnell did his survey, 743 people occupied the village,

Tombstones at Tineida

probably attesting to the security the village enjoyed under Muhammad Ali's protection.

Today, it is a nondescript village, but the tombstones in the small cemetery to the east of the village are worth visiting. Painted white or blue, with occasional splashes of red, these unusual mud tombstones stand less than a meter high and resemble small houses. In some instances they sit at both the head and foot of the grave, which is also outlined in stones and decorated with palm fronds.

Burial in the oasis varies from village to village, as do the designs of the tombstones. There is another cemetery near Mut with tombstones that resemble modern sculptures. Where in Mut a person is placed in a straightforward pit, in other villages, like Huwarna and Tineida, a shelf for the body is cut into the side of the pit. The cemetery in Tineida is located along the right side of the road just east of the village. Large sheikhs' tombs, a common feature of the oasis, are also found in the cemetery.

Naqb Tineida, located beyond the village, is the pass which leads to the Darb Ain Amur. The road leaves Tineida and heads for the escarpment. At the foothills of the scarp is a Roman *mahatta*, watering place. The Darb skirts the northern scarp to the east, passing through the Wadi al-Battikha, and up the escarpment of the Abu Tartur Plateau. The pass leading up the plateau was called Akabet es Sekhawy, Ascent of the Soft Place, by Drovetti and Akabet al-Unak, Ascent of the Neck, by Cailliaud. There are several other *mahattas* on the way to Ain Amur (see Kharga Oasis for details).

Ain Birbiya

One of the most exciting finds of the eventful past decade in Dakhla is the almost buried temple of Amun-Nakht at Ain Birbiya, between the villages of Tineida and Bashindi. It is a stone temple surrounded by an enclosure wall and has a gateway similar to Qasr al-Zayyan in Kharga Oasis. The temple is decorated with reliefs, many of which are still buried under the sand. The members of the Dakhla Oasis Project are excavating slowly in order to unearth and conserve the temple simultaneously. It was mentioned by both Drovetti and Cailliaud. Rohlfs saw it and called it a Roman castle.

Bashindi, or Ezbet Sheikh Ahmad Sanusi

Bashindi was named by joining the words of the name Pasha Hindi, the medieval sheikh whose tomb is found here. It is an ancient site and the modern village, probably begun during the Christian era, sits atop the ruins. The houses in this village, complete with square pillars, porches, and balconies, are considered to be of pharaonic design. Among the sites to visit in Bashindi are the tomb of Pasha Hindi and the hot springs.

There are many **Roman tombs** at Bashindi. The majority of them form the foundations of the modern day houses, but eight are accessible. One, to which an Islamic dome has been added, is venerated as the burial place of Pasha Hindi. Under the Islamic dome is a Roman stone dome visible from the inside of the building. A second is the square **Tomb of Kitines**, which is richly decorated with funeral reliefs dating to the second century. The sandstone tomb consists of six rooms and is decorated along the door jambs, in the sanctuary, and at the tomb entrance. This tomb has been continuously inhabited and in this century was used by Sanusi soldiers in 1914–1918, and later by a Bashindi family.

Ain Asil

Nearby is Ain Asil, Spring of the Origin. Ain Asil is an Old Kingdom settlement, dating from the Sixth Dynasty, and its discovery provides the first evidence linking Dakhla to the Nile Valley during the Old Kingdom. Called "Our Root is Lasting in the Oasis," in Egyptian hieroglyphs, there is evidence that it was continuously inhabited for decades, if not centuries. Ahmed Fakhry, who excavated here in the 1970s, believed that Ain Asil was the capital of Dakhla Oasis during the Old Kingdom and the First Intermediate Period. The fact that it sits on the Darb al-Tawil, the only direct link from the oasis to the Nile Valley, supports this theory.

Excavations have revealed that the settlement covered a large area and centered around a major fortress that was later adapted to other uses as the area became less rural, larger, and more stable. The entire structure was later replaced by a newer urban

Bashindi pharaonic house

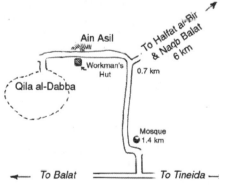

Ain Asil

building. Among the abundant pottery shards in the area were found a unique set of hieratic tablets listing names of men probably recruited to work in the community. The clay tablets have no parallels in the Nile Valley, where papyrus was employed. They are believed to be from the Sixth Dynasty.

The town that developed shows evidence of an enclosure wall and a canal. Habitation at Ain Asil ended abruptly. Since there is no evidence of disaster or war, it is possible that it was simply abandoned before the Ptolemaic era.

Qila al-Dabba

Qila al-Dabba (entrance fee), 1.5 kilometers (1 mile) west of Ain Asil, is a large burial area that was in use for an extended period of time, and was probably the necropolis of the town. There is evidence to suggest that it began in the Sixth Dynasty of the Old Kingdom. The burials of Qila al-Dabba were rich in funeral equipment. Wooden or ceramic coffins were used by the wealthy, whereas the bodies of the poor were simply enclosed in a sack.

Within the necropolis are no less than five large mastabas, a style of burial monument used by important dignitaries from the Old Kingdom. The large mastabas rise from the ground in layers like the Step Pyramid at Saqqara. They are in various stages of ruin, but all were dressed with limestone and at least one stands 10 meters (32 feet) high. Three of the mastabas have been identified as the final resting place of Old Kingdom governors of the oasis and offer us the first real evidence that Dakhla Oasis was not only known by the rulers of the Old Kingdom, but was important enough to have its own governor.

Ahmed Fakhry excavated here in 1971 and found four of these mudbrick mastabas. Recent work by French archaeologists discovered a fifth. In this mastaba, with a forecourt, courtyard, corridor, and antechamber, the governor's mummy was found. These tombs are open to the public.

Halfat al-Bir

Halfway between Ain Asil and the Naqb Balat, along the escarpment, is Halfat al-Bir.

It is located in the foothills: to the north the scarp, to the south sandstone ridges. Within the area are sandstone outcroppings. All of these natural barriers are incised with graffiti from various eras of history, showing, like the graffiti at Gebel al-Teir in Kharga Oasis and those close by at Tineida, extensive traffic in the area through the centuries. Among the giraffes, ostrich, and human figures in pharaonic garb is a drawing of a boat, an unusual image to find in the middle of a desert. Lisa L. Giddy in her book *Egyptian Oases* maintains that the boat could relate to one of the titles of the governors of the oasis during the Old Kingdom—Captain of the Ships/Marines Brigade.

Getting There: To visit Ain Asil, Qila al-Dabba, and Halfat al-Bir, turn off the main road at the turn to Bashindi. Enter the village and in front of the new mosque (to the left of the road) turn left, then right. You should be headed toward the escarpment. Seven-tenths of a kilometer later there is a fork in the road. The right fork goes to Halfat al-Bir while the left fork goes to Ain Asil, 0.5 kilometers away. After visiting Ain Asil, continue along the same road for another two-tenths of a kilometer and turn left. One kilometer beyond is Qila al-Dabba (see map).

Balat or Belat

Casuarina trees line the road at the village of Balat, the Palace. Like other Islamic villages in Dakhla, Balat contains an interesting old city with covered, narrow streets. The villages built during Mamluk and Turkish times all had such streets, not only for coolness and protection from the sand laden winds, but so the horses and camels of invaders could not penetrate the city and

Sheikh's tombs at Balat

warriors were forced to fight on foot. Balat has sprawled beyond these fortressed walls and one must pass through the modern village to visit the older one perched on top of a hill. Ornate carved door beams decorate the entrances to some of the old houses. In 1897, 1,784 people lived here.

Balat was a major Old Kingdom town and an extensive populated area once existed around its perimeter. First Intermediate Period (c. 2181–2040 B.C.) governors' tombs and residences have been found in the area, as have prehistoric sites. A good way to tour Balat is to circle the village via the first road left before Balat and exit the village by a similar road on the other side. Then stop along the center road, park your car, and walk up the hill directly into the old village via one of the covered streets. It is a treat. Edmondstone used Balat as his headquarters when he was in Dakhla.

Naqb Balat is 15 kilometers (9.3 miles) from the village of Balat, to the north of the main road over the flat depression floor. It is a single rise, fairly easy to follow, for steep cliffs line either side. There are a number of foothills and some dunes. Naqb Balat joins Darb al-Tawil on top of the escarpment. Edmondstone found a sacred tomb along this darb. The belief is that a man began a summer journey with five camels. The last one died here. The man took this as an omen and lived here. Passing caravans gave him dates, rice, and water and in return he protected the camels. When he died he was elevated to sainthood and caravans continued to leave food. Whenever a camel died, an offering of its cordage and fodder was left on this spot in honor of the saint. No one ever touched it and the mound has grown over the years.

Just southwest of Balat are five **fossil spring** vents, largely deflated. These vents indicate an ancient spring and surrounding them are signs of Early and Middle Paleolithic tools. They were explored by the Combined Prehistoric Expedition in 1972 and 1976. This is one of the few sites in the Western Desert where the earliest known human habitation can be found. Here it was the Late Acheulian.

Ain Tirghi

Five kilometers (3.1 miles) south of Balat is the cemetery of Ain Tirghi, whose excavation has produced more questions than answers. Used over an extended period of time, the cemetery contains several tombs with as many as twenty to forty burials each. The mummies are stacked one on top of the other, some in their original coffins and wrappings. Most intriguing is that the dead appear to come from an extended period encompassing the Late to the Roman periods. Whether this cache is similar to those found at Deir al-Bahri at Thebes, where the dead were brought for safekeeping from tomb robbers, or whether the tombs belonged to individual extended families, is unknown. But it is certain that the cemetery was in existence as early as the Second Intermediate Period (1782–1650 B.C.) and reused from the Late to Roman periods.

Two bodies found in awkward positions indicate young tomb robbers killed when the roof of the tomb collapsed. The coffins at Ain Tirghi include wood, which was considered the most expensive, and ceramic. Each coffin has an effigy painted on the lid. Most are primitive and many grotesque.

Western Dakhla

A stretch of desert separates Balat from its western neighbor Asmant, or Smint. This natural demarcation may have played an important role during ancient Egyptian times, for though there is much evidence emerging that the eastern section was heavily inhabited by the Egyptians of the Old Kingdom, no evidence has come to light to suggest that they even knew of the existence of the western portion of the oasis.

Sheikh Muftah

Sheikh Muftah, Sheikh of the Key, is a village 3.2 kilometers (2 miles) down a paved road 4.8 kilometers (3.1 miles) east of the village of Asmant. There is nothing of note in the small village, but all around it are ancient sites. About a kilometer to the east is a track which leaves the main road and leads to a number of ruins including the fortress Drovetti called **Qasr al-Halakeh**, Castle of

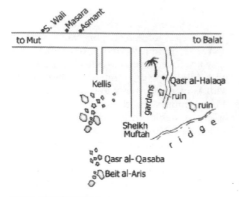

Kellis and Environs

the Ring. Winlock photographed it in 1908, and it appears to have changed very little. In addition to the fortress there are a number of other ruins in the area. We do not know what they are, yet.

To the south of the village of Sheikh Muftah additional sites exist, including the **Beit al-Aris** cemetery, with well over 100 burials and nine vaulted, mudbrick tombs. The tombs are in a very good state of preservation. **Qasr al-Qasaba** is one of the few Roman fortresses identified in Dakhla. Whereas Kharga is dominated by these outposts, Dakhla, further west, less accessible, and perhaps less prone to invasion, has no evidence of garrisons. After the extensive and interesting ruins of Kharga, the fortress at Qasr al-Qasaba, nearly leveled, is of little interest.

Asmant (Smint)

Eleven kilometers (6.8 miles) east of Mut or 5 kilometers (3 miles) west of Sheikh Muftah, along the main road from Balat, is Asmant, or Smint. Sprawling down to the road, the modern village is uninteresting but further back, on the hill, is the older Islamic village, which provides us with another view of a fortress town. In 1897, 1,037 people lived in Asmant. The exterior walls of the village still dominate, rising high, smooth, and solid. It is worth a look. The Darb al-Khashabi, which makes its way due north out of Dakhla, begins at Asmant.

But the most interesting site at Asmant, and one of the three major historical sites of Dakhla, is the ruin of the old Roman and Coptic city of **Kellis**.

Kellis or Asmant al-Kharab, Asmant the Ruined
N 25 31 081 E 29 05 707

Kellis is considered by many the most exciting archaeological site in the Western Desert. Year after year archaeologists are discovering important artifacts that are opening the doors to religions and histories thought to have been lost. There are tombs, temples, early mudbrick Christian churches, houses, baths, and several Roman aqueducts at Kellis, all in a good state of preservation. It appears that the site was inhabited for seven centuries.

The town of Kellis spreads over a fairly large area. In addition to the public buildings, there are farmhouses and pottery kilns. Two

Qasr al-Halaqa

Ruins at Kellis

of the buildings have yielded interesting finds. In one of the large southern buildings is a colonnaded hall with Corinthian capitals and painted walls. The collapsed ceiling was also painted and although the fragments must be pieced together, Dakhla Oasis Project field reports indicate that these wall paintings, "better preserved than in most areas of the Mediterranean . . . are of great art historical importance."

The Temples

Located southwest of the main settlement are two temples standing side by side. The eastern and larger temple, composed mostly of stone with mudbrick surrounding wall, has painted scenes which appear to be from the second and third centuries. The second temple, of lesser interest, has a sandstone doorway. During the 1996 field season, underground chambers were discovered. One of the temples is in honor of Tutu, one of Egypt's oldest gods.

The Churches

Three churches, built of mudbrick with white plastered walls, have been unearthed at Kellis. In one, a cache of bronze Roman coins bearing the head of Constantine the Great and other Roman emperors was uncovered. There is also graffiti.

Most important of all is that one of the churches can be specifically dated to the fourth century A.D. and is heralded as the oldest Christian church in Egypt. Although still covered for preservation, the church is "extremely well-preserved" and coins found inside date to 350 and 400 A.D.

Codexes and Papyri

Wonderful discoveries have taken place at Kellis, and it has as yet been barely explored.

In addition to well over 2,000 papyrus text fragments in Greek and Coptic, three wooden codices have been discovered. These codices, the keys to unraveling the transformation between pagan Rome and Byzantine Christianity, are hopefully the beginning of additional finds. Discovered in the corner of a room in one of the houses, the first codex consists of nine wooden boards upon which are written three literary pieces. They form a treatise and political instructions by Isocrates.

The second codex is a single board written in Greek which is a contract for the sale of a house in the settlement. It is from this board that we know the site was called Kellis and that Dakhla existed as a separate administrative center from Kharga.

Important as the second document is, the third is, by far, one of the most important discoveries in Dakhla. It is a codex of eight boards giving four years of farming accounts from the 360s A.D. Once it is fully studied it will shed much light on third century Dakhla. The location and the number of boards and tools lead us to believe that this was the home of the board maker. There were pieces of timber, probably willow, from which the tablets had been cut; recycling material to convert old books into new ones; and enough ancient clutter to show that Romans valued their books and the ancient publishers worked hard at their trade paying close attention to size of book as well as width of page. All of these items can be seen in the Kharga Museum in Qasr Kharga.

More impressive is the discovery of 5,000 fragments of rare testaments of Manichaeism, a religion established by the Gnostic prophet Mani in the third century. It spread from Babylonia to China and eventually dissolved in the fourteenth century. A smaller group of texts, written in Coptic, were found at Medinet Madi in the Fayoum, but these texts, written in Syriac, an ancient Middle Eastern language, number in the thousands. These fragments tell us that Kellis was inhabited in part by Manichaeans, and is an extraordinary find for the religion was banned from the Roman Empire in the fourth century. It could well have lasted here until the seventh century. Was this a place of banishment?

In the cemetery, 80 mummies in pit burials were unearthed during the 1996 field season.

Getting There: From the east, the ruins of Kellis, or Asmant al-Kharab, lie before the modern village of Asmant and about 2 kilometers (1.2 miles) to the west of Sheikh Muftah (see map). To find the road from Asmant, begin at the cemetery and sheikhs' tombs on the eastern edge of the community.

Two kilometers (1.2 miles) later there will be a dirt road leading south from the main road. Less than a kilometer down the dirt road, accessible by regular vehicle, visible from the road, stand the ruins.

Sheikh Wali is one of the newer communities in Dakhla. There is little to attract the tourist. The same is true of **Masara**. After Asmant it is a short drive to Mut and the end of the tour.

TOUR #3

Mut to Qasr Dakhla

- 2x2
- 1.5 to 2 hours
- easy

			km	total km
Mut	N 25 29 685	E 28 58 797	0	0
Fish pond	N 25 31 294	E 28 57 662	4	4
Al-Dahuz	N 25 33 280	E 28 56 825	4	8
Rashda	N 25 34 503	E 28 55 905	2	10
Deir Abu Matta	N 25 35 630	E 28 54 784	3.4	13.4
Sheikh/Jinn Tree	N 25 36 402	E 28 54 647	1.5	15
Budkhulu	N 25 37 790	E 28 55 39	4.5	20

There are two routes west from Mut to Qasr Dakhla, the first northwest along the main road and the second a loop through the desert. This is the main road.

Fish Pond

Less than 4 kilometers (2.5 miles) northwest of Mut is a large artificial reservoir, which when it reaches full capacity will cover 400 feddans. This lake, called the Fish Pond by locals, is being created in an effort to develop a fishing industry in the oasis. Filled, like the new lakes in Wadi Rayyan, by the extra drainage water from crop irrigation, the fish project of Dakhla Oasis is a joint effort between the Egyptian and German governments. In 1998, it covered an area of 300

feddans. Unfortunately, fishing is not permitted because the pesticides in the water are harmful to the fish and to the people who eat them. No swimming either.

Al-Dahuz

Next stop is the Bedouin village of al-Dahuz on the outskirts of the cultivated land. There is nothing much to see, except a coffeeshop along the road and the al-Dahuz Camp located beyond the village atop a small hill, with a great view overlooking the entire area.

Rashda

Rashda, located 3 kilometers (1.8 miles) west of the fish pond and a kilometer from the main road, is known for its fruit orchards, which include apricot, date, and olive trees. There is an ancient acacia tree at Rashda called the Tree of Sheikh Adam, which is believed to possess a soul. Lying close to the cliff upon which the village is built, the tree will not burn when set afire. Though of medieval origin, Rashda appears strikingly modern, a result perhaps of the local custom that insists that when a man marries he must build a new house for his bride. At the eastern end of the village are the Roman ruins of Ain Umm al-Masid. In 1897, the population of Rashda, spelled Rashida by Beadnell, was 1,191.

Two kilometers (1.2 miles) beyond Rashda, on the right-hand side of the road, is the Bedouin village of Ezbet Abu Asman.

Deir Abu Matta

Deir Abu Matta, also called Deir al-Saba Banat, Monastery of the Seven Virgins, is a mudbrick ruin 3.4 kilometers (2.1 miles) northwest of Rashda. It is a Christian basilica of the fifth or sixth century. The walls, still standing, once contained nine rooms. Around the area is a cemetery. Earthenware coffins from the Christian period were uncovered at this site. Artifacts found in the vicinity date from as late as the seventh century.

Deir al-Saba Banat features in desert lore and has long been thought to be a place of hidden treasure. Harding King, in *Mysteries of the Libyan Desert*, reported that residents would dig in the area looking for treasure and that one of the treasure books had the following instructions: "Go to Deir al-Banat, near it you will find a hollow place, three mastabas, a round hill and three red stones. Burn incense here."

In the 1830s, when Hoskin's came to visit, all four walls were standing some to a height of three stories.

Beadnell identified a well 4 kilometers (2.5 miles) south around Qalamun as Ain al-Nasrani, the Christian's Spring. Drovetti describes two additional ruins in the area as al-Salib, the Cross, and Buyut al-Nasara, Houses of the Christians. Evidently there was a Coptic community in this area of Dakhla.

Sheikh's Tomb

Less than 2 kilometers (1.2 miles) beyond Deir Abu Matta on the northern side of the road stands a solitary acacia tree shading a whitewashed **sheikh's tomb**. Villagers throughout Egypt visit and pray at similar tombs, the graves of pious persons, hoping that the blessings of the sheikh will assist them. If a jinn tree, a tree with a spirit living in it, is nearby (like this one), the women often write notes and attach them to the twigs of the tree in a mixture of pagan and religious belief.

Sheikh's cults are common in Egypt. Here in Dakhla they are especially important. A person becomes a sheikh because he has performed miracles for the living after his death: healings, ending famine, protection from enemies, drought, and bad weather. They also give blessings. In Gedida, small pieces of wood are left at a particular sheikh's tomb, so he will protect all the wood on a person's property.

Budkhulu

The gardens of Budkhulu lie on either side of the road for a couple of kilometers before the entrance to the village. Almost every type of fruit tree is represented and they arch over the roadway, offering welcome shade and cooler temperatures in the summer.

Although there is evidence that Budkhulu, 4.5 kilometers (2.8 miles) west of the Sheikh's tomb, was occupied during pharaonic times, the present structures date from the Islamic era. In 1897, 583 people lived here. The old village contains a wonderful minaret, covered streets, and door beams like those seen at Qasr, Balat, and Qalamun. The mudbrick town was of great importance during Islamic times, when the customs along the Darb al-Ghubari were assessed and paid here. One Turkish house, Beit Khalat al-Malik, reputedly belonged to the aunt of the king, though no one seems to remember which aunt of which king.

The most striking feature of the village is the Turkish cemetery located on a hill west of the town and visible from the main road. According to the mayors of Budkhulu, Mushiya, and Rashda, the cemetery was once the site of a Sanusi prison.

Today Budkhulu is an agricultural village growing mainly oranges, lemons, olives, and apricots, and its new buildings, all of mudbrick, surround the old village.

About one kilometer after Budkhulu there is a cold spring for tourists, along the west (left) side of the road. Then come a series of small villages several kilometers apart, including Ezbat Fiteima, Beit Kolo, Ezbat al-Qasr, and Ezbat Giza. Then comes Qasr Dakhla.

You can continue with Tour #4, or return to Mut along the loop, or just return to Mut the way you came.

TOUR #4
Around Qasr Dakhla

- 2x2, 4x4
- 1/2 day

			km	total km
Bir al-Gebel (at paved rd)	N 25 42 003	E 28 54 685	0	0
Tombs/Babs	N 25 41 934	E 28 53 251	2	2
Qasr Dakhla	N 25 41 695	E 28 52 924	c2	4
Muzawwaqa (at paved rd)	N 25 41 361	E 28 50 243	2.2	6.2
Deir al-Hagar (at paved rd)	N 25 41 513	E 28 48 438	5	11.2

Bir al-Gebel
N 25 44 315 E 28 55 252
Bir al-Gebel, Well of the Mountain, is about 7 kilometers (4 miles) after Budkhulu. At this point, a road to the north (right) marked with a sign, leads to Bir al-Gebel, one of the prettiest springs in the entire Western Desert. The road runs for 5 kilometers (2.5 miles), past a hot spring, a small picturesque village, interesting yardangs, lush fields, and wonderful dunes to the foot of the escarpment. The spring is in a small palm grove.

Islamic Tombs and Bab al-Qasmund
About 2 kilometers (1.2 miles) before the village of Qasr is a dirt track on the northern side of the road. It passes through a dramatic cemetery of domed tombs before it forks. The cemetery is an old one, probably Turkish, but maybe Mamluk. The tombs are in very good condition. The western fork circles the village of Qasr and leads back to the main road.

The eastern fork is the beginning of the Darb al-Farafra, which passes through the Bab al-Qasmund, which travels up the escarpment on its way to Farafra. The Bab al-Qasmund and Bab Cailliaud are the passes through the escarpment which lead down to Dakhla from the Darb al-Farafra. All locals call these the Naqb al-Farafra. The locals also maintain that coming down from the plateau above here is okay, but it is almost impossible to go up to the plateau from here.

Islamic tombs near Qasr Dakhla

Ph. Remele, the photographer of the Rohlfs Expedition, would probably give no quarrel as he had a difficult time at these passes. He attempted to photograph here, but the wind kept knocking over his camera and scratching his plates.

Qasr Dakhla (Qasr)

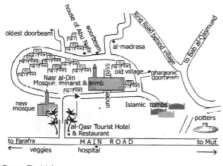

Qasr Dakhla

Built over the foundations of a Roman city, Qasr Dakhla is believed to be one of the oldest inhabited areas of the oasis and possibly the longest continuously inhabited site in Dakhla. When Cailliaud was here, he estimated that Qasr had 2,000 inhabitants. Beadnell found 3,758 in 1897.

Located on top of the Sioh Ridge and tucked just under the pink escarpment, the village is approached through a palm grove. Ten years ago there were no buildings along the road and no utility poles (there was no electricity), so the view was much more dramatic. Once passed the 'new Qasr,' things improve. It is a delight to roam among the twisting lanes of the old part of the village. Exotic four- and five-story buildings, many with carved door beams, still exist. The oldest door beam in the oasis, dating from A.H. 925 (A.D. 1518), is found in Qasr at Beit Ibrahim.

The community has rallied to protect the old city of Qasr from the encroachment of cement buildings. No new construction is permitted in or around the old city.

Ayyubid Nasr al-Din Mosque

This mosque, with its 21 meter (67 foot) high minaret, is typical of the types of religious buildings erected during the Ayyubid period. Beside it is the madrasa, or school, where the Quran was once taught to young boys. The main room of the madrasa also served as a town hall and general public building, and the stake near the door is where criminals were once shackled. The madrasa is still used as a school and a venue for town meetings. It contains an extensive library of old books.

House of Abu Nafir

The House of Abu Nafir, recently restored by the Egyptian Antiquities Organization, is a typical Islamic building. It has a tall mudbrick facade with a pointed arch over the doorway and a wonderful studded wooden door. It stands on the site of an ancient, probably Ptolemaic, temple, whose stones are incorporated into the house and surrounding buildings. Not only does the lintel of the doorway have an exciting carved wooden door beam but the door jambs are covered in ancient Egyptian hieroglyphs.

Kilns

Ancient kilns recently discovered in the village show that pottery has been made in Qasr since antiquity. Today the descendants of these ancient craftsmen sit in a small potter's garden near the base of the hill upon which Qasr is built. Here hundreds of pots dry in the sun while the potters sit in the small mudbrick hut

Islamic doorway at Qasr Dakhla

nearby throwing new pots on foot-driven wheels (see crafts above for details).

Ain al-Hamiya
Although there are dozens and dozens of wells in the Qasr area, Ain al-Hamiya, an *Ain Romani* located on the eastern side of the village of Qasr, was the most important one in the area. It once supported the potable water needs of the entire village and the runoff went to the adjacent palm groves to water the trees and fields. The Ain al-Hamiya was a hot spring and according to Beadnell the people used to cook eggs in its waters. In Beadnell's time the well was gushing, but as new wells were dug in the area its waters diminished. Today, it is dry.

Dunes
The main road continues west after Qasr on its way to Abu Minqar and Farafra Oasis. Just 2.6 kilometers (1.5 miles) beyond Qasr the road approaches a dune field and actually runs over the top of one of the dunes. Just to the north there is a wonderful view of a dune cascading down the side of the escarpment. It will re-form below and continue its march south. Dunes don't fall in an hour or a day, so unless one is staying around for a long time one will not see the entire process, but there is always one dune on its way down the scarp. This is a good place to come at sunset, when the color is spectacular.

Muzawwaqa Frescoes
N 25 40 839 E 28 50 314 (at tombs)
Entrance fee. There are over 300 tombs situated in the sides of small hills in this section of the Amheida cemetery, which Drovetti in 1919 named "Muzauwaken," from the Arabic *muzawwaqa*, meaning 'decorated.'

Fakhry dates the tombs to the first and second centuries. Two tombs stand out: the single-room tomb of Petubastis and the double-room tomb of Padiosiris. Both are decorated with exquisite full-color paintings which defy the ancient conventions of tomb decoration and blend second-century motifs with ancient Egyptian ritual. The result is extraordinarily powerful.

When Winlock photographed them in

Fresco at the Muzawwaqa tombs

1908, they were considerable defaced, with many of the murals decapitated, especially any animal heads. He also found broken fragments of human bodies scattered around the ground. The murals were restored before the 1980s. In the winter of 1998 the tombs were closed because the ceilings were collapsing.

Getting There: The dirt road leading to the Muzawwaqa frescoes moves south from the main road 2.2 kilometers (3.6 miles) beyond Qasr. It continues through the necropolis for about a kilometer before turning slightly east to the small parking area at the two main tombs of Petubastis and Padiosiris. Accessible by regular vehicle.

Deir al-Hagar
N 25 39 928 E 28 48 750 (at temple)
Entrance fee. As the name, Monastery of Stone, implies (in hieroglyphs it is called Setweh, Place of Coming Home), Deir al-Hagar, a lone Roman temple located south of

the cultivated area in the desert, is made of sandstone.

Erected during the reign of Nero (54–67) and decorated during the time of Vespasian (69–79), Titus (79–81), and Domitian (81–96), the temple was built in honor of the Theban triad Amun, Mut, and Khonsu, but is also dedicated to Seth, God of the Oasis. The latter god is represented with a falcon head and a blue anthropomorphic body.

Cartouches of Roman emperors appear on the temple, but there are also recent additions to the ancient walls. The temple has an eastern entrance and was once surrounded by a mudbrick wall. Although most of the temple is of sandstone, the collapsed columns from the entry court were of mudbrick. Excavators found a few small sphinx statues in these ruins, which are now housed in the Kharga Museum. Surrounding the temple is evidence of Roman farms and a large mudbrick village with priests' houses, pigeon cotes, and a cemetery

Almost every traveler who came to Dakhla in the nineteenth century left his calling card etched in the stones of this temple: Edmondstone, Houghton, Hyde, Cailliaud, and the entire Rohlfs expedition. Edmondstone was sure to record the month of his visit, February 1819, at Ain Amur as evidence of his departure from Dakhla. This was to prove he was in Dakhla before Drovetti. Drovetti, in his diary published by Jomard in France, said he took this journey "toward the end of 1818." That would make him the first. But here, at Deir al-Hagar, where Drovetti put his name only, we have the inscription *Rosingana, 26 F. 1819.* Rosingana was an ex-soldier of Napoleon's

Rohlfs' graffiti at Deir al-Hagar

who deserted in 1801, remaining in Egypt. He accompanied Drovetti on his journey to Dakhla. You figure it out. It was nearly 100 years before another foreign traveler passed by, found the inscriptions at Deir al-Hagar and Ain Amur, and offered up the proof. (Actually, the French consular correspondence had the facts almost from the beginning. Ronald T. Ridley in *Napoleon's Proconsul in Egypt: The Life and Times of Bernardino Drovetti* states, "Roussel wrote to Dessolle on 15 February, 1819, that Salt was going to the Second Cataract and that Drovetti was going to the Little Oasis.") The French were out and the English were in.

So, Edmondstone discovered Deir al-Hagar in 1819. Then, it was half filled with sand, which he tried to clear. He soon abandoned the project and measured the structure. The sanctuary still had a roof and parts of three front columns were still standing. Rohlfs tells us that Remele removed the sanctuary roof to clear the sand.

Local residents related an interesting legend to Harding King. They believed that Gerhard Rohlfs came to the oasis in search of buried treasure and at Deir al-Hagar, with the help of a treasure book, began looking for riches. When he was unsuccessful, locals believe that he sacrificed one of the workers of his group to the *afrit*, spirit, which was guarding the entrance to the treasury. Then he took the treasure and went away.

Restoration

In 1995, restoration efforts carried out by the Dakhla Oasis Project were completed. The restoration was done entirely with the technology and materials used by the original craftsmen. Many stones were replaced, as were the doors, and a fence of palm branches was erected to protect the temple grounds from encroaching sands. A visitors' center was also created, which includes photographs depicting the efforts of the restoration.

Around the Temple

All the ruins around the temple on the plain are columbariums, pigeon houses, in various stages of ruin. They probably belonged to separate farms during the Roman period.

They are each about a kilometer apart.

In the rock-cut tombs 250 meters (800 feet) northwest of temple, very crude human headed terracotta coffins of the Roman period were found. Rohlfs excavated here and found a complete terracotta coffin in one tomb and seven mummies covered with a mat in another.

Getting There: The road leading to Deir al-Hagar turns south from the main road 7.2 kilometers (4.5 miles) beyond Qasr. It moves south past some Roman ruins on the left and after 0.4 kilometers (0.2 miles) turns right, just in front of another ruin. It continues for 0.4 kilometers (0.2 miles), then turns left. Again, at 0.2 kilometers (0.1 miles), just in front of the small village, it turns left onto a dirt track. The track passes in front of the village and crosses right over a small ridge 0.4 kilometers (0.2 miles) later. Once over the ridge, the temple is visible on the right. Accessible by regular vehicle.

TOUR #5

Loop Road from Qasr Dakhla to Mut

- **2x2**
- **1–2 hours**
- **easy**

			km	total km
Qasr Dakhla	N 25 41 695	E 28 52 924	0	0
Loop road	N 25 41 655	E 28 52 713	1	1
Amheida	N 25 40 122	E 28 52 502	3	4
Mushiya	N 25 37 076	E 28 52 093	5	9
Gedida	N 25 35 124	E 28 51 544	4	13
Qalamun	N 25 32 779	E 28 54 335	7	20

The itinerary below runs from Qasr back to Mut. One kilometer (.6 miles) after the village of Qasr a paved road goes south, or left. This is the loop road back to Mut.

Amheida

Just before the loop road arrives at Qasr there is an extensive Roman ruin that extends for 5 kilometers (3.1 miles) to the west of the road. It is Amheida, one of the largest and most important ruins in Dakhla. Amheida was continuously occupied from the first century B.C. to the fourth century A.D. and is first mentioned in modern times by Edmondstone.

During Roman times Amheida was the major city of the western part of the oasis, the center of about seventy inhabited sites. Located 3.5 kilometers (2 miles) southwest of Qasr, the entire area is covered with buildings, most buried up to their rooftops in sand.

Left panel of the adultery of Aphrodite and Ares

The temple at Amheida is disappointing, a ruin of a ruin. It is in the center of the northern part of the complex and only fragments remain. Scattered over the ground, there is a piece here and a piece there. Maybe excavation will find something waiting under the ground.

Cemeteries

Cemeteries proliferate around the perimeter of Amheida. Most are small with 150 or so burials, but there is a major necropolis, located on the southern side of the settlement, which contains 2,000 to 3,000 graves. Most of the graves are pit burials, but there are a significant number of tombs. Nineteenth-century travelers gave many reports of the bones and jumble of funerary equipment lying on the ground throughout the area. Outstanding among the tombs is Tomb 33, with plaster and painted reliefs, funeral scenes, and images of ancient gods and goddesses. It dates from the Ptolemaic or early Roman period. Tomb 6 is a building consisting of mudbrick, burnt brick, and sandstone. It has several plastered chambers.

Wall Paintings

The most exquisite finds so far at Amheida are a series of wall paintings along the north and east walls of a large fifteen-room building in the center of the complex. This was an imposing two-story structure that had to be dug out of the sand by the Canadian team. One can imagine the excitement as centimeter by centimeter these magnificent images came to light. They depict Greek and Roman mythological scenes.

Along the northern wall to the left of the door is an illustration of the legend of Perseus and Andromeda. It is interesting that the first wall paintings found in Dakhla should tell this tale for much of its story is based in the Western Desert. A nearly nude Perseus, clutching the sword that killed the round-faced Medusa in one hand and carrying her snake-infested head in the other, wings his way through the sky to free Andromeda, chained to a rock on the right side of the painting.

On the same wall, but to the right of the door, Odysseus has returned from his long voyage, which brought him to the Egyptian shores. On the left side stands Odysseus, only his legs intact, while the servant woman Eurykleia is bathing his feet and looking up in a sign of recognition. To the left is the jeweled Penelope, Odysseus's wife, who at this point does not recognize her husband.

Along the east wall are additional scenes, broken into two registers, which is more in keeping with the traditions of Egyptian art. In the lower register are three scenes. The first is an allegorical interpretation of the city. Polis, a female figure, holds the scepter of authority in her left hand, while her right gestures toward a city. Upon her head is a turreted crown, equivalent to the city walls. The middle scene in the register is the adultery of Aphrodite and Ares. Here Aphrodite's husband Hephaistos is calling on the male gods to witness his wife's transgression. On the left, with their names written above the figures, are Poseidon, who is gazed upon by his nude neighbor Dionysus. Beside Dionysus is the laurel-wreathed Apollo, followed by Hercules and finally Helios. On the right is a nude Aphrodite accompanied by her lover Ares.

Mushiya

Mushiya, a few kilometers south of Amheida, may not look impressive, but it is a pleasant village to visit for, like at Budkhulu, homes are still being erected in the traditional mudbrick. The deeper one goes into the village the more picturesque it becomes. Of course, you have to turn off the main road. The village road forms a loop that returns to the main road. Mushiya is famous for its mangoes and dates.

In the repertory of the storyteller of Mushiya is the saga of the great plot the villagers hatched to free themselves from the tax collectors of the Sanusi army in 1916. When they arrived in the village the collectors were treated to the best of oasis hospitality. In the meantime a group of village men hurriedly began a defensive tactic some kilometers away. When gunfire was heard in the village the collectors, about to be fed the great feast, were told the British were coming. They dashed away in a great rush and the villagers were free from the dreaded tax. This is probably an oral interpretation of the bombing of the area around Mut by the British in 1916 in order to frighten away the Sanusi soldiers who had captured the village. Whatever really happened, the Sanusi left.

Mushiya is now the home of a soap factory.

Gedida

Young as far as oasis towns are concerned, Gedida, meaning 'new,' was founded about 200 years ago. One of the nicest areas of the village is the market where the fruits and vegetables of the entire oasis are laid out for sale in front of small mudbrick kiosks. Open from 9 to 2 and again from 5 to 10, the picturesque market, shaded by giant eucalyptus trees, is famous for dried dates, apricots, olives, and peanuts. In fact, in 1908, its olive oil was imported to the Nile Valley.

The market no longer sells the mats and baskets for which Gedida is famous (see crafts above for details). In addition, the women seldom have the old dresses and other traditional ornaments. Gedida is considered a wealthy village by people in the oasis, not only because it is a market town, but because its men go to work in Cairo. They do this in shifts and often two men hold the same job. While one is away the other is in the village. Then they trade places.

Today it is the home of a new arabesque factory that manufactures turned wood for mashrabiya from palm ribs, created in conjunction with the German GIZ. Tours are available daily and there is a showroom where screens, chairs, furniture, pencil boxes, and other items are for sale.

In 1897 the population was 2,410.

Qalamun

In existence since pharaonic times, there are a variety of stories as to how the village of Qalamun got its name. The first is that the two words *qala*, Arabic for fort, and Amun, the ancient Egyptian God, were joined together. Others argue that the origin of the name is the Arabic word for reed beds, of which a series exist along the main road into the village. A third version is that the name means the place where the priests lost their pens.

During Islamic times the village was the administrative headquarters of the oasis and many families are descended from Mamluk and Turkish administrators and soldiers. Beit al-Qadi, house of the judge, built during this time, still exists. The new town has spread beyond the hill into the desert plateau, but the old town, complete with Islamic door beams, an Ayyubid mosque, narrow streets, and many trees, is well worth the climb. There are also some Islamic tombs in the cemetery, dating from Mamluk and Turkish times. The entire village, both old and new, is built of mudbrick. Dunes are encroaching on the village from the west.

Like Qasr, Qalamun is protected by the antiquities department. In 1897, it had 1,704 people.

5

Farafra

Dakhla to Farafra via Darb Abu Minqar (one day)

			km	total km
Ezbet Mahub	N 25 41 556	E 28 48 167	0	0
Gharb Mahub	N 25 52 250	E 28 31 966	30	30
Abu Minqar	N 26 29 872	E 27 40 470	230	260
Farafra arch	N 27 03 102	E 27 58 120	75	340

Dakhla to Farafra is a 310 kilometer (194 mile) journey (from Gharb Mahub) over the longest, most desolate drive of the loop between the four oases. This was the first road paved in the New Valley scheme to join Farafra to Dakhla.

The modern village of **Gharb Mahub**, created as part of the New Valley project, is 30 kilometers (18.7 miles) from Qasr Dakhla. It is a Bedouin settlement and has a fine hot spring near the road called Bir Ashra, Well Ten. This village was once outside the Dakhla Oasis, but now has become a part of it. Just beyond Gharb Mahub the road was under construction for over ten years before it was finally completed.

Ezbat Mahub and Migma
Founded in this century, **Ezbat Mahub** is located on the road to Farafra, about 8 kilometers (5 miles) from Qasr. The families here came with the Sanusi from the Gebel al-Akhdar in Tripolitania to establish a *zawya*. Their ancestors were Ahmad and Muhammad al-Mahub.

The nondescript village of **Migma** appears on the right 8 kilometers (5 miles) later. Then, for over 200 kilometers (125 miles) there is nothing. Flat, soft sand sits on either side of the road, the pink and white escarpment keeps you company on the right, and finally the eastern edge of the Great Sand Sea becomes visible on the left. With no car behind as far as the eye can see, no oncoming traffic, and a silence that can be heard, you might feel yourself to be at the end of the earth. This is a pastel environment, with a big, pale blue sky forming the backdrop.

Naqb al-Igla (Pass of the Ox)
N 26 00 920 E 27 55 842
This pass is not a pass in the manner we have come to understand in the Western Desert, but a small hill. It received its name from the carcass of a mummified cow that had wandered into the desert, locals say from Farafra. Placing it upright atop the small hill it overlooked the road, a lonely sentinel serving as a reminder that the desert can kill.

Abu Minqar
Abu Minqar, Place of the Beak, comes into view a good 5 kilometers (3.1 miles) before you reach it. It shimmers in a liquid mirage, the only dark spot in the entire landscape. The Romans cultivated the area around Abu Minqar and some of

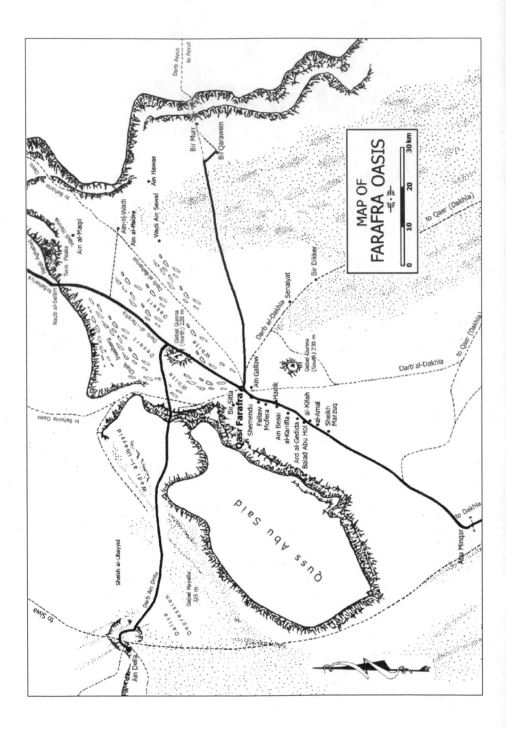

MAP OF
FARAFRA OASIS

their plowed fields can still be seen in outline.

Abu Minqar is 230 kilometers (143 miles) from Qasr Dakhla and only 100 kilometers (62 miles) from the Libyan border to the west. It sits at the eastern edge of the Great Sand Sea.

Where once this was a major checkpoint in the Western Desert, with a border patrol that asked for passports and car papers, in 1998 no checkpoint existed. Instead, the small village at Abu Minqar with a restaurant and first aid station has grown into a community. It, too, is under development, for underground water also exists here. Homesteaders are given ten free feddans and a house with free electricity and water.

From the checkpoint it is only 5 kilometers (3.1 miles) to the base of the escarpment. As the road snakes its way to the top take time to look back on the fine view, for a few kilometers later the road plunges down again and you are in the Farafra Depression.

A short distance after the descent into Farafra is **Belle Vue** at N 26 32 444 and E 27 51 853. It looks like a great place to camp and is certainly a great place to go off road and explore. At Belle Vue you are 75 kilometers (47 miles) from the arch at Qasr Farafra. There are a number of villages and small garden oases before the arch. They are all described below in Tour #2.

To Qasr Farafra from Bahariya Oasis (2–4 hours)

			km	total km
Escarpment	N 27 46 369	E 28 31 448	0	0
Sheikh Abdullah Muhammad	N 27 40 833	E 28 27 337	23	23
Crystal Mountain	N 27 39 718	E 28 25 761	3	26
Naqb al-Sillim	N 27 30 106	E 28 14 997	24	50
White Desert (middle)	N 27 21 260	E 28 09 314	c10	c60
Qasr Farafra checkpoint	N 27 05 001	E 27 68 584	32	c92

The road between Bahariya and Farafra was paved in 1978. Until that time the Darb al-Bahariya (if coming from Bahariya it is called Darb al-Farafra) and the difficult Naqb al-Sellim were used. Those old caravan routes lie to the southeast (left) of the modern road and, with a good guide, offer an off-road alternative route to Farafra. When almost to the Farafra escarpment a single, lonely roadsign in English and Arabic marks the kilometers as 125. (N 27 26 208 E 28 27 645.)

This itinerary is for the paved road. Once out of the Bahariya Depression, the scenery changes dramatically. Where Bahariya was all yellow sand and black-topped hills, this new area is dotted with white chalk cliffs, a taste of the majestic chalk escarpments that await the visitor in Farafra.

Qarat Sheikh Abdullah Muhammad

Qarat Sheikh Abdullah Muhammad is located 23 kilometers (14.3 miles) from the top of the escarpment leading out of Bahariya. This tiny spot on the right side of the road might at a distance be mistaken for a checkpoint, but is thought by some to be the final resting place of a prominent Sanusi sheikh from Farafra. In truth, the sheikh is buried on the Darb al-Bahariya, the old route from Bahariya to Farafra about 30 kilometers (19 miles) to the southeast. Once the new road was built, someone thought to move the site so pilgrims wishing favors from the sheikh would have easier access. The new location has been carefully tended: flags fly from small wooden masts, saplings have been planted in the hope of offering shade, and there is a *zir* filled with water available for any passing stranger. There is also a prayer circle outlined by rocks on the ground for Muslims to pray.

Crystal Mountain

Three kilometers (1.8 miles) beyond the sheikh's tomb is a small mountain less than ten meters (32 feet) from the left-hand side of the road. Just beyond the mountain, on the western side, as the road goes, is a small quartz crystal rock with a large hole in the center. This is Gebel al-Izaz, Crystal Mountain, also known locally as Hagar al-Makhrum, Rock with a Hole. There are plenty of quartz crystals lying about and several mountains in the area are laced with the mineral.

Naqb al-Sillim

The Naqb al-Sillim, Pass of the Stairs, appears 50 kilometers (30 miles) after ascending the escarpment at Bahariya and 24 kilometers (15 miles) after Crystal Mountain. This is the main pass descending the escarpment into Farafra Depression. Actually, the original Naqb al-Sillim is the pass to the southeast along the Darb al-Bahariya N 27 25 088 E 28 26 853. This pass was just renamed the same thing when the new road was built. Just before the descent is a very tall communications tower which serves as a good landmark while offroad in the Farafra desert. Beside it is one of the dozens of First Aid Stations recently erected along the desert routes.

Twin Peaks

As the roadway tumbles down the slope, a series of outlier hills, sometimes called sugarloaves because of their bowl-like shape, creates a dramatic backdrop to the southeast (left) of the road. This area is called Aqabat, 'the difficult.' At the end of the sugarloaves, isolated though easily recognized by its two flat-topped peaks, sits Twin Peaks, one of the most prominent landmarks in Farafra. See illustration on p.169.

White Desert and Inselbergs

After 10 kilometers (6.2 miles) the famous and beautiful white chalk of Farafra Depression comes into view. Prominent steep-sided hills, standing alone and rising from the level plain, they continue along the escarpment to the northwest (right) of the main road for 20 kilometers (12.5 miles). White, and of a considerable height, the inselbergs rise majestically in this area and together with the White Desert, comprise one of the unique natural wonders of Egypt. It is hoped that they will someday be the centerpieces of a National Park.

There are inselbergs on other planets in our solar system and scientists have come to the Western Desert to better understand the function of these outstanding conical hills on Mars. On Earth, they are created when plateaus begin to breakdown. Then, areas that are topped with bedrock remain behind. Erosion continues around them until they become free standing, steep-sided, flat-topped, or conical, hills. These shapes vary based on the aridity of the area. In semi-arid deserts, where water aids erosion, they tend to crumble on one or more sides. In hyper-arid deserts, like the Western Desert, where wind alone is doing the job, they do not.

With a 4x4 or dirt bike you can detour off the road, driving beside and between the rocks. Even to walk between the peaks is a memorable experience. Dominating the inselbergs are two massive monoliths, which are worth exploring.

Farafra

Each oasis has its own personality and they are so different from one another it is amazing that they are in the same desert. Kharga bustles. Dakhla is pastoral. Bahariya seems tranquil. But Farafra is haunting. One always feels there is something Farafra wants to tell us, like it has a deep secret it wants to share, but we have to work to find it. It is the most isolated oasis and most difficult to reach; yet, there is evidence to support the theory that it binds the entire Western Desert together. It had little to offer pharaoh, caliph, or king, remaining isolated for centuries; yet it is on its way to everywhere. If you are in the deep desert, Farafra is always nearby. The joy of Farafra is its simplicity.

History

It is now accepted that Farafra went through three distinct wet phases 9000 B.C., 6000 B.C., and 4500 B.C. This is a staggering fact that may eventually rewrite the history of ancient Egypt. If the desert wasn't the desert how did that affect the Nile Valley? In addition, Farafra may yet form the link between the Egyptian Libyan Desert and the Libyan Libyan Desert. Barbara E. Barich in *Geoarchaeology of Farafra and the Origin of Agriculture in the Sahara and the Nile Valley* tells us that 10,000 years ago in the early Holocene there were violent rains in the area and that "Epipaleolithic groups moved along a rather extended circuit, connecting the various oases of the Western Desert, with excursions toward the Saharan plains." They were looking for game and pastures and it is almost inevitable that "contacts with the Saharan hinterland were established, as evidenced in the technological base of the early Holocene groups." Around 8600 B.C., the rains stabilized and so did the population.

Old Kingdom

Known in ancient times as Oasis Trinitheos, Ta-ihw, and Land of the Cow (after the ancient Egyptian goddess Hathor), a better name is probably Land of the Invaded, for though remote, Farafra lies on the road to Libya and whenever it was left undefended invasion could be guaranteed. A Fifth Dynasty statue inscription implies that Farafra, as well as Bahariya, was part of ancient Egypt at that time. During the Intermediate Period, the text of the Eloquent Peasant refers to "rods of Farafra" as part of the produce carried from Wadi Natrun to the Fayoum. We do not know what they are.

New Kingdom (c.1570–1070 B.C.)

Ascherson found a stela dated from the Eighteenth Dynasty, but it sheds no light on activities at that time. There is written evidence in the Court of Ramses II at Luxor Temple that precious stones were sent to the Nile Valley from Farafra for Ramses' massive building plans, but no ancient mining sites have been found. We do not know what these precious stones might have been: emeralds, lapis, malachite, turquoise, or perhaps something like alabaster. Farafra was captured by Libyan invaders in the Nineteenth Dynasty, during the reign of King Merenptah (1223–1211 B.C.). This conquest allowed Farafra to be a stepping stone to the Nile Valley for the Libyans.

Third Intermediate (c. 1069–525 B.C.) and Late Periods (525–332 B.C.)

Although there is no supporting evidence, it is possible that Farafra was important during the Third Intermediate Period when Libyans ruled Egypt. Closer to Libya than to the Nile Valley, the wells of Farafra could have served as important way stations for armies and caravans. There are several major caravan routes going west in the Farafra area. If this happened, the secrets are well kept. One thing is sure, this period spawned one of the great mysteries of the world, the whereabouts of the lost Persian army.

Cambyses

There is a legend told by the Greek traveler Herodotus about the Persian conqueror Cambyses, son of Cyrus the Great. After defeating the pharaoh Psamtik III at Pelusium in 525 B.C., Cambyses entered Egypt, founding the First Persian Period. After establishing himself on the throne of Egypt, Cambyses' thoughts turned to repaying old debts. Furious with the Oracle at Siwa, Cambyses vowed to lay waste the entire oasis. While he was on an ill-fated invasion of Ethiopia, he sent a portion of his army from Thebes to Siwa through the Western Desert. Although the exact route of Cambyses' army is not certain, most sources maintain it headed first to Kharga Oasis and from there set off for Siwa, never to be seen or heard from again.

According to Siwan legend, while the 50,000 men, accompanied by all the trappings of a military force, were paused for lunch somewhere in the Western Desert mid-way between Kharga and Siwa a great storm arose and the army was buried forever beneath the sand.

In the oral history of Siwa the desert defeated the army of more than one enemy. Whether the legends began with the ill-fated army of Cambyses is uncertain, but the idea that 50,000 men could disappear in a sandstorm is not as absurd as it might sound. Though storms of such magnitude are rare, archaeologists record that in a severe storm more than a meter of sand can fall on an excavation in less than an hour, and nineteenth-century travelers reported battling storms for hours on end to keep their tents from being completely obliterated.

Our friend Hagg Zaki from Farafra remembers just such a storm when he was on his way to Bahariya. Douglas Newbold also records a storm in "A Desert Odyssey of a Thousand Miles" in *Sudan Notes and Records*: "we rode for nearly 50 miles at one stage in the teeth of a sand blizzard such as must have overwhelmed Cambyses' army." John Ball learned early to respect sandstorms. He tells us: "In the case of a camp standing for eight windy days in the same place, the arrest of the air's motion by the tent caused the deposit of a dune 8 meters [25 feet] in diameter and 30 centimeters deep on a spot previously perfectly clear of sand." If the men journeying to Siwa were caught in such storms, it is possible that they all died. Time and the desert wind would have done the rest.

Other large groups have perished in the desert. In 1881, the French explorer Colonel Paul Flatters, ten officers, and eighty-six Chaamba tribesmen met a fate that could have been similar to Cambyses' soldiers. They were massacred in the Hoggar Mountains in Algeria while trying to find a good route for a trans-Saharan railroad. Then there was the Foureau–Lamy Expedition in 1898. An infantry army of 250 soldiers left for the desert, a year later only a handful returned. Everyone assumes that a storm finished off the army. How about a *ghazya*, a desert raid? Could the Persians have encountered a raiding tribe in the desert? We know people other than the ancient Egyptians lived in the desert. We know they raided settlements to sustain their meager livelihood. An army with all its provisions would be quite a trophy. There is another legend that is too similar to Cambyses' tragedy to go unmentioned. In 1810, the sultan of Waidai sent a caravan to Dakhla to establish negotiations and potential trade. According to Rohlfs, this caravan got lost north of Darfur. Everyone perished when they could not find water, among them the sultan's mother on her way to Mecca.

Where did Cambyses' army meet its end? This question continues to perplex. Arguing that no commander would send an army through the desert from Thebes to Siwa when they could travel up the Nile and head to Siwa via Memphis, Rohlfs asserted that the army was in fact headed to Dakhla, where there was also a temple dedicated to Amun. Disagreeing, Ascherson maintained that the temple in Dakhla hadn't been built at the time of Cambyses' invasion and that the distance from Memphis or Thebes to Siwa was about the same on ancient maps. Beadnell argued that the army did not go to

Kharga at all, but proceeded to Siwa via Bahariya or Farafra, leaving the Nile around Asyut.

Hoskins presented the likely theory that the guides hired to lead the army to Siwa had no intention of seeing the famed Oracle and its temples destroyed; therefore, they purposely led it to its death. This is similar to what happened to Flatters. His expedition was ambushed by their own Tuareg guides in the valley of Tin Tarabin at Bir Garama in what is now Algeria. The majority managed to escape, but they were so disoriented that they made too many bad decisions and one by one began to perish. The few that did reach the wells at Amjid were killed by the Tuaregs, who were waiting for them. Could the Persians have met a similar fate?

Hoskins seemed to know the route, too. He says, "had I time, I would follow the route of the army of Cambyses, and might, perhaps, have greater success in reaching the Oasis of Amun." Of course, he does not tell us where it is.

The quest to locate the lost army intrigued explorers during the late nineteenth and early twentieth centuries. Almasy, the Hungarian explorer, sought Cambyses with an airplane, repeatedly crossing the Great Sand Sea in the 1920s and 1930s. Wing Commander Penderel believes the army got lost in the Great Sand Sea, too. In 1932, a Bedouin brought a horseshoe into Siwa with the story that there were "many dead horses and mules" in the desert. At first everyone got excited, for Cambyses' army is the first thought to come to mind. Until someone realized horseshoes did not exist during Cambyses' day. But everyone went looking anyway. They found nothing. Murray, who always seems to have had a theory, conjectures that almost certainly these were remains of stragglers of the Sanusi army as it fled from Bahariya in 1916.

In 1960, Hennemann and Hergenhahn also went to the Great Sand Sea in search of Cambyses. Neither solved the mystery. In 1982, Giancarlo Ligabue of the Ligabue Studies and Research Center in Venice and Gary Chafez, of the Peabody Museum at Harvard, joined the quest.

Modern research concurs with the early explorers and places the army somewhere to the west of Farafra and to the north of Ain Della in the Great Sand Sea. If the missing army is in this isolated area the storm, disorientation, lack of water, and a host of other dangers could have caused a long and agonizing death for the soldiers and the litter of bodies and machinery may be strewn over a much larger area than one would expect. Combined with all this is the fact that the area known today as the Great Sand Sea may have been different 2,500 years ago. Just where were the dune fields during Cambyses' day? And if the army lies under the dunes, it may well be buried too deep to be detected by modern equipment.

Let us add one more piece to this puzzle. Lisa Giddy in *Egyptian Oases* skeptically points out that a Farafra–Kharga desert route may have existed during the New Kingdom. As evidence she points to the tribute bearers and text on the walls in the Ramses II court of Luxor Temple. Her doubts are based upon the inhospitable terrain and the lack of water in this part of the desert. But, let us point out that what is waterless today need not have been waterless then. Outposts similar to the forts in Kharga or simple water stations could have existed further north than we suppose. There could have been wells that dried up or for some reason were destroyed (which was a common occurrence). They could have been destroyed by the ancient Egyptians specifically to kill Cambyses' soldiers.

Since all else has failed, perhaps everyone has been looking in the wrong place for this army. How did they get so far west? Thebes to the Great Sand Sea is a great distance. Let us propose that the army never went west of Kharga at all, never went near Dakhla. Let us propose it went north from Kharga near Ain Umm Dabadib and then headed northwest to dissect the caravan trails of Darb al-Tawil, Darb al-Khashabi, and Darb

Asyut. Edmondstone tell us of hillocks "resembling artificial heaps" along the Darb al-Tawil which he believed similar to those that Belzoni imagined as the tombs of Cambyses' army." This puts us right in the middle of the space in question.

The world would be a less interesting place without its great mysteries. The where-abouts of Cambyses' army has sparked the imagination of more than one person through the years and has entertained more than one generation in its telling. It will continue to intrigue people until someone solves it once and for all. At the moment one thing is certain: Herodotus said Cambyses sent an army to Siwa, and it disappeared.

Roman Period (30 B.C.–A.D. 323)

The earliest antiquities found in Farafra date from Roman times, though they are far from numerous. We originally thought that Farafra had little to offer Rome, but that is not true. The scarcity of water rendered great agricultural schemes untenable, unless the Romans knew of the underground water we have just discovered. The oasis was at the center of Rome's Africa holdings, linking Egypt's oases and the Nile Valley to Libya's oases like Jalo and Kufra. If the area was secure, there would be no reason for fortresses like at Kharga. One would have served, and that may well have been the original Qasr at Farafra.

The only Roman sites found so far in Farafra are at Ain Della, which is really a separate depression to the north of Farafra; in Wadi Hinnis, along the main caravan route to Bahariya; and at Ain Besay, a small garden to the south of Qasr Farafra. After the Romans, Farafra faded from sight.

In the Byzantine period, Farafra became Christian and remained Christian far into the Islamic era. A number of Coptic inscriptions have been found in Farafra as well as Christian houses and a cemetery of the tenth century. We do not know if it was a place of banishment like Siwa and Kharga.

Islamic Era (641–1798)

When Islam swept into the desert it did not come from the Nile Valley, it came from North Africa. Farafra, according to Cailliaud, was the first Western Desert oasis conquered by the Arabs. The first Arabic reference to Farafra is the *Kitab al-Buldan* by al-Yaqubi in the ninth century. He tells us Farafra was inhabited by people of "all descent." But conversion to Islam was slow in Farafra and probably happened in the tenth century. Once the invaders, the Fatimids, had secured the Nile, they maintained a relatively large desert army and a governor of the Bahnasa Oasis was appointed by the Caliph al-Hafiz (1130–49). By Mamluk times (1250–1517) Farafra was depopulated. The oases has been pathetically exploited and many people immigrated to avoid the harsh rule.

When the Ottomans came to power in Egypt little changed in Farafra except more corruption and a further decline in the economic situation and population. According to W. B. Kubiak, during the Ottoman era there was a total decline in secular literature and for three centuries no information about Egypt, especially its oases, was recorded.

Throughout the centuries Farafra was the victim of desert raids, *ghazwas*. These raids were carried out not only by desert peoples but also by government troops who should have been protecting the oases and collecting taxes. Once the Europeans began to appear on the scene they described raiders as coming at night and ravaging the gardens to steal dates, apricots, and other food: the poor robbing the poor to survive.

Modern Times

The first known European visitor to Farafra was Frederic Cailliaud from February 17 to 20, 1820. It took him thirty-two hours to get to Farafra from al-Hayz in Bahariya and he found 180 people living in a single village, Qasr Farafra. What he found was a community in poverty, abandoned by its government for centuries, victim of marauding tribes who took advantage of the lack of protection and the decline in population. Next came the elusive Mr. Pacho, and G. Wilkinson in 1843.

In 1850, the Sanusi founded a *zawya* in Farafra (see People for details). The Sanusi movement was still strong when Rohlfs visited Farafra in December and January of 1873–4, and the religious order stayed in the oasis until World War I. In fact, many of the residents of Farafra carry the surname Sanusi and the attitude and tone of the oasis retained strong Sanusi influence up to a decade ago. Once this author offered a cigarette to a man in Farafra. The refusal was accompanied by the words, "I am Sanusi." This was over seventy-five years after the Sanusi movement collapsed.

Rohlfs arrived at Farafra with 100 camels and 100 people. As he approached the oases his men began shooting off their guns. This terrified the Farafronis. Fearful of yet another *ghazya*—they had had one the year before—they got their guns, stuffed their women and children in the *qasr* for protection, and waited. Everything, of course, was sorted out, but on New Year's Eve, Rohlfs was at it again. He brought fireworks with him and began setting them off.

Rohlfs found Farafra divided into two camps: Sanusi and non-Sanusi. By this time the Sanusi owned the best wells, the best land, and the best gardens. He found the people like serfs. Farafra, which Rohlfs says means 'bubbling spring,' had a spring similar to Cleopatra's Bath in Siwa with bubbles constantly swimming to the surface. He found only 2 camels, 100 donkeys, and 300 sheep in the oasis, all owned by the Sanusi.

The New Valley in Farafra

Today Farafra Oasis is part of the New Valley. Although development has been slower than in Kharga and Dakhla, the ambitious plans for Farafra will change forever the easy, serene atmosphere that permeates this wonderful oasis. Over 60,000 acres of land are being prepared for development in a new agricultural scheme that has brought many immigrants into the area. The original school opened in 1938 now shares its tasks with dozens of additional schools. Qasr Farafra is no longer the only village in Farafra as a dozen new communities have emerged on the southwestern plains.

Anyone who wishes to settle in Farafra is entitled to a house and 8 to 20 feddans of land, depending on the person's experience, free electricity for the first five years (electricity came to Farafra in 1981), and free water. Houses are paid back over a thirty-five year period with no payment due the first five years. Each family receives a monthly stipend of cash and free flour, cheese, sugar, rice, oil, tea, butter, and other staples. Each new village is provided with a school, a hospital (the first hospital in Farafra was built in the 1960s), and a mosque. Fiber optics recently arrived, sewage disposal is being developed. That's quite a homesteading package.

New towns will require doctors, nurses, teachers, electricians, plumbers: in short a host of skilled people who are reluctant to homestead and leave the comforts of the Nile Valley. It will also require patience and adjustment. Fellahin of the Nile Valley will find the terrain hard going. And the Farafronis have to share their space. It will not be an easy task.

In addition to agriculture, tourism is being developed at Farafra. Two new hotels have been erected and are open for business. In 1979–81, about fifty tourists a year visited Farafra. Now, 2,000 are expected yearly and the hope is the number will increase as facilities improve.

Traditionally, the mayor or *umda*, is selected from the members of the most important clan of the village. Whenever a visitor came to call, it was customary to visit the *umda* first to get his permission to enter the community. Today, Farafra's mayor is appointed by the governor of the New Valley. But Farafra is blessed, for Muhammad Raifat Amin is truly the *umda* of this community. An agricultural engineer by profession, he wants only organic farming to take place here. No chemicals. No insecticides. An environmentalist at heart, he wants to keep the air pure, the eye unpolluted by debris. He values the White Desert and the work the archaeologists and other scientists are doing in his oasis. He wants tourism to thrive. He is a man for the people and this is good for Farafra.

Geography and Geology

The Farafra depression, carved out of Upper Cretaceous Khoman Chalk, looks like a draped ghost with its right foot kicking a spur of the Great Sand Sea. Spanning 90 kilometers (56 miles) east–west and 200 kilometers (125 miles) north–south, it is the second largest depression in the Western Desert. It sits at E 27 20 and E 28 59 longitude and N 26 18 and N 27 42 latitude.

The escarpment rings the depression on three sides. The eastern scarp, standing 244 meters (708 feet) high, and the western scarp are both steep-sided, formidable barriers. The dazzling white northern scarp, although lower, is actually two scarps, one behind the other. The southern part of the oasis is open. The depression floor comprises a mixture of white chalk and limestone which creates the White Desert, black iron pyrites and marcasite stones which create the Black Desert, scrub land, mud lions, and many seif dunes. South to Dakhla, the dunes run for over 150 kilometers (93.5 miles).

To the northwest of Qasr Farafra is the **Quss Abu Said Plateau**, a 10 kilometer (6.25 mile) wide snow-white limestone plateau of lower Eocene–upper Cretaceous origin. West of Farafra and separated from it by the Quss Abu Said Plateau is the uninhabited **Daliya Depression**. 80 kilometers (50 miles) wide, the floor is covered entirely by sand dunes. A major tectonic fold that also crosses the Bahariya Depression (see Bahariya for details), cuts through Farafra in a northeast/southwest direction.

There is ample evidence of a dry lake bed, or playa, which is under investigation by the Rome University Project.

Mountains and Hills

There are three major mountains in Farafra. Two bear the same name, **Gebel al-Gunna**. The first is 10 kilometers (6.25 miles) northeast of Qasr, just to the right of the main road. The second is 12 kilometers (7.5 miles) south of Qasr along the road to Bir Dikker. The third, **Twin Peaks**, is a major landmark. It sits to the southeast of the road just below the main descent into the oasis from Bahariya.

Perhaps the most outstanding mountain features in the Western Desert are the white chalk inselbergs, a 20 kilometer (12.5 mile) long series of free standing hills, all steep-sided but of various sizes, that look like icebergs standing in front of the northern escarpment.

Water

Water, a major problem in Farafra, is one of the reasons it remained so primitive for so long. While Dakhla has over 520 wells in its 410 square kilometers (256 square miles) Farafra, up to 1989, had under forty. Through the centuries agriculture was limited to a few acres around Qasr and its outlying gardens, creating subsistence farming in limited crops like dates and olives.

Now all of this has changed. Recent exploration has determined that there is plenty of water in Farafra, enough for the development of a major agricultural scheme. South of Qasr Farafra the land has the appearance of a boom town as well after well is sunk and town after town planned. Only the people are missing. The New Valley Governorate is slowly luring people from the Nile Valley out to this desert frontier to set down roots and cultivate the land.

Caravan Routes and Roadways

Darb al-Farafra is called Darb al-Bahariya when in Farafra and Darb al-Farafra in Bahariya. It was the major caravan route linking Farafra to Bahariya and the Nile Valley before the construction of the macadamized road. It runs through the desert about 35 kilometers (22 miles) east of the macadamized road and enters Farafra through the Naqb al-Sillim.

Darb al-Dakhla, the old caravan route from Qasr Dakhla to Qasr Farafra, is 200 kilometers (125 miles) in comparison to the 300 kilometer (187 mile) modern roadway, but since it passes through difficult terrain it has remained a dirt track. It leaves Qasr Farafra, moves south to Bir Dikker and drops into Dakhla near Qasr Dakhla. (See below for tour.) Caravans would take four days to cover the distance. Blundell used it in the 1890s.

Darb Asyut is the old caravan route which links Beni Adi, Dashlut, and Mayr, all near Asyut in the Nile Valley, to Farafra. It is one of the shortest routes to Farafra, covering about 280 kilometers (175 miles), but the terrain is difficult and it often took seven or eight days by camel. The Abu Muharrik dunes cut through the darb in a north–south direction. Along its route is a wonderful cave. It was first brought to the attention of Europeans by Gerhard Rohlfs and was rediscovered in this century by Carlo Bergmann. This road is in the process of being paved.

Despite the fact that **Darb Ain Della** led to a single spring in the middle of nowhere, it was one of the most important routes in the entire Western Desert. Originally running due north of Qasr Farafra for 75 kilometers (46 miles), at Ain Della it linked with additional routes to Libya, Siwa (via Bahrein and Areg), and Bahariya, forming a strategic crossroad. Lisa Giddy in *Egyptian Oases* proposes that an ancient text from the First Intermediate Period about products traveling over desert routes via Wadi Natrun could indicate that this Della–Siwa route was in use at that time. Rohlfs used it in 1874; Jennings-Bramley in 1898. Today the road has been macadamized (See Tour #5 below).

The **Abu Minqar–Kufra Camel Track** is an ancient route that skirts the southern tips of the Great Sand Sea and links Farafra with Kufra Oasis in Libya. In the 1950s, when Gamal Abd al-Nasser was trying to stop caravans from crossing the border with illegal products over this track, he bombed them.

The People

There is a good deal of Libyan blood in Farafra, and a lot of the population have the surname Sanusi. (See People for details.) There is also more Bedouin blood than in the other oases. The population is very small and, until recently, agriculture was centered on Qasr Farafra, the few gardens on the hillside to the south, and the gardens in the nearby oases.

Rohlfs gives us an extensive report on the people of Farafra. They ate dates and mush (polenta) for breakfast and dates and fruit for lunch, and more polenta for dinner. For meat they ate mice, camel—but only if it died naturally—and jackals. They kept goats and sheep for the milk and wool, and chickens for the eggs. Today the Farafronis eat like the people in Bahariya. They place a small, short-legged table in the center of the floor and put pillows around the perimeter for seating. A tray of bread, white salty cheese, honey or jam, and halawa is prepared for breakfast. For lunch or dinner potatoes in tomato sauce, peas and carrots in tomato sauce, rice, bread, and sometimes a boiled or stewed meat dish is served. There is always a bowl of olives, usually pickled by the family. People sit around the table and use the bread to dip into the food. Sometimes a spoon is provided. The meal is often ended with fresh fruit.

Rohlfs said the women were uncircumcised, and old and unmarried ones did not cover their faces. The dead were buried naked, and pottery, filled on the day of the death with water, wheat, and dates, was placed at the head and foot of the grave.

The Vanishing Past Time, a Polish study on Farafra, tells us the Farafronis come from four families that migrated to the oasis within the past 500 years. Blood ties oblige the people to care for their own, so no one goes hungry or faces adversity alone.

Agriculture

The past was agriculture in Farafra and so will be the future. New wells (at a million Egyptian pounds each) are being drilled everyday, eleven new villages are planned with seven already created.

Three new olive presses are in the oasis. And now the oasis produces more than it needs and is exporting dates, olives, apricots, wheat, rice, and beans to the Nile Valley. New plants currently being developed include medicinal and perfume plants. New watermelon plantations are developing in several locations.

The Crafts of the Oasis

There is little here to tempt the traveler. The people were poor, the outside world always far away. The pottery, similar in design to other oases, was distinguished only because it was unfired. Not thrown on a potter's wheel, it was hand-shaped by the women and baked in the sun. There is practically no jewelry and the dresses are mostly undecorated. There was a nosering, but made of base metal and long gone.

Wall painting at Qasr Farafra

Despite the lack of major crafts two skills are worth mentioning: wall paintings and wool. The houses in Qasr Farafra are beautifully decorated by the local artist Badr. Interestingly enough, spinning is a man's occupation in this oasis and men can often be seen in the main square, spindle in hand, working and talking. Then the men knit the wool into hats, gloves, and scarves, all for sale by a delightful personality dubbed 'Mr. Socks,' who can be seen riding his motorcycle around town with a scarf or two dangling behind.

The Tour

For travelers to Farafra it is wise to stay on the main road and only venture into the desert with a local guide. Farafra is one of the most beautiful places in the world but, like many beautiful things, it can be deadly. It is far into the Western Desert, hundreds of kilometers from a large city with modern services, and unlike Bahariya, where the depression is long and narrow and a trek in either direction from the main road is hemmed in by the escarpment, the main road in Farafra hugs the northwestern escarpment, leaving the rest of this large depression uninhabited, a true wilderness. The eastern and western scarps are so far apart that they cannot serve as markers. The south has no end, but stretches on forever to places that have seldom seen human footsteps. For the professional as well as the amateur desert traveler, misjudgment in such a place can lead to disaster. It isn't easy to keep one's bearings amid the dunes and rock-strewn plains of such a place. And heading in the wrong direction can become a life threatening situation.

TOUR #1

Qasr Farafra

Qasr Farafra was once the only inhabited village in the entire depression. Never heavily populated, in 1819, there were 180 people in Qasr with a total of 600 throughout the oasis. In 1874, there were just 345 people living in 111 houses. By 1892, the population had grown to 542. In 1936, about 600. In 1968, 1,118. In 1993, there were 3,000 in Qasr and a total of 5,000 in the entire oasis. The village sits atop a 10 meter (32 foot) hill of hard white chalk which rises gently from the desert floor.

Qasr Farafra is 80 kilometers (50 miles) from the southwestern escarpment and 54 kilometers (33 miles) from the northeastern one. The main road passes Qasr Farafra along the bottom of the hill. It is here that new buildings are growing at a rapid rate. There is a cafeteria, a bus stop, and several small kiosk-type restaurants which offer ful, canned beef, cheese, and bottled water. And there is a hotel.

Badr's Museum

Badr is a local artist and entrepreneur who has fared rather well in recent years. His original small but interesting museum, which was located in the village of Qasr itself, has been abandoned for a wonderful mudbrick structure that the artist built himself. Inside is everything from taxidermy to sculpture, and

paintings are on display. It is Badr who is responsible for the unique wall decorations found in the village.

The Fortress

The fortress of Farafra dominates the top of the hill. Like its counterparts in other oases, it was once a walled city used by the inhabitants as protection from invaders. The villagers would hasten to the fortress for safety, each family occupying a designated room where they had stored provisions. At other times, a single occupant guarded the interior. Cailliaud records the fortress was 35 feet high and 350 feet in circumference in 1819. In 1909, when Harding King visited the oasis, the fortress had around 125 rooms (earlier travelers record as many as 226 rooms) and the tower was still standing. Damaged by heavy rain, the fortress began to crumble in the 1950s and collapsed considerably in 1958. Currently it has two large entrances and, uniquely amongst buildings of this type, it is still partially inhabited.

Harding King believed the fortress was originally erected by the Romans and was much the same as the fortresses in Kharga Oasis. He is probably correct. In the fifteenth century, probably when desert raids intensified, it was either enlarged or rebuilt. By the

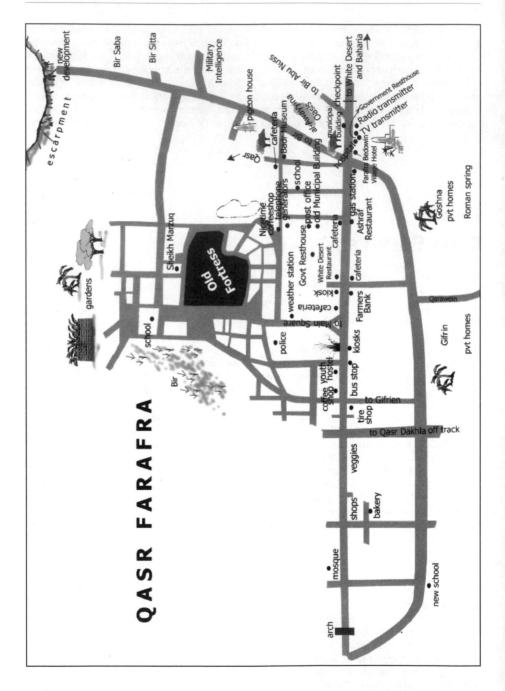

time King visited the oasis the fortress was empty, guarded by a single watchman who was responsible for protecting the goods of the various families that used it as a storehouse.

Beyond the fortress the square widens and to the left once stood the **mosque**. This was an old Sanusi mosque, with a stone in one of the corners that acted as a sun dial. When the people built a new mosque at the bottom of the hill, they saw no reason to keep the old one, so they tore it down. What a pity!

Bir Sitta
N 27 04 273 E 27 55 738
Bir Sitta is the hot spring designated by the people for tourists to use. Do not jump into the springs within the vicinity of Qasr. The road leading to the *bir* is 3.3 kilometers (2 miles) from the beginning of the road to the Military Intelligence Camp. Turn right. The *bir* is visible at the top of the hill to the left of the new hotel.

Goshna and Gifrin
Suburban sprawl has reached Farafra and the once empty oasis of Goshna is now crowded with homes. Some of them are owned by foreigners who find the oasis a perfect place to spend their vacations. The open plain that once separated Goshna from Farafra has all but disappeared.

Gifrin is still empty. Gifrin has a proper track exiting Qasr by a left-hand turn opposite the cafe along the main road (see map).

Farafra fortress in 1839 (after Cailliaud)

TOUR #2
Toward Abu Minqar

			km	total km
Farafra arch	N 27 03 102	E 27 58 120	0	0
Shemendu	N 27 01 242	E 27 57 455	3.5	3.5
Ain Gallaw	N 27 00 931	E 27 57 330	4	7.5
18	N 26 54 734	E 27 53 464	12.1	18.6
Ain Besay/Abu Hul	N 26 52 818	E 27 52 522	3.5	22.1
Al-Kifah	N 26 52 214	E 27 52 291	0.8	22.9
Petrol station	N 26 51 806	E 27 52 149	0.7	23.6
Wahat al-Amal	N 26 50 594	E 27 51 759	3	26.6
Ain Sheikh Marzuq	N 26 49 033	E 27 51 759	2.9	29.5
Abu Horaya	N 26 46 808	E 27 49 833	5.7	35.2

Though much of Farafra looks as it did in antiquity, this stretch of desert, where subterranean water was recently discovered, is a mixture of old and very, very new. Most of the new agricultural development is taking place here. Springing up between the old gardens are new villages which are changing the face of this isolated oasis. A number of small oases are stretched out for over 30 kilometers (18.7 miles) along the only paved road heading toward Dakhla.

Shemendu
The first oasis, only 3.4 kilometers (2 miles) along the road, is Shemendu, located on the right, or northwest side of the road close to the escarpment. It has an ancient spring.

Ain Gallaw
Shemendu is followed a kilometer later by Ain Gallaw, visible a distance from the road on the left. A few rock tombs and some Coptic inscriptions attest to its habitation in the past. The tombs are unfinished and one was once occupied by a Christian hermit who painted red crosses inside. There is an ancient aqueduct here.

Fallaw and Mofera
Ain Gallaw is followed after 5.6 kilometers (3.5 miles) by two oases, Fallaw and Mofera, lying one after the other on the right side of the road toward the escarpment.

Ain Besay and Hadiq
Ain Besay, on the right, and Hadiq, on the left, are opposite each other 3.7 kilometers (2.1 miles) after Fallaw. The latter has little to interest the tourist, but Ain Besay has a few archaeological sites. Ahmed Fakhry maintained that the ruins at Ain Besay make it the most important site in Farafra. They consist of an ancient cemetery, two mudbrick buildings, a few rock tombs, and a small chapel located 150 meters (480 feet) northeast of the tombs. Little is known about these ruins.

Local lore maintains that one day a spring in this small garden exploded causing smoke to come out of the hole. The people of Farafra, afraid of the spirits of the place, threw an entire family and all their belongings into the spring to appease the spirits. The well became strong again.

Ard al-Gedida and Balad Abu al-Hul
The land here is flat, once a long stretch of nothing. Four kilometers (2.5 miles) later, the road to the right is to the new village of Ard al-Gedida, New Land, followed a kilo-

meter later, again on the right, by the new Balad Abu al-Hul, Sphinx Village.

Al-Kifah and Wahat al-Amal
Sphinx is followed after a kilometer by the village of al-Kifah, the Battle, on the left. Here we have an ancient *jub*, aqueduct, which was rebuilt in the 1990s and functions perfectly today. Parts of the original tunnel had collapsed so they were replaced. The shafts are 20 to 40 meters (64 to 128 feet) from each other. The rebuilt *jub* has 49 shafts covering 280 meters (896 feet) in total length. Water flow is 80 cubic meters (249 cubic feet) per day supplying water to 8 farms. (See Kharga Oasis for more details about aqueducts.)

Wahat al-Amal, Oasis of Hope, appears three kilometers (1.8 miles) later, again on the left.

Ain Sheikh Marzuq
Finally one comes to the old garden of Ain Sheikh Marzuq, three kilometers (1.8 miles) beyond the Oasis of Hope, on the left side of the road. It took Rohlfs seven hours to reach here by camel from Qasr Farafra in 1874. He found it to be the only other inhabited village in the oases. Among its several springs is one of ancient Roman origin. The Sanusi built a *zawya* here and in the 1920s when Harding King visited Farafra this oasis was still inhabited. Today, a few families still live here and it has acquired electricity.

The White Desert

There is no perfect time to see the White Desert of Farafra. Each day offers a new treat. Each hour a new change. First there is the color. It intensifies under certain light. It elongates, deepens, lightens, and bursts forth into unimaginable shades of white and blue and bubbling gold. At dawn, the huge monsters are awakening to a new day. They lazily and delicately dance a slow-motion ballet to welcome the sun. At dusk, tired but contented, they stretch and shimmer in the long golden rays of the sun as it caresses them like the lyrics of a lullaby. When the moon is full, they do not sleep. Instead they dance to a different ballad, an exotic ballad, creating unimaginable images that seem enchanted.

In the soft light of winter they appear romantic. In the harsh sun of summer they nearly disappear in the trembling mirage of liquid air. When clouds fill the sky they appear to turn gray, seem smaller, and turn pensive and foreboding. No, there is no perfect time to see the White Desert. It wears too many faces and too many moods. It encounters each hour donning a different mask, one that pleases while it torments, exalts as it humbles, electrifies to the point of terror. The White Desert of Farafra is a haunted, troubled soul that like the sirens of old pulls one into a world from which it is hard to escape.

Local guides designate a small area of the desert between Qasr Farafra and the escarpment to the northeast as the White Desert, but in fact most of the desert floor beginning 8 kilometers (5 miles) northeast of Qasr has white outcroppings and the entire area could be called the White Desert.

Monoliths (inselbergs) of the White Desert

As beautiful as it is, the chalk can also create severe problems. Twenty kilometers (12.5 miles) NORTH-NORTHEAST of Qasr, the hard white chalk has been churned to powder by the elements and covers the ground to a depth of 30 to 50 centimeters. Heavy winds can lift the powder into the air creating a fog-like storm. Unlike sand, which settles quickly after the winds subside, the fine powder can hang in the air for days. When Beadnell was surveying here in the 1890s he encountered just such a storm. This powdery chalk penetrates some of the springs in the area and makes the water all but undrinkable.

The White Desert is a paradise for rock hounds and amateur geologists. The small quartz crystals scattered on the desert floor are used by Bedouin to help quench thirst in the dry, hot desert climate. The procedure is straightforward. Find a crystal and pop it into your mouth. It helps salivation and keeps the mouth moist.

There are hundreds of thousands of iron pyrites and marcasite in a variety of shapes

Iron pyrites

and sizes. Some are like broken twigs, others like starbursts, still others like turds. The black color is caused by a chemical change from sulfide to oxide. The desert floor also contains many fossils, including *Terebratulina*, casts of *Terebratula*, *Terebratella*, *Radiolites*, and *Spirorbis*.

The off-road driving can be precarious, but regular vehicles can travel a little of the way, while 4x4s and dirt bikes can cavort at will. For the less adventuresome this surreal forest is very close to the road and walking amid the strange monoliths is an experience not to be missed.

TOUR #3

Easy Access White Desert

- walking, 2x2
- 1–2 hrs
- easy

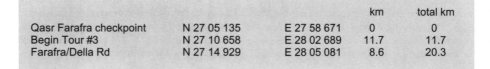

			km	total km
Qasr Farafra checkpoint	N 27 05 135	E 27 58 671	0	0
Begin Tour #3	N 27 10 658	E 28 02 689	11.7	11.7
Farafra/Della Rd	N 27 14 929	E 28 05 081	8.6	20.3

This area is good for walking or two-wheel driving. The formations are not only close to the road, but on both sides. Some are situated around the base of the mountain and taking photos in this area is great. The outcroppings run along the side of the road for 4 kilometers (2.5 miles).

Ten kilometers (8.1 miles) after leaving the checkpoint at Qasr Farafra the magnificent

white chalk sculptures begin to appear on the right-hand or south side of the road. Here is an entire cast from the Theatre of the Absurd. Some of the formations are surrealistic, others, locked into distinct shapes: sunbathers in sunglasses lifting their faces to the sun, squat Mexicans in broad brimmed hats, bull-fighters with their capes wrapped around their legs after a pass. The desert winds keep changing the sculptures, clipping a bit here and there, chipping away, eroding the ridges and creating newer, stranger shapes which lie beneath the surface of the stone.

TOUR #4

Inselbergs, Hummocks, and Monoliths of the White Desert

			km	total km
Farafra/Della rd	N 27 14 929	E 28 05 081	0	0
Inselbergs begin	N 27 16 976	E 28 06 345	5.7	5.7
Hummocks	N 27 18 023	E 28 06 947	2.2	7.9
Monoliths	N 27 21 260	E 28 09 314	1.1	9

After Tour #3 there is the military road to Ain Della (see below). Beyond the road on the left side of the Farafra road the entire panorama of inselbergs comes into view. This is easy going, safe, 4x4 travel. You cannot get lost if you keep the two roads in place and do not wander into the canyons of the escarpment. There is good camping here. Try to put your camp out of sight so others can enjoy the scenery without you in it.

Hummocks

Less than 20 kilometers (12.5 miles) beyond the beginning of the White Desert, the ground on the right side of the road turns to brown sand and is covered with hummocks, hills shaped by the small trees that sit on top of them. In the tree's quest for survival in this harsh environment its roots are forever searching for moisture. The hummock is the twisted root blended with tufts of grass and desert sands. Some are small with pathetic looking trees, others, especially after there has been plenty of moisture through heavy fogs, dews, or rare rains, are topped by miniature trees, much larger than, but reminiscent of, the bonsai trees of Japan.

Monoliths

A little over a kilometer after the hummocks, to the left side of the road, the inselbergs grow larger and more dramatic. Their white cliffs are almost vertical and they stretch high into the sky. They look like they could sink the Titanic.

This is a great place to walk among the giants. Within their canyons are a number of valleys that make excellent camping. In this area the ground is littered with the finest selection of black pyrites and, most amazing of all, embedded in the chalk cliffs are small, medium, and large seashells of all varieties. Look but don't touch.

TOUR #5

Quss Abu Said, al-Ubeida Playa, and Ain Della

			km	total km
Farafra/Della rd	N 27 14 929	E 28 05 081	0	0
Yardangs	N 27 16 102	E 28 04 286	2.8	2.8
Outlier hills	N 27 17 848	E 28 02 456	4.2	7
Al-Ubeida Playa	N 27 22 404	E 27 47 094	26.7	33.7
Infidel Rock?	N 27 18 145	E 27 37 785	17.3	51
Sphinx Valley	N 27 17 312	E 27 34 848	4.7	55.7
Ain Della Pass	N 27 18 855	E 27 25 810	15	70

You must have permission to visit these sites from the military authorities in Cairo. They may require one of their officers to accompany you. This is not a hardship as they can give you a lot of interesting information. DO NOT VISIT THESE SITES WITHOUT PERMISSION OR YOU WILL BE BREAKING THE LAW.

Although Ain Della is only 75 kilometers (46 miles) from Qasr Farafra via the old desert track, the new paved road covers 120 kilometers (74 miles). It is the only paved road leading northwest from the main road,

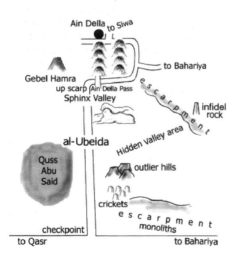

20 kilometers (12.5 miles) north of Qasr Farafra. Although the road is paved, it is often covered by a heavy blanket of sand and a 4x4 or dirt bike is recommended for this journey.

The road to Ain Della is a visual feast. Immediately after passing the military checkpoint the white chalk inselbergs that mark the northern escarpment come into view to the right and left of the road.

Yardangs

A wonderful set of symmetrical yardangs sits on the right looking like a small group of crickets, their heads just above the ground. There are also a few dunes toward the escarpment. Wonderful formations continue all the way to the escarpment.

Outlier Hills

Here is an excellent example of how the earth erodes. Notice the many hills in this area. They all have the same height and are all capped by a hard substance. Ground level was once the tops of the hills, but wind erosion over millions of years has broken down the loose earth and blown it away. Protected by a covering of hard rock, too hard for the wind to destroy so quickly, the hills remained behind. On the west rise the cliffs of Quss Abu Said Plateau, to the right the main Farafra escarpment.

Tertiary Period   erosion by wind and rain   present day

Erosion caused by wind and rain over millions of years

Quss Abu Said Plateau

Named by Cailliaud, the 250 meter (800 foot) scarp which forms the side of the plateau offers an excellent opportunity for geologists and amateurs to study the history of the earth's development. Starting from the top it consists of a 5 meter (16 foot) layer of white fossil-filled limestone (lower Eocene), followed by nummulite-filled greenish yellow limestone to 25 meters (80 feet), greenish marl with limestone and gypsum to 100 meters (320 feet), and green shale for the remaining 100 meters (320 feet).

The track up this scarp to the top of the plateau passes through a canyon of mainly limestone before finally climbing the scarp 20 kilometers (12.5 miles) north-northwest of Qasr. The walls of the high cliffs of the canyon contain many fossils, especially of large *nautili*. If you want to climb the cliffs, you must have a guide.

The Bahr Playa Basin is in the northern section of the Quss plateau and has been under study for nearly a decade. It was inhabited from the early Holocene and heavily populated in the mid-Holocene. There are plenty of sickle-knives, knives, and tranchets for working wood. Similar materials have been found at Qattara.

Al-Ubeida Playa

Discovered by the University of Rome Archaeological Expedition in the 1990s, this site is approximately 55 kilometers (34 miles) from Qasr Farafra. The archaeologists are hoping further study will help link Farafra to desert history and create a link through Farafra between the Sahara and the Nile Valley. There are several sites here:

A prehistoric village, dubbed **Hidden Valley** is surrounded by the white karstified chalks so evident in Farafra. There is evidence of Holocene and Pleistocene inhab-

itants who settled around the northern beaches of a small lake. The occupation was of some length and hearths, postholes, and lithic artifacts are plentiful.

The **Wadi al-Ubayyid Cave** is currently under study. So is its rock art. B. E. Barich in *The Wadi al-Obeiyid Cave, Farafra Oasis: A New Pictorial Complex in the Western Desert of Egypt*, tells us the drawings are engraved, but there are also painted hands. The hypothesis is that the art was done by two different groups: those who passed by and local people who did the animals. Located 50 meters (160 feet) above the valley floor about 2 kilometers (1.2 miles) north of Hidden Valley Village, the cave has three chambers. It is currently off limits to travelers.

Infidel Rock or Church of the Spirits of the Lost Persian Army

At 54 kilometers (33 miles) into the journey there is a large pillar on the right that sits atop the depression escarpment like a lonely sentinel. This could be the rock referred to as Infidel Rock or the Church of the Spirits of the Lost Persian Army on nineteenth-century maps and texts. The first name is in reference to the fact that the rock is reputed to sing on Sunday (that day being the 'infidels'' holy day). The second name is an obvious reference to Cambyses' missing army and lends credence to the theory than the army is buried somewhere nearby. (See above for details.)

Hagg Zaki, a ninety-four-year old elder of Qasr Farafra, remembers many people coming to the village and asking about this rock, which he calls Kafir Port Said, Infidel of Port Said. This may seem a strange name for a rock formation in the Western Desert hundreds of kilometers from Port Said on the Suez Canal, but if one looks closely at the rock through binoculars it is obvious that it looks like a lighthouse. This author has unearthed no evidence to support the theory that this is in fact Infidel Rock, and no one in Bahariya or Farafra seems familiar with such a name, but it is a possibility.

Sphinx Valley

The formations along the escarpment and on either side of the road are wonderful here, so reminiscent of the sphinx that they are probably what it looked like before anyone thought of carving a face on it.

At the base of the escarpment, 59 kilometers (37 miles) from the checkpoint, stands **Gebel Hamra**, Red Mountain (also known as Guma Sukkar), which is the guardian of the pass out of Farafra Depression. The ascent is smooth and fast, as the road is paved. Once atop the plateau the terrain is flat and uninteresting. It is a short distance, less than 15 kilometers (9.3 miles), across the top before coming to the descent into the Ain Della Depression.

Ain Della Pass

After traveling over the top of the plateau, one comes to Ain Della Pass. At the top of the pass the entire Ain Della depression is laid out and Ain Della, almost straight ahead, is visible beyond the dunes. The road does not pass in a direct line to Ain Della, but skirts the dunes to the right. Twelve kilometers (7.5 miles) along the depression floor at a bend in the road, the dirt track that exited Bahariya Oasis at Ain al-Izza joins the main road. Directly in front of Ain Della, the road is joined by the dirt track from Siwa Oasis. Twenty-three kilometers (14.3 miles) from the top of the escarpment, one climbs the small hill of Ain Della.

Jennings-Bramley was heading into the unknown when he left Farafra and, true to travelers in the interior of the desert at that time, he headed one way to deceive the inhabitants of Farafra and once out of sight headed in another direction. He tells us he left January 10, 1898, with "two camels, his servant, and a very useless guide named Murzuk." He was looking for Nesla as it was marked on Rohlfs' map. His useless servant told him Dal was the real name for Nesla. Of course, he was headed for Ain Della which he found exactly where his useless servant said it would be.

Restricted Area

Ain Della is off limits to travelers who do not have proper military permission. The military installation has been placed here to look for smugglers, so every vehicle coming into the area is under surveillance and suspect from the time they reach the top of the pass. (See Practical Information about acquiring permission.)

Ain Della

Ain Della, Spring of the Shade, has always been a strategic location for travelers in the Western Desert. Located less than 200 kilometers (120 miles) from three of the major oases (Siwa, Bahariya, and Farafra), the same distance from Kufra Oasis in Libya, and at the edge of the Great Sand Sea, its position makes it a vital desert outpost. Ain Della is surrounded on the north and east by cliffs and to the south and west by dunes. The major mountain in the area is Gebel Sufra, Table Mountain. There is a second cave, also called Ubayyid, in the hinterland.

Such a strategic spring must have had a major part in desert travel throughout history. One can only guess at the number of people whose lives were spared because of the water at Ain Della. As a further dividend, the water is clear and pleasant to drink, not discolored or brackish at all.

In modern times Ain Della played a significant role in helping Libyan citizens during the Italian colonization of their country. Arms and men went west, while Libyan immigrants came east. Prince Omar Toussoon, the Egyptian explorer (see People for details), provided provisions and improved the wells at Ain Della in an effort to help the Libyans who passed in either direction. Ahmed Fakhry tells us that in 1939, when he went to Ain Della, he found Prince Toussoon's wooden kiosk, twenty tins of petrol, digging tools, and baskets.

The Long Range Desert Group of the British Army used Ain Della as a major storage area and a jump off place for infiltrating behind the desert lines of the Italians and Germans during World War II. They also traveled to Kufra via Big Cairn. In *Long Range Desert Group*, W. B. Kennedy Shaw claims, "Easy Ascent Dump [marked such by P. A. Clayton, but in fact not so easy] was used till April, 1941, whenever patrols went across the Sand Sea, [and] according to the Dump Book there are still 1,200 gallons of petrol there for any one who cares to collect them."

Ain Della's location made it a major port of call for all sorts of people, including hashish smugglers. Once borders were established in the desert, smuggling became a major problem. The pharaohs were plagued by it, the Romans sent legions into the desert to capture the culprits, the modern Italians, desperate to keep gun runners from aiding the Libyan patriots, built a barbed-wire fence from the Mediterranean Sea to Kufra Oasis, and the British established a very effective frontier administration to keep smuggling under control.

In 1907, a five-hundred-man Coastguard Camel Corps existed in all towns with customs houses. Consisting mainly of Sudanese, the coastguard had a mandate to prevent smuggling, especially of hashish and salt, maintain security in the deserts, and prevent the illicit landing of pilgrims on the Red Sea Coast. In the Western Desert they had headquarters at Abu Sir, Amriya, and Sidi Abd al-Rahman, and controlled all of the desert region by regular patrols. Great chases took place in the desert. Once the soldiers tracked a caravan of hashish smuggled by the Beni Amar over 402 kilometers (250 miles), ending at the Giza Pyramids where they confiscated two thirds of the contraband.

The smugglers were very clever. They hid the goods in the false tops of tarbushes, hollowed out walking canes, and when near water, dropped the goods overboard weighted down with salt. As the salt melted the package rose to the surface and was picked up.

Just as it is today, hashish smuggling was a big problem in the Western Desert during the British occupation. The illegal contraband was brought in from Greece on the yacht *Basiliki* at every new moon and conveyed through the desert by camel. Caravans, on their way to the Nile Valley from the Mediterranean coast, would go as far south as Farafra and Dakhla to avoid

capture. Hashish was taped to the long hairs of the camel, or placed in zinc cylinders which the camels would swallow.

Although Greeks and Lebanese where very much involved in hashish smuggling, one of the most colorful hashish czars of modern times was Abdel Ati al-Hassuna (al-Maghrabi) of Algeria. Educated in France, he was considered handsome and vain and in the end this was his undoing. Sly as a fox, Abdel Ati enjoyed the game of smuggling more than the money; he equipped his men with the latest rifles, the best camels, and gave them good pay.

And the Coastguard enjoyed chasing him. It was cat and mouse in the sands of the Western Desert. Coastguard troops under the control of the British had a shoot-out at Ain Della with one of Abdel Ati's hashish caravans. One day while exploring the Great Sand Sea around Ain Della for tracks, nothing was found except a small broken mirror which the men of the Camel Corps attributed to the vain Abdel Ati. The trackers, wading knee-deep in sand, continued investigating until they uncovered a formerly unknown smuggling route.

Time finally ran out for Abdel Ati along a lonely desert track south of Siwa, which is still called Darb Abdel Ati. The colorful criminal was killed by the Coastguard Camel Corps. He was buried on the spot and in 1920, C. Dalrymple Belgrave maintained his grave could still be distinguished, marked by rough stone cairns. Hagg Zaki tells a story that the history books do not know. After his death, Abdel Ati's brother went to his grave, cut off his finger, and took his ring.

André von Dumreicher, head of the coastguard patrol in the Western Desert under the British administration, records the activities of another famous hashish smuggler, Abu Bakr. He was so crafty that one time he came to the patrol and told them he knew of a caravan of hashish coming via Mersa Matruh, agreeing to lead the patrol to the spot. When the patrol got there, Abu Bakr went into the desert to spy. He never returned. It seems the caravan was his, and he kept the patrol busy on a wild goose chase so the caravan could have free passage. Swearing that he would capture Abu Bakr, Dumreicher found himself in the Fayoum. At his hotel the room to one side was occupied by Abu Bakr, the room on the other side by Fereig, another smuggler. Dumreicher tried to get Fereig to spy on Abu Bakr for him, only to discover Abu Bakr was Fereig's uncle.

Once the salt monopoly was introduced by the British government in Egypt and a duty was declared on tobacco, these items became prime commodities for the smugglers. The salt monopoly was difficult for the poor people. In Wadi Natrun the Bedouin who had lived there for centuries were suddenly forbidden to take one pinch of the salt that had always been theirs. The same was true on the fringe of the desert all along the Nile. Villagers were persecuted with a vengeance by the patrols, who were paid with the money collected as fines. They were merciless. Illicit salt caravans came over the Darb al-Arbain from Bir al-Sultan in Sudan until the coast-guard set up troops at a vital well and put a stop to smuggling along this route. Smugglers also came from the interior of the Western Desert. It became so bad that one day while Dumreicher was at a train station in Asyut he saw many peasants carrying illegal salt. Trying to avoid the issue, Dumreicher turned away, only to be thumped so soundly by a sack of salt that he fell from his mount into the mud. When the man was brought before him he came leading his parents and said, "Praise be the Lord, the four eyes of my parents are blind, my left eye is blind, and the sight of my right eye is nearly lost. By the glimmer of that right eye I must provide the daily bread for my whole family. If I do not steal salt, how can my family eat?" Dumreicher gave him a few shillings and freed him.

Today the Egyptian army maintains a desert patrol at Ain Della and their duties are the same as those in the past, controlling smuggling through the Western Desert via this strategic waterhole. Patrols roam 160 kilometers (100 miles) into the Great Sand Sea on four-day excursions, then they are off for three days

The sweet water spring is the reason why this site is so important. Situated atop a mound of its debris, it was once shaded by several palm trees and a wooden hut. When the source is clear, as it is today, water flows at three to four gallons a minute. In Roman times the spring was lined by a stone shaft and, in this century, Prince Omar Toussoon cleared it, ran a pipe into it, and covered it all with a roof. In 1946, it also received attention. Today the well has been newly fortified. The clear water from the spring has been channeled, via a clever system of rubber hoses, to the barracks for showers. The soldiers maintain that if one stands on a particular spot near the spring the water level in the well rises.

Fakhry reports that there are several antiquities at Ain Della including two ancient houses, probably from Roman times, but a quick investigation found no traces of them today. They may well be buried under the sands surrounding the spring.

TOUR #6

Mushrooms, Acacia, and Ain Hadra

- walking, 2x2, 4x4
- 1–5 hours
- easy to difficult

			km	total km
Bir Regwa	N 27 20 797	E 28 08 804	0	0
Mushrooms	N 27 20 546	E 28 09 934	2.5	2.5
Tent	N 27 20 842	E 28 10 326	1.7	4.2
Track/2nd tent	N 27 20 487	E 28 11 361	1.9	6.1
Acacia	N 27 21 272	E 28 12 387	3.2	9.3
Ain Hadra	N 27 22 269	E 28 13 213	c2	11.3

The first part of this tour is the trip the desert guides routinely give as the White Desert Safari. There is something for everyone on this desert trip: walking, 2x2, and 4x4. You can make it a short excursion, stopping in the mushroom area, or a longer one, stopping at Ain Hadra, or go for broke and travel over the very rough terrain to reach the spectacular Ain al-Wadi and sugarloaves of Tour #7. You can spend an hour, a day, or camp overnight. You can always return the way you came. Remember the paved road is just below the escarpment on the northwest.

The tour begins 33 kilometers (20 miles) from Qasr Farafra at Bir Regwa.

Bir Regwa

Also known as al-Bir al-Akbar, the great well, it sits at the right side of the road. It is now a landmark, for just beyond, over the tiny rise, is a track leading southeast into the desert between a large array of white sculptures.

Mushrooms

There are hundreds of images here, each one reminiscent of an animal, a sphinx, camels, tents, and even a huge whale. For a good view of the area be sure to climb to the top of the white chalk hill, called the tent. You can walk this area or use a regular vehicle. If you look to the left from atop the white hill you

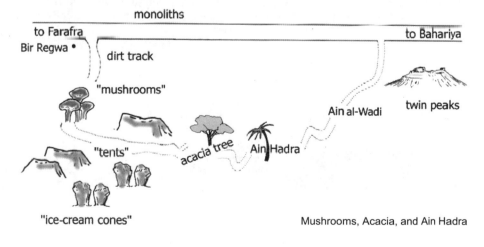

Mushrooms, Acacia, and Ain Hadra

will see the acacia tree and Ain Hadra. To visit them, a 4x4 is recommended.

Just in front of the tent, bear left.

Track and Second Tent

This is a very pretty area and the track is well defined as it passes to the right of another large, tent-like white rock. To the left are dozens and dozens of small white outcroppings looking like ice cream cones.

Acacia (Wadi Sunt)

You will soon see the acacia tree ahead of you. It sits atop a small hill. Try to find and stay on the tracks as this is very rough going. The slabs are killing to your tires. This acacia, in bloom in November–December, twists and turns and spreads out like an umbrella and the shade under its magnificent canopy is a welcome haven. Unfortunately, while building a fire one evening one of the guides set the tree on fire and it is half of what it once was. Fortunately, it was not completely destroyed. The track serpentines around the acacia and comes up from behind. You can climb to the top of the hill with your 4x4 and enjoy the view.

Ain Hadra is visible a very short distance beyond Wadi Sunt to the northeast. This is more rough crossing. Follow the tracks if you can find them for they offer the easier route.

Ain Hadra

Ain Hadra is recognized by a single palm tree jutting out from atop a hill of green fronds on a small knoll. It is the highest point in the area. The source of the spring is found around the southern side of the hill within the dense vegetation. There is a bucket with which to draw the sweet water and a palm trunk blocks the spring so people will not fall in as they gather water. At the base of the spring is a watering trough for the animals.

The ground is littered with shards from ancient travelers, everything from rough oasis ware to Roman and Coptic pieces. Facing the trough, the hill to the right holds tombs and a broken coffin is still in situ.

This is a small but vital source on the Darb al-Bahariya, 45 kilometers (28 miles) from Farafra. As has been noted earlier, the Darb al-Bahariya journeys from Farafra to Cairo via Bahariya. When one passed from Bahariya to Farafra it was called the Darb al-Farafra. It is not the macadamized road, but runs about 30 kilometers to the south of the road along the top of the plateau and descends the escarpment well to the south of the sugarloaves. From Ain Hadra it is one day's journey to Qasr Farafra by camel.

This darb, which you have been following more or less for the last few kilometers, sometimes becomes very obvious as it turns into a graded track. From here it goes on to Wadi Hinnis where caravans would pause for the second day. Then it climbs the escarpment in the area called Aqabat and heads for Bahariya. If one looks northwest one can see the radio tower atop the escarpment where the main road crosses. It is a good landmark. Keep it ahead and to the left, more or less.

Do not plan to camp here, especially in summer. There are mosquitoes and, more dangerous, a lot of horned vipers. They usually sleep in winter, but if disturbed will wake up.

You can return the way you came or continue with Tour #7.

Ain Hadra

TOUR #7

Ain al-Wadi, Wadi Hinnis, and Twin Peaks

- **4x4**
- **difficult**

			km	total km
Ain al-Wadi (at rd)	N 27 24 506	E 28 10 821	0	0
Ain al-Wadi	N 27 23 415	E 28 13 799	c3.3	15.3
Wadi Hinnis	N 27 23 415	E 28 13 799	on route	
Twin Peaks	N 27 25 279	E 28 14 678	c4.7	19.3
Paved rd and Naqb	N 27 29 133	E 28 14 501	c7.14	26.3

Just after Ain Hadra, the track to Ain al-Wadi begins to the west-northwest. The track appears immediately. At the first fork bear right and within a few meters bear right again at a second fork. Follow the car tracks as much as possible for the terrain is rough once again.

To enter from the main road and begin a new tour: The watermelon road to Ain al-Wadi begins at the asphalt road 20 kilometers (12.5 miles) from the Ain Della Road. Follow it to the wadi.

Ain al-Wadi

Ain al-Wadi sits in a small depression by the same name 12 to 13 meters (38 to 41 feet) deep and 8 kilometers (5 miles) long. Within this area are the oldest exposed beds (Danian) in the entire depression of Farafra which, according to Ball, can only be seen at this point. There is no track and one travels, as before, amid outcroppings and rough terrain before suddenly coming to the depression of the Wadi. Along the western edge is Witaq Abu Tartur, a miniature scarp, which holds the remains of a Roman house. The wadi itself is exquisite and well worth the hard work it takes to get there. The sand is golden and small shrubs and palms dot the wadi floor. It is in such contrast to the rest of the area that some geographers have designated it as an entirely separate depression.

They are growing watermelons in Ain al-Wadi at the present time. The project will eventually cover 150 feddans. Some residents of Farafra and a few desert drivers are upset that this wadi is being occupied. Some predict the project will fail. It could be worse. Someone could buy the land and build a factory that belches smoke and pollution. Watermelons are still agricultural and will return to the earth if left untended, with little

Twin Peaks

harm done. Besides, they look like they belong there. The straw is even the same color as the sand.

Wadi Hinnis and Twin Peaks

Between Ain al-Wadi and Aqabat (the sugarloaves and Twin Peaks at the escarpment) is the Wadi Hinnis, Valley of John. The Bedouin say no dog barks or person speaks in this desolate place. It is soft like the Ain al-Wadi, broken only by an occasional sand dune and contains numerous rock-covered, heavy going areas. Again, try to follow the tracks, they mark the easier routes. The closer you can get to the sugarloaves in front of you without getting into the dunes at their base the better. First head for the sugarloaves, then turn west keeping the sugarloaves and Twin Peaks to your right, and head for the northwestern escarpment. Eventually you will find the track left by travelers before you. The paved road is directly in front and running parallel to it. If you panic, remember to find the communications tower at the top of the escarpment. It marks the road on the plateau above.

TOUR #8

Qarawein

- 4x4
- 4–5 hours
- difficult

			km	total km
Farafra	N 27 03 600	E 27 58 392	0	0
First aid station	N 27 02 137	E 28 25 518	46	46
Bir Qarawein	N 27 06 383	E 28 33 956	30	76
Plantations	N 27 07 036	E 28 31 556	5	81
Bir at dunes	N 27 11 740	E 28 28 960	8.8	89.8
Sand dunes	N 27 18 705	E 28 25 377	14.2	104
Sugarloaves	N 27 25 365	E 28 14 678	en route	
Paved road	N 27 29 133	E 28 14 501	30	134

To be safe, it is wise to begin this tour along the paved road leading to Qarawein and the watermelon plantations and then go off road to the northwest, keeping one escarpment to your right and heading for the second escarpment and the paved road. If you reverse it and miss Qarawein you are headed into the deep desert.

This is the most difficult off-road journey in Farafra. Lots of loose sand. Toward the end of the journey you will be at Aqabat and face the limestone slabs once again. They will reduce your speed to zero and your tires to ribbons. You could walk the end of this journey faster than drive it. **Take a local guide.**

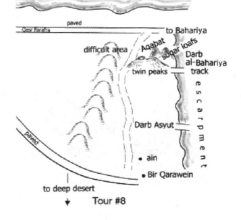

Tour #8

They know a lot of interesting stories about their desert.

The paved road to Qarawein begins at Qasr Farafra across from the White Desert Restaurant. It continues 62 kilometers (39 miles) to the worker's village at Qarawein. At Qarawein, turn north into the desert.

Qarawein

A new agricultural project is well underway at Qarawein. The first well has been drilled, the first road has been paved, the first watermelon patches are in place, and all that remains is for the entire 35,000 feddans to fall under cultivation.

The area is so unpolluted and untouched that not everyone is happy it is being developed. It was a true wilderness and few people had journeyed to it. Now it will become a community and absorb all the debris that accompanies people wherever they go.

Bir Qarawein

The ancient *bir* that made this place a stop for caravans on the Darb Asyut will soon become insignificant as well after well is drilled in the area. Rohlfs found Qarawein a very unpleasant place, full of mosquitoes. But it is beautiful here. There is no resemblance to the White Desert. Everything here is a delicate beige, both sand sheets and dunes. Bir Qarawein is about 600 meters (21,153 feet) to the NW of the waypoint reading above.

Bir Murr

Bir Murr was covered over when Rohlfs was there. As its name implies, its water is bitter. Rohlfs saw many nummalites in the area and some of the hills around the sand dunes are made almost entirely of rubble and nummalites. There is another well by the same name along the Darb al-Arbain, just south of Kharga Oasis.

Darb Asyut

Just beyond Bir Murr, the Darb Asyut, called Asyuti by the oaseans, climbs down into the oases. The Naqb leading down from Darb Asyut to Farafra is called **Naqb al-Faruj**, Pass of the Chicken (*faruj* is oasian slang for chicken), and is 12 kilometers (7.5 miles)

from Bir Qarawein. Rohlfs found it a difficult pass, very broken, and with plenty of dead camels to testify to its terrors.

Our friend Hagg Zaki began working the caravan routes when he was thirteen years old and stopped when he was eighty-two. Now in his nineties, he recalls how difficult things were. He would head for Asyut with dates, olives, and apricots along the Darb Asyut. It would take two weeks and he would come back with flour, tea, and sugar. (For more information on the Darb Asyut see Caravans and Roadways above.)

Rohlfs traveled the Darb Asyut on his way to Farafra and discovered the **Gara Cave**, which he called Djara. He marked it on his map and describes it in his book as a "wonderful stalactite cave." He was impressed with the clarity of the stalactites, which are mostly pure white. It was Christmas Day 1873. Rohlfs believed there were other caves in the area, but they were full of sand. It was rediscovered by Carlo Bergmann in 1991. Bergmann has traveled a good part of the Western Desert looking for its old darbs.

The cave begins as a fissure in the ground. It is entered by climbing down and then through a very narrow corridor. It has one large room and two small ones. There is a crack in the floor and one must be careful to avoid the snakes and scorpions that surely live there. There are two major problems: the crack is growing so the floor will probably collapse in the not-too-distant future, and the Ghard Abu Muharrik blocks the way to the cave from the west.

It is foolish to attempt to visit this cave without proper preparation and a local guide. If you want to go, ask for a guide in Farafra and get permission from the military authorities in Cairo. They know the way. Remember a major dune belt stands in your way.

North to Aqabat

Now the trek begins. It is about 35 to 40 kilometers (22 to 25 miles) to the paved road. As long as you keep the sand dunes to your left and the escarpment to your right you cannot get lost. Enjoy this wonderful off-road drive. It is exceptional.

Sand Dunes

These dunes reportedly run all the way to Dakhla. What is so special about them is that every so often a tree is growing up out of the sand. There are probably more of them hidden underneath, whole groves, inundated by the ever-marauding dunes.

Aqabat

Aqabat, the 'difficult,' is the name given to the area where the outlier sugarloaves and Twin Peaks stand near the pass out of Farafra. Here, too, one can surf the sand and weave in and out of the sugarloaves. Be careful, it is easy to get disoriented. The paved road is less than a kilometer from the last of the sugarloaves.

Additional Tours with local guides

1. Ain Sirwal

N 27 22 194 E 28 20 838.
Ain Sirwal is very similar to Ain Hadra.

2. Ain Abu Hawas (Makfy)

N 37 27 931 E 28 20 920
Named after a family that once lived here, Ain Abu Hawas is a perfect place to camp as there are no snakes and so few mosquitoes in winter one can almost say there are none. There are a number of palm trees in the area, but the spring is the largest grouping. Someone has pruned the fronds so that a nice sandy cave exists where one can spread blankets. There are stones in place for fires, and someone always seems to leave a little wood behind in case you have not gathered enough.

Look around you. All the small outlier mountains are the same size and they all are flat topped. This is the perfect example of how the earth breaks down and erodes. The surface here was once at the tops of these mountains. The wind, one cannot say water erosion in the Libyan Desert, eroded the loose earth, leaving only what you see today. These will erode further over the centuries until only small pillars, yardangs, and mushrooms remain.

3. Darb al-Farafra

Farafra to Bab al-Qasmund
The Darb al-Farafra is the old caravan route to Dakhla Oasis used by traders and explorers since antiquity. It is much shorter than the circular road via Abu Minqar, but it is unpaved.

Despite the massive influx of vehicles during the Pharaoh's Rally, the difficulty of the terrain, the lack of good markers, and the remoteness of the area indicate that a journey along the Darb al-Farafra must be approached with extreme caution. At least two 4x4 vehicles in excellent condition and carrying plenty of spare parts should undertake this journey. And under no circumstances should the trip be undertaken without an experienced guide or the permission of the military authorities in Farafra or Dakhla.

The route begins easily enough at the second turn south from the main road after the restaurant in Qasr. It continues uninterrupted through the desert with a few landmarks to guide the way: at 9 kilometers (5.6 miles) is a dry well to the southeast called Ain Mufaddal where an ancient underground aqueduct called a *jub* exists; at 17 kilometers (10 miles) Gebel Gunna comes into view on the right; at 24 kilometers (15 miles) is the sanded up well of Senayyat. It isn't until reaching 32 kilometers (20 miles) that one enters the sandy area that continues for most of the distance to Qasr Dakhla. This is the largest dune field in the depression and 55 meter (176 foot) high dunes lie to either side of the road.

Bir Dikker

Located amid the dunes, 34 kilometers from Qasr Farafra, is Bir Dikker, which is marked by two palms and the skeleton of a camel. This skeleton, reminiscent of the mummified cow that once stood along the Darb Abu Minqar, serves as a reminder of the dangers of this route. Rohlfs found the water here sweet. He also found plenty of fossil casts in this area, some in greenish clays and others along the surface of the road. Ph, his photographer, lost 200 of his glass plates here when one of the camels slipped.

Black Valley

The Black Valley is the name of an area that begins 96 kilometers (60 miles) outside Qasr Farafra. Surrounded by high yellow dunes, which form a corridor 1.5 kilometers (0.5 miles) wide, the Black Valley extends for over 43 kilometers (27 miles). It gets the name Black Valley because the ground is covered by millions and billions of tiny black stones, mostly pyrite, in a variety of wonderful shapes that turn the terrain completely black. However, if one digs just below the surface, white powdered sand forms the base of the roadway. Both the pyrites and the white powder are tough on any vehicle.

Marble Labyrinth

The Black Valley is followed by the Marble Labyrinth, a maze of limestone rocks and sandsheets, located 150 kilometers (93 miles) outside Qasr Farafra. Nearly impenetrable, the sharp stones cut tires and do not allow for a straight route, but a twisting and turning one through soft sand.

Bab al-Qasmund

Finally, after covering 173 kilometers (117 miles), one descends the desert plateau through Bab al-Qasmund into Dakhla Oasis. The Bab was named by Gerhard Rohlfs who passed this way in 1874. It is named in honor of the German consul to Egypt Dr. von Jasmund, who arranged with the Khedive Ismail to provide Rohlfs with 4000 Egyptian pounds to mount his expedition. Rohlfs wrote the name in Arabic and Roman letters on the eastern wall of the pass. It takes several kilometers to reach the depression floor and along the route is a series of unusual sand dunes. The next pass Rohlfs named **Bab al-Cailliaud** in honor of the man who had passed this way before him.

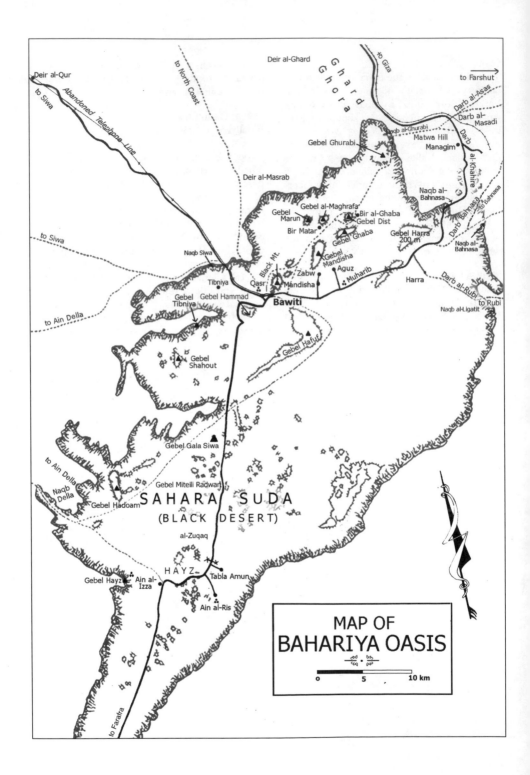

MAP OF
BAHARIYA OASIS

0   5   10 km

6

Bahariya

From Cairo to Bahariya

			km	total km
Alexandria/Fayoum rd	N 29 59 398	E 31 07 735	0	0
Fayoum–Bahariya rd	N 29 56 865	E 31 05 960	5	5
Halfway rest	N 29 24 948	E 29 43 496	155	160
Managim checkpoint	N 28 29 752	E 29 09 711	150	310
Bawiti arch	N 28 20 936	E 28 53 257	40	350

The journey to Bahariya begins at the Giza Pyramids. Take the Cairo Alexandria desert road a short distance to the first intersection and turn left onto the Fayoum road. Continue along this road, which soon climbs out of the Nile Valley to the desert plateau. A few kilometers later, almost at the top of the plateau turn right onto the dual carriageway. The sign says Wahat (oases). Bahariya is 350 kilometers (219 miles) ahead.

Twenty-two kilometers (14 miles) from the beginning of the road, the railway from Helwan joins the road and follows it all the way to Managim, just above the Bahariya depression. After 68 kilometers (41 miles) there is a small depot and railroad maintenance station, one of several to be found along the route. There is a second after 113 kilometers (70 miles).

Midway in the journey at 155 kilometers (97 miles) is a rest stop with a gas station and a cafeteria. The toilets are modest and the only foods available are biscuits and candy. The resthouse is half way to the oasis, but Bawiti, normally the end of the journey, is an additional 40 kilometers (25 miles) into the depression. The halfway rest stop has a gas station, but it is often out of gas.

At 185.5 kilometers (116 miles) the paved desert road from **al-Alamein** on the northern coast cuts into the Bahariya road. It is marked by a bevy of signs announcing the petroleum companies that are located along its route.

Then the **al-Bahr** depression is reached. It is the first breakdown of the land and exposes Middle and Upper Eocene rocks sometimes capped by dark Oligocene grits and sandstones. Unfortunately, the pastel of the desert is marred by the tar, barrels, and debris left behind by the road builders.

At 257 and 277 kilometers (169 and 173 miles), very near to the right side of the road, are two large hills filled with sea fossils and shells. Both present good places to stop and stretch. All along the perimeter can be found nummulites, brown-colored fossils the size and shape of fifty-cent pieces. There is a third (and probably a fourth and a fifth) hill at the side of the road just under 30 kilometers (19 miles) later. It is directly beside a high-tension-wire tower and the hum is very strong.

Managim

At 310 kilometers (193 miles) stands the checkpoint marking the beginning of the community of Managim. This is the major checkpoint into the oasis. The guard will write down the car license number and may ask to see passports and car papers. He will want to know your destination.

Managim, which begins through an avenue of oleander, is a mere 9 kilometers (5.6 miles) northeast of the escarpment. As its name implies, it is a mining town, erected for workers at the nearby iron ore quarries. Although there is nothing of note in the town, provisions such as freshly baked Shami bread can be purchased in the stores. Ten percent of the population of this oasis live in this town.

The mines themselves are another matter. They are the main source of iron ore for Egypt and the railway that transports the ore back to the Nile Valley runs through the desert and directly across the Nile to the steel mill at Helwan. The main entrance to the mines is located beyond the town where the road forks. The right-hand fork continues to Bawiti and the left-hand fork is the entrance to the mines. There is a small museum in the administrative building.

The importance of the mineral wealth of Bahariya was first mentioned by Frederic Cailliaud, a Frenchman who came to Egypt at the request of Muhammad Ali, to modernize and industrialize the country. By 1956, a ministry of industry was established and in 1960, the Geological Survey was working in Bahariya looking for the iron ore beds. The iron ore comes from middle Eocene limestone and is located in four major deposits, all here, just north of Bahariya Oasis. The four deposits are called al-Gedida, Ghurabi, Nasser, and al-Hara and they collectively extend over 11 kilometers (9 miles). They possess four different types of ore: hard, friable, banded-cavemous, and pisolitic. A combination of all four is delivered to the steel mills in Helwan.

The best of them is the al-Gedida deposits. Not only is the quality good, but the bed is the largest. At a rate of consumption of 3,178,000 tons a year, Gedida is expected to supply raw materials for the Helwan steel mills until the year 2010. The industrial site for preparing the ore can do 1,108 tons an hour. Loading on the rail is accomplished by three excavators.

The railway links the iron ore deposits with the Nile Valley. It is a company railroad and no coaches are used, so it is of no use to tourists. It was preceded by the Bahariya Military Railway constructed by the British during World War I. The earlier route began at Bahnasa, along the Bahr Yusif in the Fayoum, moved through Shusha Camp, a British Military facility, and ended at a place in the desert called B6, just before the great dune belt, the Ghard Abu Muharrik. Camels were used to cross the dunes. One more camp stood atop the escarpment above Hara.

When there is no gasoline in Bawiti, which is rare these days, it can sometimes be obtained at the Managim mines. (See Practical Information.)

Conical Hills N 28 25 648 E 29 09 253
Beyond Managim, the main road continues to Bawiti. At 316 kilometers (197 miles) the terrain changes once again as small conical hills begin to emerge.

Descent to Bahariya N 28 23 746 E 29 06 976
At 323.6 kilometers (202 miles) the drop through the escarpment to Bahariya Oasis begins. Expectation runs high as one approaches these descents, and the reward is worth the effort. As the car slowly descends (there is no reason to speed through such a moment) the entire oasis comes into view. The best time to descend the pass is morning, when the light is behind you.

Bahariya

Bahariya is the closest oasis to Cairo in kilometers, but the most distant oasis in time. Although Siwa remained closed to the outside world until the last decade, its modernization has been rapid. Kharga and Dakhla, the major oases in the New Valley Governorate, have grown and expanded at an equally amazing rate. Farafra is exploding. But Bahariya Oasis, part of the highly populated Giza Governorate, has been slow to move into the modern world. Of course, for the traveler in search of the past this is wonderful; for the people of Bahariya it must be very frustrating.

History

Like all the other oases, Bahariya has had many names through the centuries: Northern Oasis, the Little Oasis, Zeszes, Oasis Parva, and the Oasis of al-Bahnasa. It has plenty of ancient sites to illustrate its importance in antiquity. Unfortunately, these ruins have yielded little information as too few of them are being excavated. No foreign mission operates in Bahariya. Local antiquities inspectors move at a very slow pace. The only comprehensive study of the antiquities of Bahariya was carried out by Ahmed Fakhry, the twentieth-century Egyptologist, who did extensive work in the Western Desert over sixty years ago. Fakhry published a number of books related to these excavations and most of the factual material known today was first presented in Fakhry's works.

Middle (c. 2040–1782 B.C.) and New Kingdoms (c. 1570–1070 B.C.)

We know practically nothing about life in Bahariya before the Middle Kingdom. If early peoples lived and hunted amid the mountains of this oasis the evidence is still hidden in the cliffs and hills. If the pharaohs of the Old Kingdom, ruling from what is modern-day Giza, had governors in this oasis as they did in Dakhla, we have yet to discover the evidence. In short, the early history of Bahariya is unknown.

In the Middle Kingdom, Bahariya, known as Zeszes, was under the control of the pharaohs. Caravans between Bahariya and the Nile Valley were common. Donkeys (the camel was not introduced to Egypt until the Roman period) laden with goods, especially Bahariya wine, made their way regularly to the Nile Valley and its awaiting populace. Just as today, agriculture was of major importance in Bahariya during the Middle Kingdom and if there was agriculture there must have been large estates, houses for the landowners and laborers, military garrisons to keep marauders at bay, and all the services required to keep such establishments functioning.

Under Thutmoses III, the great warrior pharaoh of the Eighteenth Dynasty of the New Kingdom, Bahariya was under the control of Thinis (Abydos), to which it paid tribute and from which it received government services. According to Fakhry, Thutmoses controlled all of the oases and brought about many changes. It was a time of great improvements with agriculture increasing, new wells being dug, and a rise in the population. Tomb scenes in the Nile Valley depict tribute being paid to the governor by people from the Northern Oasis. The most interesting scene related to Bahariya is in the tomb of Rekhmire, Thutmose III's vizier. Here the people of the oasis, shock-headed and wearing striped kilts, are shown presenting gifts of mats, hides, and wine. By the Nineteenth and Twentieth Dynasties the mineral wealth of Bahariya was receiving attention in the Nile Valley. Such is the abundance of iron ore that it supports a still vital industry today.

Third Intermediate (c. 1069–525 B.C.) and Late Periods (525–404 B.C.)

It was in the later dynasties that Bahariya emerged as a major center in ancient Egypt and evidence for its importance exists in the antiquities found throughout the oasis. By the Twenty-sixth Dynasty, Libyans sat on the throne of Egypt and the expanse of desert that separated the Nile Valley from the Libyan homeland became a main artery of trade and traffic. Bahariya, situated in the center of this route, flourished. Fakhry believes the Libyans first captured Farafra and Bahariya, then used them as a base to conquer the rest of Egypt.

Shoshenq I, the founder of the Twenty-second Dynasty (c. 950 B.C.), took a keen interest in Bahariya when he came to the throne. His successor, Shoshenq IV, continued to develop the area and ordered that government officials were to live there. By the Twenty-sixth Dynasty, Bahariya had grown into an important agricultural and trade center with its own governors, natives of the oasis, who reported to the Libyan rulers on the throne of Egypt. The majority of ancient monuments found in Bahariya date from the Twenty-sixth Dynasty.

Roman (30 B.C.–A.D. 323) and Christian (323–642) Periods

Although prosperous, Roman times were not secure. Rule was harsh. The deserts were unsafe. Bedouin and marauders roamed and terrorized villages. Overproduction was turning once cultivated land into desert. Yet despite these problems Roman rule resulted in a number of improvements, most impressive of which is the system of aqueducts and wells, several of which, in Bawiti and Izza, are still in use today. But such is the uncertainty of this period that even these have been questioned as actually being Roman and may date from an earlier time.

However, there can be no doubting the importance of Bahariya in Roman times, when many tombs, especially those cut into the sides of the mountains, were constructed. We are sure that Roman soldiers moved between Bahariya and Oxyrhynchus in the Nile Valley. In 213, the Apriana Alae was stationed at the "Small Oasis" collecting grain. That there was heavy occupation in the northern part of the oasis to the east of Bawiti is certain, and the ruins of a major Roman city await the excavator.

By the Christian era Bahariya had a new name, the Oasis of al-Bahnasa. Enough Christians lived there for it to have its own Bishop and, according to Coptic tradition, Bahariya is where the martyrdom of St. Bartholomew took place. One of the original twelve apostles of Jesus Christ, Bartholomew was given the task of converting the oases of the Libyan Desert. According to Abu Salih, a prominent medieval Christian historian, Bartholomew met his martyrdom at Bahariya on the first day of the Coptic month of Tut (Sept 7) at a place called Qarbil (unidentified today) and his body is believed to be buried in Sohag.

When Dugald Campbell visited Bahariya in 1931, thumping his bibles, he found a Coptic monastery standing in Bawiti. He called it Dar al-Abras, the Lepers' Refuge, and described it as having paintings, old writings, and engraved crosses on the walls. He says the Christians called Bahariya Mari Girgis (St. George) and in the rock tombs he found "old baked-earth coffins of the kind made in Carthage during the Punic period." Each had the figure of a Libyan man on the lid. He took some to the Cairo Museum.

Christians remained in Bahariya until the sixteenth and seventeenth centuries, far longer than in any other oasis. In fact, in the oral tradition related by Ahmed Fakhry, the people still remember the last Christian family to convert to Islam.

Islamic Era (641–1798)

During the early Islamic period Bahariya was called the Northern Oasis and Waha al-Khas. At first deserted, Islam began to infiltrate into Bahariya as early as the seventh century, coming from two directions: Libya and the Nile Valley. An interesting theory is put forward by one of the Egyptologists in Bahariya. He maintains that the pagan cults, similar to the worship of Isis in the Nile Valley, were still strong in the oasis during Christian times and that the early inroads into conversion by Islam were among the pagans as opposed to the Christians.

There are no known monuments from the Islamic period in Bahariya Oasis. Everything in the Western Desert was in decline: the population, the fertile ground, and the wells, which were not being properly maintained. Dunes, which did not exist in the oasis in Roman times, began to encroach on the cultivated land. Taxes levied against Bahariya were now in the form of dates and olive oil. Gone was the request for wine.

The Fatimids crossed the northern portion of the Western Desert to conquer Egypt in 969, and since they had affiliations in what is now Libya, one must assume they knew and used the desert trails often. Yet there are few records that can verify activity around Bahariya. Later, during the Mamluk era the easiest access to the oasis was south of Cairo along the Darb al-Bahnasa (see below) and the oasis (up to this century) was considered a part of the Minya governorate. During the Ottoman period a tax collector was stationed at Bahariya.

There is one site in the oasis that could have shed light on events during these myste-rious centuries. Al-Marun, north of Bir Matar, has glass and pottery shards that appear to date from the Islamic era. Unfortunately, it has been flooded to form a new lake.

Muhammad Ali claimed Bahariya, including Hayz and Farafra, as early as 1813, earlier than any other oasis. The oaseans were to pay an annual tribute of 2,000 Spanish piasters. Wilkinson later says this tribute was raised to 20,000 reals. Unlike Kharga, where few soldiers were needed to maintain the peace, Bahariya was manned by 400–500 armed men. A hefty fine was levied for every native killed by another.

Nineteenth and Twentieth Centuries

In the late eighteenth and early nineteenth centuries there was a migration of fellahin from the Nile Valley into Bahariya. Once Muhammad Ali applied his rule over the oases, the explorers began to arrive.

Belzoni was probably the first European to visit Bahariya. He called the oasis Wah al-Bahnasa or Wah al-Mendeesheh. He journeyed here from the Fayoum, which he left on May 19, 1819, around the time Muhammad Ali was beginning his conquest of the other oases. He thought he was in Siwa. Shortly thereafter came Cailliaud, then Hyde visited the oasis in February of 1820. In 1823–24, Pacho and Muller came to Bahariya, followed by Wilkinson in 1825. The Rohlfs expedition arrived in 1874. Next was Captian H. G. Lyons in 1894.

In 1897, John Ball and Hugh Beadnell began the geological examination of Bahariya. Dr. Ball, along with topographer G. Vuta, began at Minya while Beadnell, with another topographer, L. Gorringe, began from Maghagha. The map they produced was 1/50,000.

As in all the oases of the Western Desert, the Sanusi had a strong presence in Bahariya. (See People for details.) They established two zawyas, one in Qasr and a second in Mandisha, where the young men in the oasis would go to school to learn reading, writing, and the Quran. They would write their lessons on wooden tablets and once the work was accomplished erase the writing with mud.

In 1916, when the Sanusi were fighting for their lives in the Western Desert, they sent an army to Bahariya and it stayed in the oasis for ten months. The British, aided by Sudanese soldiers, surrounded Bahariya in the hopes of containing the Sanusi and the final confrontation took place in the pass above Hara, where the majority of the Sanusi army was encamped. Oral tradition in the oasis maintains that the British bombed a herd of cattle thinking it was the Sanusi army. It was during these years that Captain

Williams kept his lonely vigil atop the mountain that bears his name (see Mountains below for details).

After the Sanusi were forced out of Bahariya and the rest of the Western Desert, the British established martial law and a new set of rules governed the people of the oasis. Although inhabitants who remember the era maintain that British rule was fair and just, sometimes clashes occurred. One incident relates to land once owned by the Sanusi. The wealthier landowners of Bahariya had donated land to the Sanusi to be used to serve the poor and the needs of the mosque. The British confiscated the land and held it for auction, a procedure resented by the people. At the auction the wealthy landowners purchased their own land once again and, as under the Sanusi, donated it to the mosque.

The genealogical history of the oasis is kept by several sheikhs who still dominate life in the villages. These records give accounts of births, deaths, and memorable events, including strange encounters with jinn and other supernatural creatures. Three such books are maintained: one in Bawiti, one in Mandisha, and one in the district of Hayz. There is a ritual connected with recording events in these books. When something of importance takes place in a family, a male is sent to the Sheikh and says "Iftah al-kitab," "Open the Book." The sheikh burns incense as he listens to the story and records the event.

There is electricity in Bawiti, Qasr, Mandisha, and Zabw. Generators pump energy for electricity in Aguz, Gabala, and Hara, but the villages in the district of Hayz are without electricity. Every village in the oasis has a school; there are preparatory schools (ages 6–12) at Mandisha, Qasr, Bawiti, Managim, and Hara, whilst the other villages have primary schools (ages 12–14), including four at Hayz. The village of Bawiti has the only secondary school (ages 15–17). There is one agricultural, one commercial, and two industrial schools, one at Bawiti and the second at Managim. There was once a teachers' school but today the oasis has an overabundance of teachers and the school has been closed. There are also three Islamic schools. There is a single hospital in Bawiti.

Geography and Geology

Looking like an upside down charging bull, Bahariya is completely surrounded by several rows of high escarpment which enclose a valley floor littered with hills and mountains. The depression is 94 kilometers (58.7 miles) long and 42 kilometers (26 miles) wide and contains 2,000 square kilometers (1,250 miles). Smaller than the other three major oases on this route, it is sometimes called al-Waha al-Saghira, the Little Oasis. Bahariya stands 128 meters (409 feet) above sea level with its lowest point near Qasr. This is the highest elevation of any of the oases. It sits at N27° 48' and N28° 30' and E28° 35' and E29° 10'.

The escarpment encircles the entire depression. Its lower portions, as well as much of the depression floor, are composed of Cretaceous sandstones, topped by Eocene limestone, Oligocene basalt, and dolomite. The Eocene strata, found mostly in the north, is filled with nummulites, many lying on the surface. The northern portions of the scarp, including Gebel Ghurabi, are shales, clays, and sandstones. The western scarp is 175 meters (560 feet) high, with steep slopes, and contains a number of wadis where the caravan roads are found. This scarp is really three, one following the other. The first is Nubian sandstone, the second limestone, and the third, or outer scarp, is chalk. The eastern scarp is also multilayered, actually two scarps, one behind the other. Toward the west the white chalk, which dominates the Farafra landscape, predominates. Ball and Beadnell found abundant fossils 24 kilometers (15 miles) north of Hayz.

Unlike other oases where villages were well fortified, the inhabited areas in Bahariya appear to lie vulnerably on the valley floor. However, in this instance looks are deceiving, for at Qasr and Bawiti a high cliff lies to the west of the villages with the gardens on the plain below.

Mountains

There are plenty of hills and mountains in Bahariya Depression and they form the dominant feature of this oasis. Primarily conical and cutting the depression in half on a north–south axis they are formed by Cenomanian sandstone and chalky clays. Most are capped with iron quartzites and dolorite rocks. These caps, from the Oligocene epoch, form a protective coating on the Eocene deposits that has prevented erosion. To the eye they are mainly yellow, topped by black caps. In addition there are reddish hills of ferruginous sandstone and ocherous clay laced with white limestone, the latter deposits being used to create the temples in the area.

Among the dominant mountains are **Gebel Hafuf**; **Gebel al-Ghaba**, Mountain of the Forest; **Gebel Ghurabi**, Mountain of the Crow; **Gebel Dist**, Mountain of the Pot; **Gebel al-Maghrafa**, Mountain of the Ladle; **Gebel Mandisha**; **Gebel Mayisra**; **Gebel Hammad**; **Gebel Tibniya**; **Gebel Hadoam**; **Gebel Miteili Radwan**; and **Gebel Shahut**. Details of these mountains are found in the text below.

Dunes

Dunes are not dominant in this oasis, but they do exist. **Ghard Mandisha** is a small line of short dunes lying along the asphalt road near the village of Mandisha. This is a good example of how destructive dunes can be. They are currently inundating a palm grove and homes, burying everything in their path. A dune may look picturesque, but each palm buried is a loss of income to the person who owns the grove and to a government which levies a tax on palm trees.

In addition to the Ghard Mandisha there are the **Ghard Hussein**, to the south of Bawiti; **Ghard Qazzun**, to the east of Managim; **Ghard Ghurabi**, Dune of the Crow, along the main road in the northwest before descending into the depression; and the longest dune field in the entire Western Desert, **Ghard Abu Muharrik**, Dune with an Engine. Southeast of Bahariya, this extensive dune field runs south through Kharga Oasis past Dush. It blocks the way to Bahariya from the Nile Valley and made it extremely difficult to visit this oasis in the past.

Water

Bahariya has been lucky. In the past there was no need to dig to depths of 700 meters (2,240 feet) for water, as must be done in other oases. Seven meters (22 feet) was the depth of the deepest well here. Today the digging is deep. The presence of carbon dioxide indicates that the water comes from deep in the earth, yet despite the fact that Bahariya is the highest oasis in elevation, the water makes its way to the surface through natural fissures.

Bahariya also has a number of ancient aqueduct systems which are called *manafis* locally. Today, two are known in Bawiti and Qasr and an additional one in Izza. Hoskins says, in 1843, there were four in this area, one from the northwest, one from the south, and two from the west. Caillaud found even more in the south. The one southwest of Qasr was the largest with 10 openings within 180 feet. He wrote, "The inhabitants state that they are the work of the Koofars *[kuffar]*, that is, the infidels; but they could not say where the water comes from." (See People and Kharga Oasis for more details.)

Fossils, Ferns, and Earthquakes

Fossils, best found in Bahariya in the Gebel Dist area, are primarily of vertebrates. Despite the fact that a good variety of fossils exist, no mammal has yet been found in the oasis, though reptiles, turtles, and dinosaurs have. In the 1920s and 1930s, several expeditions explored Bahariya for fossils and dozens of major finds were discovered including *Simoliophis rochebrunei*, the largest and oldest snake known. Baher al-Khashab in *Some Studies on Egyptian Vertebrates Fossils* lists a number of reptile fossils for Bahariya.

Our friend Mr. Markgraf who lived in the Fayoum and collected hundreds of fossils there, also visited Bahariya in 1911 and 1912 where he collected vertebrates. From the fossils found it has been determined that they existed under fluvio-marine conditions.

In antiquity Bahariya would pay its taxes in alum, which was exported by the ancient Egyptians. Unique to Bahariya is a water fern, *Marsilea minuta*, that is found in its wells. Ball believed an earthquake hit Bahariya around 1840 and was responsible for the destruction of the Roman arch north of Qasr drawn and described by Cailliaud in 1820. Modern technology has been able to tell us that a force-eight earthquake hit the Fayoum on August 7, 1847. In the Fayoum, 85 people died, 62 were injured, and 3,000 houses were destroyed. Evidently, Bahariya also felt the shock.

Caravan Routes and Roadways

In time past, when people from Bahariya wished to go to the Nile Valley they often waited until a caravan was passing through. The most popular caravan was the postal caravan, which left the oasis on a regular basis. Local inhabitants remember that this caravan consisted of three relay teams, each with three camels, that traveled between the Nile and the oasis in three days.

Passes (Naqbs)

Since Bahariya is completely surrounded by escarpments, every road in or out of the oasis is via a pass, a place in the escarpment which can be ascended and descended. Six main passes have been used since ancient times, but there are additional places where the escarpment can be breached. In the northeast there is **Naqb Ghurabi**, Pass of the Crow, which is also known as Naqb Khaddafi, in reference to the tomb of a holy man found at the base of the pass; **Naqb al-Qahira**, Pass of Cairo, is a new pass that is part of the macadamized road; south of the main road is **Naqb al-Bahnasa**, which climbs the scarp near Hara and forms the oasis entrance for the darb of the same name.

Southwest of Qasr is **Naqb Siwa**, the important pass that linked Bahariya with Siwa in antiquity, and beyond it, near the village of Izza in the district of Hayz, is the **Naqb Della**, leading to Ain Della. The final major pass in Bahariya is **Naqb Sillim al-Aqabat**, Pass of Difficult Stairs, where the main road crosses the southwestern scarp.

Darbs

Darb al-Qahira is the route of the modern macadamized road. It was the main route for automobiles in the 1930s, when the journey took three days. The roadway was first paved with asphalt in 1967, in conjunction with the development of the mines at Managim. At that time it extended only as far as the mines, 40 kilometers (25 miles) northeast of Bawiti. A major overhaul took place in the 1970s, when the road was extended to form a loop around the four major oases in the southern area of the Western Desert. This old caravan road began near Cairo at Kerdassa, a weaving village that served most of the oases in the Western Desert. Travelers who chose this track had a difficult time for it had no water, was continually interrupted by massive sand dunes, and was a journey of 340 kilometers (213 miles), which took nine to ten days to complete. It entered the oasis at Naqb al-Ghurabi.

Darb Asas runs from Fashut in the Nile Valley across the desert and through the

Ghard Abu Muharrik to enter Bahariya in the north. Along its route it is joined by no fewer than three other major tracks, the two Darb al-Rayyan tracks and the Darb al-Masudi. Once they join, they cross the macadamized road at a point just north of Managim and continue over the Ghard Ghurabi before descending the escarpment via the Naqb Ghurabi, near Gebel Ghurabi. Gebel Ghurabi, Mountain of the Crow, comprised of shales, clays, and sandstone topped by ferruginous, limonite beads of iron ore, and red and yellow ocher, is a spectacular sight. After descending the scarp this major caravan route continues south past Bir Ghaba and Bir Matar to Mandisha and Bawiti.

There are two main tracks leading from Bahariya to Fayoum via Wadi Rayyan. They are called **Darb al-Rayyan Bahri** (north) and **Darb al-Rayyan Qibli** (south). These routes were taken by Belzoni in 1819, Pacho in 1823, and Ascherson in 1876 on journeys that took approximately six days. The distance via either track is 240 kilometers (150 miles) and caravans that watered their camels at Rayyan took five to six days on their journey. Before the modern macadamized road these tracks were the second most important route to Bahariya. In Bahariya, the route begins as part of the Darb Asas, a single track above the escarpment 3 to 4 kilometers (1.8 to 2.5 miles) north of Managim. After some kilometers the first Darb al-Rayyan branches north from the Darb Asas and a few kilometers later the second, southern Darb al-Rayyan, moves away from the northern route. Darb Asas continues east while the other two routes continue northeast. On reaching Rayyan one route skirts the western side of the depression and heads to Qasr Qarun, up over the northern escarpment of Fayoum and on to Wadi Natrun and the northern coast. The second proceeds along the southern perimeter of Wadi Rayyan, past the monastery of Wadi Rayyan to Gharaq Sultani at the tip of the Fayoum, then veers south to Wadi Mawalih and the Nile Valley (see Fayoum).

Darb al-Masudi is the second road linking Fashut and Maghagha in the Nile Valley to Bahariya. It is well described by Ball and Beadnell in their book *Bahariya Oasis: Its Topography and Geology*. The road exits the Nile Valley at Qasr al-Lamlum Bey, going north of the Maghagha railway station. After 15 kilometers (9.3 miles) the dark limestone of Gebel Mawalih appears to the northeast (the Wadi Mawalih goes through the passes of this mountain to Wadi Rayyan). After 23 kilometers (14 miles) the road ascends the scarp. At 125 kilometers (78 miles) from the edge of the cultivation in the Nile Valley, the road runs into the al-Bahr depression. At 141 kilometers (88 miles) sand and dunes cover the area for a little over 6 kilometers (4 miles). By 146 kilometers (91 miles) the Ghard al Shubbab is crossed. Now come the Abu Muharrik Dunes, 6 kilometers (4 miles) wide at this point. Finally, at about 154 kilometers (96 miles) the black conical hills of Gar al-Hamra appear. Then more dunes at 169 kilometers (105 miles). Now the descent near Ghurabi. At Bawiti the road ends, having covered 195 kilometers (121 miles).

Darb al-Bahnasa, the desert road from Bahnasa, the pharaonic Oxyrhynchus, covers 190 kilometers (119 miles). It was once a four day journey by camel, and was in general use until 1934. There are several starting points in the Nile Valley, at Beni Mazar, Samalut, Dilgah, and Sandafa al-Far, which converge with the main track from Bahnasa (near Minya) about 15 kilometers (9.3 miles) into the desert. They enter Bahariya northeast of Hara. This route was surveyed by Ball and Beadnell in 1897. According to them the road begins in the Nile Valley along a gravel plain. At 98 kilometers (61 miles) it enters a small depression. After 124 kilometers (77 miles) it enters the sand dunes of Ghard Abu Muharrik, which it traverses for 4 kilometers (2.5 miles). After 151 kilometers (94 miles) the route crosses another depression, passing numerous white chalk hills. After 159 kilometers (99 miles) the road climbs out of this depression and enters Bahariya Depression via the Naqb al-Bahnasa, south of the main road, near the village of Hara.

This is the shortest and easiest route from Bahariya to the Nile and was used to carry mail to the oasis. Ahmed Fakhry tells us that when the mail was carried by camel it was delivered promptly every four days, but once the automobile took over (1937) it was sometimes delayed for weeks.

Darb al-Rubi is another desert track that began at Hara. It ascended the escarpment via a pass called Naqb Ligalit and continued due east to the Nile Valley, ending in the village of Rubi. Although traveled by Ascherson in four days in 1874, today locals claim it is no longer in use because it runs directly into the Ghard Abu Muharrik (though this must also have been true in Ascherson's day). It was, and probably is, the shortest distance to the Nile Valley, but its beginning in Bahariya is not easily recognized and few of the people of Bahariya seem to know of its existence.

Darb Siwa, the road to Siwa Oasis, one of the most important tracks in Bahariya, has recently been sand-paved (tar poured over sand) and is now passable by regular vehicle. Unrestricted passage is possible from Siwa, but as of this writing, travel from Bahariya is not permitted. Forming a vital link in the Western Desert, it was off limits to travelers in 1998, and persons wishing to use this route had to apply for permission from the Military Intelligence Office of the Egyptian Army (see Bahariya to Siwa for details and Siwa Oasis for permissions). This route was used by Jordan in 1874. It took him ten days to reach Siwa from Bahariya. At one time a second pass out of Bahariya was used to exit the oasis. That road joined the main route to Siwa a little bit along the way.

Darb Ain Della begins at Hayz and passes through Naqb Della in the southern portion of the oasis. This is not the route normally taken today to Ain Della (see Farafra Oasis) and travel along this route, which is in a military area, is restricted (see Izza below).

Darb al-Farafra, the main route to Farafra, passes through Naqb Sillim al-Aqabat, Pass of Difficult Stairs, and up the southwestern scarp on its way to Farafra. It was used by Cailliaud in 1820, Jordan of the Rohlfs expedition in 1874, and part of the Ball and Beadnell team in 1897. But a second road, the main route when both tracks were still natural, runs parallel to the former, between the escarpment and the cultivated land to the southeast of the modern road. This route ascends the escarpment in several places and enters Farafra Depression via a pass just to the south of the macadamized route, not far from Twin Peaks.

The People

Cailliaud found the people of Bahariya "wickedly inclined, ignorant, superstitious, and fanatical in the extreme. . . . They pillage and rob each other of the cattle that stray."

In 1897, the population of the oasis was 6,081. There were four major villages, Qasr, Bawiti, Mandisha, and Zabw. This did not include the Hayz district. In 1916, the population of Bahariya was 6,000 inhabitants. Ahmed Fakhry reported that in 1966, there were 9,791 people in Bahariya with 3,370 in Bawiti and 2,390 in Qasr. A few years ago 23,000 people lived in Bahariya Oasis with 16,000 in the capital, Bawiti. Today 27,000 are in Bahariya with only 13,000 in Bawiti. Over 1,000 people have immigrated here from Fayoum to farm.

Families have always settled together and stayed that way. Today they are integrating a little more, but usually they keep together when in larger communities like Bawiti. A family will purchase an entire city block. They will build their houses around the perimeter, facing the public streets, but the back side of each house will open onto a communal square where the women and children can visit and play safely and privately.

Although all the oases are conservative in nature, it is in Bahariya that the strong religious and social attitudes that have governed the desert for centuries are most apparent to the visitor. Tradition is the basis of all codes of conduct. Group identity is strong. Everyone knows who he is, and who he is from, in a lineage that reaches far back into time. Social law remains stronger than any legal mandate and many families such as that of "the man who killed the donkey" or "the woman who walked in the street," are known and often stigmatized by events that took place long ago.

This type of rigid social code makes the oasis a safe haven. The last murder in Bahariya occurred over two decades ago. Robbery and petty theft occur seldom and when they do, it is a disgrace for the entire family. In the past the thief was placed on a donkey and paraded through the streets of the village with children running after him crying 'al-harami tisht' ('the thief is an oaf').

Rape is non-existent among the people in Bahariya. But, as in Siwa, what constitutes provocation is drastically different than in the West. A woman walking alone in a garden could be seen as provocative. Clashes sometimes occur between local and Western moral standards, since the latter are often very different from the code of honor that governs oasis life. In one incident a tourist asked a resident to hide his suitcase so he could claim it was stolen and collect the insurance money. This was very difficult to understand and the request was refused. Another time a man approached one of the cafeterias erected for the tourists. Under the shade of the courtyard were several male tourists, their motorbikes parked nearby, their hair crewcut short in the front and falling below the neckline behind. Earrings were visible in their ears, "Are these the European crazy people?" was the question and it was evident that the man who asked it was more than a little distressed.

Tradition also has its light side. One custom, practiced throughout Egypt, is that the new bride would ride to her husband on the back of a camel in a *hawdag*, an enclosed tent. Inhabitants remember several amusing stories related to the *hawdag*. Once a camel was moving through the narrow streets carrying his special cargo when he approached a tree. The tree was short, the camel tall, and the bride, instead of being delivered to her husband, was ensconced in the branches of the tree. Another time the camel carrying the *hawdag* fell into one of the wells and the bride and her bridesmaids all tumbled in.

Today marriage customs have changed. Once all weddings occurred after the rice harvest and for ten to fifteen days everyone celebrated. Today the celebrations happen all year long and each lasts three days. On the first day, the friends are invited to a feast and the groom's family kills a cow. On the second day, the groom presents his bride with her gold ring and then goes off to enjoy a bachelor party. On the third day, he brings her to the new home he has prepared for her and she arrives in a white wedding dress and veil (gone is the wonderful traditional costume) in a procession of cars and trucks instead of on the back of the camels. Horns hoot, music plays, and people sing.

Frank Bliss who studied the people of Bahariya in the 1980s tells us that when prosperity began to rise in the oases in the 1970s and 1980s it was marked by an increase in Mecca pilgrimages and the acquisition of TV sets, even though there was no electricity to play them.

Today, with new developments happening everywhere in the desert, Bahariya is no exception. People from the Fayoum and Kafr al-Sheikh in the Nile Valley have immigrated to Bahariya to farm tomatoes and watermelon. This will change the face of this oasis.

Agriculture

Crops are plentiful in Bahariya. Orchards contain a variety of trees, including date, lemon, olive, mango, and guava. Gardens grow a variety of crops. Traditional cash crops include dates, olives, and apricots, while new cash crops are tomatoes, water-melon, and cantaloupe. During the date harvest, unlike Siwa, where Bedouin traveled to the oasis to transport the dates, fellahin from the Nile Valley came to Bahariya to assist in the harvest. Today, a farmer will realize about LE50 a year from a single tree.

In 1897, Bahariya had a booming export business with the Nile Valley. Dates, of course, were the main commodity. The date trees were taxed by the government and three quarters of their production was exported. Growers were paid by the camel load and the middleman made four times what he paid for them when he delivered them to the villages along the Nile. In 1897, Bahariya had 4,863 apricot trees, 5,370 olive trees, and 93,000 palm trees. There is a new lake, but no fishing industry.

When the oases were self-sufficient, before the macadamized road, wheat was a major crop in Bahariya. But once subsidized, wheat began appearing in the market, and it was cheaper to buy the wheat than to produce it. This eventually led to problems, for today wheat has become more expensive to buy than to produce and once again the people are beginning to grow the grain necessary for local consumption.

The paved road also brought disease. The importation of chickens, birds, and fruit trees brought new pests to the oasis. Camels also suffered from living in the oasis. Susceptible to a disease transmitted by flies in cultivated areas, they are mostly kept in the desert nearby. There has never been serious opthalmia, an eye disease that has plagued most of the rest of Egypt.

Food

The bread of Bahariya, called *eish al-shams,* sun bread, is hearty, thick, and wonderful. But baking is not done every day and the bread gets hard as a rock. It is softened by placing it in water. Then it is soggy and not so appetizing.

The people also enjoy certain dishes they believe unique to Bahariya: *Kishki* is a dish of sour milk and wheat. *Sakuti* is red rice cooked in oil with onion and tomato. *Balayya* is rice and lentils, usually eaten on Friday. But *ruz wahi* is their speciality. It is a brown rice that has a slightly crunchy, nutty flavor when cooked. It is in limited supply as it takes a lot of water to grow. It also takes longer to cook and needs more water than traditional rice. It is cooked the same as regular oasis rice, but is also used in a soup, or to stuff pigeons.

Each family pickles the olives from their trees for family use. They appear at every meal and are tasted and judged by guests with great interest. Everyone in the oasis knows which families have the best olives.

In Bahariya you can have *shay masri,* Egyptian tea, which is a mild tea for the oaseans, but pretty strong for foreigners, or *shay wahati,* oasis tea, which is very, very strong and needs lots of sugar to cut the bitterness.

The Crafts of the Oasis

Despite the fact that Bahariya Oasis is still a traditional place, indigenous crafts are not abundant. Tools used by workmen are similar to those found in the Nile Valley. Houses have decorations similar to those found in Kharga and Dakhla. Baskets are not unique, nor are the pots. Even the older women are no longer cloistered and do not wear the nose ring and traditional costumes.

Dresses

The traditional women's dress of Bahariya Oasis is one of the most beautiful in the Western Desert. Simply called a *gallabiya,* it is a black loose-fitting garment falling to well below the knees with straight sleeves to the wrists. The bodice is embroidered in red

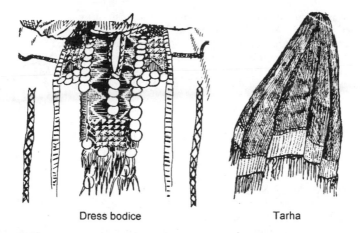

Dress bodice   Tarha

and yellow tiny cross-stitch with a lot of authentic Islamic coins sewn into the pattern below the breast. The design ends in red tassels. On the remainder of the dress, lines of embroidery two centimeters wide fall from the shoulder to the hem at spaced intervals. This dress is seldom seen today. Instead, a bastardized version with brighter colors and bigger stitches is made not only to sell to the tourists, but for use by the people, too. There are few coins on these dresses.

There was a second dress for everyday wear. Similar in shape to the first, it too was black, but the red and yellow embroidery was replaced by silver threads that form a pattern around the bodice. It is disappearing too. Instead retail shops have appeared in the oasis with clothes to buy. This is a luxury that never existed before.

Over their heads the women traditionally wore the *tarha*, a black rectangular scarf with a red silk border. Now colorful scarves imported into Bahariya are the fashion. Attached to the back of the head and dangling down the back the women wore the *aguz*, or *uqus*, red plaits with metal rings and silk tassels at the ends similar to the *dindash* worn by the women in Dakhla. The women often attached small money pouches to the *tarha* for safekeeping.

Jewelry

Where women in the cities wore Islamic jewelry with origins in Greek and Roman traditions, the poor people adopted Ottoman traditions in their jewelry. Since Ottoman jewelry was influenced by Byzantine designs, this was a jewelry tradition that followed an ancient pattern.

In Bahariya, jewelry was part of the dowry given to the woman by the man's family: *khulkhal*, silver ankle bracelets for each ankle, *halqan*, earrings, and *dimlig*, bracelets, one for each arm.

In the early twentieth century, two Coptic silversmiths from Upper Egypt opened a shop in Bahariya. They remained in Bahariya until the 1950s. One died, the other, Abd al-Malik, according to Frank Bliss, went to Cairo to work.

Up until ten years ago, women still wore the traditional jewelry. Now one would be hard pressed to see any. The most interesting piece of jewelry is the *qatra*, a nose ring made of gold. It comes in a variety of sizes, the larger the nose ring, the more affluent the family, but the design is always the same. They were purchased at the time of the wedding by the bride's family, often by the bride from her inheritance.

Qatra

(Bliss points out that women must, by law, receive a portion of their father's estates.) When the woman ate or drank she would have to pass the food or glass to one side of the ring and push it away from the mouth toward the cheek. Older women sometimes had to move the nose ring to the other nostril for years of wear caused the original hole to elongate and break through the bottom of the nostril.

Ten years ago necklaces were made of glass or tiny multi-colored beads reminiscent of the bead work of sub-Saharan Africa. They are called *bigma* and were a relatively new addition to the women's adornment. The beads came from Cairo and the girls and women designed the patterns themselves.

Bigma

One distinctive necklace, common in, but not exclusive to, Bahariya, is the *zar* pendant, or *galagil*. The *zar* was probably brought to Egypt by Abyssinian slaves in the early 1800s. It is performed to exorcise evil spirits. Women play the leading role in the exorcism, which includes a number of therapeutic traditions including dance, music, and aromatherapy. To appease the evil spirit a number of different amulets, such as this one, are used. The amulet is dipped in animal blood and worn by the afflicted person to keep the evil spirit away once it has been expelled. It is worn with the picture toward the body and the Quranic verse facing out. When used in *zar* ceremonies, the pendants must be made of silver and have tiny bells, the *galagil*, attached to them. This made the hallmark on each metal very important. It also enables collectors to date each piece, for Egyptian hallmarks consist of three stamps: the silver percentage, the year given with an Arabic or English letter, and a symbol, which was a cat before 1946 when it was changed to a lotus. Silver content is usually 60 percent, but can also be 80 or 90 percent.

Galagil

Frank Bliss maintains that the pendants in Bahariya, especially the larger ones, may be patterned after the *zar* pendants, but are unrelated to the *zar*, which is almost unknown in Bahariya. The Bahariya women, who call them *higab*, meaning amulet, adopted them and wore them daily, strictly for ornamentation. One popular drawing is the *zar* demon Yawri Bey, depicted as a Turkish officer with a fez. Other popular motifs are the sultan and Quranic inscriptions.

In the ears the women wore the *halaq*, usually gold or gold plated though occasionally made of silver or base metal. Unique in design, these earrings rank with Siwan jewelry as prized collectors' items. They have a circular center rising in layers that narrow as they extend upward and outwards. The pinnacle of this conical structure is decorated with a stone, often a turquoise. Attached to the lower edge of the cone and extending below are tiny dangling hands or round discs.

At their wrist the women wore two *dimlig*, one on each wrist. These are large 4–5 inch wide silver bracelets decorated with bird and fish motifs, similar to those worn by Bedouin women throughout the Libyan Desert. They are influenced by Berber jewelry, especially bracelets found in Tunisia where even the decorative motifs are very similar.

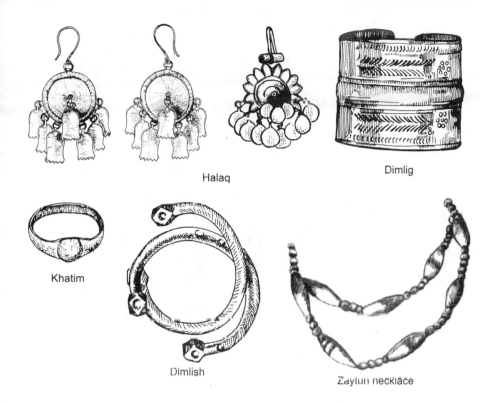

Halaq

Dimlig

Khatim

Dimlish

Zaylun necklace

They also exist in the Nile Valley. Also very common in Siwa, the bracelets peek out from under their long-sleeved dresses as the women go about their work.

A small, plain silver ring with an oval stone, a *khatim*, was the only ring worn by women in Bahariya. It is unique to Bahariya and was probably originally produced here. Finally, on the ankle were the *dimlish* or *khulkhal*, ankle bracelets common throughout the Middle East. In Bahariya ankle bracelets are heavy and plain with designs only on the ends. The hallmarks show a Libyan or Nile Valley origin.

Today the preference is gold: *zaytun* necklaces and *makhrata* earrings from the Nile Valley are very popular. The *zaytun* is a 22-carat gold string of beads that, like their name suggests, resemble olives. The *makhrata* is an earring that looks like the vegetable cutter after which it is named. It comes from the Nile Valley, where once each village or group of villages had a distinctive earring to wear. This earring has become very commonly worn throughout Egypt.

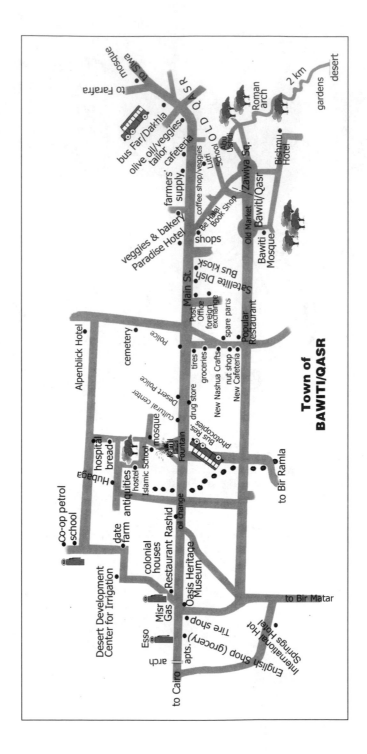

Town of
BAWITI/QASR

TOUR #1

Bawiti

- bike, walk, 2x2
- 1.5 to 2 hours
- easy

Almost all the sites in Bawiti and Qasr lie at N 28 21 and E 28 51. The minutes and seconds are so close and the streets so narrow the GPS is useless. Take a guide. He will be very happy to jump into your car or walk you around. All hotels provide this service. Inexpensive guides are available from the Tourist Information Office.

The two villages of Bawiti and Qasr, called collectively Wah al-Gharbee by Belzoni, have merged into one village in modern times. Qasr was the ancient capital of the oasis, and held 800 inhabitants when Cailliaud visited in 1819–20. Bawiti, with 600 people according to Cailliaud, did not come into existence until Islamic times, when it was named after a sheikh of the same name. In 1897, Qasr had 1,712 people and Bawiti had 1,713. Qasr, at 113 meters (361 feet) above sea level is the lowest point in Bahariya.

Today one enters the oasis from a new road into the newest part of the community. Traditionally, the descent to Bawiti and Qasr

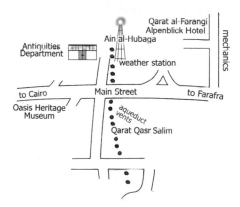

was made from Naqb al-Ghurabi. The track followed the depression floor and could be viewed by the people of the village as they had the high ground, situated as they were atop a cliff. The visitors had to thread their way through the gardens and up the twisting paths to reach the houses. The old parts of the two cities, of course, still exist and so does the cliff. Because the new road enters the town from atop the cliff it looks as if Bawiti and Qasr were not built with protection in mind. This is far from the truth.

The older sections of the villages of Bawiti and Qasr are slowly being abandoned as people move into more modern houses. These older homes, close to and tumbling down the cliffside into the gardens, are the traditional oasis communities and unless someone realizes their value and restoration work is considered, they will soon fall to ruin.

Bawiti lies directly over a more ancient settlement and it is probable that a great many antiquities are buried beneath its foundations. Fragments of temples and tombs are found in the walls of houses and a few sites have been found intact. Most of the ancient ruins date to the Twenty-sixth Dynasty.

We know even less of the Islamic era in the two communities. Up until a few years ago, almost everything of note excavated in Bahariya was done by Ahmed Fakhry but now local Egyptian Antiquities personnel have been uncovering new and exciting finds.

Oasis Heritage Museum

Entrance fee. Opened upon request: call 011 802 970 or 803 666. Mahmoud Eed, the artist, is self taught and the garden at the entrance to his museum shows the workings of his magnificent, surreal mind: a full-size mud camel with lightbulbs for eyes looks at an oasis character while at their feet ancient pots grow like flowers. The interior has five rooms filled with treasures, each scene depicting life in the oasis, with the statues bearing the actual caricature of the current weaver, potter, basketmaker, etc.

But the biggest treasures are the small faces Mahmoud does so well. Some of them are also surreal, with heads growing out of heads, growing out of heads. Mahmoud fires his own statues like the Romans once did. He builds a fire of wood and places his statues around it. He fires each piece twice and tells us the type of wood determines the final color of the piece. If he fires with cow dung the piece is very strong and becomes dark red.

Antiquities Headquarters and Museum
Since the discovery of the Valley of the Golden Mummies, a number of sites formerly closed are now open to the public. For a fee you will see five sites including Muftilla, the Temple of Alexander the Great, the museum, and two tombs. The Antiquities department is easy to find (see map). The museum contains some of the gilded coffins from the Valley of the Golden Mummies. The inspectors are excited about a new find in the oasis which they call the Temple and Tomb of Hercules, but no information is forthcoming at this time, for the work, as usual in Bahariya, is incomplete. Being a part of the Giza governorate has its pros and cons.

Ain al-Hubaga
Ain al-Hubaga is an ancient spring with an extensive aqueduct system that runs for 3 kilometers (1.8 miles) through the village of Bawiti and down to the gardens below. This is one of several springs in Bahariya that have such underground galleries. A second gallery still functions in Qasr and another at Ain al-Izza at Hayz (see below). Here these ancient aqueducts are called *manafis*.

The *manafis* have not been investigated at all in Bahariya and this is unfortunate, since there are probably more manafis in Bahariya

Aqueduct vents at Ain al-Hubaga

than in any other part of the Western Desert. When Cailliaud was here in 1820 he found plenty. At Mandisha, he saw ten *manafis*, of which eight were still working, one with 14 openings. There were at least 30 *manafis* in the southern part of Bahariya Oasis and Cailliaud tells us, "Four of these discharged their water into a huge excavation 70 meters diameter and 12 meters deep." By 1898, when John Ball was surveying Bahariya for the Geological Survey of Egypt, he only found two at Bawiti and Qasr and one in the south. The latter had dried up. As noted in the Kharga chapter, similar systems also exist in Afghanistan, Iran, Oman, and Algeria (see People and Kharga Oasis for a full description).

What all this tells us is that Bahariya has a history we know nothing about. Because we know so little about the aqueducts, we cannot use them to help us.

Ain al-Hubaga is located in the heart of Bawiti, which makes it easy to access. Most of the other locations are in the desert. The shafts serve as a good illustration of the way in which galleries and shafts were dug at the springs in the oases. Although most explorers in the Western Desert believed these galleries were introduced by the Romans, Fakhry maintained they were probably of Persian origin or earlier.

Ain al-Hubaga begins just behind the Antiquities Department and the Weather Station to the east of the main road (see map). Follow it across the road. In a few meters it runs along the edge of the ridge at Qarat Qasr Salim (see below) into the village of Qasr. As it reaches the cliffs at the edge of the village it deepens and is open at the top. It is owned by a single family and in order to keep the water flowing through the tunnels it must be cleaned each year, a task to which all males in the family must lend a hand. This is not easy as the cool, dark, recesses are hiding places for snakes and scorpions. Within the tunnels the maiden hair fern grows. Although it plagues the farmers, who weed it out, it is a beautiful plant.

Qarat Qasr Salim

Qarat Qasr Salim is a small hill within the village of Bawiti along the path of the Ain al-Hubaga. It is the major antiquity and although it, like all the other antiquities in Bahariya, is closed to visitors, a drive to the area provides some information. This is probably Ball's Qasr Alam visited by both Wilkinson and Ascherson and described as a "rectangular crude brick structure on a slight eminence." At that time, it was a ruin with only the lower walls remaining.

The rise was probably created from the debris left by centuries of occupation. Standing on top of the mound are two tombs, one, the **Tomb of Zed-Amun-ef-ankh** is only accessible via a large pit with steep sides. Fakhry describes the tomb as having traditional religious texts and distinguishes it by an abundance of false doors and pillars. The free-standing pillars are circular, whereas most of the tombs in Bahariya have square pillars.

The second tomb atop Qarat Qasr Salim is the **Tomb of Bannentiu**, the son of Zed-Amun-ef-ankh. This tomb is completely surrounded by a mud-brick wall and is one of the easiest to enter, for in recent years the authorities of the mine at Managim have donated an iron stairway leading down into the entrance of the tomb. The interior is painted in yellows and reds, the colors of the sandstone found in the oasis.

In addition there are seven Late Period tombs, none with inscriptions, discovered around the perimeter of the mound a decade ago.

Burial Gallery of the Sacred Ibis

Located at **Qarat al-Farargi**, Hill of the Chicken Merchant, the Burial Gallery of the Sacred Ibis is probably the most extensive antiquity in Bahariya. It received its unusual name because the modern inhabitants thought the small mummies found within the burial chambers were chickens. Unfortunately, at the time of writing it could not be visited. It stretches far into a small ridge in a series of tunnels with small chambers extending to either side. Within the chambers are tiny recesses cut into the walls where the small mummies were laid to rest. In ancient Egypt people would buy sacred animals from vendors who often sold their wares directly in front of sacred buildings. The mummified corpses were then offered to the gods, sometimes as petitions. Often buried along with the mummies were other offerings in the form of statues, amulets, and charms, many of which have been found within the gallery at Bawiti. The gallery was probably in use from the end of the Twenty-sixth Dynasty through to the Roman period.

Getting There: (see map) Take the first road left, up the hill, to the south of the Military Intelligence Office. Less than a half kilometer later there is an auto repair on the right and a modern cemetery on the left. The Burial Gallery of the Sacred Ibis lies under the modern cemetery.

Tombs at Qarat al-Subi

Since Ahmed Fakhry first excavated these tombs in the first half of this century, the entrances have disappeared. As strange as this may sound, it is not an unusual occurrence in the archaeological history of Egypt. Many tombs in such well-known archaeological sites as Saqqara and the Valley of the Kings were discovered in the nineteenth century only to become lost to us in the twentieth. They had to be rediscovered, just as these tombs in Bahariya will have to be. In this instance the tombs lie within, around, and under the village of Bawiti and as houses are built, remodeled, or torn down, everything changes.

However, four of the tombs of major historical significance to Bahariya were well documented by Fakhry in several publications. Information found within the hieroglyphic inscriptions indicates that the occupants were native to Bahariya and held important national positions. They are: the Tomb of Pedashtar, a high priest living in Bahariya during the Twenty-sixth Dynasty, whose tomb consists of four rooms which were reused during the Roman era; the Tomb of Thaty, the grandson of the high priest Pedashtar; the Tomb of Ta-Nefert-Bastet, the wife of Thaty; and the Tomb-chapel of Zed-Khonsu-ef-ankh, the governor of Bahariya during the reign of the pharaoh Amasis during the Twenty-sixth Dynasty. All the tombs are decorated. Fakhry believed that there remain many additional undiscovered tombs in the area.

TOUR #2

Qasr

- walk, bike, 2x2, 4x4
- 3–4 hours
- easy

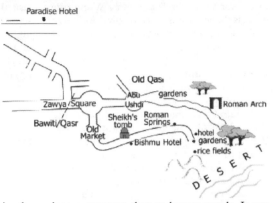

Abutting Bawiti to the southwest is the ancient village of al-Qasr, the capital of Bahariya in pharaonic times. Obviously, Qasr has had a long and continuous occupation and its tiny streets, picturesque houses, and main square are much more interesting than Bawiti. Until the building of the modern roadway, the main caravan route passed through the heart of Qasr and into its main square where the goods were unloaded.

There are plenty of monuments in Qasr, but as in Bawiti most of them lie under the present village and cannot be excavated. Fortunately ancient Qasr was larger than its present day counterpart and the ruins of the ancient city extend for 3 kilometers (1.8 miles) to the west of the present town.

As with Bawiti, many structures described by the nineteenth-century travelers to Bahariya no longer exist, or are in such a sorry state that they are of little note. One is the Temple of the Twenty-sixth Dynasty, of which only a few walls can be identified. Another is the Chapel of King Apries, first reported by Steindorff in 1900. Dedicated to the Theban gods Amun-Re and his son Khonsu, the chapel was but one section of a larger structure that no longer stands. It was erected by Wahibrenefer, a priest, and Zed-Khonsu-ef-ankh, the governor of Bahariya under the pharaoh Amasis, also described by Steindorff. It is an enclosed structure and the only decoration is on the roof, which, fortunately, is still intact.

Zawya Square

This square sits in the heart of Qasr where the old caravan route came into the city. In one corner of the square the old Sanusi mosque and *zawya* still stand (see The Sanusi in People for details). Although a new mosque is rising beside it, the old mosque and minaret are now in the hands of the Antiquity Department and hopefully they will not succumb to the same fate as the splendid mosque of Farafra, which was torn down.

To visit the remaining sites requires a short, pleasant walk: from the Old Market to the Roman Spring is 300 meters; another 100 meters to the gardens; ten minutes' walk from the gardens to the rice fields and another short walk to the sand dune. The return is mostly uphill. One can also take a car.

Old Market

Once the caravans entered the town they unloaded their goods in the old market, where the people anxiously waited. But the market, of course, was active every day of the week for it was here that people brought their produce to be sold, or bartered for cloth, sugar, and tea, or for services like ironwork, clothing, and shoemaking and repair.

Today, sadly, this historic place that served so many people for so many centuries is deserted. It needs someone to buy it up and restore it with shops, traditional crafts, and live-in artisans.

At the edge of the old market stands the old Bawiti mosque and suddenly the edge of the cliff. Now, for the first time the gardens for which Bahariya is so famous come into view. They are worth the entire trip and are not to be missed at any time of the year.

Ain Bishmu and Ain Bardir (Roman Springs)

Ain Bishmu and Ain Bardir are sometimes called the Roman Springs. Fakhry thought Ain Bishmu the most beautiful in the Egyptian deserts, but one wonders if he ever saw Ain al-Gebel in Dakhla Oasis. The hot spring flows out of a fissure in the main cliff along the border of Bawiti and Qasr. As it cascades down the cliff the water falls into a natural basin just large enough to serve as a bathtub and which is often occupied by one of the men of the village. Ain Bishmu runs into Ain Bardir, a colder spring, at the bottom of the cliff. It, too, runs into the natural basin, so there is hot and cold running water. Here women and young girls are often found washing clothes and dishes in the warm water. After the two springs join and flow into a cataract the water is dispersed to the low-lying fields. Foreigners do not bathe in these springs.

The Gardens

The gardens are by far the most pleasant part of visiting Bawiti and Qasr. They are forever green and something is happening in every corner of every garden all year long. In February, the *mishmish* (apricot) blossoms are already in bloom, by March the date trees have been pollinated, and by April and May

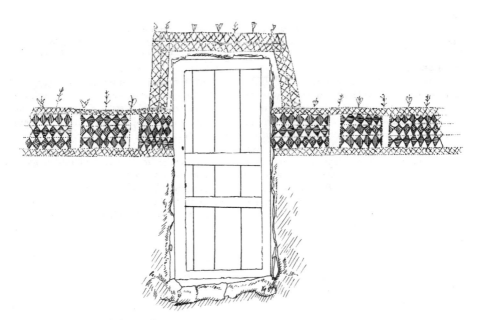

Doorway and wall painting at Qasr

the green dates are beginning to grow. There are lemons, oranges, mangoes, and olives, all in season. In October, the date harvest begins. Then the trees are pruned and prepared for the next season.

Rice Fields and Sand Dune

The rice fields are picturesque and have a delightful location. At various times of the year different activities can be seen here. Beyond them is the sand dune.

In addition to the pleasure of climbing, lying down on, and just enjoying a sand dune, the most important reason for visiting this particular sand dune is the view. Turn around. There is the old village visible on its perch with its wonderful gardens in front of it. Spectacular!

Al-Qasr Old Town

Return to Zawya Square and your vehicle before continuing the tour. Of course, feel free to walk for there is another garden to visit. Old Qasr is in the gardens today and Cailliaud's Roman Arch is tucked in there too. This part of the village used the ancient stones for building so look carefully at the structures to see if you can find an antique stone with some pharaonic writings or designs on it.

Roman Arch

The most impressive monument to greet the eyes of former travelers to Bahariya was the Roman Triumphal Arch. It was drawn by Cailliaud, who first described it. When he saw it, it had four arches. Ascherson, of the Rohlfs Expedition saw only two. It has been described by various travelers, including Belzoni, who thought it was the Temple of the Oracle at Siwa Oasis. Bits and pieces of the ancient structure can be found in the adjoining homes where they were used in construction. For a description of what the arch once was Ahmed Fakhry quotes Hoskins, who never visited Bahariya, but read Cailliaud. So, here it is fourth hand:

"The most imposing ruin in the Oasis Parva is a triumphal arch, evidently Roman. It stands on a platform, 33 feet in height above the level of the plain and 128 feet in length, being formed of rough stones thrown without any order into the cement; surrounding which is a wall 7 feet thick, very much inclined, and curiously constructed of hewn stones, placed alternately crossways and lengthways. The longer side of the stones being three times the measurement of the shorter, one stone of the row placed lengthways apparently covers three of those beneath. The cornice, which appears to have extended all round the platform, is rather of a good style, being surmounted with triglyphs and dentils. Above it is a kind of attic, with its cornice three feet high, forming a parapet to the platform. This latter is uncovered on three sides; but on the fourth side, the ground of the village of Kasr [Qasr] is now and appears to have been always on a level with it. The principal facade is toward the north.

"The triumphal arch, situated in the middle of the north facade of the platform, is 25 feet in length. Only the center arch now remains, from which a staircase leads to the ground beneath. The facades are ornamented with small columns. A winding staircase leads to the terrace, the outlet to which is under the arch. . ."

Today the arch is tucked into a garden behind an iron fence.

Continue beyond the arch through the gardens for another 200 meters. You can continue to Dist, Bir Ghaba, etc., or return to the villages.

TOUR #3
Tibniya and Environs

- bike, 2x2, 4x4
- 2–4 hours
- easy

			km	total km
Darb Siwa	N 28 20 917	E 28 51 658	0	0
Muftillah	N 28 21 378	E 28 50 858	1.6	1.6
Alexander	N 28 20 542	E 28 49 344	5.5	7.1
Hilwa (from road)	N 28 20 341	E 28 51 00	10	17.1

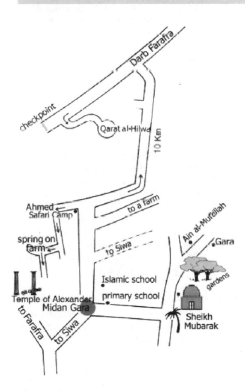

This tour begins where the Darb al-Farafra and Darb Siwa part company at the south-western edge of Qasr/Bawiti. A right onto Darb Siwa takes one to Midan al-Gara.

Palm Tree

When you make the right turn out of Midan al-Gara a primary school will be on your left. Directly in front of you, appearing above the buildings, is a single palm tree, its fronds extended toward the sky. This tree is the highest tree in Bahariya. Turn left at the palm, pass the tomb of Sheikh Mubarak, and turn right at the next fork. Muftillah is straight ahead and the sand dune called Gara is on the right.

Chapels of Ain al-Muftillah

First, of course, there is the spring. Then the temple. Four chapels exist to the south of Ain al-Muftillah. They are arranged in an unusual way, not conforming at all to traditional Egyptian temple construction. Each is independent of the other, orientation seems not to have been a factor, and the decorations are particularly odd. One was discovered by Steindorff in 1901, and the other three were excavated by Ahmed Fakhry.

In recent years the chapels have been re-excavated, but for the sake of preservation they have been purposely recovered by sand. All four sandstone and plaster chapels have religious inscriptions on the interior walls and are from the Twenty-sixth Dynasty. Two are special. One is dedicated to the god Bes, patron of musicians and dancers. Bes is portrayed as a dwarf, and is seldom given such prominence as to have a chapel dedicated to him. All that remains of his image is a foot and tail.

The second chapel has images of a series of gods arranged in a register on opposite walls of the open court. The court leads to an area that could have been a sacrificial altar. The sequencing of the gods is what is so mysterious. They are not all gods related to the rituals of death and burial, nor are they sky gods. To date, their association and the reason for their grouping is unknown.

Another interesting feature of temples in Bahariya is the color of the sandstone. Instead of the solid grey stone that is found throughout Egypt, these temples are streaked with ocher and sienna, colors that form the dominant hues in Bahariya. Although pretty in the landscape, the yellow and orange do not lend themselves well as background for the motifs of Egyptian art and because the sandstone is soft, the walls flake when touched.

The entire area of the temple is fenced in with barbed wire. Again, special permission to visit these sites must be obtained from Cairo. (See Practical Information.)

On the rise to the side of the temples just over the single dune is a wonderful panorama of the entire oasis including the villages of Qasr and Bawiti, Bir Matar, and most of the mountains in this area. Known as Gara, this site is perhaps most impressive at dawn or sunset.

Darb Siwa

Return to Midan Gara and turn right onto the road to Darb Siwa. You will pass a small hospital where the new doctor is a woman. Now all the women in the oasis come to this hospital. It is followed by an Islamic School. It is as big and as impressive as the schools donated to the oases by the United States. There are three Islamic schools in Bahariya Oasis.

About a kilometer after the Islamic School, the Darb Siwa turns right and heads for the escarpment. If you look at the escarpment you will see two roads to Siwa, one, paved, dead ahead and a second, unpaved, to the right. Do not turn onto Darb Siwa. Continue

straight ahead. Just beyond the Ahmed Safari Camp, turn left.

This entire area is known as al-Tibniya and is very pleasing to the eye and to the spirit. Turn left at the next dirt road into a small farm. Then turn right over a spring and immediately left. Head straight for the desert. Less than half a kilometer ahead is the Temple of Alexander. The farmer is the custodian of the temple and you must obey him. You cannot go to this temple without a pass.

Temple of Alexander the Great

Located at Qasr al-Migysbah, to the northeast of Qasr, this small, two-chamber temple is the only place in Egypt where Alexander the Great's effigy and cartouche have been found. Why these things were found in Bahariya is perplexing, as is the fact that to date nothing has been found from Alexander's visit to the Oracle at Siwa (see Siwa Oasis for details). As we have discovered, Bahariya is linked to Siwa by an ancient track and the temple overlooks the pass at the beginning of the route. Did Alexander pass this way and request the construction of the temple?

Ahmed Fakhry was the first to recognize Alexander's link to this temple in Bahariya. He excavated here from 1938 to 1940. The temple is on the flat depression floor and subject to the sand and wind storms that often descend from the north. Its fragile sandstone facade, blasted by centuries of harsh winds, is in a sorry state and today both Alexander's face and his cartouche have been eroded away. Rising to a height of several meters, the temple is a part of a much larger site which remains to be explored.

Desert Drive

The Qarat al-Hilwa is along the Darb Farafra not far from the checkpoint. To reach it from the Temple of Alexander one can enjoy a short 10 kilometer (6 miles), sometimes off-track, desert road. A 2x2 can do it. From the Temple of Alexander return to the Ahmed Safari Camp. With the camp on your right do not turn right, but go straight along a dirt road for about 200 meters. In the area to your left a number of gilded mummies were recently unearthed.

Valley of the Golden Mummies

Several years ago a donkey fell into a hole and unearthed a spectacular mummy with a gilded coffin. Kept under wraps as excavations continued, the find was recently announced to the world as the Valley of the Golden Mummies. It is believed the site may contain as many as 10,000 intact burials from the Roman period. The site will remain closed to visitors while excavations continue, but a few mummies will be on view in the antiquities museum once it is opened.

You will hit a paved road. Turn left onto the paved road. It will become a track. You are traveling west-southwest. Continue for about 3 kilometers (1.8 miles). You will hit the Darb al-Farafra. Turn left. You are now headed back to Bawiti. (If you turn right you will be headed to al-Hayz.) Five kilometers (3 miles) later a small dirt track goes left. You will see the small rise of Qarat al-Hilwa ahead.

Qarat al-Hilwa

Qarat al-Hilwa, Hill of the Beautiful One, is a sandstone ridge 3 kilometers (1.8 miles) south of Qasr to the northwest of the Darb al-Farafra. In pharaonic times the area was used as a burial site, similar to the Valley of the Kings in Thebes, where pharaohs were buried in rock tombs cut into the side of a mountain. Here, in Bahariya, the most important person was the governor, and the tomb of Amunhotep, governor of the Northern Oasis, is the only inscribed tomb at Qarat al-Hilwa. Not to be confused with the pharaohs of the same name, this Amunhotep was a native of Bahariya who was appointed governor during the New Kingdom, probably during the Eighteenth or Nineteenth Dynasty. It is the only known tomb from this era, and the oldest tomb so far discovered in the oasis. It is one of the few sources of information on New Kingdom activity in Bahariya.

The tomb, consisting of a forecourt and

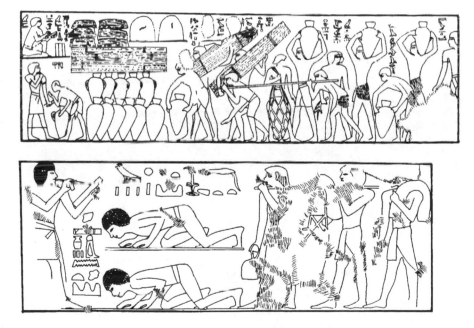

Tribute scenes from the Tomb of Rekhmire at Thebes in the Nile

Tribute scene from Qarat al-Hilwa

two chambers, includes traditional burial and religious scenes, but has also important agricultural scenes that show corn and wine being prepared for tribute to the ruler in the Nile Valley. Similar scenes can be found at Thebes in various tombs of the nobles including the Tomb of Rekhmire, vizier of Thutmose III. These agriculture scenes are found on the east wall of the second chamber of Amunhotep's tomb. Today the tomb is filled with sand and in a sorry state.

TOUR #4

Mountains, Desert, and Far Gardens

- walk, bike, 2x2, 4x4
- 2–4 hours
- easy

			km	total km
Black or English Mt	N 28 20 774	E 28 54 083	0	0
Gebel Mayisra	N 28 21	E 28 54 710	3.6	3.6
Garden road	N 28 22 329	E 28 54 728	1.3	4.9
Bir Matar	N 28 23 082	E 28 54 747	1.5	6.1
Bir Ghaba	N 28 25 856	E 28 56 494	c2	8.1
Gebel Dist	N 28 25 911	E 28 56 074	c1	9.1
Good view	N 28 22 340	E 28 53 450	c12	21.1
Sheikh Ahmad	N 28 22 114	E 28 52 949	c1	22.1
Lake at al-Marun	N 28 24 491	E 28 52 382	c2	24.1

This tour is a leisurely, easy excursion on the plain in front of Qasr and Bawiti including portions of the Darb al-Asas. It is a good test for 4x4 vehicles and their drivers for it is easy desert driving. It will test your metal for the difficult journeys in Farafra and Kharga.

From the center of Bawiti follow the main road out of town past the gas station and tire repair shops toward Cairo. Pass through the newly erected arch and just beyond Black Mountain a desert track leads off to the left. Turn onto the track and follow it for about one kilometer to the base of Gebel Mayisra. You will pass a new hotel. Then the route hugs the base of this mountain with the gardens of the village of Aguz visible about

1 kilometer to the right. Continue along the route for another 2 kilometers (1.2 miles). It will join the route from the gardens. As the roads meet, Gebel Mandisha is on the right. It follows alongside the track for 4 kilometers (2.5 miles).

Black or English Mountain

This mountain is distinguished by a ruin at its summit. It is not difficult to climb the mountain and the view from the top offers a panorama of the northern part of the oasis. At one corner of the summit are the ruins of a World War I lookout post, which was manned by Captain Williams, after whom the mountain is sometimes called. Williams was posted to Bahariya to observe troop movements by the Sanusi. The house, consisting of three rooms and a bath, is now in ruins. This is the same Captain Claud Williams of the Light Car Patrols for whom Williams Pass along the border of Libya and Egypt is named.

Gebel Mayisra

Gebel Mayisra is a long triangular hill found to the north of Gebel Mandisha. A black capping of dolorite and basalt volcanic rock tops its 50-meter (160 foot) summit. At the top it is 3 kilometers (1.8 miles) long and 1 kilometer wide.

Gebel Mandisha

Located between Bawiti and Mandisha, Gebel Mandisha divides the cultivated land. It has a black capping of dolorite and basalt volcanic rock, is four kilometers (2.5 miles) long, three kilometers (1.8 miles) wide, and 25 meters (80 feet) high According to local legend it is named after the daughter of a Roman king who converted to Islam. Since the Roman and Islamic periods are centuries apart, the legend is suspect.

Garden Road

When the track meets the asphalt you have reached the garden road. You are on the Darb al-Asas (see Caravans and Roadways above). The left goes to the lake and gardens, which you will do at the end of this tour. For now, bear right and head toward Gebel Dist, which appears to be straight ahead.

Bir Matar, Spring of the Airport

There is a lot happening at Bir Matar. A new well is being dug as I write. They have already drilled over 1000 meters. The further they dig, the greater the guarantee that the spring will be hot. That means there will be a hot and cold spring side by side here and they will probably both be available for the tourist. The spring of cold water is used by both tourists and locals as a swimming hole. It is cool and refreshing on hot desert days. When the British occupied the oasis they built a landing strip and set up their tents here. They also had an outpost at Naqb Siwa.

Nearby are camping facilities, called Chalet Bir Matar. At the present time they are maintained by the Tourist Information Office, but they are looking for prospective buyers to transform the facility. Anyone can camp here for a few pounds. There are tents, a kitchen, and toilets. It is not a bad spot.

The paved road ends after Bir Matar but as one continues toward Gebel Dist the desert track is negotiable by regular vehicle. On the far left palm trees appear in the distance. This is **Bir al-Marun** where the new lake is located.

After another three kilometers (1.8 miles) there is a fork in the dirt track. The route to the right leads through the forest, the route to the left through the desert, and both end at Bir Ghaba. The long mountain to the right of the forest is called **Gebel al-Ghaba**, Mountain of the Forest.

Bir Ghaba

Bir Ghaba, the Well of the Forest, is a hot-water well north of Bawiti located in a grove of eucalyptus trees. It is situated along the main caravan route through the oasis and is a major campsite for tourists. One can enter the depression via Naqb Ghurabi and head straight to Bir Ghaba.

Today the area in front of Bir Ghaba has been homesteaded by Fayoumis who grow watermelons and tomatoes. That means, of course, that the area is not as secluded as it once was. At Bir Ghaba there are a number of grass huts developed by a former tourist company but now under the control of the

Alpenblick Hotel. You can use these facilities for a fee. Unfortunately, too many tourists and not enough clean-up is happening at Bir Ghaba. If you go, do a little litter control. This route requires a 4x4 or dirt bike, but is easy to follow, being well marked with rocks. Once amid the trees the temperature drops dramatically as the shade offers a welcome respite from the hot sun on summer days. After a kilometer of twisting and turning, the cold water Bir Qasa, Well of the Bowl, is on the right at a fork in the track. Take the left-hand fork. Continue for over a kilometer through a wonderful tree-lined track to another fork. Again take the left fork. Another half kilometer leads out of the trees and to another fork. Both forks lead to Bir Ghaba, the right easier to manage, but longer.

Gebel Dist

Gebel Dist, Mountain of the Pot, is an Oligocene ferruginous mesa, shaped like a pyramid. It is 50 meters (160 feet) high and 800 meters (2560 feet) in circumference at the base narrowing to 30 meters (96 feet) circumference at the top. Locals call it Magic Mountain because of the way the light plays on the texture and material of the mountain during the different hours of the day. Because Dist can be seen from most places around Bawiti, it is a good landmark.

Gebel Maghrafa

Gebel Maghrafa, Mountain of the Ladle, and Dist (they are 50 meters apart) dominate the plain around Bir Ghaba. Maghrafa, the smaller of the two mountains, is an Oligocene ferruginous butte, 600 meters (1920 feet) round at the base and 15 meters (48 feet) at the top.

Paralititan stromeri (Stromer's Tidal Giant) is the name of the dinosaur that was redis-covered recently by a Penn/Egyptian Geological Museum team. It is named not only for its location along the shores of an ancient sea, but for its size, being the largest and heaviest dinosaur known, and for the man who first found dinosaurs in Bahariya, the German scientist Ernst Stromer. Stromer found the giant creature in 1914 at the base

of Gebel Dist. His research and samples were lost during World War II when his Munich museum was destroyed by Allied bombing. The modern scientists found five tons of material including 16 bones of the giant, some in fragments, but one arm bone 169 centimeters long. They estimate the beast to have been about 25 meters high and to weigh 50 to 80 tons. It ate plants and enjoyed life along coastal lowlands amid mangrove trees about 93–99 million years ago in the Cenomanian stage of the late Cretaceous period. No other dinosaur has been found enjoying mangroves. The dinosaur is not the only find in the area. Fish, turtles, a crocodile and a lot of vegetation tell us that the surroundings were subtropical.

Simply retrace your steps back to the place where the desert and garden routes meet and turn right along the garden route. As one continues along the road the entire plain comes into view on the right. With mountains as the backdrop there are fields, desert, and long vistas. A good place for photos.

Sheikh Ahmad

Not too far away on the right-hand side is the tomb of Sheikh Ahmad. The farmers believe that the Sheikh lights the way for them when they return from the fields at night. Here one makes almost a U-turn and follows the road to the lake.

Lake al-Marun

Local legend says that no one should go to Bir al-Marun alone because the *afrit* (mischievous spirits) hold parties at night, and sometimes the beating of their drums can be heard in the other villages. In fact, there is probably an old Islamic village in this area, or at least a caravan stop from the days of the Hagg.

Paralititan stromeri

TOUR #5
Northern Bahariya and Environs

- bike, 2x2, 4x4
- 2–4 hours
- easy

			km	total km
Arch	N 28 20 936	E 28 53 257	0	0
Aguz	N 28 20 650	E 28 54 434	2	2
Ghard Mandisha	N 28 20 558	E 28 55 658	2	4
Mandisha	N 28 20 639	E 28 56 388	1	5
Gabala	N 28 20 552	E 28 57 709	2	7
Qaseir Muharib	N 28 20 617	E 28 58 494	1.2	9.2
Hara	N 28 21 830	E 29 04 273	9	18.2

A series of villages and ancient sites can be visited by traveling north of Bawiti toward the escarpment along the macadamized road.

Aguz

The foundation of the village of Aguz, the Old One, is an interesting story. Unlike the other villages, Aguz is inhabited by 'foreigners' to Bahariya Oasis. Ahmed Fakhry tells us that it was founded by families from Siwa whose women were banished from that oasis for having loose morals. Just as rulers of the Nile Valley used Kharga as a place of banishment, the people of Siwa may have sent their unwanted citizens to Bahariya.

Descendants of the Badromani family, the original founders of Aguz, deny Fakhry's claim. According to the family history, which is written on a gazelle skin and held for safe keeping by the elder of the family, the Badromani family originally came from Yemen. They traveled to Minya and ultimately to Bahariya. Their intention was to settle in Jaghbub near the Sanusi center. When they got to Bahariya they stayed and made annual pilgrimages to Jaghbub instead. On one of these pilgrimages they bought several slave families from Siwa to cultivate their land around Aguz.

Cailliaud, who came to the oasis in 1819, remarked on the new colony. In 1876, many

of the villagers still spoke Siwan. Descendants of all these families still live in Aguz.

Aguz is built over an ancient site which has yet to be excavated. The old village is typical of a medieval oasis town similar to Qasr. It is abandoned today. The newer part, which is the first to be entered, offers little of note except for the Bedouin Cafeteria where Abdul Sadek Badromani sings and recites poetry.

Getting There: Just after passing Black Mountain, Aguz is visible on the left. Take the first paved road to the left.

Ghard Mandisha

This dune field is small by comparison with other fields in the Western Desert and the dunes are not very high, but their close proximity to the main road offers an opportunity to stop for a visit. The sand dunes lie on the northwest side of the road and extend for 2 kilometers (1.2 miles) toward the village of Mandisha.

Mandisha

This charming village with a wonderful name that rolls off the tongue is one of the oldest villages in Bahariya. It descends gently down the hill into the palm groves below. There are no antiquities in Mandisha, but it is a charming, friendly place and visitors are welcome.

Cailliaud says 600 people lived in Mandisha in 1819, while Ball and Beadnell in their survey of the oasis in 1897 found 1,798 people in Mandisha. This was the largest population of the Bahariya villages at that time. He also saw a number of aqueducts *(manafis)*, at Mandisha.

Getting There: Mandisha is 7 kilometers (4.3 miles) north of Bawiti. Turn left on the paved road. You immediately pass through the newly developed section of the village. The old, traditional homes are located further on. Just beyond is the village of Zabw.

Zabw

Zabw lies less than a kilometer beyond Mandisha. Its main claim to fame is the Qasr al-Zabw, a rock along the Darb al-Bahnasa which was once inscribed with what Ahmed Fakhry called "the richest collection of Libyan graffiti in our Western Desert." In fact, with the discovery of so much graffiti along the Darb al-Ghurabi and points south, Fakhry was wrong. He dated some inscriptions to the twelfth and thirteenth centuries.

Unfortunately the rock has been badly damaged as stone has been quarried for building material. However, there are a number of inscriptions worthy of note including that of Hyde, who left his name everywhere in the Western Desert.

When Cailliaud was here in 1819, there were 400 people in the village, which he called Zubbo. He also discovered the people dipped their white cloth in a particular stream which dyed them black in a day. Ball and Beadnell found 858 people in Zabw in 1897. This figure includes fifty people from Hara.

Southeast of the village are a number of ancient sepulchers and catacombs. The sarcophagi, according to Hoskins, are of burnt clay and rounded at the two ends. Belzoni saw them too, and says they are 2 inches thick with flat lids with heads of either a man, woman, or an animal placed above the head of the mummy. The antiquities department has found additional coffins.

Getting There: Take the road to Mandisha and pass through the village to the second village, Zabw. At Zabw, bear left at the first fork and pass through a palm grove.

This is a good place to see the damage that can be done by dunes as they encroach on a village, for the Ghard Mandisha is enveloping the palm groves of Zabw. Passing beyond the village the road heads for the escarpment and less than a half a kilometer later a dirt track leads to the right. The graffiti is located on the lone rock along this path.

Gabala

Returning to the main road and continuing north, the next village is Gabala, where a few rock tombs have been found in a small Late Period or Roman cemetery on a hill called Qarat Maghrabiya. There are a number of uninscribed rock tombs in the area. One, fairly large and easily accessible, is a tomb with three rooms. In the ceiling are small pieces of wood caught within the stone in some ancient era. Not a major site, the tombs are of little interest to most tourists.

Getting There: Continue north beyond Mandisha for a kilometer and turn left through the village of Gabala. After a kilometer turn right and immediately left and continue for an additional half of a kilometer. The tombs are on both sides of the road.

Qaseir Muharib

Probably the most impressive ruin in Bahariya is Qaseir Muharib, Fortress of the Fighter, an extensive Roman/Christian village. There are quite a number of impressive ruins here, some rising to two stories and most in a good state of preservation. Only one or two structures are visible from the road, but the village cascades down the slope and there is a good view of the plain below.

The village, probably garrisoned and built with defense in mind, sits to the north of the capital Qasr, commanding a strategic view of the caravan routes from the north. That there was extensive agriculture in the area is attested by the aqueducts and the condition of the soil around the ruins. There are ten to twelve structures still standing in Muharib, including a small mudbrick fortress, a stone temple, a church, and several aqueducts. This is probably Hoskins's Kasr Nosrani, Castle of the Christians, a Coptic village Hoskins maintains was 1,700 feet in circumference.

Often tucked into the corner of one of the buildings are a number of small white flags with written spells or petitions attached to them. Here we meet the pagan beliefs that still exist in remote areas of Egypt. Women from the oasis come to this site as their sisters in Qurna on the west bank of the Nile at Luxor visit the sacred lake of the Ramesseum, to petition the ancient gods to grant them children. They come in the dark of night, often using a candle to light the way, and place their petition next to those of other women who have done the same thing.

Fakhry was the first to investigate the area, and no major work has been done on the site since that time. To visitors who are accustomed to the grand and eloquent monuments of the Nile Valley it is worth mentioning that many of the more popular monuments looked much like these desert sites only a few decades ago. Here in the oases one sees raw ruins. In the Nile Valley the ruins have been in the hands of archaeologists for a long time. They have been painstakingly reconstructed, their foundations cleared of the debris of centuries, and walls rebuilt to their original height. In the oases we see the remains of the past in their natural condition, at times a little rough around the edges, but always filled with the spirits of those who came before.

Getting There: Muharib is located just over a kilometer north of Gabala on the north, or left, side of the road.

Hara and Environs

Hara is 134 meters (429 feet) above sea level. At first sight the village of Hara, meaning 'narrow streets,' doesn't seem to have much to offer, but like every village in the desert it has its own personality and treasures. Although inhabited during Roman times, the current residents of Hara came from the village of Mandisha. The first part of the village is new and called Ain Gedid, new spring, but about half a kilometer later the old mudbrick village of Hara begins. Here

the asphalt road ends and one steps back in time.

Everything is level at Hara for the village lies on the depression floor with no mountains around it. After another kilometer the road begins to wind through the gardens. Date trees line the narrow road and the ripening dates are within reach of the ground. In fact, one can reach out of the window and grab a handful.

The road exits the gardens to another cluster of houses, past a school, and out to Ain Yusif, only a kilometer away. Ain Yusif is surrounded by small lakes and is an excellent place for birdwatchers. There are plenty of farmers in this area who welcome a visit by strangers. Some will ask people to join them for tea, in most instances hoping you will say no for their stores are meager, but if you have time to spend, it is a delight to be a guest in the home of one of the villagers in the oases. Offer something in return: candy, sugar, tea.

Watermelon is the new crop for Hara and the locals tell us that fifty cars a day go to the Nile Valley to deliver the new produce from this oasis.

Wadi al-Gamel

Beyond Ain Yusif a 4x4 or dirt bike is needed. The area between the northeastern escarpment and Ain Yusif is called the **Wadi al-Gamel**, Valley of the Camel, and as the name implies the valley is used by Bedouin to graze their herds. If the visitor is lucky, both the Bedouin and their camels will be in residence. Once, one saw 3,000 to 4,000 camels in a single herd. This is becoming a rare event.

Ruins

Near the village of Hara are two ancient ruins, neither excavated. The first is a mudbrick building at Ain al-Wadi, Spring of the Valley, and the second is a Roman cemetery at Ain Gedid, New Spring.

TOUR #6

Sahara Suda (the Black Desert)

- 2x2, 4x4
- all day
- easy to difficult

			km	total km
Bawiti checkpoint	N 28 20 546	E 28 51 257	0	0
Umm al-Iffa	N 28 17 295	E 28 47 459	8	8
Tomb of René Michel	N 28 16 325	E 28 47 170	1.6	9.6
Gebel Gala Siwa	N 28 14 113	E 28 46 605	4.5	14.1
Gebel Miteili Radwan	N 28 11 130	E 28 45 631	5.5	19.6
The Pyramids	N 20 09 643	E 28 44 976	2.7	22.3
Gebel al-Zuqaq	N 28 09 441	E 28 44	2.2	24.5
Gebel al-Nuss	N 28 08 802	E 28 44 740	unavailable	

If you can take only one tour in Bahariya, this should be it. Landscape is the main feature, and the landscape of Bahariya is dominated by dozens and dozens of small black-topped mountains. These mountains are part of a major fold that cuts sharply through the oasis in a northeastern direction from the western to the eastern scarp. Almost 200 meters (640 feet) thick, the fault begins 14 kilometers (8.7 miles) northwest of Hayz and can be followed to Gebel Hafuf. by a line of cup-shaped limestone hills. Ball and Beadnell set the date of this faulting as post-Eocene, or Pliocene, when great upheavals created the landscape of Africa and Asia.

Two kilometers (1.2 miles) outside of Bawiti is the first of a series of military checkpoints. Half a kilometer beyond on the east (left) side of the road is **Bir Wali**, a good place to stop for orientation. The small mountain near the road straight ahead is the 125 meter (400 foot) high **Gebel Hammad**. As you will see, it is actually to the left of the road, but at this point, before the road curves, it appears to be on the right. Local guides tell us that an old airport exists on top of this mountain. On the left of the road, looking like the escarpment, is Gebel Hafuf, the largest mountain in Bahariya. To the right, near the far escarpment, is **Gebel al-**

Tibniya and Naqb Siwa. The naqb looks like a black snake climbing the escarpment in the distance.

Gebel Hafuf

Gebel Hafuf is a narrow, ridge-like hill of limestone, 15 kilometers (9 miles) long and 72 meters (230 feet) high, located southeast of Bawiti. Composed of dolorite and basalt tertiary volcanic rock, its black mass offers the best evidence of tectonic folding in the oasis.

Umm al-Iffa

Eight kilometers (5 miles) beyond the checkpoint between Gebel Hafuf and the escarpment are a number of sand dunes known as Umm al-Iffa. This is an excellent place to have some fun or to camp. Some of the local safari groups hold parties here at night.

Tomb of René Michel

Only 1.6 kilometers (1 mile) later, on the right, or northwest side of the road is the tomb of René Michel. René was a French-speaking Swiss who retired and came to the oases in 1981. He lived here and helped start modern tourism in Bahariya by making safaris into the desert. He named the Alpenblick Hotel because of the mountain terrain in Bahariya, which he thought looked like Switzerland. He died in 1986. The short road to his grave was recently constructed by government workers who thought the grave was a sheikh's tomb.

Gebel Shahut

As you face the grave from the road look to your right. Behind is Gebel Shahut. There is an interesting legend about how this mountain got its name. A man considered to be the best driver in the entire oasis and known for finding his way when other men got lost, got lost here. When he found his way back, the people named the mountain after him.

Sahara Suda

Now all the mountains are spread out for you in an almost straight line along the horizon. We are approaching Sahara Suda, the Black Desert, a favorite safari destination for local tour groups. The ground to the right and left of the road is covered with black stones. Weaving in and out of these mountains is great fun. Although a skilled 2-wheel driver can manage most of it, there is a good chance the car will eventually get stuck. Take a guide—they are not expensive and can tell you things you will never discover by yourself.

Gebel Gala Siwa

Gebel Gala Siwa is 4.5 kilometers (3 miles) beyond on the west (right) side of the road. This pyramid mountain served as a lookout station for caravans coming from Siwa Oasis to the north. When a caravan was expected, someone would climb to the top of Gebel Gala Siwa to observe Naqb Siwa visible to the northwest. Then, while the caravan was busy making its way slowly down the escarpment, the lookout would hasten to Bawiti to spread the news.

Gebel Miteili Radwan

Five kilometers (3 miles) beyond Gala Siwa is a black-topped conical mountain on the east (left) side of the road. It is named after a man who often traveled to Farafra before the creation of the road. Radwan used this mountain as a landmark to help him find the way.

The Pyramids

A little under three kilometers (1.8 miles) later are two mountains on either side of the road. Tourists have named them the pyramids because when you stand between them, the one on the left, east, looks like Chephren's pyramid with its covered top, and the mountain on the right, west, looks like the Step Pyramid. From a distance these descriptions do not apply.

Gebel al-Zuqaq

Only two kilometers (1.2 miles) later is a mountain called "the alley." The mountain is not really the al-Zuqaq, but marks the entrance to it. The al-Zuqaq is a favorite off-road tour for the Black Desert. First, note the brilliant strata of colorful limestone at the base of the mountain. Red, orange, yellow, and gold glisten within the white and beige stone. Looking up at the mountain itself, on one side you can see a thin line of yellow sand reaching to the top. Tourists climbing this mountain have created this path.

At the end of this tour you can return to Bawiti or continue on to al-Hayz and Farafra. Do not travel the desert at night.

TOUR #7

Al-Hayz

- 2x2, 4x4
- all day
- easy

			km	total km
Checkpoint	N 28 01 379	E 28 41 893	0	0
Ain al-Ris	N 28 01 713	E 28 41 166	2	2
Mud lions	N 28 01 625	E 28 40 571	1	3
Ain al-Izza	N 28 01 797	E 28 38 417	4	7
Checkpoint	N 28 01 594	E 28 38 388	0.2	7.2

Thirty-seven kilometers (23 miles) beyond the checkpoint at Bawiti is Awwal al-Hayz, the beginning of the district of Hayz, marked by yet another checkpoint. Hayz is not a single place, but a collection of small hamlets, each bearing a different name. It is more a district, and some of the people in Bahariya refer to it as a separate oasis. During the Roman era this area was very prosperous. Many of the current families were originally from Libya. They came to Bahariya before the Sanusi.

Ain Gumma and Tablat Amun

The checkpoint is at Ain Gumma, Spring of Friday, and Tablat Amun, Drum of Amun. At the checkpoint turn east (left). The road which leads directly past Ain Gumma is a pretty drive through scattered trees and shrubs to the gardens of the village 3 kilometers (1.8 miles) beyond. Although rumor has it that there are antiquities in the area, the villagers know nothing about them.

Ain al-Ris

Returning to the main road, Ain al-Ris is 2 kilometers (1.2 miles) later and here the antiquities speak for themselves. Visible from the main road they are located in a beautiful valley well worth the effort of having fought the traffic in Cairo to get permission to visit. Turning southeast (left) from the main road

continue along a well-paved road to the watchman's house. He will escort you on your visit. Near the watchman's house is the church, and on the opposite side of the road is the Qasr, or Deir. Beyond is a dried-up salt lake and the escarpment. It is a very peaceful and beautiful area.

This area was inhabited in Roman times, when a fairly large settlement existed. It ranks with Qaseir Muharib as one of the keys to unraveling the history of Roman and Christian Bahariya, but to date, other than early work done by Ahmed Fakhry, the area has not been investigated.

Church of Saint George

The Church of Saint George is one of the most important monuments in the Western Desert. Built between the fourth and fifth centuries, its only rival is the Christian church at Bagawat in Kharga Oasis. Together these two churches mark an important chapter in Christian history. Abu Salih, the medieval Christian historian, maintained that the relics and headless body of Saint Bartholomew, one of the disciples of Jesus, were buried here. The church still stands, although the roof is gone. It is of mudbrick and follows the traditional plan of an apse with several side aisles. No frescoes remain, but there are several decorations either incised into stucco or raised in sharp reliefs.

Ruins at al-Hayz, after Cailliaud, 1820

When the first European explorers visited the area around 1820, the head of a horse could still be seen.

Deir al-Ras
Five hundred meters (1,600 feet) to the south of the church is the Deir al-Ras, Monastery of the Head. There is no way of knowing exactly if the name of the monastery refers to Bartholomew, but one must suppose it does. The monastery is a ruin hardly rising above ground level.

Qasr Masuda
The Roman fortress, Qasr Masuda, an imposing structure with thirteen rooms, is separated from the church and monastery by the modern road. Its presence attests to the importance of the area, garrisoned in Roman times. We know the area was highly developed, agriculture being a major occupation. The foundations of several Roman mansions have been unearthed and farms must also have existed in the area. There was ample water, and evidence suggests a major settlement.

Mansaf
Returning to the main road and continuing south, a mere kilometer beyond Ain al-Ris is a small depression to the southeast (left) of the road, filled by a small group of mud lions, with the wonderful mountains of Bahariya as a backdrop. Although there are no trees for shade, a problem in the summer, and no hot spring for a refreshing bath, it is a well-protected area and a wonderful place to stop and spend a little time, perhaps even to camp.

Ain al-Izza
Four kilometers (2.5 miles) beyond Mansaf is Ain al-Izza, an inhabited village on the western (right) side of the road. There are several ancient sites here including an ancient village, in a sorry state of preservation. Rock tombs exist in the ridge to the northwest of the village, but by far the most interesting site at Ain al-Izza is the ancient aqueduct, an underground gallery similar to those found at Bawiti and at Ain Umm Dabadib in Kharga Oasis. Izza is the terminal village for the Darb Ain Della, which climbs the escarpment and heads west to Ain Della.

Church of Saint George, after Cailliaud, 1820

TOUR #8

Darb Siwa

- 4x4
- all day or overnight
- easy to difficult
- restricted, requires permission

			km	total km
Darb Siwa			0	0
Sitra Oasis	deep desert		144	144
Nuwamisa	deep desert		30	174
Bahrein	deep desert		22	196
Areg	deep desert		54	250
Checkpoint	N 29 14	E 25 32	154	404

Darb Siwa, the ancient caravan route from Siwa to Bahariya, was of major importance in the past. Joining the northern coast with the central desert, it eliminated travel to the Nile Valley for caravans that wished to move south through the desert. This route formed an important desert link for travelers and in 1874 it was traveled by Jordan on a ten-day trek as part of the Rohlfs expedition.

John Ball found the lakes on this journey quite perplexing. He asked in his article "Problems of the Libyan Desert," "Why have not certain lakes, such as Areg, Sitra, and Bahrein, situated as they are in an almost rainless region, long since dried up?" Well, he answered his own question and believed they are fed by underground springs.

Darb Siwa

Darb Siwa leaves Bahariya via a pass in the escarpment to the northwest of Qasr. From Bawiti follow the main road west to the edge of town and at the first fork in the road take the left-hand route. Continue for less than a kilometer to a second fork. The left-hand route leads to Farafra and the right-hand to an area called al-Qara (the high place). Take the right-hand fork. Continue for another kilometer along the main road. A road forks to the right. Avoid it and continue along the main route (it eventually leads to the village

of Tibniya) for an additional four kilometers (2.5 miles). Here the Darb Siwa turns right toward the escarpment (about 2 kilometers [1.2 miles] away) and the Naqb Siwa, which is visible climbing up the scarp. There is a military checkpoint along this road where permissions must be shown. Then it is a straight drive along a paved road to Siwa.

The first 43 kilometers (27 miles) of the journey to Siwa are unimpressive, but then one encounters the Ghard Kebir, the great dunes, which are slowly making their way south and will eventually reach the southern portion of Bahariya Oasis. The dunes are to the north of the road, which at this point turns west to avoid them.

Sitra Oasis

The descent into Sitra Oasis begins approximately 144 kilometers (90 miles) from the Naqb Siwa checkpoint and approximately 88 kilometers (55 miles) from the beginning of the Ghard Kebir. Sitra is crossed east to west, cutting through 20 kilometers (12.5 miles) of the lower half of this large depression. Along the roadway it is unimpressive, but to the west, where the lake is, it is more interesting. To visit the lake one needs a 4x4 or dirt bike. The lake is about 22 kilometers (14 miles) long and 5 kilometers (3 miles) wide. It is highly salty.

Evidently Nuwamisa (see next entry) is not the only mosquito-infested oasis in this area. In 1931, Dugald Campbell had a nasty mosquito experience at Sitra. He tells us, "As the sun sank away in the west, and night came on, we were attacked by swarms of mosquitoes. They bit, drawing blood; the men kept a smoky fire going to protect themselves, and I huddled up on the side of the dune with a mosquito-net covering my face and hands. As night deepened, and darkness thickened, swarms of gnats and mosquitoes filled the air. A jackal barked on the other side of the lake, a solitary night bird screeched, and our camels thumped their feet on the sand to shake off the blood-sucking insects that bit them."

These oases were great smugglers' routes as they were close enough for protection and much needed water, yet remote enough to make continuous posts impossible. This was the case in June of 1907, when the Camel Corps came upon the infamous smugglers of the Beni Amar tribe (see al-Diffa for details) bringing a load of hashish into Egypt from Greece.

The smugglers were well on their way to the Nile Valley with their cargo when a patrol out of Matruh found tracks at Areg Oasis. They jumped ahead of the smugglers to Sitra where the small patrol of two officers, five men, and two guides hid in ambush and totally surprised the Bedouin. They arrested twenty-six smugglers and confiscated thirty camels, 2,470 kilos of hashish, and some guns. The remaining smugglers escaped and seeing the small number of men who had attacked them, decided to get back the contraband. The next day they were in hot pursuit. But they were out of luck. Another Camel Corps patrol, this one with eleven men out of Dabaa, joined the chase. A few days later they found the Bedouin on the cliffs overlooking Bahariya Oasis. They were surrounded, captured, and an additional eight camels with 293 kilos of hashish were confiscated (as were twenty new camels the Beni Amar had stolen from some poor soul who was grazing them in the area).

At 170 kilometers (106 miles) from the checkpoint at Naqb Siwa the road climbs out

of Sitra. Thirty kilometers (18.7 miles) later, or 200 kilometers (125 miles) from the first checkpoint, Nuwamisa Oasis appears on the left.

Nuwamisa Oasis

The entrance to Nuwamisa Oasis, Oasis of the Mosquitoes, slopes gently down from the main road to the blue salt-lake shore. This is a beautiful place with hundreds of palm trees surrounding the lake and rounded cliffs with small bays (ideal for campsites), forming the backdrop. It is also an empty place, uninhabited for centuries, with only a few caves and tombs left over from Roman times. Unfortunately, what does live at Nuwamisa are the billions of mosquitoes that lend their name to the site. They descend at sunset in thundering hoards and this writer got at least one hundred bites in less than ten minutes. We thought we were smart and moved well away from the lake to camp in a small bay. The instant the sun was gone the mosquitoes began. We were in the process of heating a wonderful beans and sausage casserole made and frozen in Maadi days before. Our helper was pitching the tents. All was for nothing. One could not eat for the mosquitoes outnumbered the beans and had drowned themselves in the stew. The tents were as full as the outside so one could not hide within. If we opened the door to get in the car we would bring a million mosquitoes in with us before we could close it again. All that was left us was to wrap ourselves in whatever protective material we could find: sleeping bags, extra clothing. If one piece of skin was exposed, it was bomber time in the Western Desert. After an experience like this, one understands how people go mad in the desert.

Bahrein Oasis

Continuing northwest along the main road, after 22 kilometers (13.7 miles) are the temporary quarters of the Bahrein Water Well Pavement Company. Bahrein Oasis, Oasis of the Two Lakes, lies only a few kilometers to the left or south of the road. Larger than Nuwamisa and as deserted, it too was inhabited in Roman times. Although it is a depression one does not have the feeling of entering for the way in is over a sloping terrain. The western lake, shimmering blue in the sun, is a dangerous trap, for near the shore, without any warning, is mushy sand where a vehicle can sink up to the axle even while standing still. It is a small lake with vegetation growing in the marshy area to the east. The eastern lake, at least 8 kilometers (5 miles) beyond, gleams white with salt left behind during evaporation. There are some uninscribed tombs at Bahrein. They are visible on the small escarpment between the two lakes. Examined by Ahmed Fakhry, they are of little interest to anyone but specialists.

The main road reaches the eastern edge of Pancho Mountain 254 kilometers (159 miles) from Naqb Siwa. It turns north with the escarpment on the west (left) and Areg Oasis on the east.

Areg Oasis

Unlike Nuwamisa, which is visible from the main road, and Bahrein, which slopes gently down to the lakes, Areg has a formidable escarpment which must be descended to reach the soft, sandy, depression floor. Eight kilometers (5 miles) after making the turn north from Bahrein there are several tracks leading east to the top of the escarpment of Areg.

Beautiful as Nuwamisa and Bahrein are, Areg is by far the most spectacular oasis in this area. The white chalk cliffs of the escarpment form the dominant color, highlighted by the buff of the dunes and, in winter, the rich blue of the sky. There is a lake and some tombs. The sandy descent is steep, but fairly easy for a good 4x4, though getting out of the depression can be a problem. Also the floor

of the depression is not only soft sand, but crusted sand with water underneath. This can be deadly. It is not a place for the novice and even the experienced 4x4er may have problems. Never, never, never, venture into such a place with a single vehicle. In fact, three vehicles are recommended.

Most of the early travelers knew of and visited this oasis: Cailliaud in 1819, Pancho in 1826, and Rohlfs in 1874. When Jennings-Bramley was there in October 1896 he worried so much about the robbers that he did not light a fire and said, "The Arej [Areg] bears so bad a reputation that strangers are looked upon with suspicion. . ."

There are tombs at Areg. From Areg the main road continues north, making its way over dune fields into Siwa Oasis and on to Zaytun and finally Shali, the first inhabited area since leaving Bahariya.

Rock tombs at Areg Oasis

7

Fayoum

Named after the Coptic word *phiom* or *pa-yom*, meaning lake or sea, the triangular depression of the Fayoum looks like a delta. Near to Cairo, and easily accessible along several well-paved highways, the Fayoum can be explored in a series of pleasant day-trips and offers a wide variety of activities ranging from boating, swimming, and fishing, to visiting antiquities, bird watching, and looking at fossils. The lake, hemmed in on the far shore by a rugged escarpment, creates a unique desert landscape. Ancient water-wheels churn and groan, lifting the water that rushes throughout the Fayoum over an intricate and ancient canal system. The farmers toil in lush green fields at tasks that seem to imitate the drawings and reliefs of ancient tomb paintings. Ancient ruins stand at the desert fringes as haunting reminders of the long and interesting history of the Fayoum. Shards, beads, ancient tools, household utensils, and other artifacts litter the ground at many of the historic sites. From scientist to sightseer, there is something for everyone in the Fayoum.

History

In prehistory more people lived in the Fayoum than in the Nile Valley. The land was lush and there was an abundance of water. During the Qarunian period (c.7200 to 6000 B.C.) Southwest Asians, whom we call Epi-Paleolithic Qarunians, migrated to the area and established residence. Hunting and fishing were the main occupations and plants and animals were just beginning to be domesticated. This all took place around a much larger lake.

In Neolithic times (c. 5500 to 4000 B.C.) two distinct groups existed around the lake shore: Early Neolithic Fayumian and Late Neolithic Moerian. During these periods the first known agricultural communities flourished and they dined on gazelle, hartebeests, or catfish, cooked in rough faced bowls or cooking pots, and served their friends and family on red polished rectangular earthenware dishes.

Around 4000 B.C. the climate changed and the Fayoum began to dry. Over a period of many years, the people left their drought stricken homes and migrated to the Nile Valley. By 3500 B.C., some were living east of the Nile in what is now Maadi–Digla, a modern suburb south of Cairo. From the debris left behind in the Fayoum, we know they had grain silos, made pottery, and used sickles, but we have yet to find any shelters.

Once the Nile Valley became dominant, the Fayoum was all but abandoned, for life was easier along the river, especially because of the summer floods. Then the Fayoum became a hunting and fishing paradise as well as a place to be mined for its salts, limestone, and chert.

Pharaonic (2686–332 B.C.)

During the Old Kingdom (c. 2686–2181 B.C.) the Fayoum was known as Ta-she, or She-resy (the Southern Lake) and was dedicated to the crocodile god. That god was Sobek to the ancient Egyptians, Souchos, Pnepheros, Petesouchos, and Soknopaios to

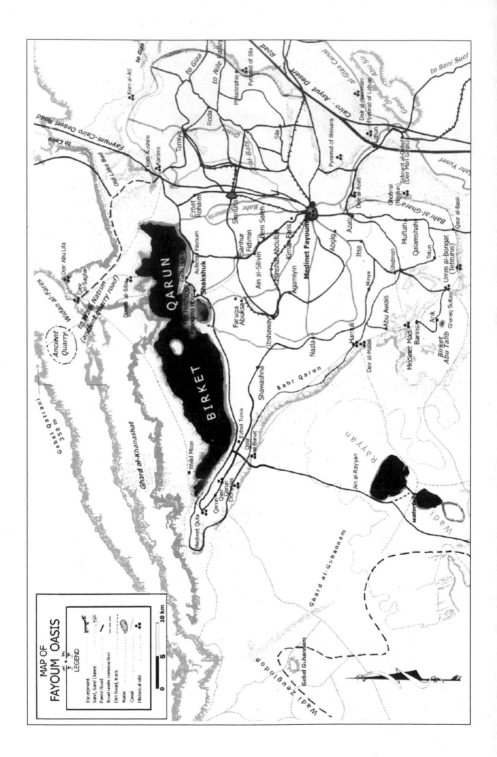

MAP OF
FAYOUM OASIS

LEGEND

Escarpment
Sand, Sand Dunes
Paved Road
Road under construction
Dirt Road, track
Water
Canal
Historical site

0   5   10 km

the Greeks and Romans. In fact, the crocodile god played a pivotal role in life in the Fayoum until the Christian era. It was believed that the lake was the primeval ocean where life in all its forms began. The crocodile was the power of that creation.

But it was not until the Twelfth Dynasty of the Middle Kingdom that great prosperity came to the Fayoum. It was during this era that the pyramids at Lahun and Hawara were built and the lake, now called Mi-wer, The Great Lake, was artificially expanded by the Nile. Some sources argue that the lake was not expanded during the Middle Kingdom but the Nile water, still permitted to enter the depression, was used to carry out drainage and land reclamation.

Greek Period (332–30 B.C.)

Although less is known about the Fayoum during the New Kingdom (c. 1570–1070 B.C.), great changes took place in the area during the Greek and Roman eras and many of the ancient ruins, especially on the desert fringes, come to us from this period. During Greek times the Fayoum was known as "the Marsh," before it was named the Arsinoite nome by Ptolemy Philadelphus in honor of his second wife (and sister). It was divided into a number of *merides* (districts), including Heracleides in the north, Themistos in the west, and Polemon in the south.

New settlements grew throughout the Fayoum including Karanis, Bacchias, Philadelphia, and Dionysius. Under Greek rule there were 114 villages in the Fayoum (only sixty existed in 1809). Sixty-six of them had Greek names. It is interesting to note that a few of the villages had Jewish names (for example, Magdola—modern Medinet Nehas—and Samareia) There was rivalry between villages and sometimes open hostility. They stole crops, good soil, and water rights from each other, just like Greek citystates, medieval European towns, and modern nations everywhere.

We know a great deal about life in the Fayoum during Greek and Roman times because of hundreds and hundreds of papyri that have been discovered throughout the area during the past century. Mummies were wrapped in old papyrus scrolls so old cemeteries were and are excellent places to discover new histories. We have everything from census records to household accounts to fictional stories and details about the army.

Not only do we know the names of towns, but also the district and street names. We know the Fayoum had running water and that it was pumped from the Nile by Archimedean screws, with men working in shifts day and night. We know men married around eighteen to twenty years old, women around fifteen. We also know the Greeks practiced infanticide, especially if the child was female. One letter written June 17, 1 B.C. states, "If you are delivered of child, if it is a boy keep it, if a girl discard it."

As now, there was a thriving tourist industry in the Fayoum. One of the lures was to feed the sacred crocodiles with fried fish and honey cakes. The food was sold by the priests. By the time of Ptolemy Euergetes II, the Fayoum was in decline. The land was being reclaimed by the desert as canals clogged and the population diminished.

Roman Period (30 B.C.–A.D. 323)

The Romans, after the defeat of Antony and Cleopatra, ruled Egypt as a province, not an independent nation, as was the case during Greek rule. What they found in the Fayoum was a Hellenized landowner gentry in the towns of the Fayoum and Egyptians working and inhabiting the fields and villages. They also found clogged canals and broken dikes. Augustus ordered the Roman army into the Fayoum to clean and repair the water system. Once done, the Fayoum began to thrive once more.

In fact tourism became an industry. In Napthali Lewis's *Life in Egypt Under Roman Rule*, we have an interesting quote from a Roman document from 112 B.C.:

Lucius Memmius, a Roman senator, who enjoys a position of great dignity and honour is making the voyage from Alexandria to the Arsinoite nome [Fayoum] to see the sights. Let him be received with special magnificence, and see to it that the guest houses are made ready at the proper places and that the landing stages leading to them are in working order, also that the welcoming gifts listed below are presented to him at each landing place, that the furnishings of each guest house are ready for him, as well as the titbits for Petesouchos [the crocodile god] and the [live] crocodiles, and the necessaries for viewing the labyrinth, and the offerings for the sacrifices. And in general take the greatest pains for the visitor's complete satisfaction, and show the utmost zeal . . .

Egypt had to produce one third of the grain needed by Rome each year and the Fayoum, with nearly ten percent of the cultivable total, earned the epithet "breadbasket of the Roman empire." Crop variety and rotation was ignored in favor of grain. Farmers had to share their harvest with the state in the form of a tax. In addition, trades were taxed and there was a type of sales tax. The people of the Fayoum had a high per capita income, but also had to pay the highest taxes, including twice the average poll tax of any other place in Egypt.

Eventually Rome exacted too much from the farmers of the Fayoum. Always rebellious, its population declined and the people, unpaid and overtaxed, were forced into serfdom. In 165, a plague descended on Egypt and the major villages in the Fayoum suffered considerably. By the third and fourth centuries, communities like Philadelphia and Bacchias stood abandoned.

Christian (323–642) and Islamic (642–1798) Fayoum

By the middle of the third century there was a large Christian community in the Fayoum. Thirty-five monasteries existed during the Middle Ages, many secluded in the surrounding deserts. Unlike other areas of the Western Desert, which fell quickly to the Arab invaders in 641, the Fayoum remained a hotbed of rebellion and did not come under Arab control until much later. New settlements sprang up as Bedouin came to settle on the land. Times were again hard.

The invading Fatimid armies, sweeping into Egypt across the Western Desert in 969, ruined the Fayoum and it continued to decline into the Ottoman era. In 1245, Nabulis, the Ayyubid governor of the Fayoum, issued a report on the status of the Fayoum with a focus on the hydrology. At that time the area was almost entirely abandoned.

Fayoum from 1798 to 1882

Napoleon's army came to the Fayoum in 1798, heralding the beginning of the modern era. The French troops had been in pursuit of Murad Bey and his Mamluk army since the Battle of the Pyramids. Murad, knowledgeable about the desert, and gathering arms and men from Minya and Beni Suef, had been playing cat and mouse with the French, who were under the command of General Desaix.

Time was on the side of Murad for the French soldiers were falling victim to eye infections, dysentery, hunger, and venereal disease. They were running out of ammunition, their uniforms were in tatters, and their shoes disintegrated until they fell off their feet. Finally, the two sides met. At first there were minor skirmishes, but on October 7, 1798, at the Monastery of Sediman, the French routed the Mamluks and marched into the Fayoum.

Under the rule of Muhammad Ali (1811–1848), the Fayoum began to recover from the devastation of centuries, mainly through the efforts of M. Linant de Bellefonds. Roads were built, telegraph and telephone systems installed, and general prosperity returned to the fertile oasis.

British Occupation (1882–1954)

The British swept into the Fayoum like any other conqueror. Toward the end of the nineteenth century a group of English engineers arrived in the Fayoum from India to "improve the wealth and agricultural prosperity of the country"—one more invasion force bent on increasing productivity in the 'breadbasket.' They brought the railroad to the Fayoum in 1893.

During the the second decade of the twentieth century the British established camps within and around the perimeter of the Fayoum, including outposts manned by the infantry and yeomanry to protect it against the Sanusi, a threat that never materialized.

Despite the heavy British presence, as late as the 1920s there was no road from Cairo to the Fayoum. In fact, Bagnold claims to have made the first car tracks "of what afterward became King Fouad's road to the Faiyum."

Fayoum Today

Today, the Fayoum is still a prosperous, growing province. As in the past, agriculture is its main industry. Produce from the Fayoum has a special status on the Egyptian market. The tomatoes always seem to be bigger, oranges sweeter, ducks and turkeys plumper and more tender.

Coptic monasteries, abandoned for centuries, have been revitalized and restored. In many of them, where once a single monk lived amid the ruins, full religious communities are creating important centers once again. Leisure tourism is on the increase around the lake and historical tourism at the ancient sites has grown in the past years.

The Fayoum has five major population centers with five cities, 163 villages, and 1,620 hamlets. Over 1,989,000 people live here, 51% of which are men. Over 340,000 feddans are under cultivation with an additional 12,613 now under reclamation. In addition to agriculture its industries include cotton and tourism. Today tourism boasts seven hotels with 243 rooms. There are ten schools of higher education, fifty hospitals, and five cultural centers.

Recently the government has instituted a program to help head of household women, who comprise 16% of the population in the Fayoum (22% in Egypt as a whole). They are guaranteed a regular income and given small loans at low interest to start small businesses.

Geography and Geology

The Fayoum has had a fascinating and turbulent geological history. Just as the landmass that is Egypt was pushed slowly into place at the crossroads of the world, the area that is the Fayoum was a fulcrum of geological change. During prehistory the area was covered and uncovered by ancient seas, crisscrossed by ancient river systems, and shaken by great upheavals. Like the other depressions in the Western Desert, it progressed through a series of changes over hundreds of millions of years from marine to marshland to high forest and then savannah, to reach its present environment.

Make no mistake, the Fayoum is a depression: its floor is well below the average level of the Western Desert and well below sea level. It is surrounded by escarpment, rainfall is scarce, and it relies on springs and canals for its water. It is more habitable than other oases simply because it is the closest depression to the Nile Valley and its escarpment is at its lowest and narrowest in the southeast corner, near the Nile. This allowed the river to break through the barrier and rush into the depression, depositing rich silt and vital water, creating a fertile agricultural area.

In the distant past some faulting occurred in the Fayoum, but it was minimal compared to Bahariya and Farafra oases and was localized along the northern escarpment 10 kilometers (6.2 miles) north-northeast of Qasr al-Sagha. It ran northwest and southeast for 6 to 7 kilometers (3 to 4 miles). In addition, there was some faulting west of Qasr al-Sagha, which affected several 100 meter (320 foot) sections.

The western and southern boundary of the Fayoum is a small scarp that separates it from Wadi Rayyan, and the eastern boundary is a wide ridge which separates the depression from the Nile Valley. This ridge extends as far as the Giza plateau on the southern edge of Cairo. Ten kilometers (6.2 miles) wide in the north, the ridge narrows to 2.5 kilometers (2 miles) in the south. It reaches its highest level east of Sersena and its lowest point at three places: northeast of Tamiya, where the railroad crosses the scarp; between Lahun and Hawara, where the Bahr Yusif enters the depression; and south of Qalamshah.

The northern desert region beyond the lake rises from the lowest point in the depression to a height of 340 meters (1,088 feet) along the major escarpment. The plateau above the scarp consists largely of brown pebble desert containing several dune fields, including the Ghard al-Khanashat, running north-northwest to south-southeast. The field begins just south of Wadi Natrun and ends 24 kilometers (15 miles) from the edge of the scarp above the western edge of the lake.

Mountains and Wadis

One of the most interesting mountains in the entire Western Desert is **Gebel Qatrani**, the Tar Mountain, a 350-meter-high (1,120-foot) sandstone mountain beyond the northern scarp above Qasr al-Sagha. Not only is it a major landmark for travelers in the northern desert, but, as we shall see, it contains an abundance of fossils.

To the west, actually beyond the boundaries of Fayoum, is **Gebel Guhannam**, Hell Mountain. (See Wadi Rayyan below for details.) Within the southeastern corner of Fayoum is **Gebel Naqlun**, where the Monastery of Malak Ghubrayal is located.

There is a single wadi in the area (two if one counts Wadi Rayyan which is really a separate depression), the picturesque **Masraf al-Wadi**, Drain of the Valley. Located near the village of Nazla, which cascades down its banks, in the southwest section of the depression, the Masraf al-Wadi is often covered in flowers and makes an interesting contrast to the usually flat depression floor.

The Lake

Located in the northwestern and lowest section of the Fayoum depression, Birket Qarun covers approximately 214 square kilometers (135 square miles), stretches 40 kilometers (25 miles) from east to west, and is 45 meters (144 feet) below sea level. The modern lake is ten times smaller than it was a million years ago, in Pleistocene times.

In 1927, Elinor W. Gardner proved there was more than one lake involved in the Fayoum. The first lake was the 23-meter (74-foot) lake that dried up before the historic period. Then there was a Neolithic lake which was 64 meters (102 feet) above the present level. Finally there was the present lake, the 7.5-meter (12-foot) lake. All of these stretches of water were sweet water lakes. During the past 5,000 years the modern lake was fed and kept alive by fresh water from the Nile, which entered the Fayoum through the Lahun Gap. Since there is little rainfall and no additional source of water feeds into the lake, this annual replenishment allowed it to survive.

Although Ptolemy I is credited by some with beginning the drainage of the Twelfth Dynasty lake, then called Moeris, scholars do not agree. We know the lake was smaller in Greek times than it was in the Middle Kingdom, but to date scholars do not know how it diminished in size.

The lake contains a single island, Geziret al-Qarn, Island of the Horn, located in the north central section called Batn al-Baqara, Cow Bay. Uninhabited, it is a flat, sandy, island and, although no standing artifacts remain, it offers evidence of having once been inhabited by a thriving community. Geologically, the island has produced many interesting fossils. The island was examined by Schweinfurth in 1879, then by Professor Karl Mayer-Eyman, and later by W. Dames.

Fishing is the main industry on the lake and fisherman can be seen in the early morning and late afternoon in their small, colorful, boats, casting their fishing nets and beating the waters with their paddles. There is no fishing from May to July when the fish are spawning.

Fossils

The Fayoum contains by far the earliest known and the most important fossil deposits in the world: one of Egypt's most exciting and elusive treasures. Mainly from the Eocene and Oligocene periods, they include shells, sharks, whales, marshland creatures like sea-cows, giant turtles, crocodilians, trace fossils, and mammals, including primates. Most of these fossils are found in the exposed strata of the hills and mountains within and surrounding the depression. According to Elwyn L. Simons, a leading authority in the field, the Fayoum "provides us with an unrivaled view of the evolution of Africa's early Tertiary plants and animals."

The Locations

The environment of the Fayoum during the geological periods that created the fossil beds was similar to present day Uganda: subtropical and tropical forest with plenty of trees, vines, and mangroves. Within the forests were freshwater swamps and rivers. There was plenty of rainfall. A coastal plain was probably along or near the shore of the Tethys Sea. As time passed the environment changed, dried, and encountered upheavals until this strata was buried. What was trapped in the soil fossilized.

Today, the fossils are exposed in layers in the escarpments surrounding the depression, especially to the north of the lake. They come from four main formations: the Birket Qarun Formation, the Qasr al-Sagha Formation, the Fluvio-Marine Formation, and the Gebel Qatrani Formation.

Birket Qarun Formation

The Birket Qarun Formation, named after the lake, is an Upper Eocene stratum found mainly north of the lake and to the west of the depression at Gebel Guhannam. Within this are Upper Eocene mammalian and reptilian remains like whales.

Qasr al-Sagha Formation

The Qasr al-Sagha Formation is a series of stratifications in the escarpment which are loaded with land animal fossils, but is marine in nature. The Qasr al-Sagha Formation covers a 154-meter (493-foot) stratum along the wall of the scarp and is considered a true bone bed created when the bodies of land animals were washed into this area by flowing water. It runs the length of the northern scarp and continues for 20 kilometers (12.5 miles) west of the lake, where land fossils increase. In this area, the Qasr al-Sagha Formation forms the summit of Gebel Guhannam.

Fluvio-Marine Formation

Still in the northern escarpment, but above the Qasr al-Sagha Formation, is the Fluvio-Marine Formation, consisting of petrified wood, crocodiles, and tortoises. This series also contains true bone beds, probably caused by a river in Pliocene times. The Fluvio-Marine Formation begins in the east of the depression at Widan al-Faras where is it 23 meters (73.6 feet) thick. At Tamiya, in the heart of the Fayoum, it is 40 meters (128 feet) thick. Beyond the lake, northwest of Qasr al-Sagha, the Fluvio-Marine Formation is the highest point of the scarp and is an impressive 210 meters (672 feet) thick. In these beds are to be found *Potanides, Scalaroides, Potamides, Tristiatus, Cerithium, Tiarella,* and the most exciting fossil of all, *Arsinoitherium* (see below).

Gebel Qatrani Formation

The Gebel Qatrani Formation gets its name from the mountain found about 15 kilometers (9 miles) north of the escarpment. In the strata of Lower Oligocene deposits of this mountain are some of the richest fossil deposits in the world. The abundance of shark teeth, ray mouth parts, and mangrove rhizoliths (root trace fossils) support the theory that it was probably close to or along the southern shore of the Tethys Sea in Miocene times.

The Fossil Hunters

In 1845, A. B. Orlebar described the very first fossil found in the Fayoum, a petrified tree. In 1879, Georg Schweinfurth, the German geologist, went poking around the Geziret al-Qarn, the island in the middle of the lake, and found some shark teeth and bones. He continued his explorations in what was to become known as the Qasr al-Sagha Formation and found an ancient whale which he named *Zeuglodon osiris.*

In 1898, Hugh Beadnell surveyed the Fayoum for the Geological Survey of Egypt. Charles Andrews, a paleontologist with the Museum of Natural History in London, joined Beadnell in 1901. He and Beadnell collected an abundance of fossils and produced a plethora of publications. One day a Bedouin came into camp with some fossils. Upon investigation it was found that he had found *Palaeomastodon,* the oldest known elephant. It was the first land mammal fossil discovered in Egypt.

The first primate ever discovered was also found by a layman. Richard Markgraf came to live in the Fayoum and collected artifacts to sell to European and American museums. In 1906, he found a pocket of fossils which included the jaw of a primate later identified by Osborn as *Apidium phiomense,* believed to be a dawn ape. He continued to uncover large and small mammals until he died in 1916 in Sinnuris.

Eberhard Fraas looked for fossils in the Fayoum in 1905. In 1907, the American Museum of Natural History in New York began its long term association with the Fayoum. When Walter Granger and his assistant, George Olsen, left the port of New York it was the first time American paleontologists had left the continental United States looking for fossils. They were accompanied by Henry F. Osborn, curator of the Department of Vertebrate Paleontology. They stayed in the Fayoum for a number of months and left in late May. When they sailed out of Egypt on June 15, they took twenty-seven cases of fossils with them.

Things languished during both world wars, then in 1947, the Pan African Expedition under Wendell Phillips of the University of California at Berkeley collected a number of fossils. It wasn't until 1961, when Elwyn Simons came to the Fayoum that interest in the fossils intensified. Work has been in progress ever since with many amazing discoveries. Between 1961 and 1986, seventeen expeditions collected fossils. It is estimated that tens of thousands of specimens were collected by Simons. They were divided between the Cairo Geological Museum, where many can be seen today, and two American institutions, Yale Peabody and Duke University Primate Center—the former from 1961 to 1967, the latter from 1977, when Simons changed his affiliation. (There was no access to the site between 1967 and 1976.)

Since the 1980s, work has continued by Bowm and Rasmussen. Because of this extensive work, Simons calls the Fayoum "the best known Paleogene site in Africa."

Warning

Mention must be made of the fact that some people come to the Fayoum fossil beds on weekends and cart away enormous quantities of fossils and prehistoric artifacts. They are devastating the area while scientific study is still in progress. It has gone so far that local tourist agencies offer trips to the Fayoum and tell people to bring their shovels and Geiger counters.

Even a well-intentioned soul is tempted to take away some memento when standing in front of an impressive artifact. One would think one little artifact would be enough. But trunk loads of booty, the vertebra of the precious whales on someone's coffee table, is beyond comprehension. Some people collect only to dump their booty in the trash when they leave Egypt, or end their trip. Really folks. Let it be. One small item lying on the surface fully exposed should be a no-no, let alone digging things up. Do not dig anything up. Do not take away anything that looks like a skull or a vertebra, an important link that scientists have not yet made.

The Fossils
Petrified Wood

Petrified wood is all over the Western Desert. Here in the Fayoum it is very diverse and we can trace the types of trees. Simons and his colleagues maintain that in the Gebel Qatrani Formation these trees existed beside free-flowing, gravel-bottom, streams. When they fell into the water, the force of the water carried them. When the force of the water diminished, the trees stopped moving and remained in place. They were eventually covered and through the centuries, petrified. The types of wood are indicative of a wet tropical climate.

Trace Fossils

A trace fossil is not an animal or plant, it is the trail or debris from activity of an animal or plant preserved as a fossil. When it is an animal trail it is called an ichnofossil, when it is the root of a plant it is a rhizolith. Trace fossils exist almost everywhere on earth and although they are exceptionally prolific in the Fayoum, it is not the abundance but the variety that amazes scientists.

Thomas M. Bowm, an authority on Fayoum trace fossils, has found fifteen types of ichnofossil, which have been classified into four categories: communal nesting social insects like termites and ants; burrowing invertebrates; worms; and excavators. Most have been found in the Gebel Qatrani Formation, which Bown maintains contain the "most important assemblages as yet described from fluvial rocks of the world." He calls them the first wholly fluvial ichnofauna from Africa and the first from an ancient tropical and coastal alluvial regime.

Mangrove rhizoliths are found along the base of the Gebel Qatrani Formation at Madwar al-Bighal to the northwest of both the Fayoum and Wadi Rayyan. This is further evidence of the coastal plain.

Reptiles

Gigantophis is a mid-Eocene snake. Found to be 9 meters (29 feet) long, it is perhaps the longest snake ever. It was found in the Eocene Qasr al-Sagha Formation. A second snake, also in the Sagha formation is *Pterosphernus*, a sea snake. A third reptile of the Sagha formation is the *Tomistoma*, which is not extinct but can only be found today in Borneo.

Turtles are the most common reptiles in the Fayoum. *Testudo ammon*, a land tortoise as large as those on the Galapagos Islands today, was first discovered by Charles Andrews around 1900. *Podocnemis blanckenhorni*, and *Stereogenys pelomedusa* are both river and tropical land turtles.

Birds

Simons and Rasmussen tell us "the bird fauna of the Fayoum is very diverse and represents the best known Paleogene record of the class in Africa." There are thirteen bird families, only two extinct (meaning they have no known living descendants). Today, to find the remaining species alive and living together in one place one must go to "a limited area of Uganda bordering Lake Victoria and the upper Nile River." There the climate is as it was in the Fayoum millions of years ago, when our fossils were alive.

The earliest known record of ospreys (*Pandionidae*) is in the Fayoum, as is the earliest record of a gigantic shoebilled stork (*Balaenicipitidae*). There are fossils of jacanas (*Jacanidae*), sometimes called lily-trotters, herons, egrets, rails (*Rallidae*), cranes (*Gruidae*), flamingos (*Phoenicopteridae*), storks (*Ciconiidae*), cormorants (*Phalacrocoracidae*), and a form of ancient eagle (*Accipitridae*). Many of their living offspring still haunt the waters of the Fayoum. It is not unusual to approach a small canal and have a large heron take wing a few feet away from you.

Mammals

There are over twenty orders of mammal fossils in the Fayoum, some endemic to Africa, others immigrants from Eurasia. They range from the very small to the very large and form an impressive array for scientific investigation. The most common is *megalohyrax eocaenus*, a large hyrax.

Arsinoitherium is from the order *Embrithopoda* and although it resembles the rhinoceros, it is extinct. It was formerly believed to exist only in the forests of the Fayoum during the Lower Oligocene 25 to 45 million years ago, but the Granger Papers Project maintains that it has recently been discovered in Romania and Turkey.

Named for the Ptolemaic queen of the Fayoum, Arsinoe, *Arsinoitherium* is a 3.4 meter (11 foot) long, two-horned mammal the size and shape of a rhinoceros. It has a five-toed foot, forty-four high-crowned teeth, and was probably a semi-amphibian. It ate foliage and probably lived in marshy areas. *Arsinoitherium zitteli* was discovered by Beadnell in 1902, and named after one of the members of the Rohlfs expedition. *Arsinoitherium andrewsi*, one third the size of the former, was discovered by Andrews and Lankester in 1903. The two species have presented a host of questions still being discussed by scientists. One thing is certain—they could not have coexisted. Excellent skeletons of this mammal, and many of the other fossils named in this section, can be found in the Egyptian Geological Museum in Cairo.

Moeritherium, the Dawn Elephant, was once thought to be the direct link with the

Arsinoitherium   Redrawn from a catalog by Charles Williams Andrews

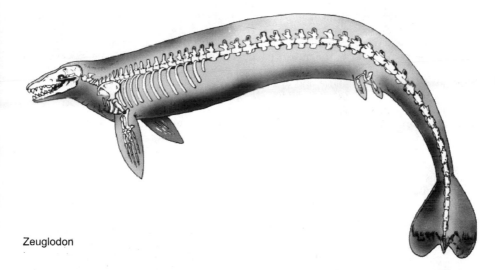

Zeuglodon

modern elephant. It is found in both marine deposits of the Eocene in the Fayoum and the ancient beds of Lake Moeris (north of Wadi Natrun). It was a heavy, fat, one meter (3 foot) high animal with a short snout, and lived in swampland. It had short, heavy legs with wide feet and flat hooves. It did not have a trunk but its upper lip was elongated and highly mobile. It had cusped teeth. It lived in the thickets around the lakes and marshes during the late Eocene, 36 to 45 million years ago.

Palaeomastodon and *Phioma* are early mastodons with four tusks, a short trunk, and long necks and skulls, both descendants of *Moeritherium*. Unlike the modern elephant, which has two tusks, these early elephants had two pairs: one pair in each of the upper and lower jaws. The *Palaeomastodon* was 1.5 meters (8 feet) tall at the shoulder. The *Phiomia* was 2.4 meters (7.6 feet) high with long legs, a bulbous skull, and perhaps a trunk.

All of the mammals above were prey for the *Apterodon, Pterodon,* and *Hyaenodon,* who, with teeth as sharp as knives, probably found the slow-moving ancient elephant- and rhino-types easy prey.

Zeuglodon, the *Basilosaurus isis,* is an ancient whale, and over 240 skeletons have been found in an 8-square-kilometer (5-square-mile) area in the Wadi Zeuglodon, obviously named in its honor. The Wadi Zeuglodon was once a bay and the whales died here in great numbers. (See Wadi Zeuglodon below for more details.)

Primates

The most studied fossils of the Gebel Qatrani Formation are Eocene and Oligocene primates, which swung through the treetops in the tropical forests of the Fayoum between 28 and 35 million years ago. This extensive and diverse grouping is unique to the Fayoum and when first discovered were believed to be the earliest relatives of apes and monkeys. Their continuous study has dramatically changed scientific theories about primate evolution.

As noted earlier, Richard Markgraf found a piece of what became the first discovered Fayoum primate in 1907. The find, called *Apidium,* was published by Henry Osborn in 1908. At the time they were not sure it was a primate, but several primate fossils were sold by Markgraf to the American Museum of Natural History and the Naturalkabinett in Stuttgart, Germany. For the next nearly 100 years the work has continued, until today we know a great deal about primates in Egypt.

From a review of primate work in the Fayoum by Elwyn L. Simons and D. Tab Rasmussen we learn that primates lived under forest conditions in the Eocene and Oligocene times and that there are two distinct groups of primates in the Fayoum fossil beds, lower sequence primates and upper sequence primates. The lower primate is the least known and most rare. It includes *Oligopithecus savagei* and *Qatrania wingi*. The former's teeth patterns identify it as a link between Eocene prosimians and Oligocene anthropoideans. Of the early *Oligopithecus savagei* we only have a jaw and a few teeth discovered by Simons in 1962. Of *Qatrania wingi* we have three small jaws.

The second group of primates, from the upper sequence, have been found in abundance in the Fayoum. We have been able to identify eleven species. Scientists know of no other site in the world where these primates appear in such diversity.

After discoveries by Simons in 1989 and 1990 the oldest known Fayoum primate is *Catopithecus browni* and *Proteopithecus sylviae* of the late Eocene. The second oldest is *Oligopithecus. Apidium phiomense*, discovered by Osborn in 1908, and *Apidium moustafai*, discovered by Simons in 1962, are next. They are short-faced monkeys, the former being the most common mammal in the upper sequences of the Gebel Qatrani Formation, the latter being the smallest Fayoum primate. The *Parapithecus fraasi*, discovered by Schlosser in 1911, and the *Parapithecus grangeri*, are like squirrel monkeys. Because of fiber found in its diet, the latter is thought to have been the most folivorous. It was discovered by Simons in 1974 in upper-level quarries. Variances in its teeth set it apart from the *Apidium* and associates it with Old World monkeys.

Now come the "dawn apes." They are *Aegyptopithecus zeuxis* and four species of *Propliopithecus*: *P. chirobates*, *P. ankeli*, *P. haeckeli*, and *P. markgrafi*.

Aegyptopithecus zeuxis is the largest of the Oligocene primates, twice the size of the types listed above, and has a short tail and low brow. Simon says it is comparable to a howling monkey. It is more than 28 to 30 million years old and Leakey and Leakey, comparing it to *Afropithecus*, found remarkable similarities in facial cranium and mandibles. Simon calls this the "first striking indication of a strong link between a particular species of Oligocene primate with a species of ape from the succeeding Miocene epoch."

Aegyptopithecus zeuxis
Drawn from reconstruction by
Margaret L. Estex

Of the *Propliopitheci*, *chirobtes* is the smallest and has a different tooth structure from *haeckeli* and *markgrafi*. The latter two were written about by Schlosser in 1911, but actually found by our friend Richard Markgraf. Of all the primates resurrected in the Fayoum, these two bear the closest resemblance to human beings; they are, with some argument, the "earliest known hominoids."

This all gets rather confusing. Our *Aegyptopithecus zeuxis* possibly begat *dryopithecines* which begat orangutans, chimpanzees, and gorillas. *Haeckeli* and *markgrafi*, as hominoids, begat *ramapithecines* which begat "Lucy," or *Australopithecus afarensis*, and perhaps the *Homo habilis* of the Leakeys. Then came *Homo erectus*, which leads to us, *Homo sapiens*. At least, this is the current consensus.

Water

Water is the *baraka*, blessing, of the Fayoum. There is plenty of it. So much in fact that the drainage alone has created two large lakes in nearby Wadi Rayyan. There are two lakes in Fayoum, the salty Birket Qarun, the largest lake in the Western Desert, and Birket Abu Talib, a tiny lake at the southern extreme of the depression. The former supports a small fishing industry and is being developed for tourism, the latter, once part of a larger swamp, is too small for any kind of development (for details about both lakes see below).

Unlike other depressions in the Western Desert, the Fayoum does not obtain its water solely from wells and springs, but from a system of canals. The feeder canal is the **Bahr Yusif**, the Sea of Joseph, dug during the pharaonic era and linking the Fayoum to the Nile River. Brown tells us that the Bahr Yusif is not an artificial canal but a naturally formed channel caused by Nile flood waters. A second explanation of its wonders is given to us by Linant de Bellefonds who maintained, in his time, that during summer the water in the canal is just as forceful as in winter due to springs in its bed.

Originally, the Bahr Yusif diverted Nile water at Beni Suef, but when the Ibrahimiya Canal was built to water Ismail's sugarcane plantations in the late 1800s, it collected the water and diverted it to the Bahr Yusif. The Bahr Yusif enters the Fayoum through the Lahun Gap at the village of Lahun, where it diverges into several channels. Once the Bahr Yusif reaches Medinet Fayoum it breaks into eight main canals which send the water throughout the depression.

All canals in Egypt are cleaned and repaired in January, and the Bahr Yusif and its tributaries are no exception. At this time of year dredgers clean the sludge out of the canals and the famous waterwheels are dismantled and repaired. It is said that the prosperity of Egypt can be measured by the condition of its canals. When the canals are allowed to silt and clog, the country is in decline.

Caravan Routes and Roadways

Today the Fayoum can be approached by three main roads: from Cairo over a four-lane highway (dual carriageway), from the new Cairo–Asyut Desert Road, and from Wasta. The first route runs 60 kilometers (37 miles) from the Alexandria–Cairo desert road at the Forte Grand Pyramid Hotel. It enters the Fayoum at Kom Aushim, along the north-eastern edge of the depression. Flinders Petrie, one of the major explorers of the Fayoum in the nineteenth century, tells us that the road from Saqqara to the Fayoum, which runs almost parallel to, and sometimes is, the main road today, was an ancient Roman road. It had Roman milestones along the way: larger tablets for each *schoenus* (7 kilometers, 4 miles) and smaller posts or pillars for each 1000 cubits or third of a mile. It is along this road that the ruins of the city of Bacchias (Kom al-Atl) are to be found.

Darb Wadi Natrun

The track linking Wadi Natrun to Fayoum is part of a larger desert route from Alexandria and the Mediterranean Coast to Wadi Rayyan and points south. It passes into the Fayoum from the north, east of the Ghard al-Khanashat and descends the scarp above the western edge of Birket Qarun. It continues to Qasr Qarun and on into Wadi Rayyan.

Darb al-Rayyan Bahri and Qibli

There are two desert tracks that link Bahariya Oasis to the Fayoum, both called Darb al-Rayyan (see Bahariya Oasis for details). Passing through the Wadi Rayyan, the first cuts north along the western side of the lakes and goes to Qasr Qarun and beyond to Wadi Natrun. The second passes south of the lakes to the south of Gebel al-Deir and the monastery and enters the Fayoum at Gharaq Sultani.

The People

The Dawn Apes, the oldest known common ancestor of both ape and humans lived by the lake 26 to 28 million years ago in the Oligocene epoch. Much later the Fayoum was settled by Paleolithic humans, the remains of whom are found mainly to the north of the lake (evidence of life to the south of the lake is buried under modern agriculture and villages). These people were followed by the more sophisticated communities of Neolithic humans: hunters, farmers, and fishermen, who left evidence of the earliest agricultural communities in the world. The northern shore is littered with hundreds of these early communities. But Neolithic humans disappeared.

Gertrude Caton-Thompson, an anthropologist who excavated in the Fayoum in the 1930s, speculated that these early farmers may have been conquered by a less developed group of people and as the size of the lake began to diminish they, along with their skills, vanished from the area. Soon there were new developments in the Fayoum as Nilotic predynastic peoples came into the area. Evidence of their villages is also found along the northern shore of Birket Qarun.

Calling themselves Fayoumi, the people of the Fayoum are mostly farmers. The Fayoumi have always had a reputation for being clannish and rebellious. H. V. Morton in *Through Lands of the Bible* reports that murder was the most frequent crime in 1938, and the police were frustrated because everyone knew who committed the crime, but no one would talk. Most of the murders were clan incidents.

Agriculture, Fishing, and Industry

Farming is the main occupation in the Fayoum. Farmers plow the land with the ancient pharaonic plows and till the soil with the pharaonic hoe. With an intricate canal system there is plenty of water to allow the fertile land to drink and the yield in the Fayoum is abundant; there is no subsistence farming here. The variety of crops is probably the largest in Egypt. The orchards, found mainly in the western portion of the depression, are among the finest in the country. The date is not king in the Fayoum, nor is the olive; instead oranges, lemons, apricots, mangoes, and guava are grown and harvested for markets throughout the country. In the late nineteenth century almost all crops were delivered to the Nile Valley by rail, with an occasional camel caravan picking up odds and ends. Today, it is the trucker who has taken over the disbursement of Fayoum goods to the Nile Valley.

The Fayoum is known for its domestic poultry, believed to be the best in Egypt. In the late afternoon vendors sit along the Cairo–Fayoum road selling ducks, turkeys, and chickens. Chicken farms, selling eggs as well as birds, often advertise by painting their houses into wonderful, full-color billboards. Honey is another famous product in the Fayoum and thousands of blue wooden beehives are found throughout the cultivated areas. Flowers are also a major crop and the Fayoum has been called the land of roses. They are grown for florists in the Nile Valley, but are also picked, dried, and shipped to perfumeries in Europe and America.

With a huge lake and plenty of canals, fishing is a major industry. The lake fishermen can be seen at early morning and late afternoon in unique boats that are built in the Fayoum along the lake shore. The boats are wide canoe-types, some with sails. Fishermen cast their nets and then beat the water with their flat oars, frightening the fish into the nets.

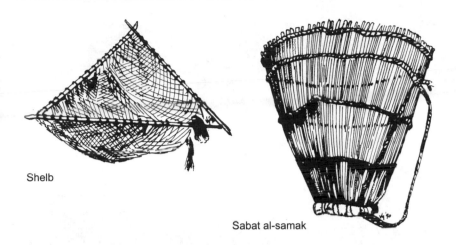

Shelb

Sabat al-samak

Morton tells us how the Fayoumis caught ducks. When the flocks came to the lake in winter, the fishermen placed decoys among the reeds in five-foot water, scattered rice, slipped their feet into stone stirrups, and crouched under water breathing through a blowpipe. When a duck came for the rice, they grabed it by the legs.

Along the canals, especially in January when the water is low, everyone is a fisherman. Young boys can be seen using the *shelb*, a triangular fishing net attached to a thin wooden frame or the *sabat al-samak*, an unusual fish trap shaped like a basket and made of twigs.

There is a cotton mill, canning plants, a Coca Cola factory, a hydroelectric station, and, in recent years, mining and quarrying in the desert areas.

The Crafts of the Oasis

Crafts are thriving in the Fayoum. The most populated oasis in the Western Desert, it is also the most fertile and the most productive. Its crafts industry reflects this abundance.

Baskets

Sturdy, utilitarian, cleverly designed, and meeting contemporary needs, the craft of basketweaving was never threatened with extinction in the Fayoum. Mostly made in the villages of Alam and Agamiyin, they are among the best baskets in Egypt and the variety of shapes and sizes is staggering.

The *tabaq* is a large, flat basket with short sides that is used to serve food. Varieties of this basket exist throughout Egypt. A smaller version of the *tabaq* is the *saniya*, which is used to serve fruit. A third type of flat basket is the *tabaq sukhna*, which has no sides and is used as a hotplate. The *tabaq falder* is a flat, rectangular serving dish.

There are two types of breadbaskets, both called *sabat eish*, one with a lid and one with side handles and no lid. Smaller, yet with the same shape and handles is the *sabat khudar*, used to hold spices. An elongated circular basket with a handle called *sabat sukkariya* is a container for sugar. For clothing there is a large, deep basket called a *gasier* and the same shape with open sides is a *wada*, used to hold fish. The *tabaq firakh* is a smaller version of the *wada* used to hold chickens. Some modern designs and uses for baskets are the *shanta khurug*, looking like and used as a handbag, the *sabat beebe*, a cradle for the baby, and the *sabat telefun* used to hold the telephone. There are even tiny

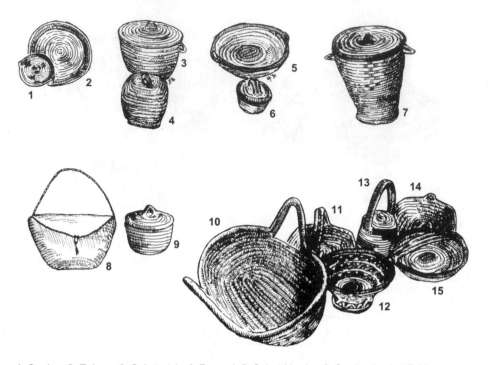

1: Saniya; 2: Tabaq; 3: Sabat eish; 4: Farauni; 5: Sabat khudar; 6: Sewing basket 7: khurug;
8: Shanta; 9: Aisha; 10: Sabat beebe; 11: Wada; 12: Fruit basket;
13: Sabat sukkariya; 14: Tabaq falder; 15: Sabat telefun.

sewing baskets used to hold threads and needles. The fanciest basket in the Fayoum is the *farauni*, 'pharaoh's basket,' a rectangular basket with a small opening on the top used to hold special items like jewelry.

A good selection of baskets is usually on display at the waterwheels in Medinet Fayoum, in front of the Panorama Hotel along the lake, and at Ain al-Siliyin. Bargaining is part of the game in buying a basket, but they are inexpensive.

Pottery

The picturesque village of Nazla, meaning 'going down,' produces most of the pottery in the Fayoum. The pots are on sale each Tuesday in the *suq* at Medinet Fayoum. Most of the pots created by the traditional craftsmen, like the *zir*, are similar to those found in the Nile Valley, but there is one pot that is distinctive to the Fayoum, the *bukla*. This pot comes in a variety of sizes depending upon its use: small pots for butter and cheese, larger pots for water. All are circular with a wide lip and two handles.

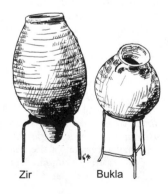

Zir   Bukla

Dresses and Jewelry

Surprisingly, there is not a wide variety of objects of adornment in the Fayoum. Women's dresses are similar to those found in the Nile Valley from Beni Suef to Asyut. They are short, falling to just below the knee, have a waist line, which is very unusual in women's dresses throughout Egypt, and have no decoration. Nose rings are seldom found. There is a bracelet that is distinctively Fayoumi. Heavy and made of silver, it is about 5 centimeters in width, with a raised rectangular design.

Woman's traditional dress

Traditional silver bracelets

Roman Fayoum Portraits

Representatives of an ancient Roman craft in the oasis, the famous Fayoum Portraits are not only beautiful, but many show a high degree of artistic merit and have opened the door to our understanding of Roman portraiture. They were found all over Egypt: Antinoopolis along the Nile had forty-one; at Panopolis (Akhmim) hundreds were excavated (only forty were saved); and at Marina al-Alamein along the northern coast, a single portrait was unearthed in 1991. A few portraits were even found at Thebes (Luxor). In the Fayoum, portraits have been found at Philadelphia, Karanis, and Hawara.

In general, Fayoum portraits date from the end of the fourth century. They were painted for the wealthy and the semi-wealthy and were mainly images of soldiers, priests, coiffured matrons, schoolteachers, and small children. We do not know if the portraits were commissioned as exact replicas of the deceased, or whether a person could go into an atelier and buy a ready-made portrait from a wide selection, or both. One beautiful portrait from Hawara, now in Copenhagen, is of a young man with a strong and sensual face. It was found on the body of an octogenarian with "little hair, gnarled joints, a hunched back and worn-down teeth." It could have been commissioned during the deceased's lifetime and decorated the home until death, when it was sent with the body for wrapping. It could have been commissioned for one person and used by another. There are even examples of portraits being repainted.

Fayoum Portrait

Fayoum Portrait
Redrawn from J. E. Berger

Once the mummy was wrapped and the portrait put in place, the mummy was sometimes brought back to the home, where it was given a place of honor until it was eventually buried. It could well have been kept in a family chapel and then interred en masse with other family members.

The artists typically used sycamore, acacia, and fig wood for ordinary portraits with cedarwood as a high-end item. The wood was about 40 to 44 centimeters (15.8 to 17.5 inches) high and 21 to 24 centimeters (8.25 to 9.5 inches) wide. The back was rough and often had plaster and bitumen attached to it, while the front was highly finished with a vertical grain. Occasionally the paint was applied directly to the wood, but usually a white gesso was used. The portraits were painted with tempera in a variety of colors and then covered with wax.

The ancient peoples placed a high value on immortality and the Fayoum portraits are one more attempt to live forever. It was important that the name of the person be known, for "to speak the name was to make the person alive." These names, when they accompany a portrait, are called portrait inscriptions.

Wildlife

Thousands of birds inhabit the Fayoum. The egret, Abu Qirdan, is probably the most visible bird in the fields, while various species of ducks and gulls abound along the lake. Spur-winged plovers, snipes, owls, and even flamingos can be spotted by birdwatchers. The most unusual and delightful bird in the Fayoum is the desert peacock, who struts the highways and byways at will, its plumage spread wide. Birds of prey soar through the skies over the Fayoum, catching the thermal currents along the northern shore of the lake. These birds are hunted illegally by local farmers since they command a high price from falconers in the Gulf states and Libya. But it is the water birds that comprise the bulk of the bird population in the Fayoum, especially in winter when millions of them migrate south to escape the cold northern climate. The Fayoum is now a restricted area and signs are posted prohibiting hunting.

TOUR #1

Eastern Edge of Fayoum

- **2x2, 4x4**
- **3–4 hours**
- **easy**

			km	total km
Kom Aushim/Karanis	N 29 31 093	E 30 55 577	0	0
Bridge	N 29 30 699	E 30 53 742	1	1
Bacchias (at rd)	N 29 32 122	E 31 00 198	11	12
Philadelphia (rd)	N 29 26 977	E 31 04 958	14	26
Pyramid (at rd)	N 29 23 004	E 31 02 500	8	34

Kom Aushim and Karanis

The first village to greet visitors upon arrival from Cairo is the small hamlet of Kom Aushim. People tend to get confused about Kom Aushim and Karanis. Although the names are often used interchangeably, Kom Aushim is a small village a few kilometers north of Karanis.

Kom Aushim Museum

Daily 8:30 to 3:30. Entrance fee. Small and newly renovated with a marble façade and dramatic entrance, the Kom Aushim Museum was originally erected in 1974. Since then, the grounds have been converted into a friendly oasis. Exhibiting artifacts dating from prehistoric to Roman periods, by far the best object in the museum is the solitary Fayoum Portrait, left in its native

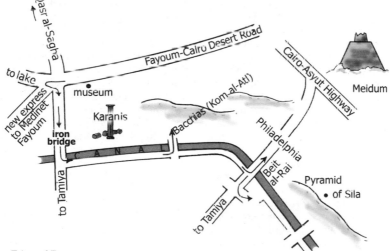

Eastern Edge of Fayoum

Fayoum when the other famous portraits were taken to the Egyptian Antiquities Museum in Cairo. (For details of these portraits see above.)

The museum is a good place to pick up guides to all parts of the Fayoum, especially to Qasr al-Sagha and Dimeh. (The road to Qasr al-Sagha begins across the highway from the museum.) Fees are minimal and the guides provide good, courteous, and friendly service.

The ruins of Karanis are entered from the museum grounds. Between the museum and the ruins is the former residence of the British High Commissioner, Sir Miles Lampson.

Karanis

Karanis, 'the Lord's Town,' is one of the largest Greco-Roman cities in the Fayoum. Founded in the third century B.C. and originally inhabited by the mercenaries of Ptolemy II's army, Karanis, with a population of about 3,000, prospered for seven centuries. It declined only during the turbulent times of the fourth and fifth centuries. It had two main north–south thoroughfares, while houses, numbering in the hundreds, were grouped together in small clusters.

Through most of the centuries, the population was poor and it held a good mix of nationalities. Early, it was predominately Greek soldiers. In 165, Karanis, like all of Egypt, was visited by the plague and the population fell considerably. In the year 171, fourteen percent of the population were Roman army veterans. They lived in simple mud-brick houses, the more affluent with stone lintels, all with courtyards for work and recreation under the warm winter sun. Most of the houses were multi-storied, including a basement used for storage. They had small windows cut high into the walls to let in the light and help the house stay warm in winter and cool in summer. They also had stone steps. Some had small gardens.

The community thrived for many centuries, so many occupations were represented. A fair number of people worked on state-owned property. Some were well educated, the majority were not. One family

made pots from Nile Valley clay. Another imported pots, especially Brindisi amphora. These were sold to other merchant families who filled them with wine and olive oil and reexported them. There were wool shearers, weavers, fullers, and wool sellers for a complete textile industry. While excavating, 3,500 pieces of textiles were uncovered.

Carpenters made everything from tools like mallets, axes, and drills to furniture, household equipment, and doors. They also made wooden toys like rattles, horses on wheels, tops, and dolls. There may also have been a glass factory. Many of these trades had makeshift shops along the outside walls of the temples, much like merchants in Cairo's medieval city did until this century. There were also public buildings in which the business of the community and the state took place, and hot and cold public baths, where a person could relax and enjoy a sauna and the companionship of friends.

But the vast majority of the villagers (94 percent in the second century) were farmers who farmed not only their own land and sites in nearby villages, but also state-owned fields throughout the Fayoum. In addition to the mandatory grain, they grew fruit, grapes, and olives, which were pressed for oil in at least two presses. In addition to domestic animals we know like dogs, cows, pigs, mules, camels, pigeons, and horses, they also kept antelope and crocodile.

And they paid taxes; too many of them and always in kind in exchange for government services. A textile manufacturer paid in cloth, a potter in pots, and, one assumes, a fisherman in fish. Grain, of course, was the most important tax. They also paid a meat tax, which was used to feed the troops in the area. *Karanis: An Egyptian Town in Roman Times* by Elaine Gazda records that Karanis supplied "twenty-four tunics and eight cloaks for the years A.D. 310–311." It took the community three years to make them. The temples were once maintained by donation but by Roman times, this, too, was a tax.

It was the duty of the centurions to keep the peace. Petitions by the people to the centurions, found within the ruins of the *grapheion* at Karanis, give us some local color at this time: a petition tells of an assault in the year 71 on the assistant of an estate manager; in the year 192, there was vandalism at a threshing floor; in 198, a dispute with a violent tax collector took place; at an unknown date, there was a robbery of a woman whose brother was in the army; in 214, a fire destroyed a field of crops; and in 216, burglary and vandalism of a house took place. Just people, doing what people do in almost any period of human history.

The two temples in Karanis were dedicated to forms of the crocodile god. Living crocodiles were kept in the sacred lakes of these temples and were fed grain, meat, and wine mixed with milk and honey. They participated in ceremonies and were mummified after death.

The Northern Temple

Excavations on the Northern Temple were begun on March 17, 1925, by a team from the University of Michigan. Facing north and built on older ruins, the structure is mainly gray limestone. It was once surrounded by a thick, mudbrick *temenos* wall, of which a small portion can be seen north of the temple. The four outer corners of the temple are decorated with slender columns. It has two pylons. By the middle of the third century, it had been abandoned.

House of the Banker

The stone entrance on this otherwise mudbrick building attests to the wealth of the owner, in this instance a banker. Twenty-six thousand coins in jars and cloth bags were unearthed here.

The Granaries

There are ten large granaries and seven small ones in Karanis. The large ones mostly housed the grain for taxes to Rome and were well guarded, with Roman soldiers' barracks erected adjacent to one of them.

As the grain was harvested, it was stored here. Then it was transported to Alexandria where is was stored in further granaries before shipping. Grain became such an important commodity that guilds existed in Alexandria to oversee the shipments to

Rome. In the first century, the grain of Egypt fed Rome for four months out of the year, so the arrival of the ships was a happy occasion. The arrival of the fleet in the Bay of Naples is recorded by Seneca: "Suddenly there came into our view today the Alexandrine ships—I mean those which are usually sent ahead to announce the coming of the fleet. . . . The Campanians are glad to see them; all the rabble of Puteoli stand on the docks. . . . Everybody was bustling about and hurrying to the waterfront."

Dovecotes

Six dovecotes were uncovered at Karanis, a number of them attached to the upper stories of homes. Like many of the dovecotes still in use along the byways of the Fayoum, these were made of mudbrick in which pots were placed for the pigeons to nest, one bird per pot. Two of the structures were big enough to house 1,250 birds. These families were vendors, selling manure and pigeons. The smaller dovecotes were for the family needs only.

The Southern Temple

Located in the southern part of the ancient town, the limestone Temple of Pnepheros and Petesouchos is the larger of two temples found on the site. Dedicated to the crocodile gods Pnepheros and Petesouchos, it was erected in the latter part of the first century on the site of an earlier temple erected in the first century B.C. It is situated at the eastern edge of a large square. Directly in front of it, but facing north, is the Gate of Vespasian. The entrance to the temple, which faces east, is surmounted by the Gate of Claudius, with an inscription on the lintel that indicated the temple was dedicated by Nero and usurped by Claudius. The temple proper has three rooms.

The Baths

The large Roman Bath contain ample evidence of the splendor in which the Romans bathed. First there was a cold water bath, then a hot water chamber much like a steam bath, then another hot, but dry bath, much like a sauna. Bathers would pass through the various chambers and finally into a large area where they could recline and rest. The baths were heated by ceramic pipes, still in situ.

Archaeological History

Karanis was uncovered when Fayoumi farmers were digging in the area to collect the rich *sibakh*, decomposed organic debris, left by the ancient occupants. They found papyri, which someone sold to collectors and museums. The papyri became one of the most coveted treasures from Egypt and it was not long before the site received serious archaeological attention.

The Fayoum was rich in such treasure because the desert desiccated abandoned sites. Allowed to dry in this manner for centuries, the documents were preserved. Unfortunately, they also made good *sibakh*. Here at Karanis, the sale of *sibakh* was big business, big enough to warrant the construction of a railway to remove it. When archaeology finally arrived here, the archaeologists tried to stop the loss. An agreement was reached with the Italian company that was processing the fertilizer. The archaeologists would provide enough *sibakh* to keep the company and the railway working. And, in what Alston calls "an early example of rescue archaeology," the papyri were hastily removed between 1928 and 1935.

The excavation of Karanis was begun by Bernard Pyne Grenfell and Arthur Surridge Hunt in 1895. It was the first Greco-Roman site ever excavated in Egypt. The two gentlemen found little as they were excavating too far north, and left the site the following season. In 1920, Francis W. Kelsey came to Egypt from the University of Michigan and following in the footsteps of Sir Flinders Petrie (see below) he began intensive archaeological excavations. In November of 1924, the team arrived at Karanis, where the *sabbakhin* had been hard at work removing fertilizer since the site was abandoned by Grenfell and Hunt in 1895. The Michigan team worked here for eleven seasons, much of their work documented and the results now on view in the Kelsey Museum in Michigan.

In all, the Michigan team found five datable levels of debris at Karanis and three areas: the north temple, the south temple, and the residential district. Karanis was later excavated by Cairo University, and most recently by the French Institute.

Getting There: Today the Fayoum is spreading beyond its traditional eastern edge and it will continue to move east as new canals are being created in the desert. The Kom Aushim Museum is tucked into a small garden almost hidden from view just in front of the junction of three roads—the main road, the road south to Tamiya, and the new highway south to Medinet Fayoum.

Bacchias (Bakchias) or Kom Umm al-Atl
N 29 32 382 E 31 00 412

A short distance away from the larger community of Karanis stood the small community of Bacchias, or Kom Umm al-Atl (Kom al-Atel, Umm al-Atel), located along the ancient caravan road from Memphis to Medinet Fayoum (Arsinoe at the time).

Once containing approximately 700 mudbrick houses and about 3,000 people, it, like Karanis to the northwest, was founded in the third century. Although most of the houses are now rubble, several interesting ruins are still standing. The site is almost always deserted, but the local guard will arrive in short order. One is free to roam at will through the ancient buildings, which include a mudbrick temple dedicated to Sokanobkonneus, a local crocodile god. It was in this temple that the papyri were found. A few Fayoum portraits were found here, too. A badly looted cemetery exists to the north of the settlement.

The site was visited by Petrie in 1889–90, and Grenfell and Hogarth excavated here for seven weeks in 1896. Among other things, like papyri and domestic objects, they found three jars filled with 4,300 coins. In 1992 and 1993, the site was excavated by an Italian-Egyptian team from Bologna and Lecce. Although the site was almost destroyed by looters, many prehistoric tools were found by the first probe and new streets and buildings were unearthed by the second.

Getting There: From the Kom Aushim

Museum head west and almost immediately turn left on the first road going south (it requires a U-turn). Continue for half a kilometer to a mosque followed by an iron bridge. Cross the bridge and turn east (left) on the dirt road. There is a canal to the left of the road and a small rise that holds the southern slopes of Karanis. The road proceeds between the desert and the cultivated fields on a picturesque journey past dozens of small artificial waterfalls (on the left), at least ten bridges, and several villages. Follow the road for 11 kilometers (6.8 miles) to the village of Gharay. There are no English signs announcing this village. Just ask. Even if you do not speak Arabic, roll down your window, say hello (very important), and say "Gharay." The person will point the way. At Gharay, turn left across the cement bridge, go straight through the very small village, and head for the desert.

Philadelphia or Kom al-Kharaba al-Kebir, Great Hill of Ruins

Philadelphia was an important frontier town between the eastern escarpment of the Fayoum and the western edge of the Nile Valley during Hellenistic times. It was founded as an agricultural community by Ptolemy II Philadelphus for his wife/sister, Arsinoe.

Now totally leveled, this once prosperous and famous city offers nothing for the visitor except ground litter. But to the archaeologist, Philadelphia is a treasure trove. Many papyri have been found here, including the archives of Zenon, the estate manager for Apollonius, and the treasurer of Ptolemy II, who owned acreage in the area. These archives, filled with details of production and management, shed light on daily activities in the Fayoum during Ptolemaic times. Then it was a garrison town with a town plan similar to Alexandria. It lay along the Bahr Wadan irrigation canal and was higher than most of the Fayoum and therefore cooler. It had small, mudbrick homes with courtyards. The citizens enjoyed two temples, athletic games, and festivals.

The community still thrived during the Roman era. We know that one fifth of the community were Roman army veterans who purchased property here in the third century. They were not always welcomed by the Egyptians, but they lived in many villages in the Fayoum. By the fourth century the irrigation system was a shambles and Philadelphia was abandoned.

Philadelphia was also the site where the largest number of Fayoum portraits were discovered. At first the location was unclear because the grave robbers had shown their cache in a cave, but later evidence pointed to a cemetery at Philadelphia. According to Euphrosyne Doxiadis in *The Mysterious Fayum Portraits: Faces from Ancient Egypt,* they were found by locals looking for fertilizer, who began to sell them to Theodor Graf, a Viennese antiquities dealer. This was one year (1887) before Sir Flinders Petrie found his cache at Hawara. Through the years, Graf acquired at least 350 such portraits. (For a description of the portraits see Crafts above.) When they were first discovered, a number of the portraits were exhibited by Graf in Munich, Paris, Brussels, London, and Berlin.

There is a little intrigue connected with Graf and the portraits. He wanted to sell them and needed to date them. Scholars, eager to study them, gave various dates from Hellenistic to Roman. Everyone joined the fray: H. Heydemann said they were post-Hadrianic, Georg Ebers said they were not Roman, but perhaps Jewish and Hellenistic; and Petrie, finding additional painting at Hawara, determined Graf's portraits to be second-century, Roman, and Hadrianic; Graf picked Greek, and then made a big mistake. He suggested they were portraits of the Ptolemies themselves, and marketed them as such. Of course his identification was wrong. A scandal erupted and the authenticity of the portraits was brought into question. After all, if he had lied about the subjects, he could well be lying about the origin. But he was not. Of course, Graf's portraits are genuine, and he sold them to museums throughout the world.

Caravans left Philadelphia for the Nile Valley regularly. Today, Philadelphia is still on the edge of the cultivated land, and the small village of Beit al-Rai before it almost looks like a toll gate. One expects to wait in line to be assessed for a desert patrol tax, as was a man called Diogenes on September 16, A.D. 147. "Paid at the toll house of Philadelphia, for the desert patrol tax: Diogenes exporting fresh dates, one donkey load, and wheat, one donkey load."

The area was excavated by Viereck and Zucker in 1908–9 and also by Ludwig Borchardt.

Getting There: After visiting Bacchias, return to the dirt track. If you wish to go home, turn right, and return the way you came. To continue on to Philadelphia, turn left. After 14 kilometers (8.7 miles) one reaches the picturesque checkpoint of Beit al-Rai. Turn left, cross the canal, and just beyond, a mere half kilometer past the trees, is Philadelphia. To the right, along a dirt track beginning just before the checkpoint, is the road to the Pyramid of Sila. At the checkpoint pick up a guide to both places. After visiting Philadelphia and Sila you can return to the Nile Valley and the pyramid of Meidum by returning to Philadelphia and driving straight. The new Cairo–Asyut Desert Road is another 4 to 5 kilometers ahead. A left-hand turn on the new highway will take you to Cairo.

Pyramid of Sila

There are of course plenty of pyramids in Egypt, but most are located in the massive cemeteries on the desert fringes of the Nile Valley and serve as burial chambers for kings. However, there are seven interesting pyramids in the Nile Valley that do not follow the pattern of the mortuary complex. Lacking subsidiary buildings, they are devoid of inscriptions, and seem to have no burial chamber. The Pyramid of Sila is one of these (the others are located at Elephantine, Edfu, Hierakonpolis, Ombos, Abydos, and Zawyat al-Mayitin).

Archaeologists are not sure of the function of these pyramids, but their locations, in this instance overlooking both the eastern half of the Fayoum and a large portion of the Nile Valley near Meidum, may indicate that they served as lookout posts. Another theory is that the pyramids provided the royal *ka*, or spirit of the deceased king, with a sanctuary when it visited the land of the living.

Discovered and investigated in 1898 by a team from the German Archaeological Institute, the Pyramid of Sila, like its six cousins, is believed to have been erected by Huni, a king of the Third Dynasty of the Old Kingdom. A step pyramid built of limestone, all that remains are the bottom levels, the first buried in rubble. During additional excavations, the Egyptian Egyptologist Nabil Swelim found the remains of two stelae bearing the name of Snefru, the first king of the Fourth Dynasty. Currently, the pyramid is under the care of Wilfred Griggs of Brigham Young University.

In the desert plain below the pyramid are Christian and Roman rock-hewn tombs. Although mostly uninscribed, they have yielded thousands of papyri which have played an important role in deciphering the ancient history of the Fayoum.

Be sure to enjoy the wildlife along this canal: spur-winged plovers, egrets, and herons predominate.

Getting There: To get to the Pyramid of Sila from Beit al-Rai turn right just before the checkpoint then follow the road for 8 kilometers (5 miles) along the edge of a small canal. Turn left over the bridge. This bridge can be distinguished from other bridges because there is a waterfall under it and an industrial complex on the other side of the canal. Once across, in front of the bridge is a Muslim cemetery and atop the scarp, not visible at this point, is the Pyramid of Sila. To reach it turn left and follow the base of the scarp, heading back toward Beit al-Rai on a well marked desert track. After about a kilometer the track skirts the Egyptian Antiquities Organization building and around the bend are the yellow signs identifying the site. Immediately to the right are the Christian and Roman rock tombs, and beyond, again following a track, is the road to the base of the mountain. To follow the road requires a dirt bike or a 4x4 and a guide. You can also walk. After less than 2 kilometers (1.2 miles) the track ends and visitors must climb the escarpment along the visible path. The pyramid is at the top of the hill.

The Lake District

Over the centuries people have had their way with Birket Qarun. It was enlarged considerably in the Twelfth Dynasty to create a large pleasure lake that rose to 18 meters (58 feet) above sea level and was fed by the Nile. In the third century, under Greek rule, it was lowered to 2 meters (6 feet) below sea level. The lake shore shrunk, allowing for the reclamation of rich, fertile land and the development of new communities around a new lake shore. Ptolemies I and II modified the Lahun Embankment diverting the Nile waters and the level fell to 5 meters (16 feet) below sea level. The reclaimed land was given to Greek and Macedonian soldiers called *cleruchs*. This, coupled with the lack of rainfall, and the intense evaporation caused by the desert climate, has seen the lake slowly decrease in size and depth.

Under the Romans, the feeder canals were allowed to clog and the lake dropped to 17 meters (54 feet) below sea level by the third century, perhaps accounting for the mass migration of the late period.

The decline continued during Islamic rule. When Nabulsi governed in 1245, the lake was 30 meters (96 feet) below sea level, under Muhammad Ali (1805–1848), 40 meters (128 feet) below. It was replenished by Nile floods breaching the protective gates in 1360, and 1817–18. In his *Memoires* of 1673 Linant de Bellefonds states that "Vansleb, who was in the Fayum in 1673, said that one embarked at Sanhur to pass to the other side of the lake." Today Sanhur is 6 kilometers (4 miles) from the lake shore.

Major R. H. Brown, a royal Engineer, tells us in *The Fayum and Lake Moeris* (1892) that the lake level fell from March to October and rose from November to January. He, too, recorded its decline. In March of 1885, the lake was 39.80 meters (128 feet) below sea level. By March, 1892, it was 43.32 (138.5) below.

Interestingly, up to the twentieth century it was still a freshwater lake. Georg Schweinfurth of the Royal Geographical Society tested the water in 1879, and was so surprised at its freshness that he believed that a subterranean outlet existed. Unfortunately, substantial evaporation has turned the fresh water, once used to irrigate crops and support a fishing industry, into salt water that supports only a small variety of fish. Birket Qarun is a dying lake with a salinity count of 3 percent. The cycle begun in the Pleistocene is continuing. Only 7.6 meters (24 feet) deep in mid-March and even lower toward the end of summer, the shape of the lake currently resembles a crocodile, the patron god of the Fayoum during pharaonic times.

Several local legends relate to the lake. Transmitted orally from generation to generation many are composites of different legends incorporated into one tale. One tells of a pharaoh who lived during the time of Moses. The pharaoh inhabited a castle called Qarun and had rooms and rooms full of gold and other riches. But the pharaoh was greedy and became mean and vicious. Then, with all his possessions, he was cast into the lake. The treasure is still believed to be hidden in the lake and treasure hunters still search to find it in the dark waters.

TOUR #2
North of Lake Qarun

- 4x4 all offroad
- 6–8 hours
- easy to hard

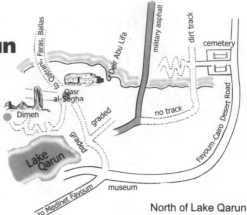

North of Lake Qarun

			km	total km
Kom Aushim Museum	N 29 31 093	E 30 55 577	0	0
Qasr al-Sagha	N 29 35 366	E 30 41 052	24.6	24.6
To Dimeh				
Qasr al-Sagha	N 29 35 366	E 30 41 052	0	0
Road	N 29 35 338	E 30 40 912	0.3	0.3
Lake view	N 29 34 358	E 30 41 197	4	4.3
Dimeh	N 29 32 165	E 30 40 168	4.5	8.8

The Northern Shore and Scarp

The northern shore is desert and should be approached with caution. No matter how sure or how experienced a person is, within a minute the desert can turn into a hostile enemy. Landmarks change, rock formations collapse, new tracks break off from the old, and everything looks different. Time of day and season of the year also affect how the desert looks, and what was once familiar will look foreign. In addition, people are encroaching on the desert.

The best and surest way to visit the northern shore is with a guide. You will get more out of your trip, for not only will he lead you

Qasr al-Sagha

through the desert, he will point out other interesting sites along the way. Guides are available at the Kom Aushim Museum. The cost is minimal.

Qasr al-Sagha

Qasr al-Sagha, the Golden Fortress, is an unusual Middle Kingdom building situated north of the lake, half way up the escarpment. At one time the northern shore of Lake Qarun stood close to the temple. The temple is constructed of limestone slabs fitted together like a jigsaw puzzle complete with oblique corner joints. It is a marvel of construction so well built that it still stands, as it has for centuries, without the help of any mortar. Never completed, it has a series of rooms with one completely enclosed and having no entrance. The function of this unusual building is unclear, but it certainly had a strategic view of the surrounding area. Be sure to find the peephole in the east door.

Qasr al-Sagha stands on a small, flat, natural platform on the side of the northern escarpment and below it are extensive remains of the village that once stood nearby. The area is well worth exploring for in addition to the village to the southwest there is evidence of an ancient roadway, an unusual platform that resembles a causeway, hand-hewn rock caves, and several prehistoric villages. The prehistoric sites are located on the flat plain to the south of the temple. Judging from the ground litter the northern villages seem to have been inhabited by hunters, while the southern sites, nearer the ancient lake, were inhabited by farmers and fishermen.

Quay

Almost immediately to the southwest of Qasr al-Sagha (about 800 yards) there is a large amount of rock that looks as if it was built into an ancient quay. Caton-Thompson believes it was a dumpsite for the rock mined at Widan al-Faras and was either awaiting transport to the Nile Valley or was to be used to build a monument on the site.

Discovered by George Schweinfurth in 1884, and sometimes referred to as Schweinfurth's Temple, the area was also studied by Flinders Petrie, Hanbury Brown, and Gertrude Caton-Thompson.

Getting There: It is 24.6 kilometers (15 miles) to Qasr al-Sagha from the main road. It takes about an hour and requires a 4x4. The beginning of the track to Qasr al-Sagha and Dimeh is on the left (north) side of the Cairo–Fayoum road, across from the Kom Aushim Museum just after the checkpoint. An oil company sign marks it. When quarrying began the track was graded for easy access and you will meet many trucks. Follow the track. At 20 to 21 kilometers (12.5 miles) from the beginning of the road the destinations are in sight. Ahead, Dimeh rises out of the desert floor like the monoliths of Stonehenge. A little to the right, half way up a flat-topped peak on the scarp, is the temple of Qasr al-Sagha. At the right, below the summit of Gebel Deir Abu Lifa, are the barely visible ruins of the monastery. Continuing, at 22.5 kilometers (14 miles) there is a sign for Qasr al-Sagha and at 24.6 (15.2) the road bears right. The road climbs up the scarp to the Qasr and a parking space directly in front of the monument awaits.

Neolithic Sites

Neolithic sites exist throughout the area north of the lake, from the Cairo–Fayoum road in the east to the west edge of the lake and well into the desert. Gertrude Caton-Thompson is the person most associated with early Neolithic exploration in the Fayoum. She was an English archaeologist who dedicated her life to Africa. Along with Elinor Wright Gardner, she undertook the first archaeological survey of the Fayoum. It was Caton-Thompson who hypothesized that there were two distinct ancient cultures inhabiting the area, one around 5000 B.C. and the second around 4500 B.C. She went on to work in Kharga and published three books, *The Desert Fayum*, *Kharga in Prehistory*, and an autobiography, *Mixed Memoirs*. She lived to nearly a hundred and died in 1985.

Deir Abu Lifa

Two kilometers north-northeast of Qasr al-Sagha, high on the southeastern slope of the escarpment where it protrudes into the plain, are the ruins of the rock-hewn Deir Abu Lifa, Monastery of Father Lifa. Probably founded by St. Panoukhius, the monastery was in use from the seventh through to the ninth centuries and was a haven for Christians during troubled times.

Visited in 1936 by Henri Munier and André Pochan, the entrance to the monastery is cut into the mountain. Inscriptions date the monastery as early as 686. Predictably, Fayoumi legend relates that there is buried treasure at this monastery, for when the monks of Fayoum abandoned nearby monasteries it is claimed they took their possessions and buried them at Deir Abu Lifa.

Dimeh al-Siba (Soknopaiou Nesos)

Dimeh al-Siba, Dimeh of the Lions, was a Ptolemaic city believed to be founded by Ptolemy II in the third century B.C. on a site that shows evidence of habitation from the Neolithic period. In Ptolemaic times it was at the shore of the much larger lake, nestled at the edge of Moeris Bay and the beginning of the caravan routes to the Western Desert. According to Caton-Thompson, it was Ptolemy who reduced the size of the lake to provide land for the settlement of retired Macedonian soldiers and their families.

Serving as a port and perhaps once an island, judging by its Ptolemaic name Soknopaiou Nesos, Island of Soknopaios (from the Egyptian Sobck-cn-Pai), the site is currently 65 meters (208 feet) higher and 2.5 kilometers (1.5 miles) beyond the water's edge (Caton-Thompson maintains it was never an island).

During the turmoil of Roman rule, Dimeh reached both its zenith and its nadir. Although Roman soldiers were stationed here, no documents suggest that Romans made the community their home. It was on the fringe of the desert away from the culti-vated lands on the south side of the lake. It was like a frontier. Retired Roman soldiers preferred to live in the villages to the south like Philadelphia and Karanis.

Richard Alston in *Soldier and Society in Roman Egypt* paints life at Soknopaiou Nesos through a number of petitions for justice presented by various members of the community to the Roman centurions: In A.D. 11, a dispute arose over land tenure; in 12, a request for protection from a person defeated in a lawsuit; in 101, an assault on a priest who was attempting to collect a debt; in 148, the disappearance, in suspicious circumstances, of a person to whom land was rented; c. 167, a priestess and defenseless widow make an appeal; in 184, a woman was assaulted and threatened with death by a man she lived with and owned property with. It all sounds familiar.

Goods from the Fayoum were transported across the lake by boat to be unloaded at the docks of Dimeh, stored, or carried up the Avenue of the Lions, assessed for a customs fee, and reloaded on animals for desert cara-vans. These caravans moved north over Gebel Qatrani, and probably via Wadi Natrun, to the Mediterranean and on to Rome.

Egypt had the reputation throughout the Mediterranean of being plagued by desert bandits. Here at Soknopiaou Nesos, as in other desert outposts in the Western and Eastern deserts, and along the northern coast, security systems were in place to protect caravans. They did not always

succeed. Dimeh was inhabited for six centuries and was finally abandoned by the middle of the third century.

The ruins contain two temples, houses, underground chambers, streets, and 10-meter (32-foot) high walls. The ground is strewn with debris. There must be billions of shards covering the entire temple mound. You drive over them, sit on them, walk on them. They are inescapable.

The city itself spread for a great distance through the desert, and the mudbrick walls that are still standing do not contain the entire community, but only the temple area. To the north were the agricultural fields, separated by long irrigation canals. To the south was the Gate of Soknopaios, at the end of the Avenue of the Lions, which ran down to the edge of the lake where the docks were located. Today one can still see the remains of this road, which ends about a kilometer to the south of the ruins at a quay. The quay has two limestone piers and steps leading south, presumably to the water's edge.

The houses are located along the proces-sional Avenue of the Lions, inside the walls, and on the plain surrounding the temple mound. At one time they reached several stories, had painted walls similar to those recently excavated at Amheida in Dakhla Oasis, and had underground chambers which were used for storage.

There are two temples at Dimeh. Of the northern one, which was constructed of stone, only the foundations remain. The brick and stone southern temple may date from the Christian era. A Roman cemetery lies 900 yards southwest of the city.

When Belzoni arrived here, he confused Dimeh with Bacchias, located on the south-eastern shore. The Dimeh area was excavated by a University of Michigan archaeological team under the direction of Professor Zuker in 1931. Prior to that it was plundered by local Bedouin, people looking for papyrus scrolls, and farmers who value the rich soil of ancient sites as fertilizer.

Getting There: The walls of Dimeh stand as sentinels along the northern shore of the lake in Fayoum. They can be seen for kilome-ters. With Qasr al-Sagha behind, drive south for about 700 meters and at the fork take the right-hand road. Ignore the well-graded road on the right. The correct road tops the rise and eventually turns west while the other stays on the plain. At 2 kilometers (1.2 miles) from the beginning of the road, the top of the rise is reached. Keep an eye open for the unusual rock formations in the area. The slabs of stone look like Swiss cheese, with holes cut through the rock by wind erosion. At 4 kilometers (2.5 miles) the lake comes into view and, in addition to enjoying the spectacular view from this vantage point, one can see how far the lake has receded in recent times. For the next 3 to 4 kilometers (2 to 2.5 miles) as the road weaves and turns, the moonlike landscape of Dimeh pops up to the right, left, and then right again. It becomes evident that the ruins sit atop a mound of their own rubble. At 8 kilometers (5 miles) Dimeh is on the right and the lake is on the left. It is a good place to enjoy the panorama. The island in the lake is visible at this point.

Widan al-Faras

Widan (or Qadan) al-Faras is a mountain. It is two conical outlier hills capped by black basalt standing about 340 meters (1,088 feet) above sea level. From the top, one can see a grand panorama from Lahun in the east across to Wadi Rayyan in the southwest. It was once an Old Kingdom quarry. Here the pharaoh's workmen mined the precious basalt that was used to make pots and statues. At Widan al-Faras it was easy to extract, for it broke off from the hillside and fell onto the desert floor in large chunks. It simply had to be loaded onto sleds and transported down the escarpment to the waiting boats at the quay at Qasr al-Sagha.

The roadway that led to the quarry was constructed of basalt stone and petrified wood during the Old Kingdom. This quarry road begins at Qasr al-Sagha, turns north, and climbs the escarpment. It moves across the plain, and directly to Widan al-Faras, 8 kilometers (5 miles) away. Then it skirts the second escarpment to Gebel Qatrani. At points the road is 3 meters (7 feet) wide.

Scientists used this road to measure the erosion of the desert. Once flat with the surrounding desert, the road now stands nearly one meter (3 feet) above the surface. They estimate that the wind takes away 3 cm per century.

Gebel Qatrani

Gebel Qatrani sits atop the northern scarp enclosing the Fayoum Depression. It is made of sandstone and clays and topped by a thick bed of hard black basalt. Many, many fossils exist here.

Abu Ballas

To the northwest is Abu Ballas, Father of Pots, first discovered by Prince Kamal al-Din in his desert wanderings early in this century. Located on the caravan trail that linked Wadi Rayyan and points south with Wadi Natrun and points north, Abu Ballas was obviously a major station where caravans stopped to rest. It sits 64 kilometers (38 miles) from Qasr al-Sagha in the middle of the desert. The pots scattered around this area date from the Roman era and consist mainly of smashed amphorae. There is a second Abu Ballas southwest of Dakhla on the way to Gilf Kebir and Kufra Oasis in Libya.

Getting There: To reach these sites put Qasr al-Sagha at your back and face the lake. There are three tracks in front of you: the original track veering left, a second that cuts off from this track and heads slightly to the right to Dimeh, seen in the distance at about 1 o'clock, and a third track that turns right. The third track is the old quarry road to Widan al-Faras. One kilometer from Qasr al-Sagha the road heads north and passes in front of a modern mudbrick building. To the right, tucked into the foothills, are a series of uninscribed, hand-hewn rock caves. Follow the track heading up the scarp. Pause along the way, for the journey is 3.3 kilometers (2 miles) to the top. At the top the ground is strewn with shells and fossils. On a clear day the Giza pyramids are visible to the northeast, Saqqara to the east, and all of Fayoum to the south. The trail continues along an ancient quarry road built of stone and petrified wood on its way to Widan al-Faras. To the west, along the cliff, is Gebel Qatrani.

TOUR #3
Southern Shore of Lake Qarun

- 2x2
- 2–6 hours
- easy

			km	total km
Kom Aushim	N 29 31 125	E 30 53 889	0	0
Old Sinnuris rd	N 29 30 255	E 30 53 123	2	2
Lake	N 29 28 978	E 30 49 262	7	9
Duck Island	N 29 28 574	E 30 47 902	3	12
Sinhur/Fayoum rd	N 29 28 097	E 30 46 751	2	14
Auberge Fayoum	N 29 28 083	E 30 46 229	1	15
Shakshuk	N 29 27 824	E 29 26 279	5	20
Wadi Rayyan rd	N 29 24 635	E 30 28 447	27	47

The contrasts that are perpetual in Egypt stand out yet again on the shores of Birket Qarun. Where the northern shore is barren and desolate desert, the southern shore is lush, green, and productive. While the north is mined for minerals, the south is cultivated for crops. The north is uninhabited, the south is heavily populated.

Because the current southern shore was underwater in ancient times there are no monuments in the immediate area. It has been developed mainly as a tourist site. The lake is a popular day trip for middle-class Egyptians trying to escape the noise and bustle of Cairo, and the beaches in this area are crowded, especially on Fridays and holidays.

Getting There: Ten kilometers (6.2 miles) from Kom Aushim Museum the road forks: the northern road leads to the lake, while the southern road (to the left) leads to Medinet Fayoum via Sinnuris (the old route). Three kilometers (1.8 miles) later the lake begins.

The first part of the lake shore is overly developed with day beaches and resorts. One must move beyond the resorts of Alla a Din, Auberge Fayoum, and Panorama and passed the village of Shakshuk to the quite, agricultural lakefront of the western half of the lake. (For details, see Practical Information.)

Shakshuk, less than a kilometer beyond the Panorama Hotel, is a fishing village. Boats can be hired for a ride on the lake, or a trip across it to Dimeh. Vendors are easily spotted for the fishermen unfurl their sails along the road and hawkers call out for customers. At the fork in the road at the Egyptian Salts and Minerals sign, bear left, continue for one block, bear left again and head south. Continue for about 2 kilometers (1.2 miles) and turn right through the cement arch to drive to the southwestern end of the lake. Here the new road to Wadi Rayyan that bypasses Shakshuk joins the road. To avoid Shakshuk, take the fork to the left that announces Wadi Rayyan just before the village. It will join the road from Shakshuk at the cement arch.

A few timeshare beach resorts and electrical wires now mar the landscape of this once pristine area. Otherwise, it is as it was centuries ago. The serene pastoral atmosphere continues for 20 kilometers (12.5 miles). High on the hill to the left of the road, on the bench mark of the former lake, rise the two newly developed communities of **Ezbat Tunis** and **Haggar al-Gilf.** The Islamic style homes are the residences of affluent families who find this section of the Fayoum a good place for a second home.

Just beyond the village, as the road reaches the crest of a hill is the road to Wadi Rayyan. Accessible by regular vehicle, simply follow it to Wadi Rayyan (for details about Rayyan see below).

At this point it is only 10 kilometers (6.2 miles) to the end of the lake. There are a few places where tracks lead down to the shore, good spots for bird watching (especially for flamingos on the far shore). Swimming and sailing are fun too, although it must be noted that the winds in the Fayoum are whimsical and early morning and mid-afternoon are often calm and not good for sailing at all. The beaches are usually empty and provide

good spots to enjoy a picnic away from the crowds. Remember there is no fresh water, no shade, and no concession stands. Although these beaches are nearly deserted, remember to dress modestly. Nude bathing is absolutely out of the question.

At the edge of the lake the road turns south. Shortly after is a road to the right, turn north (right) on any of the dirt tracks and head for the scarp. There are a few villages and some cultivated fields, but the northern shore of the lake is near. Wander at will. In some places there is a leisurely climb to the top of the escarpment. A 2x2 can navigate most of this.

TOUR #4
Western Edge of the Fayoum

- 2x2, 4x4
- 4 hours
- some entrance fees

			km	total km
Medinet Quta	N 29 24 941	E 30 22 928	0	0
Qasr Qarun	N 29 24 508	E 30 25 232	1.6	4.6
Cross Rayyan rd	N 29 24 122	E 30 28 524	5.4	10

Medinet Quta

The road north from the village of Qarun leads to the very edge of the scarp, a good place to climb nearly to the top. This is a hike. Another problem is that an abandoned car may be vandalized. However, the trip up the escarpment is a wonder. There are plenty of small fossils, and probably bigger ones too along the edges of the cliff. The wind howls over the crest of the ridge and can be strong enough to knock one down. Just below the top of the escarpment there is a ridge riddled with what appear to be white bones. Closer examination reveals large limestone rocks embedded in the soil. The view is to the south overlooking Fayoum: palm trees, cultivated fields, and the giant lake stretched out to the left, the Wadi Rayyan straight ahead, and the beige, empty Western Desert on the right.

After descending the scarp continue east at the base of the cliff to Medinet Quta. The only hope of finding it is to ask the farmers. When they see a car in the area they know the destination.

The Ptolemaic city of Medinet Quta, now a ruin, marked the western edge of the inhabited area of the Fayoum in antiquity. There are ruins of houses, inscriptions, and furnishings sitting atop a mound at the base of the scarp and the edge of the cultivated land. Little excavation has taken place at this site, which is difficult to find for the road goes through a modern-day labyrinth of irrigation ditches, twists and turns, and axle breaking ruts. At some points it narrows to a pathway, almost too narrow for a car. However, you don't need a 4x4 if you are willing to leave your car in a field and hike a bit. Just keep asking.

Qasr Qarun (Dionysias)

Entrance fee. Qasr Qarun, the ancient Dionysias, stood at the Fayoum terminus of the caravan route coming north out of the heart of the Western Desert through nearby Wadi Rayyan. Here the caravans paused before continuing along the western edge of the lake, to climb the escarpment at the Naqb al-Garw and continue on to Wadi Natrun. Today, Wadi Rayyan can be entered via a track behind the temple, but it is one of the longer and more difficult passages and a guide and 4x4 are necessary.

Founded in the third century, the community sprawled between a Roman fortress and the temple, which was located atop a rise. A thriving community for at least a century, it was probably abandoned by the fourth century.

The Temple

Built of yellow limestone, the 'temple of stone' at Qarun is dedicated to Sobek-Re, yet another form of the crocodile god. It has a good view of the desert to the west. One of the most interesting aspects of this temple is that the roof is still in place, offering us a sense of the atmosphere that once prevailed in all the temples of the Western Desert. The uninscribed exterior, minus its damaged portico, looks like a square box. The interior of the temple is a labyrinth of rooms and stairways complex enough to be confused by early travelers with the real labyrinth at the Hawara Pyramid. There are vestibules, a sanctuary, and a few additional chambers. There is also a stairway to the roof, which is worth the climb for the splendid view.

The Town

The town spreads north and south of the temple. Mostly in ruins a few structures are worth mentioning. The Roman bath is a mere outline on the ground as are most of the houses, but a few still stand, at least partially, and some, like the Roman villas in Amheida in Dakhla Oasis, have fresco decorations on the interior walls. The most noteworthy is located just east of the fortress. Thermal baths with frescoes were discovered here in 1948, but the desert has long since reclaimed them.

The Fortress

Located to the west of the temple, the fortress, constructed during the reign of Diocletian as protection against the Blemmyes, is now a ruin. Its foundations indicate that it was similar to the forts still standing in Kharga Oasis along the Darb al-Arbain and it is reasonable to assume the fortress served the same purpose. Dionysias, an outpost community receiving caravans from the Western Desert, had to be garrisoned and the caravans bivouacked when they were in the area. These procedures required organizers and guards. In addition, Dionysias was open to invasion from the west. As the first outpost in Fayoum, it required good fortifications. Built of mudbrick it was about 90 by 80 meters (255 feet) with square towers at each corner and semicircular towers on the sides. Within the ruins of the fortress are the remains of a Christian basilica. There are some stone capitals, a few with Corinthian design.

Records indicate that at some point Roman soldiers for this fortress were probably conscripts. Toward the end of Rome's rule, soldiers were not as eager to serve. Military service became compulsory for sons of soldiers and upon enlistment all soldiers received tattoos so they could be identified if they deserted.

Local lore maintains that Qasr Qarun was the home of the pharaoh who now lies at the bottom of the lake and that there is a tunnel under Qarun leading to treasure.

During the British occupation, Qarun was garrisoned by a cavalry brigade.

Dionysias was cleared by a Franco-Swiss archaeological team in the 1940s and 1950s and an epigraphic survey was done in 1976.

Getting There: As you drive along the western shore, instead of turning north to the northern scarp of Medinet Quta, continue along the main road. A few kilometers later you will be in the center of the village of Qarun. Friday is market day in this town and the market is laid out directly on the road. To avoid passing through the heart of the crowded kiosks, turn south on the east side of the canal and cross over to the main road on a small bridge approximately one kilometer or so south of the city. There is a gas station at the end of the second village (Karabit al-Shimi) on the right-hand side.

Nazla

Nazla is a potters' paradise. Located along the Masraf al-Wadi, the valley drain, one could almost pass by thinking it just another village. There is no indication that the far end of the village sits atop a ravine and that cascading down the slope are the potters' kilns. It is a magnificent site, perhaps the best in the Fayoum.

Unfortunately many travelers tell of nasty experiences in this picturesque village. Children and even men outshout and intimidate visitors with an eternal cry for baksheesh (tip). Combined with a disregard for Western ideas of private space, the experience can be overwhelming. Although a visit to the village is a must to see the kilns, it might be best to drive through and not stop. In any event, the pots are sold at the market in Medinet Fayoum on Tuesdays.

Getting There: To reach the potters turn off the main road beside the mosque in Nazla. After a short distance the Masraf al-Wadi appears on the right, as do the kilns.

Hamuli

Hamuli is the site of the Coptic monastery Deir Archangel Michael, now a ruin. In 1910, a collection of ancient Coptic documents, known as the Hamuli Manuscripts and dating from 823 to 914, were discovered by farmers digging for fertilizer in this ruin. The manuscripts are currently in the Pierpont Morgan Library in New York City.

Getting There: Hamuli is south of Qasr Qarun and in the desert. It is difficult to find and requires a guide. Ask at any of the villages south of the village of Qarun or north of Barins.

Medinet Madi

Medinet Madi, City of the Past, is considered by some to be the most important ancient site in the Fayoum. Located on a small hill commanding a strategic position guarding the southwestern entrance to the Fayoum, the site was probably occupied in prehistory. Excavators have found two distinct towns in the archaeological debris.

The Temple

The most interesting structure to the layperson is tucked into a wadi and not visible from the road. It is a Middle Kingdom temple, built in the Twelfth Dynasty by Amunemhet III and IV and dedicated to Renenutet, the serpent goddess. Expanded during Ptolemaic times, the temple fights to stay above the sands that encroach from all sides. Facing south, the artifacts include an avenue of sphinxes, lions, and on the ruined temple walls, now only a few meters high, a few reliefs and hieroglyphic inscriptions. To the east of the temple are mudbrick storerooms and foundations. Ancient debris litters the entire site.

During the 1995 season, a Ptolemaic limestone gate was discovered east of the latter temple. Upon further excavation it was revealed that a second temple lay under the debris. In front of the gate are two crouching lions and a sphinx. The mudbrick temple has sandstone doorways and its ruins rise to about 4 meters. Among the debris, tablets and papyri have been found, the most important to date are four Third Century oracular demotic documents.

In the medieval romance poem the *Story of Abu Zayd*, which was told and retold in coffeeshops throughout the Middle East, Medinet Madi was destroyed by Abu Zeid when the king refused him and his soldiers food and shelter.

An Italian team from the University of Pisa has been working here since 1966. They have done epigraphic work and visual graphics of the temple, uncovered a large Roman town, and ten churches of the sixth and seventh centuries. In nearby Khelua (Kom Ruqayya) they have excavated and restored Middle Kingdom tombs.

Getting There: Follow the road southeast from Qasr Qarun. At the small village of Menshat Sef, cross over the canal and head for the desert (through a cemetery). Once atop the rise the temple is visible 4 kilometers (2.5 miles) away. The route is accessible by regular vehicle.

TOUR #5

Medinet Fayoum

N 29 18 775 E 30 51 607

- **2x2**
- **4 hours**
- **easy**

Known as Crocodilopolis in Greco-Roman times, the capital of the Fayoum sits in the center of the depression like the hub of a wheel, with roads, railroads, and canals radiating to all parts of the oasis. R. Neil Hewison tells us in his *Fayoum: A Practical Guide* that some modern Fayoumis believe the medieval city was built in 1,000 days, or *alf yawm,* and that is how the city got its name.

Canals are the major feature of the city. Straddling the Bahr Yusif and its eight tributaries, the city is the Venice of Egypt. (Two canals actually divert from the Bahr Yusif within the city and the remaining six at the western edge of town.) There are bridges everywhere, crossing and recrossing the canals.

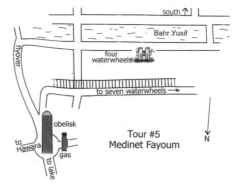

Tour #5
Medinet Fayoum

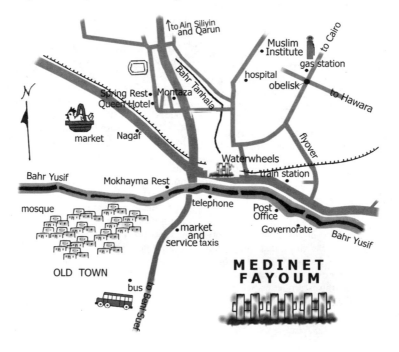

MEDINET FAYOUM

The Obelisk

Moved from its former site in the village of Abgig, the red granite obelisk created in honor of Senusert I of the Twelfth Dynasty now stands at the northern entrance to Medinet Fayoum. Although it is called an obelisk, its form is more that of a stela. An obelisk is a tall, thin, four-sided monument tapering as it rises and ending in a four-sided pyramid. A stela is usually much shorter, rectangular, and rounded at the top.

Kiman Faris

The ancient capital of the Fayoum from the Old Kingdom to the Roman era, Kiman Faris, the Horseman's Mounds, is now a ruin. Known by the various names of Shedty, Crocodilopolis, and Arsinoe, it was the cult center of the crocodile god Sobek and covered 4 kilometers (2.5 miles) in its heyday. Although at the beginning of this century it still covered 300 feddans (each roughly equal to an acre), now less that 10 feddans of rubble remain. The rest have been covered over by the expanding modern city. There is not much to see, most of our knowledge of Kiman Faris is contained in the numerous papyri found in the area.

Waterwheels

Center city waterwheels	N 29 18 499	E 30 50 688
Bahr Sinnuris wheel	N 29 19 644	E 30 50 648
Set of four	N 29 19 788	E 30 50 697
Last pair	N 29 20 49	E 30 50 961

Among the most interesting sites in the Fayoum are the ancient waterwheels. Over 200 of them straddle the canals. Unique to

Waterwheels under repair along the Bahr

the area, the wooden wheels are driven by the fast-moving water of the canals and were introduced into the Fayoum during Ptolemaic times.

They are 4 to 5 meters (12 to 14 feet) in diameter and coated with black tar to protect the wood. Each waterwheel can lift the water 3 meters (10 feet), spilling it onto higher ground. January is the month set aside throughout Egypt for cleaning the canals. The sluices are closed and in the Fayoum all the functioning waterwheels are cleaned and repaired. Although created centuries ago, each wheel has a life expectancy of only ten years and many parts have to be repaired each season.

In addition to the four moaning and groaning in the center of the city, the famous seven, hallmarks of the Fayoum, are located in the countryside along the Bahr Sinnuris. There are additional waterwheels on various canals in the area.

Getting There: To reach the seven waterwheels from the main square, cross over the railroad tracks behind the cafeteria and turn west, left. Continue for six or seven long blocks until you see a blue tourist sign along the right-hand side. Continue to the Bahr Sinnuris. Cross over the canal and turn left. The road leads out of Medinet Fayoum into the picturesque countryside along the ancient canal. The first wheel is found after 3 kilometers (1.8 miles). Less than 100 meters later a set of four wheels straddle the canal under giant willow trees, and a short distance beyond come the final pair.

Getting There:
Kom Aushim to Medinet Fayoum

Kom Aushim sits at the eastern entrance to the Fayoum. Directly ahead is the lake and to the south is Medinet Fayoum, the capital of the oasis. To reach Medinet Fayoum turn south at the second turn immediately after Kom Aushim. This is the new highway and it bypasses all the villages, taking you directly to the obelisk.

Auberge to Medinet Fayoum

			km	total km
At lake	N 29 28 110	E 30 46 740	0	0
Sanhur	N 29 24 647	E 30 46 215	6	6
Fidimin	N 29 23 298	E 30 46 519	2.7	8.7
Ain al-Siliyin	N 29 22 708	E 30 47 633	2.3	11
Crossroad	N 29 19 952	E 30 49 470	5.2	16.2
M. Fayoum	N 29 18 777	E 30 51 116	5	21.2

The road south from the lake to Medinet Fayoum is found 2 kilometers (1.2 miles) to the east of the Auberge. This is a drive through orchard country. The village of **Sanhur** is 7 kilometers (4.3 miles) from the beginning of the road. From the main crossroad in the center of town, the route east leads to Ibshaway, west to Sinnuris, and south to Medinet Fayoum. A mere 2 kilometers (1.2 miles) south is **Fidimin**, where a weaving school for children was begun recently. Open Monday through Thursday from 8 to 2 it features weaving, tapestry, embroidery, and beadwork.

Two kilometers (1.2 miles) beyond Fidimin is the famous spring **Ain al-Siliyin**. Located across the road from the village of Siliyin, the area around the natural spring has been converted into a pleasure park with bridges, a swimming pool, chalets, cafeterias, and a windmill. Extremely popular on Fridays and holidays, it is pleasant to visit the park during the week, when it is empty. The next community is **Beni Salih**. The brickmaking industry is located along this road. They still make bricks in the traditional way. Four kilometers (2.5 miles) to the south the main road veers left. Although the right fork also goes to Medinet Fayoum, the left is the preferred route. (The former passes through Mishat Abdullah on its way to Kiman Faris, the ancient city of Medinet Fayoum.) Less than a kilometer later the road crosses the small canal called Bahr Tirsa. Look to the left down the canal to see a pair of waterwheels. The dual carriageway leading to the city is about 2 kilometers (1.2 miles) later.

Shakshuk to Medinet Fayoum

Villagers along this seldom used route are not accustomed to seeing foreign visitors and their zeal, especially that of the children, can be overwhelming, but the drive is a pleasant one through farmland and fields of flowers. The road twists and turns through the fields and villages. Many of the small hamlets have interesting colonial houses leftover from the time when the land was owned by rich families and the farmers tilled the soil, planted and harvested the crops, and were subject to a feudal way of life. Five kilometers (3.1 miles) after leaving Shakshuk one comes to a crossroads: left goes back to the Auberge, straight leads to Sanhur, and right to Ibshaway. Turn right, and after a kilometer is the village of **Abud**. Three kilometers (1.8 miles) later there is a fork in the road. Right goes to Qarun and left to the village of **Faruqa**. At the entrance to the village is a marvelous old mansion surrounded by exquisite trees and a lovely garden. Beyond the mansion is the railroad crossing and the village of **Abuksa**, with an old railway station.

Less than a kilometer from Faruqa, there is a crossroads. Left goes to Medinet Fayoum, right to **Ibshaway**. One of the nicest things about Ibshaway is the row of colonial houses lining either side of the road as one enters the town. They are followed by orchards which give way to the main city, entered through a tree lined street leading to an old railroad station. Ibshaway is a large city as far as Fayoum goes and is a pleasant place to wander around. Continue down the main street, cross over the railroad tracks and take a left. Less than a kilometer later, still in the city, cross over a small bridge and take the right fork. Soon fields of flowers come into view. These flowers, harvested for sale to perfumeries in Europe and America, vary with the season. They continue in patches on either side of the road for over 3 kilometers (1.8 miles). Petals are collected and can be seen strewn in huge heaps on the ground; then they are crated for shipping. At a picturesque traffic stop the road comes to a dead end. A right turn goes to Qarun and a left to Nazla, the pottery village. From Nazla the road continues through Minya and Abgig to Medinet Fayoum.

TOUR #6

Hawara Pyramid

- **2x2**
- **2 hours**
- **easy**
- **entrance fee**

			km	total km
Obelisk	N 29 18 941	E 30 51 156	0	0
Hawara Pyramid	N 29 16 225	E 30 53 999	8	8

If visitors are looking for spectacular pyramids, then the two major pyramids in the Fayoum will be disappointing. Where most of the pyramids in the Nile Valley were built in the Old Kingdom, dubbed the Pyramid Age, the two in the Fayoum were built in the Middle Kingdom, when the art of pyramid building had declined. Both have mudbrick cores, and both have fallen to ruin. Hawara is not hard to find, but Lahun is next to a nightmare.

There is an entrance fee to this site.

Hawara

Hawara (Great Mansion) or Arsinoiton Polis, City of the Arsinoans, was the site of the pyramid complex of Amunemhet III, built on what may have been the shores of Birket Qarun during the Twelfth Dynasty. The pyramid, its casing removed in Roman times, looks like a heap of rubble. But the site was one of the most important archaeological discoveries in Egypt.

The Labyrinth

The mortuary temple of the pyramid of Hawara was excavated by Sir Flinders Petrie in 1888 and 1910 under such terrible conditions that he exclaimed he was "up to his nose in water." Until Petrie saw the value of everyday objects such as bowls, jewelry, and tools in piecing together everyday life in ancient times, scholars and archaeologists were throwing them aside for papyri.

The mortuary temple was the labyrinth that so amazed Herodotus: "I visited this place and found it to surpass description," he said. The labyrinth was believed to have been hewn from a single rock and contained over 3,000 rooms (perhaps an exaggeration). It is mentioned by almost every ancient traveler including Strabo, Diodorus, and Pomponius Mela, who claims Psammetichus erected it and that it contained a thousand houses and twelve palaces enclosed within a single wall (just like Shali). By the nineteenth century it was gone. Certainly it was larger than any known site in Egypt, including Karnak.

Unfortunately, Herodotus's find, like its pyramid, is also rubble. Sadly, bit by bit, the labyrinth was chipped away and used as quarry stone throughout the Fayoum. Today looking at the site it is difficult to imagine what it was once like. But even the most devastated site can yield interesting finds and Petrie's artifacts were the greatest treasures to be discovered in Egypt until the discovery of the tomb of Tutankhamun in the Valley of the Kings. Among them were the famous Fayoum portraits.

The Portraits

Here at Hawara 146 Fayoum Portraits were found in the cemetery north of the pyramid of Hawara. A few Fayoum portraits can be seen at the small museum at Kom Aushim and in the Egyptian Antiquities Museum in Cairo. (For a complete description of the Fayoum Portraits, see Crafts above.)

Getting There: From the obelisk at the

entrance to Medinet Fayoum, turn left, east. Cross the railroad tracks and at the dead end turn left. Continue along this road for about 8 kilometers (5 miles) until it comes to a dead end. You will pass through several villages. Turn right at the dead end. The pyramid is in front of you.

TOUR #7
South of Medinet Fayoum

			km	total km
Medinet Fayoum	N 29 18 775	E 30 51 607	0	0
Waterwheels	N 29 16 508	E 30 50 413	5	5
Deir al-Azab	N 29 15 930	E 30 51 201	2.4	7.4
Deir Ghobrial (return to rd)	N 29 11 799	E 30 52 406	8.3	15.7
Cairo/Asyut rd	N 29 14 719	E 30 54 837	5	20.7
Lahun locks	N 29 12 214	E 30 58 184	7	27.7
Lahun Pyramid	N 29 13 716	E 30 58 004	3.8	31.5

The best way to reach the roads to the south of Medinet Fayoum is to take the flyover at the entrance to the city and turn right at the sign to City Center. Then follow the signs to Beni Suef for about a kilometer. The road S-turns (left and right) and you will pass the vegetable market and service taxi stands on your way out of town.

Four kilometers (2.5 miles) after leaving the city there is a pair of waterwheels in the fields on the left side of the road. A kilometer later is a fork in the road. The right fork goes to the villages of Azab, Muftah, Qalamshah, Totun, and beyond (see below), and the left fork continues past the monasteries and the pyramids, under the new Cairo–Asyut Desert Road, and on to Beni Suef.

Deir al-Azab (St. Anba Abraam)
Founded either in the twelfth century by Peter, the Bishop of the Fayoum, or in the thirteenth century by the Patriarch Cyril III, Deir al-Azab was uninhabited from the eighteenth century until recently. Today, the monastery has come to life again and is a thriving Christian center of pilgrimage. There are new facilities, including new churches, guest accommodation, and gift

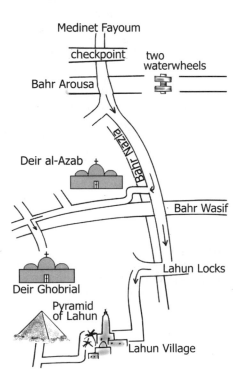

shops. From August 15–22 each year a mulid celebration is held to mark the Assumption of the Blessed Virgin Mary.

Getting There: Located 6 kilometers (3.7 miles) south of Medinet Fayoum. At the fork in the road bear left. The monastery is only 2 kilometers (1.2 miles) ahead on the right-hand side along the Bahr Nazla.

Deir al-Malak Ghobrial (Deir al-Naqlun)

The Deir al-Malak Ghobrial, located at Gebel Naqlun, is one of the oldest Coptic monasteries in the Fayoum. According to the Christian historian Abu Salih, it is where Jacob (grandson of Abraham by his son Isaac, and father of Joseph, builder of the Bahr Yusif) lived and worshiped.

The monastery was probably founded in the fourth century by Bishop Aur and remained a functioning monastery until the sixth century. According to tradition, Aur was the illegitimate son of the daughter of a Middle Eastern queen and her lover, Abrashit the Magician. He was guided by the Archangel Gabriel to this spot and erected the church in the archangel's honor. Gabriel is reported to have said to Aur, "Send none away. . . . Many marvelous things shall be performed. . . . This mountain shall prosper, and shall become as crowded as a dovecote. . . . People shall come to visit it from all countries of the earth and their prayers shall mount up to God."

From the fourth to the sixth century the monastery was the leading Christian center in the Fayoum. Saint Samuel lived here until he established the Monastery of Saint Samuel in Wadi Mawalih (see below). By the fifteenth century it was in ruins, with only the churches still standing, and up to 1968 the monastery was only used once a year on the celebration of the mulid, or saint's day, of Gabriel. Today the monastery is thriving.

The Church

The monastery contains the Church of Saint Gabriel, which is decorated with six columns with Corinthian capitals, and has a wooden ceiling with geometric designs. Its development is unclear, but the relics of Abba Kaw, a martyr of the Diocletian persecution, were known to have been kept in this church as late as the fifteenth century.

The Laura

Southeast of the monastery along the upper ridge of Gebel Naqlun is the Laura, a group of individual caves once inhabited by monks. Founded by Aur, these caves, some plain, others plastered, contain one or two rooms and serve as living quarters. At the Laura is a tower called the Modsellet Jacob, the Tabernacle of Jacob, which, according to tradition, was where Jacob lived.

Excavations are underway here both at the mountain and the monastery. Coptic, Greek, and Arabic papyri have been discovered.

Getting There: The turn right to the monastery is less than a kilometer beyond Deir al-Azab. The dirt road, accessible via regular car, continues for 7 kilometers (4.3 miles) to a bridge over the canal. Turn left and head for the desert.

Lahun

Entrance fee. You can access the Hawara pyramid before reaching Lahun, but it is easier as directed above. The town of Lahun has been dominated since ancient times by the Bahr Yusif, the canal which diverts water from the Nile and carries it to Lahun where it is dispersed throughout the Fayoum. In fact, an ancient papyrus indicates that the name of the town is taken from the ancient Egyptian Ra-Hunt, meaning the opening of the canal. Originally named after the biblical Joseph who, legend maintains, was responsible for its construction when he was vizier of Egypt, the Bahr Yusif diverts to a second canal, the Bahr al-Wasif, at Lahun. At Medinet Fayoum, the Bahr Yusif finally disperses into the eight different canals that water the entire depression.

Like Hawara, the pyramid complex of Senusert II is also rubble. Built by Anupy for Senusert II in the Twelfth Dynasty, this pyramid precedes that of Hawara by several generations. Its base is a natural rock outcrop that was cut to accept a pyramid top. Nearby was a Middle Kingdom town, which when excavated by Petrie yielded incredible treasure, the most abundant find of its time.

Among the finds in the tombs near the pyramid was the jewelry of Princess Sithathorinit. The jewelry, mostly gold and silver and decorated with precious stones including lapis lazuli, can be seen in the Egyptian Museum in Cairo and at the Metropolitan Museum of Art in New York City.

Getting There: You have to be desperate to go to Lahun. The village is dirty and unpleasant and there is no other way, you have to cut right through it. Tour buses do not take tourists there. Return to the main road after the Deir Ghobrial. Turn right, or south on the main road to the Lahun Canal. After crossing the canal, turn left immediately. Follow the main street through the village to a dead end. Turn left. Follow the road, until it comes to a dead end at the pyramid. Your must return through the village. If you want to leave the Fayoum, once you recross the canal you can turn left, retracing your route, and head for the Cairo–Asyut Desert Road not too far ahead. Although the pyramid of Hawara is just on the other side of the Cairo–Asyut Desert Road, you cannot access it from here. (See above.)

Located 5 kilometers (3.1 miles) beyond the Pyramid of Lahun is the picturesque monastery of Deir al-Hammam, which was founded between the sixth and eighth centuries.

TOUR #8

South to Tebtunis and Environs

- 2x2, 4x4
- 4–5 hours
- easy

Route #1

			km	total km
Obelisk	N 29 18 941	E 30 51 156	0	0
Azab	unavailable		16	16
Muftah	N 29 11 721	E 30 50 132	9	25
Qalamshah	N 29 10 043	E 30 50 361	3	28
Totun	N 29 09 225	E 30 49 101	2	30

Route #2

			km	total km
Obelisk	N 29 18 941	E 30 51 156	0	0
Itsa	N 29 13 526	E 30 46 565	7	7
Shidmoh	N 29 12 07	E 30 45 371	5.3	12.3
Totun	N 29 09.225	E 30 49 101	unavailable	
Qasr al-Basil	N 29 68 89	E 30 49 114	2	2

Route #1

None of the villages south of Medinet Fayoum on this route have much to offer the visitor. One simply must pass through them to get to the historical sites. They form a loop and one can exit Medinet Fayoum via one route and return via the other. Between the villages is the farming area of the Fayoum. This is worth seeing. The village of **Azab** is 1 kilometer south of the fork. Next comes

Muftah, the Key, 9 kilometers (5.6 miles) along the route, followed by **Qalamshah** 12.2 kilometers (7.8 miles) from the fork. After 13.8 kilometers (8.5 miles) the road comes to a dead end at a canal. To the right is the road to Totun, only 2 kilometers (1.2 miles) further along.

Route #2

From the flyover at the northern entrance to Medinet Fayoum the road continues across the Bahr Yusif. Immediately after the canal, turn right to the city center. After one kilometer the road goes left to Beni Suef and S-turns (right and left) past the vegetable market and service taxi stands. It is approximately two kilometers (1.2 miles) to the village of **Abgig,** where Senusert I's obelisk once stood. Pass straight through Abgig and continue about three kilometers (1.8 miles) to the village of **Minshat Rahim,** Merciful, continue another kilometer to **Abu Sir,** and a final kilometer to **Itsa,** where there is a gas station. At the southern end of the town the road left leads west through small villages for 10 kilometers (6.25 miles) to the desert's edge, Medinet Madi, and Wadi Rayyan. The road to the right continues south through the village of **Shidmoh** to Totun and Qasr al-Basil.

Qasr al-Basil

Totun is the gateway to the village of Qasr al-Basil, 2 kilometers (1.2 miles) south. It was the home of Hamed Basha al-Basil, a Bedouin who supported Saad Zaghloul in his bid for Egyptian independence from British rule in the early part of this century. While

Pigeon house

Zaghloul was operating in Cairo, Basil led an uprising in the Fayoum on March 12, 1919. Basha al-Basil's *saraya,* palace, still dominates the town. Located along a canal at the beginning of the village, the palace, in a sorry state, is being used by the military and is off limits to visitors, but even from the outside remains a visual treat.

The village itself is small and has a wonderful pigeon house on the outskirts of the desert track that leads west. This track goes to Tebtunis (Umm al-Burigat), but the drive along the canal is more interesting. At the palace, turn west and follow the dirt path through the fields along the northern side of the canal. Here the Fayoum countryside comes to life. Young boys fish with handmade *sabat al-sammak*s, fishing traps, and *shelb*s, triangular framed fishing nets (see Agriculture, Fishing, and Industry above). Farmers are working the fields with pharaonic-style plows. Acres and acres of verdant cultivation set amid palm groves lie to the right and to the left. The desert that marks the end of the Fayoum is to the south. Five kilometers (3.1 miles) later is the turn south to Umm al-Borigat, a Bedouin village, and its ancient ruin Tebtunis. This entire area was heavily populated during Ptolemaic times with a number of villages, including, in no specific order, Kerkeosiris, Theogonis, Talei, and Berenikis Thesmophorou. (A second route to Tebtunis via Totun is not as picturesque).

Tebtunis

Probably founded in the Twenty-second Dynasty, Tebtunis, meaning 'round head,' grew to be one of the largest towns in Greco-Roman Fayoum. Although it was less prosperous during the general decline of the Fayoum in the fourth century, it was still inhabited in Islamic times. It was here on January 16, 1900, that the first papyrus scrolls were found by an unsuspecting worker with the Egypt Exploration Fund and the University of California's joint expedition. In disgust at finding yet another crocodile mummy in the vast crocodile cemetery, a worker kicked it, revealing a treasure of papyri. It was the beginning of the discovery of many such caches throughout the Fayoum. It is mainly through these texts, written in Demotic, Latin, or Greek that archaeologists have been able to piece together the history of the Fayoum.

Tebtunis must have been quite a place in Roman times. At least the petitions for justice found in the papyri make it sound like a riproaring town: in 167, attempted murder by a gang; in c. 184, the village elders were extorting grain; two hunters were missing, presumed murdered; 222, the ass of the tax collector was stolen and killed; and finally, land was embezzled from the city.

Kerkeosiris, Gharaq Sultani

Returning back to the canal, turn west (left). Eight kilometers (5 miles) later, after passing through several small villages, is the large village of **Gharaq Sultani**. Called the swamp, it was a papyrus thicket in pharaonic times and a starting point for caravans to the Western Desert (see Wadi Rayyan below). Dominic Rathbone in 'Towards a Historical Topography of the Fayum,' an essay in *Archaeological Research in Roman Egypt* (Vol. 19) hypothesizes that Gharaq Sultani sits on the Ptolemaic village of Kerkeosiris, Settlement of Osiris, a village whose kidney-shaped territory covered nearly 13 kilometers (8 miles). Papyri known as the Tebtunis Papyri by Menches, a local scribe during troubled Ptolemaic times, give us a great deal of information about Kerkeosiris from 120 to 111 B.C. There were two villages called Kerkeosiris in the Fayoum—our village was located in the Polemon division, in the south. As with most villages in the Fayoum, it was agricultural. And, like many others, it was settled by retired soldiers who had received grants of land.

Kerkeosiris also had a number of dovecotes, including one with 1,000 pots for nests.

Today, it has little to offer the visitor. Note the houses of Gharaq Sultani. Instead of the traditional mudbrick, they are built of slabs of limestone. At the edge of the village the dirt road ends at a paved road. To the right the road passes through the heart of Gharaq Sultani and continues on to Shidmoh; to the left it continues to Birket Abu Talib and points west.

Abu Talib, Berenikis Thesmophorou

Four kilometers (2.5 miles) after Gharaq Sultani is the small lake of Abu Talib. It was a much larger lake in antiquity and the area of Berenikis Thesmophorou probably sat on its shore and might be the site of the modern village of Kom al-Khamsini (again by Rathbone). The lake is on the left of the road beyond a small but interesting cemetery. In the middle of the cemetery, tucked under a glorious spreading acacia tree, is the tomb of Sheikh Abu Talib, after whom the lake is named. The road to the lake passes through the cemetery. Legend says this small lake is bottomless and haunted.

Rathbone believes that a number of ancient villages can be identified in this area: the modern village of Kom Medinet al-Nehas is probably the ancient Magdola, which lay next to Ibion Argaiou; Tell al-Maraka could be Ibion Araiou; Kom Ruqayya could be Theogonis. We know of a number of other ancient villages also located here and waiting to be found: Lyusimachis, Areos Knome, and Kerekesoucha Orous.

The road continues north to Ank, al-Barins, Hamuli, and western Fayoum.

Wadi Rayyan

The Bedouin believe Wadi Rayyan was named after a king who is buried with all his gold and riches somewhere in the wadi, a myth similar to the Qarun myth of nearby Fayoum. This has made Wadi Rayyan the object of scores of treasure hunters. Arab historians credit the name to that of a pharaoh during the time of Joseph. Known to be occupied during Roman times, Wadi Rayyan has had a constant stream of visitors including Cailliaud in 1819, Letorzec in 1820, Belzoni in 1824, J. J. Rifaud 1824, John Gardner Wilkinson in 1840, G. A. Schweinfurth in 1886, G. Steindorff in 1900, and Ahmed Fakhry in 1942 and 1944.

During the British occupation of Wadi Rayyan, the American Cope Whitehouse suggested it as an ideal place for a reservoir. To this end a British officer named Colonel Western was sent to explore the area. It had been examined by Sir William Willcox when he was evaluating the irrigation resources of Egypt before settling on Aswan as the site to build the Aswan Dam. The Rayyan project was shelved for many years and it wasn't until 1966 that the idea of creating a water reservoir at Wadi Rayyan became a reality.

Today Wadi Rayyan has been transformed from dry desert with a few springs into a fertile valley for agriculture, industry, and tourism. Through the efforts of the Ministry of Agriculture and Land Reclamation 15,000 feddans of desert are destined to be converted into productive agricultural land.

To date, although the infrastructure has nearly been completed and several small communities have been constructed, little is happening in the wadi. For one thing, the second lake has begun to turn from fresh water to salt water. This is a great blow to any agricultural development. Of course, it might lead to a better understanding of what happened to the other fresh lakes in the Western Desert like Qarun and Maryut. Both lakes were once freshwater and are now salty.

Geography and Geology

Wadi Rayyan is a depression in its own right separated from the Fayoum by a limestone ridge. The depression is 42 meters (134 feet) below sea level and covers 673 square kilometers (1,076 square miles) with a 30 meter (96 foot) thick limestone floor. It has one mountain, Gebel Rayyan (Gebel al-Deir), located 24 kilometers (15 miles) west of Gharaq.

The Tour

The diverted drainage water from the Fayoum, fed into Wadi Rayyan by underground pipes, has created two deep blue lakes, one after another from north to south. The lakes have been well stocked with fish and a small, but growing, fishing industry is beginning as part of the development of the area. They have also attracted wildlife, especially birds.

The Western Shore

The western shore has become the major access area to Wadi Rayyan. A new paved road makes access very easy and small arrow signs announce all the important sites, including the waterfall. Near the beginning of the lake road a toll booth has been established and a sign announces that foreigners must pay five Egyptian pounds to enter.

TOUR #1

The Waterfall

			km	total km
Shakshuk	N 29 27 824	E 30 43 309	0	0
Rayyan rd	N 29 24 635	E 30 28 447	27	27
Crossroad	N 29 23 075	E 30 28 754	3	30
Gate	N 29 21 393	E 30 27 215	5	35
Waterfall (at rd)	N 29 13 837	E 30 24 503	14	49

Getting to the waterfall is easily managed by regular vehicle. To get to the other sites at Wadi Rayyan is not so simple. However, good help is at hand. There is an excellent safari group to lead you. You can call them in Cairo and prebook your trip. You can come in a regular car and they will take you 4x4ing on any safari you want. You can bring your 4x4 and they will lead you in theirs. They welcome GPSs. The point is, you can do the waterfall by yourself, but not the other tours and Wadi Zeuglodon is one of the best safaris in the Western Desert. Take a guide.

The Waterfall
N 29 13 837 E 30 24 503
The waterfall sits between the two lakes. The entrance is well marked along the main road. Access is for everyone. Once the domain of explorers and rally drivers, the area has been transformed into a not so pretty day trip from Cairo. Tourists come by the bus loads and at least three picnic pavilions have been erected. The route over the top of the waterfall has been closed.

TOUR #2

Magic Spring and the Monastery

- 4x4
- 2 hours
- moderate

			km	total km
Waterfall (at rd)	N 29 13 837	E 30 24 503	0	0
Al-Mudawara	N 29 11 412	E 30 21 839	7	7
Offroad entry	N 29 07 331	E 30 19 183	12	19
Magic Spring	N 29 04 798	E 30 18 099	6	25
Monastery	N 29 04 937	E 30 17 099	2	27

Al-Mudawara
Seven kilometers (four miles) south of the Waterfall, along the left or eastern side of the road, is a picturesque area known as al-Mudawara, The Lookout. There are three mountains along the lake shore. It is a favorite picnic area.

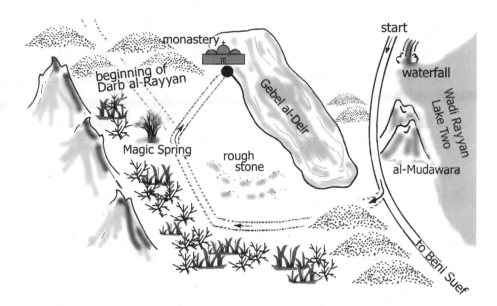

Gebel al-Deir

Gebel al-Deir, Mountain of the Monastery, looms almost dead ahead and to the right or west side of the road. Dunes, similar to those at the Gilf Kebir, attempt to climb its side just before one rounds the eastern edge of the mountain. It is worth stopping to look at this marvel for it attests to the power of dunes. Even mountains will not stop them.

The Gebel al-Deir separates Wadi Rayyan from the deep desert and on its far side is Magic Spring and the Monastery of Wadi Rayyan.

Magic Spring

Almost immediately after turning into the desert, the scrub- and dune-studded wadi that forms the entrance to Rayyan from the deep desert comes into view. It stuns you, as one does not expect all the vegetation. At the edge of the mountain, one spectacular dune knifes its way from the valley floor to the summit. After seeing only sand and water in Rayyan, this wadi surprises the visitor with its almost impassable scrub. The scrub has many medicinal plants used by the Bedouin and they often come here with their camels and goats to graze and collect herbs.

This is the terminus of the Darb al-Rayyan from Bahariya Oasis. There are three springs here. The one called Magic Spring is our destination. If one stands at the source of the spring and claps several times, the water emanating from the source slowly begins to jump, or dance, to the rhythm of the claps. Of course, when the spring is silted up after a storm, it does not dance. Thanks to the local Safari Camp, it is unclogged regularly.

Monastery of Wadi Rayyan

The Monastery of Wadi Rayyan sits on one mountain and on the far side of the second mountain, directly across the wadi, is the Monastery of St. Samuel (see below).

In October of 1960, a group of monks inhabited the caves in Wadi Rayyan and began to live as the desert fathers had centuries before. Sustained by a camel caravan from Gharaq Sultani in the Fayoum, these monks, all university graduates, lived alone in ten individual caves, meeting once a week for prayers.

As one approaches the monastery it looks new. But the work of the 1960s is in front of the old hand-hewn caves. There is even an old oven, or *furn*, where the monks baked their bread. Today, the old monastery is abandoned.

Getting There: Getting to the monastery is easy if you cross the wadi in the right place. If not, you will be on hard, tough, rock with prickly edges. From the Magic Spring follow the tracks. You can climb to the monastery door with your vehicle.

TOUR #3
Gebel Guhannam and Wadi Zeuglodon

- 4x4
- 6 hours
- easy
- entrance fee

			km	total km
Waterfall (at rd)	N 29 13 837	E 30 24 503	0	0
Enter desert	N 29 11 766	E 30 20 340	12	12
Flat plain	N 29 14 922	E 30 19 058	8	20
Graded road	N 29 10 042	E 30 15 938	5	25
Gebel Guhannam	N 29 18 747	E 30 09 598	18	43
Zeuglodon entrance			12	55
Whales			4	59

Gebel Guhannam

Gebel Guhannam, Hell Mountain, is located 28 kilometers (17.5 miles) west of Lake Qarun. To reach it from Rayyan, one travels northwest. It is flat topped.

Getting There: The drive is easy. After crossing over the canal to the right of the roadway, Gebel Guhannam becomes visible dead ahead after a few kilometers. It takes over 30 kilometers (19 miles) to reach it. A few twists and turns because of the terrain and you go down a gentle slope to its base.

Wadi Zeuglodon

Wadi Zeuglodon (also known as Wadi al-Hitan, Whale Valley) is more beautiful than the White Desert. That is a mouthful. The closer one gets to its entrance, the more astonishing the surroundings. Once inside the high valley, huge, beautifully-caramelized, surreal boulders capped with imaginary icing or thick oozing syrup which runs down their sides in great globs seem to have been flung about the landscape by some ancient event during the creation of this lunar landscape.

The bonus is that this magnificent landscape is in the middle of an 8 square kilometer (3 square mile) area where the fossil remains of *Basilosaurus isis* have been found.

In this wadi, you are at the southern shore of the ancient Tethys Sea. The valley around Gebel Guhannam is part of the Upper Eocene Birket Qarun Formation. The top of Gebel Guhannam is of the Qasr al-Sagha Formation, which holds some land mammals washed there by free flowing water, but an abundance of sea creatures who were stranded when the sea receded. Wadi Zeuglodon sits at the top of the escarpment as high as Guhannam. It, too, is of the Qasr al-Sagha Formation. It, too, sat on the southern shore of the Tethys Sea.

The valley is named after the whales known as *Zeuglodon. Basilosaurus,* which means 'King of Reptiles' is an old (1835) mistake, as *Zeuglodon* is not a reptile, but a mammal. It averaged 20 meters (64 feet) in length, had a slender, eel-shaped body, and saw-edged teeth. Just one of its fossilized vertebrae

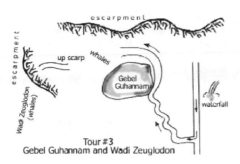

Tour #3
Gebel Guhannam and Wadi Zeuglodon

may weigh as much as 45 pounds. It existed in the Fayoum over forty million years ago. For a comparison, the earliest known whale in the world is *Pakicetus*, fifty million years old.

The most amazing thing about *Zeuglodon* is that it had feet. Sometime in the ancient past mammals migrated into the sea. Some returned to the land, others did not. As the ancestors of modern whales entered the sea their front legs began to change into flippers, their backs elongated, and their hind legs disappeared. Only nubs remain on modern whales to indicate where these hind legs were. *Zeuglodon* does not have nubs. Ten million years after whales entered the sea, *Zeuglodon* had small, fully-developed hind legs with a femur, patella, tibia, fibula, and four toes.

These legs were discovered by Philip Gingerich and Holly Smith, a husband and wife team from the University of Michigan

on an expedition to Wadi Zeuglodon in 1989. Some early conclusions are that *Basilosaurus* was an 'evolutionary dead end' in the whale family and is probably not related to modern whales. But it teaches us a lot about the transition of whales from land mammals to sea mammals.

There is a second whale in Wadi Zeuglodon, called *Dorudon*. Much smaller at 3–5 meters (12–15 feet) long, it may prove to be the link to modern whales.

Meanwhile, let the whales rest in peace. Look, photograph, but do not touch. Scientific work here is just beginning. Don't hinder its progress. The good news is the future of this ancient wonder looks bright, as it is now part of the Egyptian Environmental Affairs Agency's Wadi Rayyan Protected Area. Visitors pay an entrance fee and park rangers are on patrol to protect not only the whales but the environment as well. A visitors' center with fossil exhibits is planned.

Getting There: Wadi Zeuglodon is located 12 kilometers (7.5 miles), more or less, west-southwest of Gebel Guhannam. Circle behind the mountain and continue left. The plain has small mounds of debris, each an ancient sea creature, so do not race by. The closer one gets to the end of this wadi, the more beautiful it becomes. The escarpment turns to sugarloafs, then sphinx-like outcroppings, and the color moves to a rich coffee-cream tan. The ascent to Wadi Zeuglodon is easily managed by 4x4. Once at the top, bear right. Now, at the top of the mountain, you have entered paradise.

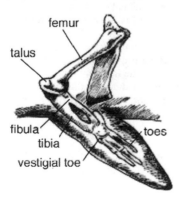

Zeuglodon's amazing feet

Wadi Mawalih

Located south of Wadi Rayyan, and separated from it by an escarpment of rock and sand, the Wadi Mawalih, Valley of Citrus Fruits, is 18 kilometers (11.2 miles) long and stretches in a northwest–southeast direction. The entrance is guarded by a conical hill of whitish, hard, fossiliferous limestone where fossils can be found.

Practically inaccessible until the new Cairo–Asyut Desert Road was built, the Monastery of St. Samuel is now easily reached. Simply follow the paved road until you see the monastery sign.

Monastery of St. Samuel
N 28 43 815 E 30 38 563 from Cairo–Asyut Road

The main feature of the valley is the Deir Anba Samwil, Monastery of St. Samuel. Built near the springs of Ain Samar and Ain Burdi during the fourth and fifth centuries, the monastery is approximately 33 kilometers (20 miles) from Qayyat.

This monastery, like many of the monasteries in the Fayoum, has had a varied history. Once abandoned, it has recently been reinhabited and is a thriving community. The original portion of the monastery is in ruins, but the newer sections are being renovated.

There are three churches at Deir Anba Samwil: the nine-domed Church of the Blessed Virgin Mary to whom the monastery was originally dedicated three centuries before Samuel lived there; the Church of Saint Misail; and the Catacomb Church, the oldest of the three. The latter is probably from the fourth century and is mostly underground.

St Samuel lived at the end of the fourth century and spent 57 years of his life as a monk. Surviving persecutions, floggings, and capture by Bedouin he sought refuge here in Wadi Mawalih. His relics are found in the monastery. His cave is located 15 meters (48 feet) from the top of Gebel Qalamun, which means you have a long 180 meter (576 foot) climb to reach it. It is a large cave, 35 meters (111 feet) deep but very low, so Samuel could not have stood. At the end of the cave is a small depression that protected the monk from the elements and a small spring. It is currently used as a chapel. Today there is a stairway, but it is just as long and just as staggering as before the stairs were cut.

It is 2 kilometers (1.2 miles) from the main gate east of the monastery. Additional caves used by the monks are to be found in the hills surrounding the Wadi Mawalih.

Getting There: There are 4 routes into Wadi Mawalih: from Wadi Rayyan, from Gharaq Sultani in the Fayoum, and from the Nile Valley and from the newly constructed Cairo–Asyut Highway.

From Gharaq Sultani: The Darb al-Rayyan heads south from Gharaq Sultani and reaches Wadi Rayyan in the extreme south below the lakes. Here it branches. One track continues southwest passed Magic Spring to Bahariya and the second kicks southeast to Wadi Mawalih. This is 4x4 and dirt bike territory. One should also have a guide. It is 32 kilometers (20 miles) to the monastery in Wadi Mawalih.

From the Cairo–Asyut Highway: By far the easiest way to reach the monastery is via this newly constructed highway. From the Pyramids Road turn onto the Cairo–Alexandria Desert Road and then on to the Fayoum Road. From the Fayoum Road travel about 13 kilometers (8 miles) to the Asyut highway. N29. 47.519/E31.02.661. Travel down the highway for 163 kilometers (102 miles) to the sign that announces the monastery and turn right (west) into the desert. N28.43.815/E30.38.563.

8

Al-Diffa
(the Northern Coast)

Al-Diffa is a term used by the Shiheibat Arabs to identify the tract of land running from Alexandria to Benghazi (in Libya) between the Mediterranean and the area approximately 40 kilometers (25 miles) inland. The area has been called by many names, including the Cyrenaican Plateau, the Libyan Desert Plateau, and the Marmarika.

G. W. Murray, the director of the Geological Survey from 1932 to 1948, accepted the Shiheibat definition and calls al-Diffa "a wonderful ham-shaped country of nothing at all—no mountains, not even hills—no rivers, not even wadis—no oases, no springs—just nothing but nothing and plenty of that." In 1938, he began the mapping of the Egyptian portion. For our purposes, then, this area is called al-Diffa, despite the fact that it has many other names. We have divided its Egyptian portion into the three classical regions, all named by the Romans: Agube Major, from the Libyan border to Mersa Matruh; the Marmarika, from Mersa Matruh to Mareotis, just west of Alexandria; and the Mareotis itself, which is the present Lake Maryut and surrounding territory. The name Marmarika has been used interchangeably with al-Diffa by some people, but we will limit it to the definition above.

While we are on the topic of names, let us deal with one more confusion about names in the Libyan Desert: they don't remain the same. Alexandria is Alexandria is Alexandria, but Mersa Matruh is Ammonia is Paraetonium, and Abu Sir is Taposiris and Hammam is Halmyrae, and on it goes. Nor are any of the names for the oases, or villages along the Nile, the same as they were in antiquity. Thebes became Luxor, Syene became Aswan. Each conquering nation brought its own names. The Greeks had their names, the Romans had theirs, the Arabs theirs. In fact, when Bayle St. John trekked across the northern coast on his way to Siwa in the 1840s, hardly a name existed that we use today. That was less than 200 years ago. Known history in the area is more than 5,000 years old. A single site may have had ten different names over those fifty centuries.

John Ball in *Egypt in the Classical Geographers* spends a great deal of time trying to figure out what Herodotus and the historians, Ptolemy and the geographers, and such works as the *Antonine Itinerary* and the *Notitia Dignitatum* are referring to when they mentioned a place. St. John thought he was following in the steps of Alexander when he turned south to head to Siwa at a place he called Mudar. But Alexander turned south at a small camp that he named Paraetonium. So, just where is Mudar? And where is Paraetonium? And what are they called today? Nice puzzle, isn't it?

Then there are the references to the Arabs' Tower. As far as can be figured, at least three places along the northern coast are referred to as the Arabs' Tower by travelers: a lookout on an island called Marabout in the harbor of Alexandria; the lighthouse at Abu Sir; and the village of Burg al-Arab. Travelers had a field day getting these three places mixed up and unless some other hint appears, we do not know which of the three locations is in question.

There are a hundred puzzles like these along the northern coast, and hundreds more throughout the Western Desert. We'll see if we can work some of them out. In the meantime, I have listed as many of the known names to a site as I can without being too tedious.

History

Either we know more about events along the coast than in the interior of the Western Desert, or more happened here. Whatever the case, the history of the coastline of Egypt is both fascinating and familiar. The drive from Alexandria to Sollum is along the edge of Africa, where the continent slips under the Mediterranean Sea without making a ripple. This is ironic because the two plates holding the continents of Africa and Europe crashed violently together as evidenced by the Atlas Mountains in Algeria and the Alps and other mountains in Europe. Yet, here, along the Egyptian coast, all is placid and there is little or no evidence of such violence.

Al-Diffa's white sand dunes, red and purple salt flats, and perfect white clouds are the backdrop to a long and fascinating journey into history. This famous coastline covering 500 kilometers (310 miles) from Alexandria to the Libyan border may lack an abundance of good harbors and anchorages; but it has been the route of the most famous travelers and invaders in history. In every century, in every epoch, in every decade, something outstanding happened along this mostly barren waterfront. It sits at the center of the world and is the broad forehead that holds in place the 'horns of Egypt.'

Once a vehicle swings west at Alexandria it can move straight as an arrow (almost) to Morocco on the other side of the African continent. In fact, there is a sign in Morocco, where the road is called the Trik al-Sultan, that reads Oudjda, 400 kilometers; Oran, 618; Alger, 1022; Tunis, 1917; Tripoli, 2709; Benghazi, 3778; Alexandrie, 4880. What a journey!

Pharaonic

The Egyptians have a long history of war with the Libyans. As early as the Sixth Dynasty of the Old Kingdom the Egyptians were hostile to the people on their western frontier. They encouraged Yam (Sudan) to invade Temehu (Libya).

Things were no different in the New Kingdom. This time however it was the Libyans that were on the move. The Libyans were forced east by invaders from the sea. They were not welcome in Egypt. Seti I, his son Ramses II, and his son Ramses III, each tried to stop the ever increasing migration. The Libyans just kept coming. The battles to keep the Libyans out of Egypt were fought here at the coast, in the delta, and around Lake Maryut. They were not minor encounters. They were major battles. Despite the resistance, the persistence made it inevitable that the Libyans would finally succeed and establish their own dynasties in Egypt. Then they moved along the coast at their leisure.

Greek and Roman Periods

The Greeks founded Cyrene (in Libya) in the 630s B.C. and the Libyans were pushed east once again. Now Apries sent his army to Cyrene. He lost the battle. Then came Alexander. (See Matruh and Siwa for details.)

If there is one era that is well known, it is that of the Roman presence along the northern coast. But, except for the high profile romances between Cleopatra and Julius Caesar and Cleopatra and Mark Antony, we hear of little else. Queen Cleopatra and her Roman lovers not only cavorted here, but fought for glory. Antony brooded on his defeat in the desert around Matruh, lost his fleet in its harbor, and Cleopatra gave up her life somewhere in her palace, now believed to lie in the waters of Alexandria's bay.

The Romans populated the coast, probably in the first occupation of this land. They built communities, opened harbors for the great grain boats, dug enormous cisterns to save water for irrigation, and established farms where grapes, grain, and other crops were grown.

In 115, there was a great Judaic uprising in Cyrenaica. The Jews had been present in Alexandria and Cyrenaica for centuries. They despised the Greeks for there pagan worship. The Greeks tolerated them as merchants and money lenders. Under Roman rule things were the same. When Trajan took troops from Cyrenaica to fight elsewhere, the Jews revolted. The pent-up rage of centuries exploded as they massacred over 200,000 gentiles, Greeks, and Romans. They destroyed pagan temples, defensive fortifications, and public buildings as they swept out of Libya and across the North African coast as far as Alexandria.

The Alexandrian Jews also rebelled. They, too, had been fighting with the Greeks for years. They were unhappy about Jewish refugees. When the Romans came they did not like the choice of governor, and were unhappy when Caligula tried to get them to worship his statue. When the Jews of Cyrenaica flooded into Egypt, the Jews of Alexandria joined them. Before it was over the city was burned and the Serapeum was destroyed. Hadrian rebuilt the city and a goodly portion of the coastal highway, which was also destroyed.

Islamic Era

A new plague, invasion, dominated the seventh century: first the Nicetas in 609, then Khusraw in 619, and finally Amr ibn al-As. After Amr's conquest of Alexandria, he made a treaty with the Berbers that enabled him to strike out along the northern coast into the Maghreb. Although under the domination of the Byzantines, the area had been in rebellion for decades. The Arabs defeated the forces of the Prefect Gregory and Byzantine rule came to an end. But the conquest of the west was not complete. In 683, the Berbers rebelled and threw the Arabs out. The Arabs came back stronger. The Berbers rebelled again. This time Mussa ibn Nusayr swept west in 708. This is when Siwa was conquered. It took seventy years for the Arabs finally to subdue the entire northern coast of Egypt and Libya. It has been said this saved Europe from an Arab invasion.

Two centuries later the Fatimid Dynasty of North Africa sent expeditions against Egypt, in 913, in 914, and again in 918. Then the northern coast was abandoned. Finally, the Fatimid ruler al-Muizz sent General Guhar. Guhar spent two years digging wells in the Western Desert to sustain his troops. When a time of famine and plague weakened Egypt, a hundred thousand men came running. In five months they covered 1,500 miles from Tunis and on July 6, 969, they took Fustat (Cairo) and the Fatimid rule of Egypt began.

British Occupation

Like the Romans, the British developed the northern coast during their tenure in Egypt. They established administrations, reconditioned the ancient Roman cisterns, created their own water resources to irrigate the desert, built roads and railroads, explored the desert, and established outposts which sometimes flourished into communities.

It all paid off when two great wars threatened their empire. But first there was the matter of the Barbary pirates.

1805 Tripolitania War

For centuries the Barbary (a possible corruption of Berber) pirates controlled the shipping lanes in the Mediterranean and exacted tribute from European traders along the Barbary Coast from Morocco to Tripoli. Great Britain paid the tribute for its colonies, but after the Revolutionary War, the United States had to deal with the problem. When the young American traders attempted to trade in the Mediterranean, they fell easy prey. Treaties had to be reached individually with each Barbary state (Morocco, Algeria, Tunisia, and Tripoli) and by 1795, the Americans had paid in excess of $900,000. to the pirates.

This unsatisfactory situation festered. The Americans had disassembled their makeshift navy after the Revolutionary War. Now, due largely to the Barbary pirates, and at the urging of Thomas Jefferson, they were forced to rearm themselves on the sea. In 1803, twenty-two American ships bombarded and blockaded Tripoli harbor. Tripoli was controlled by two brothers of a long standing ruling family, Yusif and Hamet Karamanli. The former threw the latter out of the country and he ended up in Egypt (as almost every exile manages to do).

The Americans had a number of responsible men in the Barbary countries including William Eaton, Consul to Tunis. Eaton backed Hamet and devised a plan which would restore him to power if he helped launch a land attack against Derna. Thomas Jefferson approved the plan.

Thus a detachment of US Marines led by William Eaton but under the command of Presley Neville O'Bannon (Lieutenant of Marines), arrived in Alexandria aboard the ship *Argus* on November 27, 1804, to begin preparations for America's first land battle on foreign soil. It was at Burg al-Arab on March 4, 1805, (another source says February 23) that a convention between the two men was formally signed and witnessed. The fourteen provisions included Hamet's restoration as ruler of Tripoli, the release of all American prisoners in Tripoli, and the launch of an expedition against Tripoli with Eaton as its leader. They further agreed to move west from Alexandria to the Gulf of Bomba in Libya, where three American ships would supply them with reinforcements and supplies. They would then move en masse to Derna and attack. The makeshift army was soon complete. They left Burg al-Arab on March 6, 1805. It became a trip into hell.

Eventually they attacked Derna from the land while three American ships attacked by sea. And they were successful. But Eaton and company were forced to give back the land as another American envoy had successfully negotiated a different agreement with Yusif, Hamet's brother, while Eaton was on his long trek across Egypt.

Coastguard Camel Corps

At the beginning of the twentieth century, the British established the Coastguard Camel Corps along the northern coast. Its mandate was to prevent the smuggling of contraband like hashish and salt, maintain public safety in the desert, and prevent pilgrims from landing without permission on Egyptian shores, especially at the Red Sea. The Corps consisted of mostly Sudanese soldiers.

Prior to its establishment, the only guards along the coast were those associated with customs houses, but with a rise on the duty on tobacco and the advent of a salt monopoly by the British government, more stations were needed. Three districts were established: the Northern Directorate, responsible for the coast from Damietta to Alexandria; the Eastern Directorate, from Damietta to the Suez Canal; and the Desert Directorate, responsible for the entire Western Desert including the northern coast from Alexandria to Sollum. The headquarters were in Alexandria, Port Said, and Ain Shams, respectively.

By 1907, 500 men were employed in the Desert Directorate under the leadership of André von Dumreicher, who eventually wrote the most entertaining *Trackers and Smugglers in the Deserts of Egypt*. Dumreicher viewed his work as "a boy's book of adventure," and relished with gusto a good chase through the desert, a sudden ambush, spies, counterspies, and intrigue. There were times when he got carried away.

The tax on tobacco made it unprofitable to smuggle, for too much would be lost if it were confiscated. In place of tobacco, smugglers imported hashish, and made huge profits. The hashish was grown in Greece and exported by "intelligent" Greeks, "some of whom treated the whole business as a sport."

Salt was once traded ounce for ounce with gold in North Africa. It was a major product for the huge caravans that ran the desert routes in Algeria and Libya. Salt mines were well protected and guarded enterprises that existed far earlier that the Romans. Desert dwellers were accustomed to collecting it at will from certain remote oases and selling it in the market place. This was all brought to a halt by the British salt monopoly. The consequence was smuggling. Caravans, fifty camels long, wove their way along desert trails headed from the northern coast to the Nile Valley. This "illicit trade" led to an expansion of the Camel Corps to include all of the Western Desert.

The Camel Corps had regular patrols over the more obvious routes, so smugglers had to move into the deep desert to get their goodies to the markets in the Nile Valley. They headed south, the Camel Corps in hot pursuit. Among the most famous smugglers were the Beni Amar, a Bedouin tribe living in the village of Zawiyet Amar to the east of the Cairo–Alexandria Desert Road, north of Wadi Natrun and south of Maryut in the Beheira province, They did not wait for the hashish to come to them, but went to Greece to get it. Then they smuggled it into Egypt and sent it by caravan through the Western Desert. The Camel Corps had several pitch battles with Beni Amar caravans, one between the oases of Bahariya and Farafra, another near the pyramids, "after a chase which had begun 250 miles west of the Nile valley," and a third near Sitra Oasis. (See Sitra Oasis for details.)

If the Beni Amar were successful in smuggling the hashish through the desert, Dumreicher reports, "The whole village was hung with flags, the only two cabs of Damanhur were hired, in the first of which drove a brass band and drummers, and in the second the choicest scoundrels of the tribe; they drove round the village several times, the harem sang the 'Zaghrada' and received them as heroes' sheep were slaughtered and the whole population kept festival for several days." If they were unsuccessful, as they were on July 26, 1907, when they were caught at Maghra Oasis by a Dabaa patrol and the entire convoy was captured ("7 men, 1,338 kilos of hashish, 17 camels, 8 rifles, and 590 cartridge."), they were ill treated by their women. They were called cowards, and jeered. So they went back to Greece for more hashish.

The World Wars along the Northern Coast

Over a hundred years after the Battle of the Nile and General Eaton's doomed mission, two bigger battles raged along the northern coast. The first was World War I and the second World War II.

World War I

During World War I the Egyptian Expeditionary Force garrisoned the northern coast, including a number of stations along the Maryut Railway, one called al-Alamein.

W. T. Massey in *The Desert Campaigns* says the soldiers were bored beyond belief and to keep in shape they "played football with their helmets on, lest an afternoon sun should decrease their fighting qualities." The British blockaded the coast to prevent supplies from reaching the Sanusi, but could not or did not blockade the desert trails.

Throughout the growth and expansion of the Sanusi, the ruling power in eastern North Africa had been the Ottoman Empire, which the Sanusi acknowledged. In turn, the Turkish Porte gave the Sanusi a charter in 1856.

However, increasingly threatened by the European designs on empire, the religious movement was left with little choice. The French, who already controlled the Sahara and West Africa, were moving north from the Congo into Waidai and Lake Chad, and the Italians, in their desire to colonize Libya where most of the Sanusi *zawyas* were located, were squeezing the Sanusi into the interior of the desert.

The Italians were ruthless in their pursuit of Libya. They cemented shut vital wells along caravan trails. They were the first to use tanks, and then airplanes, in desert warfare. In the first World War, the Sanusi, in an attempt to throw out the Italians, aligned themselves with the Turks. Their German advisors ordered Sayyid Ahmad, the Sanusi leader, to invade Egypt. He was reluctant, for many of his followers were scattered in the Egyptian oases and along the Northern Coast. By 1915, he had no choice. In three battles around Mersa Matruh, the Sanusi were defeated. Sayyid Ahmad went to Turkey in exile. Details of the fighting will be found throughout this chapter. (For detailed information about the Sanusi, see People.)

World War II
During World War II there was no time for the soldiers to be bored. It was a much deadlier campaign. The Battle of North Africa, from September 1940 to March 1943, took place all along the North African coast from Tunisia to al-Alamein. While battles in Europe were fought in inches, the Battle of North Africa was fought in miles. Twice Rommel traveled 1,500 miles (2,400 kilometers) east, and twice the British moved 1,500 miles (2,400 kilometers) west.

Two legendary armies emerged: the 8th Army, which went on to fight in Europe and see the end of conflict, and the Afrika Korps, which was born and died on the sands of North Africa. Like their armies, two men emerged. The first was Bernard Montgomery, a lean and tough British general who took the reigns of control of the 8th Army just before al-Alamein and, although a teetotaler, planned his victory in the bar of the Cecil Hotel in Alexandria. He turned the many British defeats in North Africa into one glorious victory. The second was Erwin Rommel, the famed Desert Fox. It is to Rommel that most of the victories of North Africa belong.

The desert was a major player in this deadly game. It offered what armies only dream about, a chance at pure warfare. It offered wide open spaces with few fixed points from which armies could take a stand or be resupplied. It created the battle strategy where the tank emerged as king. It enabled the armies to fight without the interference of cities, forests, rivers, and civilians.

During the North African Campaign, most of the battles took place in Cyrenaica, the easternmost part of Libya. Italy had colonized Libya in 1923. In June of 1940, the Italian 10th Army under Marshall Rudolfo Graziani left Fort Capuzzo in Libya and invaded Egypt. Meeting little resistance from the small British force, the Italians marched past the border town of Sollum and halted at Sidi Barrani. It was September 16, 1940.

In December, Sir Archibald Wavell, commander-in-chief of Middle East Forces, launched a British counterattack with only 30,000 men. In what was to be known as the Battle of Beda Fromm, Sollum fell on December 17, Sidi Barrani a few days later, and Bardia on January 5. The Italians withdrew to Tobruk. Tobruk was surrounded by the 7th Armored Division of the British Army, which took it on January 21, 1941. Graziani retreated to al-Agheila (Mersa Brega) where he set up a defensive line.

Mussolini turned to Adolph Hitler for men and supplies. Enter Rommel. In March of 1941, the Axis retook Libya and halted at Sollum. A small Allied force remained under siege at Tobruk until, after two unsuccessful attempts, they were liberated on December 10. At this point neither army had the men or the means to conclude the African campaign because soldiers from both sides were being sent to the Russian front.

On January 1, 1942, the German and Italian armies launched another attack. In May, the Allies were defeated at the Battle of Gazalah and withdrew to al-Alamein, where they halted the German advance and set up a defensive line through the desert between al-Alamein and the Qattara Depression. The stage was set for one of the most important battles of World War II. (For details on the battle, see al-Alamein below).

Today

Today the northern coast is enjoying yet another development. Having lain dormant since the departure of the British, its pristine beaches are being occupied by elegant resorts. Every inch of land is being gobbled up and just like the Libyans were forced east by invasions, the Bedouin are being forced south, away from the sea and into the interior of the desert.

Geography and Geology

Al-Diffa is divided into two geological zones: in the west a Miocene plateau and in the east, gravel and sand hills. It is bound in the north by the Mediterranean Sea and in the south by the Siwa and Qattara depressions. At Qattara, the plateau is 200 meters (640 feet) high and forms a sharp barrier. From that point the land slopes northward toward the sea. There are no major mountains in the area.

Water

Water is the major problem of the northern coast. The main water sources are cisterns, limestone caves used to trap ground water, many of them first excavated and plastered by the Romans. During the British Occupation, a number of these cisterns were restored and used, but after the British, they fell into disrepair. Unlike the interior of the Western Desert, it is not possible to drill wells along the northern coast as the Qattara Depression blocks much of the underground water flowing north from equatorial Africa. Of the wells that do exist, two thirds are close to the sea, not more than 24 kilometers (15 miles) inland.

Caravans Routes and Roadways

Alexandria–Sollum

Originally called the summer road and ending at Abu Sir, this roadway follows the sea all the way to Sollum and into Libya. In fact, one can follow it all along the northern coast of Africa as far as Morocco. For most of its life it was but a track, sometimes, after a rain, barely distinguishable. We can thank the 8th Army for paving the route as far as Mersa Matruh. They set its course into the next century. In fact, in the 1950s, the road was still good from Alexandria to Mersa Matruh, but it was not uncommon for travelers to be told "Follow the telegraph posts to Sidi Barrani."

Interior Road

The second major east–west route follows the railroad, about a kilometer south of the shore. It is the older route, the one most travelers took through the centuries.

Wadi Natrun–al-Alamein Road

About 20 kilometers (12.5 miles) after the halfway point along the Cairo–Alexandria Desert Road a new road directly to al-Alamein turns west into the desert. From the turn it is only 102 kilometers (64 miles) to al-Alamein. It cuts off the entire northeastern corner. It will eventually go all the way to Mersa Matruh.

Maryut Railway

In 1858, Said Pasha constructed the first rail line along the northern coast. By 1909, it had been transformed into a standard gauge rail, but still had not reached Mersa Matruh. In 1915, the Maryut Railway reached as far as Bir Fuka, 208 kilometers (130 miles) west of Alexandria. After World War II the railhead was at al-Dabaa, a lot less. The Egyptians wanted the line to run to Sollum, but this was vetoed by Lord Cromer. Martin S. Briggs tells us in *Through Egypt in Wartime* that the railhead at Sollum would cut two days off of steamship travel to Egypt. He also maintains that the Khedive wanted to continue the railroad to Siwa for the date harvest.

There are dozens of desert tracks leading to the interior. See Siwa Oasis for details on most of them.

The Tour

Alexandria to Mersa Matruh

Today the coast is strewn with beach resorts and visitors travel in cars instead of chariots or tanks. But the history of the place is ever present in the ghosts of Greek gods and gorgons that haunt the lagoons, in the ruins of the greatest empires that ruled the Western world, and in memorials erected to the dead of a quarter of its nations.

TOUR #1

Agami to al-Alamein

- 2x2
- 2–4 hours
- easy

			km	total km
Agami	N 31 40 668	E 29 44 70	0	0
Abu Sir	N 30 56 863	E 29 31 35	30	30
Al-Alamein	N 30 50 170	E 28 57 488	53	83

The 116 kilometer (72.5 mile) beach front between Agami and Sidi Abd al-Rahman faces the Gulf of Plinthine, also known as the Bay of the Umayd. Along this bay, between Alexandria and Abu Sir, are some of the finest beaches in the eastern portion of al-Diffa.

Moving west are a series of old resorts that, like Agami, have existed along the northern coast for years. They were erected in an area known in antiquity as Taenia, where such sites as Nicium and Oktokaidekaton once existed. In modern times, Said Pasha erected a number of square towers called martellos in the area.

Getting There. Turn west off the Cairo–Alexandria desert road 3 kilometers (1.8 miles) after the community of Amriya. Do not turn at the sign marked Burg al-Arab, but continue up the hill and when descending the other side take the first left. For Agami turn right just before the first checkpoint onto the main street of the town. All other resorts and beaches, located to the right of the main road, are announced by signs.

Agami

Two kilometers (1.2 miles) after turning onto the coast road, one finds one of the oldest and most popular beach resorts in Egypt. Popularized in the early part of the twentieth century by the Egyptian elite, in the past two decades the quiet community has turned into a bustling city with residential areas, hotels, restaurants, and shops. Private villas and apartments are available to buy or rent by the week, season, or year.

Napoleon's army landed here upon arrival in Egypt in 1798. In the 1930s, two forts existed in Agami, al-Ayyana and al-Agami. They were located on the ancient site of Chersonesus Paiva.

Note: Kilometer readings always vary from odometer to odometer. The readings given in the following section are from the turn-off to the coastal highway and not from Alexandria. The roadside markers give the kilometers from the center of the city of Alexandria and will not be the same as the readings in this book. Most resorts do not have a street address but are identified by their official kilometer reading from Alexandria.

Abu Sir (Taposiris Magna)

The impressive ruins of Taposiris Magna dominate a limestone ridge to the south of the roadway 32 kilometers (20 miles) along the coastal highway.

History

Taposiris was a Ptolemaic city located between the Mediterranean Sea to the north and the freshwater Lake Maryut to the south. It had a port on each waterway. Visited by Alexander the Great on his way to Siwa, the temple and the nearby lighthouse are the only remaining ancient ruins still standing on the northern coast of the Western Desert.

Southern view of the Lighthouse

Lighthouse at Taposiris

The temple was used as a quarantine station for Muslims going to and coming from the Hagg, the pilgrimage to Mecca, along the Pilgrim's Road. When Bayle St. John was here in 1847, Signor Giovanni Sciarabati was its superintendent. St. John asked him to find men to accompany him on his journey. He asked for someone who was "the least of a rogue and had cut fewest throats." Such was the perceived danger. A Coastguard Camel Corps wooden barrack for fifteen men was constructed here around 1900.

The American expedition led by William Eaton in 1805 (see History above) made their camp here at Abu Sir in March of 1805. The next day Sheikh al-Tayeb, head of the Bedouin and owner of most of the camels, demanded pay in advance. Eaton wisely said no. The Arabs mutinied. Eaton said he would return to Alexandria and end the journey and no one would be paid. The journey continued.

The Tour

A climb to the ridge of the limestone hill, either to the temple or the lighthouse (it is hard to cross from one to the other once atop the hill), is a must. The view is not only beautiful, but confirms the wisdom of placing the city atop the ridge, a short distance from its port. The view north encompasses all of the Bay of Plinthine, while the view south takes in the ancient bed of Lake Maryut, which has receded far to the east today.

Plinthinus, Kom al-Nugus

The seaport was called Plinthinus (Plinthine by Herodotus). Little remains of its busy docks and warehouses where the produce of Egypt, especially grain, was loaded onto ships to be sent across the sea. Maryut was as much a producer of grain as the Fayoum and the Nile Valley. One record shows a fifteen-fold yield of barley for five consecutive years in the area (as opposed to five- or six-fold in Italy and Sicily). Ancient sources maintain that grapes were first cultivated here at Plinthinus. A roadway directly opposite the temple of Osiris at Abu Sir leads north from the coast road and continues to the sea (about a kilometer) and the ancient ruins.

The Temple of Osiris

By Nile Valley standards, there is not much to see at the Temple of Osiris except for the enclosure walls build in the fourth century B.C. There is an interesting assortment of small rooms in the interior of the gutted temple and a tunnel that may lead to additional chambers. St. John calls it the Temple of Augustus.

It was used as a Christian church around 391. Because it commands a strategic point atop the limestone ridge, the Arab rulers used the temple as a fortress, while it made an excellent hideaway for Bedouin brigands who committed daring highway raids. Eventually the British used it as a coastguard station. De Cosson tells us that the remains of a 2 meter (6 foot) thick wall could be seen to the west of the temple in the 1930s. He maintains this was "erected across the Taenia against the Barbarians," probably the Libyans, at right angles to the sea. Today the ruins are called the Palace of Abu Zayd al-Hilali by the local Bedouin, who believe the legendary Islamic hero of romance stayed here during his exploits.

The Lighthouse

More important than the temple is the nearby lighthouse located in the midst of an ancient cemetery. From the sea, the eastern portion of al-Diffa, with a few exceptions, is barely visible as there is no elevation at all in many places. Water becomes sand in a single step without missing a stride, and if a ship had wheels it would just keep rolling, merely replacing its form of momentum. This invisible coast line presented many dangers over the years and the string of lighthouses was absolutely necessary on any type of elevated land. Here, at Abu Sir, we have elevated land.

Built in Ptolemaic times, the lighthouse is reached by a dirt track that leaves the coast road and runs to the top of the hill. This lighthouse was part of a chain that stretched along the northern coast from Alexandria to Cyrene (Libya), and it is the only one still standing. In the latter point lies its significance, for the lighthouse is a smaller version, believed to be one-tenth the size, of the famous Pharos lighthouse of Alexandria, one of the seven wonders of the ancient world. (Parts of the Pharos have recently been discovered in the harbor of Alexandria.)

Both lighthouses had three stages: a square bottom surmounted by an octagonal middle, and a circular elongated top. It is often suggested that this unique architectural combination influenced the early builders of mosques, where the combination is repeated in minarets.

One can enter the lighthouse through the window on its northern side. Wooden steps rise to the first level, where a cement stairway circles the outside of the structure and spirals to the top. Around the base of the lighthouse are natural caves, including a rather large one on the south side. The south side is reached by driving along the coast highway past the temple and turning south toward Burg al-Arab. Less than a kilometer later a track turns left (east) and weaves through the ruins of the ancient city.

The City

The ancient city slopes to the south of the temple where ruins of a winery and wine press, enclosure wall, kilns, tombs, and public baths built by Justinian are awaiting excavation. There was once a busy harbor directly on the lake, where goods and people, especially pilgrims, were loaded and unloaded. The first of these pilgrims were pagan worshipers of Osiris bound for the temple atop the hill, then came Christians on their way to Abu Mena, and finally Muslims on their way to Mecca.

St. John, on his trek to Siwa, also saw an *odeion*, and a very clear outline of the "lock of a canal with a double dike, by which water from the Nile was distributed through the gardens." He also saw catacombs: "about an hour's walk from the temple, beyond the limits of the city, is a ridge of hills containing some large catacombs and a very extensive and deep excavation in which the workmen of old had commenced rooms and galleries of tolerably regular architecture."

E. M. Forster, in his wonderful guide to Alexandria, tells us that during the British occupation tourists would take the Maryut Railway from Alexandria to Bahig Station and walk the 8.8 kilometers (5.5 miles) to Abu Sir. If they were lucky enough to visit the area in the spring, they would be greeted by a carpet of marigolds cascading down the hill from the temple. And in Lawrence Durrell's *Alexandria Quartet*, Nessim built a summer home for Justine at Taposiris Magna and would often go duck hunting at Lake Maryut.

Today, all the ghosts are silent. Only the wind whistles about the lighthouse and the tiny bells on a few goats jingle as they clamber about. There is no trace of the flying snakes rumored to inhabit the temple and tower at the beginning of the twentieth century.

Lake Maryut (Mareotis)

Below the town are the remains of the once large and beautiful Lake Maryut. It was a freshwater lake approximately 2.5 meters (8 feet) below sea level, separated from the Mediterranean Sea in the north by a strip of land where Alexandria now stands. Covering 12 percent of the Mallahat–Maryut Depression floor, it was fed by the Nile until the twelfth century, when the Canopic Nile and the Asara canal (which joined it to the Fayoum) silted up. Thus the lake was part of the Nile system, and feluccas would sail into the lake from either the Fayoum or Cairo, heavy with cargo destined for Mediterranean ports. They would sail across the lake and discharge their goods at maritime harbors on the northern shore. There they may have picked up goods imported into Egypt from those same ports.

With the silting up of the Canopic branch of the Nile, the lake fell into obscurity. With its fresh water supply cut, like Birket Qarun in the Fayoum, Maryut became increasingly saline. This process was accelerated when water from the Mediterranean Sea was purposely let into the lake on three separate occasions. The first time was just after the March 21st battle between the British and the French in Alexandria in 1801. When they squared off against each other during the Battle of the Nile, a great portion of the lake bed was dry.

Despite the naval victory in Abu Kir Bay during the Battle of the Nile, the French had to be driven out of Egypt to complete the victory. Sir John Hely-Hutchinson, the British general, in order to cut off fresh water to Alexandria and secure the western flank of the army while it pursued activities to the east near Rosetta, cut a canal to the sea allowing sea water to enter the Canal of Alexandria and the freshwater lake bed of Mareotis.

One must understand the geography as it existed at that time. Alexandria was on the sea, but behind it was water, too. It was almost an island. To the east was the salt lake of Abu Kir, which opened into the sea, and to the west was the freshwater lake of Mareotis, which was fed by the Nile through several canals, but was beginning to run dry. The two lakes were separated by a small amount of land through which the Canal of Alexandria flowed. This canal, which came into Alexandria from the southeast and turned west to flow behind the city, brought fresh water to the city. It was seven feet wide and lined with bricks.

Thomas Walsh, a captain in the 93rd Regiment of Foot and aide-de-camp to Major-General Sir Eyre Coote, is very specific about the cutting of the dike in his book *Journal of the Late Campaign in Egypt*: "General Hutchinson having determined to carry on the active operations of the army on the Rosetta side, it became necessary to secure our present position, which was intended to remain merely on the defensive, as much as possible against any future attack. For this nothing could be of greater utility than letting the waters of lake Aboukir into the bed of the Mareotis; and our left would

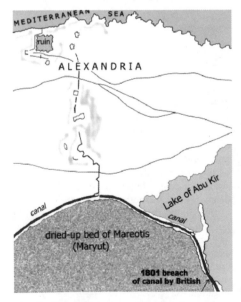

The English Cut

thus be rendered more secure, since to turn it would become impracticable; and at the same time our gunboats would be enabled to get in, and annoy the enemy. . . . Accordingly on the 12th [of April], a working party began to cut through the canal; and on the 13th, the water rushed in with impetuosity through seven channels made for the purpose, to the great satisfaction of the whole army. The violence of the water, flowing in through the cuts in the canal, was so great, as not only to destroy every thing in it's way, but to unite four cuts of the seven. By this the gap was rendered too wide to admit a bridge, and the communication was supported by means of boats stationed near the opening, in which the Arabs coming with provision were ferried over."

By cutting the canal, the British not only destroyed the lake, its fishing industry, its vineyards, and 150 villages, but the canal itself. The force of the water was so great it simply wiped the canal away.

By early May, the two lakes were practically balanced and the current stopped. Only a few islands of land remained above water. One of these islands had been fortified by the French and dubbed Isle Mariout. General Coote launched six gunboats onto the 'new' lake. This first breach was repaired in 1804.

The second time Lake Maryut was flooded was in 1807. It was the British again. This time they flooded the lake to protect their back. They were in Alexandria and Muhammad Ali was going to attack them. So, in May they flooded the lake and placed twelve gun boats there. By the end of the year the British had left Alexandria. In February, of 1808, the canal was repaired again.

The third time the lake was flooded it was to turn portions of the lake into a drainage basin for the new system of canals in the area. Lake Maryut was expendable. Today Lake Maryut is a salt lake which often dries in summer. The vacillation of the water supply is being checked by the construction of a pumping station which will attempt to maintain a shallow water level.

Villages

In antiquity, this area was very beautiful. Fig, date, almond, and fruit trees climbed up the hillsides. Eight islands dotted the lake and they were the favorite spots for the wealthy to erect villas. From their verandahs they could watch thousands of flamingos vie for space with pleasure boats, working sail boats, and the occasional crocodile. There were over forty-eight towns scattered on the shore including Nicium, Plinthine, Taposiris, and Mareotis. It was the most important place in the region.

Once Alexandria was built, the lake shore kept its resort atmosphere. Rich Alexandrines erected villas much like rich and influential Cairenes did in Agami during the days of King Farouk. They would sit by their quays on the shore and bathe in the fresh water, perhaps at sunset they would visit a lakeside taverna to eat fish and drink good Maryut wine, or fresh beer, another famous local product.

The vineyards around the lake (the favorites of Cleopatra), produced the renowned white wines of ancient Egypt. They lined the hillsides and everyone knew that the vines along the southwestern side were not as good as the rest of the grapes. The wineries would hand-pick the grapes which were then tramped by human feet in long troughs while a flutist played tunes to keep the feet in rhythm. Then the mash was pressed into ceramic containers and set in the sun to ferment.

Upon occasion the tramp of soldiers' columns would echo through the hills, or the calm waters of the lake would be disturbed by ships of war. When Julius Caesar became embroiled in the feud between his then wife Cleopatra and her brother Ptolemy, in what we call the Alexandrine War, he marched around Lake Mareotis on his way to a victory near the Canopic Branch of the Nile.

There was also space for the eccentric. In the first century, a community of Jewish healers or *therapeutae* lived along the lake. This orthodox group of men and women practiced a severe form of religious intellectualism. In addition to a renunciation of worldly goods and a quest for solitude, they practiced chastity, obedience, contemplation, and penance. They lived separately but within a

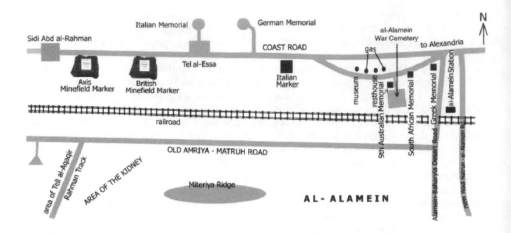

community and for six days of the week they stayed alone, eating coarse bread and water. On the Sabbath they gathered together to listen and discuss doctrines. On the fiftieth day they held a festival which included hymns, a vigil, discourse, and a meal. This was at least a hundred years before the Christian monastic movement in Wadi Natrun, a short distance south. That movement paralleled much of the *therapeutae* practices.

By the sixth century the tranquil atmosphere around the lake was disturbed and maybe destroyed by plague, and perhaps an earthquake. When the Fatimids began their exploration of the North African coast in the tenth century, Mareotis was abandoned. Maqrizi, the famous Arab historian, tells us that Mareotis was only a shadow of itself when he saw it in the fourteenth century. It appears the lake never recovered.

The community of **Burg al-Arab**, the Arabs' Tower, is directly across the lake from Taposiris. A note must be made here about the confusing name Arabs' Tower, or Tower of the Arabs. In 1801, as the British and French pursued each other over Egypt, Walsh had this to say about Marabout and the Arabs' Tower, "The fort of Marabout, on a small island at a short distance from the shore [in the bay of Alexandria] . . . is the place so well known by the name of the Tower of the Arabs, from a handsome

square white tower, which stood in the centre of the island, and served as a landmark for ships making the harbour."

This is not the lighthouse at Abu Sir. Nor is it located at the interior village of Burg al-Arab. This tower, on Marabout island, was located at the entrance to the Bay at Alexandria and was destroyed by the British during the Battle of Alexandria. "After excessive labour, two twenty-four pounders were brought against Marabout. . . . At daybreak on the 21st [August], the battery being finished, and the guns mounted, a constant and well-directed fire was opened against the fort; and at half after eleven the signal tower fell to the ground with a tremendous crash, burying a twenty-four pounder, with all the provisions, stores, etc., in it's ruins . . ."

That ends that. That Arabs' Tower is long gone. But it caused a great deal of confusion among travelers. Many confused it with Taposiris Magna and the lighthouse there. Others confused it with Burg al-Arab. So, sometimes when a traveler is telling us a tale, we are not sure exactly where he is.

Al-Alamein

By the time one nears al-Alamein, 83 kilometers (51 miles) from the beginning of the coast road, it is impossible not to question the effect of the number of resorts along the coast. As it stands, the once wild beaches, havens for wildlife and free spirits, are gone.

History

Al-Alamein takes its name from the twin-peaked hill, Tell al-Alamein, upon which it stands. Until the events of September 1940 to March 1943, when the armies of the Axis and Allied powers fought over North Africa, al-Alamein was only a stop along the modern railroad. But it does have an ancient history. Al-Alamein is the site of the Gaucum of Ptolemy and the Leucasis, Leucaspis, or Locabsis, of the Romans.

Locabsis

In 1984, when work was begun on the Markaz Marina Tourist Village, running east–west for over 2 kilometers (1.2 miles) along the shore, the construction crews unearthed a major Greek and Roman seaport. The site, located 6 kilometers (3.7 miles) east of the village of al-Alamein, covers a 3 kilometer (1.8 mile) stretch of beach and contains a town with Roman villas, two churches, and a large cemetery with Hellenistic tombs and catacombs. Two archaeological missions are currently working in the area, the Polish Center of Mediterranean Archaeology and the Egyptian Antiquities Organization. Restoration is in the hands of the Polish–Egyptian Preservation Mission at Marina.

A mummy portrait like the famous Fayoum Portraits was found here. It is dated earlier that the Fayoum Portraits and presents quite a riddle. One can visit a Hellenistic cemetery and a house with seven rooms.

The French Ships

There is also a little-known incident of Napoleon's *savants*. In 1801, a French squadron of four sail of the line, one frigate, one corvette, and five small transports, under Gantheaume anchored here in Locabsis (Lacuste) Bay by mistake. They had intended to land at Derna, in Tripolitania, and march along the coast to Alexandria (like Eaton did, but in reverse). They didn't stay long as a British fleet under Keith was approaching. By May 7, the five small transports were taken into British custody in Abu Kir Bay. According to British records, "They had no troops on board but artists of all kinds, as florists, gardeners, seedsmen, etc.

In a word, quite a small colony. There was also a company of comedians for the Cairo theatre." This small entourage was undoubtedly to supplement the *savants* who had arrived with Napoleon and were, at this time, still traipsing all over Egypt collecting, recording, and mapping.

Battlefield of al-Alamein

Protected in the north by the sea and in the south by the Qattara Depression, al-Alamein is a strong defensive position. Whoever controlled it, controlled the North African coast, which opened the way to the whole of Egypt and the trade routes to the Far East via the Red Sea and the Indian Ocean. The ancient warriors knew it and so did their twentieth century counterparts. During World War II, the Axis powers wanted to dominate Egypt in order to close Britain's sea routes to its colonial empire, which the British were desperate to protect. Starting in 1940 with the Italian invasion of Egypt via Libya, the coastal towns of al-Diffa were the scene of this ongoing battle.

Al-Alamein was the turning point of World War II. The British committed themselves, supplying their soldiers with ample equipment to secure the al-Alamein Line, the last tenable position before Cairo. Their victory convinced the Americans to enter the European war with an offensive called Operation Torch, which thrust into Morocco and Algeria.

The Eighth Army

Known as the Army of the Nile prior to the events that led to al-Alamein, the British military force had existed in Egypt since the Battle of Tell al-Kebir in 1882. Although small, it had experience in maneuvering in desert terrain, excellent British surveyor maps, and long-term reconnaissance from both the Light Car Patrols of 1915–18 and the newly formed Long Range Desert Group. By the Battle of al-Alamein, the Eighth Army had been born. It held air superiority and its tank strength outnumbered Rommel's two to one. In all, the British army had over 220,000 men. They were organized into three corps, the 10th, the 13th, and the

30th, which included Australians, New Zealanders, South Africans, Indians, Rhodesians, Americans, Greeks, and Free French.

The 10th Corps was an armored division born in the Western Desert as Montgomery's answer to the Afrika Korps. In the Battle of al-Alamein, it was held back, while the 30th Corps breached the enemy line. Then the 10th was sent through the hole for the knockout punch. The 13th Corps held reign on the southern section of the al-Alamein Line at Alam Nayal and Munassib Depression. The workhorse of the 8th Army, the 30th Corps had three dominion divisions. The 51st Highland Infantry Division were to bear the brunt of the attack across the al-Alamein Line and led the infantry charge that created the break through at al-Alamein. The 2nd New Zealand Division, the Kiwis, led by Major-General Bernard Freyberg, laid the groundwork for Operation Supercharge. The 9th Australian Division under General Leslie Morshead was considered the finest division in the 8th Army by its enemy. They had withstood the siege of Tobruk for eight months in 1941 and at al-Alamein they were hurled against the German gun line at Tell al-Aqaqir.

Then there was the Libyan–Arab Corps. When the Italians entered World War II, the Sanusi leader Sayyid Idris, living in Egypt, aligned himself with the British. Five battalions of soldiers joined the war in the Libyan Desert under the name the Libyan–Arab Corps, four with the Eighth Army, the fifth behind the lines in the desert they knew so well. When the call went out, the Sanusi warriors came from their hidden homes. (For a description of the Axis Army and the Rahman line see Sidi Abd al-Rahman below.)

The al-Alamein Line

The two armies faced each other across an almost flat expanse of desert that stretched from the Mediterranean Sea in the north, south to the Qattara Depression. The 8th Army set up its defenses at the al-Alamein Line. The train station called al-Alamein stood behind the British, and the small hamlet of Sidi Abd al-Rahman was in the midst of the Axis troops. The al-Alamein Line was fortified by a series of boxes enclosed by barbed wire and secured by minefields. There were ten boxes in all. Each was equipped with water piped from the Nile and stored in underground reservoirs near the railway at al-Alamein. Each contained two infantry battalions, and field, anti-tank, and anti-aircraft artillery. At intervals along the line were hospitals, storerooms, and headquarters.

The first box of the al-Alamein Line was the al-Alamein Box. It extended from the sea to the west of the al-Alamein station, then south below the railroad. It was manned by the 1st South African Division. Qarat al-Abd, 15 miles south of al-Alamein, held another box on the al-Alamein Line. It, like al-Alamein, was built on high ground. Ruweisat Ridge, a rocky hill 200 feet high was 12.5 miles south of al-Alamein and held the next box. The line continued south to the edge of the Qattara Depression.

Battle of al-Alamein

The Battle of al-Alamein has been divided into five phases by military historians: the break-in (October 23–24); the crumbling (24–25); the counter (26–28); Operation Supercharge (November 1–2); and the breakout (3–7). No name is given for the period from October 29 to the 30 when the battle was at a standstill.

The Break-in. Operation Lightfoot began at 9:30 p.m. on Friday, October 23, 1942. On the calm, clear evening under the bright sky of the full moon, 882 field and medium-sized guns released a barrage of fire that didn't stop until five and a half hours later, when each gun had fired 600 rounds. While the barrage was bursting, 125 tons of bombs fell on enemy gun positions.

At 10 p.m. the infantry of the 30th Corps began to move. The objective was an imaginary line in the desert where the strongest enemy defenses lay. Once the infantry reached the first minefields, the mine sweepers (sappers) moved in to create a passage for the tanks. Finally, at 2 a.m., the first of the 5,000 tanks crawled forward. By 4 a.m. the

BATTLE OF AL-ALAMEIN

lead tanks were in the minefields. They stirred up so much dust that visibility was zero and jams developed when tanks got bogged down. Entire columns went astray when the lead tank moved off course. They were seldom where they thought they were. On this night the tank units thought they had passed the first minefield and were in the second when in fact they were still in the first.

The Crumbling. The dawn of Saturday, October 24, 1942, brought disaster for German headquarters. The accuracy of the barrage had destroyed German communications. Strumme, commander-in-chief while Rommel was in Germany, died of a heart attack, and the temporary command was given to General von Thoma. The 30th Corps had dented the first minefields for the British, but not enough for 10th Corps to pass through. The British air force, responsible for so much damage to the Axis at Alam al-Halfa, plastered Axis positions all day long, making over 1,000 sorties.

The Panzers attacked the 51st Highland Division just after sunrise. By 4 o'clock in the afternoon there was little progress. At dusk, with the sun at their backs, Axis tanks from the 15th Panzer and Italian Littorio swung out from Kidney Ridge to engage the Australians, and the first major tank battle of al-Alamein began. Over 100 tanks were involved in this battle, and by dark, half were destroyed while neither position was altered.

While the Australians were fighting the 15th, the Highlanders, on their left, were entering the first tank-versus-infantry battle at al-Alamein. It was to last for two days with many casualties, but when it was over the British manned Kidney Ridge.

D Plus 2: Sunday, October 25, 1942. By Sunday, the initial thrust was over. The armies had been fighting non-stop for two days. The British had advanced through the minefields in the west to make a 6-mile-wide and 5-mile-deep inroad and sat atop Miteriya Ridge in the southeast, but the Axis were firmly entrenched in most of their original battle positions and the battle was at a standstill. Montgomery ordered an end to conflict in the south, the evacuation of Miteriya Ridge, and a swing north toward the sea. The battlefield would be concentrated at the Kidney and Tell al-Eissa until a breakthrough occurred. It was to be a gruesome seven days.

By early morning the Axis launched a series of attacks by the 15th Panzer and Littorio divisions. The Afrika Korps was looking for a weakness. They didn't find one. When the sun waned the British infantry went on the attack. Around midnight, the 51st Division launched three attacks. But no one knew exactly where they were. It was pandemonium and carnage. By morning, the British had lost over 500 men and only one officer remained among the attacking forces.

While the 51st was operating around the Kidney, the Australians were attacking Point 29, a 20-foot-high Axis artillery observation post southwest of Tell al-Eissa. This was the new northern thrust Montgomery had devised earlier in the day, and it was to be the scene of heated battle for days to come. The 26th Australian Brigade attacked at midnight. The air force dropped 115 tons of bombs and the British took the position and 240 prisoners. Fighting continued in this area for the next week, as the Axis tried to recover the small hill that was vital to their defense.

Counter: D Plus 3: Monday, October 26, 1942. Rommel returned to North Africa on the evening of the 25th. He immediately assessed the battle. The Italian Trento Division had lost half of its infantry, the 164 Light Division had lost two battalions, most other groups were understrength, all men were on half rations, a large number were sick, and the entire Axis army had only enough fuel for three days.

The offensive was stalled. Churchill railed, "Is it really impossible to find a general who can win a battle?" A counterattack began at 3 p.m. against Point 29 near Tell al-Eissa. Rommel was determined to retake the position and moved all the tanks from around Kidney to the battle site. Air and ground power poured into the area as Rommel moved the 21st Panzer up from the south. The British held the position and Rommel's troops could not retire for lack of fuel and were stuck on open ground at the mercy of air attacks.

Back at Kidney, the British failed to take advantage of the missing tanks. Each time they tried to move forward they were stopped by pounding anti-tank guns. On a brighter note for the British, the Royal Navy sank the tanker Proserpina at Tobruk. Proserpina was the last hope for resupplying Rommel's thirsty machines

D plus 4: Tuesday, October 27, 1942. The main battle was now concentrated around Tell al-Aqaqir and Kidney Ridge. The 2nd Battalion (Rifle Brigade) of the 1st Armored Division of the British was at a position called Snipe, to the southwest of the Kidney. The stand at Snipe is one of the legends of the Battle of al-Alamein. Phillips in *Alamein* exclaims, "The desert was quivering with heat. The gun detachments and the platoons squatted in their pits and trenches, the sweat running in rivers down their dust-caked faces. There was a terrible stench. The flies swarmed in black clouds upon the dead bodies and excreta and tormented the wounded. The place was strewn with burning tanks and carriers, wrecked guns and vehicles, and over all drifted the smoke and the dust from bursting high explosive and from the blasts of guns."

Mortar and shell fire was constant all day long. Around 4 p.m., British tanks opened fire against the position, killing their own. At 5 p.m., Rommel launched his major attack. German and Italian tanks moved forward. With only four guns in operation, the 2nd Battalion was able to score continual broadside hits against forty tanks of the 21st Division, knocking out thirty-seven of them. The remaining three withdrew and a new assault was launched. All but nine tanks in this assault were also wiped out. The 2nd was down to three guns with three rounds each. But the enemy did not try again.

D plus 5–6: Wednesday, Thursday, October 28–29, 1942. The Australian 9th Division was to continue pushing northwest beyond Tell al-Eissa to an enemy-held location south of the railway known as Thompson's Post and force a breakthrough along the coast road. At day's end, the British had 800 tanks still in operation, the Axis 148 German and 187 Italian. The tanker Luisiano was sunk outside Tobruk harbor. Rommel told his commanders, "It will be quite impossible for us to disengage from the enemy. There is no gasoline for such a maneuver. We have only one choice and that is to fight to the end at Alamein."

D plus 7–9: Friday–Sunday, October 30–November 1, 1942. On the night of October 30th, in a continuation of previous plans, the 9th Australian attacked. This was their third attempt to reach the paved road, which they took on this night. On the 31st, Rommel launched four retaliatory attacks against Thompson's Post. The fighting was intense and often hand to hand, but no ground was gained by the Axis forces. On Sunday, November 1, he tried to dislodge the Australians once again. Again, brutal, desperate fighting and nothing gained, only equipment and men lost. It had become obvious to Rommel that the battle was lost. He began to plan the retreat and anticipated retiring to Fuka, a few miles west. Ironically, 1,200 tons of fuel arrived, but it was too late and had to be blown up.

Operation Supercharge. Operation Supercharge began on November 2 at 1 a.m., with the objective of destroying enemy armor, forcing the enemy to fight in the open and diminish his petrol, attacking and occupying enemy supply routes, and disintegrating the enemy army. Its intensity and destruction was greater that anything witnessed so far in this horrific battle. The objective of Supercharge was Tell al-Aqaqir along the Rahman track, the base of the Axis defense. The attack began with a seven-hour aerial bombardment focused on Tell al-Aqaqir and Sidi Abd al-Rahman, followed by a 4.5-hour barrage of 360 guns firing 15,000 shells. The initial thrust of Supercharge belonged to the battle scarred New Zealanders. Freyberg had tried to free them of this chore, for they were understrength and weary. "I will lead any other infantry you like, but I will not take my New Zealanders into another assault," he had told Montgomery. But, at 1 a.m., on that cold November night with the moon on the wane, the New Zealanders moved out.

As the dawn of November 2 broke over the desert, tank after tank was hit by the German 88mm guns that kept firing through seven air attacks. The 9th never made it to their objective. In fact, they had 75 percent casualties. But they had breached the gun line, and the 1st Armored Division of the 10th Corps, under the command of Raymond Briggs, was now about to be engaged. In the heat of the noon day sun, 120 Italian and German tanks advanced for the biggest, most critical, and, to all intents and purposes, the final tank battle of al-Alamein, the Battle of Aqaqir Ridge.

The battle continued all day. "The desert, quivering in the heat haze, became a scene that defies sober description. It can be discerned only as a confused arena clouded by the bursts of high explosives, darkened by the smoke of scores of burning tanks and trucks, lit by the flashes of innumerable guns, shot through by red, green and white tracers, shaken by heavy bombing from the air and deafened by the artillery of both sides."

Rommel called up Ariete from the south to join the defenses around Tell al-Aqaqir in the last stand of the German army. By nightfall, the Axis had only thirty-two tanks operating along the entire front. While the Afrika

Korps was fighting for its life at Aqaqir, Rommel began the withdrawal to Fuka.

The Break Out. Rommel sent a message to Hitler requesting permission to withdraw. Rommel was to stand fast. Von Thoma told him, "I've just been around the battlefield. 15th Panzer's got ten tanks left, 21st Panzer only fourteen and Littorio seventeen." Rommel read him Hilter's message. He nodded, donned his medals, and headed to his command at the head of the Afrika Korps.

When 150 British tanks came after the remaining members of the nearly vanquished 15th and 21st Panzers, von Thoma stood with his men. He was in the command tank at the spot where the two panzer units joined, and there he remained until the last tank was destroyed. At the end, when all was lost, von Thoma stood alone beside his burning tank at the spot that was to become known as the 'panzer graveyard.'

Despite the desperate situation, Rommel's men stood in their positions. Entire units were destroyed, but the remnants continued to fight. A 12-mile-wide hole had been cut in the Axis line. "If we stay put here, the army won't last three days. . . .If I do obey the Fuhrer's order, then there's the danger that my own troops won't obey me. . . .My men come first!" Rommel ordered the massive retreat.

Rommel has lost 55,000 men, 1,000 guns, and 450 tanks. The British, 13,500 men killed, missing, or wounded, 100 guns, and 500 tanks. Major-General Douglas Wimberley swore, "Never again," and John Currie of the 9th Armored Brigade pointed to twelve tanks when asked where his regiments were, "There are my armored regiments." Seventy-five percent of the 100 percent Montgomery was willing to sacrifice were missing.

D plus 12, November 4, 1942. The final assaults were underway. The 51st Highland began the last infantry assault. The British 1st, 7th, and 10th armored divisions passed through the German lines and were operating in the open desert. The British had won the battle. The Axis were in retreat. This day saw the liquidation of the Italian Ariete Armored Division, the Littorio Division, and the Trieste Motorized Division. Paolo Caccia-Dominioni says of the Italians, "Names steeped in history passed out of existence alongside others newer but no less glorious. The infantry of Pavia had had a hundred years or more of life . . . . Brescia had originally been composed of volunteers of 1848; Bologna of men recruited in Venetia and Romagna in 1859. Nothing was left of them. Nor of the youthful Ariete and Littorio. Nor of the new-born Folgore."

TOUR #2

The Battlefield of al-Alamein

- 2x2
- 2–4 hours
- easy
- entrance fees at some memorials and at the museum

			km	total km
Greek memorial	N 30 50 170	E 28 57 488	0	0
British memorial	N 30 50 353	E 28 56 842	0.5	0.5
Italian marker	N 30 51 499	E 28 53 867	6	6.5
German memorial	N 30 52 594	E 28 52 316	3	9.5
Italian memorial	N 30 54 32	E 28 50 278	4	13.5
British minefield	N 30 54 765	E 28 48 941	2	15.5
Axis minefield	N 30 54 946	E 28 48 598	1	16.5

One cannot walk the battlefield here as at Gettysburg or Normandy. One can only peer into the desert, for al-Alamein is still a dangerous place. Despite the British sappers and the passage of time, land mines litter the battlefield, as do unexploded shells, including the large and deadly 88s. All have been rendered unstable by time and corrosion and they have been known to explode spontaneously, when the rusty pin snaps and the charge detonates. (Egypt did not sign the Ottawa Treaty and wants Germany and England to remove the 17.2 million land mines still here. Including the nine fields in the Eastern Desert, Egypt contains 20 percent of the world total of land mines.)

Despite the insistence of local Bedouin (eager to serve as guides) that the battlefield is safe, anyone visiting al-Alamein should be satisfied with touring the memorials and driving down the paved roads.

Each October, on the anniversary of the battle, Allied and Axis authorities hold a ceremony commemorating the dead.

Allied Monuments

All the Allied monuments at al-Alamein are centered around the al-Alamein War Cemetery erected by the British. This is Tell

al-Alamein, where two gas stations, an Egyptian military installation, a resthouse, the al-Alamein Museum, and a few other buildings are located. This is not the town of al-Alamein, which lies in the valley south of this area. The main Allied monument is the al-Alamein War Cemetery. There is no monument erected to the few Americans who fought in this conflict.

Greek Memorial

The Greek Memorial, in the form of a classical temple, stands on the south side of the road at the very beginning of the battlefield tour. It is approached via a small avenue of oleanders.

South African Memorial

The South African Memorial is less than a kilometer west of the Greek Memorial on the south side of the road. It is a simple monolith with the following dedication: "South Africans outspanned and fought here during their trek from Italian Somaliland to Germany 1939–1945."

British Memorial

About a kilometer later, still on the south of the road, lies the British Memorial. Called al-

Entrance to the cloister of the al-Alamein War Cemetery

Alamein War Cemetery, it was designed by Sir Hubert Worthington, and is maintained by the British War Graves Commission in Cairo. Here 7,367 men from Britain, New Zealand, Australia, South Africa, Greece, France, India, and Malaysia are buried in individual graves, while 11,945 men, whose bodies were never found, are honored in the cloister that precedes the graveyard. On the west side of the walkway leading to the entrance of the cemetery is the memorial to the gallant 9th Australian Division, that magnificent group of fighting men who led the final charge at al-Alamein.

Beyond the cloister are the individual graves, each topped with a white marker. Approximately 815 soldiers were identified and their names are inscribed over the graves, but the remainder of the markers read simply, "Known Unto God."

Al-Alamein Museum

The small al-Alamein Museum, about a mile west of the British memorial, is located on the north side of the road. For anyone interested in war memorabilia it is worth a stop. Created in 1965 from debris found on the battlefield, it contains uniforms, weapons, flags, and other war paraphernalia. Displays include photographs and three dimensional maps of the battle sites complete with troop placement. Each artifact has an identification tag in English and Arabic. Refurbished in 1992 for the 50th anniversary of the battle, there is a large display with an audio track describing the war. Large pieces of artillery, armored vehicles, and tanks are found in the garden.

Italian Marker

Three kilometers (1.8 miles) west of al-Alamein on the south side of the road stands a small marker erected at the easternmost advance of the Axis army in North Africa: "Manco la Fortuna, Non Il Valore [Lacking Fortune, Not Valor], 1.7.1942, Alessandria, 111."

If one stands beside it and peers south into the desert, one can barely see traces of the original Springbok Road, the main desert artery used by the Allies. Originally, the Italian and German dead were buried by the British in a single cemetery in 1943. In 1949, the Italians sent Paolo Caccia-Dominoni to reclaim the Italian dead. He searched the battlefield for ten years.

German War Memorial

Three kilometers (1.8 miles) west of the Italian marker and 9.6 kilometers (6 miles)

German War Memorial atop Gebel Alam Abd al-Gawad

from the beginning of the tour (the Greek Memorial) is the German War Memorial, a single octagonal building erected in 1959. It sits to the north of the road atop the knoll of Gebel Alam Abd al-Gawad and overlooks the sea. Patterned after the Castel del Monte in Apulia, the memorial contains the bodies of 4,280 German soldiers. At the entrance stands an impressive golden mosaic. To the right of the entrance is a small chapel where families and friends honor the dead with wreaths, photographs, and memorial ribbons. Around the courtyard are a number of alcoves, each with three stone graves honoring men from various German cities and states. At the exit there is a guest book where amid the names and addresses of visitors, one may find a poignant message like the one we found in July 1989, "A beautiful memorial. I loved one of them," a reminder that suffering lasts far beyond the final shot of any battle.

Italian Memorial

The elegant white marble Italian Memorial, the largest structure at al-Alamein, stands 5 kilometers (3.1 miles) beyond the German Memorial. It was designed by Paolo Caccia-Dominoni who served at al-Alamein and also wrote a book about it. It begins with an entry cloister containing a chapel, mosque, hall of remembrances, and small museum. In the chapel is inscribed: "To 4,800 Italian soldiers, sailors and airmen. The desert and the sea did not give back 38,000 who are missing." The main memorial overlooks the sea at the top of a oleander-lined causeway. In the interior thousands of white marble plaques bearing the names of the Italian dead line the walls.

Minefield Markers

2.5 kilometers (1.8 miles) west is the plaque commemorating the Forward British Mine Field position as of October 23, 1942 and less than a kilometer later stands another plaque, showing the easternmost line of Axis minefields. They are both on the south side of the road.

Battlefield

To cross the battle lines from east to west, return to al-Alamein and turn west on the old Amriya/Matruh road, 5 kilometers (3.5 miles) south of al-Alamein Station. At 5 kilometers (3.5 miles) the Italian marker stands along the coast to the north and Miteriya Ridge is almost the same distance to the south. At 9 kilometers (5.7 miles) the German Memorial is visible to the north and Miteriya Ridge should be coming to an end in the south. At 14.5 kilometers (9 miles) the British defenses end and a mile later the 5 mile-deep German defenses begin. At 24 kilometers (15 miles) the road enters the most critical part of the battlefield. To the south of the road stands a new addition to the memorials at al-Alamein: a pyramid to a single German airman, Hans-Joachim Marseille. Marseille lost his life when his plane crashed on this spot September 30, 1942. (N 30 53 668 E 28 41 819.) The desert track beside the pyramid is probably the Rahman Track, while running north–south in this area was the German gun line. Tell al Aqaqir is about a mile south, to the west of the track, and the Kidney is less than a mile south to the east of the track. Although you will see Bedouin grazing their animals in the area, do not wander around on your own—it is extremely dangerous.

TOUR #3

Qattara Depression

- 2x2, some 4x4 optional
- 4–6 hours
- easy to hard (Maghra)

	km	total km
Ball's rd	0	0
Amriya–Matruh rd	5	5
Italian Hospital	19	24
Naqb Abu Dweis	44	68
Maghra Oasis rd	16	84
Military checkpoint	7	91
Fork left	45	136
Fork left	9	145
Senan camp	23	168
Gas station	1	169
Cairo–Bahariya rd	104	273

Qattara Depression

Considered by some to be the greatest depression in the world, certainly the largest in Egypt and Africa, the Qattara Depression forms a formidable obstruction separating the northern coast from the rest of the Western Desert. If we combined all the oases into one place, Qattara would be seven times larger than the whole combined. It was 'discovered' by Europeans in 1926 when George Walpole was sent into the area by the Geological Survey.

History

Not until the beginning of the twentieth century was the extent of the Qattara Depression defined, and even now the history of the area is obscure. Major caravan routes traversing the interior of al-Diffa go around its perimeters and through its heart, but these routes and the dramas enacted there through the centuries are recorded only in the stories of the Bedouin, who knew Qattara better than anyone else.

P. A. Clayton did the topographical and geological survey of Qattara from 1927 to 1930. Because it is only 38 kilometers (23 miles) from the sea, John Ball suggested that Qattara was a perfect place to generate hydroelectric power. He proposed a tunnel northward to bring in sea water which would tumble over the escarpment producing a force that would generate enough electricity for all of Egypt. He believed that natural evaporation would keep the lake to a manageable size. The idea hung around a while, but in 1931 the Desert Survey underwent an acute financial crisis that ended Ball's tunnel.

During World War II, Qattara protected the Nile Valley and blocked the advance of the Axis powers, who were forced to pass through al-Alameïn. Yet Qattara was not untouched by the war. Both the Axis and Allied powers mined areas of Qattara, leaving it a dangerous place to visit.

Geography and Geology

Extending 298 kilometers (186 miles) east to west and 145 kilometers (90 miles) north to south (at its widest point) and containing

19,500 square kilometers (12,188 square miles), the Qattara Depression is larger than Wales. It is bordered by high scarps on the north and west. Qattara, at 60 to 134 meters (192 to 428 feet) below sea level, is one of the lowest places on earth and definitely the lowest point in Africa. Its lowest point is in the western section 35 kilometers (22 miles) southeast of Qara. One-quarter of the depression is covered by playas (*sabkha*), layers of mud covered by a thin salty crust that may or may not be strong enough to carry a person, a camel, or a vehicle. The major playa area is in the northeast corner of the depression. A fault runs along the northern scarp and dunes run along its southern edge.

Fossil remains in the Qattara Depression include sea creatures, reptiles, and mammals, including primates. The most important fossils found so far in Qattara are *Prohylobates tandyi*, the oldest Miocene monkey, and a Mastodon found in Maghra Oasis (for Caravans and Roadways see Qara Oasis below).

The al-Alamein–Bahariya desert road, Ball's Road of the 1920s–30s, is a pleasant journey through the heart of the Western Desert. At a length of 273 kilometers (170 miles) with two gas stations, the road can be traveled by ordinary vehicle. It also skirts portions of the al-Alamein battlefield and forms part of the al-Alamein Line, the defensive position of the Allied Forces on October 23, 1942, the day the battle began.

The road begins to the east of the Greek Memorial and drops immediately into the village of al-Alamein. To the east of the road at the railway is the al-Alamein Station, dubbed 'Heaven' by the Allied troops because it was safely tucked within the al-Alamein Box. Today the station remains as it was in 1942. Five kilometers (3 miles) later the road crosses the Amriya–Matruh road, which cuts through the heart of the battlefield.

Italian Field Hospital

At 24 kilometers (15 miles), the road enters Qarat al-Abd. Here we find one of the most interesting sites along the route, the Italian Field Hospital and defensive positions. They are located along the west of the road at the juncture with a second road. Although the field hospital is an enticing site, the traveler must use extreme caution, as evidenced by the number of installations visible along the ridges on both sides of the road. There are trenches and underground tunnels extending up the ridge and beyond.

Oil Fields

Now one enters oil country, the al-Alamein Oilfield. It was here that the first oil well in the Western Desert was discovered in 1955. Recent exploration in this area of the Western Desert indicates there is enough oil for development. Oil rigs and storage tanks dot the terrain.

Naqb Abu Dweis

At 68 kilometers (44 miles) the road arrives at the cliffs of the Qattara Depression. There is a checkpoint at the top of the descent through Naqb Abu Dweis and another halfway down the scarp. This is an 8 kilometer (5 mile) drop to the bottom of the depression floor through Minqar Abu Dweis, or Minqar Lebbuk. The area was of strategic importance during World War II and thus the pass is heavily mined. Do not wander amid the wadis in the escarpment.

The route to the Cairo–Bahariya road is dotted with landmarks. At 91 kilometers (57 miles) there is a military checkpoint; at 136 kilometers (84 miles) the road forks, go left; at 145 kilometers (89 miles) there is another fork, to the right are the Schlumberger facilities, go left; at 168 kilometers (100 miles) is the Senan Camp; at 169 the gas station; sand dunes begin at 177 kilometers (109 miles) and continue to 261 kilometers (162 miles); at 273 kilometers (169 miles) you reach the Cairo–Bahariya road. At this point it is 205 kilometers (189 miles) to Cairo and 125 kilometers (77 miles) to Bahariya.

Maghra Oasis

Situated in the eastern corner of the Qattara Depression, the uninhabited oasis of Maghra is located in a desolate, but magnificent stretch of desert. Sand dunes hem in one side, an impassable field of scrub another, and the escarpment of the depression the other two. There is a lake and five water wells dug in the 1840s at the behest of Muhammad Ali. The lake is, of course, a salt lake and is 34 meters (108 feet) below sea level.

Working for the Geological Survey of Egypt, a geologist of the Suez Canal Company named Barthoux discovered Jurassic exposures here. This is perhaps the only place in Egypt where Jurassic is found. Barthoux published *Roches ignées du Desert arabique* in 1922. Scientists have found plenty of fossils in Maghra—reptiles, fish, and mammals. We found a huge fossilized bone, probably from the mastadon family.

One of the dominant features of the terrain is the scattered heaps of petrified wood, the only movable objects in this barren area. In fact, there are several grave sites near Bir Nahad that are conspicuously outlined with petrified wood sticking up in the air like tiny stone trees. Thomas M. Bown, in an article on trace fossils in the Fayoum, provides enough evidence to place Maghra on or near the southern shore of the Tethys Sea in the Miocene. This petrified wood helps substantiate his claim.

The fossils share the oasis with the millions of mosquitoes that on one visit bit this writer during the day. Another traveler who met with Maghra's ravenous mosquitoes was Arthur Silva White, author of *From Sphinx to Oracle* (1899). White was on his way to Siwa and hopefully a hundred or so miles beyond to Jaghbub with his own caravan of seven men and six camels. (We had two 4x4s and a Bedouin guide).

He, too, encountered petrified wood. He was luckier than us, and found entire trunks 28 meters (90 feet) long. And he found "several large pieces of geyser-tubes—the blow-holes of hot vapours . . . ." He goes on

to tell us that water is so near the surface here one merely has to dig a foot or two. And that the Waled [Awlad] Ali came here for their winter camp, leaving the stormy northern coast behind.

In 1907, it was here that the Camel Corps encountered the Beni Amar smugglers with 1,338 kilos of hashish. (See History and Bahariya section for details).

During World War I a small force of British soldiers occupied what they called the Escarpment Post and watched caravan movement through the oasis. They, along with forces at Bir Hooker in Wadi Natrun and Dabaa along the northern coast, evacuated in March of 1917.

Getting There: Leaving the coastal highway just east of the Greek Memorial along the al-Alamein–Bahariya desert road one travels south through the Naqb Abu Dweis and into the Qattara Depression. At 16 kilometers (10 miles) beyond the end of the pass and 5 kilometers (3 miles) after the last checkpoint a green and white barrel marks the turn east to Maghra Oasis. The route to Maghra Oasis is difficult for even the most seasoned 4x4 driver. The road is barrel-marked for 20 kilometers (12.5 miles) and then the track disappears into open country. Cutting across country through extremely soft sand in this remote and hostile environment is extremely dangerous and not recommended for a single vehicle or without a guide. Even a guide can get lost. Twenty-three kilometers (37 miles) from the beginning of the journey Maghra Oasis comes into view in the depression below. The road has, in fact, worked its way out of Qattara and the first view of Maghra is from the top of the southeastern escarpment. You must take a Bedouin guide from al-Alamein to go to Maghra.

TOUR #4

Qara (Gara) Oasis

- 4x4
- all day
- easy to hard

Five days by camel from Siwa (70 miles) in the oasis of Qarat Umm al-Sughayyar, Mother of the Little One, is the picturesque village of Qara. A mudbrick village perched on a natural outcropping, it is one of the few remaining fortress towns to be found intact, untouched by any modern convenience. Qara is sometimes known as the Camp of Alexander because on his return journey from Siwa, Alexander paused here en route to Memphis. Modern scholars are reinterpreting Alexander's trek along the North African coast and some believe that he left the coast via Mersa Matruh but when he got lost he entered Siwa via Qara and exited going south through Zaytoun to Bahariya, where a temple was erected in his honor. The geography seems to suggest this is a possibility.

In 1819, when Cailliaud saw the village, it had one gate. Its streets were covered with boards and the best well was housed within the village. It was also a center for the slave trade and the majority of the current population is descended from former slaves.

Because of the remoteness of the area, the lack of water, the poor soil, and the limited space in the village, life was and is harsh at Qara. In the past it could only support a limited number of people. Tradition maintains the villagers made a pact that the population should not exceed a certain number. The number is unclear with various reports from travelers placing it anywhere from 40 to 145. In any event when a child was born, an older person had to leave the oasis to keep the number of inhabitants at the required level. Some sources say the people of Qara believed that the requirement was a curse because of something they did in the past. Today the sheikh maintains that ancient tradition is no longer practiced, but still only 140 people live at Qara (when White passed through in the 1890s, the count was 75). C. Dalrymple Belgrave gives the following account of how the legend originated:

"A famous religious sheikh called Abdel Sayed was traveling from Tripoli to join the pilgrim caravan to Cairo. He had with him a few attendants and some devout men who were also on their way to do the pilgrimage. When they halted at Gara [Qara] the inhabitants, instead of feeling honored and entertaining the travelers, came out of the town and attacked them. The sheikh and his followers managed to escape, and when they were safely out of the valley the venerable Abdel Sayed stood on a rock and solemnly cursed the people of Gara, swearing that there should never be more than forty men alive in the village at once. Since then, although the total number of inhabitants is over a hundred, there have never been more than forty full-grown men. When the number exceeds forty, one of them dies."

The first European traveler to visit Qara was Browne on his way to Siwa in 1792. He called it *Karet am el-Soghier* and didn't like it very much. Hornemann, in 1797, called it *Oum Essogheir*. Cailliaud and his fellow traveler M. Latorzec, making their way from the Fayoum in 1819, got closer to its name. They called it al-Garah. The Sanusi were in Qara, as was the Axis army. In the 1970s, a Russian oil company came to Qara to search for oil, but found water instead.

Geography and Geology

This oasis sits at the western border of the Qattara Depression. It is 16 kilometers (10 miles) long and 8 kilometers (5 miles) wide.

Beyond the oasis, dominating the horizon is Gebel Qarn al-Laban, Mountain of the Milky Horns, a white mountain with several outstanding peaks. There are fifteen wells in the oasis, all slightly salty and mostly dug in ancient times when the oasis may have been more prosperous. The depression floor is dotted with sandstone outcroppings, many worn away at the bottoms so that they look like giant mushrooms. One in particular is called Pharaoh's Rock. There are also a good number of caves, but Ahmed Fakhry, who visited the oasis in the 1930s, maintains there are no antiquities. Since antiquities exist in all the surrounding oases and the wells in Qara were dug in ancient times, this may not be true.

After four years of no rain, in 1982 Qara, like Siwa, was hit by a two-day storm. At that time the people still lived in their hilltop village. The rain devastated Qara. Because of the poor roads no one was able to reach the village for more than a week. After the rain the government built new housing for the people on the flat plain below the old village. In 1990, there were 57 houses, no hotels, and no school, but there was a generator that provided electricity.

Caravans and Roadways
There are no paved roads leading to Qara Oasis, but several major caravan trails connect it to the outside world. Qara is linked to Siwa in the west by the **Masrab Khidida** which passes through the Naqb Abyad, Naqb Ahmar, and Naqb Khamsa en route. In the east there are three major trails, the continuation of the Masrab Khidida which proceeds north to the coastal city of Gazalah, and the Masrab al-Dara and Masrab al-Muhashas.

The **Masrab al-Dara** leaves Qara and skirts the northern rim of the Qattara Depression. One route branches north to Gazalah, while the main route continues to Naqb Abu Dweis. There a track goes to al-Alamein on the northern coast, while another proceeds west. A third branch goes north to Abu Mena and Amriya while the main route continues to Wadi Natrun.

The **Masrab al-Muhashas**, possibly used by Alexander the Great, is a major route across the northern section of the Western Desert. After leaving Qara it crosses the Qattara Depression and points south with one branch going to Bahariya and the main track continuing up the heart of Qattara to Maghra Oasis. Here the track breaks north to Naqb Abu Dweis, Abu Mena, and Amriya, or south to Wadi Natrun and Kerdassa. Thus the Masrab al-Muhashas connected Siwa to ancient Memphis.

Sir Flinders Petrie estimated that in Roman times the roadway was 50 cubits wide with gravel embankments on either side. It was used by date caravans to Siwa in the 1800s because the Awlad Ali preferred to shun the coastline. It was a favorite of Bagnold, who claimed there was plenty of petrified wood and foot-high salt slabs to the east of Qara. White passed through it twice, coming and going from Siwa. He tells us that it took seven days by camel from Maghra to Qara.

The People
The people of Qara live in a very hostile environment and have a difficult time growing crops. They subsist on olives, dates, and a few vegetables. They have chickens, but there are no camels or donkeys and only a few goats and cows. Despite their poverty, Qara is one of the places in the Western Desert where traditional Bedouin hospitality is maintained. The village has a meeting hall where all the important matters related to the tribe are discussed. Here they entertain guests. When visiting Qara, Sheikh Hassan, offering the traditional Bedouin hospitality of tea upon arrival followed by a tour of his oasis, then a plentiful meal of chicken, rice, and mulukhiya (a leafy vegetable made into a soup), told this writer that the village needed just four things: a teacher, a doctor, a road, and a good water supply.

Getting There: Various sources place Qara 70, 120, even 150 kilometers from Siwa, but our odometer told us that from Aghurmi into the Qara Depression via Naqb Khamsa, the Fifth Pass, was a distance of 123 kilometers (77 miles). After leaving Aghurmi in Siwa Oasis, the road continues east 12 kilometers (7.5 miles) to a fork, the southern road going to Zaytun and the northern continuing 47 kilometers (29 miles) to the escarpment. It passes plenty of *karshif*, salty soil churned by some unknown force into almost impassable jagged chunks that crunch underfoot and make walking unpleasant. Luckily, there is a well-graded roadbed. The northern escarpment exposes layers of pure white chalk topped by brownish-grey stone, gleaming in the sun. Naqb Mughbara is an easy pass snaking up the scarp, and a good place to pause for an excellent view of the oasis below.

There is a story connected with Naqb Mughbara as told by Bayle St. John. It seems that one evening at sunset a caravan ascending the pass was attacked by Bedouin who were hiding behind fifty small mounds of pebbles they had erected. A battle followed and the thieves were killed. The caravan leaders buried them beside the mounds and thereafter no traveler would ascend Naqb Mughbara at sunset for fear of the ghosts of the dead Bedouin that are said to haunt the pass. In St. John's day the fifty heaps of stone still stood and his guides would not let him build a fire here for fear of trouble.

The desert floor above the scarp is uninteresting. A guide is absolutely necessary for the road winds above the scarp through mudpan after mudpan, the track visible but the horizon absolutely flat with no landmarks to guide the way. Thirty-five kilometers (22 miles) after Naqb Mughbara the descent into the Qara Depression begins at Naqb Abyad and 9 kilometers (6 miles) later at Naqb Ahmar there is a military checkpoint. The soldiers who man these checkpoints come from all parts of Egypt. They spend forty days in these lonely, desolate places before going back to Cairo for a ten day rest. Many of them are educated young men who find the harsh assignment in the desert a difficult one. Fruit, candy bars, or packets of cigarettes are appreciated. At one checkpoint a soldier asked for something to read, so even an old newspaper or magazine is useful. The final descent into Qara Depression is through Naqb Khamsa.

TOUR #5

Sidi Abd al-Rahman to Mersa Matruh

- 2x2, 4x4
- 3 hours, easy

	km	total km
Sidi Abd al-Rahman	0	0
al-Dabaa	32	32
Fuka	50	82
Gazala	5	87
Ras al-Hekma	5	92
Hanash	22	114

Sidi Abd al-Rahman, 9 kilometers (5.6 miles) beyond the last markers of the al-Alamein battlefield, is situated along the picturesque Gulf of Kanayis, where the sea is azure and turquoise and the sand is gleaming white. All the beaches in this area are exceptional. Belgrave speaks of all the booty washed ashore along the coast. In addition to sponges after a storm, one sometimes found the cargo of wrecked ships: cotton, good brown paper, casks of wine and rum.

Sidi (Saint) Abd al-Rahman was named after a Muslim saint who, according to tradition, was murdered by fellow traders on this spot. Years later, these same traders passed by again and finding a big, green, delicious looking watermelon, picked it and took it to the pasha. When the pasha unwrapped it, he found the still bleeding head of Abd al-Rahman. From that time pilgrimages were made to the Saint, who proved very gracious in granting requests. Unfortunately, local lore maintains that since the new mosque was erected by Khedive Abbas, the saint no longer helps poor people.

A wooden barracks, one of three, was constructed here by the Coastguard Camel Corps to house the fifteen men and their horses who guarded the coastline against smugglers around 1900.

Axis Forces

Sidi Abd al-Rahman was in the heart of the Axis defences during the Battle of al-Alamein. The organization of the Axis army was under the direct command of the Italian governor-general of Libya. The commander in the field throughout the North African campaign was Field Marshal Erwin Rommel, the desert fox.

Rommel brought Blitzkrieg to the African desert. He roamed the desert, turning up where least expected, just as he had done in France as commander of the 7th Panzer Division, aptly labeled the 'Ghost Division.' Once his troops arrived in Tripoli they exploded east in a lightning push that took them to the gates of the Nile Valley in a few months.

Panzergruppe Afrika

Panzergruppe Afrika was organized August, 1941, as Rommel's troops in North Africa. It was renamed Panzer Army Africa in January, 1942, and German–Italian Panzer Army in October, 1942, before the Battle of al-Alamein. Panzergruppe Afrika was deactivated on February 20, 1943 after their defeat in North Africa. The Deutsches

Afrika Korps (DAK), first organized February 19, 1941, was the heart and soul of the German army in North Africa. Operating under the symbol of a palm tree with a swastika on its trunk, it was to become the most efficient fighting machine in this theater. By the Battle of Gazalah, it had been molded into an efficient killing machine adept at the use of the ultimate desert weapon, the tank. By al-Alamein, no less loyal, no less efficient, but without the supplies needed to continue the battle, the Afrika Korps was bleeding to death.

Italians

The Italians were equal players in the Battle of North Africa. They fought in all battles, suffered the same conditions as any other player, and died in greater numbers; yet they are often forgotten when the events in North Africa are told. Rommel assessed them as follows: "The duties of comradeship compel me to state unequivocally that the defects which the Italian formation suffered. . . were not the fault of the Italian soldier. The Italian was willing, unselfish, and a good comrade, and, considering the conditions under which he served, had always given far better than average."

The Rahman Line

Rommel set up his defenses to the east of the Rahman track, which ran south from Sidi Abd al-Rahman to the Qattara Depression. Headquarters and tank repair shops were at Sidi Abd al-Rahman.

For the first time in North Africa, because of depleted mechanized divisions, British air supremacy, and lack of petrol, Rommel set up a static defense and broke up his armor divisions. Five miles deep, his deployment east to west was an outer minefield, an empty mile-long corridor, a second minefield, and the main defenses: a 5,000-yard belt of infantry implacements, dug-in tanks, and anti-tank guns.

The third line of defense ran south along the Rahman track supported by mobile tanks.

In front of this deployment stood the Axis minefields, four miles thick from the sea to the depression. They reached their eastern most edge between Sidi Abd al-Rahman and Tell al-Eissa, and ended to the east of Himeimat. Behind the Axis army stood Tell al-Aqaqir, 6.2 miles south of Sidi Abd al-Rahman. One of the major sites of this battle and the site of the final engagements, it was dubbed the 'panzer graveyard' for it saw the death knell of the Afrika Korps.

Six miles from the coast, running in a southeast–northwest direction was the mile-long Miteriya Ridge, held by the Germans. The Italian Trento Division sat atop the center section of Miteriya Ridge, with the Littorio Division behind them in the west.

Six miles northwest of Miteriya Ridge was a mile-long depression known as the Kidney. The Kidney sat between the 15th Panzer Division in the north, and the Littorio Division to its south. It was the focus of major fighting throughout the Battle of al-Alamein.

Al-Dabaa

It is said that in spring, mint, heather, sage, asters, wild violets, and white clover spread blankets of color on the white beaches surrounding al-Dabaa.

On March 13, 1805, somewhere along the edge of the Gulf of Kanayis beyond al-Dabaa, the ill-fated Eaton expedition of 1805 (see History above) met yet another problem. A messenger from Derna arrived and brought good news to Hamet which was greeted with firing guns into the air. The only problem was the Arabs at the back of the column had not heard the news and assumed their fellow Arabs were attacking the Christians and moved forward to join in the fray. It took some time before things settled down again.

After the decentralization of the Camel Corp and the erection of three Coast Guard stations and a fort at Mersa Matruh, al-Dabaa was selected as an additional station because it was halfway between Alexandria and Matruh.

There are on-and-off plans to put a nuclear reactor at al-Dabaa.

Fuka

It is 50 kilometers (30 miles) from al-Dabaa to Fuka. When the Eaton Expedition reached the area around Fuka the rains began. Here they found ruins of ancient forts, and were forced to spend a few days because of high winds, heavy rain, and thunder. They were now in Tripolitanian territory. Today there is nothing of note at Fuka. Fuka is followed by Gazala, Ras al-Hekma, and Hanash.

TOUR #6

Mersa Matruh

N 31 22 E 25 32

- walk, bike, 2x2
- half day
- easy
- some entrance fees

The Ammonia or Paraetonium of ancient times, Matruh has also been known as al-Baratun, probably a corruption of the Roman name, and during the Middle Ages and Renaissance, Portalberton, Port Alberton, Porto Alberto, all corruptions of the corruption. In the eighteenth and nineteenth centuries yet another corruption, Bareton, was used. None of this would be important except for maps. We have an abundance of them of the northern coast and very few of them carry the same names. It

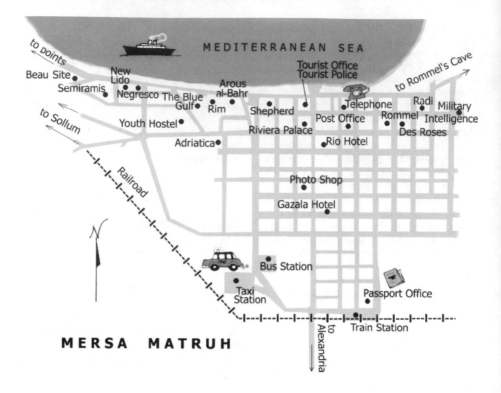

MEDITERRANEAN SEA

to points

Beau Site
New Lido
Semiramis
Negresco The Blue Gulf Rim
Arous al-Bahr
Tourist Office
Tourist Police
to Rommel's Cave
Shepherd
Telephone
Radi Military
Post Office
Rommel Intelligence
Youth Hostel
Riviera Palace
Des Roses
to Sollum
Adriatica
Rio Hotel

Railroad

N

Photo Shop

Gazala Hotel

Bus Station

Taxi Station

Passport Office

Train Station

to Alexandria

MERSA   MATRUH

current name, Mersa Matruh, popularly means 'sheltered anchorage,' but can also be interpreted as 'forsaken or deserted harbor,' as it is by Oric Bates, a noted Harvard scholar.

History

There is evidence that Cypriot traders (1500–1200 B.C.) and Libyan tribes frequented this spot, but it took Alexander the Great to place a trading town here. He paused here on his way to Siwa to consult the Oracle and it was here that he received an envoy from Cyrene to welcome him to their land and accept his leadership. Among the gifts, according to Diodorus, were 300 war horses and five teams of chariot horses.

Bates tells us that when Alexander was here he saw a large and beautiful gazelle. When the archer tried to kill it, he failed. Alexander cried, "Fellow, you have shot wide of the mark." That became its name, "Wide-

of-the-Mark," which became in Latin, Paraetonium.

The Romans considered it *Aegypti cornua*, one of the 'horns of Egypt.' The other was Pelusium, the two sat on the western and eastern borders of Egypt. Attacks on Egypt historically began at the horns.

Greek and Roman

Ancient rumor and the pen of Byron Khun de Prorok suggest that after the fall of Troy, the lovely Helen sought refuge here. If so, she was one of many beauties who came to Mersa Matruh. It was one of the favorite spots of Cleopatra, who came here after the death of Julius Caesar, swam in its waters with her new lover Mark Antony, probably gave birth to Antony's daughter Cleopatra Celene, and used its harbor to launch her fleet for the final battle against Augustus.

She and Mark Antony returned to Matruh after the battle. They wisely fortified both it and Pelusium, the 'horns of Egypt.' Cornelius Gallus came after Antony and captured Paraetonium. By this time Antony's four legions from Cyrene had mutinied and were now under Gallus's control (Augustus honored the legion faithful to him by giving it the name Cyrenaica and leaving it to guard a part of Egypt).

Antony fled the city, but rallied and returned to fight with soldiers and ships. He believed that his men would rejoin him, but when he approached the walls (yes, the city had fortified walls) to call to them, Gallus sounded the trumpets so he could not be heard. Then Gallus destroyed Antony's fleet within the western harbor. Antony turned east and went to fight Augustus, who meanwhile and predictably had attacked Pelisium, the second horn, a place Antony knew well.

Paraetonium, although often mentioned by poets like Ovid, fell from importance. Vespasian occupied it. Byzantine Matruh was the capital of the Eparchy of Lower Libya. During this time it was refortified by Justinian.

Islamic Period

During the Classical Islamic era, Mersa Matruh was an active port with goods passing from North Africa to Spain and the south of France. During the Ottoman Period, a Turkish fort guarded the entrance to the harbor and it was still standing at the beginning of World War I when the British established additional forts for the defense of Mersa Matruh. At that time Matruh was mainly a coastguard barrack with plastered houses.

In the eighteenth and nineteenth centuries it became known as Barcton and is hardly mentioned in the travel literature of the time. Most expeditions bound for Siwa bypassed it. It was von Minutoli, traveling to Siwa, who recognized that Bareton was the ancient Paraetonium.

On March 18, 1805, when the American William Eaton arrived here with his band of struggling men making their way across the Northern Coast to attack Derna, he called Mersa Matruh, Maroscah, or Massouah. Eaton found a Sheikh occupying the castle.

His problems intensified at Matruh as al-Tayyib, one of the Egyptian leaders, said he would go no further. The Sheikh maintained that Matruh was as far as he had agreed to go. Eaton had no money. He passed the hat among the non-Arabs and collected $673.50. Al-Tayyib sent all but forty camels back to Burg al-Arab. Eaton began to see that Hamet was siding with the Arabs. Eaton said he would send a courier to Bomba for news of the fleet, stop the rations to everyone except his men, and stay in Matruh for a reply. The Arabs capitulated.

British Occupation

Around the turn of the nineteenth century, Mersa Matruh came under British domination. It was the perfect spot to establish a desert headquarters for the Camel Corps that had recently been decentralized from Fort Sheffakhana in Alexandria. Three locations were selected: Abu Sir, Amaid, and Sidi Abd al-Rahman. They were to be manned by small, fifteen-man outposts. Mersa Matruh, with its deep harbor, was selected for a fort. This fort was constructed by twenty-four Sicilian masons. It was soon occupied by 125 men of the Camel Corps, almost all Sudanese, with Egyptian, English, and German officers. Their families were housed in barracks.

The Corps purchased 1,000 acres of land and constructed houses to lure settlers to the area. Unsuccessful at trying to get the sponge fisherman (see below) to settle in Matruh year round, hawkers and shopkeepers encouraged the fishermen and gradually the Bedouin of the region to settle in Matruh. Then a police station, prison, school, post office, and hospital were built by order of André von Dumreicher, the Corps director. The man who built everything was a French anarchist known only as 'E.' Dumreicher protected E. from the French Consulate in Alexandria, who wished to deport him because he was an anarchist and a deserter. Dumreicher not only found him polite and gentle in manner, but because he was the best colonist and there was "nothing to annihilate in the desert" and the "French Consulate [had no right] to interfere with my colonists" gave him protection and made him the city's architect. Thus modern Mersa Matruh was born.

The Governorate of the Western Frontier District Administration was established in Matruh and its building was erected close to what was believed to be the great villa of Cleopatra.

World War I

During World War I a military camp was set up near the harbor. Among its responsibilities was maintaining the road between Dabaa, where the Khedival Railway ended, and Matruh. In addition to the British soldiers garrisoned here, the community held a number of Italians who had fled Libya and the Sanusi.

In 1920–21, C. Dalrymple Belgrave reported no hotels in Matruh and only a dirty and uncomfortable resthouse. In the 1930s, the Libyan Oases Association operated by Captain Hillier had a resthouse here, and there were 1,410 people, with 150 houses, 140 small huts, 80 government homes, and 2 hotels.

World War II

Matruh began to change substantially during World War II. Its welcoming port and easy rail access made it important to both Germany and England and it see-sawed back and forth between the two. It was bombed several times.

In the 1950s, Matruh was "still littered with the relics of war. . . the Lido Hotel derlict." The Bedouin learned how to remove the gelignite from the mines and exploded them in the water to kill hundreds of fish at one time. German prisoners were still clearing the minefields.

Today

Today, Matruh is the capital of a governorate with a quarter of a million people (85 percent of them Bedouin). The governorate covers an area from Alexandria to Sollum and extends 400 kilometers (250 miles) south to abut the New Valley Governorate. Each summer 250,000 visitors come to Mersa Matruh. Despite the development of the city into a summer resort with dozens of hotels, Mersa Matruh still retains the feel of a frontier town.

It serves as a trading center for Bedouin in the area and is the first major port of call for travelers from Libya (when the border is open). The atmosphere is charged with the exotic, and great temptations exist in the suqs including rugs, Libyan vests, colorful boots, and shawls. Matruh is also noted for its pumpkin seeds, believed to be the best in Egypt.

Geography and Geology

Matruh is the closest Egyptian point to the islands in the Mediterranean: 400 kilometers (250 miles) to Crete and 592 kilometers (370 miles) to Cyprus. The Mediterranean is at its most beautiful at Matruh, all azure, turquoise, and brilliant blue. The white sandy beaches are accented with limestone rocks, many with caves tucked into their massive sides. Hidden below the waters are the wrecks of ships from many eras, gruesome reminders of the importance of this port throughout the ages. There is a rainy season in Matruh. Rain can be expected from November to March and owing to its proximity to the sea there is also high humidity in summer.

As with all of the northern coast, fresh water is in short supply at Mersa Matruh. John Ball, working for the Geological Survey presented a paper on "The Water Supply of Mersa Matruh" in 1937. During Ball's time there were thirty shallow wells, two ancient aqueducts (which supplied the two hotels exclusively), a few cisterns for the collection of rain water, and a daily cruiser which brought additional water directly from Alexandria. The solution recommended was the creation of a reservoir in the Wadi Kharruba, 3 kilometers (1.8 miles) southwest of Matruh. It was recommended that a dam be created at the mouth of the Wadi.

As with many small towns in Egypt, most streets in Mersa Matruh do not have a proper name. The people identify them by a prominent landmark, such as the Street of the Blue Window. Today the government is attempting to name some of them, but local residents are unfamiliar with the new labels. The main street of Mersa Matruh, running from the highway straight through town to the governorate and the sea, is Sharia Iskandariya. The street running along the coast is the Corniche. Most residents recognize these two names and since the town is laid out in square blocks, once the two streets are identified it is easy to get around.

Commerce and People

In Classical times, Bates tells us, the merchants of Mersa Matruh exported the soft white, greasy *paraetonium*, a mineral made, we believe, of solidified sea foam and mud. The Romans used it as a white wash for their walls. Bates believes it to be limestone.

Greek and Maltese sponge divers were heirs to the ancient task of collecting the famous sponges lying at the bottom of the Mediterranean from Mersa Matruh to Sollum. They were harvested from May to October each year. There are two types of sponges at Matruh: the cup-shaped and the honeycombed. The former is the most common, but the latter is the most coveted as it is considered to be the best sponge in the world.

The sponges were as coveted in ancient Greece and Rome as they are today. Then, the Greek warriors used the sponges as padding for their helmets. Divers from as far as the Cyclades and Sporades would come each season to collect the sponges and sell them in the markets of such cities as Sparta, Crete, and Athens. These divers, like their counterparts in the twentieth century, used a stone to give them additional weight, as they dove 60 to 90 meters (200 to 300 feet) to harvest the sponges along the sea floor.

Modern divers collected sponges by diving, or dredging, or by using a long-handled fork, like a trident. In most instances divers entered the water naked, so as not to get entangled and drown and would stay underwater for up to a minute and forty seconds. In later years primitive diving equipment was devised to help harvest the sponges, but these devices proved extremely dangerous and many a grave is found along the coast and on the island of Ischaila, to the west of Matruh, because the equipment failed. At the beginning of this century all such diving devices were banned by the Egyptian government and divers reverted to the use of a stone to take them to the bottom of the sea.

In the early part of this century as many as 2,000 divers a season would gather in Matruh for the annual harvest. Coming from all over the Mediterranean, they added an additional touch to the already festive summer season as they celebrated their own holidays by singing traditional songs and decorating their sponge boats in gay colors and national flags. A Greek church was erected in Matruh by the divers, and some of them are buried in the nearby cemetery.

With the advent of territorial waters, the sponge harvesting industry became regulated and permits to harvest the sponges had to be obtained from the Egyptian government. Sponge harvesting stopped in the early 1980s.

The Tour

Archaeologically, compared to the rest of Egypt, Mersa Matruh offers little. Historically, it competes with the best. With the ghosts of Cleopatra and Mark Antony haunting the lagoons and visions of great naval battles along its shores, Matruh is magical.

In our time, Mersa Matruh was first investigated by Harvard ethnologist and archaeologist Oric Bates in 1913–14. He published a number of papers that tell of sites from the Late Bronze Age to the Byzantine.

During World War I, the Reverend L. Goodenough, the military chaplain at Matruh, investigated the ruins and wrote an extensive report that was passed from hand to hand, from expert to expert, but was never published. In 1990, it was given to Donald White who incorporated some of its information in his own report for the *Journal of the American Research Center in Egypt* the following year.

The Lagoon

North to south one finds: the Mediterranean, the entrance to the lagoon, the lagoon, and the modern city of Mersa Matruh. In antiquity the lagoon had four parts: the western

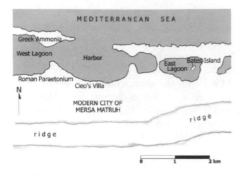

lagoon, the harbor, a small eastern section to the harbor, and the East Lagoon, completely separated from the other lagoons. Bates's Island was in the East Lagoon.

Western Lagoon

The western lagoon was the site of ancient Paraetonium. The Greek town was located along the northern shore, the Roman town on the southern shore. It was here that Mark Antony's fleet met its final defeat in 31 B.C. Having been defeated at Actium, Antony came here. He regrouped. His army mutinied. He left. Cornelius Gallus took Paraetonium. Antony returned. The death knell came when Antony's ships entered the harbor. Gallus had secretly strung chain-cable across the narrow harbor entrance, lowering it to allow Antony's ships to enter. Once inside, he pulled tight the chain-cables, locking the fleet within. The fleet was destroyed, many ships sinking to the bottom of the harbor.

Cleopatra's Villa

No longer believed to be the residence of the mysterious Cleopatra, this structure, also thought to be a Byzantine bath, is, in fact, a small Byzantine basilica.

First excavated by Bates, then Goodenough, it was described by Briggs, after World War I. He found the "ruins of a stone building of some description, with a well or subterranean passage communicating with the beach. One of the chambers in this structure appears to have had apsidal ends. It is commonly called Cleopatra's Villa. Before the winter of 1915, there was probably a

considerable portion of the building intact, but a large part of the stone seems to have been utilized in the construction of an adjoining redoubt." Stone was also pilfered in medieval times.

Although we have pictures and drawings from Bates's excavations, the site was destroyed and absorbed as part of an enlargement of the old governor's residence around 1929. It, in turn, was destroyed during a bombardment of Mersa Matruh during World War II.

City Beaches

The city beaches include Rommel, Lido, Gharam, and Beau Site. One must take note that swimming after dark is forbidden. Smuggling is a serious problem in Egypt and the shores are carefully guarded. People wandering along the shore may be mistaken for smugglers and shot.

There is a small traditional museum in the governorate building. Boats, some holding twenty people, are for hire during summer and travel along the coast from Rommel's Beach to Ubayad.

Bates' Island

We are not talking big here. The island is about 135 meters by 55 meters (432 feet by 176 feet) and can be reached by wading from the shore. But we are talking important. This island is a microcosm of Mersa Matruh. Mostly uninhabited and uncoveted through the centuries, some of the history of the rest of the city, now lying under modern buildings, can be read in the barren earth of the island. More importantly, discoveries are beginning to tell us that this area played an important role during the New Kingdom.

Donald White concludes that the island had five major occupation phases: Late Bronze Age, Archaic/Classical, Hellenistic, Roman, and Recent Historical times. It was probably occupied until the New Kingdom, when in all probability the residents were driven out by the wars of Ramses II and III against the encroaching Libyans.

The pottery on the island, studied by Donald M. Bailey of the British Museum, concurs. The pottery dates from the post–

Bronze Age (8th–7th centuries B.C.) to the late Roman period. It includes Greek, Saite, and first Persian period pottery fragments along with some local wine amphorae. It is suggested that oil was imported from the Aegean and Antioch in some of these containers.

Among the Archaic walls are to be found Bronze Age worked stone implements, Iron Age and Greek shards, and a Roman wall. The most interesting find on the island is Cypriot white slip ware pottery. The design on these pots is very similar to that found on the small white drinking cups and incense burners produced in Siwa today.

There are also shards from Canaanite jars, Levantine lamps, and Minoan and Mycenaean potsherds. They indicate a fair amount of trade in ancient times; but no pottery of the Nile Valley has been found, which caused White to conclude that "almost certainly it was the Libyans with whom the islanders were trading." As of 1985, White was still speculating as to who inhabited the island during the New Kingdom and what their relationship was to the Sea People. His belief is that further excavations around Mersa Matruh will provide interesting information about its importance during the New Kingdom.

Bates' Island is named after Oric Bates, who did extensive research in the area around 1915. His assistant was W. J. Harding-King, who went on to do a lot of exploration on his own (see Dakhla and Kharga). Bates referred to the island as Gezirah-t el-Yahudy, Island of the Jews, after two burials found there. It was also excavated in the 1980s by Donald White.

British Occupation

There is also ample evidence of occupation during World War II, including bullets and shrapnel. There are no land mines, although the island was shelled during the war and several disfigured bodies have been found.

Until 1950, sponge divers (see above) used the island. Today hunters use the island to shoot migratory birds. Each year they erect new blinds, some of them within the ruins of the Bates house.

Southwestern Matruh

Three first and second century male marbles were found here and are now in the Greco-Roman Museum in Alexandria. Nearby is a small bath with seven baths. Here a fourth to fifth century marble of the Good Shepherd, also in the Alexandria Museum, was discovered.

Cleopatra's Bath

Cleopatra's Bath where the fabled queen reportedly brought her Roman lover Mark Antony, is 7 kilometers (4.3 miles) west of Matruh, to the sea side of the western horn of the bay. The name, probably a misnomer for a chapel to Poseidon, God of the Sea, applies to a special rock formation, one of many limestone rocks that hug the shore at this point. These large rocks break the shoreline east and west. Cleopatra's Bath has two openings, one facing the sea, the other the land. Both have been hewn open for better access, but must originally have been created by natural forces. Inside the rock is a natural bath where water accumulates. At low tide the water is calm and still, but at high tide the sea rushes into the outer opening passing through the bath, to exit on the landward side. A climb to the top of the dune opposite Cleopatra's Bath leads to the recently excavated Roman ruins of a small beach-front community. White credits a British 8th Army soldier with the name Cleopatra's Bath.

Getting There: Follow the Corniche west past the Hotel Beau Site and along the causeway of the western side of the harbor. Just before the end of the causeway turn left and left again. Continue past all the Naval military camps for 3 kilometers (1.8 miles) and turn right. After 3 kilometers (1.8 miles) look for an opening in the dune field on the left. This opening offers the only view of the sea. Park the car and walk toward the sea. Cleopatra's Bath is the large rock to the west.

Rommel's Cave

This extensive cave was the headquarters of the Commander of the Afrika Korps during his short stay in Mersa Matruh. Rommel is remembered fondly by local inhabitants for his humane treatment of both local people and prisoners of war. The limestone cave is a deep tunnel-like natural opening in the white rock. Used in Roman times to store grain awaiting shipment to Rome, this particular cave, commanding an excellent view of the Matruh harbor, has been turned into a museum in honor of Rommel. Manfred Rommel, the general's only son, donated several of the commander's personal possessions, including the overcoat he wore during the North African Campaign, several photographs showing him with his men in North Africa, his compass, and six maps, some marked with battle plans in Rommel's hand. They include plans for the Battle of Tobruk. Reconstructed maps show the collapse of the Gazella Line and the Battle of Alam al-Rum.

Since the creation of the museum, members of Rommel's Afrika Korps visit Matruh on the anniversary of the Battle of al-Alamein and lay a wreath at the foot of the white marble bust of Rommel found at the entrance to the museum. Sources maintain that the wreck of a U-boat is barely visible above the surface of the sea, lying in 3 meters (9.6 feet) of water, but this writer has never found it.

Getting There: To get to Rommel's Cave take the Corniche east to the eastern horn of the bay. The cave is located near the end of the roadway.

TOUR #7

Mersa Matruh to Sollum: Agube Major

- 2x2
- 6–8 hours
- easy

	km	total km
Matruh	0	0
Aqueduct	8	8
Ubayad	6	14
Apis	6	20
Sidi Barrani	100	120
Sollum	95	215

The ancient nome of Marmarika ends at Mersa Matruh where Agube Major begins. A string of attractive beaches run west of Mersa Matruh, many of them under development.

Roman Aqueduct
Eight kilometers (5 miles) west of Mersa Matruh are the remains of an ancient Roman aqueduct discovered in 1933 by G. F. Walpole of the Geological Survey of Egypt. At that time it was a limestone tunnel 300 meters (960 feet) in length and two meters (6 feet) high that fed 280 tons of water a day to the Lido Hotel in Mersa Matruh.

Ubayad Beach
Ubayad Beach is 14 kilometers (8.7 miles) west of Mersa Matruh along the shores of a pleasant bay. There are several resorts here including a private military resort and Badr Tourist Village, an exotic facility with an enormous game room-cum-lobby, chalets, tents, and camping facilities.

It was in this area that the fortunes of

William Eaton and the American Expedition seemed to change (see History above for details). On March 22, 1805, they encountered thousands of Awlad Ali tribesmen who were eager to fight against the Libyans, even for free. They were there because the rains had filled the wells and attracted game, including ostrich. Eighty horsemen joined the expedition and the expedition horses were fed. Unfortunately, the men were living on hard bread and rice. Al-Tayeb continued to threaten to leave.

On March 26, a messenger from Derna brought bad news and al-Tayib gathered his men and marched away. Then Hamet deserted. Eaton continued his march west. Hamet returned. On the 29th, the Bedouin left. They came back on the 30th. Next it was discovered that al-Tayib had kept all the advance money and did not share it with Sheikh Muhammad. Muhammed left. Hamet went after him. Al-Tayib tried to take control of the expedition from Eaton. And on and on went this never ending nightmare

Apis

The ancient Apis, from where Strabo maintains caravans left the northern coast for Siwa, is 20 kilometers (12.5 miles) west of Mersa Matruh. Known today as the Zawyat Umm al-Rukham, the temple fortress of Ramses II is located here.

This temple fortress, between the beaches of Ubayad and Agiba, was one of a series of fortresses extending from Alexandria to Sollum. Additional forts were built at Marea, south of Mareotis, al-Gharbaniyat, and al-Alamein. This fort built by Nebre, Ramses's head bowman and overseer of foreign lands, is dedicated to Ptah. It marked the northern port of the western boundary of ancient Egypt.

The inscriptions on the gateway tell of throwing the Libyans (Temehu) out of the Delta and across the Western Desert. Within the chapels in the southern part of the excavation stirrup jars from Cyprus or Crete, Canaanite amphorae, and Syrian and Egyptian wine jars have been found. First explored by Labib Habachi in the 1950s, it is now under excavation by Steven Snape. It is currently off limits to visitors.

Sidi Barrani

Sidi Barrani, over 120 kilometers (75 miles) west of Mersa Matruh, is the ancient Aenesiphyra (Ennisyphora) of Strabo. It was a major terminus for caravans from Siwa Oasis in Egypt and Jaghbub Oasis in Libya. It was named after one of the leaders and missionaries of the Sanusi religious order, Sidi Muhammad al-Barrani. Barrani was killed in Kanem near Lake Chad by the invading French in 1906.

Sidi Barrani played a vital role in the various wars of the nineteenth and twentieth centuries. Yet, despite its importance, in the 1920s it had a single police barracks, a resthouse, and a few bungalows occupied by Greek traders.

By the time William Eaton arrived at Sidi Barrani in 1805, his ranks had swollen to about 1,200 men, women, and children. Food was running out, and there was little water. The Bedouin wanted to send an expedition to Siwa to collect dates. After much discussion the main body moved on while a smaller party was sent to Siwa. It did not rejoin the main body until Bomba.

During World War I, the final battle in the Western Desert was fought at Agagia, about 22 kilometers (14 miles) southwest of Sidi Barrani, on February 26, 1916. The Western Frontier Force consisted of Dorset Yeomanry, Bucks Yeomanry, Notts Battery, 1st South African Infantry Brigade, and Royal Scots, all under the command of General Peyton. The Sanusi commander was General Gafar Pasha.

On their march to reinforce Sollum, the British took Barrani and used it as a supply depot. Once this was accomplished they discovered that the Grand Sanusi and his army were encamped at Agagia. While General Lukin was resting his troops in anticipation of an attack on the Sanusi forces, the Sanusi attacked him. It was the last battle of the coast campaign. The Bedouin of the area were left starving. The women tried to sell their silver for food.

Eaton's hoard moved inland in this area and camped at several sites including Bir Toalim, 16 kilometers (10 miles) south of Sidi Barrani; Suani Samaluth, with nine wells; and at an ancient castle which he describes as 180 feet square.

World War II

Sidi Barrani featured prominently in the North African Campaign of World War II, passing back and forth between the Axis and Allied armies. In June of 1940, at the same time that the British Army left Europe via Dunkirk, Benito Mussolini declared war on France and Britain. By September of the same year, the Italian 10th Army under Marshall Rudolfo Graziani left Fort Capuzzo in Libya, crossed the wire, and invaded Egypt. Meeting little resistance from the small British force, the Italians marched past the border town of Sollum and halted at Sidi Barrani, 96 kilometers (60 miles) into Egypt. It was September 16.

In December, Sir Archibald Wavell, commander-in-chief of Middle East forces, launched a British counterattack with only 30,000 men. Sollum fell on December 17, Sidi Barrani a few days later, and Bardia on January 5th. The Italians withdrew to Tobruk with less than half their original force. That was the beginning of what was to become the Battle of al-Alamein.

In the 1950s, with the war over, Wilson MacArthur, still saw plenty of soldiers and encampments in this area.

Sollum

Sollum is the Banaris, Plynus Portus, Catabathmus Magnus, and Catabathmus Minor of antiquity, the Aqaba of the Arabs, and the Porto Rio Soloma on the Catalan map of 1375. It lies along the western edge of the Bay of Sollum, 95 kilometers (60 miles) west of Sidi Barrani. It is the westernmost town in Egypt and sits close to the border with Libya.

At Sollum the escarpment that has separated the coast from the interior desert comes north to the edge of the sea and Sollum is perched atop a 137 meter (600 foot) cliff overlooking the Mediterranean while its port is on the shore below the cliff. It is in an excellent defensive position.

William Eaton's American expedition arrived at Sollum on April 6–7, 1805, after a journey of nearly a month. Fifty horses had been stolen, and the remaining animals had not had water for over forty-two hours. The next day they headed west and new troubles erupted: camp was made without permission; Hamet, the reason they were all in this mess to begin with, decided to desert. The Egyptians tried to seize the supplies. Eaton formed a defensive line. The stand-off was defused by Hamet. In a show of strength Eaton had his Marines perform the manual of arms. The Arabs thought the Christians were going to attack them, and charged the line. O'Bannon and Midshipman Peck stood firm in front of the line, and the Arabs wheeled about at the last minute. Again Hamet restored order.

Eaton was in real trouble. He had only six days of rice rations left. When they reached Bomba on April 15, the ship *Argus* was not there. Eaton had signal fires lit. They were spotted by the crew of the *Argus*, the ship having anchored in a better harbor to the west. On April 20, supplies were landed by the schooner *Hornet*.

World War I

The British, who built a system of resthouses along the northern coast, established a small military post at Sollum. At that time Sollum had "three houses on the flat shore of a beautiful bay." It became the base for the Light Car Patrols of World War I, whose task was to keep the Sanusi from joining the Turks against the British.

Despite the beauty of the sea, boredom was the biggest enemy of the few men stationed here and at outposts like it. One man was so bored he asked the adjutant if he could be shot "at the first convenient opportunity." Some soldiers, according to Briggs, visited the enemy over the frontier in Libya. One day they had dinner with an Italian Captain, eating spaghetti, drinking vino di Capri, and smoking Tuscan cigars.

In 1915, the Italians had joined the Allies against the Turks. They joined with the British Western Frontier Force in a joint military operation against the Sanusi. At the same time the Germans were landing "officers, munitions, and money at the little harbours near the Anglo–Italian frontiers so frequently and regularly that the Senussi were able to commence and carry on the war."

The British set up a blockade. By mid-August of 1915 a submarine was driven ashore just west of Sollum. The Sanusi returned the crew and apologized. In November, the patrol boat *Tara* was torpedoed off Sollum and the crew captured. Sayyid Ahmad, the Sanusi leader, said he knew nothing of their fate. Soon another boat, the *Morrina*, met a similar fate. Both crews were captured by the Sanusi and taken inland some 192 kilometers (120 miles) to Bir Hakim. Then an Egyptian coastguard cruiser was sunk in Sollum harbor by the Germans and the Sanusi attacked three coastguard posts. The war was underway.

A Turco–Sanusi force attacked Sollum and Sidi Barrani on November 23, 1915. Over 10,000 men advanced as far as Mersa Matruh. They were defeated. De Casson remembers, "The wretched Beduin of the Maryut and farther west, who had been enticed away with their herds to the Senussi early in November 1915, soon found that they had to decide between starvation with the Senussi or to return broken to the British camp. I well remember seeing these people coming back in a half-starved state, mostly gaunt old men, women, and children. The British fed them and allowed them to pass back to their lands."

The decisive battle for Sollum was fought on March 14, 1916, when the British, who had retreated from Sollum the year before, charged up Naqb Halfaya and recaptured the outpost. The Sanusi leader Sayyid Ahmad and his troops took off for Siwa, then Dakhla, and finally into what is now Libya, on a mad dash across the desert in a final attempt to hold the empire together. He later sought asylum in Turkey.

In the meantime the British sent the Light Car Patrols across the unknown desert from Sollum to Bir Hakim to rescue the prisoners from the *Tara* and *Morrina*. Led by the Duke of Westminister, who received the DSO award for his gallantry, the prisoners were recaptured.

While all of these events were taking place, Sollum was a single street lined with huts for houses. When the Camel Corps arrived in 1920–21, two camps were established. The first was the official camp, and the second was called the Booza Camp, where about twelve Sudanese widows and divorcees made a drink from barley called *marissa*. Belgrave tells us the drink and the second camp caused a lot of trouble with the wives of the men.

World War II

A few decades later, the Axis and Allied armies fought for possession of Sollum's harbor and cliffs. During the siege of Tobruk the pass was manned by German artillery supplied with 88mm anti-aircraft guns. They had dug in along the cliffs overlooking the pass and as the British tanks began their charge up the pass, the 88s pounded them, knocking out eleven of the twelve lead tanks. The British attempted the assault five times and five times they were stopped. Sollum and its harbor remained in Axis control until their defeat at al-Alamein.

Operation Crusader, the British Army's attempt to free the besieged Australians at Tobruk and retake Tripoli, began at Sollum. Operation Crusader was the first victory for the British against Rommel. They had pushed the Axis out of Cyrenaica.

The Border with Libya

Sollum is the last Egyptian city in the Western Desert before the Libyan border. The establishment of this border makes an interesting story. The medieval Arab writer Abu al-Fida defined the border: "the common boundary of Egypt and al-Magreb is a line drawn between a certain mountain on the coast [implied to be the lesser Catabathmus] to the tract of al-Vahat [al-Wahat – oases], and hence along it to the boundary of Nubia." That is almost where the border is today. During the Ottoman Empire the border between Egypt and what was then called Tripolitania, was at Ras al-Kanayis (Hikma), over 50 kilometers (31 miles) to the east of Mersa Matruh.

During the Second Italo–Sanusi War, the

Italians erected a barbed-wire barrier along the frontier to keep the Libyan patriot Omar Mukhtar from getting supplies and escaping into Egypt to regroup. It was 9 meters thick and 1.5 meters high and became known as 'the wire.' When Rommel made his 'dash for the wire' near Sollum, this was it. It was along this line, from the Mediterranean to Jaghbub Oasis, that the Italians erected forts Capuzzo near Sollum and Maddalena further south.

The French did the same thing in Algeria in the 1950s to keep the guerrillas from crossing into Morocco. The French barbed-wire nightmare was a thousand kilometers long with concrete forts erected every few kilometers (they were within eyesight of each other).

Italy and Britain fixed the border we have today. In 1927 the two foreign powers met and signed the Italo–Egyptian Accord, which established the border. The Accord used British names created by the men of the Light Car Patrols to define the location: "west of Williams's Pass," for example. In the interior, along the Great Sand Sea, the border would be the 25th meridian all the way to Gebel Uwaynat. If they had used the meridian to the north, all the important desert towns (Siwa, Jaghbub, Kufra) would be in Libya. Clayton for the British and Campo for the Italians began the task of surveying the frontier and placing markers along the line from the Mediterranean well into the sand sea. 187 pillars were placed for a distance of 320 kilometers (200 miles).

From the sea near Sollum the border follows the winding Masrab al-Sheferzen until beyond Siwa and Jaghbub oases. Siwa was to remain in Egypt while Jaghbub was to belong to Libya. Placing Siwa in one country and Jaghbub in another was an important political decision because it stopped the desert traffic along the famous caravan trails that the Sanusi had created during the last century, and most assuredly put an end to any attempt at reviving the now practically defunct religious order. It also split families, who had to travel north to the coast and then south again to visit.

In December of 1937, masonry pillars replaced the markers of 1927. A new commission was organized to inspect the pillars.

9

Siwa

From Mersa Matruh: the Masrab al-Istabl

			km	total km
Mersa Matruh	N 31 22	E 25 32	0	0
Shali	N 29 14	E 25 32	300	300

Although the drive to Siwa is over the Masrab al-Istabl, used by Alexander the Great, it is not impressive. It is flat desert so lacking in landmarks that it is easy to understand how Alexander's guides lost their way. There may be an occasional black Bedouin tent, a herd of camels grazing on the scrub near the coast, or road signs indicating oil company camps located in the area, but on the whole there is little to break the monotony The road was paved two decades ago and is in very good condition. There is a very modest resthouse at the half-way point. The best thing about the road is that where once travelers took five to seven days to journey to Siwa, today it is three to four hours.

At the escarpment the scenery changes dramatically as conical hills begin to dot the landscape. We are told that 35 kilometers (22 miles) east, one of these hills is called Gebel Iskander by the Bedouin and they found ancient amphorae here. One more ancient water depot in the desert. The descent into the oasis via Naqb al-Migahhiz is straight and quick. Almost immediately the entire oasis comes into view: Gebel al-Mawta to the left, Shali directly ahead, Birket Siwa and Gebel Bayda to the right.

From Bahariya along the Darb Siwa

For great adventure the desert route from Bahariya is the way to go to Siwa. From Bahariya Oasis the route passes through Sitra Oasis, beside Nuwamisa Oasis with its picturesque lake, and Bahrein Oasis, with not one but two lakes. With the chalky white Areg Oasis on the left it continues north over the dunes to Siwa.

Covering 400 kilometers (250 miles), this is a route with no people and no petrol. Travelers must be extremely cautious and carry extra petrol, oil, fan belts, water, and at least two spare tires, both with rims. No one is permitted to travel this route without permission from the Egyptian military, which as of this writing is granted from Siwa to Bahariya, but not granted from Bahariya to Siwa. Both ends of the route have road blocks where the proper papers must be presented in order to pass. For those who want the adventure, but not the responsibility of such a trip, there are several tourist agencies that now offer 4x4 tours to the area. (For a description of this route, see Bahariya Oasis.)

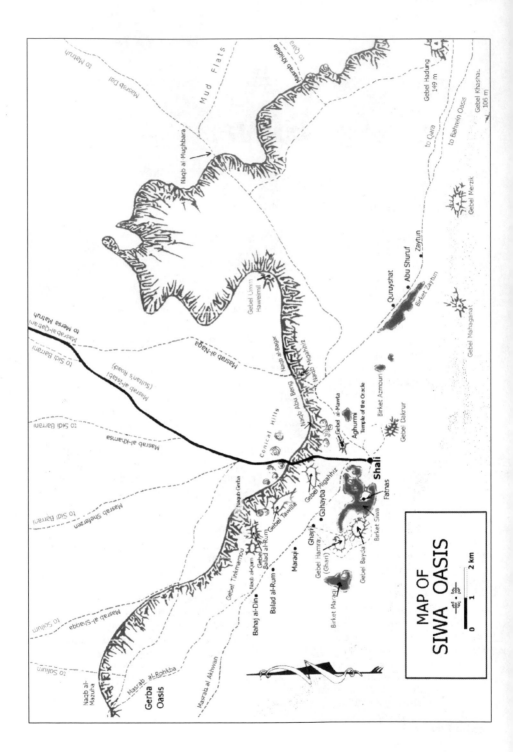

MAP OF SIWA OASIS

0 1 2 km

Siwa

Siwa is different. It is not Egyptian but North African. Most Siwans are Berbers, a people that once roamed the North African coast from Tunisia to Morocco. The Berbers are the true Western Desert indigenous people. As early as 10,000 B.C. they inhabited the area: as the land dried, they moved toward the coast; as conquerors invaded, they moved to the interior. When the Arab invaders came in the seventh century they slowly changed the sedentary Berbers until in the twelfth century the Berbers, too, were Bedouin, nomads. Because of this connection, the Siwan language, traditions, rites, dress, decorations, and tools are mostly alien to the other oases in the Western Desert. They are more closely aligned with the peoples of the Maghreb, the northern coast of Africa from Tripoli to Morocco. This is also true of the history of the oasis.

History

Wilfred Jennings-Bramley wrote that Siwa "cannot be said to have fallen from its high estate, for it is probably much as it was when Herodotus, Strabo, Diodorus, Plutarch, and Pliny though it worthy of mention; only it has stood still while the world went on."

Siwa has answered to a host of names through the centuries: it was called Santariya by the Arabs, the Oasis of Jupiter-Amun, Marmaricus Hammon, and Field of Palm Trees. Known to have been inhabited in Paleolithic and Neolithic times, Bayle St. John believed that Siwa was the capital of an ancient kingdom that included Qara, Arashieh (perhaps Areg), and Bahrein. This, according to the Siwan history, was when the oasis was called Santariya and its dominions included Nubia. During the Old Kingdom it was a part of Tehenu, Olive Land, which seems to have been a huge area extending as far east as Mareotis.

Ancient Egypt

Little is known about Siwa during the thousands of years of the ancient Egyptian civilization. No monuments from any of the three major Egyptian periods, the Old, Middle, or New kingdoms have been found in Siwa. There are indications that, along with other oases, it was colonized by Ramses III. Evidence exists from the Twenty-sixth Dynasty (663–525 B.C.) to indicate that Siwa was a part of the Egyptian empire during that time.

Once the Greeks established themselves in Cyrene (in present-day Libya), legend tells us the Oracle of Amun was discovered and elevated to a place of honor among the Greeks. One by one, great leaders came for advice and focus. Like the great medieval knights to follow centuries later, they had to endure great hardship to reach their 'quest' and once there, did not always like what they were told. The most important visitor of all was Alexander the Great.

Alexander the Great

After conquering Egypt (331 B.C.) and founding the city of Alexandria, Alexander, like Perseus and Hercules before him, made the long and exhausting eight-day journey far into the Libyan Desert to consult the famous Oracle of Amun. Alexander's journey, with only a handful of men, is recorded in a number of ancient sources including Arrian's *The Campaigns of Alexander*. The caravan got lost, ran out of water, and was caught in an unusual rainstorm. Marching across al-Diffa to Mersa Matruh, the procession cut south toward Siwa.

Arrian records that half way along the desert route the guides lost their way and the expedition was saved only by the miraculous intervention of two hissing snakes (Diodorus says crows) who led the caravan into Siwa.

But the trip was worth the sacrifice for when they reached Siwa the Oracle pronounced Alexander a god. Thereafter his name was forever linked with Egypt and upon his death Alexander's body was returned to Egypt for burial. The myth connected with his burial maintains that upon his request Alexander's body was brought to Memphis like the Egyptian pharaohs before him, but the high priest refused to bury him there, saying, "Do not settle him here, but at the city he has built at Rhakotis [Alexandria], for wherever this body must lie the city will be uneasy, disturbed with wars and battles." So he was supposedly brought to Alexandria and buried. (See Doric Temple in this chapter for details.)

Alexandria became the capital of Ptolemaic Egypt, ruled by the descendants of Ptolemy I, a general of Alexander. The last of the Ptolemy line was Cleopatra VII, the fabled queen who shook the Roman Empire. The northern coast of Egypt was Cleopatra's playground and it is possible that she came to Siwa, not only to visit the Oracle, but to bathe in the spring that now bears her name. After her, the Roman emperor Augustus sent political prisoners to Siwa, making it, like the oases in the south, a place of banishment.

Christian Era

Although many sources say there is no evidence that Christianity ever came to Siwa, Bayle St. John says it did and that the Temple of the Oracle became the Church of the Virgin Mary while monasteries were established throughout the oasis. Synesius, Bishop of Ptolemais, describes the church as a ruin in the fifth century because the desert Bedouin overran and destroyed it. Athanasius, the sometimes exiled Bishop of Alexandria, tells us that old men and bishops were banished to Jupiter Ammon from the Thebaid. Little else is known.

Islamic Era (641–1798)

Islam came to Siwa in 708, in the form of Musa Ibn Nusayr, although it had little initial success. The Siwans, now possibly Christians, walled themselves within their fortress and fought valiantly against the invaders, destroying a great part of Nusayr's army. He went away. Two years later he was followed by Tariq Ibn Ziyad of Spain. He, too, was defeated. Both men said the gates to the city were made of iron. It wasn't until 1150 that Islam was established in Siwa. (Some sources say earlier.)

In 1203, the population of Siwa had declined to fewer than 40 men. Moving from the ancient city of Aghurmi, these 40 founded the present city which the Siwans call Shali, the town. Maqrizi, the Islamic historian, tells us that Siwa was now known for its emerald and iron mines and 600 people lived in the oasis. He also tells us that it was inhabited by strange and fearsome animals and strange diseases and its fertility was legendary. Maqrizi saw an "orange-tree as large as an Egyptian sycamore, producing fourteen thousand oranges every year." Siwa exported crops to Egypt and Cyrene, but whether it had trees that produced in the abundance Maqrizi saw is questionable. At this point it may have been an independent republic.

A tale is told in the *Siwan Manuscript* of a benevolent man who arrived in Siwa at this time. He planted date trees and after a trip to Mecca brought thirty Arabs and Berbers to live in the oasis, establishing his followers in the western part of Shali. The seeds of yet another chapter in the violent lore of Siwa were sown, for the original inhabitants, who became known as the Easterners, refused to settle down peacefully with the new arrivals. (To this day western families are proud to be descended from 'The Thirty.') The battles between the Easterners and the Westerners became legendary and over the centuries, walled up together within the small confines of the fortress, their ancient enmity would sporadically surface in bursts of short, but intense, violence.

C. Dalrymple Belgrave seems to have had access to the *Siwan Manuscript* for he wrote a lot about Siwan history. Around 1700, a quarrel began because a family on the east side tried to enlarge their house. The house would have taken up a portion of the already narrow street and the neighbor on the western side objected. Everyone took sides and the battle was on.

These battles followed a time honored battle plan:

> A sheakh sounded a drum as a declaration of hostilities. The combatants then assembled to fight the battle with their adversaries. The women stood behind their husbands to excite their courage; each of whom had a sack of stones in her hand, to cast at the enemy, and even at those of their own party who should be tempted to fly before the close of the combat.
>
> At the beat of the drum, small platoons advanced successively from both sides, rushing furiously toward each other. They never placed their guns to the shoulder, but fired carelessly with their arms extended, and then retired. No person was allowed to fire his gun more than once; and when all had thus performed their part, whatever might be the number of dead or wounded, the sheakh beat his drum, and the combat ceased.

Muhammad Ali and the Europeans

Unable to assimilate dirty people, the Siwans, both Easterners and Westerners, were never able to accept travelers who encroached on their way of life. The first European known to have visited Siwa Oasis was W. G. Browne in February and March of 1792. He came with a date caravan, disguised as an Arab, and hoped to find the oasis itself and the site of the ancient Oracle. He traveled beside the Mediterranean for seventy-five hours and then, on March 4, left the coast. He passed through Qara on the way to Siwa.

The Siwans turned on Browne because he was impersonating a Muslim. He had to remain indoors at all times. Finally, on the fourth day of his stay he was permitted to venture out. He found the temple, but thought it too small to be of such importance.

Next came Frederick Hornemann, a German traveler for The African Association, who was also accosted. He, too, traveled with a date caravan. He managed to fool the Siwans and remained in the oasis for eight days. On his departure it was discovered that he was a foreigner and he was chased through the desert. His Arab interpreter ran away in fear, taking with him all Hornemann's plundered artifacts: mummies, mineralogical specimens, and a detailed account of the expedition. He allegedly buried them and they remain buried somewhere in the Western Desert today. Hornemann made his way to the Libyan oasis of Murzuk, where his bad luck continued, and he died before his journey was over.

In 1819–20, Muhammad Ali began his conquest of the oases. He sent 2,000 (Belgrave says 1,300) men under the leadership of Hassan Bey Shamashurghi to Siwa in 1819. The ensuing battle lasted three hours. The Siwans had flooded the area around their fortress, but this medieval defense, probably used for centuries, had not counted on modern artillery. Although they had enlisted the help of 100 Arabs from a Benghazi caravan, the Siwans finally had to yield to the superior force, and they had to pay a tribute of 2,000 pounds (a formidable sum to people who seldom saw money).

Accompanying Shamashurghi was the French Consul Bernardino Drovetti and his friends the artist and engineer Louis Linant de Bellefonds (who became Minister of Public Works in 1869), the physician Alessandro Ricci (an Italian doctor who sometimes worked for Belzoni), and Enegildo Frediani (a pharmacist who eventually went insane). Some sources states that the French secret agent Vincent Boutin accompanied Drovetti on this visit, but this is improbable for although he was a good friend of Drovetti, and did visit Siwa, he was assassinated in Baalbek in 1815. Despite Boutin, each of these travelers had something to say about what they saw, and they saw more antiquities than exist today. Frediani published his letters, and Drovetti wrote official notes for his files. In 1834, information about the Siwan language was discovered among Drovetti's notes and published by Jomard. In some instances their records are our only sources.

In the same year, Frederic Cailliaud, a mineralogist and envoy of the Pasha, and Pierre Letorzec, a French sailor, fared better. They tricked the Siwans by producing a firman said to be permission from the Pasha for them to visit the oasis. The Siwans welcomed them. In fact, the firman was from the Pasha of Souakin on the Red Sea and had nothing whatever to do with Siwa. Cailliaud and friends visited the tombs at Gebel Mawta and antiquities in the west of the oasis. After much bribery they were about to visit the temple of the Oracle when the party was obliged to leave the oasis in the company of a departing caravan for safety's sake. Cailliaud gave us the first scientific report on the oasis including the fact that it was below sea level. He published a book and a 470-word lexicon of the Siwan language.

The Prussian Heinrich Von Minutoli arrived in Egypt in September of 1820 and before the year was out visited Siwa. We owe the in-depth illustrations and accounts of the antiquities of Siwa, especially drawings of the Umm Ubayd temple, to Minutoli. They serve as the temple's most important record for it was blown up not too long afterwards.

Muhammad Ali continued his lengthy campaign to subdue the Siwans. He would send soldiers, the people would resist, then agree to pay tribute, then refuse to send the tribute to Cairo or permit strangers into their town, and Muhammad Ali would send soldiers again. This continued until 1829 when 600 men conquered Siwa (Belgrave says 1827 and 800 men). Eighteen sheikhs were executed, 20 were banished, the tribute was increased, and a permanent governor was appointed. Hasan Bey was ruthless. He seized money, slaves, dates, and silver ornaments as payment on the Siwan debt. He also built the first *markaz*, or government office, behind Qasr Hassuna.

In 1824, Pacho came to Siwa a number of times during his six-month North African journey. None of his findings were made known. By 1837, travel to Siwa was considered safe. The Sanusi established their first *zawya* of the entire Western Desert here in 1843. (For details on the Sanusi see the People chapter.) In 1847, Bayle St. John, the English adventurer, stayed for some time in Siwa. His fine book, *Adventures in the Libyan Desert*, published in 1849, offers us excellent information about Siwa at that time. He was permitted to see the gardens and the temple, but was not permitted to enter Shali.

James Hamilton, Siwa's next visitor, did not fare as well as St. John. His camp was invaded in 1852, by the *zaggala* (see below) and Hamilton became a virtual prisoner of Yusif Ali, an untrustworthy person who put Hamilton in harm's way only to pretend to protect him. The Siwans wanted him dead. Ali, after aggravating the situation, took Hamilton into his home and under his protection. Then Hamilton managed to have two letters smuggled out of Siwa to the viceroy. On March 14, 1852, 150 cavalry and fourteen officers approached Siwa. A week later, according to Belgrave, Hamilton was on his way out of Siwa accompanied by Yusif Ali.

You would think by this time someone would have gotten the message: the Siwans wanted to be left alone. But because of the Hamilton incident, and the failure of Siwan dignitaries to appear in Cairo as promised, the viceroy sent 200 men to the oasis. They made life very difficult for the Siwans, committed robbery, stole the women, and shot anyone who spoke out. Finally, Yousef Ali was appointed governor, a mixed blessing.

Freedom was not to be. In 1854, a new ruler took the reigns in Egypt. He gave amnesty to all the Siwan prisoners. When they arrived in Siwa they went after Yusif Ali, who was part of the reason they were all in jail. He escaped, was caught, and killed. In 1857, a new governor was dispatched to Siwa.

Gerhard Rohlfs, of whom we have heard so much in this book, came to Siwa in 1869 and 1874. Rohlfs tells us that one of the reasons the Siwans were getting into so much trouble over paying their taxes was that the Sanusi, who controlled the oasis, told them not to pay. They were stuck between a rock and a hard place. The Egyptian government was hundreds of kilometers away, the Sanusi were among them. Either way they were to pay a heavy price.

In 1896, the tribute assessed by Muhammad Ali was still in effect but it had not been paid for three years. Sheikh Hassuna Mansur fortified a fortress and refused to pay the annual tribute. Mustapha Mahr, governor of Behera Province, came to Siwa with fifty men. Hassuna was besieged. When nothing seemed to be resolved, Hassuna asked the Sanusi to intervene. They told him to surrender and pay his taxes. He did, only to die a few months later as a result of a dispute over some goats that led to another all-out Eastern and Western war.

The Widow's War began in 1898. Following the death of the *umda* (mayor) of Siwa his young wife wished to marry again, a Westerner, but her stepson had found a different suitor. She fled to Uthman Habun, a Sanusi representative. Up started the war drums. The woman returned to her stepson. Next day she disappeared again. She went to the Westerner whom she wanted to marry. Her stepson then forced her to marry his choice. Everyone in Siwa, according to Belgrave's view of the *Siwan Manuscript*, was upset and two men were killed. Up started the war drums again. The lines were drawn. By mistake a small boy was shot by the Easterners and a truce was called. The Easterners then attacked a spring. Belgrave picks up the tale:

"Then the entire Western force, led by their chief, Uthman Habun, on his great white war-horse, the only one in Siwa, surged out of the town, through the narrow gates, firing and shrieking, waving swords and spears, followed by their women throwing stones. Every able-bodied man and woman joined in the battle beneath the walls. . . . 'The Habun' found himself in danger of being captured. . . . Habun's mother, seeing her son in danger, collected a dozen women of his house and managed to get near him. He left his horse and slipped into the gardens where he joined the women. They dressed him as a girl, and with them he escaped to the tomb of Sidi Suliman. Habun sent to the Sanusi at Jugbub and they created the peace. This pattern of sporadic, but regular, violence continued until the Sanusi created order."

Siwa became a major port of call for the Sanusi caravans. Situated as it was at the desert door to Egypt, Siwa was extremely important to the slave caravans from Kufra. The Siwans participated in this trade and many of the slaves remained in Siwa either as chattels of the Sanusi, maintaining their holdings in the oasis, or as slaves of various Siwans. Many of their descendants still live in Siwa today.

The Twentieth Century

The first Egyptian ruler to visit Siwa in modern times was Abbas II. He disguised his Austrian wife as an Egyptian officer and made a state visit in February of 1904, and again in 1907. He traveled in the finest style, his vanguard alone consisting of 62 camels. The main entourage had 228 camels and 22 horses, while Abbas rode in a carriage. Water was carried from Cairo in 120 iron chests. Plenty of live sheep and fowl scurried along in the procession and the guests dined at tables laid with fresh linen tablecloths and sterling cutlery. It took seven days to trek from Mersa Matruh along the Sultan's Road. When Abbas entered Siwa, unlike the inhospitable welcomes of the past, all the inhabitants came out to meet him waving palm branches. There were banners fluttering and musicians playing as the Siwans welcomed the ruler of Egypt. In honor of his arrival, the Khedive laid the foundation for a mosque. Siwa had at last been assimilated.

C. Dalrymple Belgrave was appointed district officer of Siwa by the Frontier Districts Administration Camel Corps for 1920–21. As we have seen, he left us a vivid interpretation of the oasis in his book Siwa: *The Oasis of Jupiter Ammon*. The Camel Corps had been in existence for some time and had established their barracks and office half a mile south of Shali on two isolated rocks.

In 1929, the Italian Captain Brezzi crossed the desert from Kufra to arrive at Siwa. In 1931, the bible-thumping traveler and author of *Camels through Libya*, Dugald Campbell, visited British-controlled Siwa. He found Egyptian officials administrating the Frontier District Administration. His camels, as was the custom, were put in quarantine and he set himself up quite comfortably in the very cave previously occupied by the Grand Sanusi at Qasr Hassuna. It was during this era that Ahmed Fakhry came to Siwa.

World Wars

The Siwans did not fare well during the two world wars. They were caught between the Italians, who had colonized Libya, the Sanusi, to whom they were mostly sympathetic, and the British, who by this time had colonized Egypt. The Sanusi entered World War I on the side of the Turks, to whom they owed allegiance. After several attempts, they occupied Siwa on April 1, 1916. They entered Farafra and Bahariya in February of the same year, and Dakhla and Kharga shortly after. Kharga was abandoned after only a few days, and Dakhla was occupied until October 16, when the British dropped a bomb on the outskirts of Mut that sent the Sanusi running. The Sanusi held Siwa until it fell to the British on February 5, 1917. During all this, the Siwans adopted a new tactic. No longer able to fend off intruders successfully, they moved into the tombs of Gebel al-Mawta, welcoming whichever invader came to their town. Thus they survived.

On February 1, 1917, Massey in *The Desert Campaigns* tells us, the British set off from Mersa Matruh in grand style: "Rolls Royce armoured cars, Talbot wagons, Ford Light patrol and supply cars, a Daimler lorry carrying a Krupp gun made in 1871, and captured from the enemy in 1916, and over a score of motor lorries."

They paused 144 kilometers (90 miles) from the escarpment and General Hodgson sent out a reconnaissance to find Qirba, "a series of low hills where the enemy was hiding." Here the first battle took place. At noon the Sanusi attempted a charge, but the machine guns and heavy motorized vehicles rendered their two ten-pounders, two machine guns, and 800 guns useless. All night long sniper shots rang out. Just before sunrise the Sanusi fired two shells, threw their ammunition on a fire, and retreated. The Sanusi lost 200 men..(500 more were at Siwa.)

At 9 a.m. on February 5, the British entered Siwa and were received at the steps of the courthouse. When the British cars came dashing into Siwa, Massey tells us that the Siwans were happy to see them and offered sheep in gratitude for throwing out the Sanusi. They asked that the road up a pass be repaired as the Sanusi had blown it up to keep the enemy out and now the Siwans were being kept in. Massey found Siwa an unpleasant place and the narrow passages of Shali "slimy and slippery with accumulated filth." The whole mess was finished by February 8, when back in Sollum, the British began to plan the rescue of the prisoners of the *Tara*.

During the British occupation of Egypt, Siwa became a tourist attraction. Unlike the travelers of the past who made the journey under peril of their lives, the colonialists booked trips via the Libyan Oases Association in Alexandria, owned and operated by Captain Hillier, formerly of the Frontier District Administration. Clients had a choice of a nine-day tour by rail and coach via Mersa Matruh, or a month-long camel safari via

Wadi Natrun and the Qattara Depression. Once in Siwa they enjoyed the comforts of the Prince Farouk Hotel, also owned by Hillier. It was a small, two-story hotel situated on a spur of Gebel al-Mawta, made of whitewashed mudbrick, with red and black Bedouin rugs. Maximum occupancy was twelve guests. It also had a dining room, lounge, and verandah. Today, part of it is a small handicraft shop.

During World War II Siwa was again an important theater of war. It was occupied by Allied troops, mainly British, Australians, and New Zealanders, and closed to visitors. The Italians had introduced tank and air warfare to the desert in their successful attempt to colonize Libya and during World War II they bombed Siwa killing 100 people and a donkey. Then they occupied the oasis, where they remained for four months. During that time the Germans were also in Siwa and Field Marshal Rommel visited Siwa and had tea in the gardens with several of the sheikhs. Rommel presented the sheikhs with tea and sugar, items which were always scarce in the Western Desert, while his hosts gave him dates and the heart of a palm tree.

At one point Siwa had its own plane, which flew twice weekly to Mersa Matruh.

Today

Access to Siwa was restricted for nearly twenty years and no travelers were permitted to visit. Then in the 1980s restrictions were lifted and travel, although still hazardous, was permitted. The Siwans have opened their oasis to tourism, with restaurants, craft shops, and desert tours. Strangers are at last welcome. Along with the visitors will come change. Blending the old with the new will be a challenge for the Siwans, as it is a challenge throughout the oases. But the Siwans are accustomed to change and have proved to handle it well. Visitors, too, must take responsibility for their actions while in Siwa and other oases communities. Be respectful. Be modest. Leave your beer and hard liquor home. Try to follow the desert attitude. You just might like it.

Geography and Geology

The Siwa Depression, 82 kilometers (51 miles) long and between 9 to 28 kilometers (5.6 to 17.5 miles) wide, is the furthest Egyptian depression from the Nile Valley. Its northern escarpment comprises a system of bays and outlier mountains cut by wadis and passes. The southern portion of the oasis, including the escarpment, is inundated by dunes from the Great Sand Sea which extend over 500 kilometers (312 miles) north to south and 60 to 80 kilometers (38 to 50 miles) east to west. Some parts of the depression lie 60 meters (192 feet) below sea level. It sits at E 25 16 and E 26 7 longitude and N 29 7 and N 29 21 latitude.

There are several salt lakes in the depression, diminishing in size in the summer. Farouk al-Baz tells us that the lakes are fed from sweet water underground springs. In the west are Birket al-Maraqi, 9 square kilometers (5.6 square miles), and Birket Siwa, the largest lake in the depression at 32 square kilometers (20 square miles). The latter absorbed a portion of the former Birket Khamisa, which dried up in the 1940s. Although older maps indicate several lakes in the east, the only remaining lakes are Birket Azmuri, which is often dry, and Birket Zaytun, a 16-square-kilometer (10-square-mile) lake. Any of these could be the magic lake that Arab historians claimed is at Siwa. They believed that no bird could fly over this lake and that if it tried, it would fall into the water and could only be saved by a human hand. On the island in this lake are buried the saber and seal of the Prophet, or the ring, sword, and crown of King Solomon, depending on which legend you read.

Mountains and Hills

Identifying the mountains and hills in the oases is quite a chore, especially in Siwa where there are over 3,000 of them. Just as the people do not recognize street names in places like Mersa Matruh and Dakhla Oasis, local inhabitants in the oases call every hill al-Gebel, the Mountain, without any reference to a specific name. If asked to identify a mountain, only the most prominent like Gebel al-Mawta are recognized. In Siwa there is an additional problem because if a mountain is identified by a name, it is often the Siwan name and not the name given it by cartographers like Ball and Beadnell who mapped the Western Desert early in the 1900s.

There are four important mountains in Siwa: **Gebel al-Mawta**, **Gebel al-Dakrur** (Daran Breek, Bayle St. John's Edrar Abou Bryk), **Gebel Hamra**, and **Gebel Bayda** (Adrar al-Milal, Edrar Amelal in Siwan, Mount Khamisa, Gebel Ghaffir). All the mountains are riddled with caves. Most of the caves are uninscribed; some were used for ancient burials, others were inhabited in antiquity. Arab historians tell of great mines in Siwa where iron, lapis lazuli, and emeralds were mined. Today there is no evidence of the existence of any of these mines, but the people of Siwa are always poking around the hills looking for buried treasure.

Siwa sits at the northwestern edge of the Great Sand Sea.

In the 1970s, Apollo–Soyuz photographs from space showed a small depression 16 kilometers (10 miles) east of Siwa that no one seemed to know anything about. Upon investigation it was discovered that in addition to being totally uninhabited, it resembled Siwa in many ways. It contains weathered land forms, natural bridges, and conical hills.

Water and Salt

Water and salt are the two biggest problems in Siwa. There is plenty of water, with over 1,000 springs currently in use, but it is highly saline, cooler than in the other oases, and not good for watering a wide variety of crops. Thus the Siwans have a limited agriculture, growing only dates, olives, and a few vegetables. The lakes are so salty that no marine life survives and there is no traditional fishing industry. In fact there are no boats in Siwa, which led one European adventurer, the French secret agent Boutin, to transport his own collapsible canvas boat through the desert in an attempt to discover the treasure that was reputedly buried on an island in one of the lakes. The Siwans would not let him use it. But Byron Khun de Prorok did make it to the island of Lake Arachie in the 1920s. He found not treasure, but traces of tombs, flints, and other evidence of human habitation. Recently the Egyptian government, as the British did around the beginning of the 20th century, introduced fish into the lakes in an experiment to create a fishing industry. No one fishes.

The highly salty soil is called *karshif* in Arabic and *ererig* in Siwan, and it is used to build the traditional mudbrick houses found throughout Siwa. Herein lies another problem. The salt comes in huge chunks, like salt licks. It helps strengthen the walls, but is unhealthy, leading to rheumatism, and melts in the rain, making the houses potential death traps. Although rain is not an ordinary occurrence, because Siwa is further north than most oases, it experiences a deluge every quarter of a century or so. After a major storm in 1928, the Siwans abandoned their ancient town. Another major storm occurred in the winter of 1982, when a continuous downpour pelted the oasis for two days.

The third problem related to water is drainage. With most of the oasis well below sea level there is inadequate drainage, which creates several problems. In order to remain productive the salty soil must be washed so the salt can be drained away, but there is no place for the water to go. When it does rain flash flooding occurs. In 1982, floods damaged crops, killed livestock, and destroyed homes throughout the oasis, especially in the west.

Caravan Routes and Roadways

There are probably more desert tracks leading out of Siwa than from any other oasis. Many of them are only a meter wide and in the past camel caravans had to move along these roadways in single file because of the inhospitable terrain. Most tracks are still unnavigable by car, even by 4x4s.

Passes (Naqbs)

Each track leaves the oasis via a pass, a naqb, which usually follows a breakdown in the escarpment. Often times these passes cannot be seen by the naked eye, and some of them may take hours to climb for they are filled with soft sand. Starting in the northwest the passes include **Naqb Sharik; Naqb Mazura**, Pass of the Measure; **Naqb Qirba**, Pass of the Waterskin; **Naqb Migahhiz**, Pass that is Prepared; **Naqb Abu Beiraq**, Pass of the Banner; **Naqb al-Baqar**, Pass of the Cow; **Naqb al-Mughbara, Naqb al-Qarn**, Pass of the Horn; and **Naqb Tibaghbugh**, Pass of Bubbling Water.

Masrabs

Unlike the other oases where desert tracks are called darbs, here in Siwa they are called *masrab*s. Beginning in the northwest: **Masrab al-Ikhwan**, Road of the Brothers (after the Sanusi), begins at Bahag al-Din where it separates from the main route to the west. It climbs the escarpment through Naqb Sharik and heads toward Jaghbub Oasis in Libya and then north, to the Libyan coast. **Masrab al-Rukhba** also begins at Bahag al-Din. It moves north and climbs the scarp at Naqb Mazuha, where once a year the mulid (saint's day) of Sidi Mahdi Bahag al-Din is held. After ascending the scarp, Masrab al-Rokhba drops back into the depression and joins the Masrab al-Ikhwan on its journey to Jaghbub. Sometimes called the **Masrab Haramiya** or Thieves' Roads, these two desert tracks are the major desert routes between the two countries and were among the most traversed routes in the Western Desert during the late nineteenth and early twentieth centuries, when the Sanusi order was at its peak. In fact, the two routes began in Cairo or Alexandria, worked their way via Wadi Natrun or the northern coast across Qattara, through Qara, into Siwa and then on to Jaghbub, Kufra, and Zuila, where they joined the north–south slavers route going north to Tripoli or south to Lake Chad. One could link up with additional routes and end up in Timbuktu in Mali in West Africa. Just north of Zuila, the road is paved with what might be Roman milestones. How much more of the route was once paved we do not know.

There are several routes that lead to Sollum. The first is **Masrab al-Shaqqa** which is also known as the **Masrab Diqnash**. It runs for 310 kilometers (193 miles) from the western section of the depression, over the escarpment, and due north to Sollum. It was used by C. Dalrymple Belgrave, Commander of the Camel Corps of Siwa for the Frontier Districts Administration (see Qasr Hassuna below). The second is Masrab **Sheferzen**, which cuts off from the main road, the Masrab al-Istabl, north of Siwa. **Masrab al-Khamsa**, Road of the Five, after the five wells along the way, and **Masrab al-Qatrani**, Road of Tar, both go to Sidi Barrani on the northern coast.

The most important route to Siwa is the **Masrab al-Istabl**, the Stable Road, also known as the Sikket al-Sultan, the Sultan's Path. It begins along the northern coast at Mersa Matruh and moves south via Wadi al-Raml, Bir Gueifire, and the Naqb al-Hanayis to the halfway point known as Bir Fuad al-Awwal or Bir al-Nuss. Then it continues south to Ras al-Hamraya and enters the depression through Naqb Migahhiz. This road is the most famous route to Siwa, having been used by most desert travelers from Alexander the Great in 331 B.C. to kings Fuad I and Farouk in this century. Alexander took eight days, King Fuad, two. The first car to traverse the route was in

1917, and it took eight to ten hours. Up until the time it was paved, Siwa remained isolated. Today a car can cover the well paved 300 kilometers (187 miles) in just three or four hours. In rainy weather, water still gathers in dips in the road, just as it did when the road was a desert track full of ruts, twists, and turns. Vehicles must move slowly through these small lakes and some are deep enough to stop traffic altogether.

East of the Masrab al-Istabl, the **Masrab al-Naga** exits Siwa via Naqb al-Baqar and joins the Masrab al-Istabl in the north, while the **Masrab Dal** exits Siwa at Naqb al-Mughbara and follows its own path north to Mersa Matruh. Along the way one path cuts south to join Masrab Khidida to Qara Oasis while further along, a second path cuts northeast and heads for Gazalah on the coast. At the eastern edge of the oasis, **Masrab Khidida** climbs over the scarp and heads toward Qara Oasis via Naqb Abyad, Naqb al-Ahmar, and Naqb Khamsa. After passing through Qara it heads to Gazalah on the northern coast. This is the route used by Bayle St. John.

The **Masrab Bahariya** is the only link between Bahariya (where it is called the Darb Siwa) and Siwa oases. From Siwa it travels east via Zaytun, then drops over the southern escarpment and passes the oases of Areg, Bahrein, and Sitra. It continues south on its 300-kilometer (187 mile) journey to Bahariya, which it enters through the Naqb Siwa, just north of Qasr. This route was traversed by Jordan, a member of the Rohlfs expedition, when he traveled from Siwa to Bahariya on a ten-day journey in 1874. It is this seldom traveled route through the heart of a desert wilderness that has recently been paved to form a convenient link between the southern oases and their sister in the north (see Bahariya Oasis for details.)

The People

Aggressive, defiant, and placing a high value on their independence, the people of Siwa are descended from the Berber tribes of Zanatah and thus have a strong attachment to North Africa. True to Berber heritage some have red hair, others blue eyes. There are also a number of people in the oasis of black African origin, brought to Siwa during slave trafficking days when Siwa was one of the markets.

Although Arabic has become the official language of the oasis, the indigenous language, a Berber dialect, remains widespread, both in Siwa and parts of Libya. In fact, Claude Savary, conservator of the African Department of the Ethnographic Museum in Geneva, points out that the word Siwa itself is the "Berber ethnic denomination for the people of the oasis," Swa or Ti-Swa. The Siwans retain strong ties with Libya, only 100 kilometers (62.5 miles) to the west, and some families are split between the two countries. Smuggling is a major problem for both governments.

In an effort to bring Siwa more into line with Egyptian traditions, the Egyptian government has instituted many new programs in Siwa. Governors, teachers, and other officials have been imported from the Nile Valley, while farmers and other laborers have been encouraged to settle in the area. Industrial investments have been encouraged and several factories have emerged. The Egyptian military retains a strong presence in the area.

Building programs have changed the skyline of the oasis. The vernacular, mudbrick buildings, quaint but unhealthy, are slowly being replaced by uglier, but healthier, cement buildings, with running water and indoor toilets. These buildings, not an altogether successful choice for improved housing in a desert environment, for they are hot in summer and cold in winter, will probably come to dominate the domestic architecture of the oasis.

The population has changed through the centuries with the fortune of the oasis. In the early part of the eighteenth century, early travelers reported anywhere from 5,000 to

8,000 people. According to Robin Maugham in *Journey to Siwa*, in 1946, there were only 3,901 people in Siwa. Today 10,000 people live in Siwa, divided into nine tribes administered by nine sheikhs. The Westerners comprise only two tribes, the Esrahna and the Awlad Musa, with the Awlad Musa again subdivided into two tribes, the Eshayin and Lehwatna. The Easterners are the Hadadin, Egwasis, Shramtta, Zanyin, Lehmodat, and Bawna (in Aghurmi). The people of Qara Oasis, called Elgara, are the ninth tribe. Bedouin inhabit the outskirts of the oasis and have settled, mostly in tents, in the west.

There is an administrative mayor provided by the governorate in Mersa Matruh. There are over a dozen primary schools, one secondary school, and one preparatory school, but no trade schools. Electricity has existed in Siwa since 1957, earlier than any other place in the Western Desert. It was then that the Siwans bought their own generator. In 1966, the Egyptian government installed a new electrical system which now operates 24 hours a day.

The *zaggala*, workers in the field, were landless young men forbidden to marry until their tenure as laborers was completed, and forbidden to live in the village because they would be too close to the women of the oasis. Left to their own devices they gained a reputation for homosexuality, a practice that appears to have been a widespread and accepted part of life. Frowned upon by the government and forbidden by the religion, homosexuality is on the wane.

Once employed by landowners who provided their clothing and food and paid them in kind for harvesting the dates and olives, the *zaggala* maintained the security of the oasis—thus their name, meaning club bearers. Today, because most people own their own land, the *zaggala*, as a profession, are no longer a part of life in Siwa. The *zaggala* sang a sad song in their loneliness. The refrain was often heard coming from the gardens at night. It is a long song with many verses, often added to as the song was sung. Here is one such verse:

Afamsa kamel la neqdar issa drarin issa lebhar.
(We cannot bear our situation. It is too much.
There are mountains on one side and the sea on the other side.
We cannot escape.)

Talking to his lover a man would sing:

Igzwet na ganonawe neghlib ga nesbar felawen.
(Come down to us or we will come to you.
We have no patience to wait for you any longer.)

Agriculture and Food

Agriculture is the major industry in Siwa and the most important crops are dates and olives. The dates are the best to be found in all of North Africa. Ahmed Fakhry estimated that there were 240,000 trees in Siwa in 1938 (White estimated 300,000 in 1898) with just about half of them being the *saidi*, the king of all the dates. The Siwans, as with most of the farmers in Egypt, utilize every part of the palm tree, converting it into roof beams, furniture, mats, and baskets. In addition to eating the dates, the Siwans make a date wine, somewhat restricted today, and, as a great delicacy, eat the heart of the palm. Since the removal of the heart involves possibly killing the palm, it is reserved only for very special occasions, and to be offered such a dish is considered a great honor. Date wine, *lagmi* or *lekbi*, is made by cutting off the top of the palm at the base of the fronds and cutting slits into the topmost trunk of the tree. Soon the slits begin to ooze and the sap is collected and then fermented. It destroys the tree, which may take years to revive. Today, if the wine is made at all, it is done in secret (if that is possible in Siwa), as the oaseans do not, as a rule, drink alcohol. In the 1930s, wine and the accompanying revelry was a part of almost every festival.

In the past the extra labor for the date harvest was provided by Bedouin who would come in camel caravans to the oasis and pitch their tents in the arid areas on the outskirts of the town. In 1832, Hoskins reported 5,000 to 9,000 camel loads of dates were harvested in a season. Arthur White in *From Sphinx to Oracle*, in 1899, tells us it was a very festive time. Each tribe brought goods to barter: leather from Sudan, fly-whisks from Kufra, silver jewelry from the West, rugs, shawls, guns, spices, coffee, mirrors, glass beads, and such. The market was so overrun with camels that a sub-industry of selling camel dung for fertilizer began.

The Awlad Ali, following the coastal route, would move the dates to the Nile Valley via Kerdassa (where the Siwans still go for cloth) and return with more goods: grain, beans, knives, scissors, powder, soap, mirrors, matches, sugar, tea, coffee, dried vegetables, woolens, blue and white cloths, handkerchiefs, and leaf tobacco. Traffic to the west into Libya would be via "enterprising merchants and slave-traders," who would exchange sheep, grain, dried meats, woolen coverings, tarbushes, ornaments, and Moroccan shoes.

It would take several months and 10,000 camel loads to get the harvest out of Siwa. The harvest is still a festive time in Siwa. The Awlad Ali Bedouin no longer hold a monopoly on delivering the dates to the Nile Valley. The dates are harvested by Upper Egyptian migrants and exported by truck, many owned by the same Bedouin families who once moved the cargo by camel. Bartering is also a thing of the past, as money is now the currency of trade.

Olives have been important to the Siwan economy since antiquity, when it was called Tehenu, Olive Land. In recent times, olives were the second most important crop in Siwa, but they have recently surpassed the dates for they command a higher price on the open market. There are over 25,000 olive trees scattered throughout the oasis. Most olives are picked green, pickled in salts, and packaged in tins and plastic barrels for export. Siwan olives, like their dates, are among the best in Egypt. There are ancient olive presses in Zaytun and Qurayshat and two modern ones in operation in Abuha, a kilometer south of the market in Shali. Only the black olives, left to ripen on the trees, or allowed to fall and gathered from the ground, are used for pressing. These olives go through several processes. First they are softened between two massive stones, one stationary and one moving over the olives. The rotating stone is attached to a donkey that circles the stationary stone. This procedure takes half an hour. Then the olives are put into a press where the oil is squeezed and placed in large vats. When it settles, the excess water rises to the top and the high quality oil settles to the bottom of the vat. It is then tapped. The remaining olives are used as fodder and fuel.

Although travelers do not bear it out, locals maintain dates and olives were once the only food in Siwa. To this day, anyone may eat their fill from a date tree. Although visitors may fill their bellies, they may not take dates away with them. The trees are watered from the springs which are shared by several

Modern oil press in Abuha

families who keep a *Daftar al-Ain*, Book of the Spring, where quantity, days of usage, and other important items related to the spring are recorded.

In recent decades bees were introduced to Siwa in an attempt to develop a beekeeping industry, but the bees escaped to the villages causing havoc, and were eliminated. Hunting and trapping remains a minor practice in Siwa. There are several types of bird traps, used mainly by children and old men. One is the *alfakhkh*, a handmade trap of rope and wood. When a child is unsuccessful at his work his friends sing *Alfakhkh eba chachaoo tadalt bla hajoo* (a trap without a bird and a basket without its fruit).

Fakhkh

The Siwan diet today has expanded. They enjoy goat, mutton, and chicken. Among their vegetables are pumpkin, spinach, horseradish, and *mulukhiya* or Jew's marrow. From Mersa Matruh they import vegetables and legumes including lentils, beans, and oats, but not by caravan, by truck. Fruit is abundant and seasonal. It includes oranges, cherries, grapes, figs, and apricots.

Even though there are no fish in Siwa, pregnant women must eat fish. This is a custom from the time that Sidi Suliman was born. It seems that right before he was born his mother craved fish. Of course, none was available. Near death, the woman was spared when a pigeon flew into the room and dropped a fish on the floor. Once she ate the fish, the saint was born.

Today there are two olive-oil factories, a date factory, and two mineral water factories in Siwa.

Tools, etc.

There are a variety of tools to help the farmer at his chores. The hoe, or *iturret*, the *fas*, used to cut big branches, and the ax, or *hegari*, used to cut the stems of the palm, are similar to those used in the Nile Valley, but there are several tools unique to Siwa. The *amjir (emishir)*, a cutting knife, is used to saw, chop, stab, and do just about anything else. The *tassnat al-haded* is a 30-centimeter-long needle used in rope making and the *tahessant* is a sickle-type tool used to peel the tops of palm trees to keep the sap flowing.

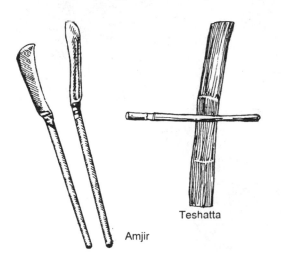

Teshatta

Amjir

Another unusual tool, used to make fire, is the *teshatta*, which consists of two pieces, the tough orange stem that holds the dates of the palm tree and a twig, *elkak*, coming from a specific type of palm tree. The former is braced and held firmly in one hand, while the latter is passed over it hard and fast like the bow of a violin to create the friction to spark the fire.

The Siwans use donkeys as their main transportation, guiding them not with bridles or reins but by tapping their necks with a stick. It is reported that only male donkeys are found in the fields and streets of the oasis and that the female donkeys are kept at Abu Shuruf and used exclusively for breeding because the Siwan men believe the male donkeys become weak with too much sex. This has created a joke among the men in Siwa, "Are you going to Abu Shuruf?" or "I've been to Abu Shuruf," alluding to sexual experiences.

The people say their donkeys are the happiest in all of Egypt for their diet is mainly dates and olives.

The Crafts of the Oasis

Siwa has an abundance of traditional crafts and they are highly prized by collectors from around the world. In 1915, British soldiers bought jewelry and baskets to take home as souvenirs, and it would not be surprising to find that ancient travelers visiting the Oracle also took a trinket or two away with them. Today, the Siwans continue to be aware of the fascination their way of life holds for visitors and well over a dozen crafts shops are open for business. Families who wish to sell their heirlooms often bring these items to the shops on consignment. Since so many items have been sold over the past decade, the quantity of authentic pieces is on the wane and their cost rising. Old items are becoming rare, though enough remain for visitors to gather an understanding of how the people once lived. Through outside interest crafts that were no longer practiced have been revived to service the tourist industry.

The Siwans, like many people in North Africa, use five dominant colors in their baskets, clothing, and other crafts: red, green, orange, yellow, and black. These colors symbolize the fruit of the date tree in different stages of maturity.

Baskets

There are a wide variety of baskets in Siwa, all finely woven by the women and young girls with coils from palm fronds. They are decorated with red and green geometric

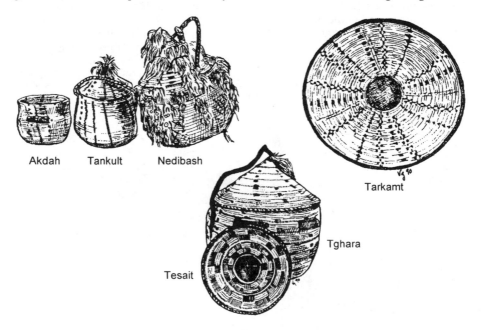

Akdah   Tankult   Nedibash   Tarkamt

Tesait   Tghara

designs and adorned with red, yellow, and green silk tassels which have been hand dyed with natural dyes. The baskets are utilitarian, each with a specific purpose. The women use two tools to help them, the *tussnat nazuma*, a 15-centimeter-long needle made of bone, and an *astten*, an icepick-type tool used to make holes for the weaving of the basket. The baskets are part of the dowry of the bride and she takes an assortment of sizes and shapes with her to her new home.

The *akdah* (*akeda*) is an open-mouthed basket without a lid used as a measure for all Siwan products including dates, olives, and grains such as lentils, peanuts, wheat, and beans. It comes in two sizes: the *akdah*, which is the full measure, and the *arbo*, a smaller basket equal to one quarter of an *akdah*.

The *agnin*, an elongated style of basket with a lid and handle, comes in three sizes. The *agnin en tankult* is the medium-size basket used as a jewelry box for the heavy Siwan jewelry. On her wedding night, the bride goes to her groom wearing the dress of the first night (see below) and all of her jewelry. She carries with her only one item—the *agnin en tankult*. The groom slowly undresses his new bride, beginning by removing each piece of jewelry and placing it in the basket. The large basket, simply called *agnin*, is used for storing flour, and the smallest basket of this design, the *arqaim*, is used for collecting the first dates of the season.

An exceptionally fine basket is the *mamura (marguna) nedibash*. It is wide-mouthed and lidded, used to commemorate a wedding, and decorated by the bride with silk tassels, leather straps, and mother-of-pearl buttons. This basket comes in two sizes. The first is used for storing personal items, collecting dates from the field, and as a lunch basket. The larger of the two is for storing candy and dried grains. The largest basket made in Siwa is the *mamura en tghara*, similar in design to the *mamura nedibash*, but with only one tassel on the top. It is used to store bread and its size is determined by the size of the family. The bigger the family, the more bread required, the larger the basket. There is also a flat woven plate called a *tarkamt* (*terkamt*), which has a red leather center and is used to serve sweets, dried fruits, and biscuits. The same style of basket is made by the women of Qara Oasis to the east of Siwa. The *tesait*, like the *tarkamt*, is a flat plate used for shaking seeds and cleaning lentils and rice.

Wooden Bowls and Boxes

Rare in other oases, the Siwans also craft items out of wood. The *al-hok na shami* (*ol hoa n'shamy*) is a small circular palmwood box with an unusual lid shaped in the form of a woman's breast with an exaggerated nipple as the handle. Painted red, with black and yellow designs, its hand-hewn interior is used to hold incense. Bettina Leopoldo, who stayed in Siwa each winter for decades, believes they are Tuareg in origin. The *tahokit* is a money box, especially for coins. It is shaped like a cylinder with a screw-on, flat-topped lid. A second *tahokit*, a small bowl-shaped box, is called the poor man's money

Shami

Tahokit

Sanduq

box. There are no banks in Siwa and although a few families possess safes, people still bury their money in what they hope will be a safe place. Most find a secret spot in their homes, but others follow the age old desert custom of burying money in the gardens, dunes, or mountain passes. The large red trunks, varying in size from a small jewelry box to a large cedar chest are called *sanduq* (Arabic) and are painted red with yellow and green designs. They are part of the women's dowry and are paid for by her father. They are used to store clothing. The smaller trunks, called *sanduq en lahli*, are used for jewelry. Some are reused ammunition boxes left in the desert by the soldiers during the two World Wars.

Pottery

Like almost everything else in Siwa the pots are unique and come in a variety of shapes and sizes. They are made out of clay, quarried by the men and then kneaded and mixed with straw. The pots are not thrown on a wheel nor are they fired in a kiln, but hand built by the women and then fired in the bread ovens. The round bottomed *trokint* (*halla*), in a variety of sizes, is a cooking pot, lidded *tajin* or unlidded, with or without handles. The *tabaklet (ulla)* is a pot with an elongated neck used for storing water, while the *maklay* is a wide-mouthed, round-bottomed bowl, often decorated with red crosstitches, used as a cup for drinking water. A special pot of similar design and decoration, but having a lip, is the *adjra (abriq)* used for washing the hands. These pots have thin walls and are light in weight.

To bake bread, large Siwan families have a big oven and small families have a mini

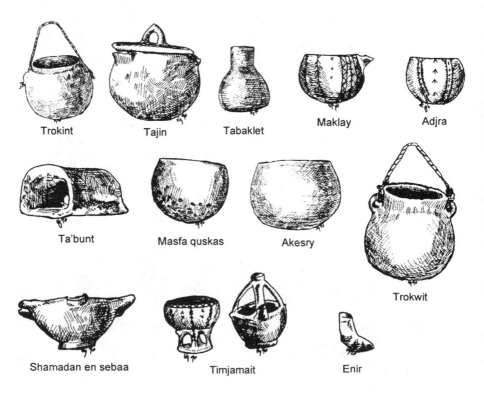

Trokint   Tajin   Tabaklet   Maklay   Adjra

Ta'bunt   Masfa quskas   Akesry

Trokwit

Shamadan en sebaa   Timjamait   Enir

portable oven. The smaller oven, called a *ta'bunt (furn) nil marhool,* bakes one loaf at a time. There is also a pottery sieve, the *masfa quskas,* with a rounded bottom pierced by small holes. The *akosry* is a large round-bottomed bowl used for kneading bread, and the *trokwit,* complete with handles, is used for storage.

A special, strange looking pot with small spoon-shaped crucibles protruding from the lip is the *shamadan en sebaa,* used for the celebrations surrounding the birth of a child. The crucibles are filled with oil that is then lit for the celebration. For incense there are two types of pots or *timjamait (tim'shamart),* both with pedestals and decorated with red cross patterns. The red cross pattern also adorns the *ajirang,* a small pitcher used for washing hands. Another oil lamp, which is used daily, is the *enir nidhan,* which has a long slim wooden handle with a pottery crucible on the end.

Clothing

At the beginning of the eighteenth century the Siwan men wore a white cotton shirt with large sleeves, a red Tunisian cap, and red shoes. In summer this outfit was accessorized by a blue and white linen cloth. In winter, the linen was replaced by a blanket. They carried a long-barreled gun and a straight sword.

The women wore a long blue linen dress, covered their heads and faces, plaited their hair, and wore silver and beads.

When a woman ventured out in Siwa, which was seldom, she encased herself in a blue and white cotton blanket woven at the looms in Kerdassa and embellished by her own embroidery. It is called a *derfudit.* The embroidery at the waist is called *tacksart achtar* and at the forehead *woshilt.*

The women's dresses of Siwa Oasis all follow the same design: wide rectangular sleeves falling below the hands, a squared neckline, and a loose flowing bodice and skirt. For daily wear the dresses come in a variety of colors and are often embroidered at the neckline. Old women, usually widows, wear the *romi,* a dark blue dress with white lines and black sleeves.

The most exciting dresses in the entire Western Desert are those worn by Siwan women during wedding festivities. The *tiddeyen lohreer* is the first night dress. Sharing the same shape as everyday dresses, it is green with red and white stripes and no

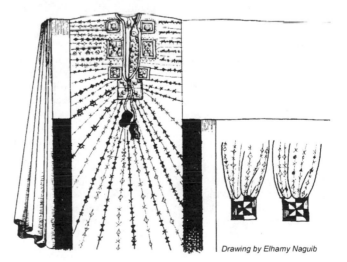

White wedding dress   *Drawing by Elhamy Naguib*

embroidery. It is worn by the bride on her visit to the mosque after bathing with her girlfriends (see Ain Tamusi below) and before going to the home of the groom.

Two other wedding dresses of similar shape are the black silk *asherah nazitaf* (*ashera nahuak*) and the white cotton *asherah namilal* (*asherah nahuak*). Both are exquisitely embroidered with small red, orange, and black designs, which are reminiscent of the sun disc of Akhenaten. They have banks of color radiating from a central disc placed in the center of the chest. The wedding dresses are heavily embellished with tiny, white, mother-of-pearl buttons and amid the buttons may be found an occasional amulet. Today, variations of the design include plastic buttons and sequined foiled leaves or flowers, all in bright colors.

The *asherah namilal* is worn by the bride the third morning after the wedding when she traditionally serves tea to women guests. Up to that time she has been secluded with her husband. Her only visitors have been children who visit by day when the husband is away. The *asherah nazitaf* is worn on the seventh day when the mother of the bride visits her daughter. The mother is accompanied by at least fifty women, who have all given her a token of money. They are received by the groom's family who have prepared small gifts of fruit for each visitor and often offer the mother-in-law the heart of a palm tree.

Beneath these wonderful dresses the Siwan women wear an equally stunning pair of trousers called *israwilen en lekhwatim* (*srauleen hatem*), pants with embroidery. They are decorated with wonderful, heavy, geometric black, red, orange, and green designs which circle the ankle. Extending up the leg are tiny patterns that end near the knee. The pants are cut to a traditional African design and tied at the waist with a drawstring belt tipped with additional embroidery. They also wear a black headscarf, the *truket*. Made of silk, it, too, is heavily embroidered with typical Siwan designs.

Although the women dye embroidery threads with their own natural dyes, in times past all the material for clothing was imported into the oasis from the village of Kerdassa in the Nile Valley. Kerdassa, a village of weavers located near Cairo at the terminus of several caravan routes, serviced many of the oases in the Western Desert. Although the Libyan weavers that once specialized in garments for Siwa have left Kerdassa and returned to Libya, and the village has become a tourist spot, the Siwan women still prize products from Kerdassa looms.

Leopoldo tells us that the mother-of-pearl buttons worn as adornment on dresses and used as decoration on baskets and kohl pots are believed to "attract energy from the sun, and transmit this to the person using the item."

Jewelry

One cannot enthuse enough over the jewelry worn by the women of Siwa. Save perhaps for the jewelry of Nubia, there is nothing as stunning in the whole of Egypt. Big and heavy, the design of Siwan jewelry is unique. Influenced not by Egypt, but by the Berber heritage of North Africa, the silver is so exceptional in design and craftsmanship that each piece has become a collector's item on the world market. There is plenty of symbolism associated with the jewelry.

Trying to trace the origin of the Siwan silver tradition is not an easy task. Frank Bliss, a German cultural anthropologist, believes the origins date to the first half of the nineteenth century and perhaps as early as the end of the eighteenth century. Bliss believes that the excellence of the silver itself diminished after 1900.

A Siwan smith, Sanusi Daddoum Aani, called Sanusi al-Gab Gab (knock, knock), is considered the master of the craft. According to Leopoldo he was born in 1868, and worked as a telephone repair man and a blacksmith. She tells us he made his first (whether it was *the* first is not clear) *aghrow* and *adrim* for his daughter for her wedding around 1920, when he was close to 60, and continued to be the silversmith of Siwa until he died in 1958, at the age of ninety. Gab Gab trained two students: Ali Bosaed and Muhammad Abugsessa. Both carried on his tradition and are now deceased. Their silver content is mostly 60 percent pure, with a few items, mostly rings, reaching 90 percent.

In a community where banks did not exist, the wealth of a family was often invested in jewelry. Because the women were secluded, adornment was a safe investment and the family's jewelry was divided among the women. Siwan women did not select a different piece to wear each day; they wore all of it at the same time. The richer the family the finer the quality of the silver, though some pieces were made out of poor quality base metal (mostly from a smith called Amin in Alexandria after the death of the Siwan smiths).

Around her neck the Siwan woman wore several *aghaiz*, necklaces, and among the most fascinating items in the entire Siwan collection are the *aghrow*

Aghrow and adrim

(aghraw) and *adrim*. The *aghrow* is a heavy, solid silver coil open at the back with a loop on one side (the vagina) and a hook on the other (the penis). A wire is wrapped nine times around the loop side representing the nine months of pregnancy. It is thicker on the loop side and slowly thins as it winds around the neck to the hook. The *aghrow* hangs to just above the breasts and is worn by young virgins seeking a husband.

Attached to the *aghrow* is the *adrim*, or *shebeka*, (*higab* in Arabic) which is a large silver disc slipped through the opening of the *aghrow* and hung on the chest. These two pieces were family heirlooms worn by one woman after another during their courting period. When a girl was eligible for marriage she would don the necklace and wear it until the night before her wedding. It was the only piece of jewelry unmarried girls were permitted to wear. Then came the traditional maiden's bath, when, accompanied by her sisters and her friends, the young woman visited one of the nearby springs for a ritual bath and passed the *adrim* along to the next eligible female of her family (early accounts maintain she would throw the disc into the water and once the party was gone young boys would dive in and retrieve it for the family). She continued to wear the *aghrow* during her married life. Women in poor families who could not afford even the basest of metals for an *adrim* would wear a red leather pouch in its place.

Although all *aghrows* and *adrims* have the same shape and size, motifs vary. Most *aghrows* are plain, but the especially fine ones have patterns incised along the spine. All *adrims* are patterned. One of the oldest designs is a cross with a star in each of the corners created by the cross. Other patterns often involve fish motifs.

Accompanying the *aghrow* and *adrim* was the *tashabat*, a silver tube decorated with flowers from which chains terminating in bells were hung. This was often worn beneath or in front of the *adrim* and was replaced by the red leather pouch by the poor.

The *aghaiz nesalhat* (*salhayat*) is another exotic fertility necklace worn by Siwan women. It is created mainly from *hilals*. The *hilal* is an unusually shaped ornament found throughout North Africa, especially Tunisia. Designs vary, as do shapes and sizes, but among the most common motifs are fish, stars, crescents, and wheels. Although the basic shape is the same, slight variations and distortions exist. The largest individual *hilals* are approximately 3.5 to 4 inches in length and 2 inches in width and the smallest are about an inch long. The *nesalhat* consists of six *hilal*s, separated by coral or plastic beads. Traditionally, whenever a woman bears a male child she breaks one of the bottom horns of a *hilal*. Bachinger and Schienerl believe that the *hilal* may be related to the apotropaic Gorgon heads of antiquity, or may stem from a Moroccan mask motif. Leopoldo tells us that only the rich women of Siwa wore this necklace and it was believed to protect them from the evil spirits. If a woman no longer wanted to have children, she removed this necklace.

Aghaiz nesalhat

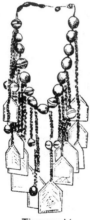

Timeznakt

Another necklace worn by Siwan women is the clanking *timeznakt* (*timiznaqt*). This copious ornament begins with a simple chain of circular balls about an inch in circumference which encases the neck in an 8- to 10-inch circle. Dangling from between the balls is a series of 6- to 8-inch-long chains and at the end of each chain is a rectangular pendant about 2 inches long and pointed on one end. The pendant is incised with a design which varies from necklace to necklace and sometimes piece to piece on the same necklace. The whole piece hangs almost to the waist.

There is one other important necklace worn by the Siwan women and it is not made predominately of silver. It is the *suwedi*, a choker of coral with both glass and silver beads, which is worn by all married women until the death of their husbands. Leopoldo says the women of Siwa believe the coral will keep them attractive. Bliss says it is worn to protect them from the evil eye In any event, the women make these necklaces themselves from material the men buy in Cairo or Alexandria.

Headdresses

The largest number of decorative pieces adorning the Siwan woman were worn on the head. First the women plait their hair into braids (*diderbulat*) much like the fine cornrows worn by African–American women in the United States in the 1990s. In Siwa, the women do thirty-three braids called *tibutibu*, which must each be divided into three strands, or ninety-nine pieces, one for each of the names of the Prophet Muhammad. Unmarried girls wear only two braids, each called a *taderbult*. When they become brides, a third braid is made down the back of the head. From this braid hangs a large silver cylinder followed by an amber ball and then a silver ring with various charms. Ahmed Hassanein saw the tiny plaits on various tribal women in the Libyan Desert on his trek of 1923. He maintains that the plaits were put into their hair at a young age and "although oiled from time to time, never combed out." This is highly unlikely since hair grows and the plaits would have to be redone at least every two years.

The *lugiyet*, or *issudan*, is a leather strap worn across the forehead and covered with mother-of-pearl buttons. Dangling from the temples along each side of the face are

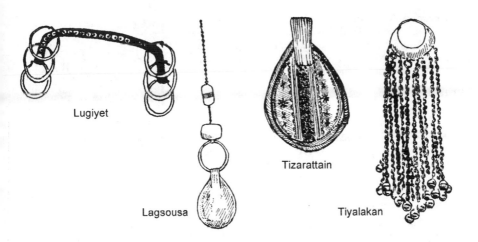

Lugiyet

Lagsousa

Tizarattain

Tiyalakan

three silver rings, the *lugiyet*. This is the rarest piece of Siwan jewelry on the market today and is Libyan in origin.

Another ornament that hangs on either side of the head is the *lagsousa* (*ligsussia*). It consists of a silver cylinder which may be followed by a piece of yellow amber, and then a silver ring from which a pendant dangles. The pendants, called *tichinchunayn*, anything that makes noise, can be a variety of things from the hand of Fatima to sleigh bells on a chain. The most outstanding bauble that adorns the end of the *lagsousa* is the extra special *tizarattain*, an oval medallion of North African origin, 5 to 6 inches long and incised with a simple pattern.

Finally, there are the *tiyalakan* (*tilakeen*), the most coveted pieces of jewelry to adorn the head. An extremely large and unusual set of earrings, the *tiyalakan* is a heavy silver ornament over 12 inches long and 4 to 5 inches wide. It begins with a crescent shaped disc, narrow at the top and full at the bottom, like a crescent moon. Attached to the lower portion of the crescent is a series of heavy, lengthy silver chains, each ending in a sleigh bell. This is the biggest *tichinchunayn* of all. A companion piece of sleigh bells strung along a 6-inch bar is hung on the back of the head. These earrings are too heavy to wear through the ears so they are attached to the head by a leather harness worn like a hat. Some of the earrings have shells and amulets attached to the chains.

Bracelets

At her wrist the Siwan woman wore several types of bracelets, *aswira*. The smallest is a narrow band of silver of Tunisian influence. It is an inch wide and has a bird motif. It is worn constantly by the women of Siwa and in pairs, two on the same wrist. It is probably the only style of bracelet to have been produced in Siwa. The remainder were imported from Matruh or Alexandria.

Bird motif bracelet

Two other bracelets, neither exclusively Siwan (also found along the northern coast and sometimes in the Nile Valley), are influenced by Libyan and Tunisian design. The first, *debelitsh*, a pair of thin 4-inch-long, highly decorated bracelets, is often incised with flowers and fish and one is worn on each wrist (see Bahariya Oasis for illustration). The second is probably the most spectacular bracelet found in all of Egypt, the *ediblidge* (*suarr nguren*). Made of heavy silver and 4 inches wide, it is incised with a splendid pattern of a central raised rosette surrounded by a circle and star type motif on a decorated background. Two bars with three raised studs adorn the sides of the bracelet.

Rings

Siwan women adorn every finger but the index finger with an *emhabis* (*mahbas* in Arabic), a ring. On the thumb they wear an *emhabis entad azoua* or *tad azar* (ring for the thumb), a small rectangular ring with a geometric pattern symbolizing the sun framed with palm leaves. There is no ring worn on the index finger because it points to God, but on the middle finger is an *emhabis entad nammas* (*tad namass*), a large disc with geometric designs, worn on a limited basis. On the third finger the women wear an *emhabis entankoutout*, a larger rectangular ring which the Siwans shaped after a favorite date cookie. This is also incised with geometric patterns. The final ring, the *emhabis entasart* (*tad hekyked*) is an oval ring worn on the little finger. In addition to the above there is a special wedding ring, the only one that has any color. Circular in design, it has small circles of red, yellow, and green enamel on its flat surface. Leopoldo tells us the eight rings represent the eight planets.

Ediblidge

1 Azouza 2 Namass
3 Entasart 4 Wedding ring
5 Entankoutout

Very few Siwan women wear the extraordinary traditional silver jewelry today. It is too heavy for their changing lifestyles and many of them now prefer gold. Since the sheer weight of the jewelry excludes the designs from being crafted in the more expensive metal, many women have abandoned the traditional designs and now prefer motifs worn in the Nile Valley.

There is one other item used by women that bears mentioning, the *tan kult* (*tangkult*), or kohl pot. A beautifully decorated piece, it begins with a bamboo tube over which red leather has been draped. Strips of leather extend beyond the tube. All is then decorated with white mother-of-pearl buttons, various colored tassels, amulets, and conch shells. The kohl is stored within the bamboo and a special applicator, made of brass and decorated with designs, has its own pouch beside the bamboo cylinder.

Tan kult

TOUR #1

Shali

N 29 14 E 25 32
- bike, walk, 2x2
- 2–3 hours
- easy

The people of Siwa have recorded the history of their oasis in a document known as the *Siwan Manuscript*. It incorporates Siwan oral history from as early as the Arab invasion of Egypt in 649 and includes family lineage, traditions, and customs interspersed with daily events in the oasis. The Siwans once denied the existence of this manuscript, but today they acknowledge that it does exist. This history, like similar documents in other oases, was maintained by a sheikh. In Siwa, the family of Sheikh Musallim recorded the events until 1960, when the practice was discontinued. Ahmed Fakhry was one of the few outsiders to see the manuscript. He tells us that Shali, the name Siwans give to their city, was founded in 1203.

The Fortress at Shali

Built on a hill inside a protective wall originally breached by a single gate, the **Bab Inshal**, Gate of the Entrance, the maze of

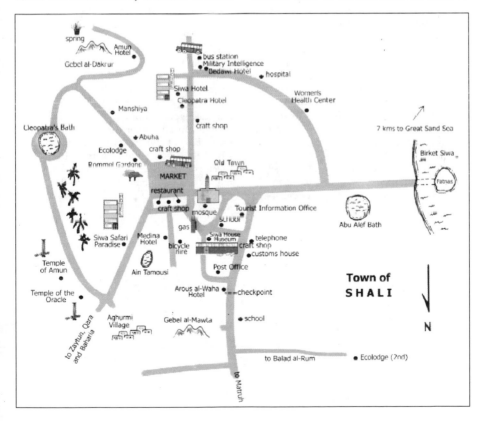

mudbrick buildings that comprises the fortress served the people of the oasis for nearly eight centuries. A second gate, **Bab Atrat**, the new entrance, was added in the 1300s and yet a third gate, **Bab Qaddumah**, was added later (White says that in 1898 it had fourteen or fifteen gates). The inhabitants had to live in narrow quarters, sharing space with their animals, which were herded into the fortress each evening. Since space was at a premium and the only place to build was up, large families often had homes of three, four, and five stories.

The Easterners and Westerners lived side by side in the small quarters, each within a self-contained community. There was a well within the fortress and legend maintains there was a tunnel cut into the sides of the well that led to the mosque in the square below. This tunnel was large enough to contain small houses. Also somewhere within the walls was a second subterranean passage that connected Shali with Gebel al-Mawta. A third underground passage is reported to link Aghurmi with Umm Ubayd.

The huge chunks of salt so prevalent in Siwa were used in the construction of the fortress, as they helped to strengthen the walls. Rain has unfortunately proved to be more destructive to the fortress than any human invaders, for when it falls the rain dissolves the salt. Fakhry notes a three-day rain in 1928, after which the fortress was abandoned, a one-day rain in December of 1930, and another in January of 1970. In each instance part of the fortress collapsed as huge holes appeared in the mudbrick,

weakening the walls and rooftops. In 1982, Siwa was hit by a two-day storm. It was devastating, not only to the fortress, but to the entire oasis, where people were forced to evacuate their homes and lost many of their possessions to floods. Walls collapsed, killing the families trapped inside.

Today the fortress is dangerous and uninhabited for no one bothers to repair it; yet it remains a majestic sight. Walk around the exterior to see the walls. Enter the gate and roam the narrow passageways. But be careful, for some of the paths are hollow underfoot and one could fall into a hole. You can hear the hollow sound as you walk. Where once the fortress dominated the landscape for miles around, today its height has diminished; it is blocked by ugly modern buildings in the square below, and with each rain it is slowly dissolving. However, at night lights now focus on the fortress and it glows golden, basking in its own self-image.

The Market

The market fills most of the space in the square in front of the old fortress. The older stands with roofs of rushes and pillars of dried mud are called *dululas*, sun shelters. They barely exist anymore. Although it is busy all week, Friday is market day, when people come to Shali from the surrounding area. Except for several recently opened kiosks that cater to foreigners and sell soap, toilet paper, snacks, and other items, the market is a traditional suq. It is in the market that one finds the restaurants that cater to tourists.

Shali in 1820, from a drawing by Von Minutoli

Siwa House

Entrance fee. It took the Siwans a while, but once they decided on a museum, they created a wonderful one. It is situated in a traditional Siwan two-story home and the interior is filled with the crafts that have become renowned throughout the world. You enter through a garden. The lower floor is a changing exhibit. There are four rooms on the upper floor. On the left, the two rooms have jewelry, musical instruments, wedding dresses, baskets, and pottery. On the right, the back room is a traditional Siwan guest room, somewhat upscale, while the front room, without a roof, is the bath and kitchen of a typical home.

Mosque

Located in the center of a huge square from which roads radiate in all directions, the mosque is dedicated to Sidi Suliman, a holy man who was one of the chief judges of Siwa. During the saint's lifetime, Siwa was invaded by a Tebu warring party and, tradition maintains, through his prayers, it was swallowed up in the desert. (Sounds like Cambyses' ill-fated fellows.)

Each year the *Mulid en Tagmigra* is held in the square surrounding the mosque. Mulids are celebrations held by both Christians and Muslims in honor of a saint's birthday. This mulid is more in celebration of the corn harvest. In Siwa, mulids are attended by men and children; the women celebrate at home. The *Mulid en Tagmigra* traditionally lasts for three days and three nights. Prior to the festivities, everything is spruced up: houses cleaned and sometimes painted. During the day festivities center around the mosque, where a great feast takes place. Food is prepared in the homes and taken to the square. There is a ritual connected with the meal. Because the fields are together and demarcation lines between neighboring fields are often difficult to ascertain, farmers encroach on each others property. In atonement, the food of one family is offered and eaten by the family that owns the adjoining field. In the evening, entertainment traditionally included the *zaggala*, who performed in the fields, and dervish, who entertained in the square. Today only the dervish performs and there is no drinking of spirits.

Women's Health Center

Created for the women of Siwa by Suzanne Mubarak, the wife of the Egyptian president, this center not only offers health services, but has a handicrafts section.

TOUR #2

Loop the Loop from Shali to Shali

- bike, walk, 2x2
- all day
- easy

			km	total km
Shali (at fortress)	N 29 14	E 25 32	0	0
Dakrur	N 29 11 346	E 25 33 219	5	5
Aghurmi	N 29 12 177	E 25 32 336	5.6	10.1
Shali	N 29 14	E 25 32	4	14.1

Gebel al-Dakrur (Takrur)

Gebel al-Dakrur, just a few miles south of Shali, is visible from all points in the oasis and its triple peaks serve as a good landmark when traveling east or west. The view from the summit of this mountain is outstanding.

When approaching the mountain, which is called Daran Breek (St. John's Edrar Abou Bryk and Hoskins's Drar Abou Beryk) in Siwan, one passes through an avenue of eucalyptus trees. The first peak on the right is **Gebel Nasra**. There is a very strong echo in the small valley between Gebel Nasra and the second peak of Gebel al-Dakrur and the Siwans often go here and sing. On the summit of Gebel Nasra, in a tiny crevice in the mountain, is a large vein of red clay which is used by the Siwans to make the decorations on their incense burners and other pottery. It is the only place in the oasis where this color exists. The crevice is so tiny that the workers must send a small boy into the interior to collect the raw material.

The second, or middle, peak is called **Gebel Tunefefan**, Mountain of the Pillars, named after three caves located on its slopes. These caves, which are three of many that dot the mountain, have been in use since classical times, some as tombs, others as living-quarters. The three large ones near the summit are decorated with pillars.

In the 1970s, a 3 meter (10 foot) thick, 20-million-year-old vein of alabaster was discovered near the summit of Gebel Dakrur.

The Siwans believe Gebel al-Dakrur is haunted and on still nights the *afrit* can be heard singing in the nearby gardens. They also believe that the entrance to the lost emerald mines of Siwa is located within one of the caves of the mountain, but it is guarded by a *jinn* and is invisible unless the person on the quest drinks from a spring in the dunes of the southern escarpment. Seventeenth-century travelers maintained that an underground passage leads from this mountain to the ruins of Umm Ubayd and the Temple of Jupiter Amun.

From half way up the slopes of Gebel al-Dakrur, one gets a marvelous view of the oasis laid out like a giant fairyland. The palm gardens form a feathery carpet of green from which the odd-shaped mountains protrude like castles and lakes shimmer like silver carpets. It is a good place for orientation. From the left the sites include Qasr Hassuna, Gebel Bayda, Shali, Gebel al-Mawta, Aghurmi, and the lake.

Sand Cures
There are three doctors at Dakrur famous for their sand cures, a treatment developed for rheumatism and arthritis. Sand baths are taken during the hottest months of the year, July through September. Patients from as far away as Sweden and Germany make the journey to Siwa for the cures, staying at one of the three clinics at the base of the mountain. Early each morning workers dig shallow graves in the sand along the slopes to allow the sun to heat the area. At midday, when the sun is most intense, the patient lies in the hollow and is covered with additional hot sand. Less sand is piled in the area around the heart. Here the patient remains for five to thirty minutes, depending on the prescribed treatment. Then the patient is removed to a nearby tent, wrapped in hot blankets, and asked to drink herbal teas and chicken soup. The treatment continues for five to seven days during which time the patient is forbidden to bathe or drink anything cold.

Festival of Siyaha
On the Festival of Siyaha, Festival of Tourism, which always takes place at the full moon in October, the Siwans gather at Gebel al-Dakrur for a great celebration. A sheikh from Sidi Barrani on the northern coast comes to assist in the festivities and families, men and children only, come with food and bedding and spend three days on the mountain in celebration of the harvest.

Qasr Hassuna
Qasr Hassuna, historically one of the most interesting areas in Siwa, is unfortunately a military zone and therefore off limits. Two of the caves of Qasr Hassuna were used by the Grand Sanusi when he came to Siwa in 1838. It was from his base here that he lived and taught his message to the people of Siwa over an eight month period. While doing so, he hand carved a *mihrab* (prayer niche) into the rock of one of the caves. Bayle St. John called it Sid Hamet.

Years later, when the Sanusi were losing their empire to the Italians and British and had been corrupted into a military force, Sayyid Ahmad retired to Qasr Hassuna with a large entourage that included his harem. This is when the Sanusi lost the respect of the Siwans, for Ahmad, out of funds and on the run, resorted to extortion and forced conscription to keep his empire from collapsing. In less than a month he was on his way to Dakhla Oasis where, equally unwelcome, he remained two months until the British forced him out and he returned to Siwa and Qasr Hassuna. These were the last days of the greatest religious order of the North African deserts.

Nearly a year later, the British, at the Siwan's request, arrived at Siwa and attacked the Sanusi forces at Naqb Qirba. Consisting of 1,300 men, Sanusi resistance disintegrated within a few days and Sayyid Ahmad fled to Jaghbub Oasis (and then on to Turkey). The British occupied Siwa, establishing their headquarters at Qasr Hassuna. It was here that King Fuad built his resthouse in 1928.

The Cave

Near the hill is a limestone rock which contains a cave and a tunnel. C. Dalrymple Belgrave attempted to explore the tunnel when he was at Siwa. He relates the following story told him by the sheikhs:

Years ago, in the time of their grandfathers, Sheikh Hassuna, the owner of the qasr—castle—discovered, as I had, the tunnel in the rock. He naturally supposed that it was the entrance to a place of hidden treasure, but he did not like the idea of going down the shaft himself, and he could find nobody else who would. There was at this time a very venerated Fiki in Siwa, and eventually Sheikh Hassuna persuaded him to make the first descent, in order that he might exorcise the jinns and make it safe for the sheikh to secure the treasure. The Fiki was lowered at the end of a rope, with a torch, a Quran, and a supply of incense. A few seconds afterward the people who were in

the tunnel and looking into the pit were startled by a rushing of wings and a great cloud of black smoke, which was the jinns escaping from the place. When they hauled up the Fiki he told them the following tale. At the bottom of the pit there was a vast chamber hewn out of stone, and at one end of it there was an iron door. When the Fiki began to read from the Quran the door swung open and two terrible jinns passed out of it, escaped up the shaft, and another jinn, a female, with huge wings, appeared and ordered him to depart and to warn all others never to visit the place again.

Belgrave was fascinated and found a Sudanese Fiki who was living in Siwa at the time. The two of them descended into the tunnel. They found the shaft was 25 feet deep, widening as it descended, and at the bottom there was a hewn room heavily covered in rubble. At one end of the room Belgrave did not find a door, but a shaft blocked with stones. He had his men labor for several days clearing the stones, but eventually abandoned the work, disheartened by the lack of progress being made.

Today Qasr Hassuna is a holy place and most Siwans will not enter it. It is best that strangers also stay away, for reverence runs high and disrespect can lead to unpleasantness.

Cleopatra's Bath

The springs of Siwa are famous throughout the Western Desert. Most of them are surrounded by palm groves and some have interesting histories. And they have wonderful bubbles. You can watch the bubbles race through the clear water from fissures in the rocks at the bottom of the pools rising to tickle toes, belly, and nose on their way to the surface.

If the springs are not cleaned regularly, a thick algae gathers on the surface and green stalagmites form at the bottom of the sparkling clear pools. Although there are dozens of springs in Siwa in which travelers can bathe, two are famous, not only for the pleasure of swimming in their bubbling waters, but for the history and events that have taken place around them.

The Spring of the Sun, or Cleopatra's Bath, has been mentioned by travelers to Siwa since the days of Herodotus. Legend maintains that Cleopatra swam here when she visited the oasis and so, it must be assumed, did Alexander the Great, Herodotus, and every other famous traveler. The ancient travelers believed that the temperature of the water varied with the time of day, growing hotter at night and cooler during the day, but this has been disproved in modern times.

Dugald Campbell tells a wonderful story of his visit to the spring. One of his traveling companions had been wounded during the war and had a wooden leg. When he wanted to swim in the fountain, he began to unscrew the leg. The Siwans had never seen such a thing and the procedure and its aftermath caused quite a stir not only at the fountain, but throughout the entire oasis.

Aghurmi

The abandoned village of Aghurmi (Gharmy of St. John; Agremieh of Hornemann; Siwah-el-Sharjieh of Minutoli), the original settlement of Siwa Oasis, sits high on a sheer-sided rock. Inhabited well into this century, the village was the home of the most important temple in Siwa, the Temple of the Oracle. Today the houses of the modern village spread over the depression floor and the deserted rock where the ancient Oracle once attracted the greatest men of Greece and Rome is a sad ruin.

The village is still blessed with an aura of mystery. Many strange events are reported to have occurred at the nearby cemetery. There is, for example, the story of a man who lives in the village today. His mother died before he was born and she was buried in the Aghurmi cemetery. After her death and burial, the dead woman gave birth. The baby was nurtured at her breast within the dark confines of the grave for two months. One day a person passed the cemetery and heard a strange knocking. Fleeing, he soon returned with help. They dug up the grave of the woman and found the baby. The mother, her eyes open, was crying, but once the child was safe, she closed her eyes to rest in peace.

The Siwans bury in a deep trench, placing the body inside followed by a split palm trunk. Leopoldo tells us if an old person dies people eat roasted beans and peanuts at the grave as symbols of longevity.

The Temple of the Oracle

The road to Aghurmi passes through a majestic palm grove and ends around a bend where a flat rock topped by the ruins of the Temple of the Oracle comes into view. It is a spectacular sight. Built during the Twenty-sixth Dynasty, the temple and its Oracle flourished well into the Greek and Roman periods (although the Oracle's origin is reputed to be much, much older).

There are many stories related to the founding of the temple. One tells of two black priestesses (another legend says doves) from the Temple of Amun at Thebes (modern Luxor) who were banished to the desert. The first founded the Temple of Dodona in Greece where she became the voice of the Oracle. The second, after a time in Libya, came to Siwa where she became the Oracle's sibyl.

Another legend maintains the temple existed as early as 1385 B.C. and was built in honor of Ham, the son of Noah, by Danaus the Egyptian. Yet another legend relates the founding of the temple to the Greek god Dionysus. While lost in the Western Desert, Dionysus was perishing of thirst when a ram appeared and guided him to the spring at Aghurmi. In gratitude, Dionysus erected the temple.

Oracles, manifestations of the god, were highly revered in the ancient world. Able to see into the future they were consulted regularly before important decisions were made. Their abodes were usually close to a natural phenomenon, at Siwa the spectacular Spring of the Sun. Sibyls, priestesses who spoke the Oracle's message, were believed to be endowed with prophetic powers often called upon to intercede with the gods. There were ten sibyls throughout the world: Persia, Libya, Delphi, Cumae,

Samos, Cimmeria, Erythrae, Tibur, Marpessa (on the Hellespont), and Phrygia.

Ancient sources, including Quintus Curtius and Diodorus, report that the original form of the Oracle at Siwa was the bezel of a ring, which was embellished with gems including the elusive Siwan emeralds. Later the form became the head of a ram. Unlike the great complex at Karnak, wealth was not important; in fact, the Oracle strove to maintain its primitive simplicity.

The Oracle at Siwa was held in such high favor in Greece that an Athenian galley was commissioned solely to convey envoys to Mersa Matruh, then called Ammonia, where they would begin their desert trek to the oasis. In all likelihood, the Greeks learned of the Oracle after they invaded the northern coast and established Cyrene (now in Libya) in 637 B.C. Then the Oracle was absorbed into Greek religion and associated with Zeus. The Oracle is reputed to have cursed Andromeda and she was tied to a rock to be devoured by a sea-serpent. Perseus stopped off to visit before he beheaded Medusa, and Hercules visited just before he fought Busiris.

It is believed that Alexander the Great wished to consult the Siwan Oracle to seek confirmation that he was the son of Zeus, the Greek god of gods. When he and his entourage arrived, a manifestation of the Oracle was paraded through the city accompanied by eighty priests. After his visit to the Oracle, whenever his image appeared on coins, Alexander was shown with the horns of the ram, the symbol of Amun, the god of gods in Egypt.

We know that Alexander consulted the Oracle at least one more time. When his favorite, and some say lover, Hephaestion was killed, Alexander sent a request to the Oracle asking if he could "pay him divine honors." The Oracle said no.

Cambyses (see Farafra Oasis for details) wanted to destroy the Oracle and lost his army somewhere in the vast outreaches of the Western Desert, perhaps, as Pliny tells us, because the sacred stone at the temple was touched by sacrilegious hands. This would cause a dreaded sand storm to rage.

Cimon, the Athenian general, stood at Cyprus in 449 B.C. awaiting word from the Oracle before attacking Egypt. When his emissaries reached the Temple, the Oracle spoke, "Cimon is already with me!" When they returned to Cimon at Cyprus they discovered that he had died as they were speaking to the Oracle.

Pindar, the Greek poet, wrote a poem about the Oracle that is said to have been kept under the altar for six centuries. Eubotas, the famous Cyrene athlete, stopped by too. The Greek city of Sparta held the Oracle in special veneration and Lysander, the Spartan general, came to Siwa at least twice. Hannibal is reported to have visited the Oracle. The Elians were deeply influenced by the Oracle and kept a list of all their questions and the answers provided by the Oracle, which they engraved in stone upon a temple wall.

The Romans did not hold the Oracle in such high esteem. In 49 B.C. Cato asked about the freedom of Rome and according to one source the Oracle refused to answer; a second source maintains that Cato had come to challenge the Oracle and break its power, so it was Cato who refused to speak, thus lowering the esteem of the Oracle. By the time Strabo visited Siwa (during the days of Jesus Christ) he noted that the Oracle, no longer held in esteem, was in decline.

The Temple

The ruins of the temple can be reached by climbing a well-marked path up the side of the rock. The temple does not occupy the entire area, for it was located within the village, which was only abandoned in 1926 after a heavy rainstorm. Up until quite recently some families actually lived in the temple. The entrance to the site is through the village gate. The ruins of the mosque stand over the gate, its minaret still dominating the skyline. In front of the mosque is the ancient well with several niches that may lead to storage areas or subterranean passages. As mentioned earlier, it is believed that a passage led from Aghurmi to the Temple of Umm Ubayd in the valley below.

The temple is in the northwest corner. Its walls abut the cliff at the edge of the rock and are in danger of falling into the precipice below. In fact, archaeologists have buttressed the rock with steel girders to keep it from collapsing. The area in front of the temple was cleared of its mudbrick houses by Ahmed Fakhry in 1970. The facade is easily distinguished and leads to an interior of two large halls and a sanctuary. The only inscriptions are in the sanctuary. Simpson interpreted the text to say, "Life itself, legs like silver, skin like gold, hair like sapphire, and horns like emerald." There is much evidence of treasure hunters at work in the temple area. If every other mountain in the oasis is believed to contain treasure, then the rock of the Temple of the Oracle must be considered to have the greatest treasures of all.

The Temple of Umm Ubayd

The Temple of Umm Ubayd, tucked into the valley below the rock where the Temple of the Oracle stands, is a pathetic ruin. Also dedicated to the god Amun, it was joined to the Temple of the Oracle by a causeway and formed an integral part of the rituals related to the Oracle and the god. It was still standing when Browne visited Siwa in 1792. Its destruction was partly due to an earthquake in 1811, but mainly due to vandalism and treasure hunters. In 1840, the Turks had a go at it. In 1896, the local governor dynamited the temple to acquire building material.

We have drawings of this temple by various nineteenth-century visitors, and one, Minutoli, who visited Siwa from October 26 to November 12, 1820, recorded in detail a large number of the inscriptions. From his drawings it has been ascertained that the temple was constructed by King Nectanebo II of the Thirtieth Dynasty. Bayle St. John, who came in 1847, mistook this temple for the Temple of the Oracle and was disappointed that so little remained.

Today, as one passes along the track leading from Shali to Aghurmi, the Temple of Umm Ubayd comes into view amid a glorious palm grove. Its ruins are still interesting and a stop, prior to climbing the rock of the Temple of the Oracle, is worthwhile.

The last archaeologists to excavate at Aghurmi were Ahmed Fakhry in the early 1970s and a French expedition in the 1980s. There is much work to be done on the two temples and the surrounding area at Aghurmi before we can fully understand the significance of the area throughout the ages.

Ain Tamusi

The second famous spring in Siwa is Ain Tamusi, where the young bride would come with her friends to bathe on the eve of her wedding. Here she would take her silver virgin's disc, the *adrim*, from around her neck and pass it to a younger sister. Today the bride still comes to the spring, but now she is accompanied by her soon-to-be-husband and instead of bathing in the waters, they arrive by car and merely drive around the spring then zoom away.

TOUR #3

Fatnas at Sunset

- bike, walk, 2x2
- 2 hours
- easy

Shali	N 29 14	E 25 32
Fatnas	N 29 11 574	E 25 28 877

Fatnas

Fatnas is a small island in Birket Siwa that appears on the local map as Fantasy Island. Perhaps the latter name is appropriate for Fatnas truly seems to be enchanted, especially at sunset. Joined to the mainland by a causeway, the island is overgrown with vegetation and the drive into the spring is like a jungle journey. The causeway may have been built by Farag Kashif, the successor to Hasan Bey during the reign of Muhammad Ali. He forced the Siwans to work on the causeway, which was made wide enough for two camels to pass. The purpose, according to Belgrave, was to pass the salt bog at the edge of the lake and make the island accessible.

Deep in the orchard which covers the entire island, the spring sees little sun and the surface looks as black as ink. In truth, it is crystal clear. Around the perimeter of the island is a spectacular view of the lake with Gebels Bayda and Hamra forming the backdrop to the west, and the sand-strewn escarpment serene across the lake to the south. A walk in the gardens shows a variety of trees including banana, date, and olive. It is a wonderful place to sit and enjoy the sunset and local tours do exactly that. A small tea shop offers *karkadeh*, a drink derived from the hibiscus flower. Here in Siwa you have the choice of the traditional ruby red *karkadeh*, or a yellow *karkadeh*, unique to Siwa.

TOUR #4

North and West of Shali

- bike, 2x2
- all day
- easy
- some entrance fees

	km	total km
Shali	0	0
Gebel al-Mawta	1.3	1.3
Birket Siwa	9	10.3
Bayda Gardens	13	23.3
Maraqi		

Gebel al-Mawta
N 29 12 E 25 31

Gebel al-Mawta, Mountain of the Dead, is a conical mountain a little over a kilometer to the north of Shali along the main road from the escarpment. Local residents also call the mountain Gebel al-Musabbarin, Mountain of the Embalmed. Tombs from the Twenty-sixth Dynasty, Ptolemaic, and Roman periods are cut into the side of the mountain. There is no evidence of Christian burial. Most of the tombs at Gebel al-Mawta are barren, but a few have decorations.

Bones once littered the mountain and it is believed that the emerald mines of Siwa are in this area. According to G. E. Simpson in *The Heart of Libya*, Cailliaud found them at Mount Zabarah and presented ten pounds of emeralds to Muhammad Ali.

Despite the fact that the people of Siwa believe the mountain to be haunted and will not venture there at night, it is here, in times of great rains and invasions by modern armies, that the inhabitants of Siwa have gone for protection, living in the caves amid the dead. Unfortunately, they destroyed many of the caves, chipping away at the inscriptions and violating the mummies in search of amulets. The mania for buried treasure includes Gebel al-Mawta and diggers often come in quest of riches. Tradition maintains that Radwan, the king

of Siwa at the time of the Arab invasion, took the bodies from Gebel al-Mawta and threw them into many of the springs in an attempt to poison the enemy.

There are four tombs worth seeing at Gebel al-Mawta.

Tomb of Niperpathot
The Tomb of Niperpathot is a large tomb, and one of the oldest in the oasis, almost certainly from the Twenty-sixth Dynasty. It has a court with three rooms on either side and is one of the few tombs on the mountain with inscriptions, here drawn in red. Niperpathot was the Prophet of Osiris and Scribe of the Divine Documents. His tomb contains his effigy and images of Osiris and Hathor.

Tomb of the Crocodile
The Tomb of the Crocodile is a three-room tomb excavated in 1941. The decorations are poor, but depict the goddess Hathor, the god Osiris, the tomb owner, and several animals, including a fox and a crocodile. The tomb has been dated from the fourth to the second centuries B.C.

Tomb of Mesu-Isis
The unfinished Tomb of Mesu-Isis is decorated on only one wall, but has an excellent depiction of *uraiae* (rows of cobras) painted in red and blue on the

cornice of the entrance. Discovered in 1940, there is evidence that it was robbed in antiquity. The owner's name cannot be deciphered, but his wife's name is legible and the tomb is known by her name.

Tomb of Si-Amun

Ahmed Fakhry called the Tomb of Si-Amun the most beautiful in the Western Desert. Si-Amun appears to have been a wealthy oasian, perhaps of Greek origin, but a follower of the ancient Egyptian religion. The tomb contains images from the Egyptian pantheon, including an exquisite painting of the Goddess Nut standing beside a sycamore tree. Discovered in 1940, the tomb has undergone considerable mutilation by inhabitants of the area, yet there is still plenty to see.

There are many uninscribed tombs at Gebel al-Mawta and Ahmed Fakhry, who excavated here in 1938 and 1939, was optimistic that more inscribed tombs would be discovered once additional excavations were carried out.

On a spur of the mountain below the tombs an ethnographic exhibition fills the interior of a traditional mudbrick house. The display is mainly of the tools and pottery used by the people of Siwa. Beside it, in the former British resthouse, is a handicraft shop.

Scene in Tomb of Si-Amun

Masrab al-Ikhwan

The Masrab al-Ikhwan, due west to Libya, leaves the main road of Siwa 2 kilometers (1.2 miles) north of Shali. For those who are traveling by car or bicycle it is a good idea to pause after 2 kilometers (1.2 miles) for orientation. To the left is Birket Siwa, the salt lake; the flat-topped mountain beside the lake is Gebel Bayda, the White Mountain; the mountain to its right is Gebel Hamra, the Red Mountain. There are a number of outlier hills and mountains to the left along the escarpment, but few bear names. Most of the mountains are honeycombed with caves that date from ancient times.

Somewhere in this area the scientists of the Apollo–Soyuz expedition found a hill almost covered by a sand dune and the top was entirely of marble.

Birket Siwa

The shoreline of Birket Siwa, like all lakes in the Western Desert, changes with the season. During the winter the lake creeps up to almost surround the nearby mountains, while in summer it recedes, leaving space for desert tracks around its perimeter. Shimmering in the bright sunlight, it turns mauve and red at the edges where salt accumulates.

Despite the fact that Siwa is drowning in salt, there is only one salt quarry in the entire oasis. This is located on the shores of Birket Siwa 9 kilometers (5.6 miles) after leaving the main road. Mainly for domestic use, the salt is not good enough to export. A few years ago some farmers tried to cure the olive harvest with this salt, but it resulted in an inferior product and today, somewhat ironically given the fact that in ancient times tributes of salt were sent to Persia, the salt necessary to cure the olives has to be imported from Mersa Matruh.

The gardens in front of Gebels Bayda and Hamra, 13 kilometers (8 miles) from the main road, are called Ghari. There is little here, and it is all private property. There are a number of caves in the surrounding hills to the north and south of the road.

Gebel Bayda (Gebel Ghaffir)

The magnificent monolith of Gebel Bayda is a

major landmark in Siwa. Called *Adrar al-Milal* in the Siwan language it is one of the most dominant features of the Siwan landscape. In the past it was also called Mount Khamisa, named, according to de Prorok, after an ancient Ammonian queen. All white, hence its name, White Mountain, it is riddled with caves along the southern side. Once a year the festival of Sidi Ghaffir is held at Gebel Bayda. Local inhabitants claim that the Italians landed their airplanes on the flat-topped summit of Gebel Bayda during the war.

Today the mountain has received a new name, Gebel Ghaffir, and at its base a new concept in desert ecology is rising. Environment Quality International has erected its new ecovillage here. It has 25 to 30 bungalows. In keeping with traditional concepts it is all mudbrick, charcoal braziers will be used for heat, traditional Siwan beds for sleeping. The doors are all recycled from homes in the area, and the restaurant will feature local recipes.

Nearby is a large top-heavy rock balanced on shaky legs. De Prorok states that the Siwans believed that when the rock falls it will land on a mound where the queen's treasure is buried.

Gebel Hamra

Known by locals as Gebel Ghara (Siwan), Bedouin in the area believe that on top of Gebel Hamra, the Red Mountain, is a stone box that sometimes throws a light at night. Here buried treasure is to be found, but it is guarded by a *jinn*. There are desert tracks going around the base of both Gebel Bayda and Gebel Hamra and caves on the south side of both mountains. In the summer some of them are flooded by Birket Siwa, but a drive is well worth the effort for it is peaceful and a good place to have a picnic.

Maraqi

Maraqi, the administrative center of this area, was once separated from the main oasis by a pass, but this obstacle no longer exists. In recent times it was settled by Bedouin who established the present village. Although they, and most of the villages to the west, value their independence, many of the crafts noted as Siwan can be found here. Today Maraqi is a small village of new brick homes, but a few years ago, before the rain of 1982, the village was all mudbrick. Here on low ground the rains flooded the area, destroying homes, killing livestock, and forcing the people to move to the caves at Balad al-Rum.

Doric Temple

The ruins of this temple sit at the center of the recent controversy over the tomb of Alexander the Great. Described by travelers in the nineteenth century as a perfect Doric structure, it is 45 feet 4 inches long, 23 feet wide, and 19 feet 8 inches high, and lies in ruins that suggest it was toppled by an earthquake, or some other cataclysmic event. A Greek mission headed by Liani and Manos Souvaltzi announced at the Sixth International Congress of Egyptology in Turin, Italy, in September, 1991, that they had discovered the tomb of Alexander while working here. The news caused an immediate sensation around the world.

The Souvaltzis claimed to have found three Greek-inscribed tablets with the sixteen-pointed star emblem of the Macedonian rulers. On one of the tablets, no less a personage than Ptolemy himself said that Alexander was poisoned and his body was buried at Siwa.

Alexander's burial site has spun controversy for centuries. Here are the details. Alexander died in Babylon in 323 B.C. and wanted his body to be thrown into the river so his mortal remains would be of no consequence. This did not happen. His generals made other plans. After the two years it took to build a funeral cart, his body, by now mummified, was en route to an unknown destination for burial when it was seized by Ptolemy. He had been Alexander's general, but was now ruling in Egypt as Ptolemy I Soter. He took Alexander's body to Memphis for burial. It stayed their until the fourth or third century B.C., when it was moved to Alexandria and buried there either by Ptolemy or by his son Ptolemy II Philadelphus. Ptolemy IV Philopater moved the body, along with all his other ancestors, during the third century B.C.

to a communal mausoleum in Alexandria at the crossroads of the major north–south and east–west arteries of Alexandria.

It was at this site that Cleopatra and Caesar, then Cleopatra and Antony, and in 30 B.C. Octavian sans Cleopatra, viewed the remains. Octavian, to ascend the throne of Rome as Augustus, is reported to have placed a golden diadem on Alexander's head. According to Robert S. Bianchi, who provides most of this information in the article "Hunting Alexander's Tomb," the last person of note to visit the tomb was the emperor Caracalla in 215. Then the tomb disappeared as Alexandria fell into a period of political disturbances. By the fourth century no one knew where Alexander was buried.

It seems to have reappeared in the 800s and 900s, for Leo Africanus, Ibn Hakam, and al-Masudi claim to have seen the body of Alexander. None of them tell us where they saw it. Perhaps they never saw it at all, as much that they recorded is questionable. Bianchi has done a good job tracing the historical journey and he reports that the Egyptian Antiquities Organization has recognized over 140 attempts to search for the tomb, including four within the last four decades. The Polish Center of Archaeology excavated in Alexandria in the 1960s at the intersection of Hurriya and Nabi Daniel streets where a Napoleonic fort once stood. They have discovered many Roman ruins, but their quest ended at the walls of the Mosque of Nabi Daniel.

A bit of a feud has erupted between two Egyptian scholars, one who feels strongly that the tomb is under the ancient mosque of Nabi Daniel, and another who claims to have excavated two sub-basements of the mosque and feels that Alexander's tomb is definitely not there. Further complications to finding the tomb have occurred because religious leaders fear that the current mosque is too fragile for such exploration. So, if Alexander is under the mosque, he will remain there untouched. Perhaps it is his revenge for having been put on display to begin with. Liani Souvaltzi, the Greek archaeologist of the Institute of Hellenistic Studies excavating in Siwa, made quite a scandal. Word spread around the world; the Egyptian authorities were first elated and then deflated. Soon her discovery was under criticism and eventually it was rejected by everyone. If Alexander's body is in Siwa, then someone in the distant past granted Alexander his wish, for he has been undisturbed for centuries.

Balad al-Rum

Balad al-Rum, the Town of the Romans, is located at the base of the mountain opposite Maraqi. There are the remains of a mudbrick structure that has been variously identified as a Roman Fort and a Christian Church. Since the area has never been excavated the exact function of the ruin remains a mystery. In his book *Siwa*, C. Dalrymple Belgrave maintains that Coptic crosses carved into the stone were still visible at the beginning of the twentieth century. If it is Christian, it is the only physical evidence that Christianity ever reached Siwa Oasis.

As with most sites in Siwa, the inhabitants believe buried treasure is to be found at Balad al-Rum and there is ample evidence of digging. Slightly to the south in the gardens is Ain Mashindit, a crystal clear spring that bubbles out of the ground and is enclosed by a circular retaining wall.

The small mountain of Gebel Tinkmamou lies to the west of Balad al-Rum. Local lore maintains that one villager actually found treasure at Gebel Tinkmamou and is now one of the richest people in Siwa. Here too, according to tradition, a light is sometimes visible at night from the top of the mountain and in one of the caves the stones tingle like silver coins.

De Prorok maintains that a mountain to the north of Maraqi (which he called Inscription Mountain) is covered with ancient graffiti of Libyans, Ammonians (Siwans), and Tuaregs. He believed that footprints carved into the rocks at Maraqi are the same as those found in Love Mountain 2,000 miles to the west and offers them as proof that the great Tuareg empire stretched to Siwa.

The Masrab al-Ikhwan continues west, but permission to visit this area usually extends only as far as Balad al-Rum.

TOUR #5
East of Shali

- 2x2
- all day
- easy

			km	total km
Aghurmi	N 29 12 177	E 25 32 336	0	0
Azmuri	unavailable		4	4
Mughbara	unavailable		8	12
Ghashsham			10	22
Ain Qurayshat	N 29 12 415	E 25 42 728	3	25
Zaytun	N 20 09 726	E 25 46 381	10	35

Leave the Shali market from the northern exit (see map), and pass through the village of Aghurmi to head east. The road is well defined and easily managed by a regular vehicle.

Birket Azmuri

Four kilometers (2.5 miles) beyond Aghurmi is Birket Azmuri on the right, or southern side of the road. Often dry, the lake bed glimmers white as sunlight is reflected off the salt residue left behind by the evaporating water, and by the light of the full moon the landscape has an eerie, haunted quality. A kilometer later, on the left, is a single flat-topped hill with mudbrick houses on its summit. Typifying what all villages must have looked like in the past, the hill is called Tourert Nakal, Hill of the Afternoon Rest, and was used by field laborers to rest during the hot summer afternoons. Today it has been taken over by the military, who use it as a lookout post.

Naqb al-Mughbara

Eight kilometers (5 miles) later there is a fork in the road. The northern route is Masrab Dal leading up the escarpment through Naqb al-Mughbara, Dust Pass, to Qara Oasis and Qattara Depression. The southern route is the way to Zaytun and beyond through the escarpment to Areg, Bahrein, Nuwamisa, and Sitra oases. Taking the southern route, the road passes kilometer after kilometer of salty soil, entirely useless for agriculture.

A note must be made here of an interesting discovery by the Geological Survey. Ten miles north of the pass is a natural shaft 300 feet in diameter and 120 feet deep. It once had a wooden roof, but this now lies on the bottom.

Qasr al-Ghashsham

Ten kilometers (6.2 miles) beyond the turn south is the empty village of Qurayshat. Nearby is the spring by the same name and the ruins of Qasr al-Ghashsham. There is ample evidence that the area was inhabited in classical times and Fakhry maintains that in antiquity the eastern half of the oasis was more populated and more productive than the western half. Today, although there are remains of a recent village, the site is abandoned. The mudbrick village was established by Abbas II in an unsuccessful attempt to cultivate the area.

Qasr al-Ghashsham, just to the south of the modern village, has recently been excavated by the Egyptian Antiquities Organization. Among the ruins are potsherds, an ancient temple, which was standing in 1900 but is now a ruin, ancient foundations of houses, and a cemetery. Fakhry dates them to the Ptolemaic era.

The Siwans believe that a king called Ghashsham lived at this place and that gold could be found in the local stones. Like other sites it has become a favorite place in the quest for buried treasure. The *Siwan Manuscript* weaves a tale of treasures, riddles, and magic similar to those found in *The Book of Hidden Pearls*. It tells of the statue of a man standing inside a small hill that had a spring that poured its waters over the golden stones of Qasr al-Ghashsham. To see the statue and the gold a person had to drink from a spring whose location has been lost in time. Once this was done the treasure could be found.

Ain Qurayshat

Ain Qurayshat is the largest spring in Siwa, and perhaps in the entire Western Desert. Yet, today, its outflow is wasted, watering only a small, sad looking palm grove as it flows into Birket Zaytun. As with most of the major springs in Siwa, the source is enclosed by a circular retaining wall. This is a pleasant place to take a bath, for the view, with Birket Zaytun lying in a valley below the spring and the sand-covered southern escarpment beyond forming the horizon, is among the most spectacular in Siwa.

A major agricultural development scheme is currently underway in this area. A few kilometers beyond Qurayshat some new brick houses are under construction to be used by immigrant families destined to farm the poor soil of the area. The government is planning to build one hundred houses for the resettled families. Each family will receive five acres and 3,000 Egyptian pounds. The first job the new farmers will face is washing the soil to rid it of the salt. This is not an easy task. The land will have to be tilled, flooded, and drained many times before it will become productive and the process will be hampered by the fact that the water itself is salty.

Abu Shuruf

Abu Shuruf is another arid and abandoned area that was productive in antiquity. Today a bevy of mudbrick structures in various stages of decay dots the settlement. Amid the mudbrick buildings is an ancient temple dating to the first century B.C., which was examined by Ahmed Fakhry in the 1930s. To the south of the temple is an ancient cemetery. In recent times the people of the oasis donated the land in this area to the Sanusi. Currently abandoned, Abu Shuruf will also be part of the new agricultural project.

The spring at Abu Shuruf is enclosed by an oval retaining wall, unusual in this oasis where most of the retainers are circular. The water is cool and Siwans believe that the outflow from the small dam just south of the main spring has great healing properties. They come to sit in the flowing waters.

Two kilometers beyond Abu Shuruf is another abandoned settlement, this time an *ordi*, or prison. In the 1950s, a group of prisoners were sent here by the Egyptian government to cultivate the land. They were housed in the mudbrick dwellings which are still standing, and slightly to the south was the officers' resthouse. The area is fed by the Ain Nakhab.

Zaytun

Zaytun is the last of the abandoned oases in the eastern half of Siwa. In the early part of the twentieth century the Siwans gave it to the Sanusi, who settled 100 slaves at Zaytun to cultivate the date and olive trees. Jennings-Bramley tells us that all the Sanusi gardens throughout the desert were cultivated by black slaves. They were to provide food for any "member of the sect." They would pile the dates under the trees and they were free for the taking. They could not be sold.

By the 1930s, the Egyptian government decided that the Sanusi had too much influence in the Western Desert, especially in Siwa, and asked the Sanusi to trade the land for other properties near the Giza Pyramids. The land is currently owned by the Haida family, sons of Sheikh Ali Haida, a prosperous Siwan merchant who was present when Rommel stopped for tea in one of the gardens between Shali and Aghurmi on September 21, 1942, less than a month before the decisive battle of al-Alamein.

In 1988, a careless workman caused a fire

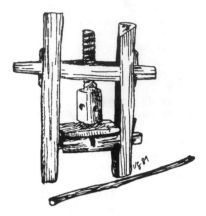

Olive press

in the garden. Left unattended and undetected, the fire burned out of control for several days, destroying over 200 date trees and 100 olive trees. Fire engines were summoned from as far as Mersa Matruh. The fire was finally brought under control, but not before it had caused a large amount of damage. Despite the catastrophe, the sturdy palm trees, bark completely charred by the fire, are sprouting green fronds once again and will probably be back in production in a few years.

The Village
Beyond the gardens is the abandoned village where the laborers of the Sanusi were housed. Although no excavations have been carried out in this village, this is an excellent place to wander for there are several interesting things to see. Entering the village from a passage in the southwestern side, take the first right to an old olive press, still intact. Circling around the outside of the village to the northeastern side, almost opposite the southwestern entrance is a low retaining wall enclosing a mudbrick building with a *mihrab* niche jutting out of its eastern wall. This was the mosque. The passage to the left of the mosque leads directly to the ancient temple. In fact, the temple can be seen at the end of the path leading from beside the mosque. At first glance it is hard to recognize for it is topped by a mudbrick structure. But it is a stone temple complete with inner sanctuary, which the Siwans call the safe because they believed it was a good place to hide money.

Fakhry, who first visited the village in the 1930s, tells us that the Italians bombed Zaytun in November of 1940. Twenty-four bombs fell on the small town, but only two exploded, neither causing great damage. The people took refuge in the temple.

10

The Darb al-Arbain Desert

The Darb al-Arbain Desert (Arbain Desert) is drier than the rest of the Libyan Desert and constitutes a separate arid region; so says C. Vance Haynes of the University of Arizona, who recently named it after the famous desert track that cuts through its belly. It extends from Wadi Howar in Sudan, north and east along the Nile to the city of Asyut, and west into Libya. It covers 400,000 square kilometers (154,440 square miles), a major portion of Egypt. It includes both Kharga and Dakhla oases and extends to the northern limits of the Great Sand Sea.

In the 1990s, this relatively new distinction has been altered and the Arbain Desert occupies only the southeastern portion of the area described above, while the newly named Uwaynat Desert covers the area to the southwest. Although all these changes have not been cemented, this book will follow their distinctions. Kharga and Dakhla have been dealt with in previous chapters.

The Darb al-Arbain Desert, a once remote area, has become most active in recent years. The changes taking place here will have long-reaching effects for Egypt.

History

The earliest known village in Egypt is in the Nabta Playa in the Darb al-Arbain Desert. It was once inhabited by cattle pastoralists from early prehistory. They took milk and blood from their cattle like the Masai of Kenya do today. For meat they ate gazelle and hares. Recently, Fred Wendorf, who has studied the Darb al-Arbain prehistoric villages for several decades, made an additional discovery about the foods of these early desert people. He tells us that they ate a variety of grasses heretofor unthought of, like sorghum. These were found in houses of three major periods of occupation, dated to 8600–8500, 8100–7900 and 7600–7400 B.C. These three periods correspond with the three major wet phases of the Libyan Desert, when people inhabited the area.

Once the wet periods were over, the desert emptied and remained empty until the ancient Egyptian kingdom dominated the Nile Valley. The ancient Egyptians came to this area of the desert to mine salt, dolorite, and other substances and sent caravans north and south through its sands to trade. As far as we know, they never established permanent settlements here. Desert peoples, lacking enough food and sustenance for survival, would raid through this desert to attack other desert peoples or richer villages in the Nile Valley, and carry away their cattle, camels, and women. This continued through the Islamic and modern eras as the desert remained too inhospitable for settlement. Slavers moved gigantic caravans north through this desert from Sudan to the markets of Cairo and Istanbul, primarily over the Darb al-Arbain.

Although Shaw, Newbold, and Murray made excursions into the area, it came under intense investigation in 1962, when Rushdi Said organized an expedition for the Geological Survey. This was at the time of the salvage programs to save the monuments of Nubia before they were inundated by the High Dam. Work has been going on ever since.

Geography and Geology

The Darb al-Arbain Desert was defined and named because it is a single geological unit. The area is primarily covered by Nubian sandstone and sand sheets.

Limestone Plateau

The Limestone Plateau abuts the Nile Valley in the east and bangs into Dakhla and Kharga oases in the north. It is mostly 450 meters (1440 feet) above sea level and contains three wells: Bir Kurkur, Bir Dunqul, and Bir Nakheila.

Nubia Pediplain

The Nubia (Nakhla–Shab) Pediplain extends from the Nile to Bir Kiseiba escarpment. In the north it extends to the rise of the scarp at Kiseiba and runs south into Sudan. It includes the Chephren Quarries, Bir Nakhla, Gebel Nabta, Bargat al-Shab, Bir Takhlis, Bir al-Shab, and Bir Kurayim.

Selima Sand Sheet

The Selima Sand Sheet, also known as the Atmur al-Kibeish, is bound in the east by the Kiseiba scarp. It is a flat expanse of land extending westward for 450 kilometers (281 miles) from Bir Tarfawi to Gilf Kebir. In the north it ends in hills 150 kilometers (13 miles) from Kharga and Dakhla. It is mainly covered with sand sheets and barchan dunes. It averages 170 meters (544 feet) above sea level and encompasses 52,000 square kilometers (32,500 miles).

Precambrian granites are found around the Chephren Quarries and Bir Tarfawi. There are a number of playas, dried-up lake beds, originally fed by surface run-off and ground water. They exist at Nabta, Bir Murr, Abu Rihewa, the foothills of the Darb al-Arbain scarp, Gilf Kebir, Bir Sahara, and Bir Tarfawi. In other words, they form a big system than once watered the entire area and created a favorable environment for both people and animals. Wendorf and Schild hypothesize that the Gilf Kebir could have been the highlands from which all the streams and water system flowed throughout this entire area. This seems to be born out by radar imaging which, according to Wendorf and Schild, shows "a labyrinth of old river channels in this part of the Western Desert."

Today there is no water. There is no rain. Most of the water sources in the region are birs, wells which have been dug at some time and maintained on a fairly frequent basis. They are not springs that flow naturally out of the ground. One important thing to remember is that the water table here is often just below the surface and water can be reached quickly.

Tushka Canal

In 1997, President Hosni Mubarak celebrated the opening of the Tushka Spillway Canal. Twenty-two kilometers (14 miles) long, the Tushka Spillway can carry 120 billion cubic meters (374 billion cubic feet) of water. It is expected to ease the water pressure on the High Dam during times of heavy floods and to open up half a million feddans of desert land to the west of the Nile to agricultural development.

In 1998, the First International Forum on the Archaeology of Tushka was held at Abu Simbel. They proposed a plan to document, protect, conserve, and excavate the archaeological sites, to create a training and research center tentatively called the Fakhry Desert Archaeology Centre, and declare areas like the Nabta Playa and the Chephren Quarries protected national sites.

Some people confuse the Tushka project with the new al-Sheikh Zayed Canal system currently being constructed. The Tushka Spillway was constructed in the 1980s and its purpose is solely to ease pressure on the dam. Eventually there will be a canal between Tushka and al-Sheikh Zayed, but that is in the future. The new canal project is 8 kilometers (5 miles) north of the spillway.

Al-Sheikh Zayed Canal

An even bigger project is the al-Sheikh Zayed Canal, the most ambitious desert reclamation project of the twentieth century. It has been a long time in planning as the first development research for a canal system from the Nile Valley to Kharga Oasis at Baris was done in the 1960s. The Ministry of Irrigation conducted an in-depth study completed in May of 1971. This study was upgraded in the 1980s. Now it is being implemented.

The canal will be 590 kilometers (369 miles) long and carry about 1.5 billion cubic meters (5 billion cubic feet) of water, which will flow from just behind the High Dam at Aswan on Lake Nasser through the desert to Baris in Kharga Oasis. Phase II will carry the water beyond Kharga to Farafra Oasis.

It is expected that 3.5 million feddans will be reclaimed by this ambitious project. The canal itself will irrigate 2.5 million feddans while the remaining irrigation will come from underground water. Six million people will move into the New Valley, new urban communities will develop as part of this project, and new governorates will be carved out of the present one. Instead of Egyptians living on 4 percent of the land, they will utilize 30 percent when the project is completed.

Construction for the project began in January of 1997. The cost is estimated to be six billion Egyptian pounds plus 120 million pounds for a 300-kilometer (188-mile) pipeline for water. It is expected to take twenty-five years to complete. The canal will begin with tunnels constructed under the lake, followed by a number of pumping stations to bring the water to the canal. The pumping stations are expected to be the largest in the world. The canal will run for hundreds of kilometers into the desert with sidecanals carrying the water to agricultural land. All along the route the Institute of Underground Water Research will dig wells to provide water beside that of the canal, to be used as a fresh water source and for additional agricultural and horticultural projects.

A lot of controversy surrounds the construction of this canal. There is no question that life in the Nile Valley, where the population continues to grow out of control, has become unbearable. In a recent article in *al-Ahram Weekly*, one of Cairo's leading English-language newspapers, guest writer Rushdi Said tells us that the air in Cairo is very unhealthy. Lead levels are 5 to 25 times higher than World Health Organization suggested levels and sulfur dioxide levels are at 114 micrograms per cubic meter instead of the recommended 50. The Nile is polluted, too. Over 500 million cubic meters of industrial waste are pumped yearly into its waters. Said's answer to the problem is the desert, too; but he does not believe this canal is the answer. He is not alone. Most scientists agree with him.

Critics point to the cost, not only in construction, but for electricity needed to pump the water through the canal. To solve some of these problems the government points out that much of the desert is at or below sea level and that the tunnels will be well above sea level, as will the pumping stations, so most of the time the water will flow by gravity. Critics also claim the evaporation rate through the desert, especially in summer will be too great. But the government maintains that the rate of evaporation will be less than 5 percent.

Egypt divides the resources of the Nile with all the countries along its path. Each country is allotted a share of the water. Some people say this project exceeds Egypt's share of Nile water. But wastage is currently taking over 30 percent of Egypt's allotment and it is hoped that with this scheme and new water usage programs, everything will balance.

Many were very critical of the Aswan Dam when the British built it. Then of the High Dam. They found dozens of reasons why it should not be built: chemical fertilizers had to be used instead of Nile silt, water tables rose and destroyed Nile Valley temples, salts began to do the same thing, crop yields diminished. But then, when there were nearly a dozen years of famine in Africa along the Nile, Egypt did not feel it at all. The only thing that happened was that the level of Lake Nasser fell. The High Dam was finally accepted as a good idea.

Caravan Routes and Roadways

The southern desert routes were as much corridors as was the river. They offered alternatives, both legal and illegal. The Nile route had its problems: cataracts on the Nile made navigation impossible and portage was extremely difficult. The Nile had a big bend between the fourth and third cataracts, and again between Luxor and Qena, while the desert routes were more direct, shorter, and often more hospitable. In addition, 'greedy' officials had to be dealt with along the river and river pirates were waiting to plunder cargoes. Often times, the desert was safer.

To the west of almost every village along the Nile there is a desert road. In most instances it links the village to its cemetery or a small factory like a stone quarry. Probably there were villages that had their own paths that no one else was permitted to use. Some of these roads join together to form a longer darb, but not often. It would be impossible to describe all of these roads. Here are four!

Darb al-Arbain

Known to have an early origin, perhaps as early as the Old Kingdom, we know little of the Darb al-Arbain's early history, not even its ancient name. By the sixteenth century it was called the Darb al-Arbain, 40 days' Road, and was a major slavers' route between Sudan and Egypt. It began in Kobbe, moved north out of Sudan to al-Shab, continued north to Kharga Oasis and then on to the Nile Valley. It covers a total of 1,767 kilometers (1,104 miles) and is the most famous desert route in Egypt. (See below for a complete description.) Parts of it are sand paved (tar poured over sand) today.

Darb al-Galaba

Lesser known that the famous and infamous Darb al-Arbain, the Darb al-Galaba, Trader's Road, begins at Dongola in Sudan and moves west to Selima, where it joins the Darb al-Arbain. The two routes run together as far as al-Shab in Egypt, where Galaba turns northeast through Kurkur and skirts the river's edge. It finally joins the Nile at Kubbaniya, 10 kilometers (6 miles) north of Aswan. Once at the river, it continues along its banks to Esna and Farshut. Murray tells us that caravans avoided the cultivated areas to avoid taxation and unfriendly villagers. He believes this is Harkhuf's "desert road." (See tour below.)

Darb al-Ishrin

Another route, noted by Burkhardt in the nineteenth century and then forgotten, is the Darb al-Ishrin, the Twenty Days' Road. Burckhardt says it ran from Mahas to Kharga, which was a slave route with a journey of twenty-three days. No other reference has been found for this route, except that Samir Lama talks of it, too.

Darb al-Tarfawi

There are two Darb al-Tarfawis today, one from Mut in Dakhla and a second from Qasr in Kharga. Both lead to Bir Tawfari, which in the past decade has seen the development of a farm called Uwaynat East. Both of these routes are now paved.

The Darb al-Arbain, the Forty Days' Road

In our time the Darb al-Arbain has become a legend. Like any legend its mysteries are difficult to unravel and sometimes we do not like what we find. The Darb al-Arbain was definitely a road of trade, probably as early as the Old Kingdom. The Romans built a string of forts in Kharga Oasis probably to guard caravans along this route. By the Islamic Period, that trade was booming. The cargo was mainly human beings. It had become, or maybe always was, a road of slavery, a via dolorosa, filled with agony and grief.

In Search of the Forty Days' Road

In the 1980s, Michael Asher, author of *In Search of the Forty Days' Road*, went looking for "The Darb," which had all but disappeared from collective memory at the beginning of the 20th century. At first he was told it was an entirely different route running west to east from Darfur to Omdurman. But Asher had done his research and knew the approximate route. He had probably read the accounts of Browne in the eighteenth century and more recent explorers like Newbold, Shaw, Almasy, Beadnell, and Ball. All gave accounts of the Darb al-Arbain in the first half of the twentieth century. He knew what the natives did not. He kept looking. When he asked a group of officials in Sudan about the Darb al-Arbain, the "portly gentlemen" laughed. One said, "Oh, I know of it. It's just that it hasn't been used for a hundred years. There's no water on that route now, and anyway there's no need to use it when the other ways are safe." They told him, "What you should do is sell your camel and . . . go by lorry."

In the 1990s, two young women traveled with Rashida camel herders along what they called the Darb al-Arbain. Their journey appears to have taken them north from Debba in Sudan through the desert near the Nile. They did not visit one site along the traditional Darb al-Arbain: not Selima, not al-Shab, not Bir Abu Hussein, not even Kharga Oasis. One cannot say they traveled the Darb al-Galaba either, for they did not pass through any of its landmarks. Today, safety is not as much an issue as in the past when true desert brigands roamed the desert killing and stealing, or the British were at war with the Sudanese, or the Egyptians were at war with the Sudanese. It is easier, close to the Nile Valley: it is shorter, less cluttered, less marred by modern roads. That is the route the Rashida take today, the easiest way. This should not, however, diminish the trek these two ladies made. It was an amazing adventure. Few could have done it. But it is not the Darb al-Arbain.

If the camel herders are calling this route the Darb al-Arbain, and they very well might be, then let us suggest they are only mimicking foreigners who, equally ignorant, believe that the Darb al-Arbain is any route north out of Sudan near the west side of the Nile. This would not be an unusual event. The people in Kharga do not know the names of the streets in their city. They never use the street names, which are a recent addition to the oasis. The people in Qasr Dakhla do not recognize the name Bab al-Qasmund for the pass descending the escarpment behind Qasr Dakhla. They call it the Naqb al-Farafra. It happens all the time in the desert.

This is not to say that the Darb al-Arbain did not vary over the centuries. It did. In someplaces it was a kilometer wide. When there was trouble one way, an alternative was chosen. One thing is sure: The Darb al-Arbain runs through Kharga Oasis. There, the Persians guarded it, the Romans erected fortresses to protect it, the Fatimids or perhaps the Mamluks built two customs ports as it entered Kharga, the Turks created small defensive fortifications, and the British built a protective system against raids. All of this was because the most important north–south route in the whole of Egypt's deserts, the Darb al-Arbain, ran through Kharga Oasis.

The Route

Here is the route as it was recorded time and time again from the sixteenth century to the twentieth century by numerous travelers, explorers, and military expeditions. The Darb al-Arbain begins at **Kobbe**, Darfur Province, Sudan, where the holding pens of the slavers existed. Kobbe was a substantial town of mud houses with a mosque and five Islamic schools when Browne visited in July of 1793. In 1803, the community could muster six thousand fighting men. In the 1980s, when Asher went to Kobbe he found one well and a few poor people for "there was nothing left of the streets and market squares except the dark patterns of their foundations left on the earth. The houses had long ago crumbled into dust, the alleys which had once swarmed with men and camels now lay under thickets of lalob and sayal trees. Kobbay [Kobbe] had become a dead town, peopled only by these few children who now toiled away at a single well where there had once been many."

Two routes run north some 400 kilometers (250 miles) from Kobbe to **Bir Natrun**. Both are obscure today, as the old names do not match any known sites. Shaw talks about them and concludes any route north had to pass through Wadi Howar and would lead to Bir Natrun. Asher claims that the true Darb actually begins at Bir Natrun (which he calls Atrun), where these two roads converge. So, to Bir Natrun, one had choices depending on the political climate and the weather.

Bir Natrun had many names: Wadi Natrun, Valley of Natron, after the salt in the area; Bir al-Malha Well of the Salt; and Bir Zaghawa, after the Zaghawa people, closely associated with the Tebu. To add a bit of confusion there are four wells here: Bir Sultan (named after Ali Dinar), Bir Milani, Bir Natrun, and Bir Nakhla. The whole area is often called al-Atrun by the Kababish and Howawir peoples of the Sudan, who frequent the area. This name was used by Asher. Idrisi, the Arab geographer, called the area Tadjerin or Tajuwin.

The ancient Egyptians once mined the natron necessary for embalming here at Natrun. Natron is bicarbonate of soda, and in this century it was still used in Upper Egypt to make soap and chewing tobacco, to clean the skins used to hold water, and to bleach linen. Salt was so important that caravans on their way north would halt here to mine salt to sell in the Nile Valley.

When Browne's caravan stopped here it met a number of Zaghawa, who often stationed men at Bir Natrun to supply caravans with overpriced goods. He tells us about one other group of people that frequented this oasis, the Cubba-Beesh (Kababish), which he calls, "a wandering tribe, who, mounted on the swiftest dromedaries, rapidly

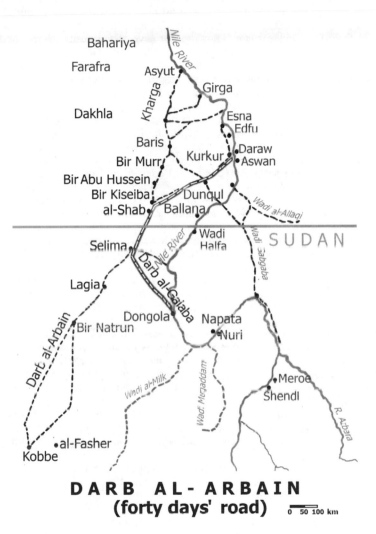

**DARB AL-ARBAIN
(forty days' road)**   0 50 100 km

traverse the desert, and live by plundering the defenceless." In 1903, Captain H. Hodgson visited the bir. In 1907, it was correctly placed on a map by Captain Coyngham. The Sudanese Camel Corps had an outpost at the turn of the century at Bir Natrun. In 1916, Howawir Arabs from Northern Kordofan were stationed here. When Shaw was here in the 1920s the Sudanese outpost was still standing, but the soldiers were long gone. They left, according to Shaw, because they had run out of food and the grain due from Dongola was late. They did not have enough water, some died of thirst, others were found by the Kababish and saved. Shaw and Newbold were at Natrun for five day in November of 1927. Kababish Arabs and a few Zaghawa and Umm Gelul from Northern Darfur were there too, collecting rock-salt. Between them, they had three hundred camels that had to be watered and loaded.

No archaeological exploration of any note has taken place here.

From Bir Natrun the Darb continued another 256 kilometers (160 miles) to **Laqya al-Arbain**. Laqya means finding, so Finding the Forty is the name of this place. One assumes it means finding the road after not being sure exactly where it was. The desert in this area was once controlled by bandits, the reason that desert travel was so dangerous. These were from the Kababish, Bedayatt, and Goran peoples, who would also harvest the dates from these empty oases. Shaw tells us that an Egyptian caravan headed for Bir Natrun to mine rock-salt was "cut to pieces by the Goran." They hid out until midnight and "crept down to cut the throats of the sleeping travellers." Only a few escaped back to Selima.

The route between Laqya al-Arbain and **Selima**, 224 kilometers (140 miles) north, is difficult. The Darb al-Galaba, moving west from Dongola, meets the Darb al-Arbain here at Selima. Selima is the closest small oasis to the Nile at the point where the Nile makes a major bend west, and two routes leave the oasis for the Nile. To the north are hills and to the south and west the Selima sand sheets. The oasis, uninhabited, has a small grove of date palms. The water source is a meter-wide hole in the ground. Gebel Tuliya, a black camelback hill, overlooks the oasis from the northeast.

When Browne traveled this way in 1793, it was the height of summer and so many camels had died of exhaustion that the merchants of his caravan were forced to bury their goods here at Selima. He says that the woman for whom the place was named was a princess who lived in a stone house here. She was a great warrior and had many followers who "spread terror all over Nubia." The building contains a lot of graffiti: names, camel brands, and Kufic text.

Charles Neufeld, a gum trader, came to Selima in April of 1887. He was not so lucky. His caravan got lost in the area and spent eight days wandering. Out of water, the people were captured by the Dervishes and Neufeld was held captive in Omdurman for eleven years.

In 1927–28, Douglas Newbold and W. B. Kennedy-Shaw met the Darb al-Arbain at Selima on their 1,000 mile camel journey. Newbold describes the building as having seven rooms and in a fair state of preservation. He found signs incised into the blocks of the building. Most of the inscriptions are Arabic, some he believed to be medieval, but most modern. Some are *wasm*s similar to those found on the rock near Tineida in Dakhla Oasis. Shaw and Newbold fixed the position of Selima astronomically. The Sudan Defense Force patrolled the area and erected grass huts in the 1920s.

Shaw came back in 1937, with a number of friends, including Mason, who maintains the oasis was named after a lady of leisure who kept a house of entertainment for the passing caravans when the Darb was in its heyday. There were no Selimas when they visited, but apparently a lot of gerbils. They also dug around a bit and found a skeleton they called Potiphar Johnson. During World War II an ordinance recovery section of the British army was stationed at Selima. It was their job to recover broken-down vehicles between Wadi Halfa and Kufra. They also helped map the area. Today, the area is under long-term study because of its Early Holocene paleoenvironment. This study centers not only on Selima but also on Merga Oasis, 500 kilometers (313 miles) to the south.

Morkot gives us one more interpretation of the building at Selima. He believes it is the remains of "an early Christian convent." So much for Selima, lady of the night. He confirms the graffiti on the stone of the convent and the knoll of the hill and believes some of it is medieval, including Tuareg writing and camel brands.

Half way between Selima and al-Shab is the Tomb of Sheikh Ambigol. We know the tomb is earlier than 1787, because Boulton's map of that year marks the spot as the tomb of a fakir. Shaw thinks this sheikh is also related to the area of the Nile east of Selima called Ambigol.

The Darb enters Egypt today as it approaches al-Shab. From al-Shab the road gets easier as the springs are closer together. It passes through Bir Kiseiba, Bir Abu Hussein, Bir Murr, and finally into Kharga Oasis at Qasr, where an ancient Roman fortress watches over it. (For a description of the Egyptian sites, see The Tour below.) Riding the desert floor past Baris, and under the watchful eye of the fortresses of Zayyan, Ghweita, and Nadura, it reaches the Temple of Hibis. From there it continues through Greco-Roman Beleida, Dabashiya, Labeka, and Sumaria, to the last outpost of the Kharga desert, Qasr Geb. After Geb, it climbs the escarpment in the north and heads to the Nile past the Wadi al-Battikha, arriving at the town of Asyut.

Ancient History

There is little recorded history about this section of the desert, especially the area known as the Darb al-Arbain. It is possible that Harkhuf from Aswan traveled this way as he explored the area, and this was the ancient Egyptian "oasis or desert road," but we have no direct evidence.

In a nutshell, the ancient Egyptians had a problem maintaining their southern frontier. They actually built a wall at Aswan during the Middle Kingdom. The Greeks and Romans had the same problem. They had formidable enemies beyond Egypt's southern frontier. Diocletian transferred the Noubades from Kharga (Oasis Magna) to Nubia. This happened after 297. We know the Blemmyes raided Kharga Oasis via the Darb al-Arbain on more than one occasion.

Kharga also fell victim to Nubian invasions. First in 747–48, a Nubian army attacked Kharga to try to stop the persecution of the Christians. Again in the fifteenth century, the King of Nubia sent an army to invade all of the oases of Egypt. He probably used the Darb al-Arbain to reach Kharga in both instances.

Islamic Era

Islam came to Darfur via the west around 1200. It was then that the empire of Kanem–Bornu around Lake Chad tried to move east. By 1240, the King of Kanem controlled not only Darfur, but the Darb al-Arbain.

From the 1600 to 1874, the Keira were the rulers of Darfur. They were slave users and slave sellers. This is when the name Darfur was born. Their rule came to an end when they were destroyed by al-Zubayr in 1874.

The incident that probably did the most to develop the Darb al-Arbain was the war between Darfur and the neighboring kingdom on the west, Waidai. The war lasted from 1700 to 1750. Prisoners were sent north to Egypt along the Darb al-Arbain to be sold as slaves. Darfur's warring nature continued throughout the century and they provided Egypt with a steady supply of slaves. This led to a tremendous hunger for slaves in Egypt, which Darfur was willing to meet. When the warring ended, another means of providing the slaves became necessary.

Europeans

We have a number of European sources for the Darb al-Arbain too. The first foreign source is the French doctor Poncet in 1698. Krump did a portion of the route in 1701, and so did du Roule in 1704. One of our primary sources for the Darb al-Arbain is W. G. Browne, who traversed it north to south and south to north with slave caravans in 1793. Browne took four months going south with traders. He left us the following report of the goods moving through the desert. Going south the caravan carried: "Amber beads; tin in small bars; coral beads; carnelian; false carnelian; beads of Venice; agate; rings, silver and brass for the ankles and wrists; carpets, small; blue cotton cloths of Egyptian fabric; white cotton ditto; Indian muslins and cottons; blue and white cloths of Egypt called Melayes [to drape over the head of women]; sword-blades, straight (German) from Kahira [Cairo]; small looking-glasses; copper face-pieces or defensive armour for the horses' heads; fire-arms; kohel for the eyes; coffee; silk, unwrought; wire, brass and iron; small red caps of Barbary; light French clothes made into Benishes; silks of Scio; silk and cotton pieces of Aleppo; shoes of red leather; black pepper, writing-paper; soap of Syria."

Going north in 1796, the caravan of 500 camels contained: "Slaves, male and female; camels; ivory; horns of the rhinoceros; teeth of the hippopotamus; ostrich feathers; gum; pimento; tamarinds made into round cakes; peroquets in abundance, and some monkeys and Guinea fowl; copper, white, in small quantity." For every ten camels carrying merchandise, one camel carried provisions, including food, in the form of beans for people and straw for camels.

By the eighteenth century the Darb al-Arbain was the main route between Egypt and Sudan. In 1817, Cailliaud saw a Darfur caravan arrive in Asyut with 16,000 people including 6,000 slaves. These are staggering numbers. The logistics of moving so many people through a mostly waterless, foodless, land for at least 40 but more likely 90 or 120 days are almost incomprehensible. He says, "They had been two months traveling in the deserts, in the most intense heat of the year; meagre, exhausted, and the aspect of death on their countenances, the spectacle strongly excited compassion." Can you imagine the chaos they presented as they hit Asyut in need of every possible item, food, water, shelter, and medical attention? The French consul-general M Drovetti traveled the Darb in 1818.

There was no mistaking that the Darb al-Arbain was the vehicle for the largest caravans of slaves headed for Egypt. And that the destination for most of these slaves was the Wakalat al-Galaba, the central slave market of Cairo. But there are no records. Reda Mowafi tells us in *Slavery, Slave Trade, and Abolition Attempts in Egypt and Sudan 1820–1882* that "the Coptic clerks who maintained a register of all the slaves imported and sold, the date of the sale and the names of the seller and buyer, burnt these registers every year."

As the twentieth century approached the Darb became a road for explorers. The portion of the Darb al-Arbain from Asyut to Kharga was mapped by Ball and Beadnell in 1898. Shaw and company traversed the entire Darb by camel. In 1924–25, Prince Kamal al-Din came south from Kharga with his by now famous caterpillar cars to Bir al-Shab along the Darb. Almasy, in 1929, was the first person to travel the Egyptian route entirely by car.

Slavery and Slave Caravans

Ten million Africans were turned into slaves by the Islamic trans-Saharan and Indian Ocean slavers from 650 to 1905. Europeans shipped seven million slaves to the New World, beginning in the seventeenth century.

It took a long time for humans to understand you cannot own another human being.

The ancient Egyptians had slaves, as did the Greeks, and the Romans. The Garamantians 'hunted' black Africans in their four-horse chariots in the sixth century B.C. The Tulunids and Fatimids had slaves and the Mamluks were slaves. Slavery existed in almost every culture in the world.

There were a number of ways a person became a slave. In the ancient world, if your country was conquered, you became a slave. In the eleventh century, if one committed a crime, the victim, or his or her family, had the choice of having the criminal killed or sold into slavery. In war, the vanquished were sold as slaves. In fact, the rise of the Darb al-Arbain happened for just this reason. As mentioned earlier, in the eighteenth century warring Darfur sent captives north to Egypt in the hundreds and thousands. Over the decades the Egyptian market became insatiable, so after the wars, Darfur had to find other ways to keep the trade alive.

The method we know most about is the slave-raid. Raiders would sneak up on a village, surround it, and take only the strong, mainly women, young men, and children. In January of 1830, the governor of Kordofan sent a raiding party into the mountains of Kordofan and took 1,400 captives. Of those, he sent 1,000 males to Egypt. In the eighteenth and nineteenth century, Darfur sent traders and raiders among pagan tribes south of Darfur in the Bahr al-Ghazal, Central African Republic, and southeastern Chad.

Slaving was strictly controlled. R. S. O'Fahey in *Slavery and the Slave Trade in Dar Fur* tells us that the sultan controlled the slave trade. Permission had to be obtained from him to make a raid, a *ghazya*. If successful, the slavers received a letter, a spear (*salatiya*), and a route. The sultan permitted 60 to 70 raids a year. Armed with the permission, the slavers received goods on consignment from local traders. In return, the traders received slaves when the raid was over. All slavers headed south at the same time and gathered at the border where they appointed one among them to be the *sultan al-ghazya*, the boss of the expeditions until they reentered Darfur. He received all slaves given as gifts, plus a portion of all slaves taken. These slaves were given as payment to everyone who made the expeditions possible.

Kidnapping was another method. It needs no explanation. And finally, people actually sold themselves or their children voluntarily in order to pay off a debt, or improve conditions for the rest of the family.

Economics of Slavery

Through the centuries the economics of slavery varied. It was always a lucrative trade, even when it was a barter system. A trader could realize 300–500 percent on the investment. At one time a slave was sold for salt, another precious commodity. Arms were also traded for slaves. The Fishers, in *Slavery and Muslim Society in Africa*, tell us that in the 1800s a boy in Liberia would sell for fifteen kegs of powder, a girl, ten kegs, or 100 sticks of salt." Hassanein, in 1923, when the trade was all but ended, found the cost of a slave much higher as they were harder to come by. In 1916, he was offered a slave girl for $24; in 1923, a slave girl was $150.

Who were the people of the caravans? We are lucky enough to have a few eyewitnesses, like Browne in the seventeenth century, who provide us with some information, but not enough to satisfy our curiosity. Who were the individuals, the humans, those that suffered the journey? Who were the slavers? They were the men who traveled year after year along the route, hauling human cargo, keeping it alive, urging it on to the valley ports. Were they less victims than the slaves themselves? Beadnell tells us, "In such caravans there is seldom more than one man who knows the particular roads to be followed; the rest are wretched underfed creatures, generally half-breeds, who for a mere pittance tramp day after day, uncomplainingly and shoeless, alongside the caravan." He was speaking of the slavers, who were, in many instances, as pathetic as their captives.

"And who were the slaves torn from their homes, condemned to a life outside of life? How did they survive such a journey? Oh, to hear voices from the past who lived it, walked it mile by mile, suffered its heat, its lack of water, its terrible terrain. Who among us are the descendants of those that survived? Did they speak of this unspeakable ordeal? What distant stories remain in an oral tradition locked away somewhere within a family's memories? The Darb al-Arbain has yet to yield any answers. Other than the carcasses of camels, few remains of these incredible treks have been found."

When Hanns Vischer was putting together his small caravan to head south from Tripoli to Bornu along yet another slavers' route in 1906 he welcomed fellow travelers, for there was safety in numbers. Among those who wished to travel south with him were freed slaves trying to get home again. One was Hadji Abdu, "an old warrior of the Sudanese army, who had served as a corporal under General Gordon at Khartoum and seen much fighting in many lands since he had been taken as a young slave from Bornu to Upper Egypt [probably along the Darb al-Arbain], some sixty years before." This gentleman said to Vischer, "I have served Gordon Pasha, now it is your duty to look after me and take me and my wife back to Bornu."

The Caravans

Slavers moved their cargo over all the great trans-Saharan trade routes (see People for details.) From the western routes slave ships moved the cargo across the Mediterranean via Malta or Crete to the Dalmation coast. In the east, they moved from Benghazi via Crete and Rhodes to Izmir and Istanbul. From Alexandria the slaves were trafficked to Istanbul following the Rhodes route, or via Cyprus to Anatolia, or directly to Damascus. In the Eastern Sahara and Libyan Desert, most of the ancient caravan routes fell under the control of the Ottomans; however, the Darb al-Arbain was Egyptian. It has been estimated that 25,000 to 30,000 black slaves, 1 percent of the population, lived in Egypt, and to maintain that number 12,500 to 15,000 had to be imported each year, primarily over the Darb al-Arbain.

According to Bagnold, with long caravans of goods headed for the markets in Cairo, slavers would often hide small children in empty water skins as they approached customs villages, like those in Kharga Oasis, in order to avoid paying taxes. Sometimes no caravan moved for a year, at other times they departed monthly. According to de Cosson, caravans left Tripoli led by Tuareg tribesmen from October to March.

Although slaves must have died on the journey, nowhere is there a grave or marker on the Darb al-Arbain. According to one source, the only evidence of their passing is the small heaps of gravel where their daily bread was cooked. It is almost inconceivable that no human bones are found along the Darb. Vischer in 1910, found plenty of them near wells along the Tripoli–Bornu trail.

Sometimes caravans traveled in the heat of summer, the caravan strung out for miles, and the slaves—as many as eight thousand—forced to walk all the way, even though the caravan would include as many as 10,000 camels. Women and children withstood the ordeal far better than men.

Captain G. F. Lyon in *A Narrative of Travels in Northern Africa in the Years 1818, 19, and 20* tells of the arrival of such a caravan in Murzuk. "These poor oppressed beings were, many of them, so exhausted as to be scarcely able to walk; their legs and feet were much swelled, and by their enormous size, formed a striking contrast with their emaciated bodies. They were all borne down with loads of fire-wood; and even poor little children, worn to skeletons by fatigue and hardships, were obliged to bear their burden. . . . Care was taken, however, that the hair of the females should be arranged in nice order, and that their bodies should be well oiled, whilst the males were closely shaven, to give them a good appearance on entering the town."

Sickness was the biggest fear of the caravan. Diseases like smallpox would make a caravan like a plague ship, adrift without harbor in a sea of sand. Raiders were another problem. Slave caravans were vulnerable and they held precious cargo. Families of slaves were known to raid caravans. They mounted expeditions and victoriously brought their sons and daughters, fathers and mothers, home again. The weather was another threat. Cold killed just as much as heat. Fear dominated most caravans. Raiders would swoop down on caravans, killing everyone in sight and carrying off the loot, be it gold, ivory, or slaves. Arabs were distrustful of Berbers. No one trusted the Tuareg.

The Slavers

Who were the traders? Almost anyone. Entire tribes dedicated themselves to slaving. Among the most famous raiders in the Sahara were the Tuareg (see People), who held dominion over as many as three of the great north–south caravan routes in West Africa and traded in slaves for centuries. During the Islamic period a new traveler joined the road—the pilgrim to Mecca. According to Robert Morkot in *The Darb al Arbain, the Kharga Oasis and its Forts*, pilgrims were not opposed to taking along a few slaves to sell to defray expenses. They made their way to Darfur from Bornu and traveled the Darb headed to Cairo to join the Egyptian *mahmal* and the official Egyptian caravan. Women were very much involved in the sale of slaves, especially in the markets of Cairo and Istanbul.

Eventually, the Europeans became traders and they were ruthless. The original lure to the Europeans was ivory (for billiard balls and piano keys); but as ivory became more and more difficult and costly to obtain, by 1854, according to Mowafi, slaves took its place. Looking for ivory was expensive and selling slaves could cover those expenses. The two trades became interwoven and then, when the ivory moved too far south, the slave trade was cheaper and more profitable.

Among the most famous slave traders along the Darb al-Arbain and Nile were Kushuk Ali, Abu Amuri, Muhammad Abu Saud Bey al-Aqqad (died 1881) and al-Zubayr Rahma al-Mansur (1830–1913). They formed trading companies with offices in Khartoum. Aqqad and Co. was the largest trading company in the Bahr al-Gabal and had offices in Cairo and Khartoum. Abu Saud, al-Aqqad's son-in-law, was the local agent. According to Mowafi, he employed 2,500 men and held a government sanctioned monopoly on trade in ivory. His 'army' exerted tremendous influence in the region and was a threat to local governments. He encouraged wars against tribes and then would take the losers as slaves. Zubayr controlled the Bahr al-Ghazal. There he was more important that the government.

Muhammad Ali and the Slave Trade

Muhammad Ali, Viceroy of Egypt, sought gold, slaves, and power through his conquest of Sudan. Egypt had just undergone a tremendous drain on its manpower. First the Mamluks had civil wars, then the French invaded Egypt (1798–1801), and then Muhammad Ali warred against Arabia (1813–18). This left a serious shortage of men to fill the ranks of the army and to labor in the large estates of the wealthy. Slaves could and did make up the shortage.

Governors of the provinces of Sudan were responsible for filling Egypt's army ranks. When raids did not get enough, Ahmad Pasha, governor-general of Sudan from 1838–43 "imposed a levy of Negroes to fill gaps. . . . A scale of contributions was drawn up by which each taxable person was required to buy and hand over one or more slaves."

The khedival holdings in Egypt were considerable and the workers who planted and harvested the crops were primarily slaves. So, too, were the public irrigation workers. When the cotton boom hit Egypt, thanks to the American Civil War, it was slaves who worked the fields.

Stopping the Trade

The death of slavery came slowly. Although the subject was broached as early as 1812, the British began exerting pressure in earnest around 1840, primarily to do away with white slavery—Circassian and Georgian. That very same year saw Muhammad Ali vow to end slavery. He closed the Wakalat al-Galaba, the Cairo slave market, in 1842. But the actual demise of the slave traffic took more than the issuing of edicts. All his efforts bore little fruit for he had no control over what was happening beyond his borders in Sudan. In fact, it made desert travel, hidden from the eyes of the administration, more frequent and more profitable. When one route was being watched, the other route took the traffic. Egypt became the most important "entrepot on the supply routes to the Ottoman markets," quite in addition to supplying their own needs.

During Ismail's reign, the great exploration of the Nile was underway and reports of appalling scenes related to slave traffic were being sent back to Cairo. Ismail put down measures to end slavery. Any slave boat found on the Nile would be confiscated and the slaves freed. The governor-general of Sudan, Muda Hamid Pasha, was ordered to stop all boats in Khartoum. By 1869, the year the Suez Canal opened, traffic in Egyptian controlled territories was on the wane. But trade on the southern river and in Darfur was not. Ismail sent two expeditions into Sudan, one via the river into the Bahr al-Gabal led by Sir Samuel Baker, the famous Nile explorer, and the second, under the leadership of Muhammad al-Bulalawi of West Africa, to the Bahr al-Ghazal, where al-Zubayr, the slave trader, was the potentate.

Bulalawi's attempt at suppressing the trade in the Bahr al-Ghazal did not go smoothly. Bulalawi was killed, and al-Zubayr's position grew stronger. Baker's mandate was to establish Egyptian authority along the White Nile as far as its source, to suppress the slave trade, to introduce legitimate commerce, to open navigation on the lakes of the Equator, and to establish a chain of military stations and commercial depots at distances of three days march. It took almost a year for the expedition to leave Cairo. In Khartoum, Baker hired Aqqad and Co. to supply his troops, a ridiculous arrangement since they were among the biggest slavers in the area. After several years, little had been accomplished. In 1874, Baker was replaced by Charles G. Gordon. In three years he suppressed the slave trade, reorganized the government, and established boats on Lake Albert and relations with Uganda.

Every trader trying to maintain the trade had moved to Darfur and the Darb al-Arbain became the main corridor. Al-Zubayr, in the meantime, thought it in his best interest to control Darfur. His preparations included a treaty with Ismail, who appointed him governor of Bahr al-Ghazal and Shaqqa. He received a garrison of troops in return for a tribute of 15,000 pounds. So Aqqad was appointed by Gordon as lieutenant-governor of Gondokoro and the Bahr al-Gabal in 1874, and al-Zubayr was appointed governor of Bahr al-Ghazal by the Khedive Ismail, in what Elbashir in *The United States, Slavery, and the Slave Trade in the Nile Valley* describes as an attempt to "neutralize [they were both major slavers] . . . and use their knowledge and influence to control the region." It failed on both counts.

On October 24, 1874, al-Zubayr attacked and brought down the Darfur government. In the chaos that followed, al-Zubayr went to Cairo to try to better his position. Ismail, who had recognized that al-Zubayr was not the best person to reign, but was the best at hand at the time, detained him in Cairo. The slave traffic was all but at an end.

The Final Curtain

Darfur and Kordofan were very unstable. From 1878, every revolt that took place was supported by people who had been slighted by the government, especially the slavers. Al-Zubayr was still detained in Cairo and his followers were not happy. Darfur rose in rebellion a number of times.

In the meantime the British were very agitated at Ismail's progress toward independence. They were fearful of the American military personnel in the Egyptian Army. When the Americans supported the mixed courts ending unlimited consular jurisdiction over resident foreigners, the British and the French dramatically opposed such a choice. Ismail was expanding his power and influence south and east, much to the annoyance of the British and French. European creditors began to squeeze him. He sold his interests in the Suez Canal to the French. The British were watching their influence and power over Ismail wane. They did not want to lose their Egyptian empire as they had lost their American colonies. They wanted American influence out of Egypt at all costs. Human beings were expendable, Empire was not. Ismail had to go.

And he did. So did his Americans. Ismail was deposed by the British and Ottoman Porte in June of 1879. Gordon, who supported Ismail, resigned as governor-general of Sudan in July and from the Egyptian service in 1880.

What did all this mean to the slave traffic along the Darb al-Arbain? It would allow it to reemerge. In a few months the caravan trade in slaves resumed along the old routes from Darfur and Bahr al-Ghazal to Egypt and the Eastern Sudan. Slave raids began again. Slave ships began to sail the Nile. The Darb al-Arbain was humming. Khartoum was in disarray and unable to cope. Muhammad Ahmad, called the Mahdi, joined the rebellion and united the rebels under his leadership. The Mahdist Revolt began.

The Mahdi

The Mahdi was the son of a boatbuilder and believed he was a prophesied new leader of Islam who would purge the faithless. Since all the changes taking place in the country were dictated by foreign Christians, it was easy for the people to believe that expelling them would solve their problems. It was difficult to understand what was wrong with slavery, as it had always been a way of life in the area.

The Mahdi could never have gained power if the slave trade did not exist and would perhaps not have gained power if Ismail had not been deposed. According to Mowafi, the suppression of this trade was viewed by the Sudanese as a Christian attempt to overthrow Islam. Slavery was also a major economic factor in Sudanese commerce and its suppression threw the country into financial ruin.

The Mahdi was able to gather together three factions: the disgruntled population, the slavers, and the Arabs of Kordofan and Darfur, who were against any type of government, especially if it intended to create taxes. Between 1883 and 1898, military posts were established at al-Shab to try to disrupt traffic on the Darb al-Arbain. Rudolf Karl Slatin was appointed Governor of Darfur in 1881. He surrendered to the Mahdi in December 1883, and Darfur was absorbed into the Mahdi's territories, as was the Darb al-Arbain.

The Mahdi's successor, Abdullah, or the Khalifa, was overthrown in 1898, and the Anglo–Egyptian government appointed Ali Dinar as sultan. This was primarily an attempt to suppress the continuing slave traffic, in which Dinar had played a role. In 1915, Dinar revolted and he was killed in the ensuing fighting in November 1916, when a British plane flew overhead and shot him dead. Darfur became part of Sudan. The slave trade greatly diminished.

TOUR #1

Riding the Darb al-Arbain

- travel restricted
- 4x4 (at least 3)
- 2–4 days
- very difficult and dangerous
- GPS, maps, all water, all food, all petrol
- guide mandatory
- permits mandatory

The Sudanese portion of this journey is restricted in 2000 as the border is closed at this point. There is no access from Egypt to Kobbe, Bir Natrun Oasis, Laqya al-Arbain, and Selima. For information on these sites see above.

Al-Shab

Al-Shab means the young man. It is here at al-Shab, 128 kilometers (80 miles) from the last oasis in Sudan and well into Egypt, that the Darb al-Arbain and the Darb al-Galaba part company. The Arbain continues north to Kharga and the latter heads northeast to the Nile via Dunqul and Kurkur oases to Aswan and on to Esna.

Al-Shab is shaded by palms and sheltered from the wind by steep encircling sand dunes. Burckhardt tells of a caravan that left slaves who could no longer keep up the grueling summer pace to Asyut here at al-Shab, with enough provisions to last until someone returned for them. In the valley they hired over a hundred camels, but when they returned to al-Shab to collect the slaves "the thoughtless slaves had been too prodigal of their provisions and several had died from hunger." One wonders how many different tribes were represented among the slaves and if those who died were of the same tribe as those who lived?

There is a two-roomed blockhouse, atop a mound on basalt on the highest point at al-Shab. The wooden ladder Shaw saw leaning aganist the outside wall in the 1920s is gone. This blockhouse was built in 1884, during the Dervish raids.

Caravans from the Nile came to al-Shab along the Darb al-Galaba to mine the alum from this oasis. Murray remembers three men from the frontier patrol whose new cars "burned out their clutches" at al-Shab. They walked to Wadi Halfa in three days with only three waterbottles between them.

The entire area from Shab to the Kiseiba escarpment carries the same ambiance. It is a very pleasant place and surely the caravans welcomed the hospitable terrain after the hundreds of kilometers of desolation they had already traversed and the hundreds more to come. Here there was shade under the dozens and dozens of stands of doum palms. Here there was water, enough for a large caravan to spread out amount the springs to water and rest.

Bir Kiseiba, Kasaba

Forty kilometers (twenty-five miles) after al-Shab is Bir Kiseiba, the Well of Gain. It is surrounded on three sides by higher ground. In the north is the escarpment, while outlier hills close in the east and west keeping the south open to the plain called Atmur al-Kibeish. The Nubia Formation scarp is vertical with only a few breaks. The Darb al-Arbain cuts it at an easy ascent. As the crow flies, Bir Kiseiba is 70 kilometers (44 miles) northwest of Gebel Nabta.

Wendorf and Schild in *Cattle-Keepers of the Eastern Sahara* tell us there are six wells within a 50 kilometer (31 mile) radius around Bir Kiseiba. Like Bir Sahara, most had to be dug and their water is highly salty. The *abyar*, with clumps of reeds and grasses around the well that indicate water is there, occur "along fault lines and the vegetation conforms to the same linear pattern [as the fault]."

Animals are few and only at the wells: beetles, camel ticks, lizards, rodents, a gazelle from time to time, and perhaps a fox. There are a fair number of birds as "occasional flocks of migrant cranes, storks, ducks, and geese pass through." But that is today. In the past there was a much greater menagerie including African wild cats, and elephants.

There were also domesticated cattle. We know they existed here as early as 9840 B.C., making it the oldest known site for domesticated cattle in the Western Desert. Kiseiba sits at the center of a region that enjoyed prosperity during one of the wetter phases of desert life nearly 15,000 years ago. That period is called the Final Pleistocene– Holocene period of playa-lake development.

The cattle may have come from the Nile Valley, but probably came from Uwaynat and central Africa. Wendorf and Schild propose that the cattle along the Nile were wild and had "a special status." The desert dwellers brought them to the desert, domesticated them, and reintroduced them to the Nile Valley at a later date. This was an important discovery because it changed the way scientists view the settlements in this area of the desert. There is evidence that the Neolithic community slaughtered and processed meat here.

The Combined Prehistoric Expedition worked at Bir Kiseiba in 1979 and 1980. Their primary objective was to learn more about the Early Holocene period in the Western Desert.

At this point the Darb al-Arbain is as much as 20 kilometers (12 miles) wide. Between Kiseiba and Abu Hussein, Murray describes a small hill which has a cairn and is covered with the graves of a Dervish raiding party. Of course, the bones of camels mark the graves.

Bir Abu Hussein

After climbing the Kiseiba scarp one travels a little over 20 kilometers to the next well. The asphalt road from Bir Tarfawi meets the asphalt road of the Darb al-Arbain at Bir Abu Hussein, the Well of the Fox. It is not in a field of dunes, as one traveler reported, but sits unobtrusively at the side of the road with only a few barrel drums to mark its place. No trees, no shrubs, nothing. But the ugliest well is the most useful, for here, where there is a modern military checkpoint, the well is free of debris and you can dip a bucket and draw up fresh, clear, tasteless water.

Bir Murr

150 meters (480 feet) above sea level, Bir Murr, the Bitter Well, is 60 kilometers (38 miles) from the top of the Kiseiba scarp along the Darb al-Arbain. There are two hollows with a well in each hollow.

There is plenty of evidence of early peoples at both sites and it is suggested that these areas could only have developed once the climate was wet enough to allow vegetation to grow in this area. Then people migrated from more secure areas like Kiseiba.

Both hollows have Holocene playa deposits attesting to lakes in ancient times. At the first hollow, called Bir Murr 1 by the Combined Prehistoric Expedition, occupation was high. Ninety hearths were discovered and dated to 6310 B.C., the Late Neolithic. No evidence exists for earlier habitation. There are many, many, ancient tools of high quality, made mostly of flint or chert. There are also grinding stones and a few ceramics.

Bir Murr II, 2 kilometers (1.2 miles) southeast of Bir Murr I shows the same type of material. Both sites are considered camps "occupied by a single group over many seasons, or by many groups sharing nearly identical tools and production techniques."

At the edge of Kharga, after traveling in almost a straight line—just like the camels whose tracks are still visible along the route (as are their skeletons)—two amazing sights are to be seen: a blue desert and a field of incredible whale dunes. The Blue Desert comes about 40 kilometers after Bir Abu Hussein. It covers a fairly extensive area: layers of blue can be seen sandwiched between other formations in the small escarpments. The most intriguing site is the Sea of Blue, where the flat rocks once covered the entire top of the hills but have now broken into hundreds of slabs, each the size of a good dining-room table. Close to Kharga, as if to herald its presence, the whale dunes appear. Kharga is extending itself and there are patches of cultivation, but these whale dunes dominate the area for over 30 kilometers. There are multitudes of them and the road runs right through the heart of the field, twisting and turning to avoid them. What a sight.

TOUR #2
Darb al-Galaba

- travel restricted
- 4x4 (at least 3)
- 2–4 days
- very difficult and dangerous
- GPS, maps, all water, all food, all petrol
- guide mandatory
- permits mandatory

The Darb al-Galaba is a bonafide caravan trail not as well known as the Darb al-Arbain, but also important to trade in Sudan. In some years it became more important to travel and trade because it was closer to the Nile. It begins in Dongola and cuts westward to join the Darb al-Arbain at Selima Oasis, still in Sudan. The two routes move north in tandem, out of Sudan to al-Shab where Galaba turns east toward the Nile Valley and the Darb al-Arbain goes west to Kharga. Galaba continues northeast via Bir Takhlis, Bir Nakhla, near to Gebel Nabta and Nabta Playa. It continues to the west of the Chephren Quarries and Quartz Ridge. It crosses a second road coming due north from Adindan south of Abu Simbel. Galaba continues on a waterless journey through the desert where it runs parallel to the Nile to Esna and Farshut, probably the route that the modern day Rashida take to deliver their camels to the Egyptian markets. The second route heads north from the crossroads to Dunqul and Kurkur oasis to Aswan.

Kharga Oasis is reached at Qasr. Here the Darb was and is more populated. The true evidence of ancient use of the Darb al-Arbain is in Kharga Oasis, where massive fortresses, placed on strategic hills, attest to an ancient security system dating at least to the Greeks and Romans and probably to the Persians. For a continuation of the Darb al-Arbain, see Kharga Oasis.

Bir Takhlis
Bir Takhlis, Well of Salvation, is 45 kilometers (28 miles) northeast of Bir al-Shab. It is a very small oasis, probably what most foreigners first envision an oasis to be, lots of sand, a few palm trees, and beautiful sunsets.

Bir Nakhla
We now enter an area known as the Nubia (Nakhla–Shab) Pediplain. It is bounded in the north by the Kiseiba scarp and in the south it flows into Sudan. It is predominately Cretaceous Nubian Formation of shales and sandstones.

Northeast of Takhlis along the Darb al-Galaba, Bir Nakhla is a little larger, with more date palms. It has no great claims to fame. It is about 35 kilometers (22 miles) southwest of the Nabta Playa area, which may prove to be very important as there is no water at Nabta.

Sidetrip to Nabta Playa
Gebel Nabta and the Nabta Playa, Basin of Little Bushes, have been pushed into the

limelight in the past decades because of what scientists are discovering about their early history. The site is 100 kilometers (60 miles) west and north of Abu Simbel, 60 kilometers (38 miles) north of the Sudanese border, 75 kilometers (47 miles) northeast of Bir Kiseiba, and 75 kilometers (47 miles) east of the Darb al-Arbain.

The **Nabta Playa** is a depression shaped like a kidney about 10 kilometers (6 miles) long and 7 kilometers (4 miles) wide. The mountain and playa areas contain plenty of Neolithic and Terminal Paleolithic remains. There is no water here. The nearest well is Bir Nakhla.

The Nabta Playa contains fossil dunes, ostrich eggshells, and large bird skeletons. It also contains the earliest evidence of man in Egypt. And it was not just a small community; Nabta was heavily populated in prehistory. Six Terminal Paleolithic sites have been located. As with other areas of the desert, like Uwaynat, Dakhla, Kharga, and Farafra, there was a super arid phase in the Nabta area around 9500 B.C. It was followed by heavy rainfalls before 9000 B.C. During the rainy period lakes were formed. A dry period followed and then before 7000 B.C., the rains came again. A new theory maintains these rains were a result of a shift in the monsoonal rain patterns of Africa. Shuttle Imaging Radar has also shown several river channels in the region.

Pottery is abundant at this site. Early Neolithic ceramics have been dated to 8100 B.C. and are among the earliest dated ceramics in North Africa. Their decoration includes a fishnet and ripple style. Some of the pottery cannot be associated with any other known site. The Middle Neolithic ceramics, 7500 to 6300 B.C., are the most plentiful. These were coil constructed.

Desert Stonehenge

The biggest and most important discovery was announced in the spring of 1998 when the oldest astronomical megalith alignment known on earth was discovered here. It is older than Stonehenge and eventually may prove to be more important. Created along the shore of an ancient lake by the nomads of 7,300 to 6,800 years ago, the megaliths, some 9 feet tall, cover almost a square mile.

Stone Calendar

In addition to the monoliths the area contains 30 rock-lined ovals and a calendar circle. The circle is 12 feet wide; two pairs of stones align north–south, two pairs of stones align east–west, two east-northeast, and two west-southwest. The latter stones cast no shadows at high noon three weeks before and three weeks after the summer solstice. In the summer the lake would flood into the circle almost submerging the megaliths, leading scientists to hypothesize that one of their functions was to announce the rainy season.

The Tombs

There are also nine circular mounds surmounted by piles of rocks, each rock weighing as much as 90 kilograms (200 pounds). One of these unusual tombs has been excavated. It contains a clay-lined roof and ritually sacrificed cattle.

The inhabitants of the Nabta Playa were cattle herders as early as B.C. 8290. Archaeological investigations were undertaken by the Combined Prehistoric Expedition from 1974 to 1977 and work has continued to today. We will hear more and more about the Nabta Playa and the southern Western Desert in the coming years. As discoveries are made it may become clear that these people moved north and constructed the first pyramids – or so scientists think.

Quartz Ridge and Chephren Quarries

Named the Quarries of Chephren (Khafre) Stone after material used to create the marvelous statue of Chephren now in the Egyptian Antiquities Museum, the discovery according to a newspaper article in *The Illustrated London News*, solved a long-standing riddle.

The stone used for the Chephren statue was used for only a short time during the Old Kingdom and never appeared in ancient Egypt again. Its origin had always been a mystery. In 1932, an army patrol, lost in a sandstorm, found just such a spot. They came into Cairo with an inscribed sample of the stone. They reported the good news back to Mr. Engelback, the keeper of the Cairo (Egyptian) Museum, and an expedition was sent out on February 4, 1933. Upon investigation they discovered two sites at this location and plenty of evidence that workers from the Old Kingdom labored here, including a cartouche of the pharaoh Khufu (Cheops).

The first site, from which the stone was taken, they named Quartz Ridge and the second, 12 kilometers (7 miles) north, marked by eight cairns, they called Stela Ridge. From the latter site were mined carnelian and amethyst.

G. W. Murray in *Dare Me to The Desert*, tells us he found the old quarry road that leads from this site to the Nile at Tushka. At 38.7 kilometers (24.2 miles) from Quartz Ridge he found Halfway cairn, a 2,000-year-old marker built of "hard silicified sandstone blocks." This road is 80 kilometers (50 miles) long and at 33.5 kilometers (21 miles) from the Nile crosses the Edfu–Halfa track. He goes on to say, "It [the track] certainly had not been used in modern times. It was found that the Egyptians had marked out the road so that there should be no chance of parties missing their way. Not only were there large, well-made cairns, mostly visible, on the hills, but very often the path in the low-lying ground was indicated by pairs of small cairns. The quarter-way and half-way cairns are exceptionally well constructed." No traces of wheeled vehicles were found.

Kurkur Oasis

Kurkur means simply valley, and its greatest claim to fame is that it is believed to have no mosquitoes or flies. There are several wells in the depression which nurture a substantial grove of acacia trees and date and dum palms. There is one mountain, Gebel Garra, and the depression is surrounded by a white chalk escarpment. It is 80 kilometers (50 miles) southwest of Dunqul.

During the New Kingdom, natives captured here (or at Dunqul Oasis below) during the reign of Ramses II, built the temple at Wadi al-Sebua, along the Nile.

Yale University surveyed this oasis looking for prehistoric information as part of the Nubian Salvage Campaign in the 1960s. In 1964, the Desert Institute in Cairo sent an expedition here to study the plant life. At Dunqul (see next entry), they found *Argun palm medemia argun*, an ancient Egyptian species once believed to be extinct.

Dunqul Oasis (Dungal)

This oasis is about 200 kilometers (125 miles) north of Abu Simbel. If there is a crossroads in the desert close to the Nile, this is it. Murray came here in the 1940s and enjoyed what he called two Dunquls— the one the caravans use is 3.2 kilometers (2 miles) north of the main one. The main one is halfway up the southward facing escarpment called the Liar's Teeth. It has palms and sweeter water. Murray drove his cars up to it and stopped for lunch.

In 1963, the Combined Prehistoric Expedition worked here as part of the Nubian Salvage Campaign. They also explored the playa as far as al-Shab.

A desert road branches 70 kilometers (44 miles) northwest to Qasr at the southern point of Kharga Oasis via Nakheila and southeast 120 kilometers (75 miles) to Tomas in Sudan along the river.

The ancient Egyptians mined minerals and hunted in this area.

Sidetrip to Nakheila Oasis

In 1925, Prince Kamal al-Din and John Ball, then the director of the Desert Surveys, arrived at Nakheila with Citröen cars. Shaw and Newbold came in

November and December of 1927 with thirty men and forty camels. Fakhry explored here, too. What they found was graffiti, including drawings of ostriches, gazelles, and snakes. But most importantly there are inscriptions from the Thirteenth Dynasty of the Middle Kingdom! At last an ancient Egyptian connection close to the Darb al-Arbain and Kharga Oasis.

Beadnell tells us Nakheila is only 60 kilometers south-southwest of Kharga and that the water at this oasis is limited to "one or two spots [and must be dug] to a depth of a couple of metres." He goes on to say the source is not ground water as are most wells in the desert, but high-level ground water like the springs at Ain Amur and Ain Tafnis.

Other reports place it 75 kilometers (47 miles) southeast of Baris. In either event it makes it 120 kilometers (75 miles) north of Dunqul. The important thing is that this is yet another desert road. It is not on the Darb al-Arbain. Nor is it to be confused with Nukheila Oasis in Sudan, which is also called Merga Oasis. A lot of riddles are waiting to be solved in this area.

11

The Uwaynat Desert

In recent years the southwestern portion of the Western Desert has been given the name the Uwaynat Desert. It is the counterweight to the Darb al-Arbain Desert in the southeast. It begins in the east around Bir Tarfawi, runs north to Dakhla Oasis and the Great Sand Sea, flows out of Egypt into Libya in the west and creeps into Sudan in the south, as the American poet Carl Sandburg says, "on tiny cat feet."

The landscape in the southwest corner is bold, dynamic, and completely different to that in the southeast. Where the Darb al-Arbain Desert is primarily a flat sand sheet, the Uwaynat Desert is pocked with craters and granite mountains, and dominated by a high plateau. It is also one of the few places in Egypt where Precambrian basement rock is exposed. The Uwaynat Desert paints a dramatic landscape.

Remote and unknown, it has been pushed center stage by the movie *The English Patient*. And now people want to visit. Well, take three steps back and count to ten. For most people a trip to the southwestern corner of Egypt is a big mistake at this time. There is no infrastructure. There are no communities. There are no amenities. When the Egyptian government talks about developing Uwaynat they are not talking about this area. They are talking about Bir Tarfawi in the center of the desert. At Bir Tarfawi an experimental farm is called Uwaynat East, and the new name is causing a great deal of confusion.

To visit the Uwaynat Desert is an ordeal. All food has to be carried. There are no gas stations, so all gasoline for the car must be carted 1,500 kilometers (938 miles) or more in gerrycans. There is no water, so all water for drinking, cooking, and bathing must be toted along. Because an emergency may require more water than available, no one bathes. In winter, it is freezing. In summer, it is boiling. Sand gets into the creases of your eyes, in your throat, in all your clothes, books, and personal items. After a week your clothes begin to smell, you smell, your companions smell. It is likely that one will not see another human being. It is likely that the wind will turn your skin to leather and you will age ten years in a few days. This is the driest most fearsome desert in the world. Unless one is willing to put up with a total lack of any type of convenience, one cannot think of coming to this region. This is probably one of the most dangerous places on earth.

Travel here in a sensible manner. Book your tour with one of the deep desert guides available through travel agencies in Cairo, or listed in the practical section of this book. **Be sure your guide has been to this part of the desert enough times to be confident**. Once you have done so, be prepared for the trip of a lifetime. Be prepared to be overwhelmed by the natural beauty and the awesome isolation.

History

There is none. Mostly, people passed through. And that is the wonder of it. Because there is evidence of rain and ancient artifacts litter the ground, we know that ancient people were here. There are no cemeteries, no permanent dwellings of any kind. At least, none have been found. All we have is a legend.

Zerzura

Somewhere within the haunting interior of the Libyan Desert is the lost oasis of Zerzura. Men have searched in vain for it. They have lain down their lives to find it. But it has always eluded them.

The first mention of Zerzura we know of is made by the medieval Arab traveler Uthman al-Nabulsi in 1447 (Almasy gives this date as 1250). The second time is in the fifteenth-century *Book of Hidden Pearls*. Buried treasure became a mania in the Middle Ages and to aid, or dupe, the treasure hunters books of treasure maps such as this were written. Often hand-inscribed by a native astrologer the books gave directions to hidden treasures interspersed with charms and magic spells. This book gave over four hundred sites where buried treasure could be found in Egypt. Anyone who was lucky enough to come across one of these books guarded it with his life, of which he spent a good part trying to decipher the magic formulae, maps, and instructions. Ibn Khaldun related how Berber students from the Maghrib, who were studying in Cairo, tried to sell counterfeit treasure documents to wealthy Cairenes, including *The Book of Hidden Pearls*. It created such a mania and so many ancient monuments were attacked that in the nineteenth century Maspero, the curator of the Egyptian Museum, agreed to have the book translated into French to put an end to the speculation. It was translated by Ahmad Kamal and published in 1907 by the IFAO under the title *Livre des Perles Enfouies*. An index to the book was published a few decades later in the *Bulletin de la Societe Royale de Geographie d'Egypte*. Maspero was convinced that once people saw the book for what it was, they would desist. They did not.

In any event, number 369 in the book, called *The City of Wardabaha* states, "In the city of Wardabaha, situated behind the citadel of al-Suri, you will see palms, vines, and springs. Penetrate into the wadi and pursue your way up it; you will find another wadi running westward between two mountains. From this last wadi starts a road which will lead you to the city of Zerzura, of which you will find the door closed; this city is white like a pigeon, and on the door of it is carved a bird. Take with your hand the key in the beak of the bird, then open the door of the city. Enter, and there you will find great riches, also the king and queen sleeping in their castle. Do not approach them, but take the treasure." So, everyone went looking, and when they did not find, the legend slowly began to disappear.

The legend sprang to life again when Wilkinson, in *Topography of Thebes and General View of Egypt*, written in 1835, mentions a number of unknown and mysterious places and gives their approximate location. He said the people of Dakhla told him of Zerzura. The hunt was on.

But Zerzura, supposedly five or six days west of Farafra and the size of Bahariya, eluded explorers and travelers. Hints and clues haunted the explorers. Gerhard Rohlfs, on his way to Siwa, found three black men who claimed they were from Zerzura. When he stepped off from Dakhla into the unknown, he did so in the knowledge that every inhabitant of Dakhla had heard of Zerzura, but none knew where it was located. Harding King was sure it lay west of Dakhla, too. Newbold believed it to be about 230 kilometers (144 miles) southwest of Bir Tarfawi. Almasy believed it to be in the Gilf Kebir. Orde Wingate, who did most of his work around Kufra in Libya, maintained the Zerzura legend also existed in Kufra. There the belief was it lay in the center of the Great Sand Sea.

The quest for Zerzura so haunted nineteenth- and early twentieth-century desert travelers and explorers that a Zerzura Club was formed and a debate was begun in the journal of the Royal Geographical Society (which sponsored many trips into the desert to find Zerzura and published an abundance of articles about the journeys).

Zerzura was never found. But the legend never died, nor did the desire to find it. Bagnold, who calls Zerzura the "wish-oasis," devotes the final chapter of his book *Libyan Sands* to the myth. He concludes:

"I like to think of Zerzura . . . as an idea for which we have no apt word in English, meaning something waiting to be discovered in some out-of-the-way place . . . Zerzura is sought in many places, in the desert, at the Poles, in the still unsurveyed mountain regions of Asia. There is no fear that the quest will end, even though the blank spaces on the map get smaller and smaller. For Zerzura can never be identified. . . . As long as any part of the world remains uninhabited, Zerzura will be there, still to be discovered. . . . [When] the time has come at last when the experts can close their notebooks, for there is nothing else unfound . . . we see Zerzura crumbling rapidly into dust. Little birds rise from within and fly away. A cloud moving across the sun makes the world a dull and colourless place."

Ball concludes "that the 'lost' oasis of Zerzura has no more real existence than the philosopher's stone."

Today the legend still persists. Some modern explorers believe Zerzura lies along the Abu Minqar–Kufra Camel Track where there is evidence that a large oasis with a waterfall once existed. Others support that mysterious Count Almasy. His quest for Zerzura is described below (Gilf Kebir section).

Exploration History

The Uwaynat Desert still belongs to the explorer. There have been enough of them through the centuries. Of course, before them were the tribes of the desert who herded there, raided there, and knew and know the terrain better than anyone. But they have not recorded or shared their information with us, so we have no record of their adventures.

The sultan of Waidai sent the merchant Shehaymah of Jalo north and he bumped into Uwaynat in the early 1800s. Harding King probably saw the Gilf Kebir on the horizon on his expedition south from Dakhla in 1909, while John Ball was at the perimeter in 1918. Ahmed Hassanein hit Uwaynat by traveling south in 1923.

Gebel Uwaynat became the destination of a series of explorers who discovered other things as they went along: Prince Kamal al-Din and John Ball discovered the Gilf Kebir in 1925 and came back in 1926; Hugh Beadnell, in 1928, established the car-route from Bir Tarfawi; R. A. Bagnold went three times in 1930, 1931, and 1938. In 1931, P. A. Clayton made a one-day survey of the west side of the Gilf, mapping it for the first time and discovering some rock art (later identified as Wadi Sura, see Wadi Sura below). This was the expedition on which Clayton discovered and helped rescue the Kufra refugees (see Tineida in Dakhla Oasis for details). Robert Clayton-East-Clayton, on an expedition with Count Almasy, flew over the Gilf Kebir in 1932, and discovered Wadi Abd al-Malik; Leo Frobenius in 1933 led the first archaeological expedition into the area and Almasy, part of that expedition, found the Cave of Swimmers in Wadi Sura. Almasy, Dr. L. E. Kadar, Hans Casparius, and Dr. R. A. Bermann surveyed the northern and western Gilf Kebir and Gebel Uwaynat, and Almasy's driver discovered the Ain Doua painted caves at Uwaynat, which were published by Count di Caporiacco. At the same time, Lady Clayton-East-Clayton, with Lt. Commander Roundell, surveyed the northern part of the Gilf. W. B. Kennedy Shaw in 1934–35 discovered rock art at the Gilf. This trip is described by Michael Mason in *The Paradise of Fools* published in 1936. Shaw, of course, published, too.

The last pre–World War II expedition was by Bagnold, who combined his efforts with the Mond Expedition sponsored by the Egypt Exploration Society in 1938. The trip was multipurpose and included Oliver Myers and Hans Winkler. Its significance to our understanding of the Libyan Desert cannot be underrated, for the scientists were able to set dates to prehistoric life in the southern desert and concluded that the culture along the desert was unified. Many publications were produced based on this expedition.

During the war, the Long Range Desert Group visited and explored the area often, as the entire desert was under their reconnaissance. The Italians commanded Libya and had outposts at Gebel Uwaynat. The Germans used it as a smuggler's route.

Then in 1962, the Royal Military Academy at Sandhurst came, followed by the US NAMRU Expedition in 1967, which was interested in mammals, insects, and plants, mainly in Karkur Murr and Karkur Talh. They were followed by the Belgian Trans Saharan Expedition of 1964–65, and the Belgian–Libyan Expedition in 1968–9 which concentrated on Karkur Talh and its rock art and prehistoric settlements. The Geological Survey of Egypt set up its camp at Wadi Wassa in 1968. The Combined Prehistoric Expedition (British Joint Service Expedition) came in 1975. The French Saviem Croisier Des Sables Expedition came in 1977. The Egyptian–American Apollo–Soyuz Expedition of 1978 came to see how similar the terrain was to Mars.

Interestingly enough, we know very little about the archaeology of the area. As pointed out by William McHugh, the Frobenius artifacts were destroyed in World War II, the Kennedy-Shaw (Shaw) collection was dispersed among several museums, but never described, and the Mond expedition artifacts, although placed in the Département de Préhistoire, Musée de l'Homme, were never fully analyzed. So there is much work to be done in the Uwaynat Desert.

Geography and Geology

This area is one of the last unknown regions of the world. Rainfall is less that a millimeter a year and may fall once every ten years at Gebel Uwaynat and every twenty years at the Gilf Kebir. (Although there are signs that the weather pattern may be changing.) It has been so dry for so long that the ancient past is strewn about the naked ground, telling the story of ancient ways of life to the knowing eye. Precambrian metamorphic rocks underlay the area intruded by granites of post Carboniferous age and surrounded by hard quartzitic sandstones of Paleozoic age. That makes the visible features of the Uwaynat Desert very old indeed.

Sand dunes are the most common landform in the region. They come in a variety of shapes and colors from near white to rusty red. The Great Sand Sea has penetrated the Gilf Kebir from the north and, although the majority of dunes pass the Gilf to the east or to the west, there are places where dunes have actually climbed the escarpment, a humbling sight.

Mountains

Mountains are a dominant feature of this area of the desert, a lot of them, and they run in and out of Egypt. Some are high cones, plugs, and dikes of Paleozoic–Mesozoic age. Three of the major mountains in the southwestern corner of Egypt stand almost in a straight line and are only 15 miles apart: Arkenu, Kissu, and Uwaynat.

Gebel Arkenu is a granite intrusion. One source says it was named for a single tree found at the entrance to one of its wadis, but another says the name means Mountain of the Corner. Arkenu is one of the few mountains in the Libyan Desert composed entirely of granite. It was discovered by Hassanein. At that time it was within the boundaries of Egypt, but when the border was fixed at E 25 degrees, it became part of Libya.

This mountain is elliptical, about 20 kilometers (12 miles) in diameter, and rises 1,435 meters (4590 feet). There are rock paintings here, located in at least eight caves. Some are similar to Uwaynat, others resemble the rock art at the Hoggar Mountains in Algeria. Arkenu contains veins of gold. It was studied by Menchikoff in 1924–25 with Prince Kamal al-Din, and again in 1926, by Sandford in 1933, and Deaio in 1931.

Gebel Babein, the Mountain of Two Gates or Doors, straddles the border. It is a granite intrusion.

Gebels Peter and Paul are still within Egypt. The twin mountains lie between the two most massive and imposing natural edifices in the entire Western Desert, the Gilf Kebir and Gebel Uwaynat. The mountains themselves are steep-sided quartz trachytes plugs. Surrounding them are old granitoid outcroppings of Precambrian basement rocks. Recent studies indicate some gold can be found here. The quantity is yet to be determined. Landmines may have been laid at and around these mountains.

Of the remaining mountains there is **Gebel Kamil**, where gold has recently been discovered, and **Gebel Kissu**, where rock art was discovered by Almasy. For in depth descriptions of **Gebel Uwaynat** and **Gilf Kebir** see below.

Craters

Recent landsat images revealed several interesting groups of craters in the Gebel Uwaynat area. The first two craters, which look as if they were created by impact (astroblemes), are located near Kufra Oasis, about 320 kilometers (200 miles) northwest of Uwaynat, in southeast Libya. Because they are similar to craters discovered on the moon, Mars, and other planets, these craters are being studied by planetologists in the hope of better understanding craters on the other planets. The craters at Uwaynat have been dated to the post Early Cretaceous period.

The second set are volcanic craters found in Egypt between Gebel Uwaynat and Gilf Kebir. These craters, circular depressions east of Gebel Kissu in northwest Sudan, were first discovered by P. A. Clayton in 1931, on the second Bagnold Expedition.

Rushdi Said thinks that springs could have caused such craters. The springs caused the ground to fall. There is no baking, and there are no meteorite remains, but remnants of springs do exist.

Clayton Craters

The Clayton Craters are a field of twenty craters. Bagnold says:

A row of seven craters rose from the level desert surface extending in line over about 5 miles . . . The crater was roughly circular in shape, measuring 1,200 yards by 1,000 yards (paced internal measurements). The walls consisted of baked and partially fused sandstone, thrust up vertically or even overturned outwards. They reached a height of about 100 feet. Inside the rim was a broad low dome of heavy greenish igneous rock, in appearance like a diorite. The rim itself was broke by several gaps, and rainwater, collecting in the crater, had escaped through one of these. A second crater about a mile to the east was smaller, but with steeper and less broken walls. In the center it contains a compound neck of basalt, which formed a low dome standing about 50 feet above the level of the plain. Again a stream bed led from the central hollow out through a gap in the rim at one point. The other craters of this group we had to leave unvisited, but from a distant view they appeared to be essentially similar to the two described.

Bagnold, Miskin, Shaw, and Sweeting Craters

This new group of craters is 130 kilometers (81 miles) east-southeast of Uwaynat. There are four craters discovered by Landsat and named "for the explorers whose tracks came nearest to them." Not yet studied, they await definition.

Wind

As with all the Western Desert, wind is the major factor in the Uwaynat Desert. The wind, coming from the north, has broken the northeastern part of the Gilf Kebir plateau into inselbergs and cones. It has pushed sand dunes up and over the valleys leading to its top. It has pitted exposed rock surfaces at Gebel Uwaynat, changing its face forever.

It has been discovered that the Uwaynat Desert has conditions similar to those found on Mars. The Viking Mission found that the drainage patterns and wadis of the Gilf Kebir are similar to those of the Ismenius Lacus region on Mars. Martian dunes are like the dunes of Kharga Oasis. On earth the land is still changing thanks to the wind and the rain. The dunes, are still marching "toward basins of deposition in the southern Sahara." On Mars, they have reached their destinations and are trapped around the northern pole. So, scientists are watching the Uwaynat region to better understand the solar system.

Caravan Routes and Roadways

Darb al-Tarfawi

There are several routes from Kharga that lead to Ain Tarfawi; none of them is this darb. This darb begins in Mut in Dakhla Oasis. It leaves Dakhla Oasis south of the city of Mut and heads southwest to the Bir Tarfawi and then into Sudan. About one eighth of the way out of Dakhla a branch moves west to Abu Ballas, Gilf Kebir, and Gebel Uwaynat. The route to Tarfawi is now paved.

Dakhla to Kufra

This is the mystery road, the long-lost road used by invaders from the south and west on the infamous *ghaswas* (raids). Soldiers out of Dakhla destroyed the water holes along the route as far as a five-day march to protect the oasis. Then the road became impassable and fell from memory. Today we are not sure where it is.

Gilf Kebir to Kufra

Along the western edge of the Gilf is a track headed northwest to Kufra. It was traveled by Hassanein in 1923.

The People

William McHugh has pieced together a profile of the ancient people based on the rock art, pottery, and tools found in the area. During the Early Holocene (8000–6000/5000 B.C.) small groups of hunter–gatherers scavenged for plant food and hunted giraffes, scimitar oryx, gazelles, Barbary sheep, and ostriches. They caught their prey with dogs, clubs, shields, wheel traps, lassoes, and bow and arrow.

In the Middle Holocene (6000/5000–3000/2000 B.C.) cattle first appeared and then became the most dominant animal. During the latter phases of this period, rock art paintings replaced engravings on the canyon walls. At the end of this time, goats appeared.

After these peoples disappeared from the desert, the area was used by herders and raiders on a sporadic basis. The Goran, Tebu, and Tuareg were among them. These tribes are described in the chapter on People.

When Ahmed Hassanein arrived at Uwaynat in 1923, 150 people lived there under a Goran chief called Sheikh Herri, the King of Uwaynat. The chief had left his home in Waidai when the French colonized it. He first settled in Kufra, but then came on to Uwaynat. By 1930, no one lived in the area, since lack of rain had dried up the lake. From time to time a herder and his family will journey to the area to graze. When conflicts arise in Libya, Chad, or Sudan, people will come to the area. But on the whole, the southwestern desert is deserted.

Rock Art

There are so many rock paintings and engravings in the Sahara and Libyan deserts that one could almost say they are commonplace. In the southwestern corner of Egypt alone over 4,000 images have been found. The rock art cuts a path from Uwaynat and the Gilf Kebir through Libya and Chad into Algeria and Nigeria and continues into Mali,

Rock art of Wadi Telisaghe

Bird goddesses of Jabbaren, Tassili n'Ajjer

Little Devils of Tassili

Mauritania, the Western Sahara, and Morocco. Some sites have become famous, others are practically unknown, and more so remote that few modern travelers have seen them and probably no one else either. Wadi Mathendous in Libya is perhaps the most prolific site in all of Africa. Here some of the engravings have heads of animals and bodies of humans, just like the ancient Egyptian art, only this is older. Perhaps the most famous sites in the world are in Algeria. The rock paintings of Tassili n'Ajjer have been protected by the establishment of the Tassili National Park. This area was explored by Henri Lhote who wrote *The Search for the Tassili Frescos*. In the book *Sahara Handbook* a good review of most North African sites is provided.

In Egypt, there is an extensive belt of rock art running from the Arabian (Eastern) Desert in the east through Kharga, Dakhla, the Gilf Kebir, and Uwaynat. The rock art of the Uwaynat region, unquestionably its greatest treasure, is as far east as cattle pastoralist rock art has been discovered. In almost every valley of Gebel Uwaynat rock art exists.

Location

Most of the art is in the wadis of Gebel Uwaynat with a few paintings and engravings found at Kissu, Yergeddah, Arkenu, and the Gilf Kebir. Many, many sites were discovered by the Italians in Libya and by the French in the Ennedi Highlands. When Hassanein was at Arkenu he asked a Goran tribesman about former residents and received a rewarding answer:

"Many different people have lived round these wells, as far back as anyone can remember. Even djinn have dwelt in that place in olden days."

Hassanein said, "Djinn! How do you know that?"

"Have they not left their drawings on the rocks?" was the answer. And the Goran told him he would find the drawings at Uwaynat "At the end of the valley, where the tail of the valley wags." Hassanein found this place on May 1, 1923. We now know it as Karkur Talh and over 1,000 drawings and engravings have been discovered. Unfortunately, today most of them are located within Sudan, which meets Egypt near the entrance to this valley.

Newbold was an important rock art discoverer, too, but mainly in Sudan. He and Shaw had two expeditions, one in 1923 from al Ubeid to Bir Natrun and back, and a second in 1927, from al-Ubeid to Halfa by Bir Natrun, Merga, and Selima. In 1923, he found rock art at Abu Sufyan, Gelti Umm Tasawir, and Zolat al-Hammad. In 1927, he and Shaw found rock art in the following places: Wara al-Gilud, Ridge of Zolat al-Hammad, Nukcila Lake (Merga Oasis), Tamar al-Gusar, Wadi al-Anag, and Burg al-Tuyur, Tower of the Birds.

Themes and Style

There are two types of rock art: paintings and engravings. Paintings are in red, white, and occasionally yellow paint. Engravings were incised with a sharp instrument. They were both done on the walls and ceilings of protected areas, especially overhangs and caves. Winkler hypothesizes that the women did the paintings and the men did the engravings.

The subject matter can also be divided in two: without cattle and with cattle. The cattle depicted differ. There are longhorn, shorthorn, and polled cattle. Longhorn cattle are the oldest known in Egypt. Shorthorn cattle replaced them, probably coming from the Near East during the Hyksos period.

There are pastoral scenes of hunting, herding, home and hearth, and in one instance, swimming. In addition to cattle, other animals are a common theme, especially ostrich, giraffes, gazelles, and a few camels. Not found are elephant, buffalo, rhinoceros, hippopotamus, or crocodile. This tells us something about the habitat.

The people are shown naked, with only belts; men in simple or double loin-cloths, and women with skirts.

Origin

Dating the rock art has not been easy as there are a number of styles and different techniques. Location also plays a part. On a larger scale the rock art of all the deserts of North Africa has been categorized into five periods: Bubalus Period from 10,000 to 7000 B.C.; the Roundhead Period from 8000 to 5000 B.C.; the Cattle Period from 5000 to 2500 B.C.; the Horse and Chariot Period from 1500 B.C. to A.D. 800; and the Camel Period from A.D. 400 to the present. Although it differs, most of the art in Uwaynat and the Gilf Kebir falls into the Cattle Period. Van Noten tells us the cattle cultures existed around 4000 B.C., but were gone from high altitudes around 2000 B.C.

Hans Winkler in *Rock Pictures at Uweinat* tells us that the rock art of Egypt, which encompasses a wider range than just that of the pastoralists at Uwaynat, spans five millennia and also spans cultures, showing Arabic, Coptic, Greek, and ancient Egyptian inscriptions. This description includes all the rock art found throughout the desert and southern Nile Valley, not just that of Uwaynat. Winkler believed that five different peoples made the early rock art of the deserts of Egypt. The first were the Eastern Invaders, with dugout canoes, and the second were the Early Nile Dwellers with papyrus boats in their drawings. Winkler thought the art of these two peoples was the best of all. Combined, he called them the Autochthonous Mountain Dwellers, who lived in southern Egypt from the Red Sea hills across the Nile to Uwaynat and beyond. In Uwaynat, he believes that the Tebu created the art.

So what was the purpose? Wellard offers two aims: to give pleasure and/or to practice sympathetic magic. The first was accomplished with gusto, as no artist or critic can quibble with the excellence of most of the art. The latter is more interesting. Seeking to have success in hunting may have required a drawing, as might success in birth, or the warding off of spirits—any of these things are possible. One would think this is more religious than sympathetic magic. It would seem that a third motive might exist. How about historical record? The persons who drew the family home, belongings, and people were saying to their world, "Here we are!" "This is how we live!" "This is how we hunt!" "This is my wife and my child!" "This is our pet ostrich!" They certainly depict life as it existed at that time. The rock art of the Uwaynat Desert is one of Egypt's greatest treasures and should be protected at all costs.

Who Found What

In addition to all the explorers who stumbled on to the rock art in the southwest corner of Egypt, there have been some expeditions that went to the area primarily for the rock art. Frobenius is probably the foremost authority on the rock art in the Fezzan in Libya and he explored the Uwaynat Desert with Almasy as guide in 1933. Interestingly, *al-Ahram* newspaper sent an expedition to Uwaynat in 1934, and they made a large collection of drawings and photographs of the art at Uwaynat, including the Wadi Sura. However, none of these drawings was ever published by *al-Ahram*. A survey was done of the existing paintings and engravings by Rhotert in the early twentieth century. The Mond Expedition's Hans Winkler came to Uwaynat in 1938 and did extensive work on the rock art especially at Karkur Talh and Karkur Murr in the south of Uwaynat. Then came World War II. It wasn't until 1968 that study was renewed on the rock art in Egypt. The Belgian–Libyan Expedition worked at Karkur Talh at Uwaynat and found thousands of images in 1968–69. They quote a total of 4,000 known works of rock art in the area.

Pottery

Pottery shards are found at a number of places in the Uwaynat Desert. These shards are important as they can be traced and hopefully the people who used them can be identified. We have found that the pots here were manufactured in a number of ways including wheel-made pots, coiled pots, and molded pots. Shapes include straight walled with rounded bases or globular bowls. They were fired in an oxidizing atmosphere. Colors run from brown through yellow to red and gray.

What is significant is that similar pottery exists in other areas of the Sahara. The Mond Expedition of 1938 was able to settle some perplexing questions about the inhabitants of the desert in prehistory through the pottery. As early as 1929 they were finding shards around Armant that they could not link to anything or anyone that they knew about. They determined it was a different group of people. The pottery did not exist north of Armant, but was abundant as far south as Edfu. The assumption was that the people came to the Nile Valley around the Sixth Dynasty from the west or from the south. The expedition came to the Uwaynat–Gilf Kebir area to look for answers.

At Uwaynat and points south they found the same types of pottery. The conclusion was that people, whom the scientists labeled the C-Group people and/or the Armant invaders, were from the Sahara, shared a common culture probably of Libyan origin, and came into Egypt around 2500 B.C. They also went to Spain around the same time. They migrated, scientists hypothesize, because the desert was drying up and they had to move on.

The Tour

Middle Arbain Desert

Bir Tarfawi

Bir Tarfawi is located along the eastern side of a basin 350 kilometers (211 miles) west of Abu Simbel along flat, desolate, and almost indistinguishable terrain. Fixing its exact location was very important at the beginning of the twentieth century for it was the farthest southwest of any known wells and there were too few landmarks to follow to get to it.

It, like the artificial Bir Sahara, 30 kilometers (18 miles) southwest, is located in a small depression less that 10 meters (32 feet) below the desert floor. The depression was formed by subsidence along a northeast–southwest axis. Both sites had lakes. Both sites were inhabited by early peoples. Both sites had several functions, including butchery.

Dum and date palm, acacia, and tamarisk extend for 15 kilometers (9 miles) in all directions from Bir Tarfawi. At the westernmost edge of the vegetation is evidence of Stone Age settlements. In the southwest are oval limestone beds of prehistoric Upper Acheulian ponds. Abundant evidence exists to support the theory of Neolithic and Early Kingdom occupancy around an extensive lake. Material from the Late Acheulian period includes cleavers and chipping tools.

The pottery of Bir Tarfawi dates only to 1160 B.C. The shapes are different and they have defined necks and rims. They were coiled, molded, and thrown on potters' wheels. One of the most important discoveries is an ancient and extensive butchery site where rhinoceros and camel were slaughtered.

Two lakes once occupied the depression. They probably existed in the last of the wet phases that inundated the land in the Paleolithic era. As with most places in the Western Desert, the area yields plenty of fossils including equid, a predecessor to the horse. Recent satellite photos have confirmed evidence of human settlements, along an ancient lake bed dating from 30,000 years ago.

East Uwaynat

East Uwaynat is a settlement located 70 kilometers south of Bir Tarfawi. In 1981, Shuttle Imaging Radar (SIR) revealed three ancient riverbeds. It convinced Farouk al-Baz of the US National Air and Space Museum that fossil water may be present. He was right. Wells have been dug and an experimental farm called East Uwaynat, eventually covering 84 square kilometers (53 square miles), was established. It is thriving.

As one can see, Tarfawi has a long history. Why anyone would want to now call it East Uwaynat is a mystery. But, big changes are in the works for Tarfawi. It is now linked to Dakhla and Aswan by paved roads.

Exploration History

The earliest record of exploration of Bir Tarfawi was in 1925 when John Ball accompanied Prince Kamal al-Din on the first of his many desert expeditions. From here the prince traveled west 400 kilometers (250 miles) to Uwaynat, marking the way with empty petrol tins.

In the winter of 1927–28, Hugh Beadnell came to Tarfawi looking for water. He believed that large quantities of water existed just beneath the surface of this barren, arid, uninhabited area. Today, we know he was correct. A month later Bagnold and company arrived on their desert adventure. On January 24, while they were headed toward Uwaynat, it rained, an event which Bagnold called "an incident to be recorded in the annals of the country."

Since the early 1970s, the Combined Prehistoric Expedition (CPE) has worked at Bir Tarfawi and Bir Sahara. They have a long history in the area, first working with the Nubian Salvage Campaign in the 1960s. The CPE is composed of scholars from Belgium, Egypt, the United Kingdom, Poland, and the United States. In 1973, they worked at Bir Sahara (see next entry), in 1974 at Bir Tarfawi, and in 1975 at Nabta.

Getting There: Restricted travel requiring permits in 2000. Needs minimum of two, 4x4 vehicles, GPS, maps, all water, all food, all petrol. GUIDE IS MANDATORY. This is true for every site listed in this chapter.

Bir Sahara

The name, given to us by Mrs. Hugh Beadnell, means, "the desert well." We can thank her husband, Hugh Beadnell, for the water here, for he dug the well in 1927. The well was started February 28, 1927, and water was found on March 19 at 17.5 meters (56 feet). Water now lies about 2 meters (6 feet) below the surface here. The well produces 440 gallons of water per day.

In the southern portion of this small depression are several fossil springs. Don't confuse this with fresh water or fossil water. These are mounds that now stand above the ground around them, but date to prehistory when they were springs. Around the springs are evidence of the earliest known humans of the desert. This was Final Acheulian.

Middle Paleolithic evidence also exists. At least five levels or periods of occupation have been found. Some of the sites, labeled Mousterian and Aterian, are too old to date with any accuracy with current scientific equipment. That means they are over 43,000 years old.

Some faunal fossils found in the area include ostrich eggshell, teeth, the jaw of a warthog, and bits of an equid (probably a donkey). Snail shells date to more than 44,700 years ago.

Exploration History

Fred Wendorf and Romuald Schilk in *Prehistory of the Eastern Sahara* tell a story about the Combined Prehistoric Expedition's stay at Bir Sahara in the winter of 1973. They had decided to bring 120 live ducks with them to eat. Each day they roamed free and at night the cook herded them into a tent. But they were noisy, especially at night or when a strange sound was heard. The cook picked two ducks for the evening meal each day, and tried to kill the noisy ones first. After a week or so there was dead silence at night among the ducks in the tent, as the 100 odd remaining ducks tried to escape their fate.

From Dakhla Oasis to the Gilf Kebir

Abu Ballas

Located 240 kilometers (150 miles) west-southwest of Dakhla, just before the southeastern tip of the Great Sand Sea, Abu Ballas, Father of Pots, was brought to the attention of Europe by John Ball when he was mapping the Western Desert in 1916. It was named by Prince Kamal al-Din because hundreds of water pots were found around its base. It is a hill rather than a mountain and was used as a storage place for water. If one searches closely one will find additional locations in this area where pots are buried at the base of hills. One thing is certain, the hill is strategic. It is one third of the way to the Gilf Kebir from Dakhla, close to the Kufra and Abu Minqar Camel Track, at the tip of the Great Sand Sea. It is a logical place to leave provisions.

The pots, once numbering in their hundreds, are huge, each holding about 30 liters of water. They are heavy. They were probably thrown on a potter's wheel. They come in two styles: tall, fat, and round-bottomed, and tall, slender, and pointed-bottomed, as in an amphora.

The history of Abu Ballas goes far beyond the day when Ball and Kamal al-Din first saw it. The route is an ancient one. There is rock art on the mountain, so prehistoric peoples roamed the area. It is possible that the ancient Egyptians had water depots throughout the desert. There is another Abu Ballas near Fayoum, and it, too, is littered with pots. There is evidence that Ibn Nusayr, traveling for the Umayyads between 695 and 700 found such a depot within the Western Desert, whether it was this one or not is unknown. The most prevalent theory, however, is that the pots were left by Tebu tribesmen from southern Libya for their frequent raids into Egypt, especially to Dakhla Oasis. This theory is supported by Prince Kamal al-Din's observation that some of the pots bear Tebu tribal markings.

Richard Bermann reported just such a theory to the Royal Geographical Society in 1934. Bermann was told that the people of Dakhla followed attackers into the desert to this place in the middle of the nineteenth century. When they found the storage supply at Abu Ballas, they broke many of the jars to stop the attacks. It is also reported that the soldiers stationed in Dakhla went into the desert and poisoned wells to stop invaders from coming across the desert. This is most likely the route. As recently as the early part of the the the twentieth century people talked about a darb, now lost, that went from Dakhla to Kufra and probably passed Abu Ballas and the north edge of Gilf Kebir. Hassanein heard of it in 1923, but its route had already been lost.

In setting forth a number of theories about Zerzura, Ball includes Abu Ballas. He explains the ancient name has been interpreted as Zerzura, the Arabic name for a small black wheatear indigenous to the Western Desert. He proposes that perhaps the word is not Zerzura at all, but similar to it. In fact, it could refer to a water jug, a *zir*, and therefore be the "water depot of the blacks."

In 1981 investigations were conducted by Dr. Rudolph Kuper of the Henrich Barth Institute of Cologne who is working in the area on a paleomonzon project. Abu Ballas has also been brought to the attention of the world by Terra X, which proposes the pots were not imported into the area at all, but were actually created on the spot. They were too heavy to be transported.

There are more theories too. In an interview, Edmond Diemer, co-contributor to *Desert Libyque*, said we cannot overlook the possibility that there is or was a small well here at Abu Ballas and that an enterprising individual filled and sold the water jars to caravans. Theodore Monod, in the same interview, maintains that waterskins were lighter and easier to handle, so why make water jugs at all.

Lots of theories, no answers. There were hundreds of pots at the base of this mountain in the past. Today few remain, and those that are there are broken. What they are and why they are there is another desert mystery.

Rock Art

There are rock pictures at Abu Ballas too! Three pictures are located half way up the mountain. They were discussed by Newbold and Shaw at the beginning of the twentieth century. One is the profile of a tall man. The second is a bearded Libyan hunter and his hunting dog chasing an antelope with a bow and arrows. The third is a cow being suckled by a calf. They were discovered by Prince Kamal al-Din.

The Great Sand Sea

In 1972, Skylab 4 studied the sand seas of the world, defining and classifying them, coordinating the terminology surrounding them, and studying regional patterns of dune morphology. One of the first things that were changed, or combined, were the names of various dune patterns. (See Natural World for details.)

Sand seas exist in deserts in at least eighteen important locations as recorded by Skylab 4 in 1972. Four of these seas exist in North Africa (See map in Natural World): Algeria has the ergs and Libya the sand seas. The Calanscio and Great sand seas begin as one, south of the northern coast. They break into the two distinct seas between Siwa and Jalo. The Calanscio moves almost due south and merges with the Rebiana south of Bilma, Libya. The Rebiana stretches east to west, jumping out of Libya into Algeria. The Great moves southeast, pouring into Egypt south of Siwa and marching into Africa to the west of Ain Della, Farafra, and Dakhla. It marches over and around the Gilf Kebir as it reaches its end.

The Great Sand Sea covers 72,000 kilometers (45,000 miles) and is larger than some countries. There are some dunes in the sea that are not only 100 meters (320 feet) high, but also 100 kilometers (62.5 miles) long. Al-Baz in *Circular Feature among Dunes of the Great Sand Sea, Egypt,* tells us these moving seif dunes sit astride stable, relatively unmoving, 2 kilometer- (1.2 mile-) wide whale back dunes. While the long seif dunes move and change, their base, the whale backs, remain in place. This explains how Rohlfs' cairn remains in situ. Dr. Ladislas Kadar found one seif dune 140 kilometers (88 miles) long. He believes this to be the longest dune in the world. Others varied from 1 kilometer to 60, but are just as awesome. Despite the fact that between the dunes the ground is nearly void of sand, the only way over them, is over them. Trying to go around them is impossible.

The Great Sand Sea sits on a rise in the desert floor. The dunes are aligned with the winds. C. Vance Haynes tells us, "Each procession of dunes maintains its alignment with the air stream whether it rises with the land or descends escarpments, most of which face southward (downwind). The barchan dunes are modern to late Holocene in age as they override the early to middle Holocene sand sheets, but the time of origin of the sand sea and its seif dunes is probably older."

Exploration History

The first European to enter the Great Sand Sea, and the man who named it, was the German explorer Gerhard Rohlfs. In 1874, Rohlfs surveyed the Libyan Desert for the Khedive Ismail. He didn't plan to explore the sea, he didn't know it existed. All he wanted to do was go from Dakhla to Kufra. Well, the sea was in his way and by the time he realized he couldn't cross it, it was too late. According to English-language texts he was exhausted and out of water, and the expedition seemed doomed. But in one of those strange twists of fate the heavens opened and rain came down in torrents in a place where it may rain a few drops every ten years. The rain saved Rohlfs' life. He replenished his water supply and headed north. Before he left, he marked the spot with his cairn and named it Regenfeld, Rainfield. In his journal he wrote, "Will ever man's foot tread this place again?"

In Rohlfs' book, *Drei Monate in der libyschen Wüste,* he tells a different story from the English-language version above. In fact, he very painstakingly describes all the preparations for the journey to Kufra. He says it rained from 7 p.m. on February 2 to 2 p.m. on February 4 for a total of 16mm. Only seven men and fifteen camels were with him, not the huge entourage he took to Farafra. Rohlfs maintained that they had provisions and water for twenty days and when he moved on he left behind some dates and German rusk. There is no hint of a problem either with logistics or with supplies. They encountered a huge dune field and changed their plans. His version is supported by Almasy, who tell us Prince Kamal al-Din, an Egyptian geographer and explorer, found the provisions left by Rohlfs.

John Ball, the English surveyor, stepped off from Dakhla Oasis and went 322 kilometers (200 miles) around the southeastern edge of the sea in 1917. Not satisfied, he came back again, this time with Prince Kamal al-Din, to continue the journey and find Regenfeld, which they did. The sea was also skirted by Hassanein on his monumental voyage from Sollum to Uwaynat in 1923. Like Ball, Colonel de Lancey Forth made two journeys between 1921 and 1924. First he followed the route used by Rohlfs, and then he approached the sea from the north via Siwa. Forth was astounded, and probably pleased, to find evidence that people had lived in this area during Neolithic times. P. A. Clayton, working for the Egyptian Desert Surveys, was the first to cross it by car from east to west. The Italians studied it from the west. The Sanusi knew it well, but did not share their information (with good reason).

The Long Range Desert Group of the British Army marched out of Ain Della and into the dunes along a 32 kilometer (20 mile) wide corridor. They describe the dunes as 300–500 feet high. Between the parallel dune ranges are corridors, many wide in the beginning, but ending abruptly in an impenetratable sea of sand. They took just such a corridor as they entered the Sand Sea. It was three miles wide in the beginning but after a day's travel, it narrowed and ended. They arrived at Siwa near Zaytun. In 1937, Shaw and company crossed the Great Sand Sea from south to north, headed from Uwaynat to Siwa. The team often traveled the route in the 1940s to spy upon the Italians in Libya and, in the hope of creating a permanent route, marked the path along the crest of the dunes with rubbish, petrol cans, and stones—many of the markings existing today, including Big Cairn. The route continued to be used in World War II and is marked on the 1:500,000 map put out by the Survey. Clayton crossed it once too often and ended up a prisoner of the Italians.

Libyan Desert Silica Glass

Among the many unsolved mysteries of the Great Sand Sea are the large chunks of silica green glass lying between the dunes. Although there is evidence that it was worked by prehistoric people, it is not manufactured glass, but a natural formation. It was first seen by westerners when soldiers saw it in the early 1930s. The glass, streaked with gray and pale green in color, can be clear or cloudy, and weigh anything from a few grams to 7.25 kilograms (16 pounds). Recently, a piece weighing 27 kilos (59 pounds) was found.

The book Désert Libyque reports that the first known mention of the mysterious Libyan Desert Silica Glass (LDSG) was made in 1846 by envoys of Hagg Hussein of Kufra and was reported two years later to the European world by Fresnel, the French consul, in the Bulletin de l'Institut de Géographie de Paris. It was also known by Zittel of the Rohlfs Expedition of 1874 and by Borchardt, who wrote about it in 1929.

P. A. Clayton rediscovered the glass in 1932. In 1934, an expedition was mounted by the Geological Survey of Egypt to bring L. J. Spencer, keeper of minerals in the British Museum, to the site. They spent nine days collecting and analyzing the glass. It is believed to exist in the small area found between latitudes N 25.02 and 26.13 and longitudes E 25.24 and 25.55 and extends to 130 kilometers (81 miles) NS and 53 kilometers (33 miles) EW in the Great Sand Sea.

Out of this collection the glass has been classified as translucent, semitranslucent, peridot-like, milky, bubbly, banded, carbonaceous, opaque, xenolithic, and granular. Before leaving the area the expedition put a piece of paper with their signatures and the dates of the expedition in a whiskey bottle filled with red sand and left it at their last camp. (Peter Clayton now has the bottle, which was given to him by a group of Italian explorers who found it in August of 1985.)

Twelve expeditions and twenty-five geologists have ventured into the Great Sand Sea to find the answers to this mysterious glass, and pieces have been sent to the Smithsonian Institute in Washington, D.C. for examination. One of the early theories was that the glass was extraterrestrial. This opened up speculation. It was estimated that to produce the glass it was necessary that the substance be heated to 1600° C for 47 days or 1800° C for one fifth of a day, or 2000° C for two minutes.

It was also proposed that the glass was a product of volcanic activity. So an expedition of eleven vehicles and twenty-three men sallied forth in December 1971 to check out the craters around the Gilf Kebir area to see if they, too, were extraterrestrial and see if there was glass at that site. Although the craters were probably formed by extraterrestrial bodies, no similar glass was found at the site.

So, if the glass was produced by a meteor, where is it? Farouk al-Baz, studying the Landsat images from space has found a candidate in the Great Sand Sea. It is 150 kilometers (94 miles) southeast of the silican glass area. Now called the al-Baz Crater, it is a 4 kilometer (2.5 mile) circular crater. Studies reveal a flat floor, "a terraced wall, a crenulated rim, and the subdued remains of an inner structure, approximately 1.6 km [1 mile] in diameter, that may have been a central uplift." All this indicates a meteorite impact. In 1991, the Geological Survey mounted an expedition and determined that the al-Baz Crater was not a volcanic crater, but did not rule out the possibility that it was created by a meteorite.

In the 1980s, new, more earthbound theories were proposed by Ulrich Jux. Since ancient lakes had been discovered in the area he proposed that super-saturated silica deposits left in the dried-up cracks of an ancient lake bed, through a complicated chemical reaction, produced the glass.

One team that has been working with the silica glass problem since 1985 is the Centro Studi Luigi Negro from Italy. In 1996, they sponsored a conference on silica glass. The varied conclusions, published in *Sahara* magazine in December 1997, bring us back to one of the original theories: silica glass was created by the intense heat of the impact of a meteorite striking the desert sand.

And now, the Italian team has more to tell us: the most astounding discovery of all. In October 1998, Vincenzo de Michele of the Centro Studi Luigi Negro was permitted to examine Tutankhamen's magnificent pectoral jewelry in the Egyptian Museum. The pectoral was an important ceremonial jewel used by the King for his coronation and for the celebration for the birth of his son. In death, it was laid on the chest of the fallen pharaoh. For years the central piece, a giant, well-polished, lime green scarab, has been listed as chalcedone, a stone not as precious as the surrounding gems embedded in the gold. Well, that stone is far more precious than all the gems in Tut's pectoral combined, for it is silica glass.

This discovery is very significant to the history of the desert. It tells us that ancient Egyptians knew of the Great Sand Sea and its silica glass. They may well have known how rare and special the glass was, perhaps even its celestial origins, for it is given a place of honor in Tutankhamen's pectoral, a very important ceremonial jewel. How many other ancient Egyptian jewels contain silica glass? How did the ancient Egyptians get it? The questions are endless.

Today the wilderness we call the Great Sand Sea is still there, as desolate as ever. But with landsat images, taken by satellites, we know exactly how big it is and exactly where it is. In fact, we can actually count the number of dunes. That doesn't make it any more hospitable; people still don't go there. It is one of the earth's last frontiers.

Regenfeld

By now the story of this site is known to the reader. If not, see The Great Sand Sea in Chapter 11. When it rained, Rohlfs marked the spot with a cairn and gave the exact location in his publication. It has become the object of a quest for true desert aficionados. You are not a desert explorer unless you have stood at Regenfeld.

Prince Kamal al-Din went looking for Regenfield in 1923 and found it. Rohlfs' marker consisted of the traditional rocks piled up one on top of the other and seven empty iron water tanks (he had taken over five hundred of these tanks into the desert: where are they now?) among which was a bottle, and inside the bottle a message. When the Prince found the cairn it was exactly where it had been left in 1874, at the base of a great dune. In fact, he discovered that the dune was not only in the same position, but was exactly the same height as recorded by Rohlfs. For over forty years nothing in this area of the Great Sand Sea had changed.

Prince Kamal read the message, copied it, added another of his own, in Arabic, and placed a new bottle at the cairn. Taking the original message and some scattered remnants of the former expedition that were lying on the ground, including bottles, an ax, a waterskin, and a basket of dates, the prince headed back to Cairo.

Ball found the area exactly as it was left. The iron tanks had "become covered with a hard dark brown film, apparently of magnetic oxide of iron, not rusted in the ordinary way." Empty wine bottles left by the Rohlfs expedition were frosted by the sandblast wherever they were exposed.

Today the messages are gone, the iron tanks are gone, and so are the wine bottles. All that remains is the cairn. Samir and Wally Lama say that in 1940, Ibrahim Lama added his name to the bottle. In the 1970s, so did Samir. Monod did the same in 1993. Others had done the same. Now everything is gone. It is to be hoped that they have been taken by somebody responsible.

Sandheim

To the north of Regenfeld is a place Rohlfs called Sandheim, where the expedition found acacia bushes in the Great Sand Sea. He left some of his iron boxes here. When he finally arrived at Siwa, Rohlfs called this journey through the Great Sand Sea "the most adventurous march ever made in the Sahara Desert." It took Rohlfs' team of ten men and twenty camels thirty-six days from the time Jordan stepped off from Dakhla to arrive at Siwa.

Ammonite Hill

Ammonite Hill, named by Zittel, is to the northeast of Sandheim. It is, as its name implies, a hill filled with the tiny fossils of the sea creatures ammonites.

Gilf Kebir

The Gilf Kebir is a flat-topped sandstone plateau 150 kilometers (93 miles) north of Gebel Uwaynat covering over 7,770 square kilometers (3,000 square miles). It rises 300 meters (1,000 feet) from the desert floor forming one of the most formidable barriers in Africa. Dozens of wadis extend into the desert around its perimeter. These wadis were formed by water erosion in a wetter phase thousands of years ago in the late Tertiary age. Then it was a great divide, draining water in all directions, north, south, east, and west.

The Gilf is 1,075 meters (3,500 feet) above sea level. The cliffs in the south and southwest are the highest. The cliffs in the northeast have been broken down into inselbergs and individual hills. Wind and water have been working away at the Gilf Kebir for over 100,000 years. Although it probably took its present form in late Tertiary, or early Quaternary time, the only reason it is still standing is its tough cap of silicified sandstone.

The Gilf Kebir sits in the southwestern corner of Egypt about 720 kilometers (450 miles) from the Nile and 960 kilometers (600 miles) from the Mediterranean, like a huge shelf the size of Switzerland. It is nearly dissected in two by a large gap.

The northern portion is drowning in sand from the Great Sand Sea. It is helping the wind break down the Gilf into inselbergs and cones. That sand is whitish. The sand at the middle of the plateau is reddish. Wadi Hamra, as its name states, is filled with red sand. The southern portion of the Gilf is 5,800 square kilometers (3,625 square miles). It has five main wadis, all of them at least 15 kilometers (9 miles) long. The sand on the western half of the southern portion is red, as are the dunes to the northeast of the Gilf.

Around 9500 B.C. the monsoonal system shifted northward and lakes formed around the Gilf. By 4500 B.C. things were arid once again.

Exploration History

Penderel, in a paper presented to the Royal Geographical Society in June of 1934, says that John Ball was the first westerner to see the Gilf, while on patrol in 1917. But credit for the discovery goes to Prince Kamal al-Din, who actually reached it, skirted its southeastern cliffs, fixed it on the maps, and named it in 1926.

After Bagnold and Clayton, another Clayton appeared on the scene. In 1932, an expedition was mounted to explore the Gilf by air. It included Sir Robert Clayton-East-Clayton, Count Almasy, P. A. Clayton, and Penderel. They discovered several valleys rich with vegetation, including what was later to be known as Wadi Hamra, Wadi Talh, and the Wadi Abd al-Malik. These valleys were used by tribesmen for grazing and some explorers believed that they were the lost oasis of Zerzura.

Archaeological work was begun in 1933 by Frobenius. Needless to say, the focus was the rock art. Prehistory work began with Bagnold's expedition of 1938, done by O. H. Myers and H. A. Winkler. This expedition was a joint effort of the Egypt Exploration Society, which supported Myers, Gray, and Winkler, and the Royal Geographical Society, which provided grant money to Bagnold. During World War II the Italians had a base in the region, while the British set up at Uwaynat. The Long Range Desert Group of the British Army were active in the area.

The Bagnold–Mond 1938 expedition spent a month working around the Gilf Kebir. They did a huge amount of survey work, archaeology, and geophysical and geological investigation. An additional month was spent at Uwaynat where Hans Winkler joined them. While Winkler was at Uwaynat, Bagnold and Peel went north along the western side of the Gilf and found two more rock art sites, one a new discovery. R. F. Peel wrote "Rock Paintings from the Libyan Desert" for *Antiquity* magazine as a result of the trip.

Recent exploration began with Misonne, the Belgian who crossed 600 kilometers (375 miles) of the high plateau in 1969. He found that sheep, foxes, and lizards lived on top of the Gilf. Issawi in 1971–72 did a geological survey, followed by Wendorf in 1974 and al-Baz in 1978. In 1976–77, the Deutsche Forschungsgemeinschaft and the Academy

of Sciences of Egypt launched an ongoing geological program under the leadership of Lkitzsch and supported by the Continental Oil Company (CONOCO).

Because of its remoteness and inaccessibility and the lack of any resources to attract people, the region was left to the explorers. It wasn't until 1976 that mapping was completed, for with the arrival of Landsat everything changed. In 1978, a new type of explorer came to the Gilf Kebir and Gebel Uwaynat, looking for answers to questions that were from out of this world. The two-week expedition of seven Americans and nine Egyptians led by Farouk al-Baz was to "verify in the field interpretations of tonal variations and surface patterns observed on Earth-orbital photographs." They wanted to compare the Libyan Desert, especially around the Gilf and Uwaynat, to photos they had of Mars.

Getting There: A TRIP TO THE GILF KEBIR IS STILL AN EXPEDITION. IT MUST BE APPROACHED WITH CAUTION AS AT EVERY TURN THERE IS DANGER. Restricted travel requiring permits in 2000. Needs minimum of two 4x4 vehicles, GPS, maps, all water, all food, all petrol. A GUIDE IS MANDATORY. This is true for every site in the Gilf.

Northeastern Side

The northeastern side of the Gilf is a bit disappointing as it has broken down considerably over the years and one does not have the sense of approaching a huge plateau with many high cliffs and wadis as one does on the southern and western sides.

In addition, and most spectacular, the southern edges of the Great Sand Sea have now reached the Gilf Kebir. This is astounding, as one can observe two great natural forces at war with one another. In two huge valleys before Lama Point they clash in an incredible phenomenon. The sand is filling up these wadis. The individual dunes climb over each other on the far side of the wadi, forming a moving, almost breathing, ladder that eventually reaches the top in the far left corner. Here the terrifying sand spills onto **Lama Point.** There must be trillions of tons of sand banked up against the far wadi wall, climbing up and over and up and over, fighting its way to the top. Never mind that the obstacle is the 1,000-foot-high Gilf Kebir, the sand slowly and patiently works its way to the top.

It is here, looking into this valley, that one must concede that sand is the ultimate conqueror, the final state of most matter. It must, in the end, win its battle and the final landscape of the earth will be reduced to fine grains of sand moving in gangs around and around the globe, propelled forward by its friend the wind, until the wind stops and the sand finds its ultimate destination.

Lama Point sits at the southwestern side of the first valley. In 1997, a team from the EEAA was at Lama Point on an expedition to look for conservation areas in the Western Desert. A short distance beyond Lama Point is **Almasy Camp**, recognized by a number of Shell gasoline tins left here by Almasy. It sits at the base of a small hill, which Samir Lama named Almasy Mountain. Shell supported many of the expeditions in the Western Desert by providing the petrol.

After the Almasy Camp at Almasy Mountain comes the second dune-filled valley. Here, too, the dunes are climbing. They look like they are eating the gilf and they have reached the top of the Gilf here. In the next decades we shall see if they succeed in breaking down the Gilf by their sheer weight. What happens once they all reach the top is anyone's guess.

The Plateau

The top of the Gilf Kebir is like the top of the world. It is gravelly, mostly featureless—at some places there are big slabs of basalt, and there is at least one riverbed. The edges of the plateau are another matter. Like a voyeur, one peers into amazing worlds filled with exotic scenes.

As one travels north-northwest along the western edge of the scarp, valley after valley can be seen from the top. It is most incredible, Egypt's Grand Canyon. Where the northeastern scarp has few true cliffs, just eroded hills and dune filled valleys that you climb slowly up, the northwestern side is all cliffs and spectacular views onto the Libyan

plain below. (One is only a few kilometers away from the border here.) There is a Black Valley, a Red Sand Dune Valley, and a valley where one can walk down to the desert floor. All of these are to the south of one of the most famous valleys of the Gilf, the Wadi Sura, the Picture Valley of Almasy.

On top of the Gilf there is flora and fauna. In January of 1998, whittiers, butterflies, and a spotted black and white fly, were observed. Acacia trees were seen, as was a field of Rose of Jericho (Kaffer Mariam) flowers, all shriveled up and waiting for enough rain to bloom. It was also easy to spot a dried-up riverbed that once had considerable force, as the rocks were large, polished, and embedded into the ground.

Northern Side of the Gilf: Zerzura?

At the extreme northern section of the Gilf Kebir stand the entrances of three wadis: Wadi Hamra on the northeast, Wadi Abd al-Malik in the center, and Wadi Talh on the northwest. These are the three valleys that Almasy claimed were the lost oasis of Zerzura.

Once the explorers saw the valleys from the air, all that remained was to visit them by land. In 1933, Almasy, Dr. Kadar, a geographer and geologist from Budapest, Mr. Casparius, a photographer and cinephotographer, Dr. Bermann, and Penderel journeyed to the Gilf once again. They took with them a new type of tire called a balloon tire and a new type of airplane compass.

Leaving Kharga on March 22, 1933, they headed to Abu Ballas, visited Regenfeld, and headed for the east side of the Gilf. It was at the same time that Lady Clayton-East-Clayton was in the field. They climbed to the top of the Gilf and found a camel route to the plain below. Almasy went looking for another wadi, the third, to round out Wilkinson's claim that Zerzura had three valleys. What they discovered was that the Gilf has two parts, a northern half and a southern half and there was a gap, which Almasy named al-Aqaba, on the western side that allowed "an easy through-route for cars."

Upon reaching the end of Wadi Hamra they climbed to the top of the Gilf. They

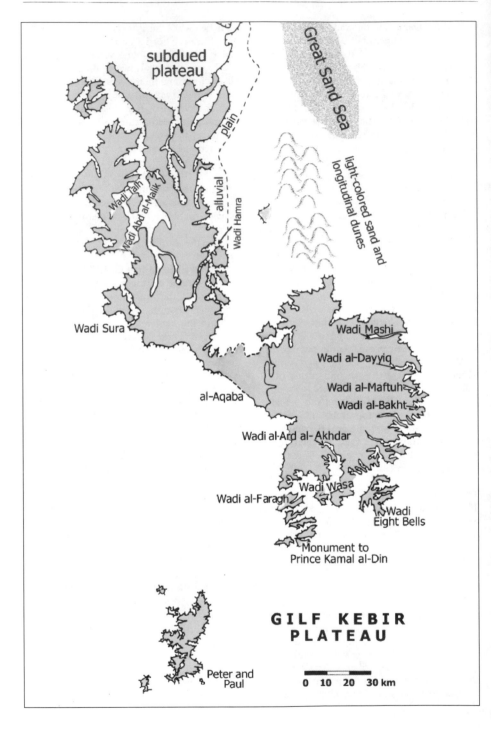

subdued
plateau

Great Sand Sea

plain

alluvial

Wadi Hamra

light-colored sand and
longitudinal dunes

Wadi Talh

Wadi Abd al-Malik

Wadi Sura

Wadi Mashi

Wadi al-Dayyiq

Wadi al-Maftuh

al-Aqaba

Wadi al-Bakht

Wadi al-Ard al-Akhdar

Wadi Wasa

Wadi al-Faragh

Wadi
Eight Bells

Monument to
Prince Kamal al-Din

GILF KEBIR
PLATEAU

Peter and
Paul

0   10   20   30 km

found it flat, gravelly, and absolutely silent. There was no wind. Nor were there any living Barbary sheep. They continued their journey from east to west across the top of the Gilf. By the third day they were close to the southern end, on the fourth day they found their way down (it is not clear where) and began moving north along the eastern side. Here they found another penetrating wadi (unnamed) and followed it for an easy ascent to the top of the Gilf once more. In one of several caves in the wadi they found rock art. The cave was large and the drawings were on the roof and consisted of longhorn cattle, men, and a cave or hut with bales and bundles hanging from the roof.

In 1933, on the next trip into the desert to do the wadi by car, Almasy talked with an old Tebu called Ibrahim Abd al-Malik, a caravan guide from Kufra who had been one of the Kufra refugees. It was Ibrahim who called the wadi Abd al-Malik, Servant of the King. He also spoke of Wadi Talh, the Valley of Acacia.

Then, on May 3, they entered Wadi Abd al-Malik. It is a long valley with plenty of acacia trees. There were sites of Tebu camps with grass huts, baskets, and a lot of camel dung.

On May 5, Almasy found a second wadi, perhaps the Wadi Talh. Then the group left for Uwaynat, where they met up with Ibrahim again. Now, the old Tebu gave up the final bit of information, there was a third valley in the group and it was called Wadi Hamra, the Red Valley. (It had already been found by P. A. Clayton). Here were the three wadis of Zerzura mentioned by Wilkinson in the 1830s.

At the lecture given by Bermann at the Royal Geographical Society one more piece of the puzzle was finally coughed up: "As to the name 'Zerzura' our Tebu friend, Ibrahim, asked where Zerzura lay, said: 'Oh, those silly Arab people, they do not know anything; they call these three wadis in the Gilf, Zerzura, but we local people know their real names.'"

Wadi Hamra

Wadi Hamra is red. Red sand dunes are *so* beautiful. Red drifts of sand cascading down the side of a black mountain are *so* beautiful.

It is said that Almasy wanted Rommel to land troops on top of the Gilf and bring them down into Wadi Hamra. Clayton found plenty of trees and many Barbary sheep. When Mason and company entered the wadi they followed it as far as it would go and almost ended up on the other side. Mason observed that the wadi "lies so far inside the Gilf Kebir that it is nearer to the western cliff than to the eastern" and that "the head of the Wadi Hamra splits up into three separate heads, the longest one reaching southward until is almost meets the head of another larger wadi which leads down to the western plain."

Wadi Abd al-Malik

The Wadi Abd al-Malik enters the Gilf Kebir from the north and runs south for almost the entire length of the northern half of the Gilf.

This is the first valley the Clayton-East-Clayton/Almasy Expedition of 1932 saw from the air but were unable to find on foot. They were sure that it was Zerzura. P. A. Clayton wrote later: "We consider it certain that this wadi is one of those whose existence and occasional occupation by Arabs has given rise to the legends of the Wadi Zerzura and Wadi Abd al-Malik. . . . I myself saw from the air, about 30 kms to the east, the edges of a large depression, and until the whole area has been explored it must not be assumed that the main Wadi Zerzura, of which the wadi discovered may be only a part, has been seen."

In 1938, Bagnold and Peel came to the Wadi Abd al-Malik to look for a weli that natives said existed but Almasy was unable to find. They looked for three days and then Peel entered a small grotto and found some more rock art. It is on the eastern side of the eastern branch of the wadi about 16 kilometers (10 miles) above the main fork. The paintings were on both walls, dust covered. They depicted some cattle and another animal, probably a dog. The paintings were dark red, red and white, and white only.

Bagnold tells us that when he was looking for this well, "there being as usual in the Gilf no possible way down for a car from the plateau to the valley within it, we had to climb down and walk. We walked a total of more than 30 miles along the soft sandy floor of that wadi, during two stifling days when a khamsin wind was blowing from the south."

Well, things change. In 1998, we did exactly what Bagnold could not do, we climbed down into the wadi with our three 4x4s. Actually, we slid down the side of a sand dune. That "climb down" is called the Lama Monod Pass.

As stated by the explorers of the 1930s, Wadi Abd al-Malik has many acacia trees and when we were there in January of 1998 some were green with foliage. There was evidence of rain within the past month with cracked mud where drainage had taken place and *zilla spinosa* bushes were green with new foliage.

As one travels north out of the Wadi Abd al-Malik, one is only 10–12 kilometers (6–7 miles) east of the Libyan border. At the northern entrance to the wadi stand three dunes—barriers, but easily managed.

The third valley of the Zerzura legend, the Wadi Talh, found by Almasy, is nearby. Although it was explored in the early part of the twentieth century, no work has been done in recent years and little is known about its environment.

The Southeastern Side
Keep in mind that the Gilf Kebir has two halves, a northern and a southern, which are separated by a narrow ridge of land, just like North America is separated from South America by the thin band of land containing Mexico.

Wadi Mashi
Wadi Mashi, the Walking Valley, was named because the mountains seem to walk, for they disappear and reappear as one journeys near. It cuts about 15 kilometers (9 miles) southwesterly into the southern Gilf in its upper northeastern corner. There are tiny bays but no side valleys. There are prehistoric artifacts here, as there are throughout the southern desert.

Wadi Dayyiq
Wadi Dayyiq, the Narrow Valley, has a major reduction station where ancient people manufactured their tools by breaking them from hard rocks and chiseling and pounding them into various shapes like knives, blades, and arrows. The site measures 12 x 20 meters (38 x 64 feet) and probably served several communities in the southeastern wadis of the Gilf.

To the east of Wadi Dayyiq a fully loaded ammunition truck from the Long Range Desert Group was found in 1992, almost 50 years after the war was over. The Bedford truck held seven to eight tons of now volatile explosives. Military Intelligence was notified and found the truck. They gave it some petrol and it started. It is now at the al-Alamein Museum. There are other war artifacts around the Gilf. A Ford cab-over-engine lorry, probably used by the Long Range Desert Group, is located to the south. A Ford lorry and a General Motors stake-bed lorry are 10 kilometers (6 miles) southeast of the southern tip of the Gilf.

Wadi Dayyiq sits below Wadi Mashi and cuts into the Gilf to the northwest. Then it turns southwest. There are three major side valleys and a few bays. It is followed by al-Aqaba al-Qadima, the Old Obstacle, another wadi cut into the Gilf.

Wadi Maftuh
Wadi Maftuh, the Open Valley, cuts deeper into the Gilf than the two previous valleys. Its entrance is rather làrge with an island in the center. There are a number of deep side valleys, but the main valley, after the island, moves northwest and then southwest. It, too, has a few smaller side valleys.

Wadi al-Bakht
The Wadi al-Bakht, Valley of Luck or Chance, extends 30 kilometers (19 miles) into the heart of the Gilf Kebir.

Over 20 km (12 miles) into its canyon-like valley, one bears left and is confronted with an enormous, and extremely dramatic, 30 meter (96 foot) high dune blocking the way. By the 1970s, when the Combined Prehistoric Expedition came to call, the dune had been breached. This dune once stood as a dam for a lake.

In 1938, four distinct concentrations of

artifacts were identified: Site Fifteen is 40 to 50 meters (128 to 160 feet) below and to the east of the dune; Site Sixteen, called upper dune and lower dune, are on the dune; and Site Seventeen is on the edge of the lake mud, 50 meters (160 feet) above the dune.

People lived here for many centuries. The entire area, including the dune face, is littered with ancient artifacts: grinding stones, pottery, ostrich eggshells, and bones. Two kilometers (1.2 miles) beyond is a Neolithic site. In all probability the people lived on the dune first, then ventured closer to the lake for settlements.

There is an abundance of pottery, mostly dated to 6930 B.C. This is of the same age as the pottery at Nabta, near the Darb al-Arbain, but the style and construction are entirely different. One shape is straight-sided, another is molded. The pottery is black, reddish-yellow, or brown, while the Nabta pottery is predominantly brown to gray.

There were also cattle. All the rock drawings in the area of the Gilf Kebir and Uwaynat show an abundance of cattle. The archaeological remains have been sparse. However the site is deep and the work has just begun. Cattle have existed in the Western Desert, especially here, at Bir Kisciba, and at Nabta from about 9000 to 9800 B.C. That's up there with other sites outside of Egypt.

The lake was probably gone by 5200 B.C. The valley has been abandoned for thousands of years.

The area was first explored by O. H. Myers in 1938. Because of the war, Myers' work was not published. In 1971, W. P. McHugh worked on Myers' papers for his Ph.D. In 1978, the Apollo–Soyuz team visited the site.

Only one ridge separates the entrance of Wadi al-Bakht from its northern neighbor the Wadi Maftuh. This valley runs fairly straight due west with a number of small bays.

Wadi Wasa

Wadi Wasa, the Wide Valley, like all of its sister wadis was created by water erosion in the distant past. It drained east. Wadi Wasa is the most amazing valley in the Gilf. It begins on the eastern side, makes its way through the Gilf in a predominately southwesterly direction and emerges on the western side. There are a few islands and dozens of major side valleys, one of them named Wadi al-Ard al-Khadra. It would be easy to get lost here and very complicated to find one's way through the valley.

The Apollo–Soyuz team, working here in 1978, made their base camp just outside the entrance, as had Bagnold forty years earlier in 1938. They believed it had not rained for twenty years in the area. There was, however, ample evidence of rain on the Gilf Kebir and in its northern valleys in January of 1998.

Wadi al-Ard al-Khadra

The Valley of the Green Earth, along the southern part of the Gilf, runs north, then curves southwest. Approximately 35 kilometers (22 miles) long, Wadi al-Ard al-Khadra is a huge steep-walled valley that emerged from within the Wadi Wasa. It has two major branches and a number of bays and smaller routes throughout.

Similar to Wadi al-Bakht, concentrations show that this valley was also blocked by a dune to form a small amphitheater basin. The dune is located 5 kilometers (3 miles) from the head of the valley. It has probably been in place since prehistory and once helped create a lake.

There is evidence of stream erosion in post-Oligocene times. When the wet phase stopped, dunes marched into the valley. Dozens of sites show human habitation. The Apollo–Soyuz team worked here in 1979.

Eight Bells

Eight Bells is the result of a huge 3,400-square-kilometer (2,125-square-mile) drainage system in ancient times which "discharged to the south hundreds of kilometers beyond the present plateau scarp." It is the only wadi on the east to drain south into a much larger water system. McCauley et al. tell us that Lake Chad, which this drainage system fed, in 5000 B.C. "filled the Bodele Depression to a level of at least 320 meters (1024 feet), extending to within about 600 kilometers (375 miles) of the south margin of the Gilf Kebir" and suggests that "the Eight Bells drainage network may have discharged from the Gilf uplands into this great inland basin." Why not!

Coming from the south one simply merges into Eight Bells from the desert plain. Coming from the northeast, Eight Bells falls out of Wadi Wasa. Coming from the southwest, Eight Bells is more difficult. Here the wadi is broken by the cliffs of the Gilf.

Western Side of the Gilf

The entire Gilf Kebir is in Egypt, but some western parts are very, very close to Libya and the terrain sometimes pushes vehicles in that direction. Although there are a number of wadis along the western side, few have been given names.

Wadi Sura

The Wadi Sura, Picture Valley, contains the now famous Cave of Swimmers. After Almasy found the rock pictures in the Giraffe Caves at Ain Doua, a wadi in Gebel Uwaynat, he came back in October of the same year (1933) with the Frobenius Expedition. They came especially to look for rock art. All along the valleys of Uwaynat they found it. Then Almasy began to explore the western slopes of the Gilf, the same area that P. A. Clayton had explored earlier. Here he found a number of

paintings and drawings including the swimmers. Their importance does not lie solely in their beauty. They attest to the presence of a lake, which does not exist at the present time. It was Almasy who named the place Wadi Sura, Picture Valley.

There are three or four caves "situated at the head of a short amphitheater-like wadi some 3 miles south of the entrance to the main wadi." Peel gives us detailed descriptions of the two caves that contain paintings. The first cave is on the right (south) as one enters the wadi. Here one group of paintings remains intact, showing two dozen figures of men and cattle all in dark red and white. In a style called "balanced exaggeration" by Winkler, the men have broad shoulders, narrow waists, triangular torsos, exaggerated rounded hips, and long, tapering legs and arms. Their feet and hands are rarely shown, while their heads are round blobs. Almost all of the figures carry bows, some of which are being used. They are all naked. The cattle in the scene have tapering limbs and long thin tails. These paintings are similar to many at Gebel Uwaynat and are undoubtedly the work of the same people: Autochthonous Mountain Dwellers.

The second cave is some twenty yards to the north, left, of the first one, and has a

Warriors of the southern caves of Wadi Sura

Thick-torsoed men of Wadi Sura

Famous swimmers in the Cave of Swimmers at Wadi Sura

larger number of illustrations, including cattle, ostrich, dogs, and giraffe. The bulk of paintings here, however, are of men, with well over a hundred figures represented. Many more paintings are damaged and the original number may well have been twice or three times that figure. Here the figures are crudely painted. The heads are round blobs, the torsos thick, the limbs clumsy, the hips narrow, and the feet only indicated. Hands appear only on the larger specimens. The colors are mostly dark red, with bands of white around ankles, wrists, upper arms, and below the knees.

Then there are the swimmers. These are small and painted in red. They are only 10 centimeters long with small rounded heads on thin necks. The bodies are rounded and the arms and legs are thin. All appear to be swimming. Some appear to be diving.

More figures from Wadi Sura

There are also figures in yellow. "A figure in dark red stands between two in yellow with an arm outstretched to each. The yellow figure on the right is small, and may be a child. The grouping may of course be accidental; but, if not, the group may be intended to represent a union between two different groups, or even a marriage, although there is no indication of sex in any of the figures."

Peter Clayton, in an interview, addressed the question of who found the Cave of Swimmers first, his father or Almasy. He believes that his father was the first to find the wadi and the other caves, but that he did not go into the second set of caves where the swimmers are located. This Almasy did. So, Clayton found the location and some caves, Almasy found the others including the Cave of Swimmers.

Bagnold tells us that Almasy spent some time copying the paintings and as he did, he dropped his cigarette butts in the sand. Later, Ronald Peel tried scooping them up and found pieces of the original pigments used to paint the pictures scattered in the sand. He left them there. YOU SHOULD LEAVE THEM THERE TOO!

Al-Aqaba

Al-Aqaba, the Difficult, is a pass leading from the desert floor up to the top of the Gilf. As its name implies it is not an easy ascent,

but it was used by the explorers in the 1930s in the Ford 2x2 cars.

Almasy believed that his friends from the Long Range Desert Group mined this pass during the war and he therefore went south in his dash across the desert in the summer of 1942. He told Clayton that he moved the mines. Shaw, on the other hand, maintains that al-Aqaba was never mined. Today we have the same story going on. Rumor has it that the Egyptian Army, in order to thwart the Libyan smugglers whose tracks are evident all over the southwestern desert, mined al-Aqaba. Is it really mined? Do you want to be the one to find out?

Between the Gilf and Uwaynat

As one travels south the sandstones that dominate the Gilf Kebir give way to the volcanic basalts and trachytes that dominate Uwaynat.

Wadi Faragh

Wadi Faragh, the Empty Valley, is another location reputedly mined by the Egyptian Army. It sits at the southern tip of the Gilf and offers easy passage around it.

Monument to Prince Kamal al-Din

This monument is a testimonial written in Arabic on the side of a wadi to commemorate the exploits of Prince Kamal al-Din. It was placed in the Wadi Faragh by Almasy.

Gebel Uwaynat

Gebel Uwaynat is a major African landmark and the highest point in Egypt. It sits at the border of Egypt, Libya, and Sudan with only its northeastern slope falling into Egypt. It is dissected by 22-degree north latitude and 25-degree eastern longitude, which are the borders between Egypt and Sudan and Egypt and Libya. It is 1,898 meters (6,073 feet) high, 600 meters (1,919 feet) above sea level, and covers 1,500 square kilometers (579 square miles). It is about 29 kilometers (18 miles) long and 24 kilometers (15 miles) wide.

Gebel Uwaynat is a multilithic structure with the western portion composed of granite, the southern of sandstone, and the northern of Nubian sandstone. The part in

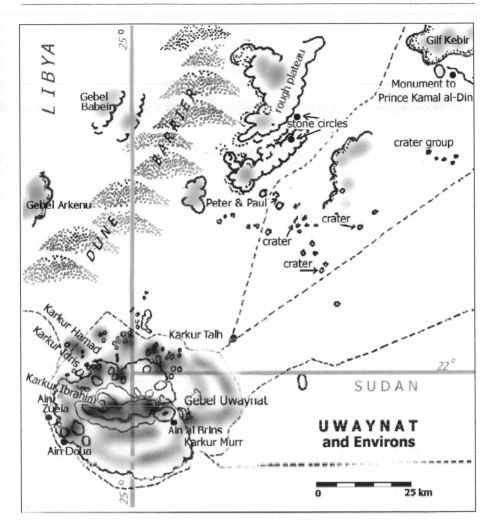

Egypt is a plug of quartz trachytes. Along the northern slope, where the wind hits the face of the mountain, erosion has created exceptionally odd formations. Gebel Uwaynat is almost entirely surrounded by sand sheets. Although located in the most inhospitable terrain of the Western Desert, when it rains, two bodies of water form at its southern base, and around the perimeter of these lakes ancient cultures have flourished.

As its name implies there are a number of 'little springs' within the mountain. Today

we know of eight such springs, with the best being Ain Doua at the southern part of the mountain in Sudan. These springs come from rain that collects in pools. When it does not rain, there is no water.

In modern times, prior to 1923, there were reports of about 250 people living at Uwaynat; Hassanein tells us of about 150 in 1923. When Shaw was there in 1930, he saw only seven men and when he went back in 1932, he found no one. In recent years the weather pattern seems to be changing and rain has been recorded at Gilf Kebir and Uwaynat. This may be the beginning of yet another wet period. If so, it will take centuries to develop fully, but how interesting it will be if people may soon be able to return to Uwaynat.

Exploration History

Uwaynat was rediscovered by Ahmed Hassanein in 1923 when he journeyed south from Kufra Oasis into unknown territory. The great era of caravan trade was over. In 1923, no one traveled where Hassanein wanted to go.

When Hassanein was setting out, he was warned, "Eight years ago the last caravan to go that way . . . was eaten up and slaughtered on the frontier of Darfur." But he insisted.

He was warned again, "This journey you propose to make is through territory where no Bedouin has passed before. . . . Your camels will drop like birds before the hot south winds. Even if you get through safely, who knows how the inhabitants of the hills over there will receive you?" But he persisted.

And again, "They do not fear God and they are under the authority of no man. They are like birds; they live on the tops of mountains, and you will have trouble with them."

Hassanein finally answered, "We are men, and we are believers. . . . Our fate is in the hands of God. If our death is decreed, it may come on the beaten track to the nearest well."

The argument heightened "The water on this route is scarce and bad. God has said 'Do not throw yourselves with your own hands unto destruction.'"

"God will quench the thirst of the true believer and will protect those who have faith in Him."

"None of my men are willing to accompany you on this route and I cannot send my camels either. It is sending them to death. If you find anybody who is willing to hire his camels I am ready to pay for them but neither my men nor my camels are going to take you on this journey."

But poor Bu Helega, who was arguing with Hassanein, had promised the leader of the Sanusi, Sayyid Idris, that he would take care of Hassanein and Hassanein now drew out this ace.

"Do what you like," he retorted, "I am going by this route. It will be between you and Sayyid Idris when he knows that Bu Helega has not kept his word."

Hassanein went through several more rounds of arguing, going up the ladder of authority until finally he won the day, the caravan materialized, and he trekked off into history.

But the mountain had a history before Hassanein. The first historic mention of the mountain in Western terms is related to looking for new caravan routes north to the Mediterranean coast in the early 1800s. According to Shaw in 1934, in the first decade of the nineteenth century, Sabun, the sultan of Waidai, was looking for a new route north for trading purposes. The old caravan route from Waidai to Tripoli had to pass through Tibesti and there were too many raids to gamble on transporting goods to the north.

The only other route was the Darb al-Arbain, but the Egyptian government took too much in tolls. Sabun had previously sent a caravan north, but it got lost northwest of Darfur (near Dakhla) and everyone died, including the sultan's mother. Then a merchant named Shehaymah came to Waidai from Jalo and said he could find a direct route to Benghazi. He was given 500 camels, and traveled 480 kilometers (300 miles) to Gebel al-Nari, which is our Gebel Uwaynat, then pushed on to Kufra. Then he returned to Waidai with a caravan. This is our first modern reference to the existence of Uwaynat, so Shehaymah discovered it, not Hassanein.

However it got lost again. It was on Shehaymah's third trip, back to Kufra, that he found the more direct route between Waidai and Kufra that was used from that time forward. The problem was a waterless 576 kilometers (360 miles) between Tekro and Kufra. The Sanusi, when they rose to power and took control of this route, solved the water problem. They constructed two wells around 1898: Bishara, 160 kilometers (100 miles) south of Kufra and Sarra, 160 kilometers (100 miles) beyond. The road was open, but the sultan did not control it. By the twentieth century this route was the only caravan route open in North Africa and the

Karkur Talh warrior

Caravan of camels from Karkur Talh

only one where, according to Boahen, "large caravans continued to move."

After Hassanein visited Uwaynat, Prince Kamal al-Din and John Ball came in 1925 and 1926. They did the "first topographical and geological studies." All the others soon followed.

There are a number of wadis, called *karkurs,* at Uwaynat, only one of them in Egypt, the Karkur Talh.

Karkur Talh

Karkur Talh, Acacia Valley, was a heavily occupied valley in prehistory. All the archaeological remains indicate a long occupation. Probably primarily agriculturists, the community was also pastoral.

Thousands of peaceful, pastoral rock-art images, both drawings and engravings, have been discovered since Hassanein made his discovery in 1923. Depicted on mostly sandstone background we have people wearing leather clothing, with colored spots on their bodies, and ostrich feathers, like other Nilotic peoples the Nuer, the Dinka, and the Nuba of Sudan.

Hassanein's first rock drawings are at ground level and depict lions, giraffes, ostriches, gazelles, and cows. They are incised. The locals believed them to be the work of jinn. What they tell us is that the climate supported these types of animals. Peel maintains that the rock art at Uwaynat belongs to the Tebu. So does Winlock, who is the authority.

Shaw published some of these drawings from the ceiling of a low sandstone rock-shelter on the east side of the valley far up from the mouth. The drawings are on the roof of the cave, which is only 3 feet from the floor. Shaw crawled in and lay on his back to record them. He found ninety pictures in all, forty in red, thirty-five in white, fifteen in both colors. Shaw compares them to those at Ain Ezzan southeast of Ghat in Algeria. Prince Kamal al-Din, Almasy, Winkler, and Myers, in addition to Hassanein all found rock art in the Karkur Talh, which today is mostly in Sudan.

Within the valley can be found the remains of reed huts and stone shelters probably belonging to the Tebu. The name Tebu means rock people and was given to them by

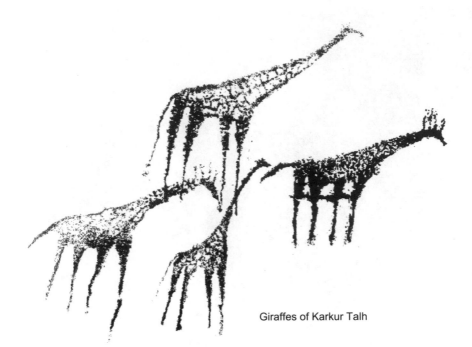

Giraffes of Karkur Talh

the Arabs. Perhaps because they came from the mountains, but more probably because they found shelter within stone walls.

In addition to the rock art in the main valley there are several smaller valleys at Karkur Talh that contain rock art. In the lateral wadi 200 paintings and engravings, probably the oldest depictions in the region, were discovered. In an area that the Belgian Expedition of 1968 called Wadi Talh I and II, they discovered over 1,000 separate locations where rock art can be found. All by itself, Kurkur Talh is an outdoor museum. One must be careful for the area is on the border with Sudan. This is not to be taken lightly.

Wadi Handal
Unnamed until the Apollo–Soyuz Mission of 1978, when C. Vance Haynes gave it the name Wadi Handal because there are plenty of green gourd plants around, this valley is just west of Karkur Talh. Dunes exist in this valley too. There is art at the head, including a baboon.

Wadi Wihish
Wadi Wihish, the Bad Valley, has eighty paintings. Their style is not the same as at Karkur Talh. In addition the rock art is on limestone, great blocks that have fallen to the wadi floor.

Western Uwaynat
The western portion of Uwaynat is in Libya and therefore off limits at the current time. However, there is much to see there in the realm of rock art.

The rock art here is painted rather than incised. Almost all are on granite surfaces. Rock art has been found at Karkur Hamid, Karkur Idris I and II, Karkur Ibrahim, Ain Zuwaya, Karkur Murr, and Ain Doua. **There is no access to this area via Egypt at the current time.**

Practical Information

When the first printing of this new edition was published I got the following comments from friends: "I just held up your book, pointed at the picture on the cover, and told the taxi driver in Kharga Oasis to take me there!" "I have two people who want to go to the Gilf Kebir. How far is it and can I take them in a regular car?" "Our trip is canceled. We are thirty people and my travel agent says only sixteen can go into the desert."

The first statement breaks all the rules about traveling to remote sites. You need permissions to visit antiquities in the desert and you must choose your guide carefully or you may just get the guide of statement number 2. This person is in the tourist business, but has no idea about the desert. By the time I heard the third statement I knew what the problem was. The desert is a new frontier and the tourist does not know all the ways to visit it, while the average travel agent does not know all the ways to package it. There is more than one way to visit the desert and people of all ages, all sizes, and all desires can be accommodated on a single desert journey.

The desert can offer up adventure in degrees, so there is something for everyone: *mild* for those who insist on a good shower and a swimming pool at the end of the day; *medium* for those who want some off-road experiences during the day and an occasional desert camp at night; *strong* for those who like to go into the wilderness but know that the paved road and the high tension lines are nearby; or *extreme*, where one tempts the fates and carries all the water, gasoline, and food necessary for a 10- to 24-day step-off-the-edge-of-the-earth escapade. Any one of these journeys is worth putting on your wish list.

Mild and Medium

The good thing about basic desert tours is that they accommodate everyone in a group: families who have a variety of interests, first-timers who are not so sure desert travel is for them, people who have both 4x4s and regular vehicles in the tour, or travelers who like a little bit of adventure, but want it peppered with modern conveniences.

There are day excursions from Cairo and Alexandria via 4x4s that can be arranged through travel agents. One can visit Fayoum in an afternoon or camp overnight in the desert. One can visit Bahariya and Farafra oases from Cairo on a three- to four-day weekend either traveling down the paved road, staying at a good hotel, and taking day excursions, or going off-road via Wadi Rayyan and camping in the desert. The same is true from Luxor for Kharga and Dakhla oases.

To 'do' the entire loop road that connects the four major oases, a traveler needs eight to ten days, a good car, a map, this book, and a sense of adventure. The on-road travel can easily be done without a guide: it is a single road going to a specific place. Once in the different oases, one may sign up for day tours into the desert. If you don't have transportation to get you to the desert, there are buses, microbuses, or tour companies in Cairo that can sign you up for this adventure without any trouble.

The loop swings out of the Nile Valley near Cairo and returns to the river near Luxor or at Asyut. It is an 1,100-kilometer (700-mile) journey that leads to four distinctly different worlds, filled with fascinating desert people, antiquities, mysteries, newly built resorts, and ample gasoline stations.

In each oasis there are a number of 4x4 groups that offer day excursions that can be booked in any of the hotels. Part of your group can go off-road for an afternoon, overnight, or for a few days. The others can wander around the old villages. Four-by-four drivers can test their mettle by joining a 4x4 excursion in their own vehicle, or they can leave their vehicle and climb aboard a desert 4x4. The choices are staggering.

Where once a desert journey began on a local bus with a backpack and ended in a sleeping bag around a desert spring, the trips mentioned above have become the standard, easy desert journeys. You can still do a backpack journey, thank God. Unlike Sinai and the Northern Coast, not all the land has been taken over by private enterprise. A wise traveler can book almost all of the journeys mentioned from agencies in Cairo, who should contact the desert hotels for good service. The desert hotels can offer the best mix of trips for groups with a variety of interests, or first-timers not quite sure what to expect. Even if you plan to do it yourself, don't think you can just drop in to a desert hotel. Those days are gone. You must book ahead.

Strong: 4x4, Hiking, and Camel Safari

If the short trip through the desert to distant forts is not enough to satiate your lust for off-road adventure, there are three other ways you can get an adrenaline rush and a sense of being an explorer without too much danger: day-tripping in a 4x4, desert hiking on foot, and a genuine Bedouin-led camel safari. Expats living in Egypt go into the Western Desert on 4x4 weekend trips all the time. Tourists can do the same on a day off from a regular Nile Valley tour. Give up a shopping trip and head for the desert for a day. If you love birds, then take a day to go birding in Egypt. There are companies that deal exclusively with watching and enjoying birds. Egypt is on the major flyway from Europe to Africa and the birds are not to be believed. This is great independent adventure and tour companies in Cairo will accommodate the traveler for any and all of them.

There is at least one tour group that offers hiking. Hiking trips are usually seven- to ten-day jaunts where hikers walk 15 to 20 kilometers (9 to 13 miles) a day through pristine terrain. Their belongings and accommodations are carted ahead of them, and a hot meal and relaxing evening awaits the walker at the end of each day.

If you want to feel like all the great explorers who came before, then a camel safari is the greatest adventure in the Western Desert. Camel safaris can be anything from a few hours in the desert from any of the oases to a fourteen-day expedition. This is as close to the nineteenth-century explorers as you are going to get in North Africa.

Neither hiking nor cameling are do-it-yourself items. You need the safari companies. Some of the best are found in the desert (as opposed to the Nile Valley agencies who end up hiring the local guys), where Bedouin, who once roamed the caravan trails, are now taking tourists to immaculate, astonishing sites like desert caves and fossilized waterfalls. Camel treks are available in all the oases.

Deep Desert Extreme

For those looking for an intense, extreme experience, the wild, uninhabited southern desert awaits. This is deep desert travel: no water, no roads, no gasoline, no food. You lug it with you. Good guides are a must, and 10 to 24 days (without a bath) are needed. You will go where few have gone. There are four major destinations to a deep desert journey: Gebel Uwaynat, Gilf Kebir, the Great Sand Sea, and the Darb al-Arbain.

These types of journeys require exceptional guides and expensive equipment. There are a number of safari companies from Europe who book such tours regularly. There are also excellent Nile Valley agencies whom most travel agents in Cairo can contact for you. It will not be long before the ultra tours will arrive in this desert: hot and cold water baths, gourmet dining, etc. For now, this world of extreme desert travel is still for the explorer in all of us.

One other point should be made: who should go to the desert? The answer is anyone: desert trips do not require the perfect body, the perfect age, or perfect health. The 'perfect' car does the work most of the time (except for hiking, which does need conditioning), so big bellies and canes are possible. All sizes and shapes of travelers come to the desert. All ages come. At 96, Thedore Monod, one of the world's great experts on the Libyan Desert, was still traveling the deep desert.

So, here it is. Hope we have cleared up the chaos of desert travel and opened up all the opportunities for you. Welcome to a new world: a world not only of adventure and excitement but of variety.

GPS and Waypoints

A new feature to this edition is the addition of GPS waypoints to the most popular places. A GPS is a Global Positioning System. It is a small hand-held device—some can be mounted on a car's dashboard—that accesses communication satellites that orbit the earth and gives your exact position in longitude and latitude, altitude. It can also note your speed and bearing, and it lays down your track so you can follow it back. When you mark your position you create a waypoint that the machine stores. On new journeys you can follow your route home by following the waypoints on your GPS. Or, you can plug in GPS waypoints before you start your journey and have fun following them to your destination, be it downtown Cairo or Kharga Oasis. With a computer you can download your waypoints onto a map.

There is no mystery here. GPS is simply longitude and latitude. It is space-age technology that does away with complicated tools and terms and gives the know-how of a scientist to an average person in a matter of minutes. GPS waypoints for the Western Desert are not as big a secret as some people think. The Geological Survey, which has been making maps and studying the landscape in the desert every day of every year since 1898, uses GPS regularly. The oil companies have been using GPS for years. The Egyptian army uses GPS. The Pharaoh's Rally participants received waypoints as part of their trip information.

All the literature on the Western Desert provides longitude and latitude to almost every place in the desert, and has done so since Frederic Cailliaud went exploring in 1820 and Gerhard Rohlfs made his gigantic exploration in 1874. If waypoints are not in the publications of the Geological Survey, then they are in the work of the desert scholars, or European desert magazines for travelers. These publications number in the thousands.

The GPS is here to stay. The GPS and its waypoints will be commonplace in a few years. Eventually they will replace the traditional map.They are already available as optional equipment on some automobiles, with routes and numbers already plugged in. GPS companies not only offer waypoints to tourist destinations, battlefields, and shopping malls, they also allow the traveler to find a friend's house in a distant and never-before visited city.

We have provided hundreds of GPS points in this book. Most are on the asphalt road to common destinations. There are a few off-road safaris where GPS points have been provided. We have not provided GPS points to the entire desert, especially deep desert and restricted travel.

Emergencies

The government has erected first-aid stations at regular intervals all along the loop road through the desert. They are usually near a satellite tower. They are equipped to handle most problems.

Warning

Throughout the text are repeated warnings about the dangers of desert travel. Take them seriously, but do not let them stop you from visiting the desert altogether.

A Few Good Tips

A *surgical mask* protects your sinuses and lungs against the wind and blowing sand of a sandstorm. *Spray bottles* are good for bathing. They conserve water, yet give you enough to get the job done. *Bathwipes* and handy wipes have a million uses in the desert. *Hard tack candy* keeps the mouth and throat moist. *Plastic baggies* have a million uses. A *flashlight attached to the head* keeps the hands free to do the task at hand.

Tours

From Europe

Many of these excellent tours offer exciting deep desert travel. Sometimes they have a seat or two available for locals: just give them a call. They are also willing to accommodate a party with their own 4x4s.

Desert Tours Egypt. Tel: +31 252 412 410. Fax: +31 252 414 102. Mobile: +31 6 51 840 656. Meeuwenlaan 3, 2162 HD Lisse, Netherlands. E-mail: *corienkortekaas@desert-tours.nl*. Webpage: *www.deserttours.nl*. A Dutch company working with the Oasis Panorama Hotel in Bahariya, their specialty is camel tours around the Bahariya area.

Lama Expeditions Tel: +49 69 447 897. Fax: +49 69 499 0767. Samir and Wally Lama. Roderbergweg 106, 60385 Frankfurt/M., Germany. *Lama-Expeditions@t-online.de*. Webpage: *http://home.t-online.de/home/Lama-Expedition/english/index.htm*. Offering six or seven tours a year from November through April, this well established desert tour agency specializes in deep desert travel with the expertise of the accepted master of the desert. They speak French, English, German, and Arabic.

From Cairo

Abanoub 12 Mahmoud Hassan, Heliopolis. Tel: 418 2671/72. All Western Desert. Booking through Sinai office: (062) 520 201/206.

Cairo International 21 Mokhtar Said. Heliopolis. Tel: 291 1495, 291 1490. Fax: 290 4554. All Western Desert including deep desert.

Dabuka Expeditions Tarek el-Mahdy, 61 Road 9, Maadi. Tel /Fax: 358 4406. Email: *el-mahdy@t-online.de*. Webpage: *www.dubuka.de*. Off-road to all Western Desert and Sinai. Speaks English, German, French, and Arabic. German office: Hubertusstr 91 1/3 D-82131 Gauting. Tel/Fax: +49 89 893 9 9572. Email: *sonje.wilhelmi@gmx.net*. Also offers *Fly and Drive*: you fly into Egypt without worrying about customs, ports, and equipment. You drive the desert in a Dabuka vehicle with all Dabuka equipment including camping gear, food, and guides.

Max Travel 5 al-Falah St., Mohandiseen. Tel: 303 5630/5125. Fax: 303 6123. Organized desert tours and 4x4 rental.

Pan Arab Tours Ahmed Moussa. 5, Saudi Egyptian Building Co., al-Nuzha St, Heliopolis, Cairo. Tel: 291 3503, 418 4409, 291 3506. Fax: 291 3506. Email: *pat@moussa.net*. All traditional and deep desert tours in all deserts.

Siag Travel Ramy Siag. Sakkara Road, Giza. PO Box 107, Al Ahram. Tel: 385 2626, 385 3013, 385 0105. Fax: 383 1444. Email: *sales@siagtravel.com*. Webpage: *www.siagtravel.com*. One of the oldest and most knowledgable desert agencies. Siag has been the sponsor of the various desert ralleys over the years. They offer all types of travel into the desert including motorcycle tours. Speak most languages.

Zarzora Expeditions Wael Abed and Ahmed Mestckawy. 12B Mahmoud Azmi Street, Zamalek. Tel and fax: 736 0350. Email: *zarzora@hotmail.com*. Webpage: *www.zarzora.com*. All parts of the desert including deep desert. Speak English, German, Italian, and Arabic.

Specialized Tours in Egypt or from Abroad

Birding (and other natural history tours)

Egypt Nature Adventures Mindy Baha el Din. 3 Aballa al-Katib St., Apt 3, Dokki, Cairo. Tel: 760 8160. Mobile: 012 218 0709. Email: *baha@internetegypt.com*. Webpage: *www.birdingegypt.com*. Mostly around Lake Qarun in Fayoum, Wadi Rayyan, Wadi Natrun, Northern Coast, Lake Nasser, and Tushka.

Study Tours

Ancient World Tours PO Box 12950, London, W6 8GY. Tel: +44 7071 222 950. Fax: +44 1483 237 398. Email: *mra@dial.pipex.com*. Website: *www.ancient.co.uk*. Unique travel experiences with noted scholars. Kent Weeks in the Nile Valley. David Rohl and rock art in the Eastern Desert. Tours to Western Desert.

4x4 Stuff

Egyptian/American Service Center. Near Maadi at Dar al-Salaam. Tel: 317-9041 (Arabic speaking only: ask for Dave). Mobile: 010 145 6439 (English-speaking). Email: *torg@intouch.com*. Maintenance for all types of 4x4s. Accessories for sale include sand mats, brush guards, lighting systems, and roof racks.

Permissions

Restrictions in the desert change with the political climate and the whims of the gods. Currently there are no restrictions to asphalt travel and one can visit any major oasis without permission. Off-road travel to deep desert destinations requires a permit. As desert travel is increasing, permissions can now be obtained from Misr Travel. They will get the necessary documents from Military Intelligence. However, they need time, so get your request in early, at least two weeks in advance of your departure date. You should be able to book through any travel agency. They, in turn, will go to Misr Travel for your permission.

Restricted areas include the Darb Siwa between Baharıya and Siwa (erratic permissions), Ain Della in Farafra, all points south of Kharga and Dakhla including the Gilf Kebir, Gebel Uwaynat, Bir Tarfawi, the Darb al-Arbain, and Darb al-Galaba.

You will need:
• List of names of all persons traveling, with passport numbers and nationalities
• Route and dates of travel
• Two photocopies of main page of your passport and visa page. Keep extra copies for checkpoints en route.

If permission includes a military escort be sure the escort has enough food, blankets, and petrol before beginning the journey, or you will have to feed and protect the escort, and provide the gas for the vehicle.

Since the discovery of the Valley of the Golden Mummies, permission requirements to visit the antiquities in Bahariya have been lifted and one can now purchase admission tickets at the museum. See Bahariya for details. In Kharga the northern desert forts still require permission.

Telephoning the Oases

Most oases now have good lines connecting them to the Egyptian telephone system. To call, you must have long distance service on your telephone (all hotels have this service). Once you dial, you may have to wait for 30 seconds to a minute for your connection. There will be dead silence on the line. Be patient.

Kharga

Tourist Information Office

Tel and fax: (092) 921 206 and (092) 921 205. The Tourist Information Office is located near the Mabrouk Fountain on Gamal Abd al-Nasser Street.

Monument Entrance Fees

As of this writing Bagawat, Zayyan, Ghuweita, Dush, and the Kharga Museum all have entrance fees: one price for non-Egyptian adults, another for non-Egyptian students, and a third for Egyptians. Summer hours from April to September are 8–6. and winter hours from October to March are 8–5. Kharga Museum hours are 8:30–5 daily, except Friday 8:30–11:30 and 1:30–5.

All other monuments require permission from the Director of Antiquities offices across the street from the Kharga Museum. The Egyptian Antiquities director is Bahgat Ahmed Ibrahim and his assistant is Magdy Hussein, (092) 921 863. The Islamic Antiquities director is Mansur Osman. Office hours are from 8–2 and 6–8. The offices are very cooperative and will request that a guide or inspector accompany you. You should tip your guide.

Places to Stay

Upper Level
The Pioneer Hotel Tel: (092) 927 982. Fax: (092) 927 983. Cairo office: Solymar Resorts and Hotels 157 26th July Street, Zamalek. Tel: 738 2016. Fax: 735 2990. E-mail: *solymar@menanet.net*. With probably the most luxurious accommodations in the desert, this five-star hotel has 102 fully air-conditioned rooms with baths, terrace, direct dial telephones, TV, music system, and satellite channels, in addition to a restaurant, lobby bar, swimming pool, pool-side coffee shop, terrace, and pergola.

Middle Level
Hamedalla Tourist Hotel Sharia al-Nada Tel and fax: (092) 920 638. Offering moderate rates, meals, and friendly service, this three-star hotel has some air-conditioned rooms.
Waha Hotel (092) 920 393. Located on the last street in the south of the town, it offers moderate rates, meals, and some air-conditioned rooms.
Kharga Oasis Hotel Sharia Gamal Abd al-Nasser. Located at the northern edge of the town in a beautiful palm grove, this hotel is currently under renovation.

Lower Level
Al-Montaz Resthouse (092) 920 820. The former resthouse of President Anwar Sadat, this is a spacious but run-down facility. It is close to all sites in the city, inexpensive, but below standard.

Camping
Nasser Resthouse Tel: (092) 927 982. Fax: (092) 927 983. Solymar Resorts and Hotels 157 26th July Street, Zamalek. Tel: 738 2016. Fax: 735 2990. E-mail: *solymar@menanet.net.* Newly Renovated. Located in a grove of casuarina trees; there are three springs that have been diverted into a large bathing area. The facilities include five bungalows sleeping four persons each, and a caravan and tent area. The Nasser Resthouse is on a dirt track 6 kilometers (3.7 miles) south of Qasr al-Ghweita and 24 kilometers (15 miles) south of Qasr Kharga. Upscale.

Gasoline
There are two 24-hour gas stations at Qasr Kharga.

Assistance
Hospital Sharia Gamal Abd al-Nasser. Tel: (092) 929 777.
Post Office Sharia Gamal Abd al-Nasser. Saturday to Thursday 9–3. International service. Open 24 hours.

Transportation
Buses leave for various locations daily from Midan Showla, next to the old city. From Cairo buses depart from al-Azhar.

From Kharga
To Asyut 5 per day at 6 a.m., 7 a.m., 11 a.m., 1 p.m., and 2 p.m.
To Cairo 4 per day at 6 a.m., 9 a.m., 7 p.m., and 8 p.m.
To Dakhla 4 per day at 7 a.m., 1 p.m., 4 p.m., and 5 p.m.
To Baris 2 per day at 12 noon and 2 p.m.
To Bulaq and Baris Multiple daily regular service.
Service Taxis can be found opposite the bus station. They offer sightseeing at a reasonable fee.
Airplanes leave for Cairo twice weekly on Sunday and Wednesday at 6 a.m., arriving at 7 a.m., and return immediately.
Train From new train station south of Qasr Kharga along the Darb al-Arbain Departure once weekly: Luxor to Kharga Wednesday (time varies); Kharga to Luxor Friday at 7 a.m. Trip takes 8 hours.

Dakhla

Tourist Information Office There are two offices in Mut. The former one at New Mosque Square (092) 820 407, fax 820 782 and the new, large, airy one on the main road to Qasr (092) 821 686, fax 820 782. English is spoken by the officer Omar Ahmed Mahmoud. Eager to help and providing useful information, the offices are open 8-2 daily, and often in the evenings. The tourist rooms at New Mosque Square are newly renovated and open at a very modest price.

Places to Stay
Upper Level
Mut 3 Chalet Tel: (092) 927 982. Fax: (092) 927 983. Solymar Resorts and Hotels 157 26th July Street, Zamalek. Tel: 738 2016. Fax: 735 2990. E-mail: *solymar@menanet.net.* This organization has completely renovated the former Hot Springs Resthouse located 3 kilometers (1.8 miles) north of Mut. There are two facilities here. The Roadside Resthouse offers a gardened villa with 4 bedrooms, 3 private

baths, and a living room. The Poolside Resthouse offers 6 chalets, each with two beds and a bathroom. The pool is a hot spring, at 42.5° C. Cafeteria at poolside.

Medium Level

El Kasr Inn Located across the road from Qasr Dakhla village. Booking exclusively via Pan Arab in Cairo. Tel: 291 3503. Fax: 291 3506, 414 1275. Five rooms with bath and hot and cold water, 2 beds per room, 10 tents for campers , showers, toilets, and jacuzzi. Restaurant.

Mebarez Tourist Hotel Third Street. Tel: (092) 821 524. Four floors of rooms with hot and cold water, showers, television, air conditioning. A cafeteria and dining room on the ground floor.

Mut Tourist Village, a hotel of traditional architecture in the center of town, it has been under construction for 10 years. Still not complete.

Lower Level

El Forsam (092) 821 347. Ehab Zacharia. 9 rooms, 27 beds, hot and cold water, and restrooms. In center of town combined with the Anwar Restaurant (see below).

Elkasr Tourist Rest House (092) 876 013. Only hotel in Qasr. 4 rooms, 2 beds per room, 2 baths, hot and cold water.

The Gardens Hotel (092) 821 577. Three floors, hot and cold water.

Nasser Camp and Hotel At Sheikh Wali, just outside of Mut. Owned by Nasser Hilal Zed. Seven rooms, bath separate. Hot and cold spring, sand dunes. English, German, and Arabic spoken. Offers safaris. Your car or his. Contact the hotel through restaurants.

Mut Tourist Resthouse North of the new mosque at New Mosque Square. In the Tourist Information Office building (use their phone numbers), this modest hostel offers 7 rooms with toilet and 8 rooms with a shared toilet. Meals are available upon request. Tel: (092) 820 407.

Camping

Al-Dahuz Bedouin Camp (092) 850 480, 850 605. Sheikh Abd al-Hamid. Hot and cold water. Choice of 20 rush chalets or tents. Inexpensive, clean, dynamite view of desert and cultivated land, evening entertainment. Safari by camel (up to 30 people) and 4x4 can be arranged to any area in the vicinity at reasonable prices.

Kamis Company Camp (092) 941 577. Currently under construction. Over 100 beds in bungalows in the dunes to the south of Mut. Will offer camel safaris.

Safaris

Best bet is still to check with the Tourist Information Office about pricing.

Ahmed Salim (092) 876 762. Tours over the various darbs (caravan roads) of Dakhla.

Anwar Muhammad Mishal (at Anwar Restaurant) (092) 941 566, 820 070. Traditional tours by car, 4x4, or camel to desert, old Islamic tombs, cold spring, Qasr, pottery factory, water wheel, and sand dunes.

Nasser Hilal Zed (092) 822 747. 4x4, camel, to all points in desert and around Dakhla. Ain Amur, Ain Umm Dabadib, White Mountains, Sand Dunes.

Sheikh Abd al-Hamid (092) 825 480. Bedouin safari by camel in Dakhla desert. Will do 4x4 in guest's vehicle.

Places to Eat (see map for location)

Abu Mohamed Restaurant (and Bike Rental) Third Street. Expensive.

Anwar Restaurant Desart Paradize (092) 820 070. In the center of town. Good food, good location, and now a hotel too.

Arabi Restaurant, 3rd Street, Mut. Arabi Hilal Zed. Two brothers run two restaurants: Arabi Restaurant and Ahmed Hamdi Restaurant. Both are clean, food is good, pricing is honest and reasonable. This brother, Arabi, ran an oil company kitchen in Saudi Arabia and has recently changed the name of his restaurant from Hamdi to Arabi.

Ahmed Hamdi Restaurant, 3rd Street, Mut. (092) 820 767. Just down the street, Hamdi runs this restaurant and wants everyone to know this was the original Hamdi Restaurant, once located in the center of town.

Gasoline

There are several gasoline stations in Mut, one at each entrance. Both are open 24 hours a day. At least six tire repair shops are located along the main road on the way to the Hot Springs.

Assistance

Mut Hospital is located beside the petrol station along the main road.

Bank Misr on Tahrir Square offers foreign exchange and will accept traveler's checks. Open daily 8:30–2. Evenings for exchange only 7–9. Closed Friday. Open Saturday for exchange only.

The **Telephone Office** is open 24 hours a day and has international lines.

Transportation

The best bus system in the oases is at Mut. All buses leave from New Mosque Square in Mut. Check with the Tourist Information Office for schedule changes.

To Kharga, 4 buses per day, connecting to Asyut.

To Cairo, 2 per day by the Upper Egyptian Bus Company. Leaves Cairo from al-Azhar station 7 a.m. and 8 p.m. Leaves Mut 6 p.m. and 6 a.m. daily; Farafra, Bahariya, Cairo.

Bus to Luxor via Asyut leaves Dakhla Friday, Sunday, Tuesday. Leaves Asyut Saturday, Monday, Wednesday.

Inter-oasis, Mut to Balat and Bashindi, 5 per day from 6 a.m. to 3 p.m. Mut to Qasr and Maghoub, 4 per day, 6 to 5.30.

Taxi rental by the day is possible. All taxis are located at the main square, or through the Tourist Promotion Office.

Dakhla Airport One flight weekly on Wednesday about 8:00 a.m. and return to Cairo immediately: Cairo, Kharga, Dakhla, Cairo. Tel: (092) 822 853, 822 854.

Farafra Oasis

Places to Stay

Upper Level

El Badawiya Hotel In Cairo: 345 8524, 012 214 8343. In Farafra: 377 4600, 377 4601. Saad Ali and Josiane Chopard. Done in Hassan Fathy style, this small hotel contains 20 rooms, 12 with bath. There is a restaurant, evening entertainment, BBQ, bicycles for rent, shisha. Offers camel and jeep safaris, walking and traditional tours.

Aqua Sun Resort Under construction. Located at the famous Bir Sitta, 75 bungalows are planned in what is intended as a spa. There will be a physical therapy center, sand, water, and aromatherapy treatments.

Lower Level

Resthouse Clean and offering sleeping accommodations (four singles to a room), a bath with cold water, and a modest kitchen. The resthouse operates on a first-come-first-served basis.

Safaris

El Badawiya Safari Owned by Saad Ali. In Cairo: 345 8524, 012 214 8343. In Farafra: 377 4600, 377 4601. This safari company offers camel and jeep safaris to all areas of the desert around Farafra. Tours run for a single day up to 12 days.

Hussein Abu Bakr and **Talaat Mohamed Hamuda**. Headquartered at the Nicetime Coffeeshop, this safari group offers trips by car, motorbike, camel, and walking. Offers traditional tours to the White Desert and Hot Springs.

Places to Eat

(All in the main square)

Ashraf's Ful and Taamiya Very cheap and open all day.

Cafeteria In the center of the restaurant district. Ownership changes each year as it is rented from the government. Maybe food, maybe not.

Nicetime Coffee Shop Coffee all day, taamiya at night. Very inexpensive.

White Desert Restaurant Kosheri all day. Very inexpensive.

Entertainment

Zikrs

On Monday and Thursday Sufi zikrs are held in the village of Qasr Farafra. There is no set location, as family homes are opened to the men for the occasion. Visitors are welcome as long as they respect the fact that they are guests in a religious rite.

Bedouin Flute

Gamal Abd al-Mogdi plays the Bedouin flute upon request in the square, at the restaurants, at your camp, and sometimes at the hotels.

Things to Buy

Mr. Socks sells camel-wool socks, gloves, hats, scarves, vests, sweaters, and blankets, all made by his family. This is a true cottage-industry success story. If you don't see him flying around on his motorcycle, just ask at any of the small cafés. They will get the word to him.

Gasoline

There are two gas stations in Farafra, one at the entrance to Qasr Farafra and a second about 20 kilometers along the road to Abu Minqar. Both have 90 gas. Although the electricity is off from 2 a.m. to 10 a.m., gas is sold in gerrycans at that time.

Hospital

There is a new hospital in Farafra at the entrance to Qasr Farafra.

Permissions

Permission to visit Ain Della may be obtained via Misr Travel (see above). At present most requests are denied.

Transportation

The bus at Farafra now runs on time. In fact, there are buses to both Dakhla and Cairo every morning and evening. Times vary by 1–2 hours.

Bahariya

Tourist Information Office (02) 847 2222. The office is located on the main street in the Municipal Building garden just as you enter the gate. If closed, ask for the manager, Mohamed Abd al-Kadar. This office operates the Paradise Hotel, practically across the street, and offers low-budget safaris.

Places to Stay
Upper Level
Beshmo Lodge (02) 847 2177. Ahmed Ibrahim and Salah Abdulla. There are 25 rooms in this new hotel, located in the palm grove at Ain Bishmu. Five rooms are up-scale, each with a bathroom and air conditioning, 20 rooms have fans and shared baths. There is a cafeteria, a restaurant, and several shops. The lodge offers safaris.

International Hot Springs Hotel (02) 847 3014, mobile: (012) 321 2179, fax: (02) 847 2322. E-mail: *whitedesert@link.net*. Peter, Heide, and Miharu Wirth. Situated at the foot of the Black Mountain on the outskirts of Bawiti, the hotel is built around a hot spring that gets its water from the nearby Bir Halfa. There are also facilities for massages, sauna, a complete gymnasium, a glorious tent for entertainment, and various patios and gazebos for relaxation. There are 36 rooms with private baths and hot and cold water. Rates are for half board. Safari company on premises.

New Oasis Hotel (02) 847 3030, mobile: 012 357 9260. Salah Ali. Located at Ain Bishmu, this hotel situated in a palm grove has 21 rooms with bath, hot and cold water, and a restaurant located on a nice patio surrounded by palm trees and morning glories. The hotel offers safaris.

Oasis Panorama Hotel (02) 847 2894, 847 2700. Magdy and Ahmed Deyab, Corien Kortekaas, Annelieke Wassenaar, and Klasske V/D Velde. Located on a spur of the Black Mountain, this double story hotel features 24 double rooms, 6 triples, and 2 suites. Each with bath, hot and cold water, some with TVs and telephones. Restaurant, patio, coffeeshop. Does safaris.

Lower Level
Alpenblick Hotel (02) 847 2184. The long-time gathering place for backpackers in Bahariya, this no-frills guest house is operated by Hagg Salah. It features 22 rooms, 6 with bath and hot and cold water.

Paradise Hotel (02) 847 2600. A government hotel along the main street of Bawiti, the Paradise has 4 double/triple rooms. The bath is shared, but has hot and cold water. Guests may use the kitchen. There is a washing machine. Safari tours are offered on asphalt, half asphalt/half off-road, or all off-road for afternoon, day, 2–3 days.

Camping
Ahmed Safari Camp (02) 847 2770, 847 3399. Fax: 847 2090. This wonderful camp is located 3 kilometers outside town along the route to Darb Siwa, in a peaceful area called Tibniya. There are 21 rooms, 20 with baths, all with hot and cold water. The camp will accommodate 13 cars and they have use of the kitchen, free electric hookup, baths with hot and cold showers. There are huts for backpackers, and people can pitch their own tents for a few pounds. Free transport offered to Bawiti all day. Free bikes are available. The hot spring is an authentic oasis spring in a natural location. Safaris include everything from a night at a nearby dune to the entire Western Desert.

Bir Ghaba Anyone can camp at the Bir (see directions in text). If you do not have a vehicle, the people at the hotels will deliver you and pick you up in the morning. Do not try to find Bir Ghaba at night without a guide.

Safaris

All the hotels offer safaris, just ask. There are a number of independent tour groups. Traditional tours include Bir Ghaba, Black Desert, White Desert in Farafra, Bawiti/Qasr, Darb Siwa. However, some guides offer tours to other oases. Walking, camel, and 4x4 tours can be arranged by any safari company.

Full Moon Safari Hamuda Kilani and Ashraf Lotfi. Tel: (02) 847 2148, 847 2704. They offer traditional tours for up to 30 people, using the travelers' vehicles. The organizers provide food, sleeping bags, tents. Sites include all the oases.

Reda Abd al-Razzoul (the Desert Fox) Tel and fax: (02) 847 2934. Reda is a geography and history teacher who has guided people in the desert for 17 years. He offers tours for all prices, in your car or in his. Once a year Reda offers a discounted week for people to join him in cleaning up the desert and the public areas of Bawiti and Qasr.

Specialized Safaris

Abdulla Abdul Kadder (02) 847 2431. Camel tour to all traditional places.

Khalid Khalifa (02) 847 2542. Long-range expeditions and exploration. Considerable experience with scientific safaris. Speaks some French. Ask at hotels and restaurants.

Naghi Family (02) 847 2061. Largest camel herders in Bahariya. Offer camel tours to all traditional places, or by the hour. Arabic-speaking only.

Peter Group (02) 847 2322. English-, Japanese-, and German-speaking guide to all traditional places. Contact through International Hot Springs Hotel, see above.

Rolou Abd al-Raouf (02) 847 2520. 10–15 day walking tours in White Desert. Speaks French, English, and Arabic.

Places to Eat

The Popular Restaurant Located off the main road near the police station, this restaurant is open from 5:30 a.m. to 11 p.m. There is no menu and the single meal prepared each day usually consists of meat, rice, and vegetables. It is the gathering place for all the desert drivers and a good place to pick up a tour.

Cafeteria al-Rahma (02) 847 2237. Across the street from the Popular Restaurant, the al-Rahma Cafeteria features oriental and occidental foods, grilled chicken, take-away, desserts, and drinks. They supply camp kitchens upon request.

Rashed Restaurant Located on the main street before the colonial houses, this is a new restaurant that offers a variety of menus including grilled chicken. It is the only place for a selection of sweets, and offers the shisha.

Gasoline and Natural Gas

There are three gas stations, and gas is available 98 percent of the time. At high season you may be left high and dry. In Bawiti (marked on the map), **Esso** has 80, 90, diesel, and oil; **Misr**, the main station, has 90, diesel, oil, brake fluid, and a car wash; **CoOp** has government 80 diesel, and natural gas for buses and vehicles running on alternative fuels.

Even when there is gas, there may not be electricity for the pumps, so always, always top your tank after each excursion. In an emergency, gas is available at Managim, from the mining company. Managim is 40 kilometers from Bawiti so save enough gasoline to get there. At Managim one must make application at the mining offices. Go to the mine (see Managim above). When passing through the entrance tell the guards you need gas (benzine, petrol) and they will send you to the administrative building. Here you must have your passport, the car papers, and money. You must know how many liters you

want. You will pay for the gas, get a receipt, and proceed to the depot where you will present the receipt. The offices are closed between shifts (2-4:30).
Tire repair and garages are marked on the map.

Things to Buy

Best buys in Bahariya include camel blankets, gloves, hats, scarves, and sweaters. Bahariya baskets are reinforced with hemp rope and are wonderful. It is very hard to find authentic dresses any more and the ones the women are wearing today are not as nice but you can buy them on the market. Also little traditional jewelry remains.

Oasis Heritage Museum (02) 847 2970. On the main road. Created by the wonderful Mahmoud Eed. You cannot miss it: gigantic camels with light bulbs for eyes mark the spot. In addition to looking at the amazing work of this self-taught artist, you can buy some of his work.

New Nashwa Handicrafts (02) 847 2276. On the square across from the police. Owner is Badri Makboul Khozam, who speaks excellent English and is also a guide to Siwa, the desert, and Wadi Rayyan. Bedouin clothes. Old silver. Camel blankets, socks, gloves, and scarves. Baskets. Desert stones. He also rents bicycles.

Saber Sanusi (02) 847 2437. Saber is a knitter and he buys his wool from Cairo. He makes the long knitted underwear the men of the oases wear under their gallabiyas to keep warm in the winter. This is a good buy for anyone camping in the desert in winter. He also makes men's and women's scarves, including the long umda scarves seen on men all over Egypt.

Entertainment

Bedouin Music Coffeeshop, Aguz. (02) 847 2431. Abd al-Sadik Badromani plays his music and recites his desert poetry here most evenings after 9. He is a self-taught musician who has been playing for 25 years and has recently become famous in Egypt and Europe. He sometimes entertains in the clubs at Giza. If you are lucky Mohamed Abd al-Latif Bodadi, known as Desert Sugar, will dance for you or play his flute.

Permissions

Antiquities One can now purchase a ticket at the museum to visit five sites around Bawiti. See museum in text for details. Al-Hayz is also open. Permission to visit any of the other antiquities in Bahariya must be obtained in Cairo from the Supreme Council for Antiquities, 4D Fakhry Abd al-Nour, Abbasiya. Tel: 284 3627, 283 8084. Daily 9–3, closed Friday and Saturday. Or from the office of the Director of Antiquities for Giza and Saqqara (next to the pyramids on the Giza Plateau).

Darb Siwa Permission to travel on the Darb Siwa may be obtained from Military Intelligence, Group 26, Sharia Manshiet al-Bakri, Heliopolis, Cairo. Best done through one of the Cairo-based desert travel agencies.

Transportation

There is ample transportation to Bahariya Oasis. Buses leave from the blue kiosk across the street from the Paradise Hotel and next to the Tourist Information Office. Travelers are advised to reserve a seat one day in advance as the bus is often booked in either direction. The cost is inexpensive enough to consider booking two seats to be more comfortable. In the microbuses you can reserve an entire row (3 seats).

Buses
From Cairo Four buses daily leave Cairo for Bahariya:
7 a.m. from Turguman near Ramses

8 a.m. from Moneeb (under the new Maadi Bridge, Giza side, book the day before)
3 p.m. from Moneeb
6:30 p.m. from Moneeb
With a stop at the halfway house, arrival time at Bawiti is 4 hours later.
From Bahariya Four buses daily leave the oasis for Cairo: 7 a.m., 12 noon (coming from Dakhla), 3 p.m., and 12 midnight (coming from Dakhla). The 7 and 3 can be reserved a day in advance.

Microbus

First come first served from the appropriately named Bahariya Café, Sharia Qadri, Sayyida Zeinab. With the front of the Sayyida Zeinab mosque behind you, continue to the end of the square and turn right. A good 100 meters down this street there is a small café on the left and there are always people with luggage there, as well as microbuses. As of this writing the buses leave Bahariya in the morning and depart from the café in the afternoon.

Fayoum

The **Tourist Information Office** is located in the center of Medinet Fayoum next to the famous Fayoum waterwheels. It has maps of the city and the oasis and offers friendly service.

Places to Stay

Alaa al-Din Resort Just at the eastern shore of the lake this new resort is under construction.

Auberge Fayoum 358 2356 / 359 5717. Five kilometers (3.1 miles) after the beginning of the lake stands the Auberge Fayoum. Once the hunting lodge of King Farouk, an avid hunter, the villa was the site of high-level negotiations between Egypt and the British, represented by Winston Churchill, in 1945. After the revolution it became the Auberge du Lac. Up to the mid-1970s it still retained the ambiance of colonial Egypt. Renovated, it is now the Auberge Fayoum, a five-star hotel offering a magnificent view and a quiet relaxing vacation. Offers a complete range of facilities, including a health center. You can expect plenty of Egyptians at the Auberge at the weekends, as day visitors.

Panorama Resort and Conference Centre Tel and fax: (084) 830 757, 830 746, 830 314. Newly renovated and expanded. Suites, junior suites, royal apartments. Under British management. Day visitors, including lunch, 9–7 daily.

Camping

Ain al-Siliyin (010) 196 1042.

Gasoline

There are more gas stations that you need in the Fayoum, but when traveling in remote areas it is best to top your tank.

Transportation

Access to the Fayoum is easy and one need not have a car to make the journey. Buses and taxis make regular runs. The cost is minimal.

Trains

One very slow train runs per day between Cairo and Fayoum.

Buses

Buses leave Cairo for Medinet Fayoum from Abbud in Shubra and Munib (under the bridge) in Giza at frequent intervals between 6 a.m. and 6 p.m. Buses leave Fayoum for Cairo from under the bridge over the railway line in the east of the town.

Service Taxis

Service taxis leave from Munib, and from near the railroad station in Beni Suef. These taxis depart when they are filled, but can be rented exclusively by paying the fare for all the places in the vehicle.

Wadi Rayyan

Safari Camp Tel and fax 258 8083. Owned and operated by Marzouk Desert Cruiser at 1 Ebn Sandar Square, Hammamat al-Qubba in Cairo.

The red signs to the Safari Camp are found all across the southern shore of Lake Qarun. This camp is also responsible for the useful arrows that point the way to important locations like the waterfall and the monastery. The camp is situated along the lake shore just south, and within walking distance, of the waterfall. Rush huts with double beds, indoor bathrooms, cold water, restaurant. All water is directly from the lake.

Safaris provided to all parts of Egypt by 4x4, camel treks to Bahariya and in Sinai. Specializes in Wadi Zeuglodon and Wadi Rayyan Monastery. Agent for Oft, Club Med, Reisen, Hekios, Emeco, and Eastmar.

Al-Diffa

The **Tourist Information Office** is in Mersa Matruh. Tel: (046) 494 3192. Open 9-2 and 4-8, the bright, well-equipped office can help with all types of information: finding a hotel, a beach, or place to eat. Located opposite the governorate building (see map).

Places to Stay

Beach resorts, beach communities, and day beaches by the dozens line the coast of the Mediterranean. There are also a number of private resorts. Here are a few.

Aida Beach Hotel (03) 990 850/855/860, 360 3888, 361 1888; fax (02) 360 5888. Ten miles east of al-Alamein, Aida Beach is a full-service resort facility, the only one along the northern coast that is open all year. Facilities include villas, apartments, chalets, and a hotel. All air-conditioned, TV, telephone, mini bar. All hotel rooms have a sea view. There is a beauty salon, sports center, sauna, and jacuzzi. Cabanas are available for the day tourist

Atic Hotel (03) 492 1340, 492 3300; 348 3428; fax 395 0718. Located at Kilometer 90. Villas for the week, month, or season. Rooms and cabanas for the day. Restaurant and coffeeshop. Closed November through March.

Al-Alamein Hotel (03) 492 1228/29/30; fax (03) 492 1232. Located in Sidi Abd al-Rahman, this facility is only open from March to October. It has the best beach.

Marakia (03) 991 313/312. This is a completely self-contained facility that includes shops, supermarkets, restaurants, bars, a swimming pool, movie house, medical clinic, and white sandy beaches. Open from April through November. The first resort built on the Northern Coast. Hotel, no day use.

Eurest Holiday Village (03) 990 487. Just before Hanoville and before Abu Sir, Eurest is operated by Wagon Lit. Small chalets are available for rent by the week, month, or season. Swimming pool, shop, gardens, beach.

Mersa Matruh

Mersa Matruh is full of hotels offering a wide range of prices. See the city map for locations. Fifty percent of the hotels close for the winter, but all hotels are open from May through October. Most are three star.

Beach House, al-Shatee Street. (046) 493 4011; fax (046) 493 3319.
Beau Site, al-Shatee Street (on the beach) (046) 493 2066 or 493 4012.
Miami, al-Corniche (046) 493 5891; fax (046) 493 2083. Has 200 rooms.
Negresco, al-Corniche (046) 494 4492. Has 68 rooms.
New Royal Palace, Corniche al-Nil (046) 494 3406. Has 170 rooms.
Radi, Corniche al-Nil, (046) 493 4828. Has 72 rooms.
Riviera Palace, (046) 933 045.
Rommel House, Galaa Street. (046) 493 5466.
Royal Palace, Corniche al-Nil. (046) 493 4295.
Semiramis, Corniche al-Nil. (046) 493 4091 / 494 4091. Open all year. Winter discounts

Places to Eat

Along the Northern Coast one must eat at one of the resorts. In Mersa Matruh, in addition to the hotel dining rooms, there are plenty of restaurants along Sharia Iskandariya, the main street of town. Most offer good fare, including sea food, grills, and traditional Egyptian dishes.

Transportation

West Delta Bus Company buses leave Cairo daily for Mersa Matruh from Tahrir Square, at 7:30 a.m. in winter, and at 7:30 a.m., 8:30 p.m., 9:30 p.m., and 11 p.m. in summer.

Service taxis leave Cairo from al-Qulali station near Midan Ramses.

Siwa

In the center of the market the Siwans have erected a sign: "Welcome to Siwa. We ask the women to respect our customs and traditions by keeping their legs and upper arms covered. . . . Enjoy your stay in this beautiful oasis. Thank you."

Tourist Information Office Phone and FAX (046) 460 2338. Located in the municipal building and operated by Mahdi Mohamed Ali Hweiti, the office is open Saturday through Thursday 8–2 and Friday 6–8 p.m. Mr. Hweiti will gladly accompany tourists around the oasis.

Places to Stay

Expensive

Adrère Amellal Desert Lodge Environmental Quality International (EQI) El Gari. Must book from Cairo at 735 0052, fax: 736-3331. There are two locations for this innovative ecolodge: one in downtown Shali, no less than 50 feet from the old fortress, called Knoz (046) 460 2399, and a second, the **Adrère Amellal Desert Lodge** at Qari at the base of a mountain. The first has 6 rooms in a traditional mudbrick building, the second 25–30 rooms and suites equipped with traditional Siwan beds, recycled doors, and charcoal braziers. The facilities include a restaurant, conference center, and spa.

Upper Level

Arous al-Waha (Bride of the Oasis) **Hotel** Facilities include private bath with hot and cold water and dining, but no air conditioning. Rates include breakfast. Expensive. Recently renovated. (046) 460 2100.

Siwa Inn Tel and fax: (046) 460 2287. Amira el Zayyat. This charming inn has 10 rooms (8 doubles and 2 triples) with hot and cold water, heaters, bath, fans, and wooden ceilings. There is a restaurant, a coffeeshop, gardens, and a spring. Food is Siwan and Mediterranean. Does local tours.

Siwa Safari Paradise Hotel Omar and Mohamed Abd al-Aziz. Cairo Office: (02) 266 7604. In Siwa: (046) 460 2289/90, fax: (046) 460 2286. Email: *mohamed@siwaparadise.com.* Webpage: *www.siwaparadise.com.* Located in a garden, this deluxe accommodation features three-, four-, and five-star accommodation including air conditioning, cafeteria, restaurant, and a swimming pool fed by a local spring. There are huts for campers. It takes VISA cards.

Middle Level

Amun Hotel (046) 460 2511. Located at Dakrur and used primarily by patients seeking hot sand cures.

Hotel Yusef In the market. (046) 460 2162.

Cleopatra Hotel Near Military Intelligence, features hot water, chalets, fans, screens, and a bug zapper. (046) 460 2148.

Lower Level

Alexander the Great Hotel Located in Mosque Square. (046) 460 0512.

Bedawi Hotel Small hotel at Military Intelligence.

Palm Trees Hotel In the market. (046) 460 2304.

Safari

There are now 18 safari cars in the oasis and many of them can be booked through the various hotels, restaurants or Tourist Information Office. They include Omar Genawi, Ibrahim Mashri, Said Abu Seif, Abdulla Adas, Mohammad Mashri, Soliman Mashri.

Safari Paradise Tours Omar and Mohamed Abd al-Aziz. Cairo Office: (02) 266 7604. In Siwa: (046) 460 2289/90. Siwa, Great Sand Sea, Farafra.

Abdulla Baghi From his craft shop in the main square of Shali, Abdulla provides almost any service including excursions to desert springs and oases.

Places to Eat

Expect to dine on plain and inexpensive fare in Siwa. There are few restaurants and they offer traditional Egyptian dishes: ful, rice, potatoes, and chicken. Ful, a horse bean prepared in a variety of ways, is inexpensive and loaded with protein. There is no alcohol in Siwa. Restaurants come and go. Here are a few that have been around for a long time. They are all located around the market: Kelani and Sons, Abdul's (460-2243), East West, Sohag, Alexanders, and Alexander the Great. Knoz restaurant is recently opened.

Assistance

There are two gas stations in Siwa, one beside the mosque in Shali and the other behind the Arous al-Waha Hotel. It is best to top your tank regularly.

There are no banks. Visitors can exchange money at the Siwa Safari Paradise Hotel. The telephone office, post office (8–2), and police are all located across the street from the Arous al-Waha Hotel. Electricity is now 24 hours a day.

Permissions

Permission to visit Siwa is no longer required, but permission to visit certain sites is. Permission to visit Bir Wahid and all oases to the south like Areg must be obtained in Siwa. Stop at the Tourist Information Office with your passport to receive a letter, then go to the Military Intelligence to get permission. You must have a photocopy of your passport.

Transportation

Getting around Siwa without a vehicle can be difficult, especially in the summer.

Carettas, small colorful carts pulled by donkeys, can be rented with driver. They accommodate four people comfortably.

Bicycles are available from the market.

Pick-up trucks have also entered the transportation business. Usually running to points west, they charge one pound one way.

There were two **local buses** that covered a 45-kilometer circle (28-mile) from Shali to Maraqi in the west, one leaving Shali at 7 a.m. and returning at 10 a.m. and the second leaving at 2 p.m. and returning at 5 p.m, but as of this writing the local driver has retired and no one wants to take his place, and the bus is broken.

To Siwa

Regular from Alexandria, leave 8, 11, 3 all air-conditioned, modest prices.

From Matruh, leave 7 a.m., arrive Siwa 11 a.m.

From Siwa

Leave Siwa 7 a.m., arrive Matruh 11 a.m.

Leave Siwa 7 a.m., arrive Alexandria 3 p.m.

Leave Siwa 10 a.m., arrive Matruh 2 p.m. and Alexandria 6 p.m.

Leave Siwa 2 p.m., arrive Matruh 6 p.m.

Leave Siwa 10 p.m. arrive Alexandria 6 a.m.

There is no bus service from Siwa to Bahariya; the road is bad and you will need 4rx4; you can rent a 4x4 with driver for LE900.

Selected Reading

General

Almasy, Ladislaus E. *Schwimmer in der Wüste*. Innsbruck: Haymon Verlag. 1997.

Alston, Richard. *Soldier and Society in Roman Egypt: A Social History*. London: Routledge. 1995.

Bagnold, R. A. "Early Days of the Long Range Desert Group." *Geographical Journal* 105 (1945): 30–46.

Bagnold, Ralph. *Libyan Sands: Travel in a Dead World*. London: Michael Haag Limited. 1987.

Bagnold, Ralph. *Sand, Wind and War: Memoirs of a Desert Explorer*. Tucson: University of Arizona Press, 1990.

Ball, John. *Egypt in the Classical Geographers*. Cairo: Government Press, Bulaq. 1942.

Ball, John. "Problems of the Libyan Desert." *Geographical Journal* 70 (1927): 21–38, 105–120, 209–224.

Barth, Henry (Heinrich). *Travels and Discoveries in North and Central Africa*. 3 vols. New York: Harper and Brothers Publishers. 1857.

Boahen, A. Adu. *Britain, the Sahara, and the Western Sudan*. Oxford: Clarendon Press. 1964.

Bovill, E. W. *Caravans of the Old Sahara: An Introduction to the History of the Western Sudan*. London: Oxford. 1933.

Briggs, Martin S. *Through Egypt in War Time*. London: T. Fisher Unwin, Ltd. 1918.

Campbell, Dugald. *Camels Through Libya*. Philadelphia: Lippincott. 1935.

Charlesworth, M. P. *Trade Routes and Commerce of the Roman Empire*. 2nd ed. revised. Cambridge: Cambridge University Press. 1976.

Clayton, Peter. *Desert Explorer. A Biography of Colonel P. A. Clayton*. Cornwall: Zerzura Press. 1998.

Dumreicher, André von. *Trackers and Smugglers in the Deserts of Egypt*. London: Methuen and Co. 1931.

Glen, Simon. *Sahara Handbook*. Brentford, Middlesex: Roger Lascelles. 1990.

Jenner, Bob and David List. *The Long Range Desert Group*. London and Vanguard: Osprey Publication Series. 1983.

Lewis, Napthali. *Life in Egypt under Roman Rule*. Oxford: Clarendon. 1983.

Massey, W. T. *The Desert Campaigns*. New York: G. P. Putnam's Sons. 1918.

Murray, G. W. *Dare Me to the Desert*. New York: A. S. Barnes and Company. n.d.

Nachtigal, Gustav. *Sahara und Sudan, Ergebnisse sechsjähriger Reisen in Afrika*. 3 vols. 1879–89. Reprinted Graz, 1967.

de Prorok, Byron Khun. *Mysterious Sahara*. Chicago: Reilly and Lee Company. 1929.

Ridley, Ronald T. *Napoleon's Proconsul in Egypt: The Life and Times of Bernardino Drovetti*. London: The Rubicon Press. 1988.

Rohlfs, Gerhard with P. Ascherson, W. Jordan, and K. Zittel. *Drei Monate in der libyschen Wüste*. Berlin: Cassel, Verlag von Theodor Fisher. 1875. Reprinted by Köln Africa Explorata I Heinrich Barth Institut. Cologne. 1996.

Sers, Jean-François. *Theodore Monod Désert Libyque*. France: Editions Arthaud. 1994.

Starkey, Paul and Janet. *Travellers in Egypt*. London: I.B. Tauris. 1998.

Thomas, B. E. *Trade Routes of Algeria and the Sahara*. Berkeley: University of California Press. 1957.

Vischer, Hanns. *Across the Sahara from Tripoli to Bornu*. London: Edward Arnold. 1910.

Wellard, James. *The Great Sahara*. New York: E. P. Dutton and Company. 1967.

White, Arthur Silva. *From Sphinx to Oracle: Through the Libyan Desert to the Oasis of Jupiter Ammon*. London: Hurst and Blackett, Ltd. 1899.

Winkler, Hans A. *Rock Drawings of Southern Upper Egypt I and II*. London: The Egypt Exploration Society. Oxford University Press. 1939.

Zsolt, Torok. *Salaam Almasy*. Budapest: Elte Eötvös Kladó. 1998.

Kharga and Dakhla

Ball, John. *Geological Survey Report 1899. Kharga Oasis: Its Topography and Geology*. Cairo: National Printing Department. 1900.

Beadnell, Hugh. *An Egyptian Oasis: An Account of the Oasis of Kharga in the Libyan Desert with Special Reference to its History, Physical Geography and Water Supply*. London: John Murray. 1909.

Beadnell, H. J. L. *Dakhla Oasis: Topography and Geology*. Cairo: Geological Survey Report. 1899. Survey Department, Public Works Ministry. 1901.

Caton-Thompson, G. *Kharga Oasis in Prehistory*. London: Athlone Press. 1952.

Edmonstone, Archibald. *A Journey to Two Oases of Upper Egypt*. London: John Murray. 1822.

Fakhry, Ahmed. *The Necropolis of al Bagawat in Kharga Oasis*. Cairo: Government Printing Office. 1951.

Giddy, Lisa L. *Egyptian Oases: Baharia, Dakhla, Farafra, Kharga During Pharaonic Times*. Wiltshire: Aris and Philips Ltd. 1987.

Hoskins, G. A. *Visit to the Great Oasis of the Libyan Desert*. London: Longman. 1837.

Kennedy, D.L. and Riley, D. *Rome's Desert Frontier from the Air*. Austin: University of Texas Press. 1990.

Winlock, H. E. *Ed Dakhleh Oasis: Journal of a Camel Trip Made in 1908*. New York: Metropolitan Museum of Art. 1936.

Bahariya and Farafra

Ball, John and Hugh Beadnell. *Baharia Oasis: Its Topography and Geology*. Cairo: Survey Department, Public Works Ministry. 1903.

Fakhry, Ahmed. *The Oases of Egypt: Bahriyah and Farafra Oases*. Cairo: The American University in Cairo Press. 1973.

Fayoum

Crawford, Dorothy J. *Kerkeosiris: An Egyptian Village in the Ptolemaic Period*. Cambridge: Cambridge University Press. 1971.

Doxiadis, Euphrosyne. *The Mysterious Fayum Portraits: Faces from Ancient Egypt*. New York: Harry N. Abrams, Inc. 1995.

Gazda, Elaine. *Karanis: An Egyptian Town in Roman Times*. Ann Arbor: Kelsey Museum, University of Michigan. 1983.

Al-Diffa

Applebaum, S. *Jews and Greeks in Ancient Cyrene*. Leiden: E. J. Brill. 1979.

Caccio-Dominioni, Paolo. *Alamein 1933–62*. Rome: Longanesi and Co. n.d.

Carver, Michael. *The Battle for North Africa, El Alamein*. London: Batsford. 1962.

De Cosson, Anthony. *Mareotis: Being a Short Account of the History and Ancient Monuments of the North-Western Desert of Egypt and of Lake Mareotis*. London: Country Life Ltd. 1935.

Falls, J. C. Ewald. *Three Years in the Libyan Desert*. Translated by Elizabeth Lee. London: T. Fisher Unwin. 1913.

Field, James A., Jr. *America and the Mediterranean World, 1776–1882*. Princeton: Princeton University Press. 1969.

Irwin, Ray W. *The Diplomatic Relations of the United States with the Barbary Powers 1776–1816*. Chapel Hill: The Univeristy of North Carolina Press. 1931.

Lewin, Ronald. *Ultra Goes to War*. The Hutchinson Publishing Group.

———. *The Life and Death of the Afrika Korps*. New York: Quadrangle, 1977.

Lucas, James. *War in the Desert: The Eighth Army at El Alamein*. New York: Beaufort Books, Inc. 1982.

MacArthur, W. *Auto Nomad in Barbary*. London: Cassell. 1950.

Phillips, C. E. Lucas. *Alamein*. New York: Little, Brown and Co. 1962.

Rodd, Francis Rennell. *General William Eaton, the Failure of an Idea*. New York: Minton, Balch and Company. 1932.

St. John, Bayle. *Adventures in the Libyan Desert*. London: John Murray. 1849.

Vivian, Cassandra. *Alamein*. Monessen, PA: Trade Routes Enterprises. 1992.

Walsh, Thomas. *Journal of the Late Campaign in Egypt*. London: T. Cadell, Jr. and W. Davies. 1803.

Wilson, Robert Thomas. *History of the British Expedition to Egypt*. Philadelphia: Conrad and Co. 1803.

Siwa

Belgrave, C. Dalrymple. *Siwa: The Oasis of Jupiter Ammon*. London: John Lane. n.d.

Fakhry, Ahmed. *The Oases of Egypt: Siwa Oasis*. Cairo: The American University in Cairo Press. 1973.

Leopoldo, Bettina. *Egypt: The Oasis of Amun-Siwa*. Introduction by Claude Savary. Genève: Musée d'Ethnographie. 1986.

Maugham, Robin. *Journey to Siwa*. London: Chapman and Hall. 1950.

Simpson, G. *The Heart of Libya, the Siwa Oasis, its Peoples, Customs and Sport*. London: H. F. and G. Witherby. 1929.

Darb al-Arbain and Gebel Uwaynat

Asher, Michael. *In Search of the 40 Day Road*. Oxford: ISIS Large Print. 1984.

Chittock, Lorraine. *Shadows in the Sand: Following the Forty Days Road*. Cairo: Camel Caravan Press. 1996.

Close, Angela E., ed. *Cattle-Keepers of the Eastern Sahara: The Neolithic of Bir Kiseiba*. Dallas: Southern Methodist University, Department of Anthropology. 1984.

Elbashir, Ahmed E. *The United States, Slavery, and the Slave Trade in the Nile Valley*. Lanham, MD: University Press of America. 1983.

Fisher, Allan and Humphrey J. Fisher. *Slavery and Muslim Society in Africa: The Institution in Saharan and Sudanic Africa and the Trans-Saharan Trade*. New York: Doubleday and Co., Inc. 1970.

Hassanein Bey, A. M. *The Lost Oasis*. New York: Century Company. 1925.

Lhote, Henri. *The Search for the Tassili Frescoes: The Rock Paintings of the Sahara*. Translated from the French by Alan Houghton Brodrick. New York: E. P. Dutton and Co., Inc. 1959.

Manning, Patrick. *Slavery and African Life: Occidental, Oriental, and African Slave Trades*. Cambridge: Cambridge University Press. 1990.

Mason, Michael H. *The Paradise of Fools: Being an Account by a Member of the Party of the Expedition Which Covered 6,300 Miles of the Libyan Desert by Motor-car in 1935*. London: Hodder and Stroughton. 1936.

Mowafi, Reda. *Slavery, Slave Trade, and Abolition Attempts in Egypt and the Sudan 1820–1882*. Lund Studies in International History 14. Esselte Studium. 1981.

van Noten, Francis. *Rock Art of the Jebel Uweinat*. Graz, Austria: Akademische Druck- u. Verlagsanstalt. 1978.

Toledano, Ehud R. *The Ottoman Slave Trade and its Supression 1840–90*. Princeton: Princeton University Press. 1982.

Wendorf, F. and R. Schild. *Prehistory of the Eastern Sahara*. New York: Academic Press. 1980.

Index

Abasgi battalion, 55
Abba Kaw, relics of, 251
Abbas II, 309–10, 341
Abgig, 253
Abu Amuri, 355
Abu Bakr, 165–66
Abu Ballas, 241, 375–76
Abu Boahen, 33
Abu Kir (salt lake), 272
Abu Kir Bay, 275
Abu Minqar, 15, 42, 143–44
Abu Muharrik belt, 13
Abu Nafir, House of, 137
Abu Salih, 251
Abu Shuruf, 341
Abu Simbel, 22, 23
Abu Sir, 253
Abu Sir (Taposiris), 269–70, 271
Abu Talib (lake), 225, 254
Abu Tartur plateau, 62, 64, 67
Abu Zayd al-Hilali, 245, 271
Abugsessa, Muhammad, 323
Abuksa, 248
Acheulian period, 23
African Association, 33–34, 307
African trade routes, 3
Afrika Korps, 43, 266, 276–78, 290, 298
Agagia, battle of, 299
Agami, 269
Aghurmi, 332
agriculture, 67; in Bahariya, 185–86; in
     Dakhla, 112; in Fayoum, 217; in
     Siwa, 315–18, 341
Aguz, 203
Ahmed Safari Camp, 198
Ain Abu Hawas, 172
Ain Amur, 62, 104–105, 107
Ain Asil, 109, 129–30
Ain Besay, 150, 158
Ain Birbiya, 129
Ain al-Dabashiya, 102–104
Ain Della, 45, 48, 150, 162, 164
Ain al-Dib, 81
Ain Doua, 43
Ain Gallaw, 158
Ain al-Gazar, 94
Ain Hadra, 168
Ain al-Hamiya, 138

Ain al-Hubaga, 192–93
Ain al-Izza, 209
Ain Mashindit, 339
Ain al-Muftillah, 197–98
Ain Muhammad Tuleib, 95, 96
Ain Qurayshat, 341
Ain al-Ris, 206
Ain Romani, 62
Ain Sheikh Marzuq, 159
Ain al-Siliyin, 248
Ain Tafnis, 85
Ain Tamusi, 334
Ain al-Tarakwa, 103
Ain Tirghi, 131
Ain Umm Dabadib, 40, 64, 95–101
Ain Umm al-Masid, 135
Ain al-Wadi, 169
Ain Yusif, 205
Ain Zaaf, 78–79
Ains, 14. See also springs.
Air Mountains, 30
al-Alamein, 265, 266, 267, 274–86
Alexander the Great, 3, 198, 269, 287–88,
     292, 303, 305–306, 313, 333, 338–39
Alexandria, 3, 17, 30, 34, 36, 49, 56, 57, 306
Algeria, 2, 11, 13, 28, 31, 50, 63
Ali, Kushuk, 355
Ali, Muhammad, 26, 35–37, 58, 75, 86,
     111, 179, 216, 307, 309, 355–56
Ali, Yusuf, 308–309
de Almasy, Count Ladislaus Edouard,
     xviii, 21, 42, 43–44, 47, 149, 366,
     372, 381–83, 388
Almasy Camp, 381
Almasy Hideout, 93
Alpenblick Hotel, 206
Alston, Richard, 66
Alum, 182, 358
Ambigol, tomb of Sheikh, 351
American Museum of Natural History,
     220, 223
Amheida, 138, 140–41
Ammonite Hill, 379
Amun-Re, 82, 103
Andrews, Charles, 220–21
animals, desert, 8, 18–22
Antiquities Headquarters and Museum
     (Bahariya), 192

Antony, Mark, 1, 262–63, 292–93, 296, 297
d'Anville, Bourgignon, 50
apes, fossils of, 223
Apis, 299
Apollonia, 3
al-Aqaba Pass, 388
Aqabat, 146, 172
Aqaqir Ridge, Battle of, 279–80
al-Aqqad, Muhammad Abu Saud Bey, 355
Aqqad and Company, slave traders, 355–56
aqueducts, 14, 89, 97, 99–100, 159, 181, 192, 209, 298
Arabs' Tower, 261, 274
Archean era, 5
Ard al-Gedida, 158–59
Areg Oasis, 212
Arianism, 56
Army of the Nile (British 8th Army), 275
Arsinoitherium, 37, 222
artesian wells, 14
Ascherson, P., 18, 38
Asher, Michael, 347
Asmant, 132
Aswan Dam, 15, 47, 346
Asyut, 53
Athanasius, Bishop of Alexandria, 56–57, 306
Atlas Mountains, 20, 29, 32, 38
Atmur al-Kibeish, 344
Augustus Caesar, 293, 306, 339
Aur, Bishop, 251
Australian Imperial Camel Corps, 112
Auto Saharan companies, 49
Awlad Ali, 26
Axis groups, 49
Azab, 252

Baaijens, Arita, 45
Bab Atrat, 328
Bab Inshal, 327
Bab al-Cailliaud, 113
Bab Qaddumah, 328
Bab al-Qasmund, 113–14, 136, 173
Bacchias, 234–35
Badr's Museum, 155
Badromani, Abdul Sadek, 203
Badromani family, 203

Badi Bastit, sarcophagus of, 74
Bagawat, 56, 57, 59, 61, 77–78
Bagnold, Ralph A., xviii, 18, 20–22, 40, 48–49, 366, 368, 383–84
Bagnold Crater, 368–369
Bahariya, 184, 185, 203–205
Bahariya Military Railway, 176
Bahariya Oasis, 6, 8, 35, 40, 42, 45, 46, 60, 63, 68, 175–212, (map, 174)
Bahr Yusif, 225
Bahrein Oasis, 36, 211–12
Bahrein Water Well Pavement Company, 211
Bailey, Donald M., 296
Baker, Sir Samuel, 356
al-Bakri, Abu Ubayd, 32
Balad Abu al-Hul, 159
Balad al-Rum, 339–40
Balat, 111, 130–31
Balbus, Cornelius, 4
Ball, John, xviii, 11, 13, 19, 39, 40, 42, 50, 59, 65, 73, 96, 99, 101, 148, 192, 210, 261, 284, 294, 358, 362, 366, 374, 375, 377, 379, 380, 391
Ball's Road, 285
Bani Hilal, 26
Bani Sulaym, 26
Barbary pirates, 29, 34, 70, 71, 263, 264
Barich, Barbara E., 147
Baris, 40, 58, 59, 62, 63, 85
al-Barrani, Sidi Muhammad, 299
Barron, Thomas, 39
Barth, Heinrich, 37, 111
Bashindi, 129
al-Basil, Hamed Basha, 253
baskets, 67, 68, 83, 117, 118, 227–28, 318–19
Bates, Oric, 295, 296
Bates' Island, 296, 297
al-Battikha, 92
Bawiti, 184, 191–94, 200–202, (map, 190)
al-Baz, Farouk, 11, 15, 51, 90, 311, 374, 381
al-Baz crater, 378
Beadnell, Hugh, xviii, 39, 56, 57, 59, 64, 65, 81, 84, 90, 92, 98–101, 113, 128, 138, 220, 363, 366
Beadnell, Mrs. Hugh, 374
Bedda Fromm, battle of, 266
Beit al-Aris cemetery, 132
Beleida, 103–104, (map, 103)

Belgrave, C. Dalrymple, 165, 287, 289–90, 294, 301, 307, 309, 310, 331, 335, 339
de Bellefonds, Louis Linant, 50, 216, 225, 237, 307
BelleVue, 145
Belzoni, G. B., 35, 179
Benghazi, 3, 20, 31
Beni Amar smugglers, 286
Beni Salih, 248
Bergmann, Carlo, 171
Bermann, Richard, 374, 375
Bianchi, Robert, 339
Bir Abu Hussein, 359
Bir Dikker, 172
Bir al-Gebel, 136
Bir Ghaba, 201–202
Bir Kiseiba, 23, 358–59
Bir Matar, 201
Bir Murr, 171, 359
Bir Nakhla, 360
Bir Natrun, 348, 350
Bir Qarawein, 171
Bir Qasa, 202
Bir Regwa, 167
Bir Safari, 23, 374
Bir Sitta, 157
Bir Takhlis, 360
Bir Tarfawi, 373–74
Bir Ziyyat, 108
birds, 21–22, 74–75, 222, 230, 243, 317
Birket Abu Talib, 225
Birket Azmuri, 311, 340
Birket Khamisa, 311
Birket Qarun, 8, 218–19, 220, 225, 237, 238–43, (map, 238)
Birket Siwa, 311, 337–38
Birket Zaytun, 311, 341
Black Mountain (English Mountain), 201
Black Valley, 173
Blemmyes, 56, 57
Bliss, Frank, 185, 188, 322
Blue Desert, 359
Bonaparte, Napoleon, 35, 44, 216, 275
Book of Hidden Pearls, 365
Booza Camp, 301
Borchardt, Ludwig, 236
Bornu, 34, 37, 39
Bosaed, Ali, 323
Boston University Center for Remote Sensing, 11, 51
Boutin, Vincent, 308, 312

Brandenburg Brigade, 49
Brezzi, Captain, 310
Briggs, Martin S., 93
British army, 47, 59, 179–80, 217, 266, 267, 275–76, 286, 294, 301, 310
British War Graves Commission, 282
Brown, Major R. H., 237
Brown, Thomas M., 221
Browne, W. G., 33, 59, 287, 307, 348–49, 350. 352
Brugsch, Heinrich Karl, 59
Buchheit, Gert, 44
Budkhulu,111, 135–36
Bulalawi, Muhammad, 356
Burg al-Arab, 274; battle of, 264
Burg al-Tuyur, 21, 49
Burckhardt, Jean Louis, 34, 347

Caccia-Dominoni, Paolo, 282, 283
Cailliaud, Frederic, 35, 59, 77, 88, 104, 113, 137, 150–51, 176, 179, 184, 192, 196, 203, 204, 212, 287, 308, 352
Caillie, Rene, 39
Calanscio Sand Sea, 13
Cambyses, 148–150, 163, 333
Camel Corps, 86, 211
Camp of Alexander (Qara), 287
Campbell, Dugald, 178, 211, 310
canals, 20–21, 60, 225, 246, 251, 272, 344–46, (map, 272)
Caporiacco, Professor, 43
caravan routes and roadways, 24, 25, 28–31, 115–16, 182, 225–26, 267
caravans, 1, 26, 28–31, 86
Castle of the Christians, 204
Catacomb Church, 260
Cato, 333
Caton-Thompson, Gertrude, 66, 92, 93, 99, 226, 239, 240
Cave of the Swimmers, 43, 45, 386, 387
Cella, Paolo Della, 39
Centro Studi Luigi Negro, 378
Chapel of King Apries, Qasr, 194
Chapel of Peace, 78
Chapel of the Exodus, 78
Chapels of Ain al-Muftillah, 197–198
Chephren Quarries, 23, 345, 361
Christian's Spring, 135
Church of the Blessed Virgin Mary, 260
Church of St. Misail, 260

Church of St. George, 208, 209
Church of the Spirits of the Lost Persian
    Army, 163
Church of the Virgin Mary (Siwa), 306
Clayton, Patrick A., xviii, 20, 42, 44, 50,
    127-28, 284, 366, 368, 377, 383
Clayton, Peter, 388
Clayton Craters, 368
Clayton-East-Clayton, Lady Dorothy
    Mary, 42, 43, 45
Clayton-East-Clayton, Sir Robert, 21, 42,
    43, 45, 366
Cleopatra, 1, 262, 273, 292–93, 294, 296,
    306, 339
Cleopatra's Bath, 297, 331–32
Coastguard Camel Corps, 165, 264–65,
    270, 286, 290, 293, 301, 310. See
    also Camel Corps.
Columbaria, 102–103
Coptic Museum, 75
Cow Bay, 219
Crocodilopolis, 246
Crystal Mountain, 146
Cubba-Beesh (Kababish), 348
Cyrenaican Plateau, 261
Cyril III (patriarch), 250

al-Dabaa, 291
Dabadib, 101, (map, 95)
al-Dahuz, 134
Dakhla Oasis, 6, 11, 15, 21, 22, 23, 25, 36,
    42, 54–55, 57–62, 64–69, 107–42,
    (map, 106)
Dakhla Oasis Project, 109
Dakhleh Oasis restoration, 139
Dakhakhin, 84
Darb Abu Minqar, 115
Darb Ain Amur, 64, 115
Darb al-Arbain Desert, 9, 11, 33, 343–63
Darb al-Arbain Road, 29, 31, 43, 46,
    53–54, 58–60, 64, 66, 70, 110, 344,
    347–48, (map, 349)
Darb al-Bulaq, 83
Darb al-Deir, 92
Darb al-Dush, 88–89
Darb al-Farafra, 115
Darb al-Galaba, 346, 360
Darb al-Ghubari, 64, 107, 108, 115
Darb al-Ishrin, 347
Darb al-Jaja, 59
Darb al-Khashabi, 115
Darb al-Rayyan , 225–26

Darb al-Rufuf, 92–93
Darb al-Sindadiya, 74
Darb Siwa, 198, 210–12, 303
Darb al-Tarfawi, 110, 115, 347, 369
Darb al-Tawil, 115
Darb Wadi Natrun, 225
Darfur, 4, 46, 60, 351–352, 356, 357
Darius I, 55, 77, 82
al-Deir, 59, 90–94
Deir Abu Lifa, 239
Deir Abu Matta, 135
Deir Anba Samwil, 260
Deir al-Azab, 250–51
Deir Archangel Michael (Hamuli), 245
Deir al-Hagar, 15, 138–39
Deir al-Hammam, 252
Deir al-Malak Ghobrial, 251
Deir al-Ras, 209
Denham, Clapperton and Oudney
    expedition, 38, 39
Derna, 264
Desaix, General, 216
Desert Institute (Cairo), 47, 362
Diemer, Edmond, 375
al-Diffa, 2, 9, 261–302
Dimeh al-Siba, 239–40
Dionysias, 244
Dinosaurs, 6, 202
Domitian, 88
Doric Temple at Maraqi, 338–39
Drovetti, Bernardino, 35–36, 59, 82, 113,
    128, 139, 307–308
von Dumreicher, Andre, 24, 86, 165, 166,
    265, 293
Dunqul Oasis, 362
Dush (Kysis), 63, 80, 87–88
Dust Road. See Darb al-Ghubari.

East Uwaynat, xvii, 374
Eastern Dakhla,127–134
Eastern Desert, 16, 66
Eaton, William, 19, 34, 35, 264, 269–70,
    291, 293, 299, 300
Edfu, 65
Edmondstone, Sir Archibald, 19, 21, 36,
    57, 59, 77, 82, 93. 105, 113, 114,
    115, 131, 139
Eed, Mahmoud, 191–192
Effendi, Hassan, 111, 114
Egyptian Antiquities Organization, 82, 83,
    87, 96, 137
Egypt Exploration Society, 367, 380

Ehrenberg, Victor, 36
Eight Bells, 385–86
Embadi, N. S., 13
Environmental Quality International, village, 338
Escarpment Post, 286
Esna, 8, 65
Ethnographic Museum (Mut), 126
European travelers in the desert, 58–59
Ezbat Tunis, 242
explorers, desert, 23–52, (map, 41)

Fakhry, Ahmed, xviii, 35, 63, 71, 99, 108, 130, 177, 194, 195, 197, 198, 204, 288, 310, 327, 328, 334, 337, 341, 342, 363
Fakhry Desert Archaeology Centre, 345
Fallaw oasis, 158
Farafra, xvii, 6, 23, 35, 42, 46, 60, 61, 63, 143–73, (map, 144)
Faruqa, 248
Fathy, Hassan, 84
Fatnas (island), 335
Fayoum, 5, 8, 13, 16, 22, 23, 33, 35–39, 42, 45, 46, 50, 56, 61, 66, 211–60, (map, 214)
Festival of Sidi Ghaffir, 338
Festival of Siyaha, 330
Fezzan, 2, 3, 4, 24, 25, 28, 30, 34
Fezzan-Kawan road, 29, 30,
al-Fida, Abu, 301
Fidimin, 248
Fish Pond, 134
Flatters, Col. Paul, 31, 148
Forbes, Rosita, 39, 45, 46
Forster, E. M., 271
Forth, Col. de Lancy, 377
fortresses, al-Deir, 91; Farafra, 155–57, Qasr al-Labeka, 96; Shali, 327–28,
Fortress of the Fighter, 204–205
fossils, 4, 6, 7, 17–18, 61, 113, 114, 160, 163, 181–82, 219–20, 221, 222, 223–24, 241, 258–59, 284, 286, 379
de Foucauld, Father, 31
Foureau-Lamy expedition, 148
Fraas, Eberhard, 220
Frediani, Enegildo, 307–308
Frobenius, Leo, 366, 372, 380
Fudail, Abu, 128
Fuka, 291

Gabala, 204
Gallus, Aelius, 32
Gara Cave, 171
Gardner, Elinor W., 218, 239
Gaucum (al-Alamein), 275
Gazalah, battle of, 267, 290
Gebel al-Aguz, 61
Gebel Arkenu, 46, 367–68
Gebel Babein, 368
Gebel Bayda, 312, 337, 338
Gebel al-Dakrur, 312, 329–30
Gebel al-Deir, 257
Gebel Dist, 202
Gebel Edmondstone, 113–15
Gebel Gala Siwa, 207
Gebel Ghaffir, 338. See also Gebel Bayda.
Gebel al-Ghanima, 61
Gebel al-Ghurabi, 62, 101
Gebel Guhannam, 218, 258–60, (map, 259)
Gebel Hafuf, 206
Gebel Hammad, 206
Gebel Hamra, 164, 312, 337, 338
Gebel Kamil, 368
Gebel Kissu, 368
Gebel Maghrafa, 202
Gebel Mandisha, 201
Gebel al-Mawta, 312, 336–37
Gebel Mayisra, 201
Gebel Miteili Radwan, 207
Gebel Naqlun, 218
Gebel Naqlun monastery, 251
Gebel Nasra, 320, 330
Gebels Peter and Paul, 368
Gebel al-Qarn, 62, 63
Gebel Qarn al-Laban, 288
Gebel Qatrani, 218, 220, 223, 241
Gebel al-Ramliya, 61
Gebel Shahut, 207
Gebel Shawshaw, 114
Gebel al-Sheikh, 62, 63, 101
Gebel al-Tafnis, 62, 84
Gebel al-Tarif, 40, 62, 63, 79, 100–101
Gebel al-Tarwan, 62, 63
Gebel al-Teir, 61, 63, 76, 79
Gebel Tinkmamou, 339
Gebel Tunefefan, 330
Gebel Umm al-Ghanayim, 61, 63, 65, 92
Gebel Uwaynat, 6, 16, 20, 23, 25, 43, 46, 47, 51, 388–89
Gebel al-Zuhur, 62
Gebel al-Zuqaq, 207

Geological Survey of Egypt, 16, 39–42, 47, 50
Geziret al-Qarn, 218–19
Ghadames, 4, 29, 30
Gharaq Sultani, 254
Gharay, 235
Gharb Mahub, 143
Ghard Kebir, 210
Ghard Mandisha, 181, 203
Ghari (gardens), 337–38
Giddy, Lisa, 130
Gilf Kebir, 9, 10, 13–15, 19, 20, 23, 25, 43, 45–46, 49, 51, 369, 379–81, (map, 382)
Gingerich, Philip, 259
Global Positioning System (GPS), xviii, 393
Golden Fortress, 238
Goodenough, Rev. L., 295
Gordon, Charles G., 356–57
Goshna, 157
Graf, Theodor, 235
Grand Sanusi, 27, 28, 330
Granger, Walter, 220
Graziani, Marshal Rudolfo, 266, 300
Great Sand Sea, 10, 11, 13, 15, 21, 38, 39, 45, 48, 49, 51, 61, 71, 114, 312, 367, 376–77
Grenfell, Bernard Pyne, 234
Gudenus, Janos, 44
Guhar, General, 263

Habachi, Labib, 299
Hadiq, 158
al-Hafiz, Caliph, 150
Hagedorn, H., 49, 50
Haggar al-Gilf, 242
Haida, Sheikh Ali, 342
Halfat al-Bir, 130
Halfway Cairn, 362
Hamilton, James, 308
Hamuli, 245
Hanadi, Sheikh Hassan, 100
Hara, 205
Harding-King, W. J., 297
Hassanein, Ahmed, xviii, 21, 25, 26, 27, 28, 39, 45, 46, 366, 367, 369, 370, 371, 390, 391
Hassuna, Sheikh Abdel Ati, 165, 331
Hawara, 229, 249–50
Haynes, C. Vance, 343, 391

al-Hayz, 208–209
Helen of Troy, 292
Hely-Hutchinson, Sir John, 272
Hercules, 96, 97
Herodotus, 9, 30, 31, 249
Hibis, 55, 59, 76–77
Hodgson, Capt. H., 350
Hoggar mountains, 30
Hope, Colin A., 120
Hornemann, Frederick, 34, 287, 307
Hoskins, G. A., 58, 59, 65, 66, 73, 81, 85, 149
Houghton, Maj. Daniel, 34, 36
House of Abu Nafir, 137
House of the Banker (Karanis), 233
Houses of the Christians, 135
Howard, Jean, 44
Hume, William Fraser, 39, 40
Hunt, Arthur Surridge, 234
Hyde, John, 36

Ibn Hawqal, 32
Ibn Khaldun, 32, 365
Ibn Nusayr, Musa, 306
Ibn Ziyad, Tariq, 306
Ibrahim, Bahgat, 71
Ibshaway, 248
Idris, Sayyid Muhammad, 28, 276
al-Idrisi, Muhammad al-Sharif, 32
Im-Pepi, tomb of, 75
Ima Bibi statue, 75
Infidel Rock, 163
Institute of Underground Water Research, 345
Isaac, Benjamin, 66
Island of the Jews, 297
Isle Mariout, 273
Ismail (khedive), 356–57
Itsa, 253

Jaghbub Oasis, 27
Jaja, 83–84
Jennings-Bramley, Wilfred, 164, 212, 305, 341–42
jewelry, 70–71, 123–24, 187–89, 229, 252, 322–26
Jomard, Edmé, 50
Jones, Arthur M., 113
Jordan, Wilhelm, 38, 57
Julius Caesar, 20, 273, 292
Jux, Ulrich, 378

Kababish, 26, 348
Kamal, Ahmad, 365
Kamal al-Din, Prince, 40, 43–44, 46–47, 241, 362, 366, 368, 374, 375, 379, 388, 391
Kanem-Bornu empire, 4
Karamanli, Yusif and Hamet, 34, 264
Karanis, 231, 232–34
Karkur Talh, 371, 391, 392
Kashif, Farag, 335
Kellis, 75, 132–34, (map, 132)
Kelsey, Francis W., 234
Kennedy-Shaw, W. B., 49, 350
Kerkeosiris, 254
Khalid ibn al-Walid, 32, 58, 83
Khalifa, 357
Kharga Oasis, 6, 11, 13, 16, 20, 21, 23, 31,   33, 36, 39, 40, 42, 48, 53–106, 348,   351, 359, (map, 52)
Kharga Museum, 74–75, 90, 95, 102
Kharitat al-Ajaib, 32
Khelua, 245
Khent-Ka, 75
al-Kifah, 159
Kiman Faris, 247
King, Harding, 25, 42, 65, 73, 83, 100, 108, 113, 135, 155, 365, 366
King Farouk's resthouse (Mut), 126
King Fuad, 42, 47
King Fuad's resthouse, 331
King Hussein Kamal, 47
King of Kanem, 351
Kitines, tomb of, 129
Kobbe, Sudan, 348
Kom Aushim (village), 231
Kom Aushim museum, 231–32, 238, 239, 249
Kom al-Khamsini, 254
Kom Medinet al-Nahas, 254
Kordofan, 4, 25, 26
Kossuth Revolution, 44
Kufra, 1, 14, 21, 27, 28, 30, 31, 38, 39, 42, 43, 45, 46, 49
Kurkur Oasis, 362
Kuper, Dr. Rudolph, 375

Lahun, 251
Laing, Gordon, 31, 39
Lake Chad, 25, 26, 29, 30, 39, 66
Lake al-Marun, 202
Lake Maryut, 271, 272–74
Lake Moeris, 223

Lake Nasser, 23
Lake Qarun. *See* Birket Qarun.
Lama, Ibrahim, 47
Lama, Samir, 45, 47
Lama, Waltrand, 19, 45
Lama Point, 381
Lampson, Sir Miles, 232
Laqya al-Arbain, 350
Laura caves, 251
Ledyard, John, 34
Leopoldo, Bettina, 319
Letorzec, Pierre, 308
Lewis, Naphtali, 55, 86
Libyan-Arab Corps, 276
Libyan Desert Plateau, 261
Libyan Oasis Association, 294, 310
Ligabue, Giancarlo, 149
Light Car Patrols, British, 40, 42, 47–48, 275, 300, 302
Limestone Plateau (Arbain Desert), 344
Linant, A., 34
Locabsis (al-Alamein), 275
Long Range Desert Group, 42, 44, 47, 48 49, 164, 275, 367, 377, 380, 384, 388
Lucas, Simon, 34
Lyon, Capt. G. F., 354
Lyons, Capt. H. G., 39, 50, 110, 113, 115
Lythgoe, Albert M., 93

Mabrouk Fountain, 69, 73
MacArthur, Wilson, 300
Maeories, 56
Maghra Oasis, 265, 286
Magic Spring, 256–58
al-Mahdi, Sayyid, 4, 28, 357
Mahmoud, Youssef, 75
Mahr, Mustapha, 309
Mahub, 143
Maks Bahri, 85–86
Maks Qibli, 85–87
al-Malik, Abd, 58
Mamluk beys, 26
manafis (aqueducts), 192, 204
Managim, 176
Manawar, 89
Mandisha, 45, 203–204
Mansur, Sheikh Hassuna, 309
al-Mansur, al Zubayr Rahma, 355
al-Maqrizi, 58, 306
Marabout, 27, 274

Maraqi, 338–39
Marble Labyrinth, 173
Mareotis. *See* Lake Maryut.
Markgraf, Richard, 220, 223
Marseille, Hans-Joachim, 283
Maryut Railway, 265, 268, 271
Masara, 134
Mason, Michael, 366
Masrab al-Dara, 288
Masrab al-Ikhwan, 337
Masrab Khidida, 288
Masrab al-Muhashas, 288
masrabs, Siwan roads, 313–14
Masraf al-Wadi, 218
al-Masudi, 32
Mauch, C., 50
Maxwell, John, 59
McHugh, William, 369, 385
Medinet Fayoum, 246–52, (map, 246)
Medinet Madi, 245
Medinet Quta, 243
Merenptah, King, 147
Merga, 46, 48, 49
Mersa Matruh, 19, 291–98, (map, 292),
Mersa Matruh, battle of, 266, 268
Mesu-Isis, tomb of, 336–37
meteorite record, Egyptian, 40
Michel, René, tomb, 206–207
Middleton, Paul, 92
Migma, 143
Mills, A. J., 110
Minshat Rahim, 253
Mishabit, 92
Mi-war, 215
Mofera oasis, 158
Mograbin (Barbary Arabs), 111
monasteries, 209, 215, 245, 250–51, 257
Monastery of Abu Lifa, 239
Monastery of Mustafa Kashif, 78, 98
Monastery of St. Samuel, 257, 260
Monastery of Sediman, battle at, 216
Monastery of Stone, 138–39
Monastery of the Seven Virgins, 135
Mond expedition, 49, 55, 367, 373,
        380, 384
Monod, Theodore, xviii, 375
Montgomery, Sir Bernard, 266
Morkot, Robert, 355
al-Mudawara, 256, (map, 257)
Muftah, 253
Mukhtar, Omar, 28, 302

Mulid en Tagmigra, 329
Muller, Frederic, 36, 38, 59, 113
Munira, 92
Murad Bey, 216
Murray, G. W., 19, 42, 261, 346, 361
Murzuk, 4, 30, 354
Musallim, Sheikh, 327
Mushiya, 141
Mut, 111, 112,125–26, (map, 125)
Mut al-Kharib, 126
Mustafa Kashif cemetery, 98
Mustafa Kashif monastery, 78
Muzawwaqa frescoes, 138
Myers, Oliver, 367, 385

Nabi Daniel mosque, 339
Nabta Playa, 23, 343, 360–63
al-Nabulsi, Uthman, 365
Nachtigal, Gustav, 37, 38, 50
Nadura, 76
Nakheila Oasis, 362
Nakhla-Shab pediplain, 360
Naqb Abu Dweis, 285
Naqb Abu Sighawal, 65, 92
Naqb Asyut, 54, 65
Naqb Bulaq, 65, 83
Naqb Bulat, 131
Naqb al-Dush, 65, 88–89
Naqb al-Farafra, 136
Naqb Jaja, 65, 84
Naqb al-Mughbara, 289, 340
Naqb Qirba, battle of, 331
Naqb al-Ramliya, 54, 65
Naqb al-Rufuf, 65, 92–93
Naqb Tineida, 128
Naqb Yabsa, 54, 65
naqbs, 65, 114
Nazla, 228, 245
Nestorius, Bishop, 57
Neufeld, Charles, 350
New Baris, 84
New Valley, 60, 61, 63, 67, 71, 345
New Valley phosphate project, 107
Newbold, Douglas, 21, 26, 49. 148,
        350, 371
Nicholls, Henry, 34
Niperpathot, tomb of, 336
North Africa, 1–4, 15, 26, 32, 37–38, 63,
        (map of trade routes, 29)
Nubia Pediplain, 344
Nubian invasions, 351

Nubian Salvage Campaign, 362, 374
Nubian sandstone plateau, 9
Nusayr, Musa Ibn, 32
Nuwamisa Oasis, 211

Oasis Heritage Museum (Bawiti), 191–92
O'Bannon, Presley Neville, 34, 264, 300
Old Baris, 85. *See also* Baris.
Old Libyan River, 8
Olsen, George, 220
Ondaatje, Michael, 44
Oracle of Amun, 305–306
Oracle of Delphi, 2
Oracle of Siwa, 1.
    See also Temple of the Oracle.
Orlebar, A. B., 220
Osborn, Henry F., 220, 223
Osiris (village), 254
Osiris Temple, 270

Pacho, Jean Raimond, 36, 212, 308
Palaeomastodon, 220, 223
Panzergruppe Afrika, 290.
    See also Afrika Corps.
papyrus scrolls, 133, 215, 234, 235,
    253–54
Paraetonium, 292–293, 296.
    See also Mersa Matruh.
Parrish, Anne M., 112
Peel, R. F., 380
Penderel, wing commander, 43
Persian army, lost, 147–48
Peter, bishop of Fayoum, 250
Petermann, August H., 50
Petrie, Flinders, 120, 225, 234, 235, 239,
    249, 251, 288
Petubastis, tomb of, 138
Pharaoh's Rock, 288
Philadelphia, 235–36
Philadelphus, Ptolemy, 215, 235
Phillips, Wendell, 220
Pindar, poem about Oracle of Siwa, 333
plants and animals, desert, 18–22
Plinthine, Bay of, 270
Plinthinus, 270
Pliny, 4, 56
Poncet, M., 33, 58
pottery , 67, 69, 118–20, 137–38, 228,
    241, 296–97, 299, 320–21, 373,
    375, 385
Prince Farouk Hotel (Siwa), 311

de Prorok, Byron Khun, 292, 312, 338,
    339–40
Ptolemaeus, Claudius, 49
Ptolemy I, 218
pyramids, Hawara, 215, 249; Lahun, 215,
    251; Sila, 236

Qalamshah, 253
Qalamun, 111, 142
Qara, 287
Qara Oasis (Gara), 287–89
Qarat al-Farargi, 193
Qarat al-Hilwa, tombs at, 199–200
Qarat Qasr Salim, 193
Qarat Sheikh Abdullah Muhammad,
    145–46
Qarawein, 170–171
Qarn al-Ginah, 62
Qaseir Muharib, 204–205
Qasr (Bahariya), 194–96
Qasr (Dakhla), 111, 136–377, (map, 137)
Qasr (Farafra), 155–57, (map, 156)
Qasr (Kharga), 67, 69, 70, 73–75, 80–89,
    (map, 72)
Qasr al-Basil, 253
Qasr al-Dabba, 130
Qasr al-Geb, 93–94
Qasr al-Ghashsham, 340–41
Qasr al-Ghweita, 81–82
Qasr al-Ginah, 82
Qasr Hassuna, caves, 330–31
Qasr al-Labeka, 95–101
Qasr Masuda, 209
Qasr al-Mughatta, 94
Qasr al-Nesim, 81
Qasr Qarun, 244
Qasr al-Qasaba, 132
Qasr al-Sagha, 238
Qasr al-Sumaria, 93–94
Qasr al-Zabw, 204
Qasr al-Zayyan, 82–83
Qattara Depression, 9, 11, 18, 19, 20, 26,
    284–86
Qirba, battle of, 310
Quadi Battalion, 55
Quartz Ridge, 361
Quss Abu Said, 162–63

Radwan, 207
Ramliya, 65
Rashda, 134–35

Rashida (Sudan), 20, 112
Rasmussen, D. Tab, 224
Rathbone, Dominic, 254
Raymond, André, 71
Rayyan project, 255
Rebiana Sand Sea, 13
Regenfeld, 378–79
Remele, Ph., 38
Ricci, Alessandro, 307
Rifaud, Jean Jacques, 36
rock art, 43–46, 79, 108, 370–72, 386,
        387, 391–92
Roger II, Norman king of Sicily, 32
Rohlfs, Gerhard, xviii, 21, 37–39, 59, 113,
        139, 171–73, 309, 365, 376, 377–79
Rohlfs expedition, 15, 36, 38, 46, 50, 61,
        70, 196, 210, 212
Roman fortress, Farafra, 155
Roman ruins, Amheida, 140–41;
        Bahariya, 178; Dakhla, 110;
        Dimeh, 240; Dionysias, 244;
        Farafra, 150
Roman Springs (Ain Bishmu and
        Ain Bardir), 195
Roman temple, Mut, 126
Roman tombs, at Bashindi, 129;
        Dakhla, 140; Qasr al-Labeka, 96
Roman Triumphal Arch (Qasr), 196
Rommel, Erwin, 43, 266, 290, 302,
        278–80, 311, 342
Rommel's Cave, 297–98
Rosingana, 139
Royal Geographical Society, 33, 34, 37,
        42–43, 45, 48, 49, 366

Sabun, Sultan of Waidai, 30, 366, 390
Sahara Desert, 1–3, 11, 16, 18, 25, 31, 39,
        45, (map, 2)
Sahara Suda, 206–207
Said, Rushdi, 14, 16, 42, 46, 47, 107,
        344, 368
St. Anba Abraam (Deir al-Azab), 250–51
St. Bartholomew, 178, 208
St. Gabriel, church of, 251
St. John, Bayle, 36–37, 261, 270, 289, 305,
        308, 330, 334
St. Samuel, 251, 257, 259, 260
sand dunes, 10–13, 63, 81, 100, 115, 203,
        206, 210, 359, 373, 280–81
Sandheim, 367, 369, 376–77, 379
sand seas, 12–13, (map, 12)

Sanhur, 248
Sanusi, 27–28, 30–31, 46, 47, 59, 111,
        141–42, 179, 265–66, 299,
        300–301, 310, 341–42
Sanusi caravans, at Siwa, 309
Schienerl, Peter W., 70
Schilk, Romuald, 374
Schweinfurth, Georg, 21, 55, 59, 104,
        220, 237, 239
Schweinfurth's temple, 239
Sciarabati, Giovanni, 270
Sea of Tethys, 5, 258
Selima (oasis), 11, 21, 22, 350–51
Selima Sand Sheet, 344
Senan Camp, 286
Senusert I's obelisk, 253
al-Shab, 358
Shakshuk, 242
Shali, 327–29, (map, 327)
Shamashurghi, Hassan Bey, 307
Shaw, W. B. Kennedy, 164–65, 350,
        371, 377
Shehaymah of Jalo, 30, 366, 390
Sheikh Ahmad, tomb of, 202
Sheikh Muftah, 131, 132
Sheikh Wali, 134
al-Sheikh Zayed Canal, 20, 345–46
Shemendu oasis, 158
Shidmoh, 253
Shoshenq, 55, 110, 178
Si-Amun, tomb and temple of, 337
Sidi Abd al-Rahman, 289–90
Sidi Barrani, 266, 299–300
Sijilmasa, 29
Sila pyramid, 236
Simons, Elwyn L., 219–20, 224
Sioh Ridge, 113–14
Sithathorinit, Princess, 252
Sitra Oasis, 36, 210–11
Siwa, 13, 23, 26, 30, 33, 35–39, 43, 45,
        56–57, 60, 66–68, 303–42,
        (map, 304)
Siwa House Museum, 328–29
Siwa Women's Health Center, 329
Siwan Manuscript, 327
Siyaha, Festival of, 330
Slatin, Rudolf Karl, 357
slave caravans, 352–55, 358
slave trade, 31, 70, 86, 287, 309, 343,
        346, 347, 351, 353–57
slaves, 4, 29, 30, 342, 353–56

Slaves' Road, 346
Smith, Holly, 259
Smith, Leigh, 39
snakes, in Egypt, 19
Snape, Steven, 299
Soknopaiou Nesos (Dimeh), 240
Sollum, 46, 266, 267, 300–301, 313
Southern Desert, 60
Souvaltzi, Liani and Manos, 338–39
Speke, John, 44–45
Sphinx Valley, 164
springs, 62, 166, 331–32. *See also* Ains.
Steindorff, Georg, 39, 194
Stela Ridge, 361
Stone Calendar, 361
Strabo, 31–32, 333
Sudan, 4–6, 15, 16, 25–26, 31–33, 37,
      46–49, 59–60, 71
Sudan Defense Force, 25, 350
Sudanese Camel Corps, 350
Suliman, Sidi, 329
Sultan's Path, 313
Suua, 3
Swelim, Nabil, 236
Synesius, Bishop of Ptolemais, 306
Szentirmany, Laszlo, 44

Tabid al-Darawish, 86–87
Taghaza road, 29, 30, 32
Tahunet al-Hawa, 79
Taposiris Magna, 269–70
Tashi, Abdulla, 59
al-Tayeb, Sheikh, 270
Tebtunis, 252–55
Tebu, 25, 29, 30
Tell al-Aqaqir, 291
Tell al-Kebir, battle of, 275
Temple and Tomb of Hercules
      (Bahariya), 192
Temple of Alexander the Great
      (Bahariya), 198
Temple of Hibis (Kharga), 35, 59, 76
Temple of Nadura (Kharga), 76
Temple of the Oracle (Siwa), 306, 332–34
Temple of Osiris (Dush, Kharga), 88
Temple of Umm Ubayd (Siwa), 334
temples, 133, 233, 244, 245, 270–71
Tethys Sea, 5, 258
Teuchira (Tuhra), 3
Tibniya, 197–200
Tineida, 107, 112, 127–28

Tinne, Alexine, 31, 38, 44–45
Tobruk, fall of, 266, 267
Toledano, Ehud R., 86
Tomb of Sheikh Ambigol, 351
tombs, 75, 78, 138, 158, 193–94, 202, 204,
      206–207, 212, 236, 336–37
Tousson, Prince Omar, 164
trade routes, desert, (map, 29)
Tree of Sheikh Adam, 135
Tripoli, 2, 4, 25, 29–30, 34–39, 264
Tripolitania, 3, 26, 28
Tuareg empire, 340
Tuareg people, 25, 29, 34, 355
Tuhra, 3
Tushka Canal, 344–45
Tutankhamen's scarab, 378
Twin Peaks, 146

Ubayad Beach, 298–99
al-Ubeida Playa, 163
Umm al-Iffa, 206
Umm al-Qasur, 93
Umm Sighawal, 65
Umm Ubayd, 36, 334
Urabi, Ahmed, 28
Uwaynat Desert, 9, 25, 30, 42, 364–93,
      (map, 389)

Valley of the Golden Mummies, 192, 199
Valley of the Melons, 65
Vischer, Hanns, 29, 111, 354
von der Esch, Baron, 43

Wadi Abd al-Malik, 383–84
Wadi Ajal, 24
Wadi al-Ard al-Khadra, 385
Wadi al-Bakht, 384–85
Wadi al-Battikha, 53
Wadi Dayyiq, 384
Wali Faragh, 388
Wadi al-Gamel, 205
Wadi Hamra, 383
Wadi Handal, 391
Wadi Hinnis, 170
Wadi Maftuh, 384
Wadi Mashi, 384
Wadi Mawalih, 260
Wadi Natrun, 8, 22, 24, 57
Wadi Rayyan, 225, 254–60
Wadi Sura, 381, 386
Wadi Talh, 384

Wadi al-Ubayyid cave, 163
Wadi Wasa, 385
Wadi Wihish, 392
Wadi Zeuglodon, 223, 258, (map, 259)
Wahat al-Amal, 159
Waidai, Sultan of, 25, 30, 366, 390
Walpole, G. F., 298
Walsh, Thomas, 272
Wardabaha, 365
water, 13–15, 40, 62–63; 114, 120, 150,
    181, 225, 267, 312
water projects, 344–46
Wavell, Sir Archibald, 266
Well of the Mountain, 136
wells, 114. *See also individual wells under*
    Bir ———
Wendorf, Fred, 375
West Africa, 31, 33, 38
Western Desert, 6–10, 13–17, 23, 25,
    31–32, 35–55, 59, 62–66
Western Dakhla, 131
White, Arthur Silva, 286, 288
White, Donald, 295, 296
white chalk, near Qara, 289
White Desert, 146, 159–61
Whitehouse, Sir Cope, 254
Widan al-Faras, 241
Widow's War, 309

Wilkinson, Sir Gardner, 59, 365
Wilkinson, John G., 113
Willcox, Sir William, 255
Williams, Capt. Claud, 201
Williams, R. S. Gwatkin, 19
Winkler, Hans, 108, 367, 372
Winlock, H. E., 15, 65, 113
Wolfe, R. W., 15
World War I, 28, 40, 43, 48, 59, 265–66
World War II, 3, 28, 31, 40, 43, 51, 60,
    266–67. *See also* al-Alamein.
Worthington, Sir Hubert, 282

yardangs (mud lions), 63, 83, 90, 162

Zabw, 204
Zaghawa, 348
Zaki, Hagg, 163
zar pendant, 188
Zawya Square (Qasr), 194–95
Zaytun (oasis), 341–42
Zerzura, 25, 42–45, 365–66; quest for,
    111, 365–66, 375
Zerzura Club, 365–66
Zeuglodon (fossil), 37, 223, 258–59
Zittel, Prof. Karl, 38, 61
al-Zubayr, and slave trade, 356